Hungarian Notation

Windows Programmers often use Hungarian Notation (HN) for their variables. Most of the examples in this book, as well as most sample programs provided with Visual C++, use Hungarian Notation. When using HN, the logical type of the variable is prefixed to the variable name, as shown in the following chart:

Type	Prefix	Example
int	n	nAge
char	ch	chInitial
float	fl	flAngle
double	d	dSalary
unsigned	u	uID
long	l	lHours
BOOL	b	bDone
WORD	w	wSize
DWORD	dw	dwError
pointer	p	pButton
C++ member variable	m_	m_nAge
Global variable	g_	g_hWnd
String	sz	szName
Flag	f	fChecked
Width	cx	cxCaption
Height	cy	cyClient
Rectangle	rc	rcClient
Window	wnd	wndMain
Handle	h	hInstance
Point	pt	ptMouse
List Box	lb	lbNames

Common Keyboard Shortcuts

Compiling and Building

Shortcut	Description
F7	Build project
Shift+F7	Compile current file
F4	Go to next error in build window
F5	Run in debugger
Shift+F5	Execute program

Text Editor

Shortcut	Description
Ctrl+F	Find
F3	Find next
Ctrl+F3	Find previous
Ctrl+A	Select all
Ctrl+C	Copies selection to the Clipboard
Ctrl+N	Create new file or project
Ctrl+O	Opens new file
Ctrl+S	Saves current file
Ctrl+V	Inserts text from the Clipboard
Ctrl+W	Starts ClassWizard
Ctrl+X	Cuts selection to the Clipboard
Ctrl+Y	Redo
Ctrl+Z	Undo

Resources

Shortcut	Description
Ctrl+D	View dialog box tab order
Ctrl+T	Test dialog box controls

Debugging

Shortcut	Description
F9	Sets or removes breakpoint
F10	Steps over current line
F11	Steps into current line
Ctrl+B	Edits current breakpoints

PRACTICAL

Visual C++ 6

Jonathan Bates

Timothy Tompkins

Contents at Glance

A Division of Macmillan Computer Publishing, USA
201 W. 103rd Street
Indianapolis, Indiana 46290

Practical Visual C++® 6

International Standard Book Number: 0-7897-2142-2

Library of Congress Catalog Card Number: 99-65511

Printed in the United States of America

First Printing: August, 1999

01 00 99   4 3 2 1

Trademarks

Warning and Disclaimer

Executive Editor
Brian Gill

Acquisitions Editor
Kelly Marshall

Development Editor
Matt Purcell

Managing Editor
Thomas F. Hayes

Project Editor
Tonya Simpson

Copy Editors
Kate Givens
Kate Talbot

Indexer
Kelly Talbot
Johnna VanHoose

Technical Editor
Matt Butler

Production
Stacey DeRome
Ayanna Lacey
Heather Hiatt Miller

Contents

About the Authors

Jon Bates has worked on a whole range of commercial, industrial, and military software development projects worldwide over the past 15 years. He is currently working as a self-employed software design consultant and contract software developer specializing in Visual C++ application development for Windows NT/95 and 98.

Jonathan began his career writing computer games for popular microcomputers and has since worked with a number of operating systems such as CPM, DOS, TRIPOS, UNIX and Windows, and a number of Assembly, 3rd-generation and object-orientated languages.

He has written system and application software as diverse as device drivers, email, production modeling, motion video, image analysis, network and telecommunications, data capture, control systems, estimating and costing, and visualization software. He has also written several technical articles for computing journals on a range of topics.

Jonathan lives with his wife Ruth, and dog Chaos, in the middle of cool Britannia. When not playing about with computers, he likes to sleep and dream of fractals.

You can reach Jonathan at jon@chaos1.demon.co.uk and visit his Web site at www.chaos1.demon.co.uk.

Tim Tompkins is currently the Software Development Manager for a European software house specializing in integrated management information systems. He is responsible for the design and implementation of their commercial applications written in Visual C++.

Tim's programming career began in 1986 writing statistical analysis applications using COBOL on IBM mainframes. Since then he has gained eight years experience of C and Visual C++ and worked on a
variety of operating systems including CPM, DOS, UNIX, XENIX, Windows NT/95 and 98.

He has designed and written numerous software modules, production scheduling, shop floor data collection, stock control and invoicing, estimating and costing and time and attendance recording.

Tim lives with his wife Tracey, and her horse Oliver (who stays outdoors) in England's green and pleasant land. When he can, he takes to the wheel of his sports convertible (even in the rain).

You can contact Tim at tinytim@globalnet.co.uk.

Dedication

To the biggest and best program of them all, DNA, the genetic code of life.

Acknowledgments

Special thanks to Matt Purcell and Kelly Marshall for their continual kind words of encouragement and attention to detail, which helped us through the punishing workload in a very tight schedule.

Thanks also to Matt Butler, Tonya Simpson, Kate Givens, and Kate Talbot, for their invaluable editorial support and comments, and for all the hardworking people behind the scenes at MCP.

Thanks to our families and friends who offered great support while suffering from our neglect over the past few months.

Tell Us What You Think!

As the reader of this book, *you* are our most important critic and commentator. We value your opinion and want to know what we're doing right, what we could do better, what areas you'd like to see us publish in, and any other words of wisdom you're willing to pass our way.

As the Executive Editor for the Que programming team at Macmillan Computer Publishing, I welcome your comments. You can fax, email, or write me directly to let me know what you did or didn't like about this book—as well as what we can do to make our books stronger.

Please note that I cannot help you with technical problems related to the topic of this book, and that due to the high volume of mail I receive, I might not be able to reply to every message.

When you write, please be sure to include this book's title and author as well as your name and phone or fax number. I will carefully review your comments and share them with the author and editors who worked on the book.

Fax: 317-581-4666

E-mail: Que_prog@mcp.com

Mail: Executive Editor
         Programming
         Macmillan Computer Publishing
         201 West 103rd Street
         Indianapolis, IN 46290 USA

introduction

Personal computers running a variant of the Windows operating system have become a ubiquitous sight in homes and offices worldwide. The popularization of the Internet and the multimedia capabilities of PCs have driven the growth in demand for varied and powerful application software still faster. It seems to be the current fashion to malign Microsoft purely for its success. However, Microsoft's success coupled with its commitment to standardization has allowed talented Windows programmers to trade their skills for ever greater rewards in a global marketplace. The demand for these skills, and thus the rewards, financial and otherwise, can only grow as western society accepts and integrates computers more and more into each individual's lifestyle.

What Is Visual C++ 6.0 and Why Use It?

Visual C++ 6.0 is Microsoft's latest and best release yet of its pedigree Visual C/C++ compiler. The product has become much, much more than just a compiler. It includes the comprehensive Microsoft Foundation Classes, which simplify and speed development of Windows applications. It includes sophisticated resource editors to design the complex dialog boxes, menus, toolbars, images, and many other elements of modern Windows applications. There is the excellent integrated development environment called Developer Studio that presents graphical views of your application's structure as you develop it. A totally integrated debugging tool lets you examine in minute detail every aspect of your program as it runs. These are just a few of the overwhelming number of features of Visual C++ 6.0 that will help you develop fast and feature-packed world-class application software using the very latest developments in Windows.

What's New in This Book?

Visual C++ 6.0 brings a whole host of new features, and we've packed as many of them as possible into this book.

The new controls, such as the date picker control that you might have seen in the Microsoft Outlook email application, are now available for use in your own applications (covered in Chapter 7, "Using Progress, Scrollbar, Slider, and Date Time Controls").

Images can now be associated with combo box items and are displayed in the combo selection box and drop list with the new extended combo box control (covered in Chapter 11, "Working with Images, Bitmaps, and Icons").

Those flat-looking toolbars and rebars you've seen in Office 98 and Internet Explorer 4 are now integrated into the Foundation Class library for you to use in your own applications (covered in Chapter 15, "Working with Toolbars and Status Bars").

You can now use the Internet Explorer from inside your application windows to view Web pages and HTML content (covered in Chapter 20, "Using List, Tree, Rich Edit, and HTML Views").

The powerful AppWizard can now create even more initial types of application framework so that your new application can have all the functionality of multiple-view applications like Windows Explorer before you even add a line of code (covered in Chapter 21, "Creating Multiple Views").

Component-based programming and the Distributed Component Object Model (DCOM) are new areas of major growth in modern software development (covered in Chapter 26, "Understanding OLE and COM Programming").

The very latest versions of APIs and SDKs such as the DirectX Game SDK are explained in Chapter 32, "Working with APIs and SDKs."

All these and many small and incidental features of the new Visual C++ 6.0 release are covered throughout this book.

Is This Book For You?

This book assumes that you have some experience of C++ programming. You don't need to have any experience of Windows or using the Microsoft Foundation Classes, but any knowledge you have will obviously help. You should have some familiarity with using the Windows 95/98 or NT operating systems and its graphical user interface.

You can either use this book to build your knowledge of writing Windows applications in Visual C++ from the ground up, chapter by chapter, or to dip into certain chapters to explore areas of specific interest to you.

Tim and I have both had the experience of books that seem to stop short of the particular things that we need to know in a real application. So we've pushed hard to go that extra mile to explain and show sample code that reflects problems and requirements encountered in real commercial applications from our own working experience. Armed with this book, you should be able write sophisticated and competitive software using one of the world's most flexible and enjoyable development environments: Visual C++ 6.0.

Conventions Used in This Book

To help enhance the clarity of information presented in this book, the following typographical conventions have been used:

- Words or phrases used for the first time appear in *italic* and are explained in the glossary. Any words that are displayed on the screen are shown in **bold.** Hotkeys and shortcut keys are shown with an **<u>underline</u>** denoting the significant key.

- All text that relates to code, or class names that you'll use in code, are shown in a `monotype typeface`.

- Listing lines that are too wide to fit into the width of a book page are shown on two lines connected with a code continuation character (➥). Such lines should be treated as one continuous line of code in your program.

We wish you every success and hope you enjoy writing applications in Visual C++ 6.0 with the aid of this book.

chapter 1

Designing and Creating a Visual C++ Program

Building a Windows application
using the AppWizard

Modifying the appearance of an
application using the resource editor

Adding code to customize the
behavior of an application

Many people who have never programmed a Windows application believe it to be an arduous endeavor. However, the right tool always makes a task easier, and you won't find a better tool than Visual C++ 6 to develop graphical programs. In fact, by using Visual C++ 6 it is possible to create and execute a new Windows application in less than one minute, but at first you'll take it a little slower.

Visual Studio alias

Visual Studio used to be called Developer Studio. You might also come across the term IDE (Integrated Development Environment), which is also sometimes used to refer to Visual Studio.

Starting Visual C++

To start Visual C++, from the desktop taskbar **Start** menu select **Microsoft Visual C++ 6.0**. When Visual C++ has started you will see the Microsoft Visual Studio window.

The Visual Studio window is displayed when you start Visual C++. Visual Studio is the name given to Visual C++'s user interface, which is displayed in Figure 1.1. Visual Studio is your working area or desktop. Don't be alarmed if your Visual Studio screen doesn't appear identical to our figures. Throughout the book you will learn how to locate the necessary options.

FIGURE 1.1
The Visual Studio window.

Creating a New Project

To begin a new application you first must create a project. A project is used to manage all the elements that comprise a Visual C++ program and produce a Windows application. Select **New** from the **File** menu to create a new project. The New dialog box appears as shown in Figure 1.2.

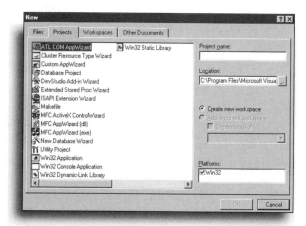

FIGURE 1.2
The New dialog box.

Selecting the Project Type

You must first specify the type of project you want to create. Click the **Projects** tab in the New dialog box if it is not already selected. This displays a list of all the types of projects you can create. For the example in this chapter, select **MFC AppWizard (exe)** from the list of project types. Selecting this option means your project will produce a standard Windows executable program.

Naming Projects and Choosing Their Locations

Every project needs a name. You specify the name in the **Project Name** box in the New dialog box. For this example, in the New dialog box type Minute in the **Project Name** box.

What does MFC stand for?

Visual C++ comes supplied with the Microsoft Foundation Class library. The MFC library is a set of predefined C++ classes. AppWizard produces a skeleton application by creating classes derived from MFC library classes. The use of the foundation classes is demonstrated throughout this book.

The **Location** box is used to specify the directory in which your project files will be placed. You do not need to change the location for this example.

The path initially displayed in the **Location** box depends on settings you chose when Visual C++ was installed. To alter the location, either edit the path directly or click the button to the right of the **Location** box. The default location is based on the project name; for example, C:\Program Files\Microsoft Visual Studio\MyProjects\Minute.

Using the AppWizard

After checking the settings of the New dialog box, click **OK** to start the creation of your project. You let AppWizard begin your coding for you. AppWizard's task in life is to create a bare-bones program for you to extend. It does this by allowing you to specify the kind of program you require and then uses the *MFC library* to generate files that together constitute a Visual Studio project.

SEE ALSO
➤ *For more details on how to create a dialog-based application see page 44*

Using the Basic AppWizard Options

The AppWizard dialog (shown in Figure 1.3) allows you to choose one of three types of application interface. For the Minute project you will use a dialog-based interface. Select the **Dialog Based** radio button. You can also select the language that will be used for your resources. You do not need to alter the setting of the **Language** combo box for the Minute program.

You have now specified all the information AppWizard requires to create the project. Click the **Finish** button. The New Project Information dialog appears as in Figure 1.4.

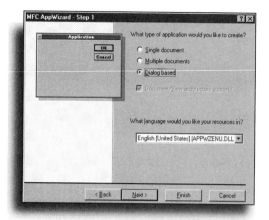

FIGURE 1.3
The MFC AppWizard –
Step 1 dialog box for
selecting the project
type.

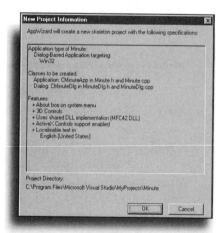

FIGURE 1.4
The New Project
Information dialog box.

AppWizard shows you this dialog box to confirm the details of the project it is about to create. You can see the names of the C++ classes in the project and the names of the files to be created. You can also see from the Features list the functionality AppWizard will provide. Click **OK** on the New Project Information dialog box.

AppWizard has completed its task and you now have the newly created Minute project open in Visual Studio. At this stage, even though you haven't even seen one line of C++ source code you have a complete and fully operational Windows application.

Starting again with AppWizard

AppWizard is used only to create new projects. You cannot return to the AppWizard option dialog boxes for an existing project. If you find you have chosen incorrectly and want to begin again with AppWizard, you must first remove the existing project. To remove a project, delete the project's directory. For example, to start again with the Minute project use Explorer to delete the C:\Program Files\ Microsoft Visual Studio \MyProjects\ Minute directory.

The left pane in the Visual Studio display is called the *workspace pane*. You can see that after the project has been created the workspace pane has three tabs: **ClassView**, **ResourceView**, and **FileView**. These tabs enable you to navigate to any part of the project. You can alter the size of the workspace pane and other panes that appear within Visual Studio by clicking the edge of the pane and moving the mouse while keeping the mouse button pressed.

Building and Executing the Application

You perform the build process to produce the Windows executable file for your project. For the Minute project the file will be named Minute.exe. After you have this file you can execute it from within Visual Studio.

Visual C++ executables are standard Windows EXE files

The Minute.exe file is like any other Windows executable file. It can therefore be executed from Explorer, or you can create a shortcut for it and place it on the desktop window.

Choosing the Configuration to Build

You can set Visual Studio to create either a *debug version* or a *release version* of the executable file. This is known as the *build configuration*. By default a debug version will be built; use this default setting in all examples unless specifically instructed otherwise. You do not need to change the configuration for the Minute program. By default, Visual Studio will build an application that includes debug information. Debug information enables you to step through the code as it is being executed and check the content of variables. However, including debug information increases the size of the executable file and produces a performance penalty. The release configuration builds the executable without debug information and is typically used when the application is shipped to a customer.

SEE ALSO
➤ *To learn more about debugging projects, see page 705*

Performing the Compile and Link Process

The build process performs the task of compiling the individual C++ files within a project and then linking the result together to form the executable file. To build the Minute project, click the **Build** button 🖮 or from the **Build** menu select **Build Minute.exe** or use the (F7) shortcut.

Minute.exe is located in the /Debug subdirectory under the /Minute project directory. This subdirectory also contains the object files of the programs within the project. A /Debug subdirectory has been created because you chose to build a debug configuration, a release configuration would place these files in a /Release subdirectory. The **Build** tab of the Output pane shows details during the build process. If the source code contained any errors they would appear on the **Build** tab as seen in Figure 1.5. Because you let AppWizard write all your code there should be no errors.

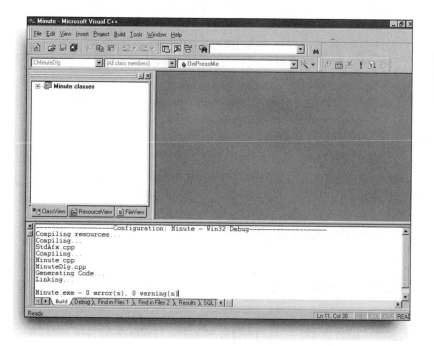

FIGURE 1.5
Building the Minute project.

Running an Application

To execute the application, click the Execute button ❗ or from the **Build** menu select **Ex̲ecute Minute.exe** or use the Ctrl+F5 shortcut. The main window of your application will appear as shown in Figure 1.6.

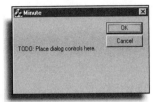

FIGURE 1.6
The Minute
application.

Understanding the Windows Interface

Congratulations! You have created a Windows application written in C++. You will see that it already includes some of the standard interface features used in virtually all Windows programs. The application window has two buttons, **OK** and **Cancel**, and displays some text. It also has a title bar that displays an associated icon, the application name, and a close button. The title bar also has a system menu and can be used to drag the window around the screen by clicking and holding down the left mouse button.

Click on the MFC image in the top-left corner of the Minute dialog. From the system menu that appears select **About Minute**. You will see that your program even has a second dialog titled About Minute to display information about itself as shown in Figure 1.7.

Click **OK** on the About Minute dialog box to close it. Click **OK** on the Minute dialog box to end the application.

FIGURE 1.7
The Minute application's
About dialog.

Modifying the Application Interface

The visual elements of a project are called *resources*. For example, dialog boxes, icons, and menus are resources. The aptly named resource editor in Visual Studio is the tool used to design the various resource types and modify what the application actually looks like.

Adding a Button Control

Before a new button can be added you must first open the dialog template.

Opening the Minute dialog template

1. Select the **ResourceView** tab of the project workspace pane. The project resources list appears.

2. Expand the list of resources by clicking the + sign to the left of **Minute Resources** and expand the **Dialog** folder. Two dialog identifiers, IDD_ABOUTBOX and IDD_MINUTE_DIALOG, appear as shown in Figure 1.8.

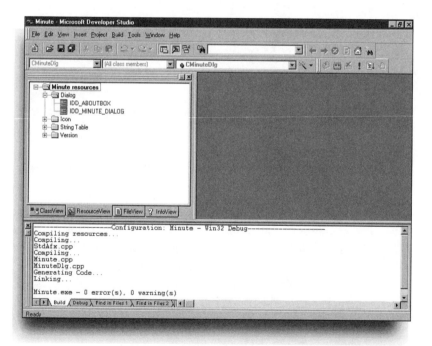

FIGURE 1.8
The Dialog item IDs in the ResourceView.

3. Double-click the IDD_MINUTE_DIALOG identifier. The template of the Minute application's main dialog window should appear and look like Figure 1.9. How the dialog appears in

the resource editor is how it will appear when you execute the program. You can now modify the dialog template using the resource editor.

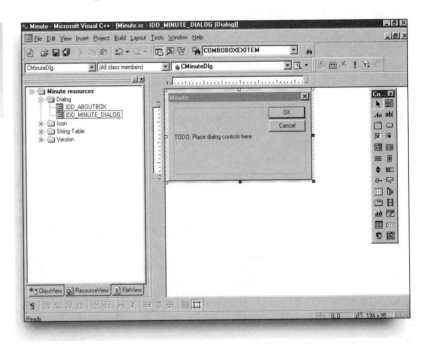

FIGURE 1.9

The IDD_MINUTE_ DIALOG dialog template resource.

Next you must add a new button to the Minute dialog template.

Adding a button to the Minute dialog template

1. Before adding the button remove the TODO static text control that appears in the center of the Minute dialog template. Click the text TODO: place dialog controls here; a formatting rectangle appears around the text (see Figure 1.10). Press the Delete key on your keyboard. The text control is removed from the dialog box layout.

2. Select the Button control from the Controls toolbox as shown in Figure 1.11.

3. Move the mouse over the dialog template. While you're over the template the cursor will change to a cross to indicate where the new button is to be placed. Position the cross

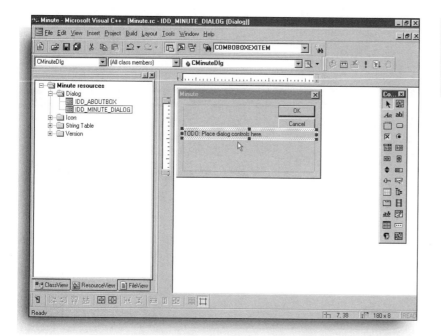

FIGURE 1.10
Removing the default text from the dialog box.

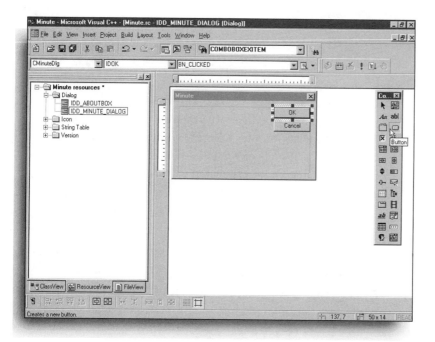

FIGURE 1.11
Selecting the Button control type from the toolbox.

away from the **OK** and **Cancel** buttons and then click with the mouse. A new button will appear labeled **Button1** as shown in Figure 1.12.

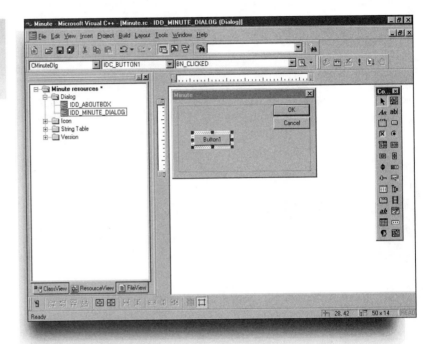

FIGURE 1.12

Adding a new button to the dialog box.

4. To change the caption of the button, first make sure you select the button with a formatting rectangle as in Figure 1.11. If the button isn't selected, select it by clicking on it. Type Press Me. As you type, the Push Button Properties dialog box will appear as shown in Figure 1.13.

5. Type IDC_PRESS_ME in the **ID** combo box on the Push Button Properties dialog box, replacing the default IDC_BUTTON1. This makes the identifier of the button more meaningful.

6. Make sure your Push Button Properties dialog box looks the same as shown in Figure 1.13.

7. Close the Push Button Properties dialog box. The label of the new button on the IDD_MINUTE_DIALOG template should now read **Press Me**.

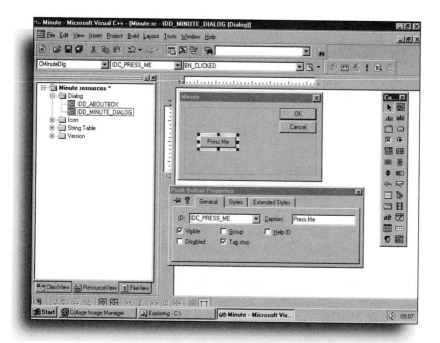

FIGURE 1.13
Changing the caption and
ID of the new button

SEE ALSO

➤ *For more information about dialog box design, see page 51*

➤ *For help on adding handler functions, see page 66*

Connecting Code to the Interface

Now that you have a new button just asking to be pressed, you
want it to react when it is. To do this you actually must write
some code, but don't get too excited because you must write
only one line yourself.

Attaching code to a button

1. Open the Minute dialog template in the resource editor. To
do this see the steps in the previous section, "Adding a
Button Control."

2. Right-click the **Press Me** button on the dialog template,
then from the context menu select the **Events** option. The

New Windows Message and Event Handlers dialog appears for the dialog class as in Figure 1.14.

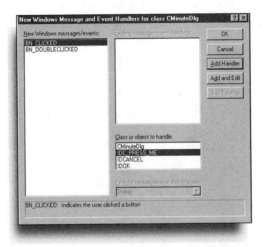

If the **Press Me** button is clicked (when the application is being executed), Windows sends the Minute dialog a message. You use the New Windows Message and Event Handlers dialog box to trap when this occurs and direct the program to specific code that handles the event.

3. Select **BN_CLICKED** in the **N**ew Windows Messages/Events list. Note that the first item in the list is selected by default.

4. Click the **A**dd and Edit button. The Add Member Function dialog box appears as in Figure 1.15. Here you are naming the function in the program that will be performed whenever the dialog box receives the BN_CLICKED message for the **Press Me** button.

5. Click **OK** to accept the default name OnPressMe. The body of the new function appears in the editor window as in Figure 1.16.

The function is added as a member of the CMinuteDlg class. This class was created and named automatically when AppWizard created the project. At the moment the function does nothing, so you must add some code.

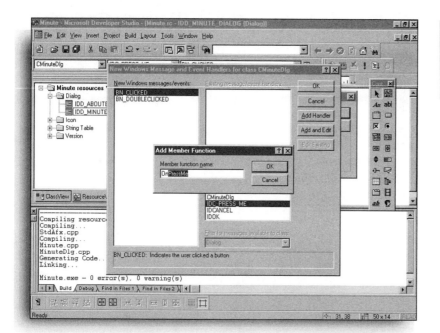

FIGURE 1.15

Naming the function that will handle the event.

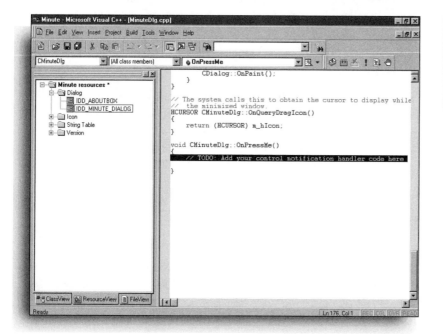

FIGURE 1.16

The skeleton OnPressMe() member function.

6. Edit the `OnPressMe` function so that it is identical to that shown in Listing 1.1.

LISTING 1.1 LST01_1.CPP—Implementing a Button-Clicked Message Handler

```
1 void CMinuteDlg::OnPressMe()
2 {
3     // TODO: Add your control notification handler code
4     MessageBox("Thanks, I needed that!");
5 }
```

You are using the predefined `MessageBox()` function to display the message `Thanks, I needed that!` in a small window whenever the **Press Me** button is clicked.

Testing the Changed Application

Changes are saved automatically when you build your project

Visual Studio automatically saves any modified files before starting to build the project, so you don't have to remember to save each file you edit.

Whenever you make modifications to a project and you want to see whether they work you must perform the build and run procedure. Click the **Build** button [⬚] or from the **Build** menu select **Build Minute.exe** or press F7. This rebuilds the window's executable file to include all changes to resources and source code.

If any errors occur during compilation they will appear in the **Build** tab of the Output pane as shown at the bottom of the Visual Studio screen in Figure 1.17. If you have errors double check that you have typed the line of code in the `OnPressMe()` function exactly as shown in Listing 1.1. Retype the line of code if necessary and click the **Build** button until no errors appear.

Click the Execute button [!] or from the **Build** menu select **Execute Minute.exe** or press Ctrl+F5. The Minute dialog should appear as shown in Figure 1.18.

Click the **Press Me** button. A message window should appear like Figure 1.19 displaying the message `Thanks, I needed that!`. Click **OK** on the message box. If you click the **Press Me** button again you will receive the message again. This happens because each time you click the button the program finds its way to the `OnPressMe()` function.

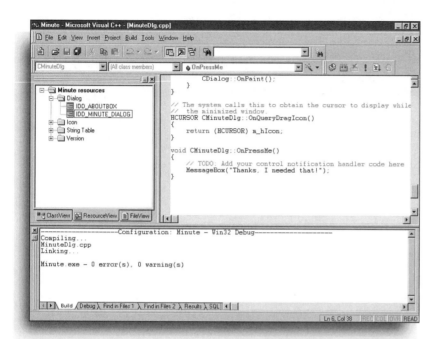

FIGURE 1.17
Errors appear in the
Build Tab.

FIGURE 1.18
Executing the Minute
application after
modifying the interface.

FIGURE 1.19
Testing that the code
responds properly.

Saving and Closing a Project

Using Visual Studio, you will get used to jumping between editing source files, modifying resources, and doing a hundred and one other things. It is a godsend, therefore, that the build process automatically saves any modifications you have made

The * modification indicator

The filename appears in the Visual Studio title bar with an asterisk next to it when there are unsaved modifications. An asterisk also appears next to the Resource folder on the **ResourceView** tab when there are unsaved resource changes.

before actually building the project. However, you can save a specific file at any time by clicking the **Save** button 🖫 . You can also save all the files you have modified by clicking the **Save All** button 🖫 .

You do not have to do anything to save a project. When you have finished working with a project you simply close it. To close a project, from the **File** menu select **Close Workspace** or simply exit Visual Studio.

chapter 2

Understanding the Development Environment

Learning the Developer Studio environment •

Navigating the Project Workspace window and its views •

Understanding settings and configurations for managing projects •

Working with Developer Studio

Customizing the Developer Studio environment

There are many ways in which the Developer Studio environment can be changed to suit the way you work. Menu options and toolbars can be customized by selecting the **Customize** option from the **Tools** menu. You can also customize the editor windows fonts, colors, and other preferences via the **Tools**, **Options** menu.

The Developer Studio environment used by Visual C++ looks somewhat complex at first. A quick count reveals there are well over 100 different menu options and almost as many toolbar buttons to choose from. Many of these lead to complicated dialog boxes and property sheets with numerous options. It's necessary for Developer Studio to be so functionally rich because it is used the world over to produce complex, professional applications. Don't be daunted. You must understand only a fraction of the overall functionality to be productive.

Opening an Existing Project

If you haven't already done so, start Visual C++ from the **Start** menu on your desktop window. In Chapter 1, "Designing and Creating a Visual C++ Program," you created a project named Minute. You'll reopen that project and use it for a guided tour around Developer Studio.

The quickest way to reopen a project is to use the **Recent Workspaces** list. To do this, click the **File** menu; then from the **Recent Workspaces** list select the required project. Note that only a limited number of projects will appear in this list.

To reopen a project that doesn't appear in the **Recent Workspaces** list, from the **File** menu select **Open Workspace**. The Open Workspace window appears, as shown in Figure 2.1.

Loading the last project on startup

The last project you worked on can be reopened automatically when Developer Studio starts. To do this, choose **Tools**, **Options**. Then select the **Workspace** tab and check **Reload Last Workspace on Startup**.

Browse to the directory used for the Minute project (if the default directory was used, the project's location should be C:\Program File\Microsoft Visual Sudio\MyProjects\Minute). Select the Minute.dsw file in the file list and click **Open**.

Whichever method you used, the project should now be open with the project title displayed in Developer Studio's title bar. Developer Studio has remembered where you were and has automatically opened the last source file edited (see Figure 2.2). To hide the Output window that appears at the bottom of the screen, click the small cross at the upper-left corner of the window (see the position of the mouse arrow in Figure 2.2).

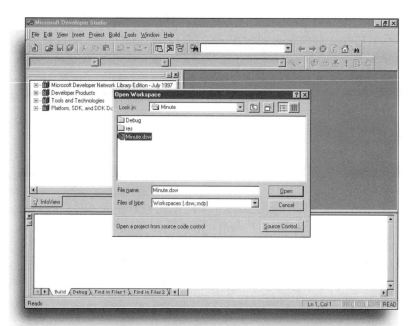

FIGURE 2.1

Opening an existing project by selecting the .dsw file.

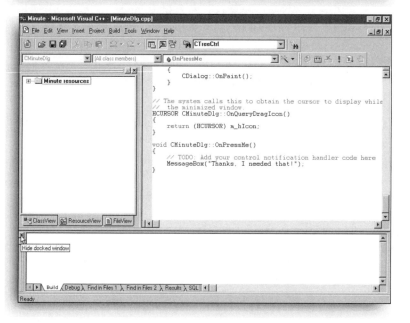

FIGURE 2.2

Developer Studio opens a project in the state it was last closed.

Using Subprojects

It is possible to have subprojects and create dependencies between projects. This way, changes to one project can cause all affected projects to be rebuilt.

You might be wondering about the term *workspace* and how it is different from a project. A workspace can contain several projects. In all the examples in this book, each workspace contains a single project, but in developing larger applications it is often convenient to manage several projects together.

The Project Workspace Window

The Project Workspace window is a dockable window. There are several of these (the Output window is one), and others appear when you are in debugging mode. To toggle between a floating or docking display, double-click the window title bar. You will probably find it easier to work with these windows docked. You can close the Project Workspace window by clicking the small close button in the top corner. To reopen it, from the **View** menu select **Workspace**. Each of the dockable windows behave similarly.

The Project Workspace window enables you to navigate between different views of your project. When a project is open three tabs are usually available at the bottom of the Workspace window: **ClassView**, **ResourceView**, and **FileView**. For projects developed for database applications there might also be a **DataView** tab.

The tabs at the foot of the window subdivide the project into its logical parts. Click a tab to toggle to its view. Each view displays a tree structure of items that represent elements in the project. You can expand or collapse the items within the tree by clicking the plus (+) or minus (-) symbol immediately to their left.

Using ClassView

Click the **ClassView** tab. The ClassView pane is displayed as shown in Figure 2.3.

This view displays all the classes used within the project. AppWizard created these classes when you initially created the project. Each item at the second level (excluding the Globals item) represents a class and displays the class name. When a class name item is expanded, each subitem represents either a member function or a member variable of that class. For example, under CMinuteDlg, you can see the OnPressMe() member function that was added in the example from Chapter 1. The small icons next to each item give additional information (see Table 2.1).

FIGURE 2.3
Selecting the **ClassView** tab enables you to manipulate the project classes.

TABLE 2.1 Icons displayed by ClassView items relate additional details

Icon	Meaning
	Class
	Public function
	Private function
	Protected function
	Private variable
	Protected variable
	Public variable

The majority of programming in a Visual C++ project relates to classes. The ClassView pane therefore is often the one used most frequently. From here you are able to navigate to any class, member function, or variable within the project. Double-clicking any item will open the relevant source code file in the editor window with the cursor positioned ready at the line the item represents.

Double-clicking a class name skips to the class definition. Double-clicking a member variable skips to the variable's definition. Double-clicking a member function skips to the top of the function definition in the class implementation file.

In addition to enabling you to maneuver around your project's classes, the ClassView pane offers many more capabilities via context menus. A *context menu* appears onscreen near the mouse pointer when an item is right-clicked. To display the context menu for an item on the ClassView tree, select the item using the right mouse button. The selected item is highlighted and the context menu appears onscreen next to it. Which context menu is displayed will depend on the type of item selected.

Click the `CMinuteDlg` class name to display the class context menu shown in Figure 2.4.

The Developer Studio title bar

The name of the file open in the active editor window is displayed in the Developer Studio title bar.

FIGURE 2.4

Selecting a ClassView item displays a context menu.

The context menu enables you to perform operations for the selected class. Selecting the **Go to Definition** option is the same as double-clicking the class name item, which skips to the class definition source file. Four options on the menu are used to add either functions or variables to the class. You'll use a couple of these in a moment, but first I'll briefly explain other options on the context menu.

Click the **References** option, and a message appears as shown in Figure 2.5.

Click **Yes** to generate the browse file. The project is automatically rebuilt. When complete, hide the Output window by clicking the small cross at the top-left corner.

Browse information makes available extra navigational aids that are available from ClassView's context menu.

The **References** option lists all the places in the project that refer to the selected item. For every reference, the source filename and line number is shown and you are able to skip directly to each line. The **Derived Classes** option displays details of the selected class and any classes derived from it. The **Base Classes** option, as you might have guessed, displays details of the selected class and all its base classes, including classes in the MFC library (see Figure 2.6).

When you click the context menu for member functions and variables, the **Calls** option lists all functions called by the selected member function, and the **Called By** option lists all places within the project where the function is called.

The **Group By Access** option on the context menu is used to sequence the members of the class. The members are listed in alphabetical order when the **Group By Access** option is unchecked; when checked, they are listed in access mode order—private, protected, and then public.

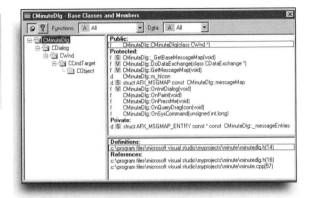

FIGURE 2.6

Selecting the **Base Classes** option shows the class hierarchy.

Adding class members without editing source code

The Add Member Variable and Add Member Function dialog boxes available via ClassView's context menu automatically add the necessary code lines to both the header and implementation source files of the chosen class.

Now you are going to modify the CMinuteDlg class. First, ensure the CMinuteDlg class is selected and the context menu displayed. Remember the context menu is displayed by right-clicking. From the context menu, select **Add Member Variable**. The Add Member Variable dialog box appears as shown in Figure 2.7. As its name implies, this dialog box is used to add a new variable to the class. You must specify the new variable type, name, and access mode.

Type int in the **Variable Type** box. Type m_nClickCount in the **Variable Declaration** box. Leave the access mode as **Public**. Here you are adding a variable of type integer called m_nClickCount to the CMinuteDlg class. This variable will be used to store a count of the times the **Press Me** button is clicked. When you have entered the details, click **OK**.

FIGURE 2.7

Adding a new member variable via ClassView.

The new variable should now be displayed in the ClassView pane as a subitem of the CMinuteDlg item. Double-click the m_nClickCount item. The editor window appears and the cursor is placed on the source code line that has been added to define the new variable.

Because this variable will count the number of times the **Press Me** button is clicked, it must have an initial value of zero. The appropriate place to initialize the variable is in the constructor of the CMinuteDlg class. To add the initialization code, double-click the CMinuteDlg constructor member function item (this is the first subitem of the CMinuteDlg class item). The editor window will skip to the relevant source file. To initialize the count variable, add the code at line 10 in Listing 2.1.

LISTING 2.1 LST02_1.CPP—Initializing a Member Variable in the Class Constructor

```
1  CMinuteDlg::CMinuteDlg(CWnd* pParent /*=NULL*/)
2  : CDialog(CMinuteDlg::IDD, pParent)
3  {
4      //{{AFX_DATA_INIT(CMinuteDlg)
5          // NOTE: the ClassWizard will add member
           ➥initialization here
6      //}}AFX_DATA_INIT
7      // Note that LoadIcon does not require a subsequent
        ➥DestroyIcon in Win32
8      m_hIcon = AfxGetApp()->LoadIcon(IDR_MAINFRAME);
9
10     m_nClickCount = 0; ──────①
11 }
```

Now the count is starting at zero; we must increment it each time the **Press Me** button is clicked. Double-click the OnPressMe() member function of the CMinuteDlg class. In the editor window, you'll see the function that you added in the Chapter 1 example. Remember that this function is performed when the BN_CLICKED message is sent to the dialog box for the IDC_PRESS_ME button.

To increment the count variable, add the code at line 5 in Listing 2.2.

LISTING 2.2 LST02_2.CPP—Counting How Many Times **Press Me** Is Clicked

```
1  void CMinuteDlg::OnPressMe() ──────①
2  {
```

continues...

Member variable naming convention

It's common practice (but not necessary) to distinguish class member variables by prefixing an **m_** to the variable name. To understand source code, it often helps to be able to pick out which variables are class members and which are local to a function. It's also common practice to identify the type of variable in the variable name. In the example, We use **n** to indicate that the variable stores a number.

① The variable m_nClickCount is initialized to zero in the dialog box class constructor.

① OnPressMe() is a message handler function that is called each time the IDC_PRESS_ME button is clicked.

② In addition to displaying a message to the user the function increments a variable to count the number of times the button is pressed.

LISTING 2.2 Continued

```
3      MessageBox("Thanks. I needed that.");
4
5      m_nClickCount++;  ────②
6  }
```

The count variable is now keeping track of the clicks. The next step is to add a new member function. Right-click the CMinuteDlg class item to display the context menu. Select **Add Member Function**. The Add Member Function dialog box appears (see Figure 2.8). This dialog box is used to add a member function to a class.

FIGURE 2.8

Adding a new member function via the ClassView context menu.

Specify the function type (this is the type of variable the function is to return). Type BOOL in the **Function Type** box. Here we are saying the function will return one of two states, either TRUE or FALSE.

We must give the function a name. Type ClickCountMessage in the **Function Declaration** box. If the new function requires parameters, these can also be typed in the **Function Declaration** box.

The **Public** access mode radio button should be selected and both the **Static** and **Virtual** check boxes should be left unchecked. Click **OK**.

The new function should now be displayed in the ClassView pane as a subitem of CMinuteDlg. The new function body should be visible in the editor window. Add the code from lines 3–18 of Listing 2.3.

Warning: adding members doesn't perform validation

No validation is performed when you add class members through the Add Member dialog boxes. For example, it's possible to create a function with a return type of BOO that will lead to compilation errors. Check that your syntax is correct before clicking **OK**.

LISTING 2.3 LST02_3.CPP—Depending on the Click Count an Appropriate Message Is Displayed

```
1  BOOL CMinuteDlg::ClickCountMessage()
2  {
3      if (m_nClickCount == 0)
4      {
5          MessageBox("You haven't clicked Press Me", "Don't Leave",
                ➥MB_ICONSTOP);          ———①
6          return FALSE;   ———②
7      }
8      if (m_nClickCount > 1)
9      {
10         CString str;
11         str.Format("Press Me was clicked %d times", m_nClickCount);
12         MessageBox(str);                                    ③
13     }
14     else
15     {
16         MessageBox("Press Me was clicked once");
17     }
18     return TRUE;   ———④
19 }
```

① The MessageBox() function has several styles. Here the MB_ICONSTOP flag is passed, which causes a stop sign to be displayed alongside the message text.

② FALSE is returned because the count variable is zero.

③ CString's Format() function is used to formulate a string message that is then passed to MessageBox().

④ TRUE is returned if the count variable is one or greater.

Here we're checking the value of m_nClickCount and using its value to display an appropriate message.

In the first call to the MessageBox() function on line 5, two extra parameters are passed. The first of these, Don't Leave, is the message box title. The MB_ICONSTOP is a flag setting that causes a stop sign icon to be displayed.

On line 10, the str variable is of class type CString, which is one of several useful utility classes provided by MFC. CString handles many common programming tasks involving text manipulation. If you're familiar with C programming, the CString Format() function (used in line 11) behaves in the same manner as the C function printf(). Finally, note the function returns FALSE (at line 6) if the count is zero and TRUE (at line 18) for any other value.

Our new function is complete but as yet it's not being used by any part of the program. This is covered in the next section.

Using ResourceView

Click the **ResourceView** tab at the base of the Project Workspace window. A list of the resources within the project appears (see Figure 2.9).

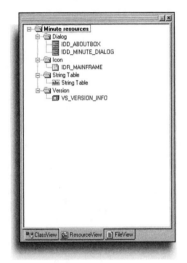

FIGURE 2.9

Selecting the **ResourceView** tab enables you to manipulate the project resources.

You have already used the ResourceView briefly to create a new button. Here is an overview of the various other types of resources.

This view displays all the resources used within the project. The term *Resource* encompasses the visual elements of a project. For example, dialog boxes are resources, as are menus and icons.

Like ClassView, the ResourceView pane displays a context menu when an item is right-clicked. From the **Minute Resources** context menu, select **Insert**. The Insert Resource dialog box appears as shown in Figure 2.10. Here you can see the various types of resources that can be used in a Visual C++ project.

An *accelerator table* is a list of associations between a keyboard combination and a program command. A common name used to describe an accelerator is a shortcut. A *shortcut* is a quicker way to perform a command than selecting it from a menu. For example, I have used Ctrl+X many times while writing this manuscript and find it far more convenient than selecting **Cut** from the **Edit** menu.

Separating resources from code

The reason resources such as menus, dialog boxes, and string table are separated from the underlying source code is so they can be altered independently from the source. This makes it much easier to produce international applications. For example, all the strings in a string table can be translated into a second language without the need to alter any source code.

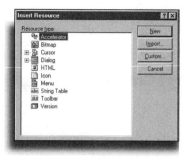

A *bitmap* resource is an image of any size that is made up of dots.
Each dot can be a different color. Bitmaps are used to display the
images you see on toolbars, and you see a larger bitmap image
on Visual C++'s startup screen every time you start it.

A *cursor* is an image resource. Cursors are primarily used as
mouse pointer images (the standard Windows cursor is an
arrow). The distinguishing feature of a cursor is that it has a hot
spot, which is used to keep track of its screen location.

An *icon* is also an image resource. The Minute project has an
icon named IDR_MAINFRAME. Double-click the IDR_MAINFRAME item,
and the standard MFC icon will open in the editor window.

A *dialog resource* is a template of a window that can contain the
other resource types, such as menus and buttons. Editing dialog
resources is covered in Chapter 3, "Creating and Designing
Dialog Boxes."

A *menu resource* contains exactly what its name implies, a menu.
Typically, an application has a menu at the top of its main window (as Developer Studio has), but an application can have several menus. For example, a menu resource could be added to a
project and used in the application as a context menu.

A *string table resource* should contain all the text items used
within an application. Each item is given a unique identifier,
which is used to refer to the string within the source code (see
Figure 2.11).

The reason all strings are entered in a string table and not
directly in source files is to make translation to different languages easier. If all the text used within an application is in a

string table, a second string table can be produced in a different language. When the application starts, the appropriate string table can be used.

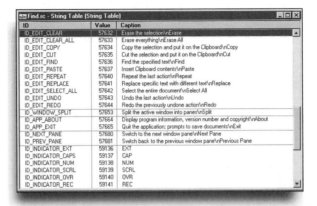

FIGURE 2.11

An example of a string table.

A *toolbar resource* contains a set of buttons. Typically, each button represents a menu command. Images can be drawn on the buttons using bitmaps, and buttons can have an associated ToolTip that is shown when the mouse hovers over the button.

A *version resource* contains data about the application such as the company that produced it, the product name, a version number, and so on. The information is in a standard format that enables it to be accessed from other applications.

New resources can be added at any time. When added, they are automatically given a unique name. For example, a new dialog box template might be given the name IDD_DIALOG1. Programmers normally alter the generated name to one that is more representative of the resource in the context of the program, as we did when we altered IDC_BUTTON1 to IDC_PRESS_ME. To view the names of all the resources in the project, select **Resource Symbols** from the **View** menu. The Resource Symbols dialog box appears (see Figure 2.12).

You can use the Resource Symbols dialog box to locate a particular resource from its symbolic name by selecting the name in the list and clicking the **View Use** button.

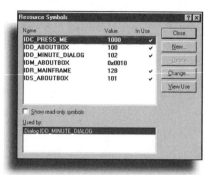

Each resource within the project can be edited by double-clicking its name in the ResourceView pane. The tools and options available within the editor window alter in accordance with the type of resource being edited. Creating and editing the various resource types is covered at the appropriate time throughout the chapters ahead.

Now we will complete the example you have been working on. Using the ResourceView pane, follow these steps.

Overriding the behavior of dialog buttons

1. Double-click the **IDD_MINUTE_DIALOG** item to open the dialog template.

2. Double-click the **OK** button.

3. The Add Member Function dialog box appears. Click **OK** to accept the default Member Function Name: OnOK. The new skeleton function is created and shown in the editor window, ready for code to be added.

4. Edit the default OnOK() function as shown in Listing 2.4.

5. Double-click the **IDD_MINUTE_DIALOG** item to open the dialog template again.

6. Double-click the **Cancel** button.

7. Click **OK** to accept the default Member Function Name: OnCancel.

8. Edit the default OnCancel() function as shown in Listing 2.5.

① This function overrides the default implementation of CDialog::OnOk(), which is the message handler for the **OK** button.

② The base class implementation of OnOk() is called, which will close the dialog box.

LISTING 2.4 LST02_4.CPP—Overriding the Default *OnOk* Function

```
1  void CMinuteDlg::OnOK()  ──────① 
2  {
3      if ( ClickCountMessage() == TRUE )
4      {
5          CDialog::OnOK();  ──────②
6      }
7  }
```

① This function overrides the default implementation of CDialog::OnCancel(), which is the message han-dler for the **Cancel** button.

② The base class implementation of OnCancel() is called to close the dialog box.

LISTING 2.5 LST02_5.CPP—Overriding the Default *OnCancel()* Function

```
1  void CMinuteDlg::OnCancel()  ──────①
2  {
3      if ( ClickCountMessage() == TRUE )
4      {
5          CDialog::OnCancel();  ──────②
6      }
7  }
```

You have added two functions. The first overrides the default CDialog::OnOK() function and the second overrides CDialog::OnCancel(). Both functions cause the dialog box to close, but now they will be called only if the ClickCountMessage() function returns TRUE. If you're still unsure about what you just did, build and run the project.

Without clicking the **Press Me** button, try clicking either **OK** or **Cancel**. You should see the message shown in Figure 2.13, and instead of terminating, the application remains running.

FIGURE 2.13

Displaying a message when **OK** or **Cancel** is clicked.

Now try clicking the **Press Me** button a few times and then click **OK** or **Cancel**. This time you should see a message telling you how many times you clicked **Press Me** (see Figure 2.14). When you click **OK**, the program should terminate.

FIGURE 2.14
Testing the count
message.

Using FileView

Click the **FileView** tab at the base of the Project Workspace
window. A list of the files included in the project appears (see
Figure 2.15).

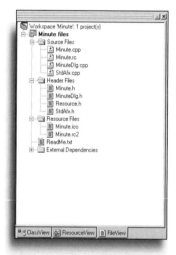

FIGURE 2.15
Selecting the **FileView**
tab lets you navigate to
the project files.

The files are organized into folders depending on their type (the
folders don't represent the location of files on the hard disk). To
open a file in the editor window, double-click the filename. If
you try opening the Minute.rc file, the ResourceView pane will
be selected because the .rc file stores information about
resources. For a list of the common types of files found in a
Visual C++ project, see Table 2.2.

Rebuilding the ClassWizard information file

If you delete the .clw file from your project directory, the next time you attempt to use ClassWizard you will receive a prompt asking whether you want to rebuild the file. This is some-times necessary if not all your classes or control identifiers are visible on the ClassWizard dialog box.

TABLE 2.2 Common file types used in Developer Studio

Extension	Type	Description
.dsw	Workspace file	Combines details of projects into a workspace.
.dsp	Project file	Stores details of a project and replaces the .mak file.
.clw	ClassWizard file	Stores class information used by the ClassWizard tool.
.ncb	No Compile Browser file	Holds details used by ClassView and ClassWizard toolbar.
.opt	Options file	Stores customized workspace display options.
.cpp	C++ source file	Contains implementation code.
.h	C++ header file	Contains definition and class declaration code.
.rc	Resource script file	Stores details of resources such as dialog boxes and menus.
.rc2	Resource script file	Used to include resources into several projects.
.bmp	Bitmap file	Stores bitmap images.
.ico	Icon file	Stores icon images.

This is by no means a definitive list. If you open a project directory with Explorer, you'll see several other types of files. Some are temporary files used by Developer Studio; others depend on the type of project and what it contains.

The **FileView** context menu enables you to perform several useful functions. You can compile individual programs or a selection of programs within your project. This is useful when you're working in a specific area and don't need to build the entire project. You can also add files to the project from other projects.

Removing files from the project

To remove a file from the project, locate the filename in the FileView tree and simply press the Delete key. Note that this only removes the file from the Visual Studio project and does not physically delete the file from the disk.

Managing Projects

Once, one of the most exacting tasks when writing applications in C or C++ was maintaining the makefile. The makefile is responsible for telling the compiler many detailed instructions on how the programs are to be compiled and which programs are to be linked in what order. Now Developer Studio manages this complex task for you in the background and most of the time you won't know it is doing it. In fact, Visual C++ 6.0 projects don't have a makefile, but you can generate one if you want by selecting **Export Makefile** from the **Project** menu.

Project Settings

You can modify the compiler settings and perform many other project management tasks using the Project Settings dialog box. To open the Project Settings dialog box, from the **Project** menu select **Settings**. You will see a tabbed dialog box as shown in Figure 2.16.

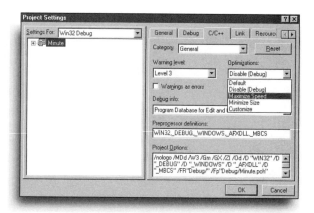

FIGURE 2.16
Compilation, linking, and other facilities are available on the Project Settings dialog box.

Here are just a few of the useful options available:

- On the **Debug** tab you can specify command-line arguments for the program to use when it is executed.
- On the **C++** tab you can add directives for the preprocessor and select compiler optimization settings.
- On the **Link** tab you can specify the directory in which the executable file is to be placed.

Additional Configurations

Our Minute project already has two configurations—a Debug configuration and a Release configuration. It's possible to create your own project configurations. For example, you could create configurations with different optimization settings for performance testing. To create or remove configurations, from the **Build** menu select **Configurations**. In the vast majority of cases, the default Debug and Release configurations are sufficient.

Creating and Designing Dialog Boxes

Editing an existing dialog box and
creating new dialog box templates

Learning how to set the display properties
of dialog boxes and their controls

Working with the resource editor tools
to position and align controls

Understanding how functionality can
be added during dialog box design

The dialog box is one of the weapons most used in the armory of any Windows developer because it's useful for a variety of purposes. Dialog boxes can be used simply to relay messages to the user, as you have already seen in the case of MFC's `MessageBox()`. However, the most common use of dialog boxes is in allowing users to enter information into the application. Normally, the user has a chance to confirm or cancel the details entered. Cancellation simply closes the dialog box as if it had never been opened; confirmation causes an action to take place using the entered data, and then often, but not always, closes the dialog box.

Creating dialog boxes used in Visual C++ applications is performed in two stages. The first stage is the design stage; this involves creating the dialog box template and adding the required controls. The second stage is the programming stage, which involves connecting the dialog box and its controls with classes and functions in C++ code. The first stage (the design stage) can be achieved without writing a single line of code, and this is the subject of this chapter.

Creating Dialog Box Templates

Use AppWizard as the starting point of your applications

The AppWizard is a powerful tool used to generate a new working project. AppWizard enables you to specify many customizable features and then build these into the source files it creates. AppWizard-generated projects are fully functional; they can be built and executed without requiring any additional code.

Although it's possible to create and design dialog boxes with Developer Studio without first creating a project, it is much more common to add and edit dialog boxes of an existing project. You will first use AppWizard to create a new project for a dialog-based application. While doing this, you'll examine some options offered by AppWizard.

Creating a new dialog-based application project

1. Click the **File** menu and select **New**.
2. Select the **Projects** tab; from the list of project types, select **MFC AppWizard (exe)**.
3. Click the **Project Name** box and enter the project name: Person. Your New Project dialog box should look like Figure 3.1.

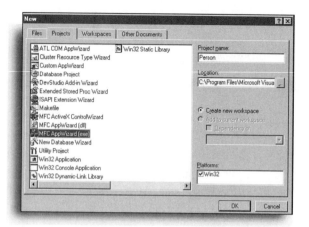

FIGURE 3.1
Creating a new project.

4. Click **OK**. Now you should see the MFC AppWizard – Step 1 dialog box.

5. Select the **Dialog Based** radio button.

6. Click **Next** to move to the MFC AppWizard – Step 2 dialog box.

   This step enables you to customize certain elements of your application before it has even been created. You can see the effect of selecting or deselecting each visual feature in the diagrams on the left side. You can also alter the title of the main dialog box. Other options deal with enabling support for more advanced features. Ensure the options are set as shown in Figure 3.2.

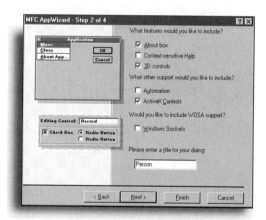

FIGURE 3.2
Choosing features and support options.

7. Click **Next** to move to the MFC AppWizard – Step 3 dialog box.

   This step asks whether you would like AppWizard to add comments to the code that it generates for you. The comments are explanatory and aid in understanding where to add your own code. I always answer **Yes, Please** to include comments.

   By default, AppWizard creates a program that uses a DLL (dynamic link library) version of MFC. This is advantageous because the executable (.exe) file resulting from the project will be smaller because it will look to other files on the disk for all the MFC functions it requires.

8. Click **Next** to move to the MFC AppWizard – Step 4 dialog box shown in Figure 3.3.

FIGURE 3.3

Reviewing the generated class and filenames.

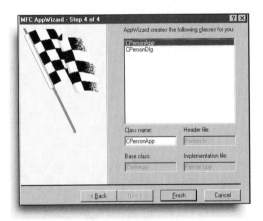

On this final step you see the class names and filenames that AppWizard will generate. If you aren't happy with these names, you can alter them using the edit boxes at the bottom of the dialog box.

9. Click **Finish**.

10. Click **OK** on the New Project Information dialog box and AppWizard will create the new project and source files.

Now you have your project and can edit its resources. To do this, on the Workspace window click the **ResourceView** tab, and then expand the items by clicking the **+** (plus) sign to their left.

You'll see under the Dialog folder that AppWizard has created two dialog box templates. The IDD_PERSON_DIALOG template is the application's main dialog box, which AppWizard created because you chose a dialog-based application. The IDD_ABOUTBOX template is the dialog box that is accessed from the **Help About** menu option, and shows the application's icon and version number. First you'll do some simple editing to the AppWizard-created dialog box; then you'll see how to insert new dialog boxes into your project and use some of the more advanced features of the resource editor.

Editing the application's main dialog box template

1. From the ResourceView pane, double-click the **IDD_PERSON_DIALOG** item. The dialog template will appear in the resource editor window.

2. Click the text **TODO: Place Your Controls Here**, and then press the Delete key. The text item will be removed.

3. Click the **Cancel** button, and then press the Delete key. The **Cancel** button will be removed.

4. Click **OK**.

5. Click the right mouse button and a context menu will appear.

6. Select **Properties** from the context menu. The Push Button Properties dialog box appears.

7. Select the **General** tab; then in the **Caption** box replace the word **OK** with **Exit**.

    Here you are changing the label of a control without affecting how the control operates within the program. Programs identify resources by their IDs. In this case IDOK is the ID that is used when adding code to respond to messages of a particular control. The IDOK is a predefined MFC control ID that causes the CDialog:OnOk() function to be called, which performs the necessary code to close the dialog box.

8. Close the Push Button Properties dialog box. The dialog box should now look like Figure 3.4.

> **The resource.h file**
>
> By default the #defines of the project's resource IDs are located in the resouce.h header file. This file can be viewed and edited by selecting the **Resource Symbols** option on the **View** menu.

FIGURE 3.4
Editing the properties of an existing control.

You have carried out some minor modifications to an existing dialog box generously created by AppWizard, but what if you want a completely new dialog box?

Creating a new dialog box template

1. Select the ResourceView pane of the Project Workspace window.

2. Right-click the **Dialog** folder. A context menu appears.

3. Select **Insert Dialog** from the context menu. A new dialog template is created and opened in the resource editor window. The new dialog box is generated with default **OK** and **Cancel** buttons.

SEE ALSO

➤ *For more information about the ResourceView tab, see page 34*

Setting the Dialog Box ID

Dialog box naming conventions

It's common practice to prefix the ID of a dialog box with **IDD_** to distinguish it from other types of resources.

On inserting a new dialog box template, the resource editor ensures that it is given a unique ID. The generated ID will be IDD_DIALOG followed by a number, and will appear under the Dialog folder on the ResourceView pane. The first thing you are likely to do after inserting a dialog box is to alter the generated ID to something more meaningful. For example, if the dialog box will be used to record book sale details, a likely ID could be IDD_BOOK_SALES, which will be much easier to recognize than IDD_DIALOG9.

Alter the ID of the new dialog box

1. With the right button, click the dialog template away from any controls (click the title bar if the dialog box has one). A context menu appears.

   By ensuring a control is not selected when displaying the context menu, you're able to access the properties of the dialog box itself.

2. Select **Properties** from the context menu. The Dialog Properties dialog box appears (see Figure 3.5).

FIGURE 3.5
Giving a dialog box a meaningful ID.

3. Select the **General** tab of the Dialog Properties dialog box.

4. In the **ID** box, replace IDD_DIALOG1 by typing IDD_PERSONALITY.

Working with Dialog General Properties

Modifying properties is one of the most common tasks of dialog box design. It is a good idea therefore to keep the Dialog Properties dialog box open by using the pin in the upper-left corner, as shown in Figure 3.6. This simply means the Dialog Properties dialog box will remain open when you click elsewhere, for example, on the resource edit window. Developer Studio has several other "pinable" dialog boxes.

FIGURE 3.6
Pinning the property dialog box open.

① The pin button is pressed to keep the dialog box open.

49

The type of selected resource determines the tabs and options available on the Property dialog box. Using the options on the Property dialog box, you can alter the characteristics of the overall dialog box and each control it contains. The second most likely property you'll change when first creating a dialog box is its caption. The dialog box caption is the text that appears in the title bar.

Alter the caption by typing `Personality Dialog` in the **C**aption box. You should see the new title appear on the dialog template in the resource editor window as you type it.

Other options available on the **General** tab include changing the font used by the dialog box. If you select a font size larger than 8, you will find that the entire dialog box becomes larger. The size of the dialog box is calculated from the average width and the height of the dialog box font. The default font is MS Sans Serif size 8 and it is uncommon for dialog boxes to use any other font.

X **Pos** and **Y** **Pos** specify the location of the dialog box when it first appears. The positions relate to the dialog box's parent window. Zeros in these coordinates mean the dialog box appears in the center of its parent window.

Using Dialog Box Styles

You'll see on the Dialog Properties dialog box there are three tabs that deal with styles. Click the **Styles** tab to select the first of these (see Figure 3.7).

Dialog units

A dialog unit is the name given to the size measurement used within dialog boxes that is based on the dialog's font. You may also come across the term DLU, which stands for Dialog Unit.

FIGURE 3.7
Selecting dialog box styles.

You must be aware that some style settings affect others. If you uncheck the **Title Bar** style, this not only removes the title bar but it also disables the system menu options and will remove your caption. If you subsequently recheck **Title Bar**, you'll need to enter your caption again. A similar problem can result if you alter the dialog border.

Warning about dialog style settings

Setting some dialog styles automatically causes other style settings to be de-selected. It is also possible to set a dialog's properties in a way that renders it unusable.

You should also be aware that it's easy to render a dialog box useless or even completely invisible by setting style options, which can be a very tricky problem to solve. If you suspect you have such a problem, the easiest way to check is to compare the style settings with a dialog box that works correctly. In the vast majority of cases, the default style settings are recommended.

Adding and Positioning Controls

Dialog boxes are nothing without controls. Whenever a dialog box template is open in the resource editor, a **Layout** menu is added to Developer Studio. You should also see a couple of extra toolbars. One is the Dialog toolbar (see Figure 3.8). The other is the Controls toolbar (see Figure 3.9).

FIGURE 3.8

The Dialog toolbar helps position controls.

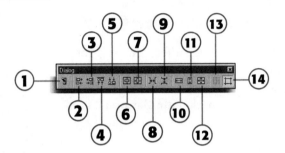

①	Test	⑧	Space Across
②	Align Left	⑨	Space Down
③	Align Right	⑩	Make Same Width
④	Align Top	⑪	Make Same Height
⑤	Align Bottom	⑫	Make Same Size
⑥	Center Vertical	⑬	Toggle Grid
⑦	Center Horizontal	⑭	Toggle Guides

FIGURE 3.9
The Controls toolbar
enables controls to be
added to a dialog box.

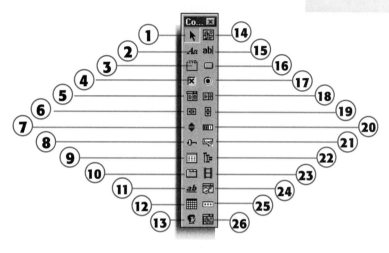

①	Select	⑭	Picture Control
②	Static Text	⑮	Edit Control
③	Group Text	⑯	Button Control
④	Check Box	⑰	Radio Button
⑤	Combo Box	⑱	List Box
⑥	Horizontal Scroll Bar	⑲	Vertical Scroll Bar
⑦	Spin Control	⑳	Progress Control
⑧	Slider Control	㉑	Hot Key
⑨	List Control	㉒	Tree Control
⑩	Tab Control	㉓	Animate Control
⑪	Rich Edit Control	㉔	Date/Time Picker
⑫	Calendar Control	㉕	IP Address Control
⑬	Custom Control	㉖	Extended Combo Box

If the Dialog toolbar or the Controls toolbar aren't visible, they can be displayed by following one of the following sets of steps.

Displaying the Dialog toolbar

1. From the **Tools** menu select **Customize**. The Customize dialog box appears.

2. Select the **Toolbars** tab.

3. In the **Toolbars** list, check **Dialog**.

4. Click **Close**.

Displaying the Control toolbar

1. From the **Tools** menu select **Customize**. The Customize dialog box appears.

2. Select the **Toolbars** tab.

3. In the **Toolbars** list, check **Controls**.

4. Click **Close**.

The new extended combo box

The extended combo box control enables you to add images to the standard combo box.

Each image on the Controls toolbar represents a different type of control. If you position the mouse pointer over an image, a small box appears describing the control type. You choose the type of control you want to add to the dialog box by clicking its image. When a control is selected, its image is drawn indented. The arrow image at the top-left of the toolbox deselects the control and returns the mouse to its normal behavior. You add a control to the dialog box by first selecting its image and then clicking the dialog box template.

Before adding some controls to your new dialog box, make the overall dialog box larger to give yourself some more space. To change the size of the overall dialog box, follow these steps.

Enlarging the dialog box

1. Click the edge of the dialog box template. A rectangle appears around the edges of the template with sizing points as shown in Figure 3.10.

2. Click the sizing point on the bottom-right corner, keeping the mouse button pressed.

   You can alter any dialog box dimension by clicking the appropriate sizing point. For example, if you want to alter the width of the dialog box, click the sizing point on the right edge of the dialog box. The mouse pointer alters to indicate which dimension(s) will be affected.

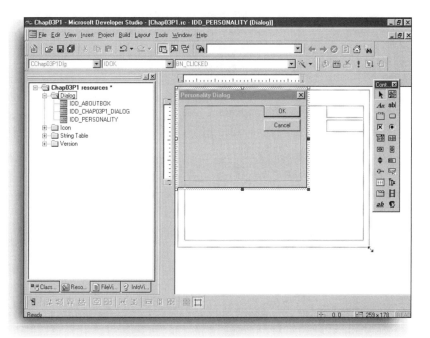

FIGURE 3.10

Increasing the size of a dialog box.

3. Move the mouse, keeping the button pressed. An outline of the new dialog box size is shown as the mouse is moved.

4. Release the mouse button when the dialog box is the required size. The dialog box is redrawn.

Now you're going to add some controls to the dialog box. To add the required controls, perform the following steps.

Adding controls to the dialog box

1. On the Controls toolbar, select the static text control.

2. Static text controls can be used simply to display some written information. Their most common use, however, is to act as labels or titles of other controls on the dialog box.

3. Click the dialog box template toward the upper-left corner. A static text control appears on the dialog box, with the default text Static.

4. Type `First name`. The text in the static control should change automatically.

5. On the Controls toolbar select the edit control.

6. Click the dialog box template to the right of the **First name** text you have just added (the exact position does not matter). An edit control appears.

7. On the Controls toolbar select the static text control.

8. Click the dialog box template under the **First name** text. A new static control appears.

9. Type `Surname`. The text in the static control should change automatically.

10. On the Controls toolbar, select the edit control.

11. Click the dialog box template to the right of the **Surname** text you just added (the exact position does not matter). An Edit control appears.

You should now have a dialog box that looks something like Figure 3.11.

The default command button

Each dialog box can have a default button, the command of which can be activated by pressing the Enter key. The default button is shown with a bold outline. The **OK** button usually is the default. You can make a button the default button from the **Styles** tab of the Push Button Properties dialog box.

FIGURE 3.11

Adding controls to a dialog box.

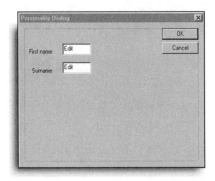

SEE ALSO

➤ *For more details about button controls, see page 66*

➤ *To learn more about using static text controls, see page 90*

➤ *For more details about edit controls, see page 97*

➤ *For more details about the new extended combo box, see page 261*

Sizing Controls

Adjusting the size of controls is handled in several ways. First, when you type the text into the static control, the size of the control changes automatically to accommodate the entered text. This is called *sizing to content* and is available for all controls that have captions.

Sizing a control according to its content

1. Click the control. A rectangle appears around the edges of the control.

2. Click the right mouse button to display the context menu.

3. Select **Size to Content**.

You can change the size of each control using the sizing points that appear when the control is selected. In our sample dialog box, the name edit boxes could be a bit larger so we'll stretch the first control and then see how to make the second the same size.

To size the Edit control next to **First name**, perform the following steps.

Sizing an edit control

1. Click the edit control to the right of **First name**. A rectangle appears around the edges of the control with sizing points.

2. Move the mouse to the right edge of the control and position it over the middle blue sizing point. When you're in the correct position, the mouse pointer will change to a left-right arrow.

3. Click and hold the mouse button.

4. Move the mouse to the right, keeping the button pressed. An outline of the control size is shown as the mouse is moved.

5. Release the mouse button when the control is the required size. The control is redrawn.

Your dialog box should now look something like Figure 3.12.

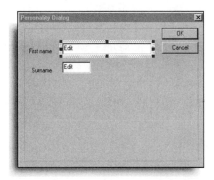

FIGURE 3.12

Sizing an individual control.

Selecting Several Controls

Using rubber banding to select several controls

You can use what is termed *rubber banding* to select serveral controls on a dialog template. Rubber banding is when you press the mouse button and keep it pressed while you drag the mouse cursor over the controls you want to select. As you drag, a dotted rectangle appears. All the controls inside the rectangle when the mouse button is released are selected.

In order to present a clean interface, it's common to require several controls to be positioned relative to one another, or for controls to be of the same size. This can be achieved by first selecting the controls that are to be positioned or resized and then choosing the appropriate sizing or alignment option from the **L**ayout menu or the Dialog toolbar.

It's important to note that when you want to perform a task such as making two controls the same size, the control that was last clicked will be the selected control (the one with the solid blue sizing points). The selected control determines what happens when the size or alignment option is performed.

To make the second Edit control on our dialog box the same width as the first, follow these steps.

Positioning several controls

When you move a control while several are selected, all the selected controls will be moved.

Editing the second control

1. Click the edit control to the right of **Surname**. A rectangle appears around the control.

2. Hold down the Ctrl key and click the other edit control.

   A rectangle appears around the control. The first control should remain selected but only the last control selected has solid blue sizing points.

3. From the **L**ayout menu, select the **M**ake Same Size submenu and then select **Same W**idth. The second edit control should now be the same width as the first.

Aligning Controls

Apart from having several options to deal with sizing controls, the resource editor **Layout** menu and the Dialog toolbar also help align controls. To align controls relative to one another, it's first necessary to select the controls (this is covered in the section "Selecting Several Controls," earlier in this chapter). When the controls are selected, numerous alignment operations can be performed. We'll examine some of these using the sample dialog box.

To align the static text controls with the corresponding edit controls, follow these steps.

Aligning the edit controls

1. Select the First Name control, and then select the edit control to its right. Both controls should have a selection rectangle, but only the edit control should have solid blue sizing points.

   If you're unsure about how to select several controls, refer to the section "Selecting Several Controls," previously in this chapter.

2. From the **Layout** menu, select the **Align** submenu and then select **Bottom**. This causes the text **First Name** to be aligned to the bottom edge of the edit control.

3. Repeat steps 1 and 2 for the second pair of controls.

4. Now select the First Name control and then the Surname control.

5. From the **Layout** menu, select the **Align** submenu and then select **Right**. This causes the two text controls to be right-aligned.

Your dialog box should now look something like Figure 3.13.

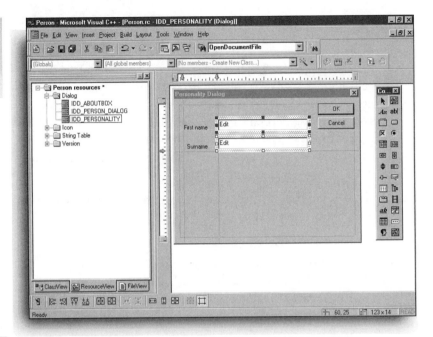

FIGURE 3.13

Aligning control edges and using guidelines.

**Controls touching guidelines
are automatically repositioned**

When the edge of a control is docked to a guideline the control can be repositioned by clicking and moving the guideline. Guidelines are displayed only during resource editing and not when the dialog layout is tested or during program execution.

Using Guidelines

To aid in the positioning of controls, you can add guidelines to the dialog box template. The dotted blue lines you see around the margin of the dialog box are guidelines. You can see these guidelines in Figure 3.13. When the edge of a control is placed on a guideline, moving the guideline also moves the control. The effect guidelines have can be seen by increasing the width of the dialog box. You'll see that the default **OK** and **Cancel** buttons stay relative to the right edge of the dialog box; this is because they are attached to the margin.

You can add your own guidelines by clicking in the rulers displayed at the top and left of the dialog box. When guidelines are added, an arrow appears within the ruler. To position a guideline, click and drag the rule arrow. Guidelines added close to existing controls snap to the edge of the control; similarly, a control added close to a guideline causes the control to snap to it.

Organizing Dialog Box Controls

Aside from adding and positioning controls, there are several other important aspects to be taken into consideration when creating dialog boxes. Group boxes can be used to keep the dialog box tidy and simplify its appearance. The order in which controls are accessed when tabbing can be specified; you can also specify any keyboard shortcuts.

Using Group Boxes

One method of producing a cleaner interface is to group controls together, giving the group a title and drawing a border around the controls. This is achieved by using the group box control. As always, the best way to understand is to see something in action, so we'll add some more controls to the sample dialog box.

Group boxes are not just for a pretty interface

Group box controls are used not only to improve the appearance of a dialog box. When used in conjunction with check boxes or radio buttons they enable a set of controls to be associated. The controls within each group box can automatically affect the state of another.

Adding a group box and several check box controls to the dialog box

  1. On the Controls toolbar, select the group box control.

  2. Add the control to the dialog box below the edit controls.

  3. Resize the group box using the bottom-right sizing point, as shown in Figure 3.14.

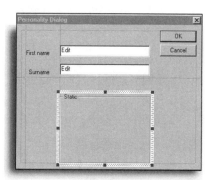

FIGURE 3.14
Grouping controls together to present a neater dialog box.

  4. Edit the caption of the group box to read `Analysis`.

  5. On the Controls toolbar, select the check box control.

  6. Add four check box controls. Position the four controls within the group box as shown in Figure 3.15.

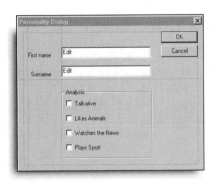

FIGURE 3.15
Positioning controls within a group box.

Adding several check box controls

You need to reselect the check box control on the toolbar after each one is added to the dialog.

7. Edit the check box captions. You can use whatever captions you like (I have devised my own personality-testing criteria).

8. Use the other sections in this chapter that deal with sizing, selecting, and aligning controls to arrange the controls within the **Analysis** group box in an orderly fashion.

SEE ALSO

➤ *For more information about using group boxes, see page* 77

Setting the Tab Order

Navigating between controls on a dialog box

The tab order is the sequence in which the controls on a dialog box receive the input focus when the Tab key is pressed. Only one control can have the input focus at any time.

The controls on a dialog box can be moved in sequence; this sequence is known as the *tab order*. To move to the next control in the sequence, the user presses the Tab key, and to move to the previous control, Shift+Tab is pressed. When a control is tabbed to, it receives the input focus. For example, when a button control is tabbed to, you'll see a dotted rectangle appear on the button face. This denotes that the button has focus.

A control can be excluded from the tab order by deselecting the **Tab Stop** property on the **General** tab of the Control Property dialog box.

Specifying the tab order for a dialog box

1. From the **Layout** menu, select **Tab Order**. The dialog box template is redisplayed with the tab sequence number by each control, as shown in Figure 3.16.

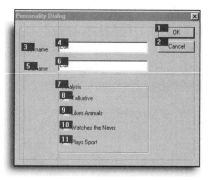

FIGURE 3.16
Modifying the tab order
sequence of controls.

2. Click the control you want to receive focus when the dialog box is first displayed. A number 1 appears next to the control.

3. Click all subsequent controls in the order you want the tab sequence to follow. Each control receives the next number in the sequence.

4. To test the tab order, from the **Layout** menu select **Test** or press Ctrl+T. Then use the Tab key to ensure the specified sequence is correct.

In test mode your dialog box appears as though it's being used within the application, allowing you to test its functionality. To terminate the test mode press Esc.

Setting Keyboard Shortcuts

A keyboard shortcut is specified for a control by incorporating an & in the control's caption before the character to be used as the shortcut mnemonic. For example, if a button control was given the caption E&xit, the button label would actually appear as **Exit** and pressing the button could be simulated by typing Alt+X or Alt+x.

If more than one control on a dialog box is given the same mnemonic, the first control in the tab order will be the one performed when the shortcut is typed. To avoid confusion, the resource editor enables you to check whether you have specified any duplicate mnemonics. To check for duplicate mnemonics, from the Resource Editor context menu select **Check Mnemonics**.

Mnemonic shortcuts

A *mnemonic* is an underlined character that can be used as a shortcut method of accessing a particular control. Pressing the Alt key plus the mnemonic character activates the shortcut. Mnemonic are specified in the resource editor by placing an & immediately before the required letter to be used as the shortcut.

If there are no duplicate mnemonics, you'll receive the message `No duplicate mnemonics found`; if there are, you'll be asked if you want the controls with duplicate mnemonics selected so you can resolve the conflict.

SEE ALSO

➤ *For more information about adding shortcuts, see page 91*

chapter

4

Using Button Controls

Utilizing the different types of buttons ●

Manipulating buttons during program
execution ●

Mapping messages to C++ functions ●

There are three types of buttons: pushbuttons, radio buttons, and check boxes. Each type has a particular use. A pushbutton represents a command that is performed whenever the button is clicked. Radio buttons allow a choice to be made from a list of mutually exclusive options. Only one item in a group of radio buttons can be selected at a time. Check boxes are used to allow a choice of whether an item is selected; unlike radio buttons, several (or no) check boxes in a group can be selected at one time.

Buttons are the most commonly used controls. You'll find them on virtually all dialog boxes. The correct use of each type makes understanding and using a program much easier.

Using Pushbuttons

CDialog implements default OK and Cancel handler functions

The resource editor adds **OK** and **Cancel** pushbuttons to newly created dialog box templates. The MFC base class of all dialog boxes is `CDialog`, and this has default implementations that handle the `BN_CLICKED` messages of these buttons; `OnOK()` and `OnCancel()`. You can override these functions in your dialog classes derived from `CDialog` to alter their behavior.

The pushbutton is the simplest Windows control. Each pushbutton represents a single command and, when clicked, invokes the action that performs the command. Almost all dialog boxes will have at least two pushbuttons: OK and Cancel.

AppWizard includes these automatically for dialog-based applications. Many dialog boxes require additional pushbuttons; you have seen that these can be added using the resource editor. The initial properties and style options for each button are also specified using the resource editor, but what happens if you want to alter any of these properties at runtime? For example, you might want to change the button caption, depending on information that is available only after the application has started. To do this, you need access to the control within the program and a method to specify the new caption. In the following example, you'll see how the `GetDlgItem()` function is used to retrieve a pointer to a `CWnd` object that represents the button control. You'll then learn how the `CWnd` pointer is used to modify the caption and other attributes while the program is running.

Use the AppWizard to create a new dialog-based project named Buttons. When you have created the new project, you must add five buttons to the Buttons dialog box. During the following procedure, you might find it necessary to increase the width of the dialog box and alter button sizes.

Football Trivia for Super Bowl XL
Seattle Seahawks VS. Pittsburgh Steelers

1. The winner of the coin toss was :

   SEAHAWKS   STEELERS

2. Once the coin was tossed, what did the calling team select?

   HEADS   **TAILS**

3. Once the coin was tossed, what actually showed up?

   HEADS   **TAILS**

4. After the ball had been kicked off and the game officially started, the first TV commercial shown was for …

FAST FOOD RESTAURANT	POP (Pepsi, Coke, etc)	**BEER (Bud, Coors, etc)**
CAR/TRUCK (Ford, GM, etc)	COMPUTERS (Dell, Gateway)	CHIPS (Frito Lay, Tostitos, etc)
CANDY (M & M's, etc)	OTHER _____	

5. The first team to score was :

   SEAHAWKS   STEELERS

6. The first points scored was a …

   TOUCHDOWN   **FIELD GOAL**

7. (Tied in with Question 6). The last name of the person that scored starts with the letter : **BROWN**

A – F	G – L	M – R
S – V	W – Z	

8. At the end of the second quarter, who had the lead?

   SEAHAWKS   **STEELERS**   TIE SCORE

9. The last team to score before half-time was?

   SEAHAWKS   **STEELERS**   NO SCORE

Adding buttons to the Buttons dialog box

1. Select the **ResourceView** tab, expand the **Dialog** folder, and double-click the **IDD_BUTTONS_DIALOG** item. The dialog box appears in the resource editor. Click on the **TODO: Place dialog controls here** text then press the Delete key to remove it.

2. Select the Button image on the Controls toolbar and add two buttons at the top left of the dialog box, as shown in Figure 4.1.

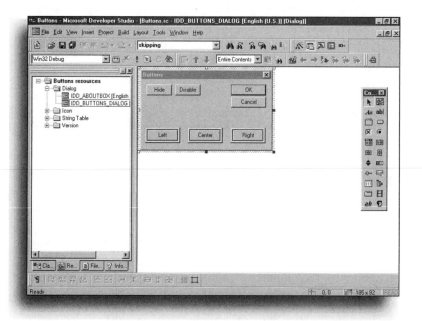

FIGURE 4.1

The Buttons dialog box layout.

3. Select the first of these buttons, click the right mouse button, and select **Properties** from the context menu. The Push Button Properties dialog box appears. You can keep the properties dialog box visible by clicking the pin icon in the top-left corner.

4. Enter a name in the **ID** combo box; use IDC_SHOW_HIDE for this example. Enter a label in the **Caption** box; use Hide for this example.

5. Select the second button. Enter IDC_ENABLE_DISABLE in the **ID** combo box and Disable in the **Caption** box.

6. Add three more buttons toward the bottom of the dialog box (refer to Figure 4.1).

7. Select all three buttons you just added by clicking each one while pressing the Ctrl key.

8. Click the **Extended Styles** tab of the Multiple Selection Properties dialog box. Check the <u>C</u>**lient Edge** and <u>M</u>**odal Frame** options.

9. Select the far-left button. Enter IDC_LEFT for the <u>**ID**</u> and Left for the <u>**Caption**</u>. Select the center button. Enter IDC_CENTER for the <u>**ID**</u> and Center for the <u>**Caption**</u>. Select the far right button. Enter IDC_RIGHT for the <u>**ID**</u> and Right for the <u>**Caption**</u>.

10. Close the Push Button Properties dialog box. Your dialog box should now look like Figure 4.1.

SEE ALSO

➤ *For details of how to create a dialog-based application, refer to page 44*

➤ *For more information about dialog box design, see page 51*

Adding Handlers for Button Click Events

The pushbutton control, like all other Windows controls, sends messages to its parent window when an event occurs. When a pushbutton on a dialog box is clicked, the BN_CLICKED message is sent to the dialog box. In order for the program to respond with the appropriate action, a handler function must be created for the BN_CLICKED message.

By the end of the Buttons example, each of the five added buttons will have a handler function. The function of the IDC_SHOW_HIDE button will toggle the visibility of the three buttons at the foot of the dialog box and toggle the button's caption between **Show** and **Hide**. The function of the IDC_ENABLE_ DISABLE button will toggle the enabled state of the three bottom buttons and toggle the button's caption between **Enable** and **Disable**. When a button is disabled, its caption is dimmed or grayed and it can't receive input from the mouse or keyboard.

The **Left**, **Right**, and **Center** buttons will all respond by altering the title of the dialog box.

Here you will add the BN_CLICKED handler function for the first button and then move on to the next section, which deals with writing the code and adding handlers for the other buttons.

Adding a button click handler function

1. Double-click the **Hide** button. The Add Member Variable dialog box appears.

2. Click **OK** to accept the default **Member Function Name**, OnShowHide. The new skeleton function is created and shown in the editor window, ready for code to be added.

OnShowHide() will be called each time the IDC_SHOW_HIDE button is clicked, but how exactly does this happen? To answer this, I'll need to digress and explain a little about message maps.

Understanding Message Maps

The *MFC framework* uses a system known as message mapping to connect Windows messages with specific C++ functions. A *message map* can be added to any class derived from MFC's CCmdTarget class. The hierarchy of the CButtonsDlg class is shown in Figure 4.2.

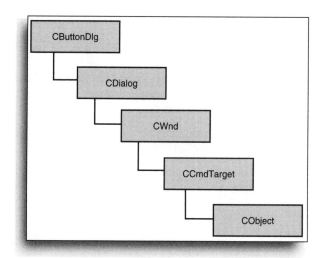

FIGURE 4.2
The CButtonsDlg class hierarchy.

Message maps are provided by
`CCmdTarget`

A message map is the mechanism that directs which C++ function is performed in response to a Window message. In order to implement a message map a class must be derived from `CCmdTarget`.

Much of the code behind message maps is hidden away in macros, which are added and updated by the Visual C++ tools. The `CButtonsDlg` class definition (in ButtonsDlg.h) includes the following line:

```
DECLARE_MESSAGE_MAP()
```

AppWizard inserted this statement when the class was created. The macro actually declares some additional variables to maintain *message map* entries and functions that route messages to the correct C++ function.

When the `OnShowHide()` handler was created, the following three things happened:

1. The implementation function was created, which looks like this:

```
void CButtonsDlg::OnShowHide()
{
  // TODO: Add your control notification handler code
  ➥here
}
```

2. The function declaration was added (in CButtonsDlg.h), which looks like this:

```
afx_msg void OnShowHide();
```

   The `afx_msg` prefix is nothing clever; it just serves as a reminder that this is a message-handling function.

3. An entry was added to the `BEGIN_MESSAGE_MAP` macro to couple the message with the function. The macro, in the CButtonsDlg.cpp file, looks like this:

```
1 BEGIN_MESSAGE_MAP(CButtonsDlg, CDialog)
2 //{{AFX_MSG_MAP(CButtonsDlg)
3 ON_WM_SYSCOMMAND()
4 ON_WM_PAINT()
5 ON_WM_QUERYICON()
6 ON_BN_CLICKED(IDC_SHOW_HIDE, OnShowHide)
7 //}}AFX_MSG_MAP
8 END_MESSAGE_MAP()
```

You can see in line 6 that the OnShowHide() function has been given an entry in the *message map* macro. When Windows sends the BN_CLICKED message to the dialog box for your IDC_SHOW_HIDE button, the entries are searched and, if a handler function is found, it is called. AppWizard created the other entries, which are for a different type of message; these and other message types are covered in later chapters.

SEE ALSO
➤ *To learn more about reacting to Windows messages turn to page 176*

ClassWizard's special comments

The special comment //{{AFX_MSG_MAP is used by C++ tools such as ClassWizard to understand the code structure. If you remove them or edit the code between them incorrectly ClassWizard might cease to function.

Modifying Pushbuttons at Runtime

The resource editor is very flexible when you are designing a dialog box layout, but sometimes it isn't flexible enough. For example, if you were asked to develop an application that designed electronic forms, one of the requirements would be the capability to customize buttons. To modify the properties or style of a pushbutton (or any other control) while a program is running, you must gain access to the control's object. This is done easily for dialog box controls by calling the GetDlgItem() function and passing the ID of the desired control. The function returns a pointer to the CWnd object that represents the control; this pointer can be cast to the appropriate class and then used to get and set the control's attributes.

GetDlgItem() returns a CWnd pointer because a button is really a window itself. A button might look vastly different to a dialog box because of its style, but both are windows and a CWnd object can be used to represent either.

For the OnShowHide() handler function to toggle the visibility of the three buttons at the bottom of the dialog box, enter the code shown in Listing 4.1 after the //TODO comments.

The CWnd class provides basic windows functionality

The CWnd class *encapsulates* a window and provides basic window functionality. It is important to note that the CWnd object is a C++ object and not the window itself. The Windows window is a separate entity accessed via CWnd's member functions. The CWnd object is constructed before the window is created, and the window can be destroyed by calling DestroyWindow() while the CWnd object remains valid.

LISTING 4.1 LST04_1.CPP—Toggling the Visibility of Buttons with *ShowWindow()*

```
1 void CButtonsDlg::OnShowHide()
2 {
```

continues...

① GetDlgItem() returns a pointer to the CWnd object. **IsWindowVisible()** is a CWnd member function that returns TRUE if the window is currently visible.

② The visibility of each button window is toggled by calling **ShowWindow()** and passing either the **SW_SHOW** or **SW_HIDE** flag.

③ SetWindowText() is another very useful CWnd member function that in this case alters the button's caption.

LISTING 4.1 Continued

```
3     // TODO: Add your control notification handler code
4
5     // ** Check if the Left button is currently visible
6     BOOL bVisible = GetDlgItem(IDC_LEFT)->          ①
      ➥IsWindowVisible();
7
8     // ** Toggle the visibility of each control
9     GetDlgItem(IDC_LEFT)->ShowWindow(bVisible        ②
      ➥? SW_HIDE : SW_SHOW);
10    GetDlgItem(IDC_CENTER)->ShowWindow(bVisible
      ➥? SW_HIDE : SW_SHOW);
11    GetDlgItem(IDC_RIGHT)->ShowWindow(bVisible
      ➥? SW_HIDE : SW_SHOW);
12
13    // ** Toggle the show/hide button's caption
14    GetDlgItem(IDC_SHOW_HIDE)->SetWindowText(bVisible ③
      ➥? "Show" : "Hide");
15  }
```

Using the pointer returned by GetDlgItem()

The CWnd pointer returned by GetDlgItem() might not remain valid for too long. You should not store this pointer; instead, call the function again to retrieve its memory location. The GetDlgItem() function will return NULL if there is no window with the ID passed to it.

The GetDlgItem() function call in line 6 is passed the resource identifier IDC_LEFT and therefore returns a pointer to the CWnd object of the **Left** button. The returned pointer is then used to call the IsWindowVisible() function, which returns TRUE or FALSE accordingly. The result is stored in the local BOOL variable bVisible. Because all three buttons will either be visible or not, only one needs to be checked.

In lines 9, 10, and 11 the GetDlgItem() function is called to retrieve the CWnd pointer for the three buttons in turn. For each control the ShowWindow() function is called and (depending on the value of bVisible) is passed either SW_HIDE, which hides the window, or SW_SHOW, which makes the window visible. This has the desired effect of making all three buttons disappear with one click and making them reappear on the second click.

Line 14 uses the GetDlgItem() function again, this time passing IDC_SHOW_HIDE, which is the ID of the button that was clicked. The SetWindowText() is the CWnd member function that is called to change the button's caption. The string passed is either Show or Hide, according to the value of bVisible.

At first glance it might appear that the caption will say **Show** when the buttons are visible and **Hide** when they are not, which would be backward. Remember that `bVisible` was set at the top of the function in line 6; if the buttons were visible then, by line 14 they are invisible and the caption should say **Show**.

Add this code, build and run the program, and then try clicking the **Hide** button. This should cause the **Left**, **Right**, and **Center** buttons to disappear and the label of the button you clicked to change from **Hide** to **Show**. The buttons should reappear if you click the button again.

Now a similar handler function is required to toggle the three buttons between an enabled and disabled state.

Add a `BN_CLICKED` message handler for the `IDC_ENABLE_DISABLE` button. For help on how to do this, refer to the procedure "Adding a Button Click Handler Function" outlined earlier in this chapter (remember to select the **Disable** button).

You should now have a member function `OnEnableDisable()`. For this function to toggle the state of the three buttons, add the code shown in Listing 4.2. You can see immediately the similarity between this and the `OnShowHide()` shown in Listing 4.1, so here we will cover the differences.

LISTING 4.2 LST04_2.CPP—Toggling the State of Buttons with *EnableWindow()*

```
1  void CButtonsDlg::OnEnableDisable()
2  {
3      // TODO: Add your control notification handler code
4
5      // ** Obtain the current state of the Left button
6      BOOL bState = GetDlgItem(IDC_LEFT)->IsWindowEnabled();    ①
7
8      // ** Toggle the state of each control
9      GetDlgItem(IDC_LEFT)->EnableWindow(!bState);             ②
10     GetDlgItem(IDC_CENTER)->EnableWindow(!bState);
11     GetDlgItem(IDC_RIGHT)->EnableWindow(!bState);
12
13     // ** Toggle the Enable/Disable buttons caption
```

① `GetDlgItem()` returns a pointer to the CWnd object. `IsWindowEnabled()` is a CWnd member function that returns TRUE if the window is available to respond to being clicked.

② The enabled state of each button window is toggled by calling `EnableWindow()` and passing either the TRUE or FALSE flag.

continues...

(3) The caption of the IDC_ENABLE_ DISABLE button is set to show an appropriate caption using SetWindowText().

LISTING 4.2 Continued

```
14    GetDlgItem(IDC_ENABLE_DISABLE)->SetWindowText(bState
      ➥? "Enable" : "Disable");
15  }
```
(3)

In line 6 the IsWindowEnabled() function is called and returns the current enabled state of the IDC_LEFT button.

In lines 9, 10, and 11 the EnableWindow() function is called and passed the opposite of the current state. This has the desired effect of either enabling or disabling each control.

At line 14 a pointer to the IDC_ENABLE_DISABLE button is retrieved by the GetDlgItem() function and used to call SetWindowText() to alter the button's caption.

Now build and run the program. Try clicking the **Disable** button. This should cause the **Left**, **Right**, and **Center** buttons to be disabled as shown in Figure 4.3. A disabled button can't receive mouse or keyboard input. You will see that a button's enabled state can still be set even when the button is invisible.

FIGURE 4.3
Disabling buttons.

To round up the Buttons example, a handler function is required for the three remaining buttons. Each function has just one line of code, a call to another new function ChangeDialogTitle(). This alters the dialog box title to show which button was clicked. It also stores the ID of the button so the title reflects whether a button is clicked twice. All the code is shown in Listing 4.3.

Add a BN_CLICKED message handler for the IDC_LEFT, IDC_CENTER, and IDC_RIGHT buttons. For help on how to do this, refer to the procedure "Adding a Button Click Handler Function" earlier in this chapter.

Inserting member variables and functions with ClassView

1. Select the **ClassView** tab of the Project Workspace view.

2. Right-click the `CButtonsDlg` class to show the class context menu.

3. Choose **Add Member** **V**ariable to display the Add Member Variable dialog box.

4. Enter a **Variable** **T**ype of `UINT`; then press the Tab key to move to the next field.

5. Enter `m_nIDofLastButton` as the **Variable** **D**eclaration; then click **OK**.

6. Right-click the `CButtonsDlg` class to show the class context menu.

7. Choose **Add Member** **F**unction to display the Add Member Function dialog box.

8. Enter a **Function** **T**ype of `void`; then press the Tab key to move to the next field.

9. Enter `ChangeDialogTitle(UINT nID)` as the **Function** **Declaration**; then click **OK**.

You now have a variable in the dialog box class to store the ID of the clicked button. You also have a function that accepts a `UINT` (unsigned integer) parameter. Add the code to the four functions as it appears in Listing 4.3.

LISTING 4.3 LST04_3.CPP—Modifying the Dialog Caption to Reflect Button Click Messages

```
 1 void CButtonsDlg::OnLeft()  ——①
 2 {
 3     // TODO: Add your control notification handler code
 4     ChangeDialogTitle(IDC_LEFT);
 5 }
 6
 7 void CButtonsDlg::OnCenter()  ——②
 8 {
 9     // TODO: Add your control notification handler code
10     ChangeDialogTitle(IDC_CENTER);
```

① OnLeft() is the handler function for the **Left** button called in response to the BN_CLICKED message.

② OnCenter() is the handler function for the **Center** button called in response to the BN_CLICKED message.

continues...

LISTING 4.3 Continued

③ OnRight() is the handler function for the **Right** button called in response to the BN_CLICKED message.

④ ChangeDialog Title() is not a handler function but is called from all three handler functions. It is passed the ID of the button that was clicked.

⑤ The CString operator += appends text to the end of the existing contents of the strCaption variable.

⑥ SetWindowText() alters the text displayed in the dialog box title bar.

⑦ Store the ID of the clicked button in a member variable for later use.

```
11  }
12
13  void CButtonsDlg::OnRight()          ──── ③
14  {
15      // TODO: Add your control notification handler code
16      ChangeDialogTitle(IDC_RIGHT);
17  }
18
19  void CButtonsDlgChangeDialogTitle(UINT nID)   ──── ④
20  {
21      CString strCaption;
22
23      // ** Get the label of the button that was clicked
24      GetDlgItem(nID)->GetWindowText(strCaption);
25
26      strCaption += " was pressed";        ──── ⑤
27
28      // ** Check if the button is the same as last time
29      if(m_nIDofLastButton == nID)
30          strCaption += " again";
31
32      // ** Set the caption of the dialog box
33      SetWindowText(strCaption);           ──── ⑥
34
35      // ** Store the ID of the clicked button
36      m_nIDofLastButton = nID;             ──── ⑦
37  }
```

You can see in lines 4, 10, and 16 that each handler function calls the ChangeDialogTitle() function. Each handler passes to the function the ID of its own button.

In line 24 the ID is passed to the GetDlgItem(), which returns a pointer to the CWnd object of the relevant control. The returned pointer is then used to call GetWindowText() to retrieve the button caption. The caption is stored in the CString variable strCaption. In line 26 the += operator of CString is used to concatenate the text "was pressed" to the end of the caption.

In line 29, the ID of the clicked button is compared with the member variable m_nIDofLastButton (which holds the ID of the last button clicked); if the IDs are equal the text "again" is added to the end of the strCaption variable in line 30.

In line 33, the strCaption variable is passed in the call to SetWindowText(). Because the CButtonsDlg object is derived from CWnd, this results in calling SetWindowText() for the dialog box, which alters the text in the title bar.

In line 36, the ID of the clicked button is stored in the member variable m_nIDofLastButton.

Now build and run the program. Test your program by clicking the **Center** button. The dialog box title should say Center was pressed. Click the **Center** button again and the title should read Center was clicked again.

Using Radio Buttons

There are numerous occasions when only a single choice from two or more options is logical. For example, it's sensible that selecting the Female option in a program should automatically deselect the Male option. Radio buttons are designed for this scenario and can perform this deselection automatically. Radio buttons are almost always placed within group boxes, which enables a dialog box to have several sets of radio buttons operating independently.

Because the selection and deselection of buttons within the group happens automatically, the only thing required of the program is to find out which of the mutually exclusive options is set (when necessary). To do this, a variable is linked with the radio buttons. This can all be achieved quite painlessly—to see how we'll use another sample program. Use the AppWizard to create a new dialog-based project named CityBreak.

SEE ALSO

➤ *For details on how to create a dialog-based application, refer to page 44*

Adding Radio Button Groups

The most important thing to remember when adding radio buttons is to ensure the correct property and style settings are specified with the resource editor. When these are correct, most of the functionality of radio buttons takes care of itself.

Each radio button control in a group box must have the **Auto Style** option checked for automatic deselection to work. This option is set by default when radio buttons are added, so you shouldn't need to worry about it. The method by which controls are grouped together is via the use of the **Group** property. A control with the **Group** property checked is deemed the first control in the group; each following control (in the tab order) with the **Group** property unchecked is in the same group. The group is terminated by the next control with the **Group** property checked. You move between controls in a group by using arrow keys.

The CityBreak project uses two sets of radio buttons; the first selects a destination city, and the second selects the type of hotel required.

In the following procedure, you might find it necessary to increase the width of the dialog box and alter button sizes.

Adding radio buttons to the CityBreak dialog box

1. Open the IDD_CITYBREAK_DIALOG dialog box in the resource editor. Click the **TODO: Place dialog controls here** text then press the Delete key to remove it.

2. Select the Group Box image on the Controls toolbar; then add a group box to the left of the dialog box as shown in Figure 4.4.

3. Ensure the group box is selected; then right-click and select **Properties** from the context menu. The Group Box Properties dialog box appears. You can keep the properties dialog visible by clicking the pin icon at the top-left corner.

4. Enter Destination in the **Caption** box and check the **Tab Stop** option.

5. Select the Radio Button image on the Controls toolbar, and add four radio buttons inside the group box.

6. Select the top button. Enter IDC_LONDON for the **ID** and London for the **Caption**, and check the **Group** option.

7. Select the second button. Enter IDC_PARIS for the **ID** and Paris for the **Caption**. Select the third button. Enter IDC_NEWYORK for the **ID** and New York for the **Caption**. Select the bottom button. Enter IDC_MUNICH for the **ID** and Munich for the **Caption**.

8. Select the Group Box image on the Controls toolbar; then add a group box to the right of the **Destination** group, as shown in Figure 4.4.

9. Enter Hotel in the **Caption** box and check the **Tab Stop** option.

10. Add three radio buttons inside the **Hotel** group box.

11. Select all three radio buttons that you just added by clicking each one with the Ctrl key pressed.

12. Click the **Styles** tab of the Properties dialog box. Check the **Push-like** option.

13. Select the top button. Enter IDC_LUXURY for the **ID** and Luxury for the **Caption** and check the **Group** option.

14. Select the second button. Enter IDC_STANDARD for the **ID** and Standard for the **Caption**. Select the third button. Enter IDC_ECONOMY for the **ID** and Economy for the **Caption**. Your dialog box should now look like Figure 4.4.

FIGURE 4.4
The CityBreak dialog box layout.

The tab order is important for radio boxes to function properly because it is used to find the next logical control. To check the tab order, from the **Layout** menu select **Tab Order**. Compare this with the tab order shown in Figure 4.5. To test that the radio button groups you have added have the correct settings, enter Ctrl+T, or from the **Layout** menu select **Test**. You should be able to select only one of the cities and one of the hotel types. To exit from the layout test press the Esc key.

SEE ALSO

➤ *For more information about dialog box design, see page 51*

FIGURE 4.5
The CityBreak dialog box tab order.

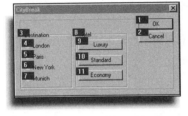

Retrieving the Selected Radio Button

> **The invaluable ClassWizard**
>
> ClassWizard is an invaluable tool that is useful time and time again during project development. ClassWizard helps you create and manage new and existing project classes. It also helps you maintain message handling functions and overrides of virtual functions implemented by the MFC library.

The purpose of a group of radio buttons is to allow a choice of one item from several. At some point in the program it becomes necessary to discover which is the selected button and then act accordingly. To achieve this, a variable is associated with the group of radio buttons. The variable is actually associated with the first radio button in the group (the one with the **Group** option checked). In the CityBreak example, these are IDC_LONDON and IDC_LUXURY.

You use the ClassWizard tool to add these variables and attach them to the correct radio button. For the CityBreak example a variable is required for each group.

Attaching variables to radio buttons with ClassWizard

1. Press Ctrl+W to start ClassWizard, or from the **View** menu select **ClassWizard**. The MFC ClassWizard dialog box appears as shown in Figure 4.6.

2. Select the **Member Variables** tab.

3. Select the dialog class in the **Class name:** combo box; use **CCityBreakDlg** for this example.

4. Select the control ID in the **Control IDs:** list box; select `IDC_LONDON` for this example.

5. Click the **Add Variable** button. The Add Member Variable dialog box appears (see Figure 4.7). Note you can also add a member variable for a control by double-clicking the control's ID.

6. Enter the variable name in the **Member Variable name** box; use `m_nDestination` for this example. Then click **OK** to return to the **Member Variables** tab of ClassWizard.

7. Select `IDC_LUXURY` in the **Control IDs** list box; then click the **Add Variable** button to open the Add Member Variable dialog.

8. Enter `m_nHotel` in the **Member Variable Name** box; then click **OK** to add the new member variable.

9. Click **OK** to close the ClassWizard dialog box.

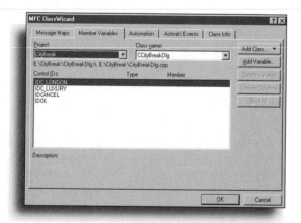

FIGURE 4.6
The ClassWizard dialog box.

Now that the variables are added, they must be initialized. ClassWizard has created code in the program that initializes the values to –1, which means that if the program is built and run at this point, none of the radio buttons will be selected when the dialog box is first displayed. This is rarely the desired effect; usually, the first radio button in each group is selected initially.

FIGURE 4.7

The Add Member Variable dialog box.

To do this you must edit the initialization code created by ClassWizard in the `CCityBreakDlg` class constructor. Select the **ClassView** tab, expand the `CCityBreakDlg` class, and double-click the first subitem. The constructor function is displayed in the editor window. Edit the two lines of code to initialize the variables to zero as shown.

```
m_nDestination = 0;
m_nHotel = 0;
```

The only thing that remains is to add some code that investigates which of the radio buttons in each group is selected. You'll do this by adding a handler for the **OK** button and displaying a Bon Voyage message. Add a `BN_CLICKED` message handler for the `IDOK` button. For help on how to do this, refer to the procedure "Adding a Button Click Handler Function" earlier in this chapter.

You should now have a member function `OnOk()`. For this function to format and display a message that takes into account which radio buttons are selected, add the code shown in Listing 4.4.

LISTING 4.4 LST04_4.CPP—Code to Retrieve the Selected Radio Buttons

```
1 void CCityBreakDlg::OnOK()
2 {
3     // TODO: Add extra validation here
4     CString strMessage;
5     CString strHotel;
```

```
6      CString strDest;
7
8      // ** Transfer data from the controls to the variables
9      UpdateData();  ————(1)
10
11     // ** Retrieve the caption of each selected radio button
12     GetDlgItem(IDC_LUXURY + m_nHotel)->GetWindowText(strHotel);
13     GetDlgItem(IDC_LONDON + m_nDestination)->GetWindowText(strDest);
14
15     // ** Format and display the message
16     strMessage = "Bon Voyage to a " + strHotel + " Hotel in "
       ➥+ strDest;
17     MessageBox(strMessage);
18
19     CDialog::OnOK();
20  }
```

(1) UpdateData() retrieves the data from the controls on the dialog box and updates their associated variables.

(2) Retrieve the caption of the selected radio button in the hotel type group.

(3) Retrieve the caption of the selected radio button in the destination group.

(4) Formulate a message incorporating the strings of the selected buttons.

The UpdateData() function in line 9 transfers the value of the control to the associated variable. After line 11, the value of m_nDestination and m_nHotel will be a number relative to the first control. For example, if **London** is selected, m_nDestination will have the value 0; if **Paris** is selected the value will be 1. These values are used to retrieve the labels of the selected buttons in lines 12 and 13. In line 16, the CString + (plus) operator is used to compose a message in the variable strMessage; this is displayed using the MessageBox() function in line 17.

Now build and run the program. Test your code by trying several combinations of destinations with hotel types. If **New York** and **Luxury** are selected when the **OK** button is clicked you should see the message shown in Figure 4.8.

SEE ALSO

➤ *To learn how dialog data exchange works, turn to page 223*

FIGURE 4.8
A Bon Voyage message.

Using Check Boxes

Check boxes are extremely common in applications; you have already used many of them to select the various properties and styles of controls in the resource editor. Check boxes enable the user to select none, one, or several options. The standard style of a check box is to display a label next to a small box. The box displays a tick (or a cross in Windows NT) when the item is checked and is blank when nothing is checked. A check box can be a *tri-state* control, having a third state, where the tick (or cross) appears dimmed. This is used when the state represented by the control cannot be determined. For example, if you are designing a dialog box in the resource editor and you select several controls that have different styles, the check boxes representing the styles will be dimmed.

Adding Check Boxes

To explore how to use check boxes, the CityBreak project can be expanded slightly. A couple of check boxes will be added to enable the vacationer to select whether she or he wants to attend a dinner dance during their stay and, if so, whether they would also like champagne.

Adding check boxes to the CityBreak dialog box

1. Open the IDD_CITYBREAK_DIALOG dialog box in the resource editor.

2. Selecting the Check Box image on the Controls toolbar and add two check boxes, as shown in Figure 4.9.

3. Select the top check box; then right-click and select **Properties** from the context menu. The Check Box Properties dialog box appears.

4. Enter a name in the **ID** combo box; use IDC_DANCE for this example. Enter a label in the **Caption** box; use Dinner Dance for this example.

5. Select the **Group** option. This terminates the **Hotel** radio button group.

Using Check Boxes CHAPTER 4

6. Select the second check box.

7. Enter IDC_CHAMPAGNE in the **ID** combo box and Champagne in the **Caption** box. Your dialog box should now look like Figure 4.9.

FIGURE 4.9
The CityBreak dialog box with check boxes.

Getting and Setting Check Boxes

As with radio buttons, the purpose behind check boxes is to allow options to be set. At some point the program must retrieve the state of the check box. To access the state of a check box, use the CButton class. This class has a member function GetCheck() to retrieve the check box state, and a SetCheck() function to set it.

The sample code demonstrates how two check boxes can be related. You can't have the champagne if you don't go to the dinner, but you can have the dinner without drinking champagne. Therefore, if **Champagne** is checked, **Dinner Dance** is automatically checked and if **Dinner Dance** is unchecked, **Champagne** is automatically unchecked.

Add a BN_CLICKED message handler for both the IDC_DANCE and IDC_CHAMPAGNE check boxes. For help on how to do this, refer to the procedure "Adding a Button Click Handler Function" earlier in this chapter.

Now that you have the skeleton functions, add the code as shown in Listing 4.5.

The CButton class

CButton is the MFC class that encapsulates the functionality of pushbuttons, radio buttons, group boxes, and check boxes. You can cast the pointer returned by GetDlgItem() to a CButton pointer to utilize its member functions. These functions enable you to check and set the state for radio buttons and check boxes and get and set the button style flags.

LISTING 4.5 LST04_5.CPP—Accessing the State of Check Boxes

```
1 void CCityBreakDlg::OnChampagne() ———①
2 {
```

① OnChampagne() is the message handler function called when the **Champagne** check box is clicked.

continues...

LISTING 4.5 Continued

(2) Retrieve a CButton pointer to the IDC_DANCE check box.

(3) Retrieve a CButton pointer to the IDC_CHAMPAGNE check box.

(4) If the **Champagne** check box is checked, make sure the **Dance** check box is also checked.

(5) OnDance() is the message handler function called when the **Dance** check box is checked.

(6) Retrieve a CButton pointer to the IDC_DANCE check box.

(7) Retrieve a CButton pointer to the IDC_CHAMPAGNE check box.

(8) If the **Dance** check box is not checked then make sure the **Champagne** check box is also not checked.

```
3       // TODO: Add your control notification handler code
4
5       // ** Get a pointer to each of the check box objects
6       CButton* pDance = (CButton*)GetDlgItem(IDC_DANCE);        ——(2)
7       CButton* pChamp = (CButton*)GetDlgItem(IDC_CHAMPAGNE);    ——(3)
8
9       // ** If champagne is checked, check dinner dance
10      if (pChamp->GetCheck())            ——(4)
11          pDance->SetCheck(1);
12  }
13
14  void CCityBreakDlg::OnDance()          ——(5)
15  {
16      // TODO: Add your control notification handler code
17
18      // ** Get a pointer to each of the check box objects
19      CButton* pDance = (CButton*)GetDlgItem(IDC_DANCE);        ——(6)
20      CButton* pChamp = (CButton*)GetDlgItem (IDC_CHAMPAGNE);   ——(7)
21
22      // ** If dinner dance is unchecked, uncheck champagne
23      if (!pDance->GetCheck())           ——(8)
24          pChamp->SetCheck(0);
25  }
```

You can see in lines 6, 7, 19, and 20 that the CWnd pointer returned from the GetDlgItem() function is cast to a CButton pointer. CButton is the MFC class that *encapsulates* the functionality of all the button types. The reason CButton was not used for pushbuttons is that it wasn't necessary; the CWnd pointer could be used directly. The difference between a pushbutton and a check box is that a pushbutton doesn't have a state. The cast to a CButton pointer is necessary in order to call its member functions GetCheck() and SetCheck().

The if statement in line 10 finds the state of the **Champagne** check box, and if checked, it calls SetCheck() for the **Dinner Dance** check box, passing 1 to set it. The if statement in line 23 does the opposite, which is to uncheck **Champagne** when **Dinner Dance** is unchecked.

Build and run the program. Check to see that selecting or dese-lecting the appropriate control automatically sets the other.

To round off the example, extend the functionality of the OnOK() function by adding the code shown between lines 19 and 29 of Listing 4.6.

LISTING 4.6 LST04_6.CPP—Adding Extra Information to the Bon Voyage Message

```
1  void CCityBreakDlg::OnOK()
2  {
3      // TODO: Add extra validation here
4      CString strMessage;
5      CString strHotel;
6      CString strDest;
7
8      // ** Transfer data from the controls to the variables
9      UpdateData();
10
11     // ** Retrieve the caption of each selected radio button
12     GetDlgItem(IDC_LUXURY + m_nHotel)->GetWindowText(strHotel);
13     GetDlgItem(IDC_LONDON + m_nDestination)->GetWindowText(strDest);
14
15
16     // ** Format and display the message
17     strMessage = "Bon Voyage to a " + strHotel + " Hotel in
    ➥" + strDest;
18
19     // ** Get a pointer to each check box
20     CButton* pDance = (CButton*)GetDlgItem(IDC_DANCE);
21     CButton* pChamp = (CButton*)GetDlgItem (IDC_CHAMPAGNE);
22
23     // ** Append to the message according to the check boxes
24     if(pDance->GetCheck())
25     {
26         strMessage += " and a Dinner Dance";
27         if(pChamp->GetCheck())
28             strMessage += " with Champange";
29     }
30     MessageBox(strMessage);
31
32     CDialog::OnOK();
33 }
```

① Retrieve the caption of the selected radio button in the hotel type group.

② Retrieve the caption of the selected radio button in the destination group.

The OnOK() function now takes into account the check box settings and will display extra information in the Bon Voyage message. In lines 19 and 20, the CWnd pointer returned from GetDlgItem() is cast to a CButton pointer. After these lines, pDance points to the IDC_DANCE check box and pChamp points to the IDC_CHAMPAGNE check box. The pointers are then used to test the state of each control in lines 24 and 27, respectively. If the IDC_DANCE control is checked, and a Dinner Dance is appended to the strMessage variable using CString's += operator. If the IDC_CHAMPAGNE control is checked, strMessage is modified further to include with Champagne.

If you build and run the application, when the **OK** button is clicked the message should include additional information depending on the check boxes (see Figure 4.10).

FIGURE 4.10

The extended Bon Voyage message.

chapter

5

Using Text Controls

Display informative text and messages
on dialog boxes ●

Manipulate text during program
execution ●

Validate data as it is being entered ●

Extend the functionality of controls by
subclassing ●

For many years, before the advent of Windows and the graphics user interface, most computers were limited to displaying about 24 lines of 80 characters of text. Predominantly the display was green on black in a single dotted font; the very unfortunate had amber terminals. Contrary to what some of the pundits espouse, these mono terminals have not yet disappeared. This is because the vast majority of information entered into, and relayed to us from computers is still textual, which enables these applications to still perform a useful purpose. Graphics user interface or no, there is still a big need for applications to display and accept text from the computer user.

On dialog boxes informative text is displayed using static text controls, and text is entered using edit box controls.

Using Static Text Controls

If you asked someone how many words one picture is worth, "a thousand" would probably be the reply, but if you show two people the same picture and ask them to come up with one word without conferring, their words likely would differ. As long as written words appear in a language the reader can understand, they are the best way to communicate exact meaning. Such informative text is regularly needed on dialog boxes. Text is often added to act as labels for other controls or to describe an option, or sometimes just to display a sentence such as a copyright message.

Formatting Text on Dialog Boxes

When simple text is required on dialog boxes you use a static text control. Each static text control can display up to 255 characters, which is entered as the caption. You can use the newline character (\n) to break the text over several lines, with left, right or center alignment. Several style settings enable raised, sunken, and various other types of borders to be added around the control. Using static text and a bit of ingenuity, dialog boxes can be made to look fairly stylish, as shown in Figure 5.1.

FIGURE 5.1

Mountain Journey:
an example of static
controls.

Combining Static Text and Edit Boxes

The most common use of static text controls on dialog boxes is to act as descriptive labels for edit boxes. *Edit boxes* are controls that enable users to enter information. Static text controls are positioned next to edit box controls as their labels because edit boxes do not themselves have captions.

You can add a static text control in front of an edit box to create a shortcut to the edit box. This is achieved using a mnemonic in the static text caption. A mnemonic gives you a way of activating a control with a keystroke. The mnemonic key is specified in the caption by preceding the letter to use as the shortcut with an ampersand (&). For example, the caption, 'Foot&ball' specifies the letter 'b' or 'B' as the mnemonic key. The caption is displayed Foot̲ball with the mnemonic key underlined. Each mnemonic on a dialog should be unique, to check for duplicates you can use the **Check M̲nemonics** option on the context menu in the resource editor.

A static text control can't receive the input focus, so when the shortcut is typed the next control in the tab order receives the focus instead. When an edit box receives the input focus, a cursor is automatically placed in the control ready for data entry.

Disabling mnemonics

If the next control is disabled when a mnemonic is entered the input focus is given to the next enabled control. To stop this behavior it is necessary to subclass the static text control.

SEE ALSO

➤ *To learn how to create edit box controls, see page 97*

Modifying Static Text Controls at Runtime

Static text controls can come in handy when all you want to do is convey a message. For example, a multiuser application might have a status dialog box that displays the current number of active users in the system. Static text controls are ideal for this type of requirement. Obviously, in this situation the number of users could vary, so the contents of the text control would have to be modified during program execution. In this section you'll create a system information dialog box. Using static text controls you'll display your computer and username and the amount of total and free memory available.

First, use the AppWizard to create a new dialog-based project called Sysinfo.

After you have the new project you must add eight static text controls and one button control to the Sysinfo dialog.

Adding static text controls to a dialog box

1. Open the dialog box, IDD_SYSINFO_DIALOG, in the resource editor. Click the TODO: Place Dialog Controls Here text then press the Delete button to remove it.

2. Select the static text image on the Controls toolbar, and add four text controls to the left side of the dialog box as shown in Figure 5.2.

3. Modify the caption of each control to read as shown in Figure 5.2.

4. Select the static text image on the Controls toolbar, and then add a text control to the right of **Computer Name**.

5. Enter a name in the **ID** combo box; use IDC_COMPUTER_NAME for this example.

6. Select the static text image on the Controls toolbar, then add a text control to the right of **Total Memory**.

7. Enter IDC_TOTAL_MEMORY in the **ID** combo box.

8. Select the static text image on the Controls toolbar, then add a text control to the right of **Free Memory**.

9. Enter IDC_FREE_MEMORY in the **ID** combo box.

10. Select the static text image on the Controls toolbar, then add a text control to the right of **Memory Load**.

11. Enter IDC_MEMORY_LOAD in the **ID** combo box.

12. Hold the Ctrl key down and select all four text controls you just added. Remove the word Static from the caption edit

box, and then select the **Styles** tab and check the **Sunken** option.

13. Select the button image on the Controls toolbar, then add a button to the bottom right of the dialog box.

14. Enter IDC_REFRESH in the **ID** combo box, and enter Refresh as the caption. Your dialog box should now look like Figure 5.2.

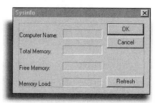

FIGURE 5.2
The Sysinfo dialog box layout.

The four sunken controls will be updated to display the relevant information each time the **Refresh** button is clicked. To do this, first associate a variable with each of them by following these steps.

Attaching variables to text controls with ClassWizard

1. Press Ctrl+W to start ClassWizard, or from the **View** menu select **ClassWizard**.

2. Select the **Member Variables** tab.

3. Select the dialog class in the **Class Name:** combo box; use CSysinfoDlg for this example.

4. Select the text control ID in the **Control IDs** list box; use IDC_COMPUTER_NAME for this example. Then click the **Add Variable** button; the Add Member Variable dialog box appears. Note, you can also add a member variable for a control by double-clicking the control's ID.

5. Ensure the **Category** combo box has **Value** selected and that the **Variable Type** has CString selected.

6. Enter the variable name in the **Member Variable Name** box; use m_strComputerName for this example. Click **OK**.

IDC_STATIC is a special identifier

By default static text controls are given the same ID, IDC_STATIC. This is a special identifier with a value of –1. This default ID must be overridden in order to attach a variable to a static text control.

7. Select **IDC_TOTAL_MEMORY** in the **Control IDs** list box, and then click the **Add Variable** button.

8. Enter m_strTotalMemory in the **Member Variable Name** box, and then click **OK**.

9. Select **IDC_FREE_MEMORY** in the **Control IDs** list box, and then click the **Add Variable** button.

10. Enter m_strFreeMemory in the **Member Variable Name** box, and then click **OK**.

11. Select **IDC_MEMORY_LOAD** in the **Control IDs** list box, and then click the **Add Variable** button.

12. Enter m_strMemoryLoad in the **Member Variable Name** box, and then click **OK**.

13. Click **OK**.

Now add a BN_Clicked message handler for the IDC_REFRESH button. For help on adding handler functions, see the "Adding a Button Click Handler Function" procedure in Chapter 4, "Using Button Controls." This should create a member function OnRefresh(). In order for this function to update the CString variable associated with each text control to display the correct information, add the code in Listing 5.1.

LISTING 5.1 LST05_1.CPP—Modifying Static Text Controls at Runtime

① The name of the computer is retrieved and stored in a string variable.

```
1  void CSysinfoDlg::OnRefresh()
2  {
3      // TODO: Add your control notification handler code here
4      // ** Variables used for getting the computer name
5      TCHAR szBuffer[256];
6      DWORD dwSize = 256;
7
8      // ** Retrieve the computer name from Windows
9      GetComputerName(szBuffer, &dwSize);  ──── ①
10
11     // ** Transfer the computer name to the appropriate
12     // ** member variable
13     m_strComputerName = szBuffer;
14
15     // ** Allocate structure to receive memory data
```

```
16      MEMORYSTATUS mem_stat;        (2)
17
18      // ** Retrieve the current memory status
19      GlobalMemoryStatus(&mem_stat);
20
21      // ** Transfer the memory details to the appropriate
22      // ** member variable variable
23      m_strTotalMemory.Format("%ld KB",     (3)
24                              mem_stat.dwTotalPhys / 1024);
25      m_strFreeMemory.Format("%ld KB",
26                             mem_stat.dwAvailPhys / 1024);
27      m_strMemoryLoad.Format("%d %%",
28                             mem_stat.dwMemoryLoad);
29
30      // ** Update the contents of controls to display
31      UpdateData(FALSE);
32  }
```

(2) The MEMORYSTATUS structure contains details of the physical and virtual memory.

(3) String variables are used to format the memory details and display them on the dialog box.

In lines 5 and 6 two local variables are declared that are then passed to the *global function* GetComputerName() function in line 9. The parameters for this function are a character buffer, which the function fills in with the name of the computer, and the address of a DWORD variable holding the maximum length of the character buffer. The character buffer variable is declared using the TCHAR macro (line 5). This macro is used to make the program compatible with both the ANSI and Unicode character sets. The Unicode character set uses two bytes to represent each character and is a standard employed to encode all possible worldwide symbols.

In line 13 the buffer contents are transferred to the m_strComputerName variable, which is associated with the IDC_COMPUTER_NAME text control.

In line 16 the mem_stat variable is declared as a MEMORYSTATUS structure. The members of this structure are shown in Listing 5.2. In line 19 the address of mem_stat is passed to the global function GlobalMemoryStatus(), which fills in the structure's variables with the current memory data. The CString::Format() function is used in lines 23, 25, and 27 to extract information from the mem_stat members and update the CString variables attached to each of the memory-related text controls.

Useful system functions

In addition to GetComputerName() you can also call GetUserName() to determine who is executing an application and GetVersionEx() to determine the operating system it is running on.

The call to UpdateData() is passed FALSE in line 31 in order to update the display of the four static text controls.

After you build and run the Sysinfo project, each time you click the **Refresh** button the memory information is updated. Try opening and closing other applications, and then click **Refresh**. The dialog box should be similar to Figure 5.3. You might wonder why the **Memory Load** figure (the percentage of memory in use) doesn't seem to add up; this is because it includes *virtual memory*, which is a file used as memory.

Virtual memory

In order for Windows applications to be able to use more memory than is physically available part of the disk pretends to be memory. This memory is called virtual memory.

LISTING 5.2 LST05_2.CPP—The *MEMORYSTATUS* Structure

```
1   typedef struct _MEMORYSTATUS {
2   DWORD dwLength;
3   DWORD dwMemoryLoad;
4   DWORD dwTotalPhys;
5   DWORD dwAvailPhys;
6
7   DWORD dwAvailPageFile;
8   DWORD dwTotalVirtual;
9   DWORD dwAvailVirtual;
10   } MEMORYSTATUS;
```

FIGURE 5.3

An example of the system information display.

SEE ALSO

➤ *For details of how to create a dialog-based application see page 44*
➤ *For more information about dialog box design, see page 51*
➤ *For help on adding handler functions, see page 66*

Using Edit Box Controls

Have you ever wondered how many characters of text are entered into computer applications around the world each day—how many people enter data of a bank transaction, order details, or inventory quantities? Well, however many characters it amounts to, on Windows it's a fair wager that most of them first arrive to an edit box.

Edit box controls are used to accept text input and display text output. Characters, numbers, and the usual symbols found on a keyboard (including accented characters) can be entered and displayed in an edit box. They also have some editing capability. For example, all or portions of the text can be selected with the mouse or keyboard and cut or copied and then pasted into a second edit box. A context menu is available by clicking the right mouse button enabling the following options: **Undo**, **Cut**, **Copy**, **Paste**, **Delete**, and **Select All**.

> **Single-line edit box limit**
>
> Single-line edit boxes are limited to a maximum of 32KB or approximately 32,000 characters.

Several useful edit box styles are available. The **Password** style hides the user input, typically by replacing the entered characters with an asterisk (*). The **Uppercase** and **Lowercase** styles automatically convert the text to a single case as it is typed. The **Number** style prevents input of non-numeric characters; note that this style will also disallow the period (.) character.

The following sections cover how you can utilize edit boxes, but first you must create a new project. Use the AppWizard to create a new dialog-based project called Edits.

You should now have a new dialog-based project open in Developer Studio.

SEE ALSO

➤ *For details of how to create a dialog-based application see page 44*

Adding Edit Boxes

As with all other controls you add edit boxes to dialog box templates from within the resource editor. Follow the steps given in "Adding Edit Boxes to a Dialog Box" to modify your Edits dialog box layout to look like Figure 5.4.

Adding edit boxes to a dialog box

1. Open the dialog box IDD_EDITS_DIALOG in the resource editor. Click the TODO: Place Dialog Controls Here text and then press the Delete button to remove it.

2. Select the static text image on the Controls toolbar, then add a text control at the top left of the dialog box as shown in Figure 5.4.

3. Be sure the text control is selected, and then click the right mouse button and select **Properties** from the context menu. The Text Properties dialog box appears. You can keep the properties dialog visible by clicking the pin icon at the top-left corner.

4. Enter a label in the **Caption** box; use &First for this example.

5. Select the edit box image on the Controls toolbar, and then add an edit box to the right of the **First** text control.

6. Enter a name in the **ID** combo box; use IDC_EDIT_FIRST for this example.

7. Select the button image on the Controls toolbar, and then add a button to the right of the edit box as in Figure 5.4.

8. Enter IDC_GET_TEXT as the **ID** and type Get Text as the caption.

9. Select the static text image on the Controls toolbar, then add a text control below the **First** text control.

10. Enter &Second in the **Caption** box.

11. Select the edit box image on the Controls toolbar, and then add an edit box to the right of the **Second** text control. Enter IDC_EDIT_SECOND as the **ID**.

12. Select the edit box image on the Controls toolbar, and then add another text control to the right of the edit box you just added.

13. Enter IDC_EDIT_SHOW as the **ID**, then select the **Styles** tab and check the **Read-only** option.

14. Extend the length of the control you just added to the right side of the dialog box. Your dialog box should look like Figure 5.4.

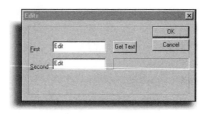

FIGURE 5.4

The Edits dialog box layout.

The Edits dialog box shows how mnemonics in static text controls act as keyboard shortcuts to edit boxes. You can test this by pressing Ctrl+T or by selecting **Test** from the **Layout** menu to display the dialog box in test mode. When in test mode, typing Alt+F should place a cursor in the edit control next to **First**. Typing Alt+S should activate the edit box next to **Second**.

Shortcuts to edit boxes

When you use a mnemonic to enable a shortcut to an edit box, the edit control must immediately follow the static text control in the tab order.

SEE ALSO

➤ *For details of how to create a dialog-based application see page 8*

Setting and Retrieving Edit Box Text

Often when edit boxes are placed on dialog boxes, the text entered in them is accessed only when required, typically when the user clicks a button such as **OK**. At this point the text is extracted from the control and stored internally by the program, or possibly written to a field on a database. You can use ClassWizard to attach a CString variable to the edit control. The wizard creates the variable declaration and invokes macros that handle the exchange of data between the variable and the control, enabling you to easily extract and update the value of the edit box's text.

Attaching a *CString* variable to an edit box with ClassWizard

1. Press Ctrl+W to start ClassWizard, or from the **View** menu select **ClassWizard**.

2. Select the **Member Variables** tab.

3. Select the dialog class in the **Class Name** combo box; use **CEditsDlg** for this example.

4. Select the control ID in the **Control IDs** list box; select **IDC_EDIT_FIRST** for this example.

5. Click the **Add Variable** button. The Add Member Variable dialog box appears. Note, you can also add a member variable for a control by double-clicking the control's ID.

6. Make sure the **Category** combo box has **Value** selected and the **Variable Type** has `CString` selected.

7. Enter the variable name in the **Member Variable Name** box; use `m_strFirst` for this example, and then click **OK**.

8. Enter 15 in the **Maximum Characters** box at the bottom of the ClassWizard dialog box. This restricts the length of the string accepted by the edit box.

9. Click **OK**.

Now that the controls are added the **Get Text** button will be used to extract the text in the **First** edit control, reverse the text, and place it back into the edit control. To do this, add a `BN_CLICKED` message handler for the `IDC_GET_TEXT` button. For help on adding handler functions, refer to Chapter 4.

You should now have a member function `OnGetText()`. Edit the function as shown in Listing 5.3.

LISTING 5.3 LST05_3.CPP—Getting and Setting Text in an Edit Box

① Ensure the string is not blank.	
② The order of the characters within the string variable is reversed.	
③ The reversed string is shown on the dialog box.	

```
1   void CEditsDlg::OnGetText()
2   {
3       // TODO: Add your control notification handler code here
4       // ** Exchange data from control to variable
5       UpdateData();
6
7       // ** Check if any text has been entered
8       if (m_strFirst.IsEmpty() == FALSE) ────① 
9       {
10          // ** Display the entered text
11          MessageBox(m_strFirst);
12
13          // ** Reverse the characters in the string
14          m_strFirst.MakeReverse(); ────② 
15
16          // ** Exchange data from the variable
17          // ** to the control
18          UpdateData(FALSE); ────③ 
19      }
20  }
```

The call to UpdateData() in line 5 uses the default parameter TRUE, which transfers text from the control to the variable m_strFirst. In line 8 the CString function IsEmpty() returns FALSE when m_strFirst is not blank. In line 13 the MakeReverse() member function of CString simply reverses the characters in the string and then UpdateData() is called again, this time passing FALSE to transfer the contents of the now changed variable back in to the control.

Responding to Edit Notification Messages

What has been covered so far allows the text to be retrieved after it has been entered. When you handle messages that are sent each time the text changes it is possible to retrieve the text as it is being entered. Windows sends eight notification messages dealing with edit controls. These are shown in Table 5.1. For example, the EN_CHANGE notification message is sent each time the text within a control alters.

TABLE 5.1 Edit control notification messages

Message	Description
EN_CHANGE	Sent to indicate that the text has changed after it has been displayed.
EN_UPDATE	Sent to indicate that the text has changed before it has been displayed.
EN_SETFOCUS	Sent when the control is receiving the input focus.
EN_KILLFOCUS	Sent when the control loses the input focus.
EN_MAXTEXT	Sent to indicate the text was longer than allowed and was truncated.
EN_HSCROLL	Sent when the horizontal scrollbar is clicked (multiline only).
EN_VSCROLL	Sent when the vertical scrollbar is clicked (multiline only).
EN_ERRSPACE	Sent when the control cannot allocate memory.

Now you'll create a message handler for the EN_CHANGE notification of the **Second** edit box. In the handler function you'll retrieve the latest entered text and transfer it into the read-only edit box. This will give the impression that text is actually being typed in two places at once. You'll use ClassWizard to add the message handler.

Until now message handlers were added using the New Windows Message and Event Handler dialog box, but like all good Windows software, Developer Studio offers several methods of performing the same task. ClassWizard can be more convenient because it is not just limited to dealing with messages, and it circumvents the need to open dialog box templates.

Creating a message handler with ClassWizard

1. Press Ctrl+W to start ClassWizard, or from the **View** menu select **ClassWizard**.

2. Select the **Message Maps** tab.

3. Select the dialog class in the **Class Name** combo box; use `CEditsDlg` for this example.

4. Select the control ID in the **Object IDs** list box; select `IDC_EDIT_SECOND` for this example.

5. Select the message in the **Messages** list box; use `EN_CHANGE` for this example.

6. Click the **Add Function** button.

7. Click **OK** on the Add Member Function dialog box showing `OnChangeEditSecond` as the new member function. The ClassWizard dialog box should now look like Figure 5.5.

8. Click **Edit Code** to start editing this new handler function.

Now you should have the skeleton function `OnChangeEditSecond()`; add the code as shown in Listing 5.4. This function will be called every time the user changes the text in the `IDC_EDIT_SECOND` control, which includes deleting characters as well as inserting them.

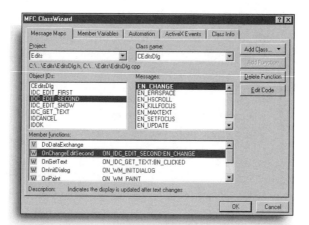

FIGURE 5.5
The ClassWizard dialog
box after adding the
EN_CHANGE handler.

LISTING 5.4   LST05_4.CPP—Capturing the *EN_CHANGE* Notification

```
1   void CEditsDlg::OnChangeEditSecond()
2   {
3       // TODO: If this is a RICHEDIT control,
4       // the control will not send this notification
5       // unless you override the CDialog::OnInitDialog()
6       // function to send the EM_SETEVENTMASK message
7       // to the control with the ENM_CHANGE flag ORed
8       // into the lParam mask.
9
10      // TODO: Add your control notification handler code here
11
12      // ** Get a pointer to each of the edit controls
13      CEdit* pEdit = (CEdit*)GetDlgItem(IDC_EDIT_SECOND);
14      CEdit* pEditShow = (CEdit*)GetDlgItem(IDC_EDIT_SHOW);
15
16      // ** Declare a varaible to hold the entered text
17      CString strText;
18
19      // ** Retrieve the text from the "Second" edit box
20      pEdit->GetWindowText(strText);
21
22      // ** Update the context of the read-only edit box
23      pEditShow->SetWindowText(strText);
24  }
```

(1) Assign pointers to each edit control.

(2) Retrieve the contents of the first edit control into a string variable.

(3) Set the contents of the second edit control equal to that of the first.

Notice that ClassWizard has added some additional comments at the top of the function regarding using rich edit text controls. However, because we are not using this type of control the comments can safely be ignored.

In lines 13 and 14, the `GetDlgItem()` function is called to retrieve a separate pointer to each of the edit controls you are dealing with. These pointers are cast to type `CEdit`.

The `CEdit` class is the *MFC library* class that encapsulates edit box functionality. Like other control classes `CEdit` is derived from `CWnd`. The `CEdit` class adds numerous functions to those already provided by `CWnd`. Some of the most useful functions are shown in Table 5.2.

The `GetWindowText()` call in line 20 gets the current edit box text and updates the local variable `strText` with its contents. This variable is then used to copy the text into the read-only edit box in line 23.

Build and run the program. Now as you type in the **Second** edit box identical text should appear in the read-only control on its right. You might notice that if you click the read-only control a cursor appears but you are not able to enter text. You can alter this behavior by adding a handler function for the `EN_SETFOCUS` notification of the `IDC_EDIT_SHOW` control. Use the steps given in "Creating a Message Handler with ClassWizard" to help you. Then in the created `OnSetFocusEditShow()` function add the following line of code:

```
GetDlgItem(IDC_EDIT_SECOND)->SetFocus();
```

Build and run. Now if you click in the read-only control the cursor will appear in the **Second** edit control instead.

TABLE 5.2 *CEdit* Member Functions

Function Name	Description
`Create()`	Allows edit controls to be created at runtime.
`GetSel()`	Gets the start and end character position of the current selected text.

Function Name	Description
SetSel()	Selects a range of characters.
ReplaceSel()	Replaces the current selected text.
LimitText()	Sets the maximum number of characters allowed.

SEE ALSO

➤ *For help on adding handler functions, see page 66*

➤ *For more information on exchanging and validating data in controls, see page 223*

➤ *For more details of the* CWnd *class, see page 66*

Subclassing Edit Controls

Often text must be entered in a specific format and also in a preferred format. For example, countries around the world have postal codes; some are purely numeric and some are combinations of letters and numbers. Windows applications that enable such codes to be entered should validate according to the applicable rules. The best time to perform this validation is when the code is being entered. To do this it is necessary to extend the edit box functionality by subclassing the CEdit class. *Subclassing* is creating a new class by inheriting the member attributes and functions of an existing class. The new class can utilize the behavior of its base class and override its functionality where required.

In this section you'll develop a new class derived from CEdit called CInitials. This new class will be used to force the entry of people's initials in a specific manner. For example, only alphabetical characters will be allowed and they will be converted to uppercase automatically. The class will also insert full stops automatically after each initial and will automatically remove them if the user presses the backspace key.

To do this you'll first need to add some more edit controls to the Edits dialog box.

What is subclassing?

A subclass is a class derived from an existing class that inherits the member attributes and functions of the exisiting class.

Adding further edit boxes to the Edits dialog box

1. Open the IDD_EDITS_DIALOG in the resource editor.

2. Select the static text image on the Controls toolbar, then add a text control at the bottom left of the dialog box as shown in Figure 5.6.

3. Enter Initials in the **C**aption box.

4. Select the edit box image on the Controls toolbar, then add an edit box to the right of the **Initials** text control.

5. Enter IDC_EDIT_INITIALS in the **ID** combo box.

6. Select the static text image on the Controls toolbar, then add a text control to the right of the edit box you just added (see Figure 5.6).

7. Enter Surname in the **C**aption box.

8. Select the edit box image on the Controls toolbar, then add an edit box to the right of the **Surname** text control.

9. Extend the length of the control just added to the right side of the dialog box. Your dialog box should look like Figure 5.6.

FIGURE 5.6
The Edits dialog box extended.

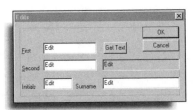

After you add the edit boxes, create the CInitials class. During the steps you might notice that ClassWizard can be used to subclass many other *MFC library* classes, not just CEdit.

Creating a new subclass with ClassWizard

1. Press Ctrl+W to start ClassWizard, or from the **V**iew menu select **Class**W**izard**.

2. Select the **Message Maps** tab.

3. Select CEditsDlg in the **Class name:** combo box.

4. Click the **Add Class** button, then from the menu that appears select **New**. The New Class dialog box appears as shown in Figure 5.7.

5. Enter CInitials in the **Name** box.

6. Select CEdit in the **Base Class** combo box.

7. Click **OK** to create the new class.

8. Select the **Member Variables** tab. Selet *CEditsDlg* in the **Class Name** combo box.

9. Select IDC_EDIT_INITIALS in the **Control IDs:** list box.

10. Click the **Add Variable** button. The Add Member Variable dialog box appears.

11. Enter m_edtInitials for the **Member Variable Name**.

12. Select **Control** in the **Category** combo box.

13. Select CInitials in the **Variable Type** combo box. The description at the bottom of the dialog box should read **Map to CInitials Member (User-Defined-Class)**.

14. Click **OK** to add the new member variable. A message will be displayed informing you that it is necessary to add an #include directive. Click **OK**.

15. Click **OK** to close the ClassWizard dialog box.

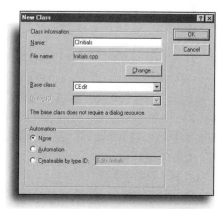

FIGURE 5.7
The New Class dialog box.

The new class CInitials should now appear in the ClassView pane. First you'll need to add the #include directive mentioned by ClassWizard. To do this, double-click the CEditsDlg class item on the ClassView pane. The header file of the CEditDlg class appears in the editor window. Edit the header file, adding a single line above the class declaration line. After you have edited the file it should look like this:

```
#include "Initials.h"
class CEditsDlg : public CDialog
{
...
```

When ClassWizard created this class for you it generated two new files and added them to the project: Initials.h and Initials.cpp. The #include directive is required in EditsDlg.h because the CEditsDlg class now has a member variable of type CInitials that is declared in Initials.h. Not entering the #include would result in compilation errors.

Now you can use the CInitials class to perform the specific task of entering a person's initials. The first task will be to reject any non-alphabetic characters, convert to uppercase characters entered in lowercase, and automatically add a period after each letter. You can do all this by creating a handler function for the WM_CHAR message. The WM_CHAR message is sent whenever a normal keyboard character is pressed when the edit control has the input focus. Unlike the notification message EN_CHANGE, the handler function for the WM_CHAR message receives the characters before they are displayed and therefore is the ideal place to perform validation. If the character is valid it can be passed to the edit control. If it is invalid it can simply be ignored.

Creating a subclass message handler function with ClassWizard

1. Press Ctrl+W to start ClassWizard, or from the **View** menu select **ClassWizard**.

2. Select the **Message Maps** tab.

3. Select CInitials in the **Class Name** combo box.

4. Select WM_CHAR in the **Messages** list box.

5. Click the **Add Function** button. OnChar appears in the **Member Functions** list at the bottom of the ClassWizard dialog box.

6. Click the **Edit Code** button.

You now have the member function OnChar() within the CInitials class. This function is called when a character is entered in the **Initials** edit box. The nChar argument contains the integer value of the entered character. The additional arguments nRepCnt and nFlags are not relevant to this example and they need not concern you. Add the code shown in Listing 5.5.

LISTING 5.5   LST05_5.CPP—The *OnChar* Handler Function

```
1   void CInitials::OnChar(UINT nChar, UINT nRepCnt, UINT nFlags)
2   {
3       // TODO: Add your message handler code here and/or call
        ➡default
4       // ** Validate the entered character is alphabetic
5       if( isalpha(nChar) ) ─────(1)
6       {
7           // ** Convert lower case to upper case
8           if( islower(nChar) ) ─────(2)
9               nChar -= 32;
10
11          // ** Call the default windows procedure as
12          // ** the value of nChar may have been altered
13          DefWindowProc(WM_CHAR, nChar, ─────(3)
14                          MAKELONG(nRepCnt, nFlags));
15
16          // ** Call the default windows procedure
17          // ** again to add the period
18          nChar = '.';
19          DefWindowProc(WM_CHAR, nChar,
20                          MAKELONG(nRepCnt, nFlags));
21      }
22      // ** If the backspace key is pressed call the
23      // ** base class function twice to remove the period
24      // ** and the letter
25      if( nChar == VK_BACK ) ─────(4)
26      {
27          CEdit::OnChar(nChar, nRepCnt, nFlags);
28          CEdit::OnChar(nChar, nRepCnt, nFlags);
29      }
30  }
```

(1) Check to see whether the character entered is alphabetic.

(2) Convert lowercase characters to uppercase.

(3) Call the default window procedure to perform standard processing for an entered character. Change the character to a period, then call the default window procedure again.

(4) Convert a single backspace into a double backspace.

The `if` statement in line 5 checks to see whether the character passed to the function in the `nChar` argument is alphabetic. In line 8 a check is performed to see whether the character is lowercase. If it is, it's converted to uppercase by subtracting 32 (the difference between lower and uppercase characters in the ANSI character set).

In line 13 the `DefWindowProc()` (default window procedure) function is called. It is necessary to call this function rather than the base class function `CEdit::OnChar()` because the latter will not note any changes made to the `nChar` argument. If you read the online help of the `CWnd::OnChar()` function you will see a note that states the function uses the original message parameters, ignoring any passed parameters.

In line 18 the value of `nChar` is replaced with a period, and this is sent to the edit control by calling `DefWindowProc()` once again.

In line 25 a check is made to see whether the backspace key was pressed. `VK_BACK` is a symbolic name that defines the virtual keycode value of the backspace key. Virtual keycode definitions exist for all keys. Table 5.3 shows a few examples. If the backspace key was pressed the base class `CEdit::OnChar()` function is called twice in order to remove both the period and the letter.

Build and run. Test the functionality of your `CInitials` class.

TABLE 5.3 Virtual keycodes

Definition	Key Description
VK_BACK	Backspace
VK_TAB	Tab key
VK_LEFT	Left arrow
VK_RIGHT	Right arrow
VK_RETURN	Enter key
VK_ESCAPE	Esc key
VK_CONTROL	Ctrl key

Using Multiple-Line Edit Controls

Edit boxes are not limited to being single lines. To create a multiple-line edit box all you must do is increase its vertical height on the dialog box template and check the **Multiline** style. You will probably also find it necessary to check the **Want Return** style. With **Want Return** checked you can press Enter within the edit box to insert a new line.

Multiple-line edit boxes handle vertical scrolling and can add scrollbars automatically when there are more lines of text that can fit within the control.

Thankfully the principles of using multiple-line edit boxes are much the same as using single-line controls. You use the CEdit class, which has several member functions specifically for multi-line operations as shown in Table 5.4.

Multiple-line edit box limit

Multiple-line edit boxes are limited to a maximum of 64KB or approximately 64,000 characters.

TABLE 5.4 *CEdit* multiple-line member functions

Function Name	Description
GetLineCount()	Gets the number of lines.
GetLine()	Gets a line of text.
FmtLines()	Turns on or off soft line breaks.
SetTabStops()	Enables tab stop positions to be specified.

The final type of edit control to mention is the rich edit control. This control is far more extensive than an edit box and allows both character and paragraph formatting. Rich edit controls are rarely seen on dialog boxes; they usually are embedded within an application view. For this reason they are not covered at this stage.

SEE ALSO

➤ *For details of the Rich Edit Control, see page 497*

6

Using List Controls

Displaying lists of information on
dialog boxes

Maintaining data in a tree structure

Handling single and multiple item
selection

Implementing dependency between
different lists on a dialog box

The presentation of information within a program has the greatest bearing on how user friendly an application is. The more user friendly an application, the more successful it's likely to be. Much of this information comes in the form of lists: directories and files, font names and styles, maybe even the list of aircraft on final approach into L.A.

The best way to display a list of data depends on exactly what information it contains and whether one or more of the items are selectable. For this reason several types of list controls are available, both textual and graphical. Each control has specific characteristics and numerous styles that can be exploited to suit any circumstance. For example, a combo box shows a list in a similar fashion to a drop-down menu, allowing only single selection, whereas a tree control can be used to show a hierarchy of items with images against each node.

Creating List Controls

List controls come in four varieties: combo boxes, list boxes, trees, and list controls. Each type suits a particular programming purpose. When adding list controls to dialog boxes, it's important to select the correct style properties because these can radically alter both the look and behavior of the control. For example, multiple selection can be allowed for both list boxes and list controls, and the combo box style Drop List enables edit box functionality whereas Dropdown does not.

Throughout this chapter the uses of the various types of list controls are explored; first you'll need to use the AppWizard to create a new dialog-based project called Lists. The project will utilize all four varieties of list control to display directory and file information.

SEE ALSO
➤ *For details of how to create a dialog-based application, see page 44*

Adding Combo Boxes

A combo box control is so called because it is actually a combination of controls: an edit box, a list box, and a button. A combo box is used to display a list of choices and enable only a single selection. Combo boxes are unique among list controls in that the selected item is always visible as it is displayed at the top of the control.

There are three types of combo box as described in Table 6.1. The type is set from the **Styles** tab of the Combo Box Properties dialog box when adding the control to the dialog template.

In the Lists example, a combo box is used to enable selection of a main directory, which is then interrogated to fill other controls on the dialog box with details of subdirectories and files.

TABLE 6.1 Combo box types

Type	Description
Simple	Combines an edit box with a list box. The list is always visible and the selected item is displayed in the edit box.
Dropdown	Combines an edit box with a button and list box. The list box is visible only when the button is clicked.
Drop List	Combines a static text with a button and list box. This is the same as the Dropdown type except the user cannot type into the control.

Adding a combo box control to the Lists dialog box

1. Open the IDD_LISTS_DIALOG in the resource editor and remove the TODO text control.

2. Remove the **Cancel** button and reposition the **OK** button at the bottom right of the dialog box. You will be required to add several more controls to this dialog box, so increase its overall width and height as shown in Figure 6.1.

3. Select the Static Text image on the Controls toolbar, and then add a text control at the top left of the dialog box.

4. Enter Main Directory as the caption.

5. Select the Combo Box image on the Controls toolbar, and then add a combo control to the right of **Main Directory**.

6. Extend the length of the combo box to the right side of the dialog box.

115

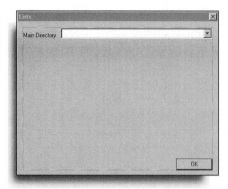

FIGURE 6.1

Adding a combo box to the Lists dialog box.

7. Enter IDC_MAIN_DIR in the **ID** combo box.

8. Select the **Styles** tab and in the **Type** combo box, select **Drop List**. Your dialog box should now look similar to Figure 6.1.

When a combo box is added to a dialog box, the **Sort** option is checked by default. This means that items added to the combo box will automatically appear in alphabetical order. To turn this behavior off, select the **Styles** tab and uncheck the **Sort** option. Another common requirement with combo boxes is to alter the size of the drop-down list box. This is accomplished by clicking the arrow at the right of the control. A formatting frame then appears to indicate the list box display, which can be resized using the sizing buttons.

After you have added the combo box control to your dialog box, use ClassWizard to attach a variable as shown in the following steps.

Attaching a *CComboBox* variable to a combo box control with ClassWizard

1. Press Ctrl+W to start ClassWizard or from the **View** menu select **ClassWizard**.

2. Select the **Member Variables** tab.

3. Select CListsDlg in the **Class Name** combo box.

4. Select IDC_MAIN_DIR in the **Control IDs** list box.

5. Click the **Add Variable** button; the Add Member Variable dialog box appears.

6. Ensure the <u>C</u>ategory combo box has **Control** selected and the **Variable <u>T</u>ype** has `CComboBox` selected.

7. Enter `m_cbMainDir` in the **Member Variable <u>N</u>ame** box and then click **OK**.

8. Click **OK** to close ClassWizard.

SEE ALSO

➤ *For details about the new extended combo box, see page 261*

The new extended combo box

Visual C++ 6 has an extended combo box control that enables you to add images to the standard combo box.

Adding Tree Controls

The tree control is unique because it is the only control geared specifically toward showing hierarchical information. A tree control has a left-to-right structure. An item on the far left of the tree is called a *root node*. An item on the far right (having no subitems) is called a *leaf node* and an item between a root and a leaf is called a *branch node*. Whether lines are displayed to connect items is configurable with styles. By default, tree controls allow only single-item selection; if you require a user to be able to select several items in a tree at one time then you'll need to write the code to do it.

In the Lists project, a tree control is used to display the files within a directory alphabetically. You will add a root node for each letter of the alphabet and then insert items to represent files under the appropriate node.

To add a tree control to the Lists project, follow these steps and then map a variable to it by performing the "Attaching a `CTreeCtrl` Variable to a Tree Control with ClassWizard" steps.

Adding a tree control to the Lists dialog box

1. Open the `IDD_LISTS_DIALOG` in the resource editor.

2. Add a static text control called Files to act as a title for the tree control as shown in Figure 6.2.

3. Select the Tree Control image on the Controls toolbar, and then add a tree control to the left of the dialog box.

4. Enter `IDC_FILES_TREE` in the <u>I</u>D combo box.

5. Select the **Styles** tab and check the **Has B<u>u</u>ttons, H<u>a</u>s Lines,** and **Li<u>n</u>es at Root** options. Your dialog box should now look like Figure 6.2.

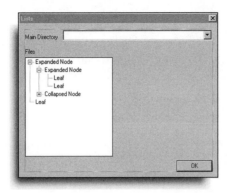

FIGURE 6.2

Adding a tree control to the Lists dialog box.

Attaching a *CTreeCtrl* variable to a tree control with ClassWizard

1. Press Ctrl+W to start ClassWizard, or from the **View** menu select **ClassWizard**.

2. Select the **Member Variables** tab.

3. Select **CListsDlg** in the **Class Name** combo box.

4. Select **IDC_FILES_TREE** in the **Control IDs** list box.

5. Click the **Add Variable** button; the Add Member Variable dialog box appears.

6. Ensure the **Category** combo box has **Control** selected and the **Variable Type** has **CTreeCtrl** selected.

7. Enter m_treeFiles in the **Member Variable Name** box and then click **OK**.

8. Click **OK** to close ClassWizard.

SEE ALSO

➤ *For more information on tree control styles and using tree controls in a view, see page 488*

Adding List Box Controls

Tree controls and multiple item selection

The CTreeCtrl class doesn't support multiple item selection but you can subclass CTreeCtrl to add this functionality if you want.

A list box in its simplest form is a straightforward list of items, but unlike the combo box or tree control a list box can support either single- or multiple-item selection. In fact, there are four types of selection available as described in Table 6.2.

TABLE 6.2 List box selection types

Type	Description
Single	Only one item can be selected. Selecting an item removes the previous selection.
Multiple	Several items can be selected by using the mouse in combination with the Shift and Ctrl keys.
Extended	Like Multiple, but several items can also be selected by dragging the mouse over them with the left button clicked.
None	No items can be selected.

As with combo boxes, the style to automatically sort items is checked by default. To turn this behavior off, select the **Styles** tab and uncheck the **Sort** option. The Lists project uses a list box to display a list of subdirectories. Several of these subdirectories can then be selected from the list box and further details about the selected items are shown in a list control. To add a multiple-selection list box to the Lists project, follow the steps given in "Adding a List Box Control to the Lists Dialog Box." The procedure refers to the style option **No Integral Height**, which is unchecked so that the height of the control is calculated to display an exact number of items. If you leave the option checked, the control could display partial items.

Adding a list box control to the Lists dialog box

1. Open the `IDD_LISTS_DIALOG` in the resource editor.

2. Add a static text control, Sub Directories, to act as a title for the list box control (see Figure 6.3).

3. Select the List Box image on the Controls toolbar, and then add a list box to the dialog box as shown in Figure 6.3.

4. Enter `IDC_SUB_DIRS` in the **ID** combo box.

5. Select the **Styles** tab and in the **Selection** combo box, choose **Extended**.

6. On the **Styles** tab, uncheck the **No Integral Height** option. Your dialog box should now look like Figure 6.3.

Now that the list box is added, map a variable to it.

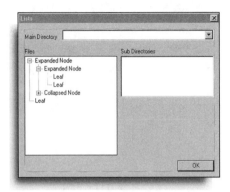

FIGURE 6.3

Adding a list box to the Lists dialog box.

Attaching a *CListBox* variable to a list box control with ClassWizard

1. Press Ctrl+W to start ClassWizard, or from the **View** menu select **ClassWizard**.

2. Select the **Member Variables** tab.

3. Select `CListsDlg` in the **Class Name** combo box.

4. Select `IDC_SUB_DIRS` in the **Control IDs** list box.

5. Click the **Add Variable** button; the Add Member Variable dialog box appears.

6. Ensure the **Category** combo box has **Control** selected and the **Variable Type** has `CListBox` selected.

7. Enter m_lbSubDirs in the **Member Variable Name** box and then click **OK**.

8. Click **OK** to close ClassWizard.

Adding a List Control

Windows Explorer uses a list control

The most famous example of the list control is found in Windows Explorer. The **View** menu shows the four different display modes.

The list control is a little confusingly named because the other three controls described in this chapter are also types of list controls. However, the list control is the most complex of the four and is more commonly used within a view than on a dialog box. A list control is capable of displaying images as well as associated text items and has four view modes as described in Table 6.3.

TABLE 6.3   List control view modes

Mode	Description
Icon	Displays large icons (32×32 pixels) with text positioned under each icon. Items are ordered across and then down.
Small Icon	Displays small icons (16×16 pixels) with text positioned to the right of each icon. Items are ordered across and then down.
List	Display is the same as Small Icon but items are ordered down and then across.
Report	Displays information in columns with column headers.

In the Lists example, the list control is used to display details of the directories selected in the list box above it on the dialog box. The list control will have three columns; the first column will contain the directory name, the second will show the number of files within the directory, and the third will display the size of the directory in megabytes. To add the list control, follow these steps. Then map a variable to it by performing the "Attaching a CListCtrl Variable to a List Box with ClassWizard" steps.

Adding a list control to the Lists dialog box

1. Open IDD_LISTS_DIALOG in the resource editor.
2. Add a static text control, Selected Directory Details, to act as a title for the list control (see Figure 6.4).

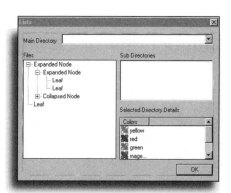

FIGURE 6.4

Adding a list control to the Lists dialog box.

3. Select the List Control image on the Controls toolbar, and then add a list control to the dialog box as shown in Figure 6.4.

4. Enter IDC_SELECTED_DIRS in the **ID** combo box.

5. Select the **Styles** tab, and in the **View** combo box choose **Report**. Your dialog box should now look like Figure 6.4.

Attaching a _CListCtrl_ variable to a list box control with ClassWizard

1. Press Ctrl+W to start ClassWizard, or from the **View** menu select **ClassWizard**.

2. Select the **Member Variables** tab.

3. Select CListsDlg in the **Class Name** combo box.

4. Select IDC_SELECTED_DIRS in the **Control IDs** list box.

5. Click the **Add Variable** button; the Add Member Variable dialog box appears.

6. Ensure the **Category** combo box has **Control** selected and the **Variable Type** has CListCtrl selected.

7. Enter m_lcDirDetails in the **Member Variable Name** box then click **OK**.

8. Click **OK** to close ClassWizard.

SEE ALSO

➤ *For more information on list control styles and using list controls in a view, see page 472*

Adding Items to List Type Controls

Because list controls are aimed at dealing with the display and selection of multiple pieces of data, the first programming requirement is to populate the control with information. Each entry added to a list control is referred to as an item. Although there are similarities between the mechanism employed for inserting items, you'll see that each control class has its own specific peculiarities.

Populating a Combo Box

The combo box is the only one of the four list controls that can be populated with items from the resource editor. This is accomplished by selecting the **Data** tab on the Combo Box Properties dialog box. An example is shown in Figure 6.5. Each item can then be typed into the **Enter Listbox Items** box. If you have cause to do this at any time, remember to press Ctrl+Enter after each item because pressing the Enter key alone will close the dialog box. It is unusual to populate a combo box this way; normally a combo box is populated at runtime and often within the OnInitDialog() function. The MFC framework calls this function when the dialog box is first opened before it is displayed.

FIGURE 6.5
The **Data** tab of the
Combo Box Properties
dialog box.

The MFC class that encapsulates a combo box is CComboBox. This class has several functions that deal with adding and removing items; these are shown in Table 6.4. Each item is given a zero-based index number when added, and this index can then be used to access the particular item.

TABLE 6.4   *CComboBox* population functions

Function Name	Description
AddString	Adds an item either to the end or in its correct sorted position
DeleteString	Removes an item
InsertString	Inserts an item in a specific position
ResetContent	Removes all existing items
Dir	Special population method for inserting filenames as items

For the Lists example, the combo box is populated from within the dialog box's OnInitDialog() function, with a list of main directories ascertained using some of Windows global

functions. To do this, first add a new member function named
`PopulateCombo()` with return type void. Then edit `OnInitDialog()`
to call this new function after the `//TODO:` comments as shown in
line 28 of Listing 6.1. Then add the code shown between lines
34 and 53 to insert items into the combo box.

① Call the
PopulateCombo
function from within
OnInitDialog.

LISTING 6.1 LST06_1.CPP—Populating the Combo Box

```
1   BOOL CListsDlg::OnInitDialog()
2   {
3       CDialog::OnInitDialog();
4
5       // Add "About..." menu item to system menu.
6       // IDM_ABOUTBOX must be in the system command range.
7       ASSERT((IDM_ABOUTBOX & 0xFFF0) == IDM_ABOUTBOX);
8       ASSERT(IDM_ABOUTBOX < 0xF000);
9
10      CMenu* pSysMenu = GetSystemMenu(FALSE);
11      if (pSysMenu != NULL)
12      {
13          CString strAboutMenu;
14          strAboutMenu.LoadString(IDS_ABOUTBOX);
15          if (!strAboutMenu.IsEmpty())
16          {
17              pSysMenu->AppendMenu(MF_SEPARATOR);
18              pSysMenu->AppendMenu(MF_STRING, IDM_ABOUTBOX,
                    ➥strAboutMenu);
19          }
20      }
21      // Set the icon for this dialog box.
        ➥//The framework does this automatically
22      //  when the application's main window
        ➥//is not a dialog box
23      SetIcon(m_hIcon, TRUE);      // Set big icon
24      SetIcon(m_hIcon, FALSE);     // Set small icon
25
26      // TODO: Add extra initialization here
27      // ** Initialize the main directory combo box
28      PopulateCombo();
29      return TRUE;  // return TRUE  unless you set the focus
        ➥//to a control
30  }
```

① (circled marker pointing to lines 21–24)

```
31
32   void CListsDlg::PopulateCombo()
33   {
34       TCHAR szBuffer[MAX_PATH];
35
36       // ** Get the Windows directory, usually C:\Windows
37       // ** and add to the combo box
38       GetWindowsDirectory(szBuffer, MAX_PATH);
39       m_cbMainDir.AddString(szBuffer);
40
41       // ** Chop off the directory to leave the drive letter C:
42       // ** and add to the combo box
43       szBuffer[2]=0;
44       m_cbMainDir.AddString(szBuffer);
45
46       // ** Get the System directory,
     ➥//usually C:\Windows\System
47       // ** and add to the combo box
48       GetSystemDirectory(szBuffer, MAX_PATH);
49       m_cbMainDir.AddString(szBuffer);
50
51       // ** Get the present directory and add to the combo box
52       GetCurrentDirectory(MAX_PATH, szBuffer);
53       m_cbMainDir.AddString(szBuffer);
54   }
```

(2) Add the Windows directory to the combo box.

(3) Reduce the string to the drive letter only and add to the combo box.

(4) Add the system directory to the combo box.

(5) Add the current directory to the combo box.

The GetWindowsDirectory(), GetSystemDirectory(), and GetCurrentDirectory() function calls shown in lines 38, 48, and 52, respectively, are global functions that fill in the string buffer szBuffer argument with the appropriate pathname. The MAX_PATH define is used to specify the maximum length of a path; in the majority of cases this is 260. After each path is retrieved, the szBuffer is then passed to the AddString() function of the m_cbMainDir member variable, which is responsible for inserting the item into the combo box. Because the combo box has the Sort style, the inserted items will be automatically placed in alphabetical sequence.

Responding to Combo Box Notification Messages

Check for errors when populating a combo box

You should check the return values of the **AddString()** and **InsertString()** functions. If an error occurs these return either **CB_ERR** or **CB_ERRSPACE**.

The purpose of a combo box is to allow one of the items it contains to be selected. When this occurs normally, the program must know immediately and respond to the changed selection. Capturing the CBN_SELCHANGE notification message, sent from the control to the dialog box whenever the selected item is altered, enables this.

Add a CBN_SELCHANGE message handler for the IDC_MAIN_DIR combo box. This should create a member function OnSelchangeMainDir(). You will also need to add a new CString member variable, m_strMainDir, to store the retrieved path. The m_strMainDir will be used in the next sections to populate both the tree control and the list box. Now add the code in Listing 6.2.

① Called when the combo box selection changes.

② Gets the index of the selected directory.

③ Gets and stores the selected directory name.

④ Calls a function to populate the tree control.

LISTING 6.2 LST06_2.CPP—Retrieving the Text of a Selected Combo Box Item

```
1   void CListsDlg::OnSelchangeMainDir()  ——— ①
2   {
3       // TODO: Add your control notification handler code here
4       // ** Retrieve the index of the selected item
5       int nIndex = m_cbMainDir.GetCurSel();  ——— ②
6
7       // ** Check the index is valid
8       if(nIndex != CB_ERR)
9       {
10          // ** Get the text of the selected item and store in a
11          // ** member variable and call functions to populate
12          // ** the other controls
13          m_cbMainDir.GetLBText(nIndex, m_strMainDir);  ——— ③
14          PopulateTree();  ——— ④
15      }
16  }
```

On receiving notification that the selected item has changed in line 5, the GetCurSel() function is called and returns the index of the selected item to nIndex. If no item is selected, the special value CB_ERR is returned, which is checked for in line 8. If the nIndex is valid, in line 13 it is passed to the GetLBText() function along with the member variable m_strMainDir, which the function fills in. You can see that a new function, PopulateTree(), is called in line 14; this is created in the next section.

Populating a Tree

When populating a tree, it's often necessary to store information about the structure of the tree in order to insert items as parents or subitems of previously inserted items.

The MFC class that encapsulates a tree is CTreeCtrl; this class has the functions shown in Table 6.5 that deal with adding and removing items. The InsertItem() function has several overloaded versions to cater for associating images and pointers to data external to the tree, if necessary. Each inserted item is given an HTREEITEM handle that can be passed to InsertItem(), making it possible to create the tree hierarchy.

TABLE 6.5 *CTreeCtrl* population functions

Function Name	Description
InsertItem	Adds an item either as a root item or as a subitem, depending on its parameters.
DeleteItem	Removes an item.
DeleteAllItems	Removes all existing items.

To populate the Lists tree, first create a new member function named PopulateTree() with return type void. The tree shows the files of the directory selected in the combo box in alphabetic sequence. The function first inserts an item for each letter of the alphabet and then a 27th item to contain filenames not starting with a letter. It then uses some functions provided by Windows to acquire the directory contents and inserts the name of each file in the appropriate place in the tree. When you have created the PopulateTree() function, add the code shown in Listing 6.3.

LISTING 6.3 LST06_3.CPP—Populating a Tree Control

① Add root items (letters of the alphabet).

② Find a file in the directory m_strMainDir.

③ Iterate through the files in the main directory.

```cpp
1   void CListsDlg::PopulateTree()
2   {
3       // ** Remove all existing tree items
4       m_treeFiles.DeleteAllItems();
5       // ** Allocate an array of HTREEITEMS
6       HTREEITEM hLetter[27];              ──── ①
7       // ** Insert items 'A' through 'Z' as root items
8       for(int nChar = 'A'; nChar <= 'Z'; nChar++)
9           hLetter[nChar - 'A'] =
                ➥m_treeFiles.InsertItem((TCHAR*)&nChar);
10
11      // ** Insert 'Other' item as a root items
12      hLetter[26] = m_treeFiles.InsertItem("Other");
13
14      HANDLE hFind;
15      WIN32_FIND_DATA dataFind;
16      BOOL bMoreFiles = TRUE;
17      CString strFile;
18
19      // ** Find the first file in the main directory                ②
20      hFind = FindFirstFile(m_strMainDir + "\\*.*", &dataFind);
21
22      // ** Continue to loop until all files have been found
23      while(hFind != INVALID_HANDLE_VALUE && bMoreFiles == TRUE)
24      {                                                              ③
25          // ** Check a file has been found and not a directory
26          if(dataFind.dwFileAttributes ==
                ➥FILE_ATTRIBUTE_ARCHIVE)
27          {
28              // ** Get the first letter of the file name
29              int nChar = dataFind.cFileName[0];
30              // ** Convert lower case letters to upper case
31              if(islower(nChar))
32                  nChar -= 32;
33              // ** If the file name starts with a letter then
34              // ** subtract 'A' to find the index in to
35              // ** the hLetter array, for others use index 26
36              if(isalpha(nChar))
37                  nChar -= 'A';
38              else
39                  nChar = 26;
```

```
40          // ** Insert the file name in to the tree
41          m_treeFiles.InsertItem(dataFind.cFileName,   ──④
            ➥hLetter[nChar]);
42       }
43       // ** Find the next file in the main directory
44       bMoreFiles = FindNextFile(hFind, &dataFind);
45    }
46    // ** Close the file handle
47    FindClose(hFind);
48 }
```

④ Insert the filename into the tree.

In line 4, the call to `DeleteAllItems()` removes all existing items; this is necessary because the tree is populated every time the directory selected in the combo box is changed. The `for` loop in lines 8 and 9 calls the `InsertItem()` function, passing in each letter A to Z; because no other parameters are passed, these are automatically inserted as root items. Each time the `InsertItem()` function is called, the returned `HTREEITEM` handle is stored in the `hLetter` array; therefore, `hLetter[0]` stores the handle of A, `hLetter[1]` stores the handle of B, and so on. An `"Other"` root item is inserted at line 12 that will contain filenames not starting with a letter.

To acquire the list of files, first a call is made to the `FindFirstFile()` function in line 20. The `m_strMainDir + "\\*.*"` is passed to this function to find all the files in the selected directory. Then to move to the next file a call is made to `FindNextFile()` in line 44. This function returns `FALSE` when there are no more files, which terminates the loop. These `Find` functions fill in the `dataFind` variable, which is a `WIN32_DATA_FIND` structure. This structure contains information about each entry found.

The type attributes of the file are checked in line 26 to ensure it is a standard file and not a directory. The first letter of the filename is extracted in line 29 and converted to uppercase if necessary in line 32. The check in line 36 ascertains whether the filename starts with a letter and if so, converts the integer value of the letter to an index into the `hLetter` array. The `InsertItem()` call in line 41 passes the filename to be inserted and the handle of the `HTREEITEM` of its parent.

Associating a tree item with application data

Sometimes it is handy to associate each item within a tree with a pointer to an object. this can be done using the `SetItemData()` and `GetItemData()` functions.

Build and run the application. The combo box should display several directories, and selecting one should cause the tree to be populated with its files, as shown in Figure 6.6.

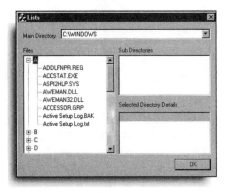

Populating a List Box

Populating a list box is virtually identical to populating a combo box because the list of items in a combo box are actually list box items. The major difference between the two controls is their display and the fact that list boxes are capable of handling multiple item selection.

The MFC class that encapsulates a list box is `CListBox`. The functions that deal with adding and removing items are identical to those shown in Table 6.4, earlier in this chapter.

For the Lists example, the list box is populated with the names of the subdirectories under the main directory selected in the combo box. To do this, first add a new member function named `PopulateListBox()` with return type `void`. Then edit the `OnSelchangeMainDir()` function to call this new function after the call to `PopulateTree()`.

Now add the code shown in Listing 6.4 to populate the list box with subdirectory names.

LISTING 6.4   LST06_4.CPP—Populating a List Box

```cpp
void CListsDlg::PopulateListBox()
{
    // ** Remove all existing list box items
    m_lbSubDirs.ResetContent();                    (1)

    HANDLE hFind;
    WIN32_FIND_DATA dataFind;
    BOOL bMoreFiles = TRUE;

    // ** Find the first file in the main directory        (2)
    hFind = FindFirstFile(m_strMainDir + "\\*.*", &dataFind);

    // ** Continue to loop until all files have been found
    while(hFind != INVALID_HANDLE_VALUE &&          (3)
    ➥bMoreFiles == TRUE)
    {
        // ** Check if a directory has been found
        if(dataFind.dwFileAttributes ==
        ➥FILE_ATTRIBUTE_DIRECTORY)
        {
            // ** Add the directory name to the list box
            // ** ignoring the "." and ".." directory entries
            if(strcmp(dataFind.cFileName, "."))            (4)
                if(strcmp(dataFind.cFileName, ".."))
                    m_lbSubDirs.AddString(dataFind.cFileName);
        }
        // ** Find the next file in the main directory
        bMoreFiles = FindNextFile(hFind, &dataFind);
    }
    // ** Close the file handle
    FindClose(hFind);
}
```

(1) Clear the list box.

(2) Find a file in the directory m_strMainDir.

(3) Iterate through the files in the main directory.

(4) Insert the directory name into the list box, ignoring the "." and ".." directories.

In line 4, the call to ResetContent() removes all existing items; this is necessary because the list box is populated every time the directory selected in the combo box is changed. For details of the `FindFirstFile()` and `FindNextFile()` functions, please refer to the section "Populating a Tree" earlier in this chapter.

The type attribute of the file item is checked in line 17 to ensure it is a directory. The two `strcmp()` function calls in lines 21 and 22 cause the directory entries `"."` and `".."` to be ignored. The `AddString()` call in line 23 is passed the filename (in this case the name of the subdirectory) that is inserted into the list box. If you build and run the application now, you should find that selecting a directory in the combo box causes both the tree and the list box to be populated.

Responding to List Box Notification Messages

Actions performed by the user on list box controls cause notification messages to be sent to the dialog box. The `LBN_SELCHANGE` message is sent if the selected item or items (for multiple selection controls) change. The way in which selection is dealt with depends on whether the control allows multiple item selection and the `CListBox` class has functions specific to each type.

The list box on the Lists example allows multiple selection. The notification handler creates a list of the selected directories in a new member variable, `m_strList`, which is a `CStringList` type. First add this new variable using the Add Member Variable dialog box.

Add an `LBN_SELCHANGE` message handler for the `IDC_SUB_DIRS` list box. This should create a member function `OnSelchangeSubDirs()`. The function must establish how many items are selected, and then retrieve the text of each one and add it to the `m_strList` variable. Finally, the function will call a new function, `PopulateListControl()`, which will use `m_strList` to insert details into the list control. Now add the code shown in Listing 6.5.

CStringList

`CStringList` is an example of an MFC helper class. It is used to manage a growable list of individual `CString` objects.

LISTING 6.5 LST06_5.CPP—Responding to List Box Notification Messages

```cpp
1   void CListsDlg::OnSelchangeSubDirs()                (1)
2   {
3       // TODO: Add your control notification handler code here
4       // ** Get the number of selected items
5       int nSelCount = m_lbSubDirs.GetSelCount();      (2)
6
7       // ** Clear the string list
8       m_strList.RemoveAll();
9       if(nSelCount)
10      {
11          CString str;
12          // ** Create an int array to store the indexes and
13          // ** initialize with the indexes of selected items
14          LPINT pItems = new int[nSelCount];
15          m_lbSubDirs.GetSelItems(nSelCount, pItems);
16
17          for(int i = 0; i < nSelCount; i++)          (3)
18          {
19              // ** Retrieve selected item text and
20              // ** store it in a string list
21              m_lbSubDirs.GetText(pItems[i], str);
22              m_strList.AddTail(str);                 (4)
23          }
24          // ** Tidy up the int array
25          delete [] pItems;
26      }
27      // ** Now populate the list control
28      PopulateListControl();                          (5)
29  }
```

(1) Called when the list box selection changes.

(2) Retrieves the number of selected items in the list box.

(3) Fills the array from the control.

(4) Adds the selected sub-directory name to the string list variable m_strList.

(5) Calls the function that populates the list control.

The GetSelCount() function in line 5 returns the number of selected items and is used only for multiple-selection controls. In line 8, all existing strings in the m_strList variable are removed using the RemoveAll() of CStringList ready for the list of strings to be rebuilt.

In line 14, an array of `int`s is allocated; this array will contain the indexes of the selected items and therefore must be equal in size to `nSelCount`. The `pItems` variable is an `int` pointer and is initialized pointing to the beginning of the array. You can see the array is deallocated in line 25, using `delete []` when it is no longer needed.

In line 15, the `GetSelItems()` function retrieves from the control the list of selected items. This list is in the form of the zero-based index. The second parameter is the address of the `int` array, which is filled in by the function.

The `for` loop in line 17 iterates for the number of selected items. Each time, `GetText()` is called, passing in the next index from the array (`pItems[I]`) and storing the text in the `str` variable. Then in line 22 this text is added to the end on the `m_strList` variable. Because each time the list of selected subdirectories alters, the sample will change, the items shown in the list control `PopulateListControl()` are called at the end of the function in line 28.

Populating a List Control

The method of populating a list control is a little different than that of the other forms of list controls covered in this chapter. It also differs depending on which type of list control is being used; there are four (Icon, Small Icon, List, and Report), which are explained in the section "Adding a List Control" earlier in this chapter. Probably the most common (and useful) type is the Report type. The Report type displays information in columns. For example, Explorer's Report view shows Name, Size, Type, and Modified as column headings and the file details are displayed in rows down the screen.

The MFC class that encapsulates a list control is `CListCtrl`; this class has the functions shown in Table 6.6 that deal with adding and removing items.

TABLE 6.6 *CListCtrl* population functions

Function Name	Description
InsertColumn	Adds a new column at a specific position
DeleteColumn	Removes a column
InsertItem	Adds a new item
DeleteItem	Removes an existing item
DeleteAllItems	Removes all existing items
SetItemText	Inserts the text of a subitem

The Lists example uses a Report Type list control with columns for the directory name, the number of files in the directory, and the accumulated size of those files. The first thing necessary is to insert the columns; because these don't change, this can be done in the OnInitDialog() function. The actual data items will be added to the control in PopulateListControl() as mentioned in the previous section. Now is the time to add this function using a void return type.

Now add the additional code shown between lines 8 and 11 of Listing 6.6 to the OnInitDialog() function.

LISTING 6.6 LST06_6.CPP—Initializing List Control Columns

```
1   BOOL CListsDlg::OnInitDialog()
2   {
3
4   ...
5       // TODO: Add extra initialization here
6       // ** Initialize the main directory combo box
7       PopulateCombo();
8       // ** Initialize the list control columns
9       m_lcDirDetails.InsertColumn(0, "Directory", LVCFMT_LEFT, 70);
10      m_lcDirDetails.InsertColumn(1, "Files", LVCFMT_RIGHT, 50);
11      m_lcDirDetails.InsertColumn(2, "Size KB", LVCFMT_RIGHT, 60);
12
13      return TRUE;   // return TRUE  unless you set the focus to a
                          ➥control
14  }
```

(1) Initialize the list control with three columns.

The first parameter of `InsertColumn()` is the zero-based index number of the column. You have a choice of `LVCFMT_LEFT`, `LVCFMT_RIGHT`, or `LVCFMT_CENTER` text alignment and the final parameter is the initial column width in pixels. The width can be altered using the mouse at runtime. Now add the code shown in Listing 6.7 to populate the control fully.

LISTING 6.7 LST06_7.CPP—Populating a List Control

① Iterate the files in each subdirectory.

```
1   void CListsDlg::PopulateListControl()
2   {
3       // ** Remove all existing list control items
4       m_lcDirDetails.DeleteAllItems();
5
6       POSITION pos;
7       // ** Iterate round the list of directories selected
8       // ** from the list box
9       for(pos = m_strList.GetHeadPosition(); pos != NULL;)
10      {
11          int nItem;
12          HANDLE hFind;
13          WIN32_FIND_DATA dataFind;
14          BOOL bMoreFiles = TRUE;
15          CString str;
16          CString strFind;
17
18          str = m_strList.GetAt(pos);
19          // ** Add a row to the list control (column 0)
20          nItem = m_lcDirDetails.InsertItem(0, str);
21
22          strFind = m_strMainDir + "\\" + str + "\\*.*";
23          hFind = FindFirstFile(strFind, &dataFind);
24
25          int nFileCount = 0;
26          double nFileSize = 0;
27
28          // ** Loop finding each file in the directory and
29          // ** total up the file count and size variables
30          while(hFind != INVALID_HANDLE_VALUE &&  ——————①
               ↪bMoreFiles == TRUE)
31          {
32              if(dataFind.dwFileAttributes ==
                   ↪FILE_ATTRIBUTE_ARCHIVE)
```

```
33              {
34                  nFileCount++;
35                  nFileSize += (dataFind.nFileSizeHigh *
                    ➥MAXDWORD)
36                                      + dataFind.nFileSizeLow;
37              }
38              bMoreFiles = FindNextFile(hFind, &dataFind);
39          }
40          // ** Close the file handle
41          FindClose(hFind);
42
43          // ** Format the text of the file count and
44          // ** insert it as column 1
45          str.Format("%ld", nFileCount);
46          m_lcDirDetails.SetItemText(nItem, 1, str);
47
48          // ** Format the text of the file size and
49          // ** insert it as column 2
50          str.Format("%-1.2f", nFileSize / 1024.0);
51          m_lcDirDetails.SetItemText(nItem, 2, str);
52
53          m_strList.GetNext(pos);
54      }
55  }
```

(2) Increment the file count and the total file size.

(3) Add the file count column details.

(4) Add the file size column details.

The DeleteAllItems() function call in line 4 removes all existing items from the list control but does not remove the columns. The for loop in line 9 iterates around the m_strList variable that was built in the OnSelchangeSubDirs() function. Each CString in the list represents a directory selected from the list box. The InsertItem() at line 20 is passed the directory name and this is added as column 0. The InsertItem() function returns the zero-based index of the newly added item and is held in nItem. You can see this is passed to the SetItemText() calls in lines 46 and 51, which inserts the text of the other two columns.

For details of the FindFirstFile() and FindNextFile() functions, refer to the section "Populating a Tree" earlier in this chapter.

Build and run the program. Test the multiple selection of the list box; you should receive results similar to those shown in Figure 6.7.

FIGURE 6.7
The Lists program.

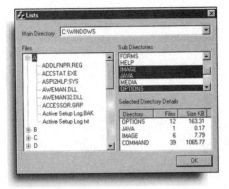

SEE ALSO

➤ *For more information on list control styles, see page 472*

chapter
7

Using Progress, Scrollbar, Slider, and Date Time Controls

Using progress controls to display
the progress of a lengthy task

Exploiting sliders and scrollbars to
specify a position and selection in a
certain range

Utilizing the new date time picker and
month calendar controls to specify
dates, times, and calendar ranges

Range-Oriented Controls

Your programs will often need to let the user specify a value from a range of values, define the endpoints of a certain range, provide the user with feedback about a current range setting, or show the progress through a lengthy task. These ranges might represent different types of data such as numeric, date, time, or some application-specific derivation such as meters or miles. Visual C++ 6 provides a variety of controls available from the resource editor's Controls palette each with MFC wrappers to provide a quick and easy mechanism for this kind of user interaction. This chapter covers these types of controls and demonstrates how you can integrate them into your applications.

Using a Progress Control

You would normally use a progress control to indicate to the user the current progress of a lengthy task. A progress control is drawn as a solid or dotted blue line that steadily fills a rectangle as the task progresses, as shown in Figure 7.1. You don't have to use a progress control just to display the progress of a task; you could also use it to represent a value in a range. For example, Figure 7.2 shows how progress controls could be used to display a graphic equalizer like you'd find on a HIFI system.

FIGURE 7.1

A typical progress control used to indicate task completion.

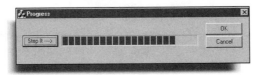

FIGURE 7.2

Progress controls used to represent range values, like a HIFI graphic equalizer.

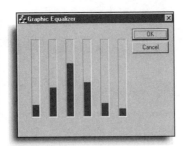

Adding a Progress Control to a Dialog Box

You can add a new progress control to a dialog box from the resource editor by dragging the progress control icon from the Controls palette and positioning it on your dialog box. You can then size the control as required. The progress control icon is shown under the mouse pointer in Figure 7.3 described by a ToolTip.

Copying and pasting controls

You can create a duplicate of an existing control (of any type) from your new dialog box or any other dialog box by using the normal copy and paste procedures (Ctrl+C and Ctrl+V). This will then create a new control that inherits the size and properties of the original copied control.

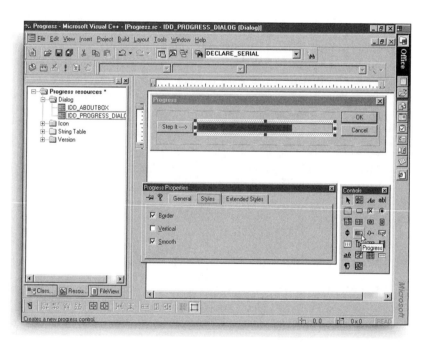

FIGURE 7.3

Adding a progress control to a dialog box with the resource editor.

Figure 7.3 also shows the **Styles** tab of the Progress Properties dialog box. You can invoke the Progress Properties dialog box by selecting the control and pressing Alt+Enter, or by right-clicking over the control and selecting the **Properties** options from the pop-up context menu.

The Progress Properties dialog box lets you change the ID of the control from the **General** tab. You should set the **ID** to a name appropriate to the control, and change any other control properties shown on this tab as required.

Default progress style settings

If you don't change the **Styles** tab of the Progress control, by default the **Border** style is set on and the **Vertical** and **Smooth** styles are set off.

The **Styles** tab of the Progress Properties dialog box lets you change the following visual aspects of the control by clicking the corresponding check boxes:

- **Border.** If checked, a thin black border is drawn around the control.
- **Vertical.** If checked, the control is draw vertically rather than horizontally.
- **Smooth.** If checked, the progress bar is drawn as a continuous bar rather than a blocky bar.

The example shown in Figure 7.1 shows how a simple AppWizard-generated dialog-based application can be tailored to display a progress bar that is incremented when the **Step It-->** button is pressed. If you want to follow this example, create the dialog-based application with AppWizard and add a progress and button control as shown in Figure 7.3. The progress control in the example has an **ID** of IDC_MY_PROGRESS, and the button has an **ID** of IDC_STEPIT. The following sections show how to map an MFC class to the progress control, and how to update the control's bar.

SEE ALSO

➤ *For more detail about dialog box editing and control properties, see page 44*

Mapping a Variable to a Progress Control

You can use ClassWizard to map a member variable to the progress control. Progress controls are mapped with the MFC CProgressCtrl class.

Mapping a member variable to a progress control

1. From the resource editor, select the new progress control to be mapped by clicking it.
2. Press Ctrl+W, or click the **View** menu and select the **ClassWizard** option to invoke ClassWizard showing the **Member Variables** tab. Ensure that the **Class Name** combo is set to the appropriate class for the new control (such as CProgressDlg).

3. You can simply double-click the new progress control with the corresponding control **ID**, or click **Add Variable** to display the Add Member Variable dialog box for the new control.

4. You can enter a name for the new member in the **Member Variable Name** edit box (such as m_MyProgress in the sample program).

5. Notice that the **Category** combo box is set to **Control**, and the **Variable Type** is `CProgressCtrl`. These are the only options available for the progress control.

6. Click **OK** to confirm the mapping for the new control and close the Add Member Variable dialog box. You should see the name of your new mapped member variable appear to the right of the corresponding ID for your control listed in the **Control ID's** list.

7. Click **OK** to close ClassWizard and add the new member variable to your chosen class.

After you've mapped the control, you can manipulate the mapped member variable to change the displayed characteristics of the control as described in the next section.

SEE ALSO
➤ *For a more detailed explanation of member variable mapping, see page 221*

Manipulating and Updating the Progress Control

You can manipulate progress controls by calling methods on the mapped `CProgressCtrl` member variable. The progress control has a range that defines the integer values which correspond to an empty progress control (0% full) to a complete progress control (100% full). It also has a current position that represents what proportion of the control should be filled corresponding to the progress through the defined range. Finally, you can set a step value to increment the control position by whenever the controls' `StepIt()` member function is called.

> **The progress common control**
> Because the progress control is one of the new common controls, you must be running Windows 95/NT 3.51 or a later operating system version to use this and the other common controls.

Setting the Progress Control's Range

Using 32-bit ranges with progress controls

The `SetRange()` function is limited to accepting 16-bit values. This means the greatest range you can set is –32768 to 32767. If you require a bigger range or larger lower and upper number, you must use the `SetRange32()` function instead, which accepts 32-bit values. This lets you set range values from –2147483648 to 2147483647.

Initially you should set the range of the progress control. You can set these values by calling the control's `SetRange()` member function, passing two integer values for the lower and upper values of the control's range. Typically you'd set the range to values that correspond directly to a task you are performing. For example, if you are calculating the prime numbers between 3000 and 7000, you can set the range values to those numbers.

You would probably set the range once when the control is initialized (although you can change it again at any time). The obvious place to initialize the control is at the end of the dialog box's `OnInitDialog()` function.

In the sample program, you can set the control's range from 0 to 10. If the position is set to 0, the control should be blank, if set to 10 it should be full. By clicking on the **ClassView** tab of the project workspace view and clicking on the plus signs next to the project name and classes, you can view the project's classes and their members. If the dialog-based application were called Progress, a corresponding `CProgressDlg` class will handle the application's main dialog box. You should also find an `OnInitDialog()` member function for this class that can be viewed in the editor window merely by double-clicking on the `OnInitDialog()` entry in the ClassView. To initialize the progress control's range, you could add the following line at the end of `OnInitDialog()` just before the return statement:

```
m_MyProgress.SetRange(0,10);
```

The progress control's range is now set from 0 to 10.

There is also a corresponding `GetRange()` function that takes two integers by reference as parameters and sets the first to the lower-range value and the second to the upper-range value. You can use this function to determine the current range set to a progress control.

SEE ALSO
➤ *For a more information about dialog box initialization, see page 123*

Setting the Progress Control's Position

After you've set the progress control's range, you can update the displayed position just by calling the SetPos() member function. This will update the position of the control to the integer value you pass SetPos() and redraw the control to reflect the position. If the value is beyond the control's upper range, the bar will be drawn as full, if below the control's lower range the bar will be drawn as empty.

In the sample program, you can add a line to set the initial position of the bar to zero immediately after setting the range with a line like this:

```
m_MyProgress.SetPos(0);
```

This initialization isn't strictly necessary because the control's position is initialized to the lower position of the range by default. You could then show the control as being half complete by adding the following line:

```
m_MyProgress.SetPos(5);
```

Rather than updating the control with an absolute value between the range endpoints, you could change the current position by a relative amount using the OffsetPos() function. When you pass a value to OffSetPos(), that value is added to the current position and the control is redrawn to reflect the change.

Setting and Using the Step Value

You can set an automatic value to increment the control whenever an update signal is received. The SetStep() function lets you set such a step value by passing it an integer increment value. You can subsequently update the progress control's position by calling the StepIt() function with no parameters to signal it.

For example, in the sample program you could add another line to the end of OnInitDialog() to set the control's step increment value to 1 with a line like this:

```
m_MyProgress.SetStep(1);
```

Then you could add a handler function for the **Step It-->** dialog button (by double-clicking on the button in the resource editor) that calls the progress control's StepIt() function like this:

> **The Fire sample application**
>
> The Fire sample application is a hot demonstration of the progress and slider controls. This sample can be obtained from the MSDN CD or the MSDN Web site at `www.microsoft.com/msdn` by searching for FIRE.

```
void CProgressDlg::OnStepit()
{
    m_MyProgress.StepIt();
}
```

If you build and run the sample program after adding this button handler code, you'll see that clicking on the **Step It-->** button advances the progress control. You'll also notice that when it has reached the end of the bar after 10 clicks, another call to StepIt() empties the control and the process repeats.

Using a Scrollbar Control

Scrollbars are often seen attached to the frame of a window to scroll the contents (as described in detail in Chapter 18, "Sizing and Scrolling Views"). However, they can also be used as controls in their own right to specify a position on a defined range. Nowadays, the slider control (discussed in the next section) largely takes over this role; even so, you should still know about scrollbars because the slider control borrows much of its underlying functionality.

SEE ALSO

➤ *For more information on using scrollbars to scroll a window, see page 458*

Adding a Scrollbar Control to a Dialog Box

The dialog resource editor lets you drag the scrollbar control onto the dialog box from the Controls palette. There are two scrollbar icons on the Controls palette, one for a horizontal scrollbar (as shown by the ToolTip in Figure 7.4), and the other next to it for vertical scrollbars. You can then position and size the scrollbar as required, and set its ID as appropriate from the **General** tab of the Scrollbar Properties dialog box (invoked by pressing Alt+Enter after selecting the control).

FIGURE 7.4
Adding vertical and horizontal scrollbars with the dialog resource editor.

The **Styles** tab of the Scrollbar Properties dialog box shows only one setting to let you configure the scrollbar alignment, called **Align**. You can set this alignment to one of three values:

- **None.** The default setting, this will draw the scrollbar to the size of the scrollbar rectangle you've set in the dialog template.

- **Top/Left.** This will draw the scrollbar with a standard width and align it at the top and left of the size of the scrollbar rectangle you've set in the dialog template.

- **Bottom/Right.** This has the same effect as the **Top/Left** setting, except that the scrollbar is aligned to the bottom and right of the rectangle.

SEE ALSO
➤ *For more detail about dialog editing and control properties, see page 44*

Mapping a Variable to a Scrollbar Control

You can map a scrollbar to a variable following the "Mapping a Member Variable to a Progress Control" step by step, earlier in this chapter. The only noticeable difference is in the **Category** combo box and **Variable Type** mentioned in step 5. A scrollbar control can only have a **Control** category setting, but a slider control lets you select either **Control** or **Value** for the category setting.

If you select **Value**, the **Variable Type** is set to int. An integer member variable mapped to the slider control is then inserted into your selected destination class. The new mapped integer member variable will then be updated by the control position in a way similar to how an integer can be updated by an edit control (discussed in detail in the "Adding Member Variables to Store Dialog Data" section of Chapter 10, "Using Dialog Boxes").

147

Using the control mapping category

Whenever you map a control using the **Control** category setting, the mapped control class (for example, `CScrollBar`) will always be derived from the **CWnd** class. This means that any operations you can perform on a window such as changing its size and position can be performed from your code using the mapped control member variable. You can see an example of an edit control resized in this way in the "Handling the Final Size Event" section of Chapter 18, "Sizing and Scrolling Views."

Scrollbar range limitations

You can pass an integer value for the minimum and maximum range values, but the difference between the two values must not exceed 32767.

If you select the **Control** category setting, the **Variable Type** will be automatically set to the MFC `CScrollBar` mapping class. You can continue the "Mapping a Member Variable to a Progress Control" step by step to dismiss the Add Member Variable dialog box and ClassWizard.

SEE ALSO

➤ *For a more detailed explanation of member variable mapping, see page 221*

Initializing a Scrollbar Control

You can initialize the scrollbar from the `OnInitDialog()` function like you did for a progress control. The scrollbar also has a range like the progress control, which you can set by calling the `CScrollBar` class's `SetScrollRange()` function and passing it the minimum and maximum position values as the first and second parameters, respectively. You also can set an optional redraw flag for the third parameter (which defaults to `TRUE` if omitted).

For example, if you've mapped the scrollbars as shown in Figure 7.4 to two `CScrollBar` member variables called `m_ScrollBar1` (vertical) and `m_ScrollBar2` (horizontal), you might initialize them both at the end of the `OnInitDialog()` function with these lines:

```
m_ScrollBar1.SetScrollRange(0,100);
m_ScrollBar2.SetScrollRange(0,200);
```

In this case, the vertical scrollbar (`m_ScrollBar1`) will have a range of 0 to 100, whereas the horizontal scrollbar (`m_ScrollBar2`) will have a minimum value of 0 and a maximum of 200. No third parameter is passed, so both scrollbars are redrawn by default (you could pass a `FALSE` value as a third parameter to inhibit redrawing). A corresponding `GetScrollRange()` function can be passed two pointers to integers that will receive the current scroll range, like this:

```
int nMin,nMax;
m_ScrollBar2.GetScrollRange(&nMin,&nMax);
TRACE("Range = (%d to %d)\n", nMin,nMax);
```

If you want to disable either of the scrollbar arrows drawn at the ends of the scrollbar, you can call the scrollbar's `EnableScrollBar()` function, passing one of the flag values shown in Table 7.1.

TABLE 7.1 Flag values for *EnableScrollBar()* to disable the scrollbar arrows

Flag Value	Description
ESB_DISABLE_BOTH	Disables both scrollbar buttons.
ESB_DISABLE_LTUP	Disables the left or up button (depending on the scrollbar orientation).
ESB_DISABLE_RTDN	Disables the right or down button (depending on the scrollbar orientation).
ESB_ENABLE_BOTH	Enables both scrollbar buttons (this is the default action if no parameters are passed to EnableScrollbar()).

Like the progress control, you can set the current scrollbar position represented by the movable rectangle portion by calling the scrollbar's SetScrollPos() function passing an integer value representing the position within the defined scrolling range. A corresponding GetScrollPos() function also returns the current position.

If you want to set the position rectangle's size so that it represents a proportion of the scrolling range (such as the size of one page in a text document), you can use the SetScrollInfo() function passing a pointer to a SCROLLINFO structure. Most of this structure duplicates the functions to set the position and range that you've seen already.

The relevant member variable of the SCROLLINFO structure is the nPage. You should set nPage to an integer value that represents the visible page size as a proportion of the entire scroll range. For example, consider that you are writing a word processor application. Your application's entire scrollbar range for the whole document may be set from 0 to 100, and the screen may display only one page at a time. So for a 2-page document, you may want to set the nPage member variable to 50 to represent that a single page is half of the document. However, for a 20-page document, you should set the nPage member variable to 5 to represent that a single page is a 1/20th of the whole document (that is, a 1/20th portion of the 0 to 100 range).

You must also set the fmask member to SIF_PAGE to inform SetScrollInfo() that the nPage member is valid, and the cbSize

The SCROLLINFO structure

GetScrollInfo() is a corresponding function to SetScrollInfo() that can be used to fill a SCROLLINFO structure with details about the scrollbar. GetScrollInfo() needs two parameters, the first is a pointer to a SCROLLINFO structure that you want to fill, and the second is a bitmask of SCROLLINFO flag values that you want to retrieve. These flag values can be a combination of SIF_RANGE, SIF_POS, SIF_TRACKPOS, and SIF_PAGE to set the nMin and nMax, nPos, nTrackPos, and nPage SCROLLINFO member variables, respectively. Alternatively, the SIF_ALL flag will set them all.

member to the size of the structure (common in Win32 structures). For example, to set the page size of the vertical scrollbar to 30, you'd add the following lines after the call to `SetScrollRange()` in your initialization code:

```
SCROLLINFO si;
si.cbSize = sizeof(SCROLLINFO);
si.nPage = 30;
si.fMask = SIF_PAGE;
m_ScrollBar1.SetScrollInfo(&si);
```

After running these lines, the size of the scrollbar position indicator rectangle will be larger for the vertical scrollbar than the default size set in the horizontal scrollbar.

SEE ALSO

➤ *For more information about using the* TRACE *macro, see page 714*

Handling Scrollbar Notification Messages

Whenever the user repositions a scrollbar, presses one of the buttons, or presses Page Up/Page Down or the up/down arrow keys, a notification message is sent from the scrollbar to its owner (parent) window. These notification messages are the Windows WM_HSCROLL and WM_VSCROLL messages for horizontal and vertical scrollbars, respectively. You can add handlers for these messages from the **New Windows Messages/Events** dialog box in the usual way. The dialog-based application's main dialog class will handle the parent window for the scrollbar, so the handler function should be inserted there. For example, if your dialog-based application were called Scroll, the main application class would be CScrollDlg; this class should be selected in the **Class or Object to Handle** list of the **New Windows Messages/Events** dialog box. (If you need help with this, you can follow the "Adding an OnHScroll() Handler Function to Catch WM_HSCROLL or WM_VSCROLL Messages" step by step from Chapter 18, "Sizing and Scrolling Views." You'll need to substitute the view class references with your application's main dialog class, and pick WM_VSCROLL rather than WM_HSCROLL.)

After you insert a new handler function for the WM_VSCROLL message, you'll see the following ClassWizard-generated handler code:

```
void CScrollDlg::OnVScroll(UINT nSBCode, UINT nPos,
➡CScrollBar* pScrollBar)
{
    // TODO: Add your message handler code here and/or call
    CDialog::OnVScroll(nSBCode, nPos, pScrollBar);
}
```

The handler function for WM_HSCROLL messages is identical in its definition and structure except that it is called OnHScroll(). If you have both horizontal and vertical scrollbars you'll need separate handler functions for both orientations.

The first parameter passed (nSBCode) is a flag that indicates the type of scrolling action taken by the user. This action depends on how he used the scrollbar control (for example, dragged the rectangle, clicked on its arrows or body, or pressed a page or arrow key). The possible values for this flag value are shown in Table 7.2. You must first determine whether you want to handle the scrollbar (in case it's a window scrollbar, in which case the CDialog's base class OnVScroll() handler will deal with it). Then you can use this flag value to decide how the scrollbar should be repositioned. If you don't explicitly reposition the scrollbar with a call to the scrollbar's SetScrollPos() function, when the user releases the drag rectangle it will spring back to the beginning of the scrollbar control!

Negative scrollbar positions

If the initial scrollbar range allows the scrollbar to represent a negative number, it is possible that nPos should contain a negative number. However, because it is passed as a UINT (unsigned integer value), large positive numbers will represent the negative value instead. If you know that this might be the case, you should cast the nPos variable to an int data type so it can represent negative values.

TABLE 7.2 Flag values passed by the *nSBCode* parameter of a scrollbar handler

Flag Value	Meaning
SB_THUMBTRACK	The user has dragged the scroll rectangle to a specific position. You can find the position from the second nPos parameter.

continues...

TABLE 7.2 Continued

Flag Value	Meaning
SB_THUMBPOSITION	The user has dragged the scroll rectangle to a specific position and released the button. You can find the position from the second nPos parameter.
SB_ENDSCROLL	The user has released the mouse button after holding it on one of the end arrows or the main body (not the position rectangle).
SB_LINEUP	The scroll box position should be decreased by one.
SB_LINELEFT	Same as SB_LINEUP, but for horizontal scrollbars.
SB_LINEDOWN	The scroll box position should be increased by one.
SB_LINERIGHT	Same as SB_LINEDOWN, but for horizontal scrollbars.
SB_PAGEUP	The scroll box position should be decreased by one (application-specific) page value.
SB_PAGELEFT	Same as SB_PAGEUP, but for horizontal scrollbars.
SB_PAGEDOWN	The scroll box position should be increased by one (application-specific) page value.
SB_PAGELEFT	Same as SB_PAGEDOWN, but for horizontal scrollbars.

WM_VSCROLL and WM_HSCROLL messages

You must remember that vertical scrollbars send the WM_VSCROLL message, which is handled by the OnVScroll() handler. However, horizontal scrollbars send the WM_HSCROLL message, and require a different OnHScroll() handler. A common mistake is to implement one handler function that handles only either the vertical or horizontal scrollbar messages. It might have been better if Microsoft had sent just one message for all scrollbars that included an orientation flag. But unfortunately, the original 16-bit restrictions in the early days of Windows necessitated two messages.

You can find out which scrollbar sent the message by interrogating the third parameter passed to the OnVScroll() handler, which is a pointer to the scrollbar that the user has changed. Probably the best and easiest way to identify the scrollbar is to use its ID. You can find this by calling the GetDlgCtrlID() function on the pScrollbar pointer. This function will return the associated ID of the control, which you can compare with your known controls to decide whether (and how) it should be handled.

The code shown in Listing 7.1 shows a sample scrollbar handler for the WM_VSCROLL message. After the correct scrollbar has been identified, the type of operation is identified and dealt with appropriately to update the scrollbar position from the current position. The horizontal scrollbar position is then also updated to mirror the changes to the vertical scrollbar, so if the user drags the vertical scrollbar, the horizontal bar position rectangle will move as well.

LISTING 7.1   LST7_1.CPP—Handling the Scrollbar Messages and Updating the Scrollbar Position

```
1   void CScrollDlg::OnVScroll(UINT nSBCode, UINT nPos,
➥ CScrollBar* pScrollBar)
2   {
3       if (pScrollBar->GetDlgCtrlID() == IDC_SCROLLBAR1)         (1)
4       {
5           int nCurrentPos = pScrollBar->GetScrollPos();
6           switch(nSBCode)
7           {
8               case SB_THUMBTRACK:
9               case SB_THUMBPOSITION:
10                  pScrollBar->SetScrollPos(nPos);              (2)
11                  break;
12              case SB_LINEUP:
13                  pScrollBar->SetScrollPos(nCurrentPos-1);
14                  break;
15              case SB_LINEDOWN:
16                  pScrollBar->SetScrollPos(nCurrentPos+1);
17                  break;
18              case SB_PAGEUP:
19                  pScrollBar->SetScrollPos(nCurrentPos-5);
20                  break;
21              case SB_PAGEDOWN:
22                  pScrollBar->SetScrollPos(nCurrentPos+5);
23                  break;
24          }
25          m_ScrollBar2.SetScrollPos(           (3)
26              2 * pScrollBar->GetScrollPos());
27      }
28
29      CDialog::OnVScroll(nSBCode, nPos, pScrollBar);
30  }
```

(1) Check the ID to ensure that the notification is for the correct scrollbar.

(2) Update the scrollbar position depending on the message sent from the scrollbar by user interaction.

(3) This line updates the second scrollbar to twice the value of the first scrollbar as the second scrollbar's range is actually double that of the first.

Line 3 of Listing 7.1 identifies the scrollbar by testing whether the ID returned from GetDlgCtrlID() is the same as the ID of the vertical scrollbar (IDC_SCROLLBAR1). If it is the correct scrollbar, the current position is found by calling the scrollbar's GetScrollPos() function and assigned to nCurrentPos in line 5.

The `switch` statement in line 6 separates the different user action codes from the `nSBCode` parameter. If the scrollbar is being dragged or has been dragged and released, the scrollbar position is merely set to the user's requested `nPos` position by calling the `SetScrollPos()` function in line 10.

If the scrollbar is moved up or down a line (by clicking on an end arrow), the current scrollbar position is incremented or decremented by one unit in lines 12 to 17.

If the user clicks on the scrollbar shaft to indicate that a page distance should be moved, the current scrollbar position is increased or decreased by an arbitrary five units to represent a page length by lines 18–23.

Finally, the other (horizontal) scrollbar mapped to the `m_ScrollBar2` variable is mirrored to the position of the vertical scrollbar by calling its `SetScrollPos()` function with the position value found from the first scrollbar in lines 25 and 26. Notice that this position is multiplied by 2 in line 26. This is because the range of the horizontal scrollbar is double that of the vertical scrollbar that you set in the `OnInitDialog()` with the `SetScrollRange(0,200)` function call.

The call to the dialog box's base class handler function, `CDialog::OnVScroll()` in line 29, lets the dialog box handle any scrollbars that it owns to scroll the dialog box itself (this is discussed in more detail in the "Scrolling Windows" section of Chapter 18, "Sizing and Scrolling Views."

SEE ALSO

➤ *For more information about scrollbar notifications, see page 465*

Using a Slider Control

A slider control lets the user set a value by dragging an indicator along a linear range and dropping it at a specific position (as shown in Figure 7.5), like a HIFI volume slider.

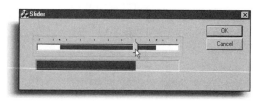

FIGURE 7.5
A slider control with tick
marks (top); the position
is shadowed by a
progress control (below).

The slider control is a sophisticated equivalent of the scrollbar control in that it also has a definable range and current position. However, the slider control allows a lot more sophisticated customization and configuration than the scrollbar control.

Adding a Slider Control to a Dialog Box

You can drag a slider control to a dialog box by dragging it from the Controls palette like the other controls (the slider icon on the resource palette is situated to the right of the progress control). As usual, you can size and position the control as required and should set the appropriate **ID** to identify the control in the **General** tab of the Slider Properties dialog box. The **Styles** tab of the Slider Properties dialog box (shown in Figure 7.6) lets you configure several details pertaining to the behavior and visual aspects of the control.

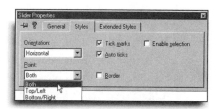

FIGURE 7.6
Setting the Slider Style
Properties in the
resource editor.

There are two combo boxes in the **Styles** tab. The first is the **Orientation**, which can be set to either **Horizontal** or **Vertical** as required. The slider is horizontal by default; if you change it to a vertical slider you might have to resize the control's window to suit the vertical aspect. The second combo box lets you set a **Point**. Normally, this is set to **Both**, which draws a rectangular block for the position pointer. You can change this from **Both** to **Top/Left,** which will display a pointer rather than a rectangle with the sharp end pointing to the top for a horizontal slider or to the right for a vertical slider. Alternatively, you can set this to **Bottom/Right** for the sharp end to point in the opposite direction than the **Top/Left** setting.

Several other check box flags can be set to mean the following if clicked:

- **Tick Marks.** If checked, the slider will display small lines at right angles to the direction of the slider away from the **Point** direction to help the user judge the current position of the slider more accurately.

- **Auto Ticks.** If checked, the tick marks are placed so that they correspond to the current increment value through the slider's range.

- **Enable Selection.** If checked, a white bar is added that lets the program display a selection range with small triangles.

- **Border.** If checked, a thin black border is drawn around the slider control.

SEE ALSO

➤ *For more detail about dialog editing and control properties, see page 44*

Mapping a Variable to a Slider Control

The process for mapping a variable to a slider control is very similar to that for a progress control. You can follow the "Mapping a Member Variable to a Progress Control" step by step, earlier in this chapter; the only noticeable difference is in the **Category** combo box and **Variable Type** mentioned in step 5. Like a scrollbar, a slider control lets you select either **Control** or **Value** for the category setting.

If you select **Value**, the **Variable Type** is set to int. This then inserts an integer member variable mapped to the slider control into your selected destination class. The new mapped integer member variable will then be updated by the control position just like the scrollbar if mapped to an integer.

The rest of this section will concentrate on the **Control** category setting, which will automatically set the **Variable Type** to the MFC CSliderCtrl mapping class for slider controls. After

---

Dynamically enabling and disabling controls

You can use the new mapped control variable (such as CSliderCtrl) to enable or disable the control programmatically. You can do this by calling the mapped variable's EnableWindow() function passing TRUE or FALSE to enable or disable the window respectively (for example, m_mySliderCtrl.Enable Window(FALSE)). You might want to do this to stop the user from changing the control in certain circumstances.

you've set the mapping variable details, you can continue the "Mapping a Member Variable to a Progress Control" step by step as normal.

SEE ALSO

➤ *For a more detailed explanation of member variable mapping, see page 221*

Initializing a Slider Control

You can set the range of the slider control by calling its `SetRange()` function, passing the minimum and maximum positions for the slider as integer values for the first two parameters. Optionally, you can also pass a FALSE value as a third parameter to stop the default automatic redraw of the control. There are also functions to set just the minimum or maximum range settings by passing an integer to the `SetRangeMin()` or `SetRangeMax()` function. The corresponding `GetRangeMin()` and `GetRangeMax()` member functions return the current range settings.

You can set the position of the slider by calling `SetPos()`, passing an integer value to represent the new position within the specified range, and retrieve the current setting from the value returned from the `GetPos()` member function.

Like the scrollbar control, the user can increment the slider by line or page values by pressing the arrow keys or Page Up/Page Down keys. However, you don't have to explicitly handle the notification messages from a slider control to update its position like you must with the scrollbar control. To let you programmatically control the increment and decrement values for the line and page movements, you can call the `SetLineSize()` and `SetPageSize()` slider control functions, passing the appropriate integer value for the line or page size. The current settings for line and page movement values are returned from the corresponding `GetLineSize()` and `GetPageSize()` member functions.

You can also programmatically set the slider control's tick marks using the `SetTicFreq()` function, passing the frequency of the tick marks. So if you need tick marks on every fifth position, you'd code the following line:

```
m_Slider.SetTicFreq(5);
```

Finding the slider's channel rectangle

The channel rectangle is the area of the slider control that the moving part of the control moves along. You can find the size and position of this rectangle by calling the `CSliderCtrl` class's `GetChannelRect()` function.

Clearing the tick marks programmatically

You can clear any tick marks drawn currently against the slider control programmatically using the `ClearTics()` function. To redraw the control immediately after clearing, pass a **TRUE** value to this function.

For the `SetTickFreq()` function to work, you must have set the **Auto Ticks** style in the **Style** tab of the Slider Properties dialog box. You can find out how many tick marks exist in the specified range from the value returned by calling the `GetNumTicks()` member function.

If you have the **Enable Selection** flag set in the **Style** tab of the Slider Properties dialog box you can use the `SetSelection()` member function to display a selection range inside the slider control, which appears as a highlighted bar on a white background under the slider (refer to Figure 7.5). You can pass `SetSelection()` the minimum and maximum selection values to represent the selected area within the current specified range of the slider. You can retrieve the current selection with the corresponding `GetSelection()` function by passing two references to integers that will hold the resulting minimum and maximum values, or clear the selection by calling the slider's `ClearSel()` function.

SEE ALSO

➤ *For more information about initializing dialog boxes, see page 219*

Responding to Slider Notifications

Slider controls notify the parent window using the same `WM_VSCROLL` and `WM_HSCROLL` messages as scrollbars. The only difference is that you don't need to explicitly set the new position of the slider because this is updated automatically for you. However, you can use this notification to perform a specific action when the user changes the slider position.

For example, if you wanted to mirror the position of a slider with a progress control as shown in Figure 7.5, you could add the two controls as shown in Figure 7.6. You could then map the slider (with the ID of `IDC_SLIDER1`) to a `CSliderCtrl` control variable called `m_Slider`, and the progress control (with the ID of `IDC_PROGRESS1`) to a `CProgressCtrl` control variable called `m_Progress`. You might then update the progress control whenever the slider control is moved by adding the following `OnHScroll()` handler function and code:

```
void CSliderDlg::OnHScroll(UINT nSBCode, UINT nPos,
➥ CScrollBar* pScrollBar)
```

```
{
    if (pScrollBar->GetDlgCtrlID() == IDC_SLIDER1)
        m_Progress.SetPos(m_Slider.GetPos());
    CDialog::OnHScroll(nSBCode, nPos, pScrollBar);
}
```

The GetDlgCtrlID() function is used to identify the slider, then the progress control position is set with the SetPos() member function from the slider position retrieved by calling the slider's GetPos() function.

If you wanted to check for specific tracking or page/line movements, you can test the nSBCode parameter for the values in Table 7.2 just like a scrollbar.

SEE ALSO

➤ *For information about control IDs and notification messages, see page 69*

Using the Date Time Picker Controls

Most users would object to picking a date or time from a slider, but until Visual C++ 6.0 there were no built-in date and time picking controls; you had to write your own date and time picking mechanism or use an ActiveX control. Now Microsoft has added two interlinked controls to the Controls palette, the date time picker and the month calendar controls. The date time picker automatically uses the month calendar control (discussed in the next section) to let the user specify a date when the drop arrow button is clicked.

You might have seen these controls used in Microsoft's Outlook email application. The date time picker can be used to pick either a date or a time (you can use two controls to let the user specify both). When used to pick a date, the date time picker usually appears like a combo box, displaying the currently selected date in a long or shortened format. When you click on the combo drop arrow, a month calendar control pops up (as shown in Figure 7.7) to let you specify the month and day. The time picker version (shown to the right of Figure 7.7) displays the currently selected time and lets you change the time by direct editing or by using the spin controls.

Finding a control from a dialog ID

GetDlgItem() is a handy corresponding function to GetDlgCtrlID() that returns a CWnd pointer to the control specified by the control ID passed as its first parameter. If no control with the corresponding ID was found on the current dialog box, a NULL value is returned. If you want to use the CWnd pointer returned as a specific control, you should cast it to the MFC class corresponding to that control.

FIGURE 7.7

The date time picker being used to specify a date and a time.

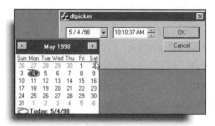

SEE ALSO

➤ *For an example of an ActiveX date control, see page 198*

Adding a Date Time Picker Control to a Dialog Box

The date time picker control can be dragged from the Control palette (shown by the ToolTip in Figure 7.8) onto the dialog template, and sized and positioned as appropriate. As with all other controls, you should set a unique ID in the **General** tab of the Date Time Picker Properties dialog box (invoked by selecting the control and pressing Alt+Enter) as shown in Figure 7.8.

FIGURE 7.8

Adding date time picker controls to the dialog box in the resource editor.

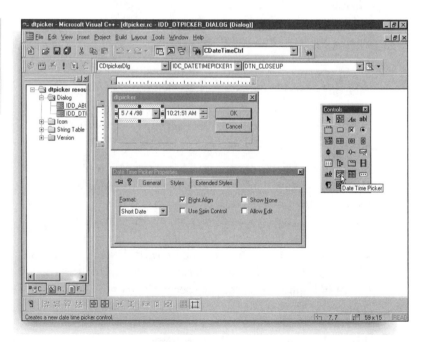

The **Styles** tab of the Date Time Picker Properties dialog box lets you set either the date, or time picking mode of the control by choosing one of the following three options from the **Format** drop-down list:

- **Short Date.** This makes the date time picker display a shortened date format (for example, 5/4/98), and displays the month calendar picker control when you click on the control's drop button to specify an exact date.

- **Long Date.** This displays the long date format in the control (for example, Monday, May 04, 1998), and again displays the month calendar picker control when you click on the drop button.

- **Time.** This displays the time in the date picker (for example, 10:21:51 AM), and displays a spin control rather than a combo-style drop button to spin the selected hours, minutes, or seconds component of the selected time.

You can also set the following style flags by clicking the specific check boxes to toggle the state of the flag:

- **Right Align.** If checked, when the month calendar control is displayed after the user has clicked the drop button the calendar will be aligned to the right of the date time picker control; otherwise the calendar will be displayed below the control.

- **Use Spin Control.** If checked, a spin control is displayed rather than a drop-combo button. The user can then click on the up or down arrow of the spin control to change the selected day, month, or year component of the date.

- **Show None.** If checked, a check box is displayed in the left of the date time picker to let the user specify that no date or time is currently selected when the date time picker's check box isn't checked.

- **Allow Edit.** If checked, your program can perform any special modification and checking of the input as the control is edited by handling the DTN_USERSTRING message sent from the control.

SEE ALSO

➤ *For more detail about dialog box editing and control properties, see page 44*

Mapping a Variable to a Date Time Picker Control

You can map a date time picker control with ClassWizard in the usual way like the "Mapping a Member Variable to a Progress Control" steps, earlier in this chapter.

Using CTime and COleDateTime

You should use COleDateTime in preference to CTime because it handles dates to be represented from 1 January 100 to 31 December 9999. However, CTime can store dates only in the range 1 January 1970 to 19 January 2038. Also, as its name suggests, COleDateTime can be handled more easily by interacting OLE and COM programs.

If you select **Value** from the **Category** combo box (in step 5), the **Variable Type** combo box will let you select either **CTime** or **COleDateTime** as the variable type to map against the control. Choosing either of these two similar date-handling classes provides a quick and easy way to set and retrieve a value from the date time picker control by using a mapped member variable of either type like you might use a CString mapped to an edit control.

If you need more programmatic control over the date time picker, you should choose **Control** from the **Category** combo box, which will automatically set the **Variable Type** combo box to the CDateTimeCtrl class (which handles the date time picker control as discussed for the rest of this section).

You can also quite legitimately map two or more variables of different types to a single control (by its ID) so that you can have the best of both worlds; control via the CDateTimeCtrl class and quick access via a COleDateTime class of variable.

When you've chosen the type of variable to map to the control, you can click **OK** to close the Add Member Variable dialog box and ClassWizard. This will add the new variable(s) to the appropriate specified class (usually your dialog handling class).

For the AppWizard-generated, dialog-based example used in this section, you can place two controls (one date and one time) like those in Figure 7.8. The date format version is referenced by the IDC_MYDATE ID and mapped to the m_myDate variable, whereas the time format version has an ID of IDC_MYTIME and is mapped to the m_myTime variable. Both variables are of the CDateTimeCtrl class.

SEE ALSO

➤ *For a more detailed explanation of member variable mapping, see page 221*

Initializing a Date Time Picker Control

Like the slider and scrollbar controls, you can set a range for the date time picker. This range is in the form of a minimum and maximum allowable date and time. You can set this range by passing the CDateTimeCtrl's SetRange() function two pointers to COleDateTime (or CTime) objects that hold the minimum and maximum allowable date-time values. For example, if you wanted to restrict a date time picker control to only allow the user to pick dates and times within the year 1998, you could add the following lines to the end of your OnInitDialog() implementation:

```
COleDateTime dtMin(1998,1,1,0,0,0);
COleDateTime dtMax(1998,12,31,23,59,59);
m_myDate.SetRange(&dtMin,&dtMax); // Set the control range
```

The first two lines construct COleDateTime objects with the parameters specifying year, month, day of month, hours, minutes, and seconds. Pointers to these two objects are then passed to the control's mapped m_myDate variable (of CDateTimeCtrl type) via the SetRange() function. When run, the user will not be able to specify any date outside 1998, and the dates shown (when the drop month calendar control is displayed) that are outside the range are grayed. A corresponding GetRange() function sets the two COleDateTime (or CTime) objects to the currently specified range.

You can also specify how the date time picker presents the selected date and time by changing its format. You pass a format string to the SetFormat() function to change the default displayed format to your specific requirements by building the string from the string part format codes shown in Table 7.3.

> **The COleDateTime time validity status**
>
> If you've constructed COleDateTime with a valid date time, the object will be marked with a valid status flag (COleDateTime::valid). Otherwise the status flag is invalid (COleDateTime:: invalid). You can check this status by calling the GetStatus() member function to return the relevant flag value, or force the flag value by passing it into the SetStatus() function.

Formatting COleDateTime **output**

You can also specify similar format codes for the COleDateTime objects (extracted from the date time picker control) using the COleDateTime's Format() function. The Format() function takes a format specification string as its first parameter.

There are a whole range of formatting codes for formatting aspects such as the month, year, day, hours, minutes, and seconds. For example, %c will produce the full date and time in the current locale like this: 04/04/98 18:05:01. Similarly, a longer form can be formatted using the %#c specification, producing a string like Saturday, April 04, 1998 18:05:01.

TABLE 7.3 Formatting codes for the date time picker control

Format Code	Description
yyy	Display the full year (for example, '1998')
yy	Display the last two year digits (for example, '98')
y	Display the last year digit (for example, '8')
MMMM	Display the full month name (for example, 'April')
MMM	Display the three-character month abbreviation (for example, 'Apr')
MM	Display the two-digit month number (for example, '04')
M	Display a single or double month number (for example, '4' for April or '11' for November)
dddd	Display the full weekday name (for example, 'Monday')
ddd	Display the three-character weekday abbreviation (for example, 'Mon')
dd	Display the day of the month as two digits (for example, '04')
d	Display the day of the month as one or two digits (for example, '4' for the 4th or '11' for the 11th)
HH	Display the hour in two-digit 24-hour format (for example, '16')
hh	Display the hour in two-digit 12-hour format (for example, '04')
H	Display the hour in one- or two-digit 24-hour format (for example, '4' for 4 AM or '16' for 4 PM)
h	Display the hour in one- or two-digit 12-hour format (for example, '4' for 4 AM or '4' for 4 PM)
tt	Display the AM/PM indicator in two-digit format (for example, 'AM' or 'PM')
t	Display the AM/PM indicator in one-digit format (for example, 'A' or 'P')
mm	Display the minutes in two-digit format (for example, '07' or '59')
m	Display the minutes in one- or two-digit format (for example, '7' or '59')

You can also add your own text sections to this string by enclosing them in single quotation marks as delimiters. For example, if you want to display the date and time in a single date time picker control for the user to specify each part, and format it like 1998/05/04 12:22:23, you could add the following line to your `OnInitDialog()`function:

```
m_myDate.SetFormat("yyy'/'MM'/'dd' 'HH':'mm':'ss");
```

Notice that the single quote character delimits the slashes, colons, and spaces. When run, this date time picker will let you edit both the date and the time at once, as shown in Figure 7.9.

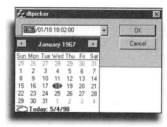

FIGURE 7.9
A custom formatted date time picker showing an initial date and time.

You might also want to set the initial time and date selection of the date time picker rather than let it default to the current system date and time. You can pass `SetTime()`, a `COleDateTime` object that contains the date and time you want to use to initialize the control.

For example, if you wanted to set the initial date and time to 2 minutes past 6pm on the 18th of January 1967, you might code the following:

```
m_myDate.SetTime(COleDateTime(1967,1,18,18,2,0));
```

When the control is displayed, you'll see the starting date and time displayed as in Figure 7.9.

You can also retrieve the current date and time setting from the control during its lifetime by calling the control's corresponding `GetTime()` function passing a `COleDateTime` variable to be set from the control. The `COleDateTime` variable can then be used or interrogated as you require.

For example, you could add the following code to display a message box showing the chosen date and time when the

Retrieving values from
`COleDateTime`

Several access functions return
parts of the chosen time such as
`GetYear()`, `GetMonth()`,
`GetDay()`, `GetHour()`,
`GetMinute()`, or
`GetSecond()`. There are also
some useful derivative functions:
`GetDayOfWeek()` and
`GetDayOfYear()`.
`GetDayOfWeek()` returns the
day of the week in the range 1 to
7, where 1 is Sunday. The
`GetDayOfYear()` function
returns a value in the range 1 to
366 starting at January 1.

dialog's **OK** button is clicked (after inserting an `OnOK()` handler
function):

```
void CDtpickerDlg::OnOK()
{
    COleDateTime dtChosenTime;
    m_myDate.GetTime(dtChosenTime);
    AfxMessageBox(dtChosenTime.Format("%#x"));
    CDialog::OnOK();
}
```

The current date and time are retrieved and assigned to the
`dtChosenTime` variable, which is then formatted with the
`COleDateTime` class's `Format()` function and displayed as a message
box.

The date time picker also lets you set the drop month calendar
control's color and font. You can pass an index and color reference to `SetMonthCalColor()` to set the color of one of the con-
stituent parts (identified by the index from Table 7.4). By passing
a valid font handle (`HFONT`) to the `SetMonthCalFont()` function,
you can change the default month calendar's font.

SEE ALSO

➤ *For information about handling fonts, see page 433*

Responding to Date Change Notifications

When the user changes a date in the date time picker, you can
handle the `DTN_DATETIMECHANGE` notification set to your parent
dialog box to perform a specific action. You can add a handler
for this notification function as follows.

Adding a date change notification handler function

1. Right-click on the specific date-time picker control you want
   to handle from the dialog template in the dialog resource
   editor.

2. Select **Events** from the pop-up context menu to display the
   New Windows Message and Event Handlers dialog box.

3. Select the `DTN_DATETIMECHANGE` message from the list of **New Windows Messages/Events**. (Alternatively, you can select one of the other notification messages if required.)

4. Click on the **Add and Edit** button to display the Add Member Function dialog box with the default handler function name.

5. Change the handler function name if required, and click **OK** to start editing the new handler function, which should resemble the sample handler function in Listing 7.2.

When you've added the new handler function, you can perform any application-specific appropriate action to take for when the date or time has been changed. The handler function passes a pointer to an `NMHDR` structure as the first parameter. Normally, you'd insert a handler specific to each date time picker; however, you can interrogate the sender control's ID from the `NMHDR`'s `idFrom` member variable. This lets you have one handler function that is shared by several date time pickers. Listing 7.2 shows such a shared handler function and its two `ON_NOTIFY` message map entries that share the same handler function. The code in Listing 7.2 changes the parent dialog box's title bar to display the current date or time whenever the user changes the date- or time-oriented date time picker controls.

LISTING 7.2   LST7_2.CPP—Handling the *DTN_DATETIMECHANGE* Notification Shared by Two Date Time Picker Controls

① The second message map handler is added manually.

```
1   BEGIN_MESSAGE_MAP(CDtpickerDlg, CDialog)
2       //{{AFX_MSG_MAP(CDtpickerDlg)
3       ON_WM_SYSCOMMAND()
4       ON_WM_PAINT()
5       ON_WM_QUERYDRAGICON()
6       ON_NOTIFY(DTN_DATETIMECHANGE, IDC_MYDATE,
        ➥OnDatetimechangeMydate)
7       //}}AFX_MSG_MAP ────────①
8       ON_NOTIFY(DTN_DATETIMECHANGE, IDC_MYTIME,
        ➥OnDatetimechangeMydate)
9   END_MESSAGE_MAP()
10
11  void CDtpickerDlg::OnDatetimechangeMydate(
    ➥NMHDR* pNMHDR, LRESULT* pResult)
```

continues...

② Depending on which control sent the message, either the date- (line 16) or time-oriented (line 20) date time picker is used to update the dialog box's title bar.

LISTING 7.2 Continued

```
12  {
13      COleDateTime dtSel;
14      switch(pNMHDR->idFrom)
15      {
16      case IDC_MYDATE:
17          m_myDate.GetTime(dtSel);
18          SetWindowText("Date:"+dtSel.Format("%#x"));
19          break;
20      case IDC_MYTIME:
21          m_myTime.GetTime(dtSel);
22          SetWindowText("Time:"+dtSel.Format("%H:%M:%S"));
23          break;
24      }
25      *pResult = 0;
26  }
```

Manually adding message map entries

Whenever you manually add a message map entry, you should be careful to ensure that your new code is outside the section enclosed by the //{{AFX_MSG_MAP comments. ClassWizard uses these comments to denote where the automatically generated wizard is to be placed, and will get confused if it sees lines that don't match up with its expectations. The best place to add your own message map code is after the second //{{AFX_MSG_MAP comment, but before the END_MESSAGE_ MAP() macro line.

The message map entry on line 6 of Listing 7.2 is the standard entry generated automatically by ClassWizard (after following the "Adding a Date Change Notification Handler Function" steps). However, the message map entry on line 8 must be added manually to share the same handler function (OnDatetimechangeMydate()).

The OnDatetimechangeMydate() handler function is implemented in lines 11 to 26. A COleDateTime variable (dtSel) is declared to hold the current date/time selection in line 13. The switch statement in line 14 must determine the control that sent the message.

If the IDC_MYDATE control sent the message, the time is sought from the m_myDate control-mapped variable in line 17 and displayed as a date in the dialog box's title bar by line 18.

If the IDC_MYTIME control was the sender, the time is instead sought from the m_myTime control-mapped variable in line 21 and displayed as a time in the dialog box's title bar by line 22.

SEE ALSO

➤ *For information about control IDs and notification messages, see page 69*

Using the Month Calendar Control

You can use the month calendar control on its own as a normal dialog control. You saw the month calendar control pop-up when the date time picker control's drop-combo style button was clicked. The control draws a calendar-style display showing the days for each month. The user can select a specific date, or change the displayed month and year. Normally the month calendar control allows a single date selection, but it can also be configured to allow the user to specify a range of dates.

Adding a Month Calendar Control to a Dialog Box

The month calendar control icon on the Controls palette is to the right of the date time picker, and can be dragged and sized in the normal fashion. You can invoke the Month Calendar Properties by selecting it and pressing Alt+Enter to change the control's default **ID** on the **General** tab. The **Styles** tab (as shown in Figure 7.10) lets you set the following flags by clicking their check boxes to toggle their state:

- **Day States.** If checked, you can specify which date is to be drawn inverted (white on black) from within your program; otherwise, the current system date is automatically drawn inverted.

- **Multi Select.** If checked, the user is able to specify a range of dates; otherwise the default behavior allows only one date selection.

- **No Today.** If checked, the red line normally drawn around the current system date isn't drawn.

- **Week Numbers.** If checked, the number of the week in a year (1 to 52) is drawn to the left of each of the displayed weeks.

> **Month calendar control style flags**
>
> These control styles are equivalent to the MCS_DAYSTATE, MCS_MULTISELECT, MCS_NOTODAY, MCS_NOTO-DAYCIRCLE and MCS_WEEK-NUMBERS style flags. You might want to use these style flags if you create the control dynamically using one of its Create() functions rather than the usual automatic dialog box template creation.

FIGURE 7.10

Adding a month calendar control to the dialog template from the resource editor.

SEE ALSO

➤ *For more detail about dialog editing and control properties, see page 44*

Mapping a Variable to a Month Calendar Control

The mapping process is very similar to the date time picker control's mapping as discussed in the previous section. You can map either a CTime or COleDateTime variable directly to the control if you select the **Value** option from the <u>C</u>ategory combo box in the Add Member Variable dialog box. If you require more control, you should select the **Control** option from the <u>C</u>ategory combo box, which automatically selects a **Variable <u>T</u>ype** of CMonthCalCtrl to map as a member variable of the selected dialog handling class.

SEE ALSO

➤ *For a more detailed explanation of member variable mapping, see page 221*

Initializing a Month Calendar Control

You can initialize the month calendar control to allow selecting within a specific range of dates by passing a minimum and maximum allowable date to the `CMonthCalCtrl`'s `SetRange()` member function as two pointers to `COleDateTime` (or `CTime`) objects (like the date time picker). A corresponding `GetRange()` function assigns the range endpoints to the objects pointed to by the two pointer parameters.

You can set the first day of the week from its default of Sunday by passing a zero-based day index representing the day number to the `SetFirstDayOfWeek()` member function (where Monday is zero and Sunday is 6). For example, if you want Monday to be displayed as the first day of the week, you could add the following line to the end of your `OnInitDialog()` function (where `m_MyMonthCal` is your mapped variable of `CMonthCalCtrl` type):

```
m_MyMonthCal.SetFirstDayOfWeek(0);
```

You can change the "today" day (ringed in red) by passing a `COleDateTime` object (holding your new today date) to the `SetToday()` function. The current today setting can be retrieved by passing a `COleDateTime` variable to the corresponding `GetToday()` function. The current today value will then be assigned to the variable.

The default colors can be changed by calling the `SetColor()` function by passing an index flag value as the first parameter (from Table 7.4), and a color reference value as the second parameter.

> **Setting the month scrolling rate**
>
> When the user scrolls the date time control, it usually scrolls by a single month each time. You can change this default using the `SetMonthDelta()` function passing the number of months by which you want the control to scroll each time. The corresponding `GetMonthDelta()` member function returns the current month delta scroll rate setting.

TABLE 7.4   Month calendar color code flag values

Index Value	Description
MCSC_TEXT	Change the main date text color
MCSC_TITLETEXT	Change the title's color
MCSC_TITLENBK	Change the title's background color
MCSC_TRAILINGTEXT	Change the header and trailing days color
MCSC_BACKGROUND	Change the background color

SEE ALSO
➤ *For details about color references and color values, see page 385*

➤ *For details about color references and color values, see page 385*

Setting the month calendar control's range

You can set the minimum and maximum allowable dates for the Month calendar control using the `SetRange()` function by passing pointers to two `COleDateTime` objects, just like the `CDateTimeCtrl` allowed. The corresponding `GetRange()` function can be used to find the current range settings.

Month Calendar Control Date Range Selection

You can let the user select a single date or range of dates depending on the **Multi Select** check box setting in the **Styles** tab of the Month Calendar Control Properties dialog box.

When set to a single selection, the initial selected date can be set by passing a `COleDateTime` object to the month calendar's `SetCurSel()` function, like this:

```
m_MyMonthCal.SetCurSel(COleDateTime(1967,1,18,18,2,0));
```

The date picked or changed by the user can be retrieved at any time during the control's life by passing a `COleDateTime` object to the calendar's `GetCurSel()` function, like this:

```
COleDateTime dtChosenTime;
m_myDate.GetCurSel (dtChosenTime);
AfxMessageBox(dtChosenTime.Format("%#x"));
```

The last line then displays the chosen date in a message box.

If you allow multiple selections, you should use `GetSelRange()` and `SetSelRange()` to get the current selected range and set a new selected range, respectively. These both need two `COleDateTime` objects passed as parameters. The first is the minimum date of the selected range, and the second is the maximum date of the selected range.

There is a further complication to range selection in that the default multiple number of days that can be selected is seven. You can change this default to any maximum allowable number of selected days by passing the restriction integer value to the calendar's `SetMaxSelCount()` function.

For example, if you wanted to initialize the month calendar control to show the first 14 days of January 1998 as selected, and allow the user to select a maximum of only 15 consecutive days, you could add the following lines:

```
m_MyMonthCal.SetMaxSelCount(15);
m_MyMonthCal.SetSelRange(COleDateTime(1998,1,1,0,0,0),
                    COleDateTime(1998,1,14,0,0,0));
```

When run, the month calendar will then display this selected range, and only allow you to select 15 days.

You could then find which range, and how many days the user has selected by adding the following lines:

```
COleDateTime dtMin,dtMax;
m_MyMonthCal.GetSelRange(dtMin,dtMax);
COleDateTimeSpan dtSpan = dtMax - dtMin;
AfxMessageBox(dtSpan.Format("You Selected %D Days"));
```

The number of days is calculated by subtracting the maximum selected date from the minimum selected date and the difference is assigned to a COleDateTimeSpan object dtSpan. A message box is then displayed showing the number of selected days.

Responding to Date Range Change Notifications

You can add a handler function to call your code when the user has changed the current date selection. The steps are the same as in the "Adding a Date Change Notification Handler Function" step by step, except that the required notification message is MCN_SELCHANGE. When you've added a handler for the MCN_SELCHANGE message, your new handler function will look like this:

```
void CMonthcalDlg::OnSelchangeMonthCalendar1(
➥NMHDR* pNMHDR, LRESULT* pResult)
{
    // TODO: ...
    *pResult = 0;
}
```

Manipulating COleDateTimeSpan objects

You can set a time span by passing the number of days, hours, minutes, and seconds as integer parameters to SetDateTimeSpan(). You can also retrieve these values from a valid COleDateTimeSpan object by calling the GetDays(), GetHours(), GetMinutes(), and GetSeconds() functions, which return long values representing each portion of the time span value. If you want to retrieve the overall time span expressed in days, hours, minutes, or seconds in one double value, you can call GetTotalDays(), GetTotalHours(), GetTotalMinutes(), or GetTotalSeconds(), respectively.

You can then add your handler code and check the NMHDR structure as shown in Listing 7.2 for the date time picker control. You can add code to find the current selection using the GetCurSel() or GetSelRange() functions described in the previous section.

SEE ALSO

➤ *For more information about control IDs and notification messages, see page 69*

Responding to Mouse Events

Coding for when the user presses and
releases mouse buttons

Responding to mouse movement with
your custom functions

Dealing with mouse coordinates and
testing for selected areas

Handling Button Messages

Often you might want to know when a mouse button was pressed or released and where it was pressed—without using a button control. An obvious example is a paint application in which a window area is used as a drawing pad and mouse clicks are used to draw in that area. As you've already seen, all input from the user arrives at your application in the form of messages (or events). The mouse-button messages are no exception to this rule. Position information is bundled with the button messages, which makes these messages very easy to use in conjunction with the Windows drawing functions.

Handling the Button Up and Button Down Events

Windows handles three mouse buttons: the left, middle, and right buttons. Some mice have only two buttons, in which case you have only left and right button events. Because of this, most applications respond to the left and right buttons, but in special circumstances, you might want to use all three. For each button, your program will receive two events from Windows: one for when users press the button and the other for when they release the button. Sometimes, handling these events is referred to as *catching*. Because these messages are normally sent down to the window base class, you are catching or intercepting them with your own code.

To catch these events, you can create a simple dialog-based application with AppWizard and name it MouseMsg. (Follow the same Step by Step from the section "Creating a New Dialog Application" in Chapter 4, "Using Button Controls.")

After you've created the dialog-based application, you should increase the size of the main application dialog IDD_MOUSEMSG_DIALOG to approximately 300 pixels wide by 200 high, using the Resource Editor. This will give you plenty of room to investigate the mouse coordinates returned. While you are editing the dialog box you should also remove the TODO: Insert Controls message so that the dialog box is a large blank area with only the OK and Cancel icons.

By following this step by step, you can add a *message handler* to catch the message sent when the user presses the left mouse button.

Adding a mouse-button message handler

1. Click the **ClassView** tab of the Project Workspace view.

2. Click the top **+** to open the view of the project classes.

3. Right-click the `CMouseMsgDlg` class to display the context menu.

4. Select the **Add Windows Message Handler** option to display the New Windows Message and Event Handlers dialog box.

5. You should select the `WM_LBUTTONDOWN` message from the **New Windows** messages/events list.

6. Click the **Add and Edit** button to start editing the new handler.

You now have a handler named `OnLButtonDown()` for the left mouse-button event. This function will be called every time the user presses the left mouse button. You can customize this function to add your own drawing code. For example, if you add the code shown in Listing 8.1, an exclamation mark icon will be drawn wherever you click the left mouse button.

LISTING 8.1 LST8_1.CPP—Customizing the *OnLButtonDown()* Handler to Draw an Exclamation Mark at the Click Position

```
1   void CMouseMsgDlg::OnLButtonDown(UINT nFlags,
    ➥CPoint point)
2   {
3       // TODO: Add your message handler code here and/or
4
5       // ** Display a message in the window title bar
6       CString strMessage;
7       strMessage.Format("Left Button Pressed at (%d,%d)",
8                           point.x,point.y);
9       SetWindowText(strMessage);
10
```

(1) The position is formatted to a string variable and displayed in the dialog title bar.

continues...

177

LISTING 8.1 Continued

② If the Ctrl key is held down, a different standard icon is selected.

③ The selected icon is drawn at the mouse click position.

```
11      // ** Choose the icon depending on the control key
12      char* pszIcon;
13      if (nFlags & MK_CONTROL)          ②
14          pszIcon = IDI_EXCLAMATION;
15      else
16          pszIcon = IDI_HAND;
17
18      // ** Draw an exclamation icon at that point
19      CDC* pDC = GetDC();
20      pDC->DrawIcon(point,
21              AfxGetApp()->LoadStandardIcon(pszIcon));     ③
22      ReleaseDC(pDC);
23
24      CDialog::OnLButtonDown(nFlags, point);
25  }
```

In Listing 8.1, notice that the OnLButtonDown() handler function is passed two parameters: the first parameter, nFlags, tells you which other mouse buttons are held down and whether the Ctrl or Shift keys are pressed, as shown in Table 8.1. These values are *bit flags*, and any combination can be set at any time. To test for a specific flag, you can use the bitwise AND operator (the C++ & operator) as shown in line 13. Here the MK_CONTROL flag is tested, which will be TRUE if you are holding the Ctrl key down when you click the mouse button.

In the listing, the pszIcon pointer is set to the standard IDI_EXCLAMATION at line 14 or IDI_HAND icon, depending on the result of the nFlags Ctrl key test. These icons are standard system icons and are used in lines 20 and 21 with the DrawIcon() device context function. (I don't want to dwell on device contexts here; they are covered in detail in Chapter 15, "Understanding Drawing in Device Contexts.") The application class function LoadStandardIcon() passed the pszIcon pointer to load the specific standard icon in line 21; other possible standard icons are shown in Table 8.2.

The second parameter passed to the OnLButtonDown() handler function is a CPoint object named point. CPoint is a class that holds a coordinate point as x and y members. Line 7 formats this point into a string that is displayed in the dialog box's title bar by SetWindowText() in line 9. This point is also used in line 20 to position the icon.

TABLE 8.1 Button flags passed as the *nFlags* parameter to *OnLButtonDown*

Flag Value	Description
MK_LBUTTON	Indicates that the left button is held down.
MK_MBUTTON	Indicates that the middle button is held down.
MK_RBUTTON	Indicates that the right button is held down.
MK_CONTROL	Indicates that the control key is pressed.
MK_SHIFT	Indicates that the shift key is pressed.

TABLE 8.2 Standard system icons available via *LoadStandardIcon()*

Icon Flag	Description
IDI_EXCLAMATION	An exclamation mark in a triangle
IDI_HAND	An X mark in a red circle
IDI_APPLICATION	The default application icon
IDI_ASTERISK	A small i for information
IDI_QUESTION	A question mark

Standard icon images under Windows 95 and NT 4.0

If you use these standard icons, you'll notice that the images don't match the names. For example, IDI_HAND draws a white cross on a red background with no hint of a hand image. This is a legacy of Windows 3.11 and NT 3.51; the icon images have been updated, but the names remain the same and no longer match the images.

If you add these lines to the handler function, as shown in Listing 8.1, and build and run the application, you'll have the world's simplest drawing program. You should be able to click the dialog box and draw either an exclamation mark by clicking the left mouse button, or a cross by clicking the left mouse button with the Ctrl key held down, as shown in Figure 8.1.

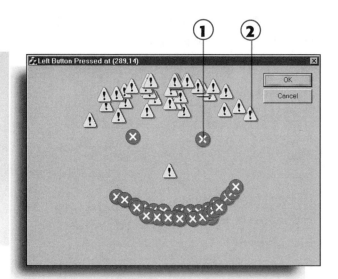

FIGURE 8.1

Drawing icons when the left mouse button is pressed.

1. The cross icon is drawn when the Ctrl key is held down.

2. The exclamation mark is drawn when the left mouse button is pressed.

Also notice that the current mouse position is displayed in the title bar from the position of the last button click. If you click near the top-left corner, you'll see that the coordinate points are relative to the top left of the dialog window and not the screen coordinates. You can obtain the screen coordinates by instead using the GetCursorPos() function, which can be called at any time to obtain the current mouse pointer position. This function takes one parameter, a pointer to a CPoint object to receive the cursor position. You can test this by adding a GetCursorPos() call in the OnLButtonDown() handler after the // TODO: ... comment, shown in line 3 of Listing 8.1, like this:

```
GetCursorPos(&point);
```

If you build and run the program after adding this line, you'll see that the coordinate position displayed in the title bar is now relative to the top left of the screen, not the dialog box. Also, the icons will be drawn at that offset. Because the drawing function expects window-relative positions, the icons will be drawn some way from the mouse pointer. To regain the proper icon positioning, you might want to remove this line after testing the effect.

You can add a handle to catch the left mouse-button up message by following the preceding step by step for adding a mouse-button message handler, but you choose the WM_LBUTTONUP message instead of the WM_LBUTTONDOWN message. This will create an OnLButtonUp() handler function. You can then add your own code to display a title bar message showing that the left button has been released, like this:

```
SetWindowText("Left Button Released");
```

If you add this line and build and run the program, you'll see that this handler is called when you release the left mouse button. This lets you write application code that can start a special mode when you press the button and stop that mode when you release it. An everyday example of this is moving windows around the desktop. Pressing the left button with the cursor over a window title bar starts the moving mode; when you release the button the window position is set, and normal functioning resumes.

There are similar handlers for the right and middle button events. Table 8.3 shows all the possible mouse-button events. You can add handlers for the middle and right buttons by following the same steps you've already used to add the left mouse-button events.

Using the middle mouse-button event handlers

Adding a handler is trickier for the middle button because Microsoft hasn't included it in the wizard to generate handler functions. You can still create your own handlers for these messages, but you must do this manually by adding a message map entry and the function definition yourself. This is to dissuade developers from producing programs that work only with three-button mice.

TABLE 8.3 Windows mouse-button messages

Message Name	AppWizard Handler Name	Description
WM_LBUTTONDOWN	OnLButtonDown()	Left button pressed
WM_LBUTTONUP	OnLButtonUp()	Left button released
WM_MBUTTONDOWN	None	Middle button pressed
WM_MBUTTONUP	None	Middle button released
WM_RBUTTONDOWN	OnRButtonDown()	Right button pressed
WM_RBUTTONUP	OnRButtonUp()	Right button released

SEE ALSO

➤ *For more information on drawing in device contexts, see page 356*

➤ *To learn how to design and change the dialog template, see pages 44*

Catching Double-Click Events

Double-clicking often has special meaning in Windows applications. It is frequently used as a shortcut operation in selection lists. The user can send a double-click event to your application by clicking any mouse button twice in rapid succession. Windows tests the timing between the clicks and sends you a WM_LBUTTONDBLCLK message if the left-button clicks are quick enough. The corresponding WM_MBUTTONDBLCLK and WM_RBUTTONDBLCLK are sent for the middle and right buttons, respectively. You can add handlers for these by again following the "Adding a mouse button message handler" step by step from the preceding section. You can add a left-button double-click handler and insert a message box, as shown, to try this:

```
void CMouseMsgDlg::OnLButtonDblClk(UINT nFlags,
➡CPoint point)
{
    AfxMessageBox("Left Button Double Clicked");
    CDialog::OnLButtonDblClk(nFlags, point);
}
```

If you build and run after adding this handler, you'll see a message box when you double-click the left mouse button. As with the other button messages, you will notice that the same nFlags and point parameters are passed so that you can determine the combination of keys and buttons held down, along with the position of the double click.

Setting the double-click speed

The interval between clicks that qualifies as a double-click can be set from the Mouse Control Panel Applet, which displays a slider for the speed and a Jack-in-a-Box image to test the double-click timing.

Limiting mouse-movement processing

Normally, application developers try to limit the processing performed when this message is captured because lots of mouse move messages might be sent in rapid succession as the user drags the mouse around. Too much processing will slow the whole system down and might cause a lag between the mouse position and any related drawing.

Tracking Mouse Movements and Position

Obtaining the position of a mouse click is useful, but there are times when you'll need to track the mouse position as the user drags the mouse. A paint program would probably need to do this to enable the user to draw freehand lines. Windows caters to this need by sending a message whenever the mouse is moved and passing the coordinates each time for the current mouse-pointer position.

Handling the Mouse Move Event

Like the mouse buttons, the mouse movements are sent to your application by yet another message, the WM_MOUSEMOVE message. You can add a handler for this message in the same way you did for the mouse-button events. Follow the "Adding a mouse-button message handler" step by step in the section "Handling the Button Up and Button Down Events" in this chapter for the WM_MOUSEMOVE message. The wizard will generate an OnMouseMove() handler for you, as shown in Listing 8.2.

LISTING 8.2 LST8_2.CPP—Displaying and Storing the Cursor Position When the Mouse Is Moved in an *OnMouseMove()* handler

```
1   void CMouseMsgDlg::OnMouseMove(UINT nFlags,
    ↪CPoint point)
2   {
3       // TODO: Add your message handler code here and/or
4
5       // ** Display the mouse position
6       CString strMessage;
7       strMessage.Format("Mouse Position = (%d,%d)",
8                                   point.x,point.y);
9       SetWindowText(strMessage);
10
11      // ** Store the point and redraw the window
12      m_ptMouse = point;
13      Invalidate();         ——①
14
15      CDialog::OnMouseMove(nFlags, point);
16  }
```

① The mouse position is stored in a member variable for use later in the OnPaint() function.

Notice that the parameters passed to the OnMouseMove() handler are the same as those passed to the button event handlers. You can test the buttons held down by testing nFlags against the values in Table 8.1, in the same way as the button handler does in Listing 8.1. The second parameter is the mouse position point; this is displayed in the title bar in Listing 8.2, lines 6–9. The Invalidate() function call in line 13 forces the window to redraw itself.

You can store this mouse position in the CMouseMsgDlg as a member variable, as shown in line 12 of Listing 8.2, to update the current dialog box display. After adding the lines in this listing, you must add the m_ptMouse member variable to the class definition. This is easily done by following the step by step for adding a member variable to the dialog class.

Adding a member variable to the dialog class

1. Click the **ClassView** tab of the Project Workspace view.

2. Click the top **+** to open the view of the project classes.

3. Right-click the CMouseMsgDlg class to display the context menu.

4. Select the **Add Member Variable** option to display the Add Member Variable dialog box.

5. Enter CPoint as the type of variable in the **Variable Type** box.

6. Enter the name of the variable, m_ptMouse in the **Variable Declaration** box.

   You can leave the Access Type at the default setting of **Public Access** for the example (allowing access to all objects). Alternatively you might want to change it to **Protected** or **Private** if you don't want objects of other classes to have access to the new member variable.

7. Click **OK** to add the new member variable.

This has added the m_ptMouse variable, which can now be used in the OnPaint() handler function to repaint the dialog using the latest mouse position. You can add code to this handler to draw a pair of eyes that follow the mouse pointer as you move it, as shown in Listing 8.3. To add this code, double-click the OnPaint() member function in the ClassView pane of the Project Workspace view. You might have to click the plus sign (+) next to the CMouseMsgDlg to display the member functions. This function already holds code that draws the application icon if the IsIconic() function returns TRUE (the application is minimized). You should ignore this and add your code inside the Wizard generated else condition braces.

LISTING 8.3 LST8_3.CPP—Drawing a Pair of Eyes That Follow the Mouse
Pointer Position

```
1   else
2   {
3       // ** Create a device context for drawing
4       CPaintDC dc(this); ———①
5
6       // ** Find the dialog dimensions
7       CRect rcDlg;
8       GetClientRect(&rcDlg);
9
10      // ** Loop twice, once for each eye
11      for(int i=0;i<2;i++)
12      {
13          // ** Find the center of the eye
14          CPoint ptEye = rcDlg.CenterPoint();
15
16          // ** Set the eye position for each eye
17          ptEye.x += i==0 ? -80 : +80; ———②
18
19          // ** Make an eye rectangle
20          CRect rcEye(ptEye,ptEye);
21              rcEye.InflateRect(40,60);
22
23          // ** Draw the eye white
24          dc.SelectStockObject(WHITE_BRUSH);
25          dc.Ellipse(rcEye); ———③
26          rcEye.DeflateRect(20,40);
27
28          // ** Use the mouse position to update the pupil
29          CPoint ptRel = m_ptMouse - rcEye.CenterPoint();
30          double dX = (double)ptRel.x *
31              (rcEye.Width() / (double)rcDlg.Width());
32          double dY = (double)ptRel.y *
33              (rcEye.Height() / (double)rcDlg.Height()); ———④
34
35          // ** Move the pupil position and draw it
36          rcEye.OffsetRect(CPoint((int)dX,(int)dY));
37          dc.SelectStockObject(BLACK_BRUSH);
38          dc.Ellipse(rcEye); ———⑤
39      }
40
41      CDialog::OnPaint();
42  }
```

① A paint device context is initialized and used for drawing.

② The eye position is set 80 pixels left or right of the center of the dialog by this line.

③ This Ellipse() function is used to draw the white section of each eye.

④ The current mouse position is used to calculate the offset of the pupils in each eye.

⑤ Here the pupils are drawn at an offset toward the current mouse position.

Listing 8.3 constructs a CPaintDC device context object to draw with in line 4. (Device contexts are discussed in detail in Chapter 15.) The dialog dimensions are found by the GetClientRect() function call in line 8 and stored in the CRect object rcDlg declared in line 7. A CRect is a class that holds two CPoint objects, one for the top-left coordinate and the other for the bottom-right coordinate. It also provides some useful function for finding the center point, width, and height and to make it bigger or smaller.

Line 11 starts a loop of two passes, one for each eye. The rectangle for each eye is set in line 14 and put left or right of center by line 17. Line 20 then makes the right size, and the white part is drawn by lines 24–25. The rectangle is made the correct size for the pupil in line 26.

The really interesting line is 29. This is where the mouse position is used to calculate the pupil position for each eye. The offset is calculated and set in lines 30–36 and then drawn by lines 37 and 38.

I haven't explained the drawing functions in much detail here because they are covered in Chapter 16, "Using Pens and Brushes."

If you build and run the application after adding these changes, you will have a dialog box with two eyes that follow the mouse position as you move it around the dialog window (see Figure 8.2).

FIGURE 8.2

The two eyes follow the mouse cursor as it's moved around the dialog box.

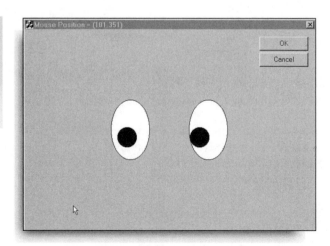

SEE ALSO

➤ *For more information on using the* OnPaint *handler, see page 363*

➤ *To learn how to draw with pens and brushes, see pages 390 and 409*

Capturing the Mouse Input

If you have built the application shown in Listing 8.3, you'll notice that there is a problem with it. All works fine until you move the mouse cursor outside the dialog window. This is because applications are normally sent only mouse move messages while the cursor is in one of their windows. When you move the mouse outside your window, another window will receive the mouse messages. There is a technique to keep the messages going to your application, referred to as *mouse capture*.

You can easily capture the mouse input by calling the SetCapture() function from the application window that must capture the input. However, capturing is antisocial to other applications that might want the mouse input, so you should always call ReleaseCapture() to release the mouse input so that normal operation is resumed.

A good place to set and release the mouse capture is in the button down and button up handlers, respectively. Using the same sample program as in Listing 8.3, change your OnLButtonDown() handler so that it captures the mouse like this:

```
void CMouseMsgDlg::OnLButtonDown(UINT nFlags, CPoint point)
{
    SetCapture();
    CDialog::OnLButtonDown(nFlags, point);
}
```

Now, whenever you press the left button, the mouse capture is set to the dialog window. You can release the mouse capture by calling ReleaseCapture() from the OnLButtonUp() handler function like this:

```
void CMouseMsgDlg::OnLButtonUp(UINT nFlags, CPoint point)
{
```

Mouse capture rules

Only a window displayed in the foreground may capture the mouse. If other background windows attempt to capture the mouse, they will see mouse messages only for the exposed parts of their window. Only one running application in the system at a time can capture the mouse.

```
        ReleaseCapture();
        CDialog::OnLButtonUp(nFlags, point);
}
```

Build and run the application after making these changes. You will find that by pressing the left mouse button over the dialog window and holding it down, you can move the pointer anywhere around the screen and the eyes still follow the pointer. This means that you are still receiving the WM_MOUSEMOVE messages, even when the pointer is not over the dialog application. Also, notice that the coordinates become negative when you are left of and above the dialog box position, because the mouse position is still relative to the top left of your window.

If you release the mouse button, the ReleaseCapture() is called, and the behavior of the eyes reverts to normal, indicating that the mouse capture mode is ended.

Setting Up a Hit Test

The cursor's hotspot

Only one specific pixel of the cursor is actually used to represent the current mouse position. This pixel is called the hotspot and is usually at the end of the arrow shape. The position of the hotspot can be specified when the cursor is created. A hit test is TRUE only when this hotspot lies within the tested rectangle.

A common requirement of free mouse movement is to be able to test whether the mouse has been clicked in a particular area, without the hassle of using a button control. For example, if you want to be able to click one of the eyes in the sample application to change its color, you set up a *hit test*.

A hit test is nothing more special than checking whether a point lies within a particular rectangle. First, you must store the position of the last button click. This is a case of assigning the point parameter passed into the OnLButtonDown() handler to a member variable:

```
void CMouseMsgDlg::OnLButtonDown(UINT nFlags, CPoint point)
{
    SetCapture();
    m_ptButton = point;     // ** Store the passed point
```

You must add the CPoint member variable m_ptButton to the CMouseMsgDlg class, as you did with the mouse position, by following the Step by Step for adding a member variable to the dialog class and using the m_ptButton as the variable name (the type is still a CPoint).

Now that the last button click has been stored, you can check whether m_ptButton lies within one of the eyes by changing the OnPaint() slightly after the // ** Draw the eye white comment, like this:

```
// ** Draw the eye white
if (rcEye.PtInRect(m_ptButton))
    dc.SelectStockObject(GRAY_BRUSH);
else
    dc.SelectStockObject(WHITE_BRUSH);
...
```

The PtInRect() member function of CRect returns a TRUE value if the specified point parameter (in this case, your m_ptButton variable) falls within the test rectangle rcEye. If the point does lie within the eye, the GRAY_BRUSH is used, rather than the normal WHITE_BRUSH, so the eye turns gray.

Build and run the application after making these changes, and you will see that clicking one of the eyes turns it gray, as shown in Figure 8.3. If you then click the other, that turns gray instead because the point now lies within the other rectangle. If you click elsewhere, both eyes turn white again because the point lies in neither rectangle.

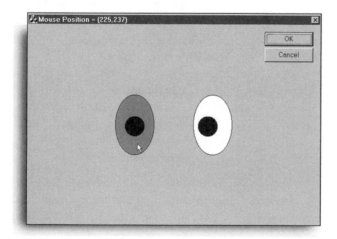

FIGURE 8.3
Hit testing turns the eye gray if the click point lies within the eye area.

SEE ALSO
➤ *To learn more about stock brushes, see page 406*

Using the *CRectTracker* Class

You might have used a rubber-banding rectangle in some applications to select several items at once. This functionality is named *rectangle tracking* and is easy to use by using the CRectTracker class. This class uses code that does its own mouse capture, enables the user to select an area, and then lets your application test points to see whether they fall within the user-defined rectangle.

You can add a CRectTracker object to the sample program to select one or both of the eyes by drawing a sizable rubber band around the defined selection area and then testing whether either eye falls within that rectangle.

To add a CRectTracker member variable named m_RectTracker to your CMouseMsgDlg class, follow the step by step for adding a member variable to the dialog class.

The first thing you should do is initialize the rect tracker with an initial rectangle and a style parameter. You can add this code to the initialization of your CMouseMsgDlg class in the constructor function CMouseMsgDlg::CMouseMsgDlg() like this:

```
CMouseMsgDlg::CMouseMsgDlg(CWnd* pParent /*=NULL*/)
  : CDialog(CMouseMsgDlg::IDD, pParent),
     m_RectTracker(CRect(0,0,0,0),
     // ** Initial rectangle
       CRectTracker::hatchedBorder +
       // ** Hatched border
         CRectTracker::resizeOutside)
         // ** Outsize handles
```

You can get to this function by double-clicking the CMouseMsgDlg() member function listed under the CMouseMsgDlg class in the ClassView pane of the Project Workspace view.

The additional (commented) lines show how the `m_RectTracker` member variable is initialized with a zero coordinate rectangle (so nothing is initially selected). The second parameter to the `CRectTracker` constructor is a style that can be combined from any of the flags shown in Table 8.4. The `CRectTracker::hatchedBorder` style will draw a thick hatched border, and this is combined with the `CRectTracker::resizeOutside`, which uses the outside area as the selection area (this will stop nasty assertions after rubber-banding if the rectangle chosen is too small).

TABLE 8.4 *CRectTracker* style flags

Style Flag	Description
`CRectTracker::solidLine`	Draws a solid borderline when rubber banding.
`CRectTracker::dottedLine`	Draws a dotted borderline when rubber banding.
`CRectTracker::hatchedBorder`	Draws a thick hatched line when rubber banding.
`CRectTracker::hatchInside`	Draws a hatched pattern over the selected region.
`CRectTracker::resizeInside`	Resizing handles are considered to be inside the rectangle.
`CRectTracker::resizeOutside`	Resizing handles are considered to be outside the rectangle.

The rubber-banding operation usually begins when the user presses the left mouse button, so the `OnLButtonDown()` handler is the obvious place to start the rubber-banding process. The whole rubber-banding process is carried out by the `TrackRubberBand()` member function of the `CRectTracker` class. You can add this to your `OnLButtonDown()` handler like this:

```
void CMouseMsgDlg::OnLButtonDown(UINT nFlags, CPoint point)
{
    m_RectTracker.TrackRubberBand(this,point,TRUE);
    CDialog::OnLButtonDown(nFlags, point);
}
```

Customizing the rubber banding operation

You can customize the action of the `CRectTracker` class by deriving your own specialized version from `CRectTracker`. There are several virtual functions such as `DrawTrackerRect()` that you can override in your derived class to perform specialized drawing of the selection area as it changes.

As you can see, the `TrackRubberBand()` function needs three parameters. The first is a pointer to the window in which the rubber banding will occur. You want the dialog box to be used as the rubber-banding window so that you can pass the C++ special `this` pointer for this argument to refer to the `CMouseMsgDlg` object itself (which is derived from the `CWnd` class and, therefore, is a window object).

The second parameter is the starting point for the top left of the rubber-banding rectangle. You can assign the button click position to this.

The third optional parameter can be set to `TRUE` to enable the rectangle to be stretched to the left and above the starting position, or `FALSE` if the user can stretch it only down and right from the starting position.

Previously, there was a `SetCapture()` in this `OnLButtonDown()` handler, which is now removed because the `rect` tracker will do its own mouse capture, with which your `SetCapture()` will interfere. Now you should also remove the corresponding `ReleaseCapture()` from the `OnLButtonUp()` handler:

```
void CMouseMsgDlg::OnLButtonUp(UINT nFlags, CPoint point)
{
    CDialog::OnLButtonUp(nFlags, point);
}
```

Finally, you must modify the hit-testing operation in the eye-drawing code in `OnPaint()` to test the `rect` tracker member rather than the point member. The `CRectTracker()` class has its own `HitTest()` function that you can call by passing the `CPoint` object to be tested:

```
// ** Draw the eye white
if (m_RectTracker.HitTest(rcEye.CenterPoint())
➥!=CRectTracker::hitNothing)
    dc.SelectStockObject(GRAY_BRUSH);
else
    dc.SelectStockObject(WHITE_BRUSH);
...
```

By passing the `rcEye.CenterPoint()` to `HitTest()`, you are asking whether the center of each eye rectangle falls within the dragged rectangle. `HitTest()` will return `CRectTracker::hitNothing` (-1) if the point doesn't fall within the selected area. If the point does fall inside the selected area, several values are returned to indicate the exact positioning of the point within the selected area. These can be any of the values shown in the enumeration (see Table 8.5), although normally it will be `CRectTracker:hitMiddle` if within the area or `CRectTracker::hitNothing` if not.

TABLE 8.5 Values returned by the *CRectTracker HitTest()* function

Return Value	Value	Meaning
`CRectTracker::hitNothing`	-1	Nothing was hit.
`CRectTracker::hitTopLeft`	0	The point is at the top left of the rectangle.
`CRectTracker::hitTopRight`	1	The point is at the top right of the rectangle.
`CRectTracker::hitBottomRight`	2	The point is at the bottom right of the rectangle.
`CRectTracker:hitBottomLeft`	3	The point is at the bottom left of the rectangle.
`CRectTracker:hitTop`	4	The point is at the top of the rectangle.
`CRectTracker:hitRight`	5	The point is right of the rectangle.
`CRectTracker:hitBottom`	6	The point is at the bottom of the rectangle.
`CRectTracker:hitLeft`	7	The point is left of the rectangle.
`CRectTracker:hitMiddle`	8	The point is somewhere in the middle of the rectangle.

When you build and run after making these changes you will be able to drag out a rectangle by pressing the left mouse button and stretching the rectangle to the desired size before releasing the button. If the middle of either eye is inside your rectangle, that eye will be selected and will turn gray, as shown in Figure 8.4.

FIGURE 8.4
Using a CRectTracker for rubber-banding selection.

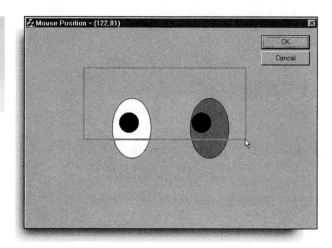

Using ActiveX Controls

Adding advanced ActiveX controls to
your project

Customizing control properties and
styles

Using data from the control in your
program

ActiveX controls and the World Wide Web

With the advent of Active Server Pages, ActiveX controls and server-side scripts can be added to Internet Web pages to make sophisticated Web-based applications.

The whole thrust of programming in the past decade has been largely focused around solving the syndrome of re-inventing the wheel that dogged programming through the '80s. Techniques such as *object orientation* and *COM/OLE* (Component Object Model/Object Linking Embedding) are the culmination of that effort. Nowadays you can buy very sophisticated *ActiveX controls* that quickly and easily integrate into your application, saving you hours, weeks, or even months of programming effort. Several controls are freely distributed or available as shareware. If you like writing controls, fine; you can distribute them freely or sell them to other developers. All in all, everybody benefits because software is quicker to develop, cheaper, and more sophisticated.

SEE ALSO

➤ *To create ActiveX controls, see page 676*

➤ *To learn more about COM and OLE, see page 648*

Selecting and Adding ActiveX Controls from the Component Gallery

The *Component Gallery* is a collection of components that you can import into your application to enhance it. Visual C++ comes with a wide selection of ActiveX controls instantly available, and you can add new controls (at any time) to extend the range. ActiveX controls are based on COM, so they can be used in Visual C++, Visual Basic, Visual J++, and a whole host of languages that can talk to COM objects. Because of this, the documentation often describes Visual Basic examples—don't be put off by this, the same methods are also available to Visual C++ applications.

Browsing for ActiveX Controls

You can create a dialog-based application to try adding and using ActiveX controls, which can be placed directly on the application's main dialog box. Create a new dialog-based project with AppWizard named ActiveX (following the same steps that were presented in Chapter 4, "Using Button Controls.")

From your new application, you can show a list of the registered ActiveX controls on your system by following these steps.

Browsing the Component Gallery for an ActiveX control

1. Click the **Project** menu and choose the **Add to Project** pop-up menu option.

2. Select the **Components and Controls** menu option from the pop-up menu.

3. Double-click the **Registered ActiveX Controls** folder from the Components and Controls Gallery dialog box.

4. You should now see a list of the installed ActiveX controls on your system similar to Figure 9.1.

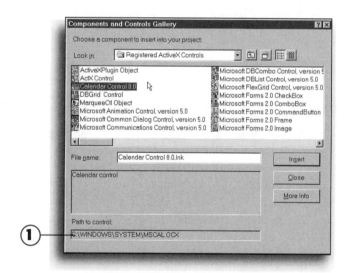

FIGURE 9.1

The registered ActiveX controls shown in the Component Gallery.

① The executable code for the ActiveX Calendar control is held in this .ocx file. (This calendar control is supplied with Office 97, you may have an earlier, or later version, or none at all depending on what programs have installed it.)

Notice that in the Components and Controls Gallery the controls are shown as normal Windows Explorer shortcuts. The code-holding file for each control is shown in the **Path to Control** box at the bottom of the window. The code for ActiveX controls actually lives in either an .OCX file or a .DLL, so if you distribute your application you must also remember to distribute these files associated with the application and register them on the target machine. Controls can be registered with the regsvr32.exe from the main **Start** menu via the **Run** option or from a command prompt like this:

```
regsvr32 C:\Windows\System\mscal.ocx.
```

This will register the Calendar ActiveX control and is necessary only when you distribute or install new controls; those that you see in the Component Gallery are already registered on your system.

If you select a control, you might see the **More Info** button become enabled. If so, you can click this button to display a standard Help dialog box that should describe the control and how to use it.

From the help pages, you'll see that ActiveX controls, like normal controls, have several properties, methods, and events. Properties let you change the appearance of the control. Methods let you set or retrieve data to or from the control. Events call your code when the user interacts with the control (for example, clicking a button).

Inserting New Controls Into the Current Project

To add the Calendar control to your dialog-based application, click the **Calendar Control 8.0** shortcut that should be near the top of your list of installed controls. When it is highlighted, you can add the Calendar control to your application by clicking the **Insert** button. You'll be prompted with an Insert This Component? dialog box; click **OK** to insert the control.

The next dialog box you'll see is the Confirm Classes dialog box as shown in Figure 9.2. This tells you which filenames will be added to your project to implement the interface classes (also known as *dispatch classes*) needed for the control. You can change the names of the implementation classes and filenames here if required. Normally you would accept the defaults, but occasionally they might conflict with classes and filenames you are already using. You can also deselect the classes to be added, but in most cases you'd add the classes shown.

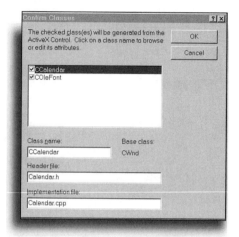

If you leave the default settings as they are and click **OK**, the new classes and their implementation files will be added to your project. You can see these new classes when you close the Components and Controls Gallery dialog box and select the ClassView pane from the Project Workspace view. The two new classes, CCalendar and COleFont, provide you with function stubs for the Calendar control and the font it uses.

What are these function stubs? If you click the plus sign next to the CCalendar class to show its member functions, and then click the GetBackColor() function, you'll see that its implementation in the editor window is just a few lines like this:

```
unsigned long CCalendar::GetBackColor()
{
    unsigned long result;
    InvokeHelper(DISPID_BACKCOLOR, DISPATCH_PROPERTYGET,
    ➥VT_I4, (void*)&result, NULL);
    return result;
}
```

The other functions are all similar to this one. These are *function stubs*, or *dispatch functions*. You can call them just like real functions, but the real implementation code lives in the .OCX or .DLL file for the control. These stub functions use a COM interface to call the real code using the InvokeHelper() function.

VBXs and Visual Basic's controls and compatibility

You might have heard about VBXs; these were Visual Basic controls and the ancestors of OCXs, and although they worked differently than OCXs, they could be used with the 16-bit Visual C++ compiler. However, VBX controls are not compatible with 32-bit Visual C++ and 32-bit programs—you must use OCXs (ActiveX controls) in modern 32-bit software.

The parameters that are passed to the function or retrieved from it are then converted to Variant parameters and are sent to or from the real code. This serves three purposes. First, it reduces the size of your application because you need the code only for these stubs in your application. Second, it means that your code is automatically compatible with later versions of the control (assuming that the control author maintains their old interfaces), so the users can upgrade their controls without the need for a new application version. Third, it protects the intellectual property of the control's author because you can't see the source code for the control.

SEE ALSO
➤ *To learn more about COM and OLE, see page 648*

Selecting, Sizing, and Testing ActiveX Controls from the Control Palette

Not only have the interface classes for the new control been added to the project, a new icon representing the ActiveX control has been added to the control's palette in the resource editor.

Adding an ActiveX Control to a Dialog Box

You can use this new calendar control in your dialog box. Select the ResourceView pane and open the ActiveX project resources to show the resource types. Then open the Dialog folder and double-click the IDD_ACTIVEX_DIALOG to edit the main project dialog box. Increase the size of the dialog box and remove the //
TODO: Place dialog controls here comment.

In the Controls palette, you should now see a new icon for the calendar control at the end of the palette icons, as shown in Figure 9.3.

FIGURE 9.3

The new ActiveX Calendar control added to the Controls palette.

①   Calendar control 8.0 icon

You can drag and add this control to the dialog box just like any other control. After the control is added to the dialog box, you can make it bigger in just the same way as normal controls. Stretch the control so that it is aligned toward the top left of the dialog box. You might need to increase the size of the dialog box because Calendar controls are quite large.

Adding ActiveX Controls from the Dialog Editor

Rather than selecting the ActiveX controls from the Component Gallery, if you know which control you need, you can use a shortcut to the process from the dialog editor. By clicking the right mouse button over the dialog template in the editor, you can display the dialog editing context menu. From this menu select the **Insert ActiveX Control** option to display the Insert ActiveX Control dialog box.

This dialog box displays a list of the installed ActiveX controls from which you can directly select a control to add to the dialog box. From this list, select the **Microsoft MCI Control, version 5** control (keep in mind that the version number might change). When you click **OK** the new control should appear. The MCI (Media Control Interface) control, which looks like a white rectangle during dialog box design, should be positioned toward the bottom left of the new dialog box.

The interface for this isn't added when you use this method, but it can be added with ClassWizard when you map the control to a member variable, as you'll see in the "Adding a Control Dispatch Class Member Variable" section later in this chapter.

The MCI control gives you a set of buttons that can be hooked into a multimedia device such as the waveaudio device for playing .WAV sound files, the cdaudio device for playing CDs, or the digitalvideo device for playing video clips.

Testing the Controls from the Dialog Editor

You can test these controls using normal dialog editor testing. To try this, click the **Layout** menu and choose the **Test** option (or press Ctrl+T). You should see the ActiveX controls as they will appear (see Figure 9.4) and can interact with them.

SEE ALSO

➤ *For more details on dialog box editing, see page 44*

➤ *To learn more MCI and using the API libraries, see page 761*

FIGURE 9.4

Testing the dialog box with the new ActiveX controls.

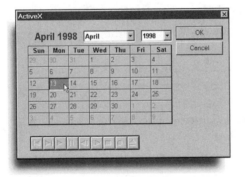

Changing the Control Properties from the Resource Editor

Like regular controls, there are several properties that you can set for the ActiveX controls arranged as pages in a property sheet. The properties are offered both programmatically by the interface class functions available when a member variable is mapped to the control, and by the settings on each of the property pages that are also implemented by the control. You can access these property pages by selecting the control and pressing Alt+Enter, or by clicking **Properties** on the context menu.

Setting Standard Properties

The **General** tab is also available. As with normal controls, in this tab you can assign an ID against the control to uniquely identify it, and set the standard enabling and visible flags. Right-click the Calendar control and select **Properties Calendar Object** to display the Calendar control properties; then change the ID from the default IDC_CALENDAR1 to IDC_CALENDAR. Do the same for the Microsoft MCI control to change its ID to IDC_MMCONTROL.

Using the Control Property Pages

The other property pages are specific to the control itself. Select the Calendar control properties again and select the **Control** page. You'll now see several properties specific to the control itself, as shown in Figure 9.5.

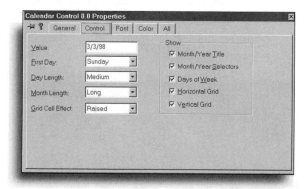

FIGURE 9.5
The Calendar control properties.

These properties let you change the look and style of the Calendar control. Try changing some of the properties and watch the effects on the displayed control (you might have to move the Properties dialog box so that it doesn't obscure the control). There is quite a bit of flexibility in the display attributes for the Calendar control.

Now select the **Font** tab. Notice that this lets you set the sizes and typefaces for the fonts used in the control. If you select the **Color** tab, you'll see that the colors can also be customized.

The final tab is the **All** tab. This is common to all the ActiveX controls, and it lists all the properties of the control along with their current settings. This list is generated from the control's published OLE properties, and they are also available from the control classes as `Get` and `Set` functions for each property. Therefore, the `BackColor` property has corresponding `GetBackColor()` and `SetBackColor()` functions that you can use to get or set these values programmatically.

Close the Calendar control properties, right-click the Microsoft MCI control, and select **Properties MMControl Object** to view its properties. If you click through the various pages you'll notice that the **General** and **All** tabs are very similar between the controls, but the other control-specific pages are very different. If you select the **Controls** page of the MCI control you'll see that the buttons can be individually enabled and set to be visible. Uncheck the `EjectVisible` and `RecordVisible` flags (see Figure 9.6). Close the control and then press Ctrl+T to test the dialog box again. You should see that those two buttons have disappeared and that the white box in the editor template view is consequently shorter.

FIGURE 9.6
The **Controls** tab of the Microsoft MCI control lets you individually select visible buttons.

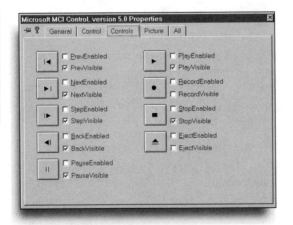

Using the Control-Supplied Classes

So far, you've done quite a bit with the ActiveX controls without adding a line of code, and indeed you could build and run the test application at this point to display and interact with the controls. As with normal controls, you will need to programmatically set data to, and get data from the control. Normally you would map the control by ID to the member variable of the control's class, and embed it in the dialog box class. This is no different for ActiveX controls, and you can use ClassWizard to help add the required code.

Adding a Control Dispatch Class Member Variable

You invoke ClassWizard from the resource editor, either by pressing Ctrl+W or by clicking the **View** menu and selecting the **ClassWizard** option. Select the **Member Variables** tab from the MFC ClassWizard dialog box to display the list of **Control IDs** that can be mapped.

You'll see that the IDC_CALENDAR and IDC_MMCONTROL IDs from the dialog box can be mapped to the CActiveXDlg dialog box class. If you select the IDC_CALENDAR and click the **Add Variable** button, you'll see the usual Add Member Variable dialog box.

You can only map ActiveX controls against their dispatch or interface class. Therefore, the **Category** combo box only allows the Control category and the **Variable Type** can only be CCalendar for the Calendar control.

Enter m_Calendar as the member variable name and click **OK** to add the member variable. Select the IDC_MMCONTROL ID and click the **Add Variable** button again. This time, you will see a dialog box informing you that the Microsoft MCI control hasn't been inserted into the project and prompting you to do this for you (see Figure 9.7).

FIGURE 9.7
The ClassWizard prompt to insert the ActiveX C++ wrapper.

Click **OK** and you will see the same Confirm Classes dialog box that appeared when you selected the Calendar control from the Component Gallery but now for the MCI control. Once again you can customize the inserted classes and implementation files if required.

205

When you click **OK** in this dialog box, you'll continue to the Adding Member Variable dialog box where you can map a `Cmci`-based member variable to the dialog class. Enter `m_MCI` as the **Member Variable** <u>**Name**</u> and click **OK** to add the new member variable.

Now that you have mapped member variables in the dialog box for these controls, you can call their functions from your code to get and set values to and from them.

Getting and Setting Control Properties Programmatically

You can now add some code to initialize these ActiveX controls in the dialog box's `OnInitDialog()` function as shown in Listing 9.1. The calendar control has a `Today()` function that sets it to today's date. The MCI control can be configured to play a .WAV file as an audio clip.

① The MCI control can be associated with a media clip file so that the buttons control the playing, stopping, and pausing of the clip.

LISTING 9.1 LST9_1.CPP—Initializing the Calendar and MCI ActiveX controls in *OnInitDialog()*

```
1   // TODO: Add extra initialization here

2

3   // ** Set the calendar to today
4   m_Calendar.Today();

5

6   // ** Set up the mci waveaudio device to play
7   // ** The Microsoft Sound.wav file
8   m_MCI.SetNotify(FALSE);
9   m_MCI.SetWait(TRUE);
10  m_MCI.SetShareable(FALSE);
11  m_MCI.SetDeviceType("waveaudio");
12  m_MCI.SetFileName("C:\\Windows\\Media\\TheMic~1.wav");  ——①
13  m_MCI.SetCommand("Open");
14
15  return TRUE;   // return TRUE  unless you set the focu
16  }
```

In Listing 9.1, the Calendar ActiveX control is set to today's date by calling its `Today()` stub function. The MCI control is a bit trickier to set up because it can be used with several devices and hence is quite configurable. Lines 8 through 13 set the MCI control to play the .WAV file called The Microsoft Sound on the waveaudio MCI device. Notice that the filename specified on line 12 has two backslash characters \\ to represent one directory folder backslash. This is because the backslash character has special meaning in C++ strings for specifying other control characters. Two backslashes together are used to represent one real backslash. The filename is reduced to its DOS shortcut name TheMic~1.wav. If you use Windows Explorer you can find this file under the C:\Windows\Media directory as The Microsoft Sound.

There is one more addition you must make. The Multimedia waveaudio device opened on line 13 of Listing 9.1 should be closed to properly manage system resources. The best place to close it is when the dialog box is destroyed. You can add the virtual member function DestroyWindow() with the following steps.

Adding a virtual function to the dialog class

1. Click the **ClassView** tab of the Project Workspace view.

2. Click the top plus sign to open the view of the project classes.

3. Right-click the **CActiveXDlg** class to display the context menu.

4. Select the **Add Virtual Function** option to display the New Virtual Override dialog box. You should see a DestroyWindow virtual function in the **New Virtual Functions** list.

5. Click the **Add and Edit** button to start editing the new handler.

This function will be called when the dialog box is destroyed; you can add another SetCommand() function call to the m_MCI ActiveX MCI control object to close the waveaudio device to the DestroyWindow() function like this:

```
BOOL CActiveXDlg::DestroyWindow()
{
    // TODO: Add your specialized code here and/or call the
    m_MCI.SetCommand("Close");
    return CDialog::DestroyWindow();
}
```

> **Directory names in Windows NT**
>
> Please note that in Windows NT, the C:\Windows part of the path should be substituted with C:\WINNT because this is where the Windows files are stored by default. If you can't find the file in Explorer, any .WAV file will work as long as the name and path are correct.

The MCI device will be closed properly, so now you can build and run the application. Notice that the Calendar control is now set to the current date (if your system date is correct) and that the play button (the > arrow icon) is enabled. If you click the play button, you should hear The Microsoft Sound. When playing, the pause button will be enabled, letting you pause and continue playing. When the sound has finished playing, you can play it again only after clicking the rewind button.

If you look through the member functions listed under the ActiveX CCalendar and Cmci classes, you'll see many more functions that you can invoke on these two controls. Also remember that help is available for these controls from the Component and Controls Gallery dialog box when you click the **More Info** button.

These are only two of the many controls available from the Component Gallery; many more can be downloaded from the Internet and are actually used in Web pages themselves. By now you should be starting to realize the power behind this simple code—the reusability concept enabled by COM.

Implementing ActiveX Event Handlers with ClassWizard

Obviously ActiveX controls would be fairly limited if you could get no messages to indicate the user has changed the state of a control. Fortunately the controls can also fire events back at your application. You can add event handlers for these controls in the normal fashion by adding an event handler with ClassWizard or by the New Windows Messages/Event Handlers dialog box.

You can add a handler to detect when the user has clicked the Calendar control.

Adding an ActiveX event handler with ClassWizard

1. Invoke ClassWizard by pressing Ctrl+W or by clicking the **V**iew menu and selecting **ClassWizard**.

2. Ensure the **Message Maps** tab is selected.

Creating ActiveX controls in the dispatch class

If you examine the class definition for the CCalendar and Cmci classes (held in the Calendar.h and mci.h modules), you'll notice that both are derived from the CWnd class. This lets your container application treat them as it would any other window (like other controls). The clever part is in the Create() function, which is defined as a virtual function in the CWnd class and overridden in the dispatch classes to call the CWnd class's CreateControl() function to actually create an OLE (ActiveX) control rather than a normal window.

3. Select **CActiveXDlg** from the **Class Name** combo box if it isn't already selected.

4. Select the **IDC_CALENDAR** ID from the list of **Object IDs**.

5. From the list of **Messages**, double-click the Click Message to Show the Add Member Function dialog box.

6. Accept the default **Member Function Name** of OnClickCalendar by clicking **OK**.

7. Click the **Edit Code** button to start editing your new handler function.

You should now see the new OnClickCalendar() handler function; this function will be called whenever the Calendar control is clicked and the date changed. You could display the new date in the dialog box title bar whenever it is changed by adding the code shown in Listing 9.2 to the new handler function.

LISTING 9.2 LST9_2.CPP—Adding a Handler for the *Click* Event Sent from the Calendar ActiveX Control

```
1   void CTestcalDlg::OnClickCalendar()
2   {
3       // TODO: Add your control notification handler code
4
5       // ** Convert the VARIANT calendar value
6       COleDateTime dtChosenDate(m_Calendar.GetValue());  ——————①
7
8       // ** Format Ole date to a sensible default
9       // ** it in the dialog title bar.
10      SetWindowText(dtChosenDate.Format("You Chose %#x"));
11  }
```

① The VARIANT struct is turned into a COleDateTime by the constructor.

In Listing 19.2, line 6 uses the GetValue() member function of the m_Calendar object to get the current selected date from the Calendar control. If you double-click the GetValue() member function under the CCalendar class in the ClassView pane, you'll see that the GetValue() function returns a VARIANT:

```
VARIANT CCalendar::GetValue()
{
    VARIANT result;
```

```
InvokeHelper(0xc, DISPATCH_PROPERTYGET, VT_VARIANT,
        (void*)&result, NULL);
return result;
```
}

A VARIANT is a structure that can hold many different types of data. It does this by having members for each type of data, which are held in a union (a union in C++ holds all the members at the same address to save space). It also has a VARTYPE member *vt* that holds a flag to represent the type of data stored in the variant.

You'll see VARIANTs and their MFC wrapper class COleVariant used quite a bit in the COM/OLE world. This enables applications to transfer data that could mean different things in different languages, thus providing a common mechanism for storing and retrieving that data. Fortunately you rarely have to deal with a variant directly because many of the MFC classes recognize VARIANTs and can convert them into the more friendly MFC classes. In Listing 19.2, this conversion is performed on line 6 where the VARIANT returned by the GetValue() call is passed directly to the constructor of the dtChosenDate object to hold it as a COleDateTime object.

COleDateTime is an object that holds and manipulates dates and times. It has a handy Format() function that can be used to turn its stored date into a nicely formatted CString by passing a number of formatting flags to it. The %#x flag is used in line 10 by the Format() function, which turns the date and time that the COleDataTime object stores into the general format: Day of Week, Month Day of Month, Year. (For example, Monday, April 21, 1998.)

This CString formatted date can then be passed directly to the SetWindowText() function that will set the dialog box title bar to the date chosen by the user.

If you build and run the program after adding these lines to the handler function, you should be able to click the calendar and see the chosen date displayed in the dialog box's title bar as shown in Figure 9.8.

Creating ActiveX controls in the dispatch class

MFC provides four classes to handle all the aspects of date and time manipulation and storage. Originally, there were just two classes, CTime and CTimeSpan, which are based on the UNIX time_t (4-byte long value) system (the number of elapsed seconds since 1970). However, granularity of only one second and a limited range of dates between 1970 and 2038 proved too restrictive for many applications. Hence, two new classes, COleDateTime and COleDateTimeSpan, are used in newer OLE applications.

COleDateTime is based on an underlying DATE structure (which is actually just a **double** value). The capacity of this storage type lets COleDateTime cover a range of dates between January 1, 100 and December 31, 9999 and down to an approximate resolution of 1 millisecond. The difference between two COleDateTime values can be represented and manipulated by the COleDateTimeSpan object.

SEE ALSO

➤ *For details about messages and event handling, see page 69*

➤ *To create your own ActiveX controls, see page 676*

➤ *To learn more about COM and OLE, see page 648*

FIGURE 9.8

Using events fired from the ActiveX control to update the date display.

10

Using Dialog Boxes

Creating your own customized application dialog boxes and handler classes

Exploiting modal dialog boxes to maintain application data

Creating modeless dialog boxes for special cases

Learning how to use and customize dialog box data exchange and validation

Creating a Dialog Class

You can create additional dialog boxes, which might be invoked from the main application dialog box or window in response to user interaction. For each additional dialog box you'll need a dialog template resource and an associated `CDialog`-derived class. You can create the dialog template using the resource editor and then use ClassWizard to create a `CDialog`-derived class to handle the dialog box's functionality. You can then add functionality to the new class to handle the dialog box's controls in just the same way as you would to extend the dialog-based application's main dialog box.

Most dialog boxes follow a standard model with which you are probably already familiar. The standard model is to display a dialog box with blank or initialized settings, enable the user to change those settings, and then apply them if an **OK** button is clicked or disregard them if a **Cancel** button is clicked. From the programmer's perspective, this generally means that the dialog box must hold a local copy of the data being modified. If the user clicks **OK**, you must apply those modifications to your main application data; otherwise, do nothing.

The standard approach is generally implemented with a modal dialog box. When a modal dialog box is displayed, the rest of the application's user interface is inaccessible, forcing the user to close the dialog box before the application resumes. These modal dialog boxes can be stacked so that one dialog box starts another, thus forcing control to the most recent top dialog box and returning to the calling dialog box when closed.

Modeless dialog boxes are an alternative to the modal model. Modeless dialog boxes are displayed while the rest of the application remains enabled. A floating toolbar dialog box such as the Controls palette is a good example of a modeless dialog box.

Modeless dialog boxes are explained in more detail later in this chapter; however, both types of dialog boxes need a C++ source class to wrap the functionality of the dialog box, which is associated with a dialog resource template used when displaying the controls.

Prompting the user with `AfxMessageBox()`

If you require a dialog box simply to prompt the user, a wide variety of functionality can be invoked by passing parameters to the `AfxMessageBox()` function. `AfxMessageBox()` has two forms, the difference being the first parameter. In the first form it's a pointer to the string to be displayed, and in the second it's the ID of the string resource to be displayed. The second parameter is an optional message box type, which specifies the style (which buttons are added and whether an icon is displayed). The third parameter lets you specify an ID for context-sensitive help. The function returns a value corresponding to the chosen button.

SEE ALSO

➤ *To create dialog template resources, see page 44*

Adding a New Dialog Template Resource

Before you create a new dialog box handler class, you must create a new dialog template resource and add your dialog box controls.

Inserting a new dialog template resource

1. Select the ResourceView pane to display the project resources.

2. Right-click the top-level item and select the **Insert** option from the drop menu to display the Insert Resource dialog box (see Figure 10.1).

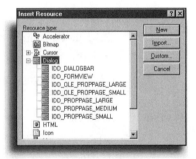

FIGURE 10.1

The Insert Resource dialog box showing the new dialog template options.

3. Select the top-level **Dialog** box item to insert a normal dialog box. Alternatively, you can add one of the specialized dialog box types by clicking the plus symbol to show the dialog box types available.

4. Click **New** to insert the new dialog box resource. You should see the new dialog template appear under the **Dialog Box Resource** heading.

5. Right-click the dialog box and select the **Properties** context menu option to display the dialog template properties.

6. You can now change the default IDD_ resource **ID** name to a more appropriate name for your dialog box.

SEE ALSO

➤ *To learn more about creating dialog template resources, see Creating Dialog Templates, page 44*

➤ *For more information about creating a dialog box application, see page 44*

Deriving a Class from *CDialog* Using ClassWizard

After inserting the new dialog template, you can add any required controls or change the default properties as required. To use the new dialog template, you must create a new class to load and display the dialog template and handle messages originating from the dialog box or its controls. The CDialog base class performs much of the work of loading and displaying the dialog template. You can derive your new dialog class from CDialog to incorporate this functionality. ClassWizard even automates this process for you.

Creating a new dialog-handling class using ClassWizard

1. Click the new resource template in the ResourceView pane to highlight it.

2. Press Ctrl+W, or click the **View** menu and select the **Class<u>W</u>izard** to invoke ClassWizard.

3. ClassWizard will detect that your dialog template is a new resource and will display the Adding a Class dialog box (see Figure 10.2).

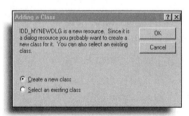

FIGURE 10.2

ClassWizard displays the Adding a Class dialog box after detecting a new dialog template resource.

4. Click **OK** to accept the **<u>C</u>reate a New Class** default option.

5. ClassWizard will then display the New Class dialog box as shown in Figure 10.3.

FIGURE 10.3
The New Class dialog box lets you assign a name for the new dialog box handler class.

6. You can enter a name for your new dialog box handling class in the **Name** box. Convention is that MFC-derived classes should begin with the letter C.

7. As you type you should see the filename of the implementation file appear in the **File Name** box. You can change this default name if required by clicking the **Change** button.

8. You should leave the **Base Class** set to CDialog unless you are implementing a property page in a property sheet.

9. The appropriate dialog box ID should be displayed in the **Dialog ID** combo box. If this is incorrect, or you want to use another dialog template, you can select the correct ID from the list of new dialog box resource templates from the combo box's drop-down list.

10. Click **OK** to create the new class, which will be created in the specified class implementation (.cpp) and header definition (.h) files.

11. ClassWizard will then display the usual **Message Maps** tab for adding event handlers to dialog box messages. You can now add event handlers and mapping variables for the dialog box and its controls as normal.

12. Click **OK** to close ClassWizard when you've finished adding handler functions or mapped variables.

SEE ALSO

➤ *For more information about creating a dialog box application, see page 44*

➤ *To learn more about message handlers, see page 69*

Initializing the New Dialog Class

After you've added the new dialog class, you'll see the new class listed in your project's list of classes in the ClassView pane. If you click the plus symbol to the left of the new class, you should see a constructor function (with the same name as the new class).

If you double-click the constructor function, you should see code similar to this:

```
CMyNewDlg::CMyNewDlg(CWnd* pParent /*=NULL*/)
    : CDialog(CMyNewDlg::IDD, pParent)
{
    //{{AFX_DATA_INIT(CMyNewDlg)
        // NOTE: the ClassWizard will add member initializa
    //}}AFX_DATA_INIT
}
```

Notice that a dialog-specific member, `CMyNewDlg::IDD`, is passed into the constructor of the `CDialog` base class. In your class definition, you should find a definition for this member as an enumerator value set to the dialog box resource ID:

```
enum { IDD = IDD_MYNEWDLG };
```

The `CDialog` base class uses this value to load the appropriate dialog box resource template when your derived class (`CMyNewDlg`) is instantiated. If you add new member variables via ClassWizard, you'll also see initialization lines for these variables added between the `AFX_DATA_INIT` comments.

You might want to add member variables to the class definition manually (that is, not using ClassWizard). These variables should be initialized to their proper default starting values in this constructor function.

When you subsequently invoke ClassWizard, you can select the appropriate class from the **Class Name** combo box. After adding

ClassWizard-generated code

You should be careful when modifying ClassWizard-generated code. The ClassWizard becomes confused easily if it finds that an expected identifier is missing. If you add your own initialization code, you should add the extra lines after the ClassWizard comments.

your new dialog class to a dialog-based application, you should see the class for your new dialog box as well as the main application dialog box listed here. Whenever you add any new member variables or message-handling functions for the controls in the dialog box, you must ensure that the correct dialog box is selected in the **Class Name** combo box. Otherwise, ClassWizard will insert these into the currently selected class (which might not be where you want them!).

Displaying a Modal Dialog Box

At this stage, it's worth considering how the new dialog box is invoked. Generally, your dialog box will be invoked in response to a user action, such as selecting a menu or clicking a button from a parent window or dialog box.

In the appropriate handler function of the parent window (which responds to the control), you can display your new dialog box by two simple stages. The first is to create an instance of the dialog class. You can do this simply by declaring a dialog class object local to the handler function, such as

```
CMyCustomDlg dlgMyCustom(this);
```

In the preceding line, `CMyCustomDlg` is the AppWizard-generated dialog class. The class will be instantiated as the `dlgMyCustom` object. The constructor is passed the special C++ `this` pointer. Because the calling handler function belongs to a `CWnd`-derived class (such as `CDialog`, `Cview`, and so on) the new dialog box will be passed the correct parent window information. Recall from the previous section that the dialog template will be automatically passed to initialize the `CDialog` base class.

So that the compiler knows about your derived dialog class when compiling the source module that instances it (`CMyCustomDlg` in the preceding line), you must remember to include the class definition header (.h file) at the top of the *instantiating* module with an `#include` preprocessor directive.

For example, if your new dialog class definition resides in the MyCustomDlg.h and you are adding the instantiating line that references the new dialog class definition to the CustomDlg.cpp

Property sheets and pages

ClassWizard also lets you create a tabbed dialog box known as a property sheet. Essentially these behave in a similar fashion to modal dialog boxes where each tab (or page) is a separate dialog template resource. To construct a tabbed dialog box, derive your classes from the `CPropertySheet` and `CPropertyPage` MFC classes.

implementation file, you should add the following line to the top of CustomDlg.cpp:

```
#include "MyCustomDlg.h"
```

The second stage is to display and start the modal operation of the dialog box. To do this, simply call the dialog box's `DoModal()` function. This will display the dialog box and its controls (from the dialog template) and wait in a local message loop, dispatching messages from the dialog box's controls to your implementation until the user closes the dialog box.

If an error occurs while displaying the new dialog box, `DoModal()` immediately returns an integer code of either `-1` or `IDABORT`. If the dialog box is displayed successfully, `DoModal()` returns when the `EndDialog()` is called, which terminates the dialog box. `EndDialog()` is passed an integer value that is then returned from the `DoModal()` as an exit code.

The default implementations of `OnOk()` and `OnCancel()` automatically call `EndDialog()`, passing the `IDOK` and `IDCANCEL` exit codes, which are then returned from `DoModal()`. For example, you might code the following call to `DoModal()` to invoke the dialog box:

```
int nRetCode = dlgMyCustom.DoModal();
```

When the dialog box is closed (usually by the user clicking **OK** or **Cancel**), the returned code (usually `IDOK` or `IDCANCEL`) will be assigned to `nRetCode`. Normally, at this stage you'd interrogate `nRetCode` to perform the appropriate action, depending on the user response, such as modifying the application data if `IDOK` was returned, with code such as the following:

```
if (nRetCode == IDOK)
{
    // Store the dialog changes
}
```

You can also close the dialog box programmatically at any time by calling the `EndDialog()` function from your code and passing it the required return code.

Terminating modal dialog boxes with `EndDialog()`

Programmatically you should always use the **`EndDialog()`** function to close a modal dialog box as do **`OnOK()`** and **`OnCancel()`** and not **`DestroyWindow()`**. **`EndDialog()`** ensures that any GDI resources used by the dialog box are cleaned up before termination. You can close a dialog box using **`EndDialog()`** even in the **`OnInitDialog()`** function, which means it will terminate before it is displayed to the user.

Adding Member Variables to Store Dialog Box Data

Most applications require that a dialog box be initialized with a copy of the application's current data (or settings). Then they allow the user to modify the dialog box's controls and thus directly or indirectly modify the local dialog box's copy of the application's data. Finally, the data should be re-applied to the application's main data set if the user clicks **OK**.

This usually means that you must pass the application current values to your dialog box object before calling the dialog box's DoModal(), and then apply the changed values in the OK condition when DoModal() returns.

You can often store the dialog box's local copy of the application's data in the control mapping variables (those that you've added with ClassWizard) and retrieve those values when the dialog box is closed. For example, you might need to display a simple dialog box that manipulates a name and age via two edit controls, as shown in Figure 10.4.

FIGURE 10.4
A simple maintenance dialog box.

You could map a CString (m_strName) variable to one of the edit controls to store the name and an int (m_nAge) variable to store the age. You could add these maps with ClassWizard, resulting in the Member Variable map for the dialog class (CMyCustomDlg) as shown in Figure 10.5.

You can then initialize the variables after the dialog box object is declared, but before the dialog box is displayed, by setting the mapped variables directly with code:

```
CMyCustomDlg dlgMyCustom(this);
dlgMyCustom.m_nAge = 31;
dlgMyCustom.m_strName = "Jon Bates";
dlgMyCustom.DoModal();
```

The user can then modify the values in the controls. You would then check that `DoModal()` returns `IDOK` and read the values from the dialog box's mapped member variables with code like this:

```
if (dlgMyCustom.DoModal()==IDOK)
{
    CString strMsg;
    strMsg.Format("New Name = '%s', Age = %d",
        dlgMyCustom.m_strName,dlgMyCustom.m_nAge);
    AfxMessageBox(strMsg);
}
```

FIGURE 10.5

ClassWizard showing variables mapped to a simple dialog box.

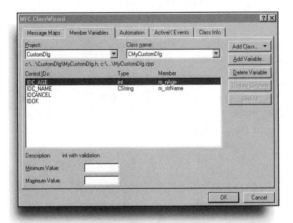

In the preceding lines, the modified name from the edit box will be set in `dlgMyCustom.m_strName` and the age is set in `dlgMyCustom.m_nAge` when `DoModal()` returns. These lines are then formatted into a `CString` and displayed in the message box. In a real application, you might want to transfer this modified data into your application's main data storage area.

SEE ALSO

➤ *To learn about adding mapped member variables to controls, see page 91*

Using Dialog Box Data Exchange and Validation

You might be wondering how the values from the member variables are transferred to and from the edit controls. Whenever you map member variables to controls via ClassWizard, code is automatically generated to perform this exchange in the dialog box's DoDataExchange() function. This function is responsible for transferring the data in both directions, to and from the dialog box controls.

The transfer process is called Data Exchange and is initiated by a call to the dialog box's UpdateData() function. UpdateData() can be passed one Boolean parameter called bSaveAndValidate. You can pass either FALSE to set the controls from the member variables or TRUE to transfer the current control values into the member variables. UpdateData() is automatically called by the CDialog base class's OnInitDialog() function to set the controls when the dialog box is being displayed. The base class's OnOK() function (called when the user clicks **OK**) is responsible for calling UpdateData() and passing a TRUE value, which transfers the values from the controls into the member variables.

> **Data exchange is not limited only to dialog boxes**
>
> The technique of using UpdateData() in conjunction with DoDataExchange() is not limited only to dialog boxes. In fact these two functions are members of **CWnd**, so you can implement data exchange and validation for any **CWnd** derived class.

The dialog box can also validate the values that were entered by the user. These validation tests are also performed by lines added to the DoDataExchange(), which is invoked via a call to UpdataData() when passed the TRUE flag for the bSaveAndValidate parameter. If the data was valid, UpdateData() returns TRUE (and the default implementation of CDialog::OnOK() closes the dialog box). If the data was invalid, the appropriate warning is issued to the user and UpdateData() will return FALSE.

Using the Data Exchange (*DDX*) Functions

You can take a closer look at these data validation lines by examining the contents of a DoDataExchange() function. For example, the DoDataExchange() from the name and age dialog box in the previous section looks like this:

```
void CMyCustomDlg::DoDataExchange(CDataExchange* pDX)
{
```

```
        CDialog::DoDataExchange(pDX);
        //{{AFX_DATA_MAP(CMyCustomDlg)
        DDX_Text(pDX, IDC_AGE, m_nAge);
        DDX_Text(pDX, IDC_NAME, m_strName);
        //}}AFX_DATA_MAP
    }
```

Notice that the function is passed a pointer to a CDataExchange object (pDX). The CDataExchange object holds all the details associated with the direction and target window for the data transfer. The pDX pointer is then passed along with a dialog box ID and associated member variable to the DDX_Text() function call (generated by ClassWizard) to implement the data transfer. There are several of these DDX_ functions that handle the various types of controls and datatypes. Some of the more common functions are shown in Table 10.1. ClassWizard automatically adds these lines for you between the // AFX_DATA_MAP comments when you map a member variable to a control from ClassWizard's **Member Variable** tab. You can also add your own entries manually at the end of the DoDataExchange() function after the ClassWizard map.

TABLE 10.1 The various DDX functions available

Name	Control Types	Associated Datatypes
DDX_Text	Edit box	BYTE, short, int, UINT, long, DWORD, String, LPTSTR, float, double, COleCurrency, COleDateTime
DDX_Check	Check box	int
DDX_Radio	Radio button group	int
DDX_LBString	Drop list box	CString
DDX_LBStringExact	Drop list box	CString
DDX_CBString	Combo box	CString
DDX_CBStringExact	Combo box	CString
DDX_LBIndex	Drop list box index	int
DDX_CBIndex	Combo box index	int
DDX_Scroll	Scrollbar	int

These functions then interrogate the passed `CDataExchange` object pointer to determine the transfer direction, held in its `m_bSaveAndValidate` member. You can check this flag and perform specific tasks depending on the transfer direction with a line such as

```
if (pDX-> m_bSaveAndValidate == TRUE)
```

The `DDX` functions implement the `WIN32` code that either sets or retrieves values from the controls using Windows messages (remember that each control is itself a window). You can implement your own custom `DDX_` functions or add code to `DoDataExchange()` to perform any customized interaction with the dialog box's controls.

You might need to call `UpdateData()` from your own code to force a transfer between the dialog box's controls and the member variables. You might need to do this if you implement any message-handler functions for the dialog box that needs the current values from the controls.

For example, suppose you wanted to catch user changes to an edit box in a dialog class to display the text as it changes in the dialog box title. You could use ClassWizard to add a handler for the edit box `EN_CHANGE` notification and use the `SetWindowText()` function to update the dialog box title.

However, without the addition of a call to `UpdateData(TRUE)` the mapped member variable won't be updated with the latest text in the control. By adding this line in the handler, you ensure that `DoDataExchange()` is called to transfer the contents of the edit control to the mapped `CString` variable.

The handler function (based on the name edit box from the name and age dialog box in the previous section) should therefore look like this:

```
void CMyCustomDlg::OnChangeName()
{
    UpdateData(TRUE);
    SetWindowText(m_strName);
}
```

When a key is pressed, `OnChangeName()` would be called and `UpdateData(TRUE)` updates the member variables including `m_strName` via a `DDX_Text` call. The updated contents are then sent to the dialog box's title bar with the call to `SetWindowText()`.

You might also call `UpdateData(FALSE)` to reset the contents of the controls to the mapped member variables. You might want to do this in response to the user clicking an undo or reset button on the dialog box to reassign the controls to their initial settings.

SEE ALSO

➤ *To learn about various types of controls, see Chapter 5, "Using Text Controls," Chapter 6, "Using List Controls," and Chapter 7, "Using Progress, Scrollbar, Slider, and Date Time Controls."*

Using the Data Validation (*DDV*) Functions

When you add some types of mapped member variables to a dialog box with ClassWizard, such as edit box to `CString` or `int` datatypes, you also must supply optional validation parameters. You can set these parameters by selecting one of the new mapped member variables from the **Member Variables** map tab in ClassWizard and changing the validation options at the bottom (as shown in Figure 10.6).

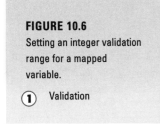

FIGURE 10.6

Setting an integer validation range for a mapped variable.

① Validation

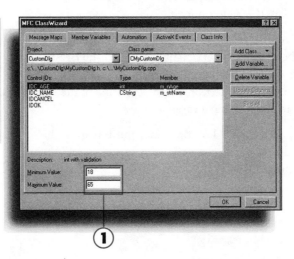

For a `CString` mapped to an edit control, you can supply a maximum character length to limit the length of the input string keyed by the user. For an `int` mapped edit control, you can supply a minimum and maximum range so that the user is prompted if an entered integer is out of the acceptable range.

When you add these validation rules, ClassWizard will generate corresponding DDV lines in the `DoDataExchange()` function. For example, the validation rule shown at the bottom of Figure 10.6 will produce the follow DDV line:

```
DDV_MinMaxInt(pDX, m_nAge, 18, 65);
```

The DDV function call will appear directly after the corresponding DDX call so that the value of `m_nAge` is up-to-date before the validation is performed. If the entered range fails the validation check, the user is informed with an appropriate message box and the `UpdateData()` call that initiates the exchange will return a `FALSE` value indicating validation failure (see Figure 10.7).

The ClassWizard-generated validation code for limiting the number of characters entered into an edit box would look like this:

```
DDV_MaxChars(pDX, m_strName, 15);
```

The available DDV validation functions are shown in Table 10.2. These validation routines can be used with any control map that supports the appropriate applicable datatype, such as edit controls, scrollbars, and radio groups. Generally, they limit the allowable numeric value to fall between the specified numeric range. You can add these DDV function calls manually, but you should be careful to place the new entries after the ClassWizard `AFX_DATA_MAP` section; otherwise, ClassWizard might become confused.

Catching the `CUserException` **thrown by** DDV **failure**

When a validation rule fails, a `CUserException` is raised. You can catch this exception to override the default message box prompt.

FIGURE 10.7
The automatic user prompt for a numeric validation failure.

TABLE 10.2 Standard ClassWizard-generated *DDV* functions

DDV Function	Applicable Datatype	Description
DDV_MaxChars	CString	Limits the number of characters entered
DDV_MinMaxByte	BYTE	Limits the number to specified range
DDV_MinMaxDouble	double	Limits the number to a specified range
DDV_MinMaxDWord	DWord	Limits the number to a specified range
DDV_MinMaxFloat	float	Limits the number to a specified range
DDV_MinMaxInt	int	Limits the number to a specified range
DDV_MinMaxLong	long	Limits the number to a specified range
DDV_MinMaxUnsigned	unsigned	Limits the number to a specified range

SEE ALSO

➤ *To learn about various types of controls, see Chapter 5, "Using Text Controls," Chapter 6, "Using List Controls," and Chapter 7, "Using Progress, Scollbars, Slider, and Date Time Controls."*

Creating Custom Validation Functions

You can create your own customized validation functions to check for special cases by writing a DDV_-style function. To do this, you must write a function that accepts the pointer to the CDataExchange object (pDX), a reference to the mapped variable to be tested, and any additional custom parameters you might need.

The first condition your custom validation function must check is that the CDataExchange object is in save-and-validate mode, and you can do this by checking that pDX->m_bSaveAndValidate is TRUE. If this flag isn't TRUE, the controls are being initialized from the member variables, so no validation checks are required and your function should just return. Otherwise, you should validate the mapped member variable according to your custom criteria.

If the mapped variable is valid, your function can return normally; otherwise, you should display a prompting message box and call the Fail() function on the CDataExchange object pointer pDX to inform the calling UpdateData() that validation has failed.

For example, if you wanted to extend the age checking of the previous example so that 31-year-olds are excluded, you might write a validation function like this:

```
void DDV_ValidateAge(CDataExchange* pDX,int& nCheckAge)
{
    if (pDX->m_bSaveAndValidate &&
    (nCheckAge < 18 ¦¦ nCheckAge > 65 ¦¦ nCheckAge == 31))
    {
        AfxMessageBox(
            "Ages must be between 18 and 65, but not 31!");
        pDX->Fail();
    }
}
```

Because the nCheckAge parameter is a reference to the calling mapped variable, you could optionally reset the value to a valid default if it's found to be incorrect.

The custom DDV_ValidateAge() function could then be called from the DoDataExchange() function after the member variable has been updated by the corresponding DDX function with a call like this:

```
DDV_ValidateAge(pDX,m_nAge);
```

Your custom validation should now accept age values between 18 and 65 excluding 31-year-olds.

> **Dialog data validation**
>
> If you add DDV_... macros to the DoDataExchange() function override they should immediately follow the DDX_...macro of the data member they validate. For a complete list of the data exchange macros provided by MFC see the header file afxdd_.h.

Using Modeless Dialog Boxes

A modeless dialog box doesn't take over the application input like a modal dialog box does. Instead, a modeless dialog box is usually displayed to complement the normal running of the application by passing messages and details back to the calling application. Modeless dialog boxes are usually used as floating toolbars, enabling the user to click the dialog box's buttons to indicate mode settings or user choices.

A modeless dialog box uses a normal dialog template resource to specify the layout of controls. However, you would normally remove the now irrelevant modal **OK** and **Cancel** buttons.

It also uses a CDialog-based handling class that can be created by ClassWizard from the template. The differences between a modal and modeless dialog box lie in the way in which the dialog box is started and closed.

Creating and Destroying a Modeless Dialog Box

Rather than entering the modal loop via the DoModal() call to display the dialog box, modeless dialog boxes can be displayed by a call to the CDialog's Create() function. You could add this call to Create() to your derived dialog box's class constructor to create an instance of the class when an object of the class is instantiated. Alternatively, you might want to separate the class instantiation and the call to Create() to allow some initialization code in between. The Create() function takes two parameters; the first is the ID of the dialog template to be created, and the second is an optional pointer to a parent window object (this defaults to the main application's window). Create() will indicate success by returning a TRUE value, or failure by returning a FALSE value.

When Create() returns indicating success, the modeless dialog box window will exist, but isn't yet visible. You can make it visible by a subsequent call to the dialog box window's ShowWindow(), passing the SW_SHOW flag to make it appear.

Whereas the modal dialog box can be safety scoped inside a handler function, you'll need to access the modeless box from other parts of the program. Therefore, the modeless dialog box should be dynamically created by the C++ new operator and its address assigned to a global or member pointer variable.

You can close the dialog box when required by deleting it with the C++ delete operator. The CDialog base class destructor will then close the dialog box window.

You could try this technique by creating a dialog-based sample program with AppWizard. Insert a new dialog template resource for the modeless dialog box with the dialog box ID set to IDD_MODELESS (this was described previously in the "Inserting a New Dialog Template Resource" set of steps. Create a handling class for the dialog box called CModeless, following the previous set of steps, "Creating a New Dialog-Handling Class Using ClassWizard."

When you've added the new class, you should see CModeless appear in the list of classes in the ClassView pane of the project workspace view. If you click the plus sign next to the class to show its member functions, you should see the CModeless() constructor function. Double-click this constructor function entry to start editing the associated constructor. You can then add the lines to call Create() and ShowWindow(), as shown in Listing 10.1.

LISTING 10.1 LST10_1.CPP—Adding the *Create()* and *ShowWindow()* Functions to the Modeless Dialog Box's Constructor

```
1   CModeless::CModeless(CWnd* pParent /*=NULL*/)
2       : CDialog(CModeless::IDD, pParent)
3   {
4       //{{AFX_DATA_INIT(CModeless)
5       // NOTE: the ClassWizard will add member initializa
6       //}}AFX_DATA_INIT
7
8       // ** Create the modeless dialog box window
9       if (Create(CModeless::IDD,pParent))          ①
10      {
11          // ** Creation succeeded so show the window
12          ShowWindow(SW_SHOW);          ②
13      }
14  }
```

① The modeless dialog box is created by calling the Create() function.

② The modeless dialog box created is displayed with the ShowWindow() function.

The additional lines (8 through 13) in Listing 10.1 convert the dialog box to modeless operation. Line 9 calls Create(), passing the ClassWizard-generated CModeless::IDD enumerator that holds the ID of the associated dialog template, and pParent a pointer to the parent window. If the Create() function returns the TRUE value indicating its success, ShowWindow() is called on line 12 passing the SW_SHOW flag to display the new dialog box.

You could then add a button to the main dialog class with an ID of IDC_START_MODELESS that will be used to start the modeless dialog box, as shown in Figure 10.8, and another with an ID of IDC_STOP_MODELESS to stop it.

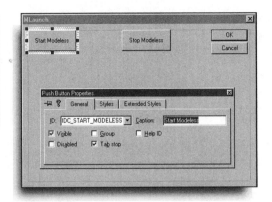

FIGURE 10.8

Adding buttons to the main application dialog box to start and stop the modeless dialog box.

You can insert message handlers for the BN_CLICKED messages from each button in the main dialog box to start and stop the new modeless dialog box. You could then add the code to implement these new handler functions and start and stop the modeless dialog box (see Listing 10.2). The OnStartModeless() handler function will then start an instance of the modeless dialog box when clicked, if it isn't already active. The OnStopModeless() handler function will destroy the modeless dialog box if it is active.

(1) You can access the global pointer from anywhere in the application, but might require an extern declaration.

(2) If the dialog box isn't active, another is created just by making a new object of the CModeless class.

LISTING 10.2 LST10_2.CPP—Creating and Destroying the Modeless Dialog Box from the Main Dialog Box Button Clicked Handler Functions

```
1   // ** include the required class definitions
2   #include "modeless.h"
3
4   // ** Declare a global pointer to the modeless dialog
5   CModeless* g_pDlgModeless = NULL; ———(1)
6
7   void CMLaunchDlg::OnStartModeless()
8   {
9       // ** Create a new dialog if the global pointer
10      // ** is set to NULL indicating that the dialog
11      // ** doesn't already exist
12      if (!g_pDlgModeless) ————————————(2)
13          g_pDlgModeless = new CModeless(this); —
14  }
15
16  void CMLaunchDlg::OnStopModeless()
17  {
```

```
18        // ** If the modeless dialog pointer is valid
19        // ** the dialog can be deleted and destroyed.
20        if (g_pDlgModeless)
21        {
22            delete g_pDlgModeless; ──────③
23            g_pDlgModeless = NULL;
24        }
25    }
```

③ The destructor will automatically close the dialog box window.

Line 2 of Listing 10.2 includes the required class definitions for CModeless from the modeless.h file. A global pointer to a CModeless dialog box (g_pDlgModeless) is declared on line 5 and initialized as NULL. A conditional check for a NULL g_pDlgModeless pointer is made in OnStartModeless() to ensure that the dialog box isn't already active before the new dialog box is created on line 13, passing the main dialog box as the parent window via the this pointer. The dialog box will be displayed immediately upon creation, as the Create() and ShowWindow() calls are implemented in the dialog box's constructor.

The OnStopModeless() function on line 16 is called when the **Stop Modeless** button is clicked. Then the g_pDlgModeless pointer is tested on line 20 to ensure that the dialog box exists (if the pointer isn't NULL). The dialog box is then deleted on line 22 (destroying the dialog box window in the destructor). Finally, the dialog box pointer is set to NULL on line 23 so that clicking the **Start Modeless** button subsequently can create another instance.

If you build and run the application after making these changes, you can dynamically create and close the dialog box by clicking between the two buttons.

SEE ALSO

➤ *To learn about creating message/event handlers for button clicking, see page 68*

Setting and Retrieving Data from a Modeless Dialog Box

You can set values or call member functions of the modeless dialog box at any point during its lifetime through its access pointer. The same rules apply for transferring data between the controls and the mapped member variables with `UpdateData()` and `DoDataExchange()`. You can set the member variables from the main application and then call `UpdateData()` passing a `FALSE` value to transfer the contents of the member variables to the controls.

You can also call functions or set member variables in other application objects from the modeless dialog box in response to user interaction with the controls. To do this, you must pass a pointer to the required application objects into the modeless dialog box (or use a global pointer) so that you can access those objects. The constructor of the modeless dialog box is a good place to pass these pointers. You can modify the constructor's parameter list to take pointers to the required application objects when you create the modeless dialog box. These pointers can then be stored as member variables local to the modeless dialog box so that any of the dialog box's functions can call back to the required application objects. You must also remember to add the required `#include` preprocessor directive to the top of the modeless dialog box's header definition file so that the compiler understands the new class declarations for the member variables.

You can add code to the sample program to demonstrate this. For example, you can add a list control to the main dialog box and send messages from two new buttons on the modeless dialog box. An edit control added to the modeless dialog box can be used to receive text set by the main application. These changes would create an application like that shown in Figure 10.9.

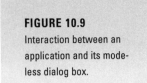

FIGURE 10.9

Interaction between an application and its modeless dialog box.

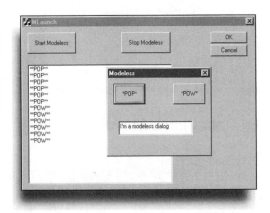

First, the modeless dialog box constructor must be modified to ensure that the parent pointer is a CMLaunchDlg rather than the current CWnd pointer. You can do this by changing the constructor definition in the CModeless class definition header module (Modeless.h) to accept only a pointer to CMLaunchDlg like this:

```
CModeless(CMLaunchDlg* pParent);    // standard constructor
```

You can edit this file by double-clicking the CModeless class in the project classes shown by the ClassView pane of the project workspace view.

So that the compiler knows about CMLaunchDlg, you must add the following #include preprocessor directive to the top of the CModeless class definition module:

```
#include "MLaunchDlg.h"
```

To store the passed pointer, you'll also need to add a corresponding member pointer variable; this can be added as a protected member after the protected operator like this:

```
CMLaunchDlg* m_pParent;
```

To store the passed pointer into this member pointer, you must change the constructor function to initialize the pointer from the passed pParent parameter, like this:

```
CModeless::CModeless(CMLaunchDlg* pParent)
    : CDialog(CModeless::IDD, pParent), m_pParent(pParent)
```

Notice that the parent dialog box, pParent, can be passed as the parent window to the CDialog base class. pParent can also be used to initialize the local member in the m_pParent(pParent) section.

You can add a list box to the main dialog box to display messages sent from the modal dialog box like the one shown on the main application dialog box in Figure 10.9. You can map this to a local CListBox variable m_DisplayList using ClassWizard, as shown in Figure 10.10.

You can then add the two buttons and edit control to the modeless dialog box resource template. The buttons can be used to provide two handler functions that can send two different

> **Terminating modeless dialog boxes with DestroyWindow()**
>
> When a modeless dialog box has an **OK** or **Cancel** button you must override the default implementation of OnOK() and OnCancel() because these will call EndDialog(), which will make the dialog invisible rather than destroy it. To terminate a modeless dialog box, call DestroyWindow(), which can be done from the OnOK() and OnCancel() overrides.

messages to the main application dialog box's new list box. You can use ClassWizard to create BN_CLICKED handlers for the two new buttons, and add a string to the main application's list box by adding lines like this:

```
void CModeless::OnPop()
{
    m_pParent->m_DisplayList.AddString("**POP**");
}
void CModeless::OnPow()
{
    m_pParent->m_DisplayList.AddString("**POW**");
}
```

FIGURE 10.10

Mapping a new list box in the main application dialog box.

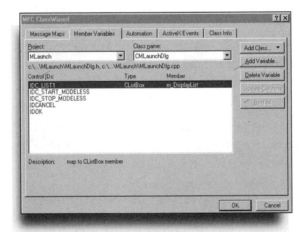

Notice that the new handlers use the new embedded CMLaunchDlg pointer, m_pParent, to access the m_DisplayList in the main application dialog box. The list box AddString() function then adds a string to the list box to show that the user has clicked one of the modeless dialog box's buttons.

To demonstrate accessing the modeless dialog box from the main application, you can add an edit box control to the modeless dialog box with the dialog template resource editor. You can use ClassWizard to map a CString to the edit control called m_DispMsg.

You can then access this mapped member from anyplace in the application when the modeless dialog box is active via the g_pDlgModeless pointer. To set the text into the control, you must force a data exchange by calling UpdateData() and passing the FALSE flag. You can do this by adding the following lines:

```
if (g_pDlgModeless) // Ensure the dialog is active
{
g_pDlgModeless->m_DispMsg=CString("I'm a modeless dialog");
g_pDlgModeless->UpdateData(FALSE);
}
```

SEE ALSO

➤ *To learn about creating message/event handlers for button clicking, see page 68*

➤ *For more detail about using list controls, see page 114*

Handling the Close Message in a Modeless Dialog Box

There is one remaining loose end to be tied up when using the modeless dialog box. Even though you have removed the modal **OK** and **Cancel**, the small cross-shaped window close button in the top-right corner remains. If you close the modeless dialog box in this fashion, the window will be closed, but if your application doesn't trap this message your global pointer to the dialog box and the memory used remains valid. This can lead to memory leak problems and you won't be able to start another instance of the modeless dialog box after closing the first instance.

To resolve this problem, you must trap the WM_CLOSE message in the modeless dialog box to delete the dialog box and reset the pointer. You can add a handler function that is called when the user clicks the close icon by using the New Windows Message and Event Handlers dialog box. This dialog box can be invoked by right-clicking the CModeless class in the **ClassView** tab and then selecting the **Add Windows Message Handler** option.

The following lines show the additions required to the new OnClose() handler function in the sample program to delete the dialog box object and reset the global pointer:

> **When to use a system modal dialog box**
>
> One of the style settings of a dialog template enables you to create a system modal dialog box. This will prevent users from switching to any other window or application until they have terminated the dialog box. Use system modal dialog boxes only to warn the user in special cases where operations by other applications might damage the configuration of the operating system.

```
extern CModeless* g_pDlgModeless;
void CModeless::OnClose()
{
    CDialog::OnClose();
    delete this;
    g_pDlgModeless = NULL;
}
```

Notice that an `extern` declaration is used to declare the global pointer; this is so the same g_pDlgModeless pointer as declared in the MLaunchDlg.cpp module is used. The handler then calls the base class `OnClose()` function to perform the default processing. When it returns, the memory for the modeless dialog box object (`this`) is deleted. Then the g_pDlgModeless pointer is reset to `NULL` so that a subsequent instance of the modeless dialog box can be restarted by the main application dialog box.

Removing the Close Option

Instead of handling the `WM_CLOSE` message, you can stop the user from clicking it by removing the **System Menu** flag from the dialog template in the resource editor (see Figure 10.11). This will remove the close icon and menu options so the user can't close the dialog box manually. You might want to do this if you must keep the modeless dialog box open.

FIGURE 10.11

Removing the System menu from the modeless dialog box with the resource editor.

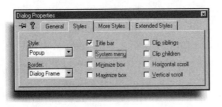

Working with Images, Bitmaps, and Icons

- Learning how to create, import, and edit icon and bitmap images

- Displaying pictures on dialog boxes

- Implementing graphical pushbuttons

- Utilizing images within list, tree, and combo box controls

Graphical images are prevalent within the Windows environment. There are several reasons for this. They can be international, they take up less space than their word equivalents, and they look good. The main purpose of using graphical images is to help the user recognize a particular program or function more quickly than scanning a lot of text.

Windows applications use several types of graphical images.

- An *icon* image is associated with the application itself and shown within Windows Explorer. The application icon is also typically displayed on the desktop to denote a shortcut.
- *Bitmap* images are used on splash screens and toolbar buttons and can also be placed on dialog boxes and other windows.
- *Cursor* images are used to alter the graphical representation of the mouse pointer. These are common in drawing packages to signify how a selected screen object can be edited or moved.

The resource editor within Developer Studio enables you to create and edit each image type. You can add as many icons, bitmaps, and cursors to your projects as you want. It is then up to you to implement the code to use the image resource how and when you see fit.

Using the Image Editor

The image resource editor enables you to design each different image type (bitmap, cursor, icon, and toolbar). You can sketch free-hand or use various options and tools that assist in drawing filled and outlined shapes. The editor window is normally split into two panes, with a true size display of the image on the left and a magnified version on the right. The magnified version makes it possible to distinguish each individual pixel for precise editing. Both views are updated automatically during editing. No matter which type of resource you're modifying, many of the graphical editing functions are identical.

The **Image** menu is available whenever an image editor window becomes active. The **Image** menu enables various drawing options. The **Invert Colors** option provides a way to invert the colors in a selected portion of the bitmap. The selected part can also be flipped and rotated. You can define and save your own color palettes using the **Image** menu.

The drawing tools are located on the Graphics toolbox and colors are selected from the Colors palette as shown in Figure 11.1. If these toolboxes aren't visible, follow these steps.

Opening the Graphics and Colors toolboxes

1. From the **Tools** menu select **Customize**. The Customize dialog box appears.
2. Select the **Toolbars** tab.
3. In the **Toolbars** list, check the **Graphics** and **Colors** items.
4. Click **Close**.
5. Alternatively, position the mouse on the menu bar at the top of the screen and click the right mouse button.
6. From the context menu select **Graphics** or **Colors**.

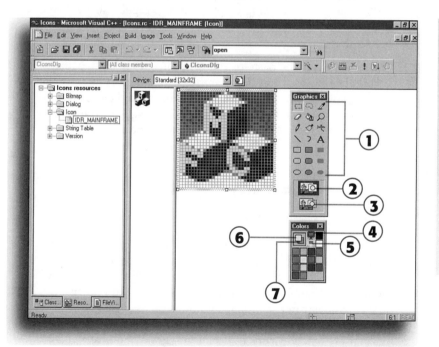

FIGURE 11.1

Editing an icon.

1. Drawing and editing tools
2. Draw opaque
3. Draw transparent
4. Screen color
5. Inverse color
6. Foreground color
7. Background color

The Graphics toolbox includes all the common editing features found in bitmap design software. For example, there is an airbrush, color selector, rectangular and irregular shape selectors, outline and filled shapes, and so on. At the bottom of the Graphics toolbox is an option selector that is used to pick brush styles, line widths, and further choices depending on the selected tool. While designing images, remember you can use the **Undo** and **Redo** options on the **Edit** menu or Ctrl+Z and Ctrl+Y, respectively.

The Colors palette enables you to select the current foreground or background color by clicking with the left or right mouse button, respectively. The currently selected graphical tool draws with the foreground color when the left mouse button is pressed and the background color when the right mouse button is pressed.

For cursor and icon images, the Colors palette shows two additional features, screen color and inverse color (see Figure 11.1). Pixels drawn with the screen color are transparent when the image is displayed, making it appear as an irregular shape. Pixels drawn with the inverse color are displayed inverted when the icon is dragged.

You can also cut and paste to and from the Clipboard from within the image editor. For example, if you want several similar images, you can select a portion of one image and paste it to another. You can choose to paste in either opaque or transparent mode by clicking the appropriate option on the Graphics toolbox or checking **Draw Opaque** on the **Image** menu.

SEE ALSO

➤ *For details about editing toolbar resources, see page 329*

Creating and Editing Icon Resources

Visually, distinguishing between icons and bitmaps is hard, but there are some important differentiating characteristics. A bitmap is an array of data that represents a color image display of pixels. An icon image is manufactured from two bitmaps; the first is the color image bitmap and the second is the mask bitmap. The merging of the information in these two bitmaps make it possible for icons to have transparent and inverted color parts.

You will often see icons that look like irregular shapes—spherical, for example. In fact, all icons are rectangular; the transparent mask enables them to appear irregular. An icon can contain several images that vary in size and number of colors for different display devices.

Modifying the Default MFC Icon

AppWizard-generated applications always insert a default icon. The image is of a three-dimensional MFC. The icon ID is IDR_MAINFRAME, and it is the icon that is associated with the application and can be seen on the About dialog box. To customize the application icon for a project, follow the steps in "Modifying the Default MFC Icon."

Typically, icons associated with an application or a particular document type have two 16-color images: standard (32×32 pixels) and small (16×16 pixels). These icon images are registered with Windows so that they can be shown from within Windows Explorer, on the desktop start menu, and on the taskbar.

Modifying the default MFC icon

1. On the ResourceView pane, expand the **Icon** folder and double-click **IDR_MAINFRAME**. The default MFC icon appears in the resource editor (refer to Figure 11.1).

2. Edit the **Standard (32×32)** image of the icon using the Colors and Graphics toolboxes. Editing an image is covered in the section "Using the Image Editor," earlier in this chapter.

3. From the **Device** combo box, select and edit the **Small (16×16)** image of the icon. If a small version of the icon doesn't exist, Windows will create one from the large version to display in Windows Explorer and on the taskbar.

SEE ALSO
➤ *For more details about registering application icons, see page 607*

Inserting a New Icon Resource

A project can have any number of icon resources. These can be newly created and drawn or imported from an existing project or .ico file. Newly created icon images are initially transparent and default to VGA device display size (32×32). To create a new icon, follow these steps.

Creating a new icon resource

1. Press Ctrl+R or from the **Insert** menu select **Resource**. The Insert Resource dialog box appears as shown in Figure 11.2.

FIGURE 11.2

The Insert Resource dialog box.

2. From the **Resource Type** list, select **Icon** and then click **New**. A blank icon is created and shown in the resource editor. Note you can press Ctrl+4 as a shortcut method to create a new icon.

3. Select the image size. To select a default size, use the **Devices** combo box.

4. To create a new image size, click the **New Device Image (Ins)** button to the right of the **Devices** combo box; the New Icon Image dialog box appears as shown in Figure 11.3.

FIGURE 11.3

The New Icon Image dialog box.

5. Select the desired image size from the **Target Device** list box or click **Custom** to specify the exact image width, height, and number of colors.

6. From the **View** menu, select **Properties.** The Icon Properties dialog box appears as shown in Figure 11.4. The properties dialog box can also be displayed by double-clicking anywhere within the image editor window except on the image itself.

7. Enter a name in the **ID** combo box. Icon IDs are traditionally prefixed IDI_.

8. Enter a filename in the **File Name** edit box. Note, this step is optional because Developer Studio generates a unique name for the icon file, which is located in the /res directory under the main project directory.

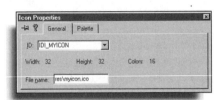

FIGURE 11.4
The Icon Properties
dialog box.

To remove an icon from a project, select the icon ID in ResourceView and press the Delete key. This doesn't remove the .bmp disk file, which you must do manually. To remove a specific device icon, select the image size in the **Devices** combo box, and then on the **Image** menu select **Delete Device Image**.

Inserting a New Bitmap Resource

Bitmap resources are put to numerous uses. They can be used for visual effect as you have already seen with the checkered flag bitmap on the last step of AppWizard. You can also display a bitmap image on a pushbutton control rather than text, which is covered later in this chapter.

Unlike the fairly limited size of icons, a bitmap resource image can be up to 2048×2048 pixels. Also unlike icons, bitmaps don't have transparent or inverse color attributes. A project can have any number of bitmap resources, which can be drawn from scratch or imported from an existing project or (.bmp) file. To create a new bitmap, follow the steps in "Creating a New Bitmap Resource."

To remove a bitmap from a project, select the bitmap ID in ResourceView and press the Delete key. This doesn't remove the .bmp disk file, which you must do manually.

Creating a new bitmap resource

1. Press Ctrl+R or from the **Insert** menu select **Resource**. The Insert Resource dialog box appears (refer to Figure 11.2).

2. From the **Resource Type** list, select **Bitmap** and then click **New**. A blank bitmap is created and shown in the resource editor. Note you can press Ctrl+5 as a shortcut method to create a new icon.

3. From the **View** menu select **Properties**; the Bitmap Properties dialog box appears as shown in Figure 11.5. Note the properties dialog box can also be displayed by double-clicking anywhere within the image editor window except on the image itself.

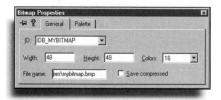

FIGURE 11.5

The Bitmap Properties dialog box.

4. Enter a name in the **ID** combo box. Bitmap IDs are traditionally prefixed IDB_.

5. Set the image size and color properties. For details on performing these operations, refer to the next section, "Adjusting Bitmap Size and Colors."

6. Enter a filename in the **File Name** edit box. This step is optional because Developer Studio generates a unique name for the icon file, located in the /res directory.

Adjusting Bitmap Size and Colors

A new bitmap resource defaults to a size of 48×48 pixels and 16 colors. To customize the size or colors, follow the steps in "Modifying Bitmap Properties." When the size is decreased, pixels are removed from the bottom and right boundaries. When the size is increased, extra pixels are added to the bottom and right boundaries and are filled with the current background color.

Modifying bitmap properties

1. On the ResourceView pane, expand the **Bitmap** folder and double-click the ID of the bitmap you want to edit.

2. From the **View** menu, select **Properties**. The Bitmap Properties dialog box appears. Note the properties dialog

box can also be displayed by double-clicking anywhere within the image editor window except on the image itself.

3. Click the **General** tab. Enter the required **Wi̲dth** and **Height** dimensions. You can also resize the bitmap by clicking and dragging the sizing handles on the outer border of the bitmap in the image editor.

4. Select the required number of colors in the **C̲olors** combo box.

5. To customize the color palette, click the **Palette** tab, and then double-click the color you want to customize. The Custom Color Selector dialog box appears as shown in Figure 11.6. Select the required color then click **OK**.

FIGURE 11.6
The Custom Color Selector dialog box.

Importing Images

If you have an artistic streak, you'll probably enjoy designing and drawing your own images. You can, however, import resources from existing files and projects and even from executable files on your system. To import an icon or bitmap from an .ico or .bmp file, follow the steps in "Importing a Resource from a File." When you build your project's executable file, it incorporates the resources. You can therefore extract these resources from your and other people's executable files.

Importing a resource from a file

1. Select **I̲mport** from the ResourceView context menu, or from the **I̲nsert** menu select **R̲esource** and then click the **I̲mport** button on the Insert Resource dialog box. The

Import Resource dialog box appears. This dialog box is a slightly customized File Open dialog box.

2. Navigate to the appropriate directory and select the file(s) containing the resource(s) you want to import; then click the **Import** button. You can use the **File of Type** combo box to filter the display to a certain kind of resource file.

3. If the selected file is of a recognized type, the resource is added to your project. A unique ID is automatically generated and a copy of the imported file is placed in the project's res directory.

Importing resources from executable files

1. From the **File** menu select **Open**. The standard Open dialog box appears.

2. In the **Open As** combo box, select **Resources**.

3. Navigate to the appropriate directory and select the executable file (.exe, .dll, or .ocx) from which you want to import; then click the **Open** button. The resources embedded in the executable file are shown in the editor window (see Figure 11.7). As a demonstration, select the Cards.dll file, normally found in the C:\Windows\System directory. It's a good idea to check the **Open as Read-Only** option when opening system files.

4. To view the resources, open the properties dialog box and click the pushpin in the top-left corner to keep the dialog box open. The **Preview** frame shows how each resource looks when selected.

5. To insert a resource from the displayed list, select it with the mouse. Hold down the mouse button and the Ctrl key and move the mouse into the ResourceView pane. Release the mouse button when you see a plus sign near the mouse pointer. The resource is inserted into your project.

6. From the **File** menu, select **Close**.

Using Images in Dialog Boxes

There are numerous ways to show images on dialog boxes. Icons and bitmaps are easily displayed on dialog boxes using a picture control and setting its properties to point to the relevant image resource. Picture controls can also be used to simply add colored rectangles or outline frames if you want to group elements on a dialog box.

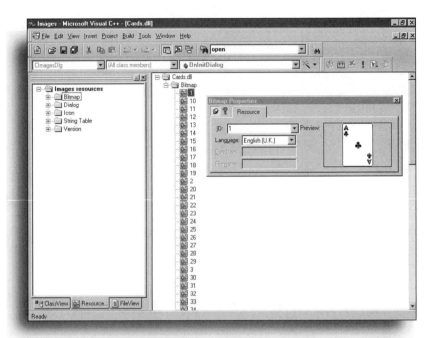

FIGURE 11.7
Importing resources from
executable files.

This chapter concentrates on how to use resource images. To draw nonresource images within the client area of a dialog box you must override the OnPaint function. This is covered in detail in Chapter 15, "Understanding Drawing in Device Contexts."

SEE ALSO

➤ *For details about using the* OnPaint() *function, see page 363*

Setting Picture Control Properties

AppWizard automatically adds the icon resource IDR_MAINFRAME to your project, which has a three-dimensional MFC image. To show the icon, AppWizard inserts a picture control on the About dialog box. Figure 11.8 shows the properties of that picture control. The **Type** combo box denotes the kind of image and, when set to **Icon** or **Bitmap**, the resource ID is specified in the **Image** combo box. Table 11.1 describes the available image types that a picture control can display.

What is an enhanced metafile?

A metafile stores a picture in a
format that is device-independent.
Apart from holding the actual
image, a metafile also contains
structures that describe the image
in terms of its size, graphics
objects it uses, and color palette.
The enhanced metafile format is
used in Win32 applications only.

TABLE 11.1 Picture control image types

Type	Description
Frame	Shows a black, white, gray, or etched border. Used for visual effect to group items.
Rectangle	Shows a solid black, white, gray, or etched rectangle.
Icon	Shows an icon resource image.
Bitmap	Shows a bitmap resource image.
Enhanced Metafile	Shows the image contained in an enhanced metafile.

Loading Resource Images at Runtime

To load an icon or bitmap resource at runtime, attach a CStatic
variable to the picture control. In order to do this you must alter
the ID of the control from the default IDC_STATIC. Table 11.2
shows the CStatic class member functions used to specify the
image displayed by a control. Each function has an equivalent
Get that retrieves the image.

TABLE 11.2 *CStatic* class functions

Function	Description
SetIcon	Defines the icon to be displayed
SetBitmap	Defines the bitmap to be displayed
SetCursor	Defines the cursor to be displayed
SetEnhMetaFile	Defines the enhanced metafile to be displayed

Before calling any of the set functions shown in Table 11.2, the resource image must first be loaded. The procedure to load an image depends on its type. Figure 11.9 shows the Images example, which loads a bitmap and several icons at runtime. To follow this example, use AppWizard to create a dialog-based application called Images. When the project is created, follow the steps in "Adding a Picture Control to a Dialog Box." When you have the picture controls, use ClassWizard to attach a CStatic variable to each, and then follow the steps in "Attaching a Variable to a Picture Control."

FIGURE 11.9
The Images example.

Adding a picture control to a dialog box

1. On the ResourceView pane expand the **Dialog** folder and double-click the ID of the dialog box you want to edit; use IDD_IMAGES_DIALOG for this example. Click the **TODO: Place Dialog Box Controls Here** text and then press the Delete button to remove it.

2. Select the picture image in the Controls toolbar and add a picture control in the upper-left corner of the dialog box.

3. From the **View** menu, select **Properties.** The Picture Properties dialog box appears. You can keep the property dialog box visible by clicking the pin icon in the top-left corner.

4. Enter a name in the **ID** combo box; use IDC_B1 for this example.

5. Select the kind of image the control is to display in the **Type** combo box; select **Bitmap** for this first picture.

6. Select the picture image in the Controls toolbar and add five picture controls to the right of the first, as shown in Figure 11.10.

FIGURE 11.10

The layout of the Images dialog box.

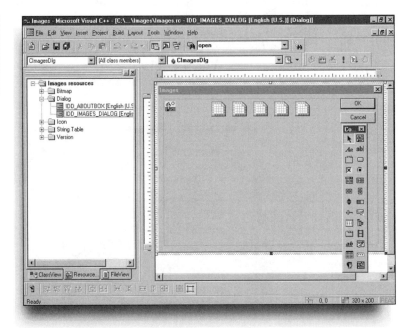

7. Select all five added controls by holding the Ctrl key down and clicking each control. When all five are selected, set the **Type** combo box property to **Icon**.

8. Select each icon control in turn and enter a name for each in the **ID** combo box; use IDC_I1, IDC_I2, and so on for this example.

Attaching a variable to a picture control

1. Press Ctrl+W to start ClassWizard or from the **View** menu select **ClassWizard**.

2. Select the **Member Variables** tab.

3. Select **CImagesDlg** in the **Class Name** combo box.

4. Select **IDC_B1** in the **Control IDs** list box, and then click the **Add Variable** button. The Add Member Variable dialog box appears. You can also add a member variable for a control by double-clicking the control's ID.

5. Enter the variable name in the **Member Variable Name** box; use m_b1 for this example.

6. Select **Control** in the **Category** combo box. Click **OK**.

7. Repeat steps 4–6 for each of the other controls from IDC_I1 to IDC_I5, giving each variable a unique name; use m_i1, m_i2, and so on.

8. Your ClassWizard dialog box should now look like Figure 11.11.

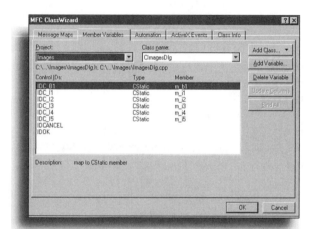

FIGURE 11.11
The MFC ClassWizard dialog box.

Because the first control is to display a bitmap, you must add a bitmap resource to your project. Figure 11.9 shows a bitmap imported from the cards.dll file. The steps to import this bitmap are described in "Importing Resources from Executable Files" in the section "Importing Images" earlier in this chapter. The image used in the example is actually number 64. When you have the bitmap, modify its ID to IDB_BEACH.

A bitmap is loaded using a CBitmap object by calling its LoadBitmap function and passing the ID of the resource. First add a member variable to the CImagesDlg class of type CBitmap (use m_bmp for the variable name). Now add the code shown in Listing 11.1 to the OnInitialUpdate function after the TODO comments.

LISTING 11.1 LST12_1.CPP—Loading Image Resources and Setting Picture Controls

①	LoadBitmap() is a member of the Cbitmap class.
②	SetBitmap() attaches the bitmap to the picture control represented by m_b1
③	Loads the application icon MFC.
④	LoadStandardIcon to load in standard icon resources.

```
1    // ** Load the bitmap resource and
2    // ** set the picture control to the loaded bitmap
3    VERIFY(m_bmp.LoadBitmap(IDB_BEACH)); ──────① 
4    m_b1.SetBitmap(m_bmp); ──────②
5
6    CWinApp* pApp = AfxGetApp();
7    HICON hIcon;
8
9    // ** Load the application's icon and
10   // ** set the picture control to the loaded icon
11   hIcon = pApp->LoadIcon(IDR_MAINFRAME); ──────③
12   m_i1.SetIcon(hIcon);
13
14   // ** Load some of the standard icons and
15   // ** set each picture control
16   hIcon = pApp->LoadStandardIcon(IDI_HAND); ──────④
17   m_i2.SetIcon(hIcon);
18
19   hIcon = pApp->LoadStandardIcon(IDI_QUESTION);
20   m_i3.SetIcon(hIcon);
21
22   hIcon = pApp->LoadStandardIcon(IDI_EXCLAMATION);
23   m_i4.SetIcon(hIcon);
24
25   hIcon = pApp->LoadStandardIcon(IDI_ASTERISK);
26   m_i5.SetIcon(hIcon);
```

The LoadBitmap call in line 3 retrieves the IDB_BEACH bitmap resource and attaches it to the CBitmap variable m_bmp. The CBitmap object is then passed to the CStatic::SetBitmap function in line 4, which informs the control associated with m_b1 which bitmap to display.

The CWinApp::LoadIcon function in line 11 retrieves the IDR_MAINFRAME icon resource and returns an HICON (handle to the icon graphic object). The handle is then passed to the CStatic::SetIcon function, informing the controls which icon to display.

Several standard icons are loaded using the CWinApp::LoadStandardIcon, as shown in lines 16, 19, 22, and 25.

You pass the ID of the icon you want and the function returns an HICON.

Now build and run the application. Your dialog box should look like Figure 11.9.

Creating Bitmap Buttons

Because pictures are often more immediately recognizable than words, it's sometimes preferable to show an image on a pushbutton rather than text. The MFC library provides the CBitmapButton class specifically for this purpose. You use the image editor to create your bitmaps and add the pushbutton controls to the dialog template in the usual manner. There are two things to remember to do when creating resources for bitmap buttons. The first is to give your bitmap a string name in the **ID** property rather than a #define number. The second is to set the **Owner Draw** property of the pushbutton control. The bitmap resource is coupled with a pushbutton via the CBitmapButton::AutoLoad function.

Use AppWizard to create a dialog-based application called Smile. In this example, you'll create your own bitmaps to display on a pushbutton. The button image will change when the state alters—for example, when it's being clicked.

First remove the **TODO** text control from the IDD_SMILE_DIALOG. Now add a pushbutton control in the center of the dialog box. Give the control the ID IDC_SMILE and the caption SMILE. Note that the size of the button isn't important because it will be resized according to the dimensions of the bitmap.

Creating Bitmaps for Button States

A pushbutton has one of four states (up, down, disabled, or focused). The state changes when the user clicks or tabs to the button, or it can be altered programmatically. Normal pushbuttons that have text captions handle the state display changes automatically. For example, the text is shown etched when the button is disabled.

Bitmap buttons are owner drawn; as the owner you are responsible for supplying an image for each state. If you supply only one image, the user won't receive any feedback when he clicks the button. You should supply images for the up and down states at least. The bitmap's IDs must be a string value (inclusive of quotation marks) based on the button's caption. For example, if a button has the caption "SMILE," the IDs of the four images would be "SMILEU" (up), "SMILED" (down), "SMILEX" (disabled), and "SMILEF" (focused). In fact, these are the four bitmaps required for the example; to create them follow these steps.

Creating bitmap button images

1. Press Ctrl+5. A blank bitmap is created and shown in the resource editor.

2. From the **View** menu, select **Properties.** The Bitmap Properties dialog box appears.

3. Enter "SMILEU" (include the quotation marks) in the **ID** combo box.

4. Edit the bitmap to look like the one shown in Figure 11.12.

FIGURE 11.12

Bitmaps for the up and down states.

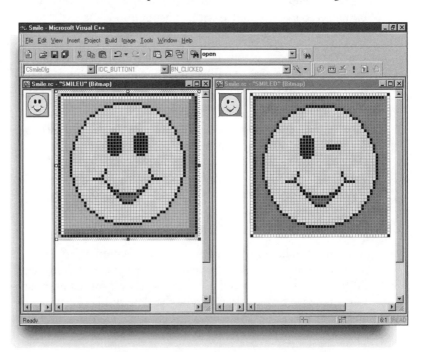

5. Repeat steps 1–4 to create three other bitmap images.

6. Enter a filename in the three other bitmaps giving them the IDs "SMILED," "SMILEF," and "SMILEX." Edit each to look similar to the images shown in Figure 11.12 and Figure 11.13.

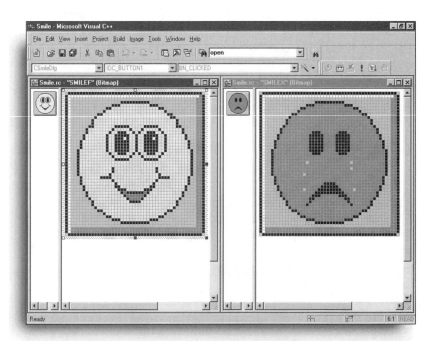

FIGURE 11.13
Bitmaps for the focused and disabled states.

Using the Bitmap Button Class

As mentioned earlier, the MFC library provides the CBitmapButton class for putting bitmaps on pushbuttons. The class is derived from CButton and has only a few member functions. It implements the virtual DrawItem function that is called for owner-drawn controls. The only function you must call is AutoLoad.

Add a member variable to the CSmileDlg class of type CBitmapButton. Use m_bbSmile for the variable name. Now add the following line of code to the OnInitialUpdate function after the // TODO: comments:

```
VERIFY(m_bbSmile.AutoLoad(IDC_SMILE, this);
```

You use the VERIFY macro to check the return code from the AutoLoad function; if this is FALSE, an assertion is thrown in

Debug mode. You can see that the AutoLoad function is passed the resource identifier of the pushbutton IDC_SMILE. From this it retrieves the caption and then loads the bitmaps with names based on the caption.

There is just one last thing to do now before building. In order to test the program, you need a way to set the button to the disabled state. You can do this by modifying the **Cancel** button. First edit its caption to read **Dis/Enable** and its **ID** to ID_DISENABLE. Now add a BN_CLICKED message handler for the ID_DISENABLE button. This should create a member function OnDisenable. For this function to toggle the enabled state, add the following line of code after the // TODO: comments:

```
m_bbSmile.EnableWindow( !m_bbSmile.IsWindowEnabled() );
```

Now build and run the Smile example. Try setting the focus to the bitmap button by tabbing; you should see the image alter when it receives and loses the focus. Also try toggling the enabled state. If you click and hold down the mouse button, the image should display as shown in Figure 11.14.

FIGURE 11.14
The Smile example.

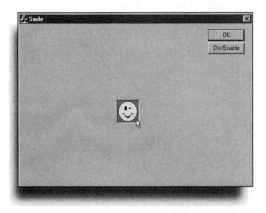

SEE ALSO
➤ *For more information on the* VERIFY *macro, see page* 717
➤ *For help on adding handler functions, see page 66*

Using Images in Controls

This chapter has already covered the use of bitmap images with pushbuttons, but several other controls also directly support the use of images: the list control, the tree control, and the new extended combo box control. All these controls maintain a list of items. Each item typically has a text attribute but can also be associated with two images, one for the nonselected state and one for the selected state. The images can be either bitmaps or icons.

Understanding Image Lists

The images shown by a list, tree, or combo box must reside in an image list. An image list is contained within a `CImageList` object. This object is created and then bitmaps or icons are added to it. All the images must be of the same size. A pointer to the `CImageList` object is then passed to the control by calling the `SetImageList` member function. When an item is inserted into the control, it's associated with an image in the image list by specifying the zero-based index of the image. Because the image list is contained in an object separate from the control, it's possible for several controls to share an image list.

To see exactly how to construct an image list and use it within a control, use AppWizard to create a dialog-based project called Shapes. After creating the project, the next thing you need are some images. When you want to add several images to an image list, the easiest way is to construct one bitmap containing all the images. The sample requires eight images; these are held in a single bitmap as shown in Figure 11.15.

Create a new bitmap resource giving it an **ID** of `IDB_SHAPES`, a **Width** of 118, and a **Height** of 16. Then edit the bitmap to look like Figure 11.15. If you're unsure of how to do this refer to the sections "Inserting a New Bitmap Resource" and "Using the Image Editor," earlier in this chapter.

Now add a list, tree, and a combo box control to the `IDD_SHAPES_DIALOG` as shown in Figure 11.16. For the list control properties, enter `IDC_LIST1` for the **ID** and select **List** in the **View** combo box on the **Styles** tab. For the tree control properties, enter `IDC_TREE1` for the **ID** and check the **Has Buttons**, **Has Lines**, and **Lines at Root** options on the **Styles** tab. For the combo box properties, enter `IDC_COMBOBOXEX1` for the **ID** and select **Drop List** in the **Type** combo box on the **Styles** tab.

Modifying image lists

It's possible to add, remove, and replace images within an image list and enable transparent drawing by specifying a mask.

FIGURE 11.15

The image list bitmap.

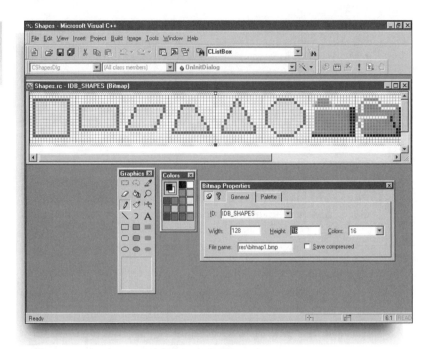

FIGURE 11.16

The layout of the Shapes dialog box.

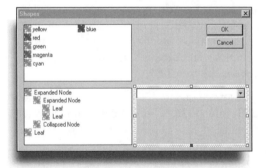

Now use ClassWizard to add a member variable to the CShapesDlg class for each control. For the variable names use m_list, m_tree, and m_combo and select **Control** in the **Category** combo box on the Add Member Variable dialog box each time. After adding the variables, the **Member Variables** tab of ClassWizard should look like Figure 11.17.

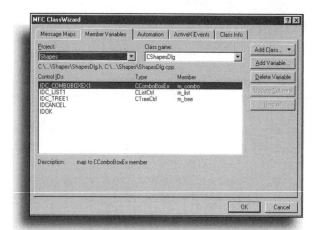

FIGURE 11.17
The MFC ClassWizard
dialog box.

SEE ALSO

➤ *For information on adding list controls to dialog boxes, see page 114*

➤ *For more information on using tree controls see page 488*

➤ *For more information on using list controls see page 472*

Creating and Using an Image List

An image list maintains a collection of bitmap images used by
controls. The image list is contained within a CImageList object.
For the example, add a CImageList variable named m_imagelist to
the CShapesDlg class. All the code necessary to create the image
list and insert items into the three controls can take place within
the OnInitDialog function. Add the code shown in Listing 11.2
after the // TODO: comments of OnInitDialog.

LISTING 11.2 LST12_2.CPP—Creating and Using an Image List

```
1   // ** Create some text names for the shape images
2   static char* shape[] = {
3           "Square", "Rectangle", "Parallelogram",
4           "Trapezoid", "Triangle", "Octagon"};
5   int nShapes = 6;
6
7   // ** Load the bitmap resource
8   CBitmap bitmap;
9   VERIFY(bitmap.LoadBitmap(IDB_SHAPES)); ————①
```

① Loads the IDB_SHAPES
bitmap resource.

continues...

LISTING 11.2 Continued

② Creates an image list specifying the width of each image as 16 pixels.

③ Sets the list control to use the created image list.

④ The image list is shared by the tree control.

⑤ Specifies which members of the COMBOBOXEXITEM structure are valid when the call to InsertItem() is made.

```
10
11    // ** Create the image list and add the bitmap
12    m_imagelist.Create(IDB_SHAPES, 16, 1, 0);  ──────② 
13    m_imagelist.Add(&bitmap, (COLORREF)0xFFFFFF);
14
15    // ** Set the list control to use the image list
16    m_list.SetImageList(&m_imagelist, LVSIL_SMALL);  ──────③
17
18    // ** Insert 6 items into the list control
19    // ** setting the image index
20    for(int i = 0; i < nShapes; i++)
21        m_list.InsertItem(i, shape[i], i);
22
23    // ** Set the tree control to use the image list
24    m_tree.SetImageList(&m_imagelist, TVSIL_NORMAL);  ──────④
25
26    // ** Insert 2 top level items into the tree
27    // ** set normal/selected images to closed/open folder
28    HTREEITEM hTetragons, hOther;
29    hTetragons = m_tree.InsertItem("Tetragons", 6, 7);
30    hOther = m_tree.InsertItem("Other", 6, 7);
31
32    // ** Insert first 3 shapes as subitems of 'Tetragons'
33    // ** and last 3 as subitems of 'Other'
34    for(i = 0; i < nShapes; i++)
35        m_tree.InsertItem(shape[i], i, i,
36            i < 3 ? hTetragons : hOther);
37
38    // ** Set the combo box to use the image list
39    m_combo.SetImageList(&m_imagelist);
40
41    // ** Allocate a combo item structure and set the mask
42    COMBOBOXEXITEM cbItem;
43    cbItem.mask = CBEIF_TEXT|CBEIF_IMAGE|CBEIF_SELECTEDIMAGE;  ──⑤
44
45    // ** Insert 6 items into the combo box
46    // ** set normal/selected to the same image
47    for(i = 0; i < nShapes; i++)
48    {
49        cbItem.pszText = shape[i];
50        cbItem.iItem = i;
```

```
51        cbItem.iImage = cbItem.iSelectedImage = i;
52        m_combo.InsertItem(&cbItem);
53    }
```

⑥ **6** Initialize the
COMBOBOXEXITEM
structure and then
insert the item.

At first sight, Listing 11.2 might look a little complex but there are in fact only 28 lines of code—the rest are comments.

In line 2, an array of strings is created called shape. The names match the first six images in the IDB_SHAPES bitmap. In lines 8 and 9, a local CBitmap is used to load the IDB_SHAPES resource; note the VERIFY function will cause an assertion if the resource fails to load.

The CImageList object m_imagelist is initialized in line 12 with a call to Create. The first parameter is the resource ID, and the second is the pixel width of each image. The third parameter specifies a grow-by number used to optimize performance. The last parameter can be passed a mask color to enable transparent images. When the image list is initialized, images are added by calling Add (line 13). Here the address of the bitmap is passed so all eight images are added.

Image list creation

Several overloaded versions of
CImageList::Create are
available. These can enable you to
pass a string of resource IDs or
concatenate two existing image
lists to create a new one.

After the image list is initialized, the controls can be told to use it. This is done similarly for each control by calling SetImageList as you can see in lines 16, 24, and 39. Apart from passing the address of the image, the list and tree controls are passed an additional parameter to specify the image list type. Tables 11.3 and 11.4 show the possible types.

Image list initialization

To add an icon to an image list, an
overloaded version of Add exists
that takes an HICON as a
parameter.

To add images directly from a disk
file, call the Read function.

TABLE 11.3 Types of image lists for a list control

Image List Type	Type Description
LVSIL_NORMAL	Image list with large icons
LVSIL_SMALL	Image list with small icons
LVSIL_STATE	Image list with state images

TABLE 11.4 Types of image lists for a tree control

Image List Type	Type Description
TVSIL_NORMAL	Image list with both nonselected and selected images
TVSIL_STATE	Image list with user-defined state images

Items are inserted into the list control within the `for` loop at line 20. The `InsertItem` function is passed three parameters. The first is the item position in the control, the second is the item text, and the third specifies the position of an image in the image list. In this case, the `i` passed is being incremented so each item is given the next image in the list.

The tree control has two root level items that both have three subitems. The two root items are inserted in lines 29 and 30. The calls to `InsertItem` are passed the item text as the first parameter. The second parameter specifies the position of the image used when the item isn't selected (in this case 6 denotes a closed folder). The third specifies the position of the image used when the item is selected (in this case 7 denotes an open folder).

Subitems are inserted into the tree control within the `for` loop at line 34. The overload of `InsertItem` here takes four parameters. The first is the subitem's text. The second and third are the non-selected and selected image positions, respectively (in this case the same image is used for both states). In the fourth parameter, either `hTetragons` or `hOther` is passed, which specifies the parent of the new item.

The combo boxes items are inserted by a different method. Here it is necessary to fill in a `COMBOBOXEXITEM` structure variable (`cbItem`) with the item data and then pass the address of this variable to the `InsertItem` function. The `mask` flag settings in line 43 specify which structure elements are valid or, put another way, which variables in the structure you are going to fill in. As you can see in line 51, both the `iImage` and `iSelectedImage` variables are set to the same image position.

Build and run your project. Figure 11.18 shows the Shapes example.

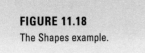
FIGURE 11.18
The Shapes example.

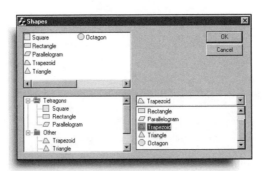

chapter

12

Using Documents, Views, and Frames

Creating a single document interface
application

Developing an application utilizing the
MFC Document/View architecture

Understanding document, view, frame,
and document template classes

Appending additional items to
the standard menu resource

The billions of dollars spent on car development has given cars a remarkably consistent user interface. That's why you can hop out of one type of car into another and be motoring along within minutes. When basic driving skills have been obtained behind one steering wheel, they are easily transferred to others, which offer virtually identical controls save for a few cosmetic aesthetics.

The popularity of Windows applications stems from the consistent user interface concept. The typical Windows application has a title bar at the top, followed by a drop-down menu and then one or more rows of toolbar icons serving as shortcuts. Below the toolbars is a main display area, and finally a status bar rests on the bottom. Even across many different types of applications, the same menu options and toolbar icons are identical and keep the same meaning. This has made it possible to hop from word processing packages to electronic mail applications and be happily processing data within minutes.

For the Visual C++ programmer, conforming to the familiar Windows look and feel is relatively effortless. The MFC library offers an enormous amount of assistance to first generate an application using AppWizard, which can automatically include a menu, toolbar, status bar, and other components and then allow easy customization of each component. The classes created by AppWizard work together to form an interrelated structure commonly termed the *Document/View architecture*.

The fundamental concept of the Document/View architecture is to separate the actual data required from the presentation of what the data represents to the user. This is achieved by retaining data in one class (the Document class) and presenting information to the user via another class (the View class), hence the term Document/View. The MFC library solution, however, provides much more than just this organizational framework. It also encompasses many user interface features and methods for loading and storing information to files.

There are two categories of Document/View applications, SDI (single document interface) and MDI (multiple document interface). This chapter concentrates on the SDI category.

The true meaning of the term "document"

The first application to use the Document/View programming technique was MS Word, the primary function of which is to produce textual and graphical documents. The word *document*, however, isn't limited to this conventional meaning. The Document class can contain any type of data, making the Document/View architecture adaptable to diverse applications.

266

SEE ALSO
➤ *For more information about MDI applications, see page 546*

Creating an SDI Application

The task of creating an application with all the familiar Windows visual interface features, such as a toolbar and status bar, would be quite daunting if AppWizard wasn't at hand to provide them for you. In fact, AppWizard does better than provide the basics; it includes several optional extras. For example, the capability to connect the application to a database is one such option; another is incorporating basic email functionality. In this section you'll create an SDI application that will be used to explore the generated classes and how the Document/View architecture operates. First, create a new project named SDICoin.

Creating an SDI application with AppWizard

1. Select **New** from the **File** menu. On the **Projects** tab of the New project dialog box, select **MFC AppWizard (exe)**.

2. Enter a name for the project (use SDICoin for this example) and then click **OK**.

3. On the MFC AppWizard Step 1 dialog box, select the **Single Document** radio button and ensure **Document/View Architecture Support?** is checked (see Figure 12.1). Click **Next**.

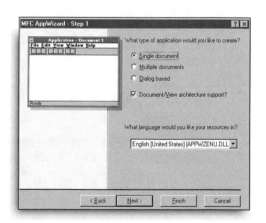

FIGURE 12.1
AppWizard step 1.

4. On the Step 2 dialog box, select the **None** radio button. The options on this step allow for various types of database support that aren't necessary for this example. Click **Next**.

5. On the Step 3 dialog box, select the **None** radio button and check the **ActiveX Controls** option. The other options on this step deal with adding OLE automation features that aren't necessary for this example. Click **Next**.

6. On the Step 4 dialog box, check the following options: **Docking Toolbar**, **Initial Status Bar**, **Printing and Print Preview**, and **3D Controls**. Select the **Normal** radio button for the toolbar style. Refer to Figure 12.2 for the correct settings. Click **Next**.

FIGURE 12.2
AppWizard step 4.

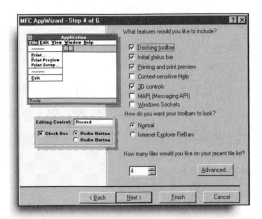

7. On the Step 5 dialog box, select **MFC Standard** for the project style, select **Yes** to generate source file comments, and select **As a Shared DLL** for how to use the MFC library. Click **Next**.

8. On the Step 6 dialog box, click **Finish**. The New Project Information dialog box appears as shown in Figure 12.3. This dialog box includes some useful information about the generated classes and names of source files. You can also check the list of features. Click **OK**. The new project should now be created and open in Developer Studio.

FIGURE 12.3
The New Project
Information dialog box.

You will develop this application so that it displays a stack of coins. Menu options will enable a coin to be added or removed from the stack. The data, which is simply the number of coins, is held in the document class and accessed by the view class in order to display the stack. Although this is a relatively simple example, it should give you an appreciation of the fundamental goal of the Document/View architecture, which is the *encapsulation* of data. With encapsulation, data is stored only in the document class and access functions are provided so the view class can render the information to the user in any chosen fashion. For example, instead of displaying a graphical stack of coins, the view class could be made to display a simple count without any alteration needed to the document class. However, before enhancing the project, some explanation of the AppWizard-generated classes is necessary.

A single document interface application has one document class derived from MFC's CDocument and one view class that can be derived from one of several MFC view classes. The different view classes reflect the range of application types that can be based around the Document/View architecture. The base view class is chosen on step 6 of AppWizard. Table 12.1 shows the available classes; the SDICoin example uses the default CView class.

Documents encapsulate the application data

The document class is derived from CDocument and its member variables contain the application data. The member functions of your CDocument derived class provide the means to act on the data. For example, the Serialize() function is used for both loading and storing the data to disk.

TABLE 12.1 Base view classes available with AppWizard

Class Name	Description
CView	The default class that implements all the important functionality associated with a view, including interaction with the document class.
CSrollView	Derived from CView and enhanced to enable scrolling in situations in which the logical area of the view is larger than the physical displayable area.
CListView	Uses a list control as the view, enabling the application to display icons or text columns.
CTreeView	Uses a tree control as the view, enabling the application to display hierarchical information.
CEditView	Uses a multiline edit control as the view class, adding scrolling and search capabilities.
CRichEditView	Uses a rich edit control as the view for more powerful text editing capabilities than the CEditView class.
CFormView	Uses a dialog box template as the view, enabling the application to appear as a database form.
CRecordView	Derived from CFormView and enhanced to connect the view with a specific database record set. This class is available only if database support has been selected.
CHtmlView	Uses the Internet Explorer view to enable the creation of a Web browser application.

SEE ALSO

➤ *For information on the* CListView *class, see page 472*

➤ *For information on the* CTreeView *class, see page 488*

➤ *For information on the* CRichEditView *class, see page 497*

➤ *For information on the* CHtmlView *class, see page 503*

➤ *For information on the* CSrollView *class, see page 458*

➤ *For information on the* CFormView *and* CRecordView *classes, see page 642*

➤ *For information on file handling with the Document/View architecture, see page 591*

➤ *For information on including database support, see page 634*

➤ *For information on OLE automation, see page 657*

Understanding the Classes of an SDI Application

The class structure of a single document interface application differs from that of a dialog-based application. You can see by looking at the ClassView pane of the SDICoin project that AppWizard created four classes that handle the structure of the application. The inheritance of these classes is shown in Figure 12.4.

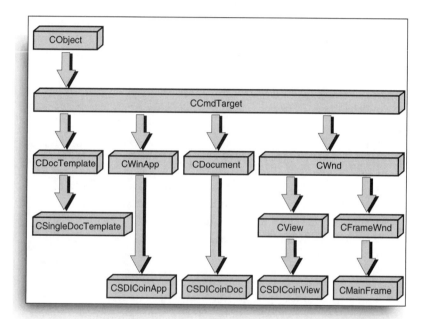

FIGURE 12.4
The class hierarchy of an SDI application.

The CWinApp-derived class CSDICoinApp has several roles and differs in implementation to that of the application object of a dialog-based project. It manages the initialization of the application. It is responsible for maintaining the association between the document, view, and frame classes. It also receives Windows messages and dispatches them to the appropriate target window.

As stated previously, with a single document interface application, only one instance of the CDocument-derived class CSDICoinDoc will ever be instantiated. The role of the CSDICoinDoc class is as the container of the application data. The data can be in any form; in the Coin example it will be a simple count, but usually the data required to satisfy the needs of the

---

CObject is a great grandparent

The CObject class is the base of all but a few of the classes provided by the MFC library. All CObject derivatives inherit the ability to check the class type of an object at runtime, output diagnostic information, and support serialization.

application is far more complex. For a word processing application, the data would include the text of the document as well as all the necessary formatting information, whereas the data of a computer-aided design package would need to store the coordinates and other details of each part of a graphical image.

How data storage is implemented in the document is the responsibility of the programmer. Ideally, an object-oriented approach should be employed so that the data is held completely independent from the user interface. Adhering to this methodology adds both flexibility and portability to the code. In the Coin example, there is only one view but you might require several views, all using the same underlying document data. The views might be of differing types; if so, careful attention must be paid to the mechanism used by the document class to supply data to each view.

The CSDICoinView class is responsible for rendering the visual representation of the document's data to the user and enabling the user to interact with the data. Each view can be interfaced with only one instance of a document, whereas a document might be interfaced with several view objects. The view class accesses the data it requires via member functions supplied by the document.

Modifying the frame window style

You can alter the style flag settings of the main frame window before it is rendered by overriding PreCreateWindow(). This function is passed a reference to a CREATESTRUCT structure that contains the style attribute, which you can modify before it is passed to the base class version of the function.

The role of the CMainFrame class is to supply a window for the application to use. It is derived from the CFrameWnd class, which is a wrapper for a simple window. By default, the window style flags include WS_OVERLAPPEDWINDOW, which gives the frame window a title bar with minimize/maximize and close buttons, a system menu, and enables the window to be moveable and resizable. The style flags also include FWS_ADDTOTITLE, which causes the name of the loaded document to be displayed automatically in the title bar. The CMainFrame class also handles the creation, initialization, and destruction of toolbars and the status bar.

SEE ALSO

➤ *To learn more about the difference between SDI and MDI classes, see page 534*

The Visual Elements of an SDI Application

Accepting the default options set in step 4 of AppWizard during the creation of an SDI project will result in an application having a title bar with the standard minimize/maximize and close buttons, a drop-down menu including print and print preview options, a toolbar, and a status bar. However, some of these visual features are optional. Refer to Figure 12.2 to see the step 4 options. More options are available by clicking the **A**dvanced button on the step 4 dialog box, as shown in Figure 12.5. These enable the frame window style to be customized.

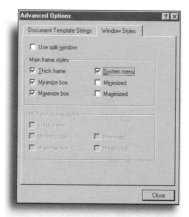

FIGURE 12.5
The Advanced Options of AppWizard step 4.

The client area of the frame window isn't actually used to implement the view. The view has its own window, which is a borderless and menuless child of the frame. This view window overrides the entire client area of the frame window (see Figure 12.6). The view is implemented this way so that the same model can be used in both single and multiple document applications, but an MDI application has different frame and child window classes. It is the frame window that receives the menu and frame window messages.

Frame window messages

Certain messages are sent only to windows with frames. These include moving, sizing, minimize and maximize, and messages sent regarding the display of the nonclient area of the application window.

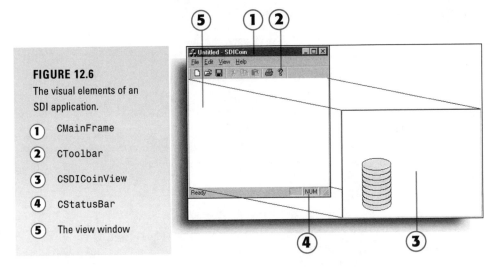

FIGURE 12.6

The visual elements of an SDI application.

(1) CMainFrame

(2) CToolbar

(3) CSDICoinView

(4) CStatusBar

(5) The view window

The following explains the different parts of the window:

- **CMainFrame.** Derived from CFrameWnd; it provides the application frame window.

- **CToolbar.** Implements toolbars docked to the frame window.

- **CSDICoinView.** Implements the view as a child of the frame window.

- **CStatusBar.** Implements the status bar attached to the frame window.

- **View window.** Overrides the client area of the frame window.

You might be wondering where the visual features such as the menu and toolbar come from. They are actually resources that AppWizard added to the project during its creation. If you select the ResourceView pane, you'll see there are four resources (an accelerator table, an icon, a menu, and a toolbar) with the same ID, IDR_MAINFRAME. Each resource can be edited by double-clicking the resource ID. There is also a special string table entry with the ID of IDR_MAINFRAME. The string has a specific format; it is subdivided into seven separate strings delimited by \n (new line). Each substring describes a specific attribute of the application's document. For example, the first substring is the application window title.

Understanding SDI Document Templates

So far, this chapter has concentrated on the individual classes of a Document/View application and the individual visual features. All these elements are brought together and managed by a document template class. If you refer to Figure 12.4, which shows the class hierarchy of an SDI application, you'll see it includes `CSingleDocTemplate`, which is the document template class used by single document interface applications.

An instance of the `CSingleDocTemplate` class is instantiated and used within the `CSDICoinApp::InitInstance` function (see Listing 12.1). The `InitInstance` function is called by the MFC framework right at the start of execution to initialize the application.

LISTING 12.1 LST13_3.CPP—The *InitInstance* Function

```
1   BOOL CSDICoinApp::InitInstance() ————①
2   {
3       // ** Note: some lines removed for brevity
4
5       // Register the application's document templates.
        ➥ Document templates
6       //   serve as the connection between documents,
        ➥ frame windows and views.
7
8       CSingleDocTemplate* pDocTemplate;
9       pDocTemplate = new CSingleDocTemplate(
10          IDR_MAINFRAME, ————②
11          RUNTIME_CLASS(CSDICoinDoc),
12          RUNTIME_CLASS(CMainFrame),
            ➥// main SDI frame window
13          RUNTIME_CLASS(CSDICoinView));
14      AddDocTemplate(pDocTemplate);
15
16      // Parse command line for standard shell commands,
        ➥DDE, file open
17      CCommandLineInfo cmdInfo;
18      ParseCommandLine(cmdInfo); ————③
19
20  // Dispatch commands specified on the command line
```

① Called by MFC at the start of program execution.

② Initializes the document template with the resource ID, document, frame, and view classes.

③ Parse the command-line arguments.

continues...

LISTING 12.1 Continued

④ Process the command-line arguments and create a new document or open a file.

⑤ Show and update the main application window.

```
21    if (!ProcessShellCommand(cmdInfo))    ──── ④
22        return FALSE;
23
24    // The one and only window has been initialized,
   ➥so show and update it.
25    m_pMainWnd->ShowWindow(SW_SHOW);    ──┐
26    m_pMainWnd->UpdateWindow();          ──┴──── ⑤
27
28    return TRUE;
29 }
```

The class factory method

The document template class is an example of a class factory, which is a class that defines how to instantiate other classes. A class factory, therefore, knows how to manufacture application-specific classes.

You can see in line 9 a CSingleDocTemplate object is created and passed four parameters. The first parameter is the resource ID IDR_MAINFRAME. In the SDICoin example, IDR_MAINFRAME identifies four separate resources: an application icon, a menu, a toolbar, and an accelerator table. The next three parameters are all pointers to runtime class information for the document, frame, and view classes, respectively. The RUNTIME_CLASS macro is used to generate these pointers. This is possible because AppWizard included support for dynamic creation of these classes by incorporating the DECLARE_DYNCREATE and IMPLEMENT_DYNCREATE macros.

The document, view, and frame objects themselves are not created at this time. This code initializes the CSingleDocTemplate object with the information needed to be able to load the resources and allocate documents, views, and frames on demand. The document template class is known as a class factory.

The document template object itself is retained in the application class. The AddDocTemplate function call (line 14) registers the newly created document template object within the CWinApp class.

The CWinApp class retains the CSingleDocTemplate object until it is destroyed itself, which happens only when the application is terminated. During its destruction, the CWinApp class will tidy up any allocated memory for the document template so you don't need to worry about it.

SEE ALSO

➤ For information on runtime class information, see page 591

Using the Document/View Framework Functions

Perhaps the hardest aspect of understanding—and therefore using—the Document/View architecture is following the creation sequence of the objects involved and the virtual function calls that happen along the way. This isn't due to complexity, but because much of the implementation takes place behind the scenes. This is a good thing because it means the framework is doing a considerable amount of work for you. However, in order to fully comprehend how Document/View ticks, a look behind the scenes is required.

Following the creation and initialization of the CSingleDocTemplate object in lines 8 to 14 of Listing 12.1, command-line parameters are dealt with and then the application window is shown.

The CCommandLineInfo class (line 17) aids in handling arguments passed to the application from the command line. The CWinApp::ParseCommandLine function (line 18) takes a reference to the CCommandLineInfo object as its parameter. A call is made to the ParseParam function for each command-line argument, filling in member variables of the CCommandLineInfo object. Table 12.2 shows the default command-line options and their purpose.

Parsing your own command-line arguments

The easiest way to cater for additional command-line arguments is to derive a class from CCommandLineInfo and override the ParseParam function.

TABLE 12.2 Command-line arguments

Argument	Purpose
NONE	Create a new document.
file	Open the specified file.
/p file	Print the specified file on the default printer.
/pt file printer driver port	Print the specified file on the specified printer.
/dde	Start a DDE session.
/automation	Start the application as an OLE automation server.
/embedding	Start the application to edit an OLE object embedded in another application.

You can see from Table 12.2 that if no arguments are passed from the command line, a new document is created when the application starts. This, of course, is what happens by default. Along with the document, the frame window and view are also created. It all takes place within the `CWinApp::ProcessShellCommand` function shown in line 21. Listing 12.2 gives an overview of the sequence of events involved. Note that the code contained in Listing 12.2 is paraphrased and has been condensed in order to focus specifically on the creation sequence.

LISTING 12.2 LST13_4.CPP—Document, View, and Frame Creation Sequence

① Called by InitInstance function.

② pTemplate is a pointer to the CSingleDocTemplate object already registered.

③ If document exists it is reinitialized.

```
1   BOOL CWinApp::ProcessShellCommand( ———①
    ➥CCommandLineInfo& rCmdInfo)
2   {
3       if(rCmdInfo.NewFile)
4       {
5           OnFileNew();
6       }
7       if(rCmdInfo.OpenFile)
8       {
9           OpenDocumentFile(rCmdInfo.strFileName);
10      }
11      ...
12  }

13  void CWinApp::OnFileNew()
14  {
15      m_pDocManager->OnFileNew();
16  }

17  void CDocManager::OnFileNew()
18  {
19      pTemplate->OpenDocumentFile(NULL); ———②
20  }

21  CSingleDocTemplate::OpenDocumentFile
    ➥(LPCTSTR lpszPathName)
22  {
23      if(m_pOnlyDoc != NULL)
24          pDocument->SaveModified(); ———③
```

```
25      else
26      {
27          pDocument = CreateNewDocument();
28          pFrame = CreateNewFrame(pDocument); ─────④
29      }
30      ...
31      pDocument->OnNewDocument(); ─────⑤
32      InitialUpdateFrame(pFrame, pDocument); ─────⑥
33
```

④ The document and frame objects are constructed using runtime class information in the template. `CreateNewFrame` also constructs the view.

⑤ Virtual function that is overridden to perform document initialization.

⑥ Performs frame window initialization by calling `LoadFrame`. Activates the view and sends a `WM_INITIALUPDATE` message that causes `CView::OnInitialUpdate` to be called.

The `CWinApp::ProcessShellCommand` function shown in lines 1 to 12 sparks a series of framework function calls depending on the result of parsing any command-line arguments. The function will call `CWinApp::OnFileNew` (line 13) if no arguments are specified. This is also the function called in response to the user selecting **New** from the **File** menu, which is hooked up automatically by AppWizard.

Listing 12.2 shows the logic for creating a new document on startup, but the difference between this and opening a file isn't great. The distinction lies at the beginning where `CWinApp::ProcessShellCommand` either finds the passed file or prompts the user to select a file via a standard dialog box. After the file is located, its path and name are passed to the same `CSingleDocTemplate::OpenDocumentFile` function (line 21) instead of `NULL`, which creates a new document.

`CWinApp::OnFileNew` immediately delegates responsibility to `CDocManager::OnFileNew` (line 15), which retrieves a pointer to the previously created `CSingleDocTemplate` object. Using the template pointer, a call is made to `OpenDocumentFile` passing `NULL` as the parameter. In this function, the real work takes place.

CSingleDocTemplate::OpenDocumentFile

The document object of an SDI application is created only once (the first time `OpenDocumentFile` is called). Subsequent calls to the function in response to selecting **New** or **Open** from the **File** menu reinitialize the open document so it can be used again. The reinitialization process takes place in the `SaveModified` function. The function first checks the modified state of the document. The CDocument class, which is the base of all document classes, has a BOOL member variable that stores whether the document has been modified. This member is set using the SetModifiedFlag function.

If the current document is modified, the user is prompted to save the document before continuing. The message box enables the user to continue with or without saving or cancel the OpenDocumentFile function. The document is saved by a call to OnSaveDocument and is reinitialized by a call to DeleteContents, both described later in this section.

If the document object needs creating, a call is made to the document template function CreateNewDocument (line 27). This uses the template runtime class information to construct your application-specific document object. The function also adds the new document to a list of current documents. When the document has been created, the frame and the view are also created by a further template function, CreateNewFrame.

The CreateNewFrame function (line 28) uses the template runtime class information to construct both the frame window and view objects. After creating the frame, the CFrameWnd::LoadFrame function is called and passed the resource ID that was specified in the template constructor. If you recall, this was IDR_MAINFRAME. LoadFrame loads each resource (menu, toolbar, icon, accelerator table, and string) and attaches them to the frame window. Please note, if the loading of any resource fails, the LoadFrame function will fail and produce a trace message: Warning: CDocTemplate couldn't create a frame. Now that all the objects are constructed, the document is initialized via the OnNewDocument function (line 31) described later in this section.

Finally, in the creation sequence the template function InitialUpdateFrame is called (line 32). This sets the newly created view as active and then sends the message WM_INITIALUPDATE to the frame window's children, which includes the view window. On receiving this message, the virtual function CView::OnInitialUpdate is called. It is a very common practice to override this function to perform specific view initialization. Please note it is normally necessary to ensure the base class version is also called.

OLE documents

If with AppWizard you specify that your application is either an OLE server or container, your document class will be derived from one of three CDocument subclasses: COleDocument, COleLinkingDoc, or COleServerDoc. Each of these three classes builds on the functionality of the previous one. Fundamentally they add the capability to treat the document as a list of OLE objects.

CDocument::OnNewDocument

This function is called during the process of document object creation. This could be at the start of an application or in response to the user selecting **New** from the **File** menu. It calls the DeleteContents function to tidy up any existing document data and sets the document's modified state to FALSE (unmodified). It also empties the string containing the document's filename.

CDocument::OnOpenDocument

This function is called during the process of opening an existing file. This could be at application startup if a file is specified as a command-line argument or in response to the user selecting **Open** from the **File** menu. The DeleteContents function is called to tidy up any existing document data. The default implementation opens the file and then calls the Serialize function to load the document data. When the data is loaded, the file is closed and the modified state is set to FALSE (unmodified).

CDocument::OnSaveDocument

This function is called during the process of saving a file. It is called in response to the user selecting either **Save** or **Save As** from the **File** menu. It is also called if the user chooses to save the document when prompted to do so after attempting to close the document while it's in a modified state. The function has one parameter, a pointer to a constant string containing the filename. The default implementation opens the file and then calls the Serialize function to save the document data. When the data is saved, the file is closed and the modified state is set to FALSE (unmodified).

CDocument::DeleteContents

OnNewDocument, OnOpenDocument, and OnCloseDocument call this function. It's responsible for removing the contents of the current document. The default implementation does nothing because document data is application-specific. You must provide an override of the function that should free any allocated members of your document and reinitialize variables.

CDocument::OnCloseDocument

This function is called when the current document is closed. In an SDI application this happens when the user chooses to open or create a new document and when the application is terminated. The function first closes all views attached to the document. It then calls DeleteContents before destroying the document object.

SEE ALSO

➤ *For information on OLE automation, see page 657*

➤ *For information on file handling and serialization, see page 591*

Using Documents and Views Together

Implementing the Document/View architecture provides the basis for a functionally scalable application. Separating data-handling code from user interface–handling code produces a modular application that is easier to maintain and enhance. For example, to present existing data in a new way is a matter of developing a new view class that uses the existing document interface to access the required information.

Designing the interaction between the Document/View class pair is of ultimate importance. A common difficulty, even for experienced programmers, is deciding exactly what information belongs in the document and what belongs in the view. There are no hard and fast rules, and largely it depends on the type of application. Ideally, the view should not maintain data itself but retrieve it from the document when it needs to. This way data changes are all handled in one place, which then notifies all views attached to the document so they are updated. However, this approach isn't always convenient or efficient. For example, text editing applications often store a copy of all or some of the data in the view class because otherwise constant accessing of the document is required (perhaps on every keypress), which impacts performance.

Numerous situations will arise where some caching of data within the view is appropriate. There is no problem with this—

you are free to code as you want, but unnecessary duplication of data will make your programming life more difficult, so avoid it if possible.

Initializing Document Data

The CDocument class is an abstract class, so you must derive your own document class from it. The members of the document class store your application's data. In all but the simplest applications, documents require numerous member variables, often in the form of allocated arrays or linked lists.

Remember that in an SDI application, the document object is constructed once and then reused for subsequent documents. Therefore, the document constructor is not always the appropriate place to initialize member variables because this will be called only once and not for each new document.

In the section "Using the Document/View Framework Functions," you saw that the document virtual function DeleteContents is called automatically from OnNewDocument, OnOpenDocument, and OnCloseDocument. These are all the situations when the current document is changing. DeleteContents is responsible for deleting the contents of the document, so after this has been performed it can be a convenient place to initialize document members.

Adding Member Variables to the Document

The document class is like any other class within the project; therefore, member variables can be added using ClassView's Add Member Variable context menu. If you're adding many variables, you might find it more convenient to edit the code directly. You can open the document class header file by double-clicking the document class name on ClassView.

In order to preserve data integrity, document variables should be *protected member variables*. A protected variable can be altered only by member functions of its own class or a class derived

> **MFC collection classes**
>
> The MFC library provides several helper collection classes for designing complex data structures such as CArray and CObList. Use this built-in functionality where possible.

Protecting document variables

Your document class should contain *protected member variables* that are accessed via public member functions.

from its own class. Prohibiting all other classes from altering document data means there is only one point of change for the variable; this makes notifying views attached to the document easier. To enable views to see protected document data, the document class must provide access functions that return references to member variables.

Now that you have knowledge of the Document/View architecture, it's time to start developing the SDICoin example. In this section, you'll deal with the document class CSDICoinDoc. The data required in the document class is the current number of coins, which can be stored in a single member variable. Whenever the view class must draw the stack of coins, it requires access to this count. The simplest way of achieving this would be to have a public member variable in the document to store the count, giving the view class direct access to it. The disadvantage of this is that it makes it possible for code in the view class to alter the value of the count, perhaps accidentally. The preferred method is to have a protected member variable store the count and for the document class to provide an access function for the view class to retrieve the count. To add the necessary code, follow these steps.

Implementing the document data storage and access methods

1. On the ClassView pane, select the CSDICoinDoc class; then from the context menu, select **Add Member Variable**. The Add Member Variable dialog appears.

2. Enter int in the **Variable Type** edit box. Enter m_nCoins in the **Variable Name** edit box and select the **Protected Access** radio button. Click **OK**.

3. With the CSDICoinDoc class still highlighted, select **Add Member Function** from the context menu.

4. Enter int in the **Function Type** edit box. Enter GetCoinCount in the **Function Declaration** edit box, and select the **Public Access** radio button.

5. Enter the following line of code in the body of the GetCoinCount function:
   ```
   return m_nCoins;
   ```

6. Press Ctrl+W to start ClassWizard or from the **V̲iew** menu select **ClassW̲izard**.

7. Select the **Message Maps** tab.

8. Select `CSDICoinDoc` in the **Class N̲ame** combo box.

9. Select `CSDICoinDoc` in the **Object I̲Ds** list box.

10. Select `DeleteContents` in the **Messages** list box, and then click the **A̲dd Function** button.

11. Click **OK** to close the ClassWizard dialog box.

12. Enter the following line of code after the TODO comments in the `DeleteContents` function:

    ```
    m_nCoins = 1;
    ```

`CSDICoinDoc` now has a protected member variable `m_nCoins`, which is initialized in the overridden `DeleteContents` function. You have also added an access member function `GetCoinCount`, which will be used by the view to retrieve the value of `m_nCoins`.

Accessing Document Data from the View

In order for the view to retrieve data from the document, it must first be able to access the document object. The MFC framework provides for this automatically by adding a `GetDocument` function to your application-specific view class. This function returns a pointer to the document object to which the view was attached with the document template. In fact, the framework provides two `GetDocument` functions. In the example you'll find the `CSDICoinView` class has a `GetDocument` implementation in SDICoinView.cpp and one in SDICoinView.h, as shown following. The two functions perform exactly the same task; the only difference is that the first is used for the debug version of the project and the second is used for the release version. The reason behind this is that inline functions are more efficient, and this function is likely to be called frequently during execution.

> **Using inline functions can improve performance**
>
> The keyword `inline` enables the compiler to replicate a function's code in each place it is called rather than performing a function call. Execution speed improves because function calls are eliminated. Note that you cannot single step through an inline function using the debugger.

SDICoinView.cpp

```
#ifdef _DEBUG
CSDICoinDoc* CSDICoinView::GetDocument()
{
```

```
        ASSERT(m_pDocument->IsKindOf(
    ➥ RUNTIME_CLASS(CSDICoinDoc)));
        return (CSDICoinDoc*)m_pDocument;
#endif // _DEBUG
```

SDICoinView.h

```
#ifndef _DEBUG // debug version in SDICoinView.cpp
inline CSDICoinDoc* CSDICoinView::GetDocument()
    { return (CSDICoinDoc*)m_pDocument; }
#endif
```

The CSDICoinView class is responsible for displaying the stack of coins. The code to actually draw an imitation coin is quite simple and takes place in the CSDICoinView::OnDraw function. AppWizard has already provided a skeleton of this function to use. The MFC framework calls the OnDraw function whenever the view must be rendered to the screen—for example, if the frame window is resized. The OnDraw function is also called to handle print and print preview processing. A different target device context is passed to the function depending on where the view is to be drawn. Edit the CSDICoinView::OnDraw function as shown in Listing 12.3.

(1) Call the view's GetDocument() to retrieve a pointer to the application document class.

(2) Retrieve a pointer to the brush currently selected in the device context pDC.

(3) Create a brush that will draw in a solid yellow color.

LISTING 12.3 LST13_1.CPP—Accessing Document Data to Render the View Image

```
1   void CSDICoinView::OnDraw(CDC* pDC)
2   {
3       // ** Retrieve a pointer to the document
4       CSDICoinDoc* pDoc = GetDocument();        (1)
5       ASSERT_VALID(pDoc);
6
7       // TODO: add draw code for native data here
8       // ** Save the current brush
9       CBrush* pOldBrush = pDC->GetCurrentBrush();    (2)
10
11      // ** Create a solid yellow brush
12      CBrush br;
13      br.CreateSolidBrush(RGB(255,255,0));       (3)
14
15      // Select the yellow brush into the device context
```

```
16        pDC->SelectObject(&br);  ─────④
17
18        // Retrieve the number of coins from the document
19        // and draw two ellipses to represent each coin
20        for(int nCount = 0;  ─────⑤
       ↪ nCount < pDoc->GetCoinCount(); nCount++)
21        {
22            int y = 200 - 10 * nCount;
23            pDC->Ellipse(40, y, 100, y-30);  ─────⑥
24            pDC->Ellipse(40, y-10, 100, y-35);
25        }
26
27        // ** Restore the current brush
28        pDC->SelectObject(pOldBrush);  ─────⑦
29   }
```

④ Select the new brush into the device context.

⑤ Loop until the correct number of coins has been drawn. The number is retrieved by calling the document access function GetCoinCount().

⑥ Draw two ellipses with offset coordinates to represent each coin.

⑦ Reselect the original device context brush.

The first two lines (lines 4 and 5) in the function are automatically provided by AppWizard. The GetDocument function returns a pointer to the document object, which is stored in pDoc. The pointer is used in the for loop in line 20 to retrieve the current number of coins by calling the access method GetCoinCount.

In line 9, a pointer to the brush currently selected in the device context is stored in pOldBrush, which is restored at the end of the function in line 28.

Lines 12, 13, and 16 create a solid yellow brush in the local variable br and select it into the device context, ready to draw the coin(s). Each coin is drawn using two ellipses, one above the other, to give a three-dimensional effect. To do this, the CDC::Ellipse function is used as you can see in lines 23 and 24.

SEE ALSO

➤ *For information on device contexts, see page 356*

➤ *For information on drawing graphics, see page 409*

Using the Standard Template Resources

As mentioned previously in this chapter, several resources are automatically added to the project to support the visual elements of an SDI application. These are the menu, the toolbar, an icon, an accelerator table, and the document string.

All these standard resources are fully functional. For example, the **New** option on the **File** menu will call `CWinApp::OnFileNew`, which causes a new document to be created, as will the New icon on the toolbar. This doesn't mean you can't alter the default behavior of these options. You can override any of the command functions and perform whatever processing you want. You might remove menu and toolbar options if they aren't pertinent to your application. However, it's far more common to leave the standard options as-is and add your own application-specific options. This is very easy to do because each resource can be edited using the resource editor and attached to command processing functions using ClassWizard.

For the SDICoin example, you must add two menu options, one to add a coin and one to remove a coin. When selected, these options will each call a function within the document class that will either increase or decrease the coin count and then ensure the view is updated. To add the menu options, follow these steps.

Adding menu options

1. On the ResourceView pane, expand the Menu folder and double-click `IDR_MAINFRAME`. The menu resource appears in the resource editor.

2. Click the **Edit** menu item within the resource editor. The drop-down menu appears.

3. Double-click the blank item at the bottom of the drop-down list. The Menu Item Properties dialog box appears as shown in Figure 12.7.

4. Enter an **ID** for the menu item. For this example use `ID_EDIT_ADD_COIN`.

5. Enter a **Caption** for the menu item. For this example use `Add a Coin`.

6. Enter a **Prompt** for the menu item. For this example use `Increase the number of coins`.

7. Double-click the blank item at the bottom of the drop-down list.

8. Enter an **ID** for the menu item. For this example use `ID_EDIT_REMOVE_COIN`.

Adding accelerators for menu options

When editing the properties of a menu option you can specify a keyboard alternative by appending it to the end of the caption. For example, the menu option caption &Toolbar\tCtrl+T indicates that Ctrl+T will perform the view toolbar menu option. You must also add `ID_VIEW_TOOLBAR` to the accelerator table defining T and Ctrl as the key combination.

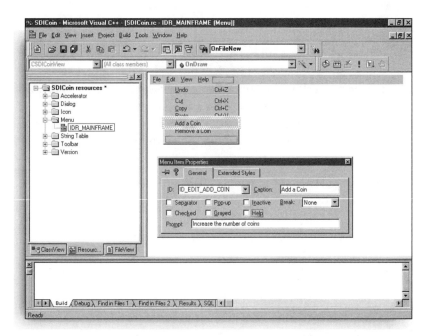

FIGURE 12.7
The Menu Item
Properties dialog box.

9. Enter a **Caption** for the menu item. For this example use
   `Remove a Coin`.

10. Enter a **Prompt** for the menu item. For this example use
    `Decrease the number of coins`.

11. Press Ctrl+W to start ClassWizard or from the **View** menu
    select **ClassWizard**.

12. Select the **Message Maps** tab.

13. Select `CSDICoinDoc` in the **Class Name** combo box.

14. Select `ID_EDIT_ADD_COIN` in the **Object IDs** list box.

15. Select `COMMAND` in the **Messages** list box, and then click the
    Add Function button. Click **OK** on the Add Member
    Function dialog box.

16. Select `ID_EDIT_REMOVE_COIN` in the **Object IDs** list box.

17. Select `COMMAND` in the **Messages** list box, and then click the
    Add Function button. Click **OK** on the Add Member
    Function dialog box.

18. Click the **Edit Code** button.

Updating the View

After any modification has been made to the document data, it's almost always necessary to reflect this within the view. This is achieved by calling functions that cause the view to be redrawn. In the previous section, you added two menu options and created command handler functions for them within the document class. Now edit the two functions as shown in Listing 12.4.

LISTING 12.4 LST13_2.CPP—Updating the View from the Document

(1) Menu command handler function called when the **Add a Coin** menu option is selected.

(2) Increment the document's member variable that records the number of coins.

(3) Causes the OnUpdate() function of views associated with the document to be called, which subsequently causes the view to be redrawn.

```
1   void CSDICoinDoc::OnEditAddCoin()        (1)
2   {
3       // TODO: Add your command handler code here
4
5       // ** Increment the number of coins
6       m_nCoins++;                (2)
7
8       // ** Update view to redraw coin stack
9       UpdateAllViews(NULL);         (3)
10  }
11
12  void CSDICoinDoc::OnEditRemoveCoin()
13  {
14      // TODO: Add your command handler code here
15
16      // ** Decrement the number of coins
17      if(m_nCoins > 0)
18          m_nCoins—;
19
20      // ** Update view to redraw coin stack
21      UpdateAllViews(NULL);
22  }
```

As you can see, each function either increases or decreases m_nCoins, which is the document data. Then a call is made to UpdateAllViews, passing NULL as a parameter. The NULL parameter means all views attached to the document are to be updated. Each view is updated by calling its OnUpdate function. This invalidates the client area of the view window and causes the OnDraw function to be called.

Now build and run the SDICoin project. Try selecting the **Add a Coin** and **Remove a Coin** menu options. The view should appear similar to Figure 12.8.

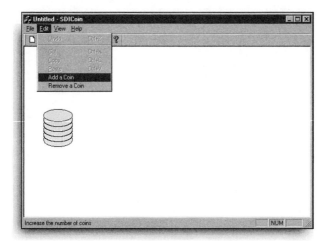

chapter

13

Working with Menus

Creating and editing menu resources

Writing handler functions for
menu commands

Learning how to implement
context menus

Dynamically creating and maintaining
menu options

Creating and Editing Menu Resources

Menus provide the backbone for user interaction with Windows applications, enabling the user to quickly navigate the high-level user interface structure. Menus have header items (seen along the top of the menu bar) and menu items (the drop-down options). Menu items themselves can have pop-up submenus to provide hierarchical routes into the application code, and can be disabled, checked, or treated like *radio controls*.

Context menus let you add specific menu items to application objects that pop up on demand when the right mouse button is clicked, thus giving the user a much quicker and clearer control of the application.

You can easily create and maintain menu resources using the resource editor. The resource editor lets you add and remove menu headers and menu items in a WYSIWYG (what you see is what you get) manner.

SEE ALSO

➤ *For more information about the resource editor, see page 34*

Dynamically created menus

If you don't use a menu resource, you can still dynamically create menus and add menu options to those menus programmatically as shown later in this chapter.

Adding New Menu Resources

Menus are normally displayed from a menu resource (like dialog box templates), which hold all the header and submenu items of the menu. You can add menu resources from the resource editor. However, if you create an SDI or MDI project with AppWizard, you'll get an initial default menu for the view with an ID of IDR_MAINFRAME. If you want to add additional menus, the procedure to add a new menu resource is described in the following list.

Add a new menu resource

1. Select the ResourceView pane to display the project resources.

2. Right-click the top-level item and select the **Insert** option from the drop-down menu to display the Insert Resource dialog box.

3. Select **Menu** from the list of new resource types.

4. Click the **New** button to insert the new menu resource. You should see the new menu template appear under the Dialog Resource heading.

5. Right-click the dialog box and select the **Properties** context menu option to display the menu properties.

6. You can now change the default IDD_ resource **ID** name to a more appropriate name for your dialog box.

7. Alternatively, you can expand the project resources and right-click the **Menu** header, which lets you pick the **Insert Menu** option to add the new menu resource, and then change the default ID as in steps 5 through 7.

SEE ALSO

➤ *For more information about creating SDI applications, see page 267*

➤ *For more information about creating MDI applications, see page 530*

➤ *For more information about the resource editor, see page 34*

Adding Menu Header Items

After you've inserted a new resource or selected an existing framework-generated resource, you can edit that resource in the main Editor window. The menu is displayed in the editor as you'd see it displayed when your application is run, with the header items shown along the top of the Editor window. You can insert a new menu header into a new or existing menu resource.

Insert a new menu header item

1. Select the menu resource from the ResourceView pane so that the correct menu resource is highlighted and the menu is displayed in the main Editor window.

2. Click the blank rectangle displayed to the right of the existing menu header items on the top of the menu bar. The rectangle should become selected by displaying a white border around the rectangle.

Using the Insert Menu shortcut key

You can skip steps 1 to 4 by using the Ctrl+2 Insert Menu resource shortcut key from wherever you are in Visual Studio. After pressing Ctrl+2, you should find the resource pane displayed with the new menu highlighted and displayed in the main editor window.

3. Type the name of the new menu header. You should see the text appear in the rectangle, and a Menu Item Properties dialog box appears as you type. Also, a menu item box will appear beneath the new header as shown in Figure 13.1.

4. Select any required property flags for the header item (these flags are explained in more detail in later sections in this chapter, and can be amended later).

5. Press Enter to complete the new menu header insertion.

6. You can now drag and drop the new menu header into any position along the menu bar to rearrange the current menu header order.

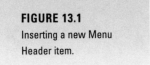

FIGURE 13.1

Inserting a new Menu Header item.

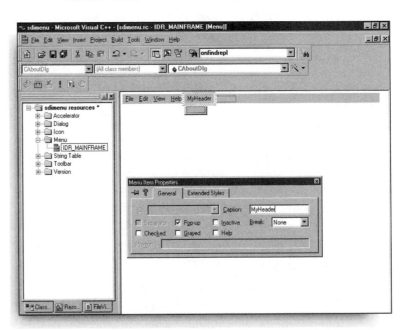

Adding Menu Items

Insert a new submenu item

1. Click the menu header item that will contain the new submenu item.

2. Click the blank rectangle displayed at the bottom of the existing submenu items. If you are adding a new menu item under a pop-up menu item, click the pop-up submenu item

to display the submenu item list. The rectangle should become selected by displaying a white border around the rectangle.

3. Type the name of the new menu item. You should see the text in the rectangle and a Menu Item Properties dialog box appears as you type (see Figure 13.2).

4. Select any required property flags for the header item (these flags are explained in more detail in later sections in this chapter, and can be amended later).

5. Click the **Prompt** edit box. You can now enter text that will appear in the status line when the menu is selected. You can also add a second string after the first that will appear in a ToolTip over an associated toolbar icon by separating the strings with a \n newline character. Such a string is shown in the **Prompt** edit box at the bottom of Figure 13.2.

6. Click the **ID** edit box. You should see a default menu ID appear based on the submenu item and header name. If necessary, change this default ID to one more appropriate to your application.

7. You can now drag and drop the new submenu item into any position anywhere in the menu (even as a new header).

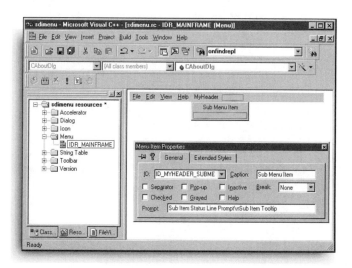

FIGURE 13.2
Inserting a new submenu item.

Assigning Command IDs

Using command IDs

The command ID you associate with each menu item will later be used to notify you that the user has selected a specific menu item. Windows sends the WM_ COMMAND message from the menu to notify the menu's parent window in your application. It bundles the command ID in with this message. The ID will then be interrogated in your window's message map by the ON_ COMMAND macro to find the appropriate handler function.

The submenu ID will be used to map a menu handler to the new menu item, as described in the "Adding a Menu Command Handler Function" section later in this chapter. If you want to assign the ID to an existing ID (such as a toolbar button), you can select the appropriate ID from the list of existing IDs by clicking the drop button of the combo box. You might want to share IDs among different menu resources. For example, you might have two different views but need both to display a common **File** menu that calls a document-based handler function. To do this, you could duplicate the **File** menu and share the IDs so that the same handlers are called.

Until you add an appropriate menu handler, all new submenu items will be disabled by default.

If you enter the Prompt string as described in step 5, the string value will be stored in the string table with a corresponding ID to the submenu item itself. When you compile your application, the prompt string will be displayed in the application status line.

Amending Menu Item Properties

You can display menu item properties by double-clicking an item or by selecting the item and pressing Alt+Enter. You can then change any of the item's properties from the Properties dialog box.

Any menu items can be repositioned by dragging the menu item and then dropping it into the new position. Insertion guide bars appear between the menu items to show where the item will be dropped.

You can delete any menu item by selecting the required item and pressing the Delete key. If you delete a menu header, all the submenu items under that header item will be deleted (although you are prompted first).

SEE ALSO

➤ *For an explanation of string tables, see page 34*

Adding Separators

You can add separators to group submenu items by drawing horizontal bars across the dialog drop box (like the Developer Studio **File** menu). To do this, double-click a new blank entry rectangle to display the Menu Item Properties dialog box; then click the **Separator** check box to set the Separator property. When you set this property, all the controls are disabled except the **Caption** edit box, which is cleared. Press Enter to close the dialog box. You'll see the new separator appear as a horizontal bar. You can drag and drop this separator to position it correctly.

Creating Pop-Up Submenu Items

You can create submenu items that act as header items in that they pop up another list of submenu items (see Figure 13.3). To create one of these pop-up menu lists, you can add a new submenu item and then click the **Pop-Up** check box in the Menu Item Properties dialog box to set the **Pop-Up** property for that menu item. When you've done that, the **ID** field is grayed and a small right-pointing arrow is drawn to the right of the menu item, pointing to another blank insertion rectangle.

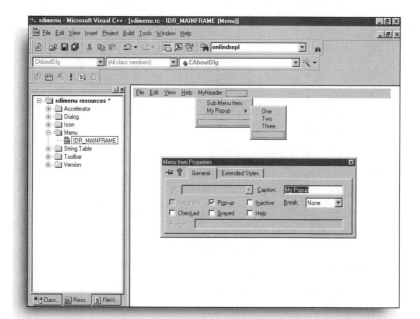

FIGURE 13.3
Creating pop-up menu items.

You can now insert new submenu items of the pop-up item as you would normal submenu items. These submenu items can also have pop-up items to form yet another sublevel menu, if required. By using these pop-up items, you can create a highly hierarchical menu system.

Adding Check Marks

Submenu items can have check marks placed to the left of the menu item text when displayed. You can set these check marks programmatically, or set them from the resource editor to appear by default against the menu item when the menu is first displayed.

To set the check mark to appear by default, you can click the **Checked** property in the Menu Item Properties dialog box for each submenu item you need to be initially displayed with a check mark.

Adding Shortcuts

Mnemonic keys

These shortcuts are also called mnemonics keys, and can be set in dialog boxes against controls to set focus and change a specific control.

You can add key shortcuts to the menu items, which enable the user to choose the menu item by pressing the associated shortcut key. These shortcut key codes are shown by an underlined style that appears on the shortcut character for each menu item.

To assign the shortcut character in the menu item text, you must insert an ampersand character (&) before the required shortcut character. When you display the menu item, the prefixed character will be underlined and the corresponding keyboard key will automatically work as a shortcut to that menu item.

For example, if you wanted to make the S of My Shortcut a shortcut key, you would enter the menu item caption as My &Shortcut, which would be displayed as My Shortcut.

If you actually want an ampersand character, you must use two ampersands together to display one. Thus, My && Am&persand, will display the text: My & Ampersand.

SEE ALSO

➤ *For more detail about shortcut keys, see page 63*

Handling Menu Commands

You can handle a menu command much like a dialog box button with a command handler function. You can use ClassWizard to create these command handlers, which will then create a message map entry for a Windows WM_COMMAND from your menu item with the ID of the selected menu item. When the user selects the menu item, Windows passes a WM_COMMAND message to the application window that owns the menu; if you have a corresponding message map entry, it will call the associated handler function.

You can also add command user interface message handlers to update the enabled/disabled status of the associated menu with another ClassWizard-generated message map and handler function.

SEE ALSO

➤ *For a detailed explanation of message maps, see page 69*

Adding a Menu Command Handler Function

After you've inserted your new menu, you can assign a handler function to be called when that menu item is selected, and start executing your code associated with the menu item. The handler function can be implemented in any class whose objects will be passed the menu selection command message when the item is selected. This would normally be either your document that sports the views or the specific view that implements the menu option. However, you can also handle the menu option in the application or frame window classes. The best guide as to where to implement the handler function is to consider where it is more appropriate in terms of accessing data and methods that it needs from the various application objects. You can use ClassWizard to add this handler.

Adding a menu command handler function with ClassWizard

1. Select the menu item for which you want to add a handler function.

2. Press Ctrl+W, or click the **View** menu and select **ClassWizard** to invoke ClassWizard. You should see the selected menu item ID highlighted in the **Object IDs** list, as shown in Figure 13.4.

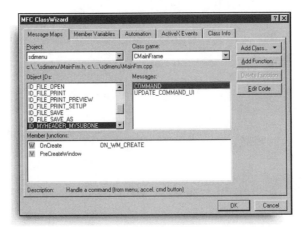

3. The **Class Name** combo box shows the destination class for your new handler function. You can click the combo drop button to list all the possible classes that can implement your new menu-handler function. You can select the required implementation class, which is normally either the view that implements the menu option or a document class, depending on which is more relevant.

4. Double-click the COMMAND message shown in the **Messages** list box to show the Add Member Function dialog box (see Figure 13.5). If you're not partial to double-clicking, you can select the COMMAND message entry and click the **Add Function** button.

FIGURE 13.5

The Add Member Function dialog box lets you change the new handler function name.

5. The default handler function name is based on the menu ID of the submenu item. You can modify this default name in the **Member Function Name** edit box before creating the new handler function.

6. Click **OK** to add the new member function.

7. You should then see the new member function appear in the **Member Functions** list at the bottom of the ClassWizard dialog box.

8. You can edit the code of the new member function by clicking the **Edit Code** button.

When you've added the new handler function, you can add your application-specific implementation code. For example, the following menu handler (implemented in the document class) just displays a message box indicating that the menu item has been selected:

```
void CSdimenuDoc::OnMyheaderMysubone()
{
    AfxMessageBox("You picked the 1st menu item");
}
```

SEE ALSO

➤ *To understand message passing in an SDI application, see page 271*
➤ *For a detailed explanation of message maps, see page 69*

Adding a Command User Interface Handler Function

When are command user interface handler functions called?

The command user interface handler functions for menus are called only after the user has clicked a menu header but just before the menu is displayed. This update-on-demand system makes menus much faster than if the menu item attributes needed to be updated whenever a program state changes, even though the user couldn't see the menu items affected.

The command user interface function is responsible for the look, style, and behavior of each specific menu item. Before the menu is displayed, the corresponding user interface handler functions are called to let your application enable or disable each item, add or remove check marks, or change the item's text.

You can change these various user interface attributes by calling the access functions of a CCmdUI object associated with the menu item. Whenever your user interface (UI) handler function is called, it will be passed a pointer to a CCmdUI object.

For example, the following UI handler enables the menu item so that the user can select it. It does this by calling the Enable() function of the CCmdUI object pointed to by the pCmdUI pointer:

```
void CSdimenuDoc::OnUpdateMyheaderMysubone(CCmdUI* pCmdUI)
{
    pCmdUI->Enable(TRUE);
}
```

The next sections in this chapter describe these aspects of the user interface in more detail.

To add such a UI handler function to your application, you can follow the steps for adding a menu command handler function with ClassWizard, discussed previously in this chapter, but you should select the UPDATE_COMMAND_UI rather than the COMMAND message from the **Messages** list in step 4.

Enabling and Disabling Menu Options

You can enable or disable menu options by calling the CCmdUI object's Enable() function. If you pass a TRUE value to this function, the menu is enabled; otherwise, the menu option will be disabled and grayed out.

You could maintain this grayed state by setting a Boolean member variable embedded in the class and passing it to the Enable() function of the CCmdUI object when your UI handler function is called with a line such as the following:

```
pCmdUI->Enable(m_bMySubItemEnableStatus);
```

By maintaining the state of `m_bMySubItemEnableStatus` in your application, the menu item will be correspondingly enabled or disabled.

Setting or Clearing the Check Mark

You can display a check mark (or *tick*) next to the menu item to indicate a Boolean status to the user that is relevant to your application. You can set the status of the check mark by calling the `CCmdUI` object's `SetCheck()` function and passing a zero value to uncheck the menu item or a one value to check it.

If you wanted to implement a simple toggle switch on a menu item by letting the user toggle the check mark on and off by selecting the menu item, you could implement the code as shown in Listing 13.1.

LISTING 13.1 LST14_1.CPP—Implementing a Toggle Switch Menu Item with Check Marks

```
1   void CSdimenuDoc::OnMyheaderMysubone()
2   {
3       // ** Flip the current toggle state
4       m_nToggleState = m_nToggleState==0 ? 1 : 0;        (1)
5   }
6
7   void CSdimenuDoc::OnUpdateMyheaderMysubone
    ➥(CCmdUI* pCmdUI)
8   {
9       // ** Enable the menu item
10      pCmdUI->Enable(TRUE);
11
12      // ** Set the current toggle state
13      pCmdUI->SetCheck(m_nToggleState);        (2)
14  }
```

(1) In response to the user selecting the menu item, flip the value in m_nToggleState between 0 and 1.

(2) Draw the check mark if m_nToggleState is 1, clear the check mark if it is 0.

In Listing 13.1, both the command and command UI message handler functions are used in combination to implement the toggle switch. The message command handler function `OnMyheaderMysubone()` implemented in lines 1 through 5 maintains the state of the toggle in the `m_nToggleState` member variable. This member variable could be defined in the class definition as a simple integer:

```
int m_nToggleState;
```

Line 4 uses the inline conditional operator ? to check whether the state of m_nToggleState is currently zero. If it is, m_nToggleState is set to one; otherwise it is set to zero, thus toggling its current state.

The user interface handler is implemented by the OnUpdateMyheaderMysubone() function in lines 7 through 14. Line 10 ensures that the menu item is always enabled by calling the CCmdUI object's Enable() function.

The current toggle state is updated to the menu item by setting or clearing the check mark status by calling the CCmdUI object's SetCheck() function in line 13. SetCheck() is passed the m_nToggleState variable to either display or clear the check mark, depending on the value of m_nToggleState.

Changing the Menu Text Dynamically

Continuing the command UI message routing

You could add a message map entry for your command UI message in two classes (the document and view classes, for example). However, normally the first handler function would stop the message from routing and reaching the second. You might want to implement a two-tier handler where in some circumstances you would want to fall through the first to drop into the second handle. To do this, you can call the CCmdUI object's ContinueRouting() function to make it carry on to the next handler function in the routing chain.

You can also use the command UI handler function to change the menu item text by passing a new text string to the CCmdUI object's SetText() function. The menu will then be changed to the new text string, including any shortcut codes set by the ampersand symbol (&).

You could make the menu item text in the previous toggle example also change the menu text to display **On** and **Off**, depending on the toggle state, by adding the following line to the end of the UI handler function:

```
pCmdUI->SetText(m_nToggleState?"&On":"O&ff");
```

In the preceding line, the inline conditional operator ? is used to pass one of the two strings, depending on the value held in m_nToggleState.

Adding Context Menus

A *context menu* is a menu that pops up anywhere on the screen (conventionally) when the user right-clicks an application object.

The user can then select menu items specific to the application object from the menu.

You can add a new menu resource to display as the pop-up context menu. This should be added with the resource editor as described in the steps earlier in this chapter, and edited as described in the "Creating and Editing Menu Resources" section.

You can implement context menus in your application by adding a handler for the Windows WM_CONTEXTMENU message, which is passed to your application when the right mouse button is clicked anywhere within your application windows. In the handler function you can load the appropriate menu resource and then start the pop-up menu by calling the TrackPopupMenu() function. Menu item command handler functions can be added as normal to implement the menu item functionality.

Starting a Context Menu

You can add a handler for the WM_CONTEXTMENU context menu message with the following steps.

Adding a context menu handler function

1. Select the **ClassView** tab of the Project Workspace window and expand the class list if necessary to show project classes by clicking the plus sign next to the top project classes line.

2. Right-click the view class to which you want to add the new context menu and select the **Add Windows Message Handler** option from the pop-up menu to display the New Windows Message and Event handlers dialog box.

3. Select the WM_CONTEXTMENU message from the **New Windows Messages/Events** list and click the **Add and Edit** button to add a new handler function for the context menu message.

4. You should now see a new ClassWizard generated, by default with the OnContextMenu() handler function. You can add your application code to this default implementation.

The WM_CONTEXTMENU message

The WM_CONTEXTMENU message is generated by the default window procedure when the WM_RBUTTONUP message is received. If you catch the WM_RBUTTONUP message but don't call the base class handler function, your application will never get the WM_CONTEXTMENU message.

When you've inserted the new handler function, you can add the code to display a context menu. You might want to display the context menu only if the mouse cursor is over a particular object, or display different context menus depending on the specific object selected. You can do this by using the `CPoint point` parameter to detect which application object or window area has been clicked to conditionally display the context menu (or a particular context menu). The techniques to do this are described in Chapter 8, "Responding to Mouse Events."

To display the context menu, you must first declare a `CMenu` object to implement the pop-up menu (the `CMenu` class is an MFC wrapper class that can hold and access a Windows `HMENU` object). Then the new `CMenu` object can be initialized with your new pop-up menu resource by calling its `LoadMenu()` function and passing the ID of the menu resource. The `CMenu` object will then be initialized with the header menu item for your new menu resource. You will only need the pop-up submenu items of this header menu item to display the pop-up menu. You can find this submenu by calling the `GetSubMenu()` function and passing zero to indicate that the first pop-up item is required.

From the pop-up menu you can call the `TrackPopupMenu()` function to display and track the pop-up menu. `TrackPopupMenu()` needs four parameters. The first is an alignment flag to specify where the menu should appear in relation to the specified position. If the mouse pointer should be to the left of the pop-up menu, you can pass the `TPM_LEFTALIGN` flag for this parameter and pass the mouse pointer position as the menu position. Other possible alignment flag values are shown in Table 13.1. The second and third parameters specify the horizontal and vertical coordinates to position the new menu. You would normally pass the `point.x` and `point.y` values passed into the `OnContextMenu()` function for these two parameters to draw the context menu at the mouse pointer position. The last parameter is a pointer to your window object, which is usually the C++ `this` operator for a pointer to the current view object.

Creating dynamic context menus

Instead of loading a predefined context menu from a menu resource, you might want to display different text associated with the specific object the user has clicked (rather than the type of object). If this is the case, you might find it better to call the `CMenu` class's `CreatePopupMenu()` function to create the menu and then use `AppendMenu()` to add menu items to the new menu. You can then use `TrackPopupmenu()` in the same way to display it. More details can be found on the `AppendMenu()` function in the "Dynamically Adding Menu Items" section, later in this chapter.

TABLE 13.1 Flag alignment values for *TrackPopupMenu()*

Flag Name	Description
TPM_LEFTALIGN	Aligns the menu so that the specified position is to the left
TPM_RIGHTALIGN	Aligns the menu so that the specified position is to the right
TPM_TOPALIGN	Aligns the menu so that the specified position is above the menu
TPM_BOTTOMALIGN	Aligns the menu so that the specified position is below the menu
TPM_CENTERALIGN	Aligns the menu so that the specified position is centered horizontally
TPM_VCENTERALIGN	Aligns the menu so that the specified position is centered vertically
TPM_HORIZONTAL	If screen space is limited, horizontal alignment is more important
TPM_VERTICAL	If screen space is limited, vertical alignment is more important

When the call is made, the pop-up menu will be displayed and the user can select one of the menu options. After an item is selected or the user clicks elsewhere, the context menu will disappear.

For example, you could implement a context menu that lets the user pick between North, East, South, and West menu options from an AppWizard-generated SDI framework. First you could add a new menu resource for the pop-up menu items as shown in Figure 13.6.

FIGURE 13.6

Inserting a new menu resource for a pop-up context menu.

When you've inserted the new menu resource, you can add a WM_CONTEXTMENU handler for the context menu message by following the "Adding a Context Menu Handler Function" steps presented earlier in this chapter. You should add this function to the SDI application's view class and implement the code for loading and tracking the context menu as shown in Listing 13.2.

① This line displays and starts the user menu selection tracking.

LISTING 13.2 LST14_2.CPP—The *OnContextMenu()* Handler Function for *WM_CONTEXTMENU* Loads and Tracks the Pop-Up Context Menu

```
1    void CSdimenuView::OnContextMenu(CWnd* pWnd,
  ⮡ CPoint point)
2    {
3        // ** Declare a CMenu object
4        CMenu menuPopup;
5
6        // ** Initialize with the context menu resource
7        menuPopup.LoadMenu(IDR_MYCONTEXT);
8
9        // ** Display and start tracking the new menu
10       menuPopup.GetSubMenu(0)->TrackPopupMenu( ————①
11               TPM_LEFTALIGN,point.x,point.y,this);
12   }
```

Line 4 of Listing 13.2 declares a new CMenu object as the menuPopup variable. menuPopup is then initialized with the menu items from the IDR_MYCONTEXT menu resource in line 7.

Line 10 calls TrackPopupMenu(), specifying left-coordinate relative alignment, and passes the mouse pointer position that was passed to the context menu handler function. It also passes the pointer to the current CSdimenuView view object using the C++ this keyword.

To display the correct menu, TrackPopupMenu() must be called from the main menu resource's contained pop-up menu. A pointer to this menu is returned from the main menu by the menuPopup.GetSubMenu(0) function call at the start of line 10.

SEE ALSO

➤ *For more information about hit testing, see page 188*

Handling the Context Menu Commands

After you've added the context menu, you can add handler functions for the menu options just as you would for a normal menu (as described in the "Adding a Command User Interface Handler Function" section earlier in this chapter).

You could use ClassWizard to add the menu command handler functions and the user interface function handlers for each pop-up menu option, like these for the **North** option:

```
void CSdimenuView::OnMypopupmenuNorth()
{
    AfxMessageBox("North");
}
```

The menu command handler function displays the word North in a message box when the **North** menu option is selected.

```
void CSdimenuView::OnUpdateMypopupmenuNorth(CCmdUI* pCmdUI)
{
    pCmdUI->Enable(TRUE);
}
```

The menu user interface handler function enables the menu option by calling `Enable()` on the pointer to the `CCmdUI` object passed to the handler function.

You could add these changes to a standard SDI framework and build and run the application. Right-clicking the mouse anywhere inside the main view will display the new context menu shown in Figure 13.7.

ClassWizard's Adding a Class dialog box

When you've inserted a new menu resource and sub-sequently invoke ClassWizard, it displays the Adding a Class dialog box because it has detected your new menu resource. You don't need to create or select a handler class, and can dismiss this dialog box by clicking the Cancel button.

FIGURE 13.7
The pop-up context menu displayed by clicking the right mouse button.

SEE ALSO
➤ *For more information about handling mouse click events, see page 176*

Accessing the menu handle

You can access the CMenu object's underlying menu handle via its m_hMenu member variable. This might be useful if you must use some of the Win32 functions rather than the MFC counterparts.

Creating and Accessing Menu Objects

MFC provides the CMenu class to wrap an underlying Windows menu handle (HMENU) and simplify menu operations. You can use CMenu to programmatically build your own menus (rather than loading them) or you can dynamically add and remove menu items from existing menus. CMenu has a whole host of member functions that handle every aspect of menu display and manipulation. The following sections describe a few of the most important CMenu functions.

Initializing the *CMenu* Object

Before you can use a declared new CMenu object, you must initialize it by loading the menu item from a menu resource, creating a new menu, or attaching the menu object to an existing Windows menu.

Each of the various initialization functions return TRUE if the function succeeds and the menu is initialized or FALSE if the menu couldn't be initialized:

- Loading the menu from a menu resource template

  You can load a menu using the LoadMenu() member function by passing the resource ID of the required menu, as shown in Listing 13.2 in the previous section. The menu template will then be loaded from the resource and used to create Windows menu items for the menu.

- Creating new menus

  CreateMenu()will dynamically create an empty Windows menu resource with no menu items. You can then add the menu items dynamically to create the new menu, as described in the next section.

Alternatively, you can call `CreatePopupMenu()` to create a pop-up menu that can be used as the pop-up from other menu items, or for pop-up context menus.

- Attaching to existing menus

  You can call `Attach()` to attach an existing Windows menu to the `CMenu` object by passing the `HMENU` handle to the existing Windows menu. You can obtain this handle from an associated `CWnd` (or derived `CView`) by calling the window object's `GetMenu()` menu function. When you've finished manipulating the menu, you can detach it from your `CMenu` object by calling `Detach()`.

After you've initialized the `CMenu` object, you can add, remove, or modify the menu items to suit your application needs as described in the next sections.

SEE ALSO

➤ *For more information about windows and views and the* `CWnd` *and* `CView` *classes, see page 271*

Dynamically Adding Menu Items

New menu items can be added to a menu by calling either `AppendMenu()` or `InsertMenu()`, depending on whether the menu item should be added to the end of the menu or inserted into the menu at a specific position.

The `AppendMenu()` menu function needs three parameters. The first mandatory parameter is a flag value that specifies the new menu item type and a combination of menu style values. Normally you'd pass `MF_STRING` as this flag value to specify that the new item holds a pointer to a normal null-terminated string (you can also use `CString` objects). Alternatively, you can create a separator item by passing `MF_SEPARATOR`. You can then combine these basic type flags with the other menu flags shown in Table 13.2 by adding the flag values with an addition (+) operator, or a bitwise logical OR (¦) operator.

You can pass the second parameter an ID for command messages or the `HMENU` handle of a pop-up menu if the `MF_POPUP` flag is specified.

Checking the uniqueness of menu IDs

You should check that your menu IDs are unique and don't conflict with any resource menu IDs. You can check this by opening your project's resource.h file (shown in the **FileView** tab) and searching for your new ID. If the ID isn't found in resource.h and isn't duplicated in another dynamic menu, it should be safe to use.

You can pass a string pointer for the third parameter for the menu item text (or leave the default NULL setting for separator items).

TABLE 13.2 Menu flags for use with *AppendMenu()* and *InsertMenu()*

Flag Settings	Description
MF_CHECKED	Sets the menu item's check mark flag to display the check mark next to the menu item
MF_UNCHECKED	Clears the associated menu check mark flag
MF_ENABLED	Enables the menu item
MF_DISABLED	Disables the menu item
MF_GRAYED	Same as MF_DISABLED
MF_POPUP	The menu item has an associated pop-up menu as specified by the ID parameters
MF_MENUBARBREAK	The menu item will be placed on a new line (or in a new column for pop-up menus separated by a vertical line)
MF_MENUBREAK	Same as MF_MENUBARBREAK but without the vertical line in pop-up menus

The InsertMenu() option function lets you insert the new menu item at a specific position, or before a menu item with a specific ID. If you want to specify the position by index, pass the position as a zero-based offset to the first parameter, and include the MF_BYPOSITION flag with your flag values passed to the flags parameter.

To insert the new menu item before an existing menu item with a specific ID, pass the ID as the first parameter, and include the MF_BYCOMMAND flag with your flag parameter value.

The other three parameters are identical to the AppendMenu() parameters. For example, instead of loading a context menu (as shown in Listing 13.2 in the previous section), you could create the pop-up menu and append the menu items as shown in Listing 13.3. This technique gives you more control over the appended menu item and lets you dynamically add menu items specific to your application. Listing 13.3 also shows some of the various ways the new menu items can be added and the effects of various flag combinations.

LISTING 13.3 LST14_3.CPP—Dynamically Creating and Displaying a Pop-Up Context Menu

```
1    #define ID_MENU_RED       5001
2    #define ID_MENU_GREEN     5002
3    #define ID_MENU_BLUE      5003
4    #define ID_MENU_YELLOW    5004
5
6    void CSdimenuView::OnContextMenu(CWnd* pWnd,
  ➥ CPoint point)
7    {
8      // Declare a CMenu object
9      CMenu menuPopup;
10
11     // Create the pop-up menu resource
12     if (menuPopup.CreatePopupMenu())
13     {
14       // Add simple menu items
15       menuPopup.AppendMenu(MF_STRING,ID_MENU_RED,"&Red");
16
17       // Insert an item at the top of the menu
18       menuPopup.InsertMenu(0, MF_BYPOSITION | MF_STRING,
19                             ID_MENU_GREEN,"&Green");
20
21
22       menuPopup.AppendMenu(MF_SEPARATOR);
23
24       // Add a checked item
25       menuPopup.AppendMenu(MF_STRING | MF_CHECKED,
26                            ID_MENU_BLUE,"&Blue");
27
28       // MF_MENUBARBREAK
29       menuPopup.AppendMenu(MF_STRING | MF_MENUBARBREAK,
30                            ID_MENU_YELLOW,"&Yellow");
31       menuPopup.TrackPopupMenu(TPM_LEFTALIGN,
32                            point.x,point.y,this);
33     }
34   }
```

(1) The unique menu IDs are defined here.

(2) If the pop-up menu can be created, the menu items can be added safely.

(3) Note this item is added by position at an index of zero (above the first item).

(4) The menu bar break flag causes a vertical line to separate the pop-up menu into columns.

Lines 1 through 4 of Listing 13.3 define ID values for the four menu items to be added. In line 9 the CMenu-based menuPopup object is declared and initialized as a pop-up menu with a call to the CreatePopupMenu() function in line 12.

A new menu item with the text **Red** is added to the menu in line 15 with the AppendMenu() function. Another menu item with the text **Green** is inserted before the **Red** item by the InsertMenu() function in line 18. A separator is added in line 22 by appending a menu item with the MF_SEPARATOR flag. The **Blue** text is added by lines 25 and 26 with a check mark set, and the **Yellow** item is added in lines 29 and 30 to the right of a vertical separator bar.

Finally, TrackPopupMenu() is called in line 31 to display and track the new pop-up menu.

You can add handler functions for your dynamic menu items by adding message map entries at the end of the view's message map for your user-defined IDs:

ON_COMMAND(ID_MENU_YELLOW,OnYellow)

(You must ensure that the #define lines for the IDs are above the message map in the code for the compiler to find them.)

The OnYellow() handler function will then be called when the user selects the new dynamic menu option with the ID_MENU_YELLOW ID. You can then implement the command handler function as normal:

```
void CSdimenuView::OnYellow()
{
    AfxMessageBox("Yellow");
}
```

If you build and run the application with these changes, you'll see the pop-up context menu shown in Figure 13.8.

FIGURE 13.8

A dynamically created pop-up menu with various flag options set.

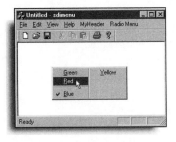

Dynamically Modifying Menu Items

You can also modify menu items while they are displayed or are valid objects by calling the ModifyMenu() function. ModifyMenu() needs four parameters.

The first mandatory position parameter works like the InsertMenu() position parameter. If you want to specify the position by index, you should pass the position as a zero-based offset to the first parameter, and include the MF_BYPOSITION flag with your flag values passed to the flag's parameter. Alternatively, to modify a menu item with a specific ID, pass the ID as the first parameter and include the MF_BYCOMMAND flag with the other flag's parameter values.

You must pass the second parameter a set of new flag values for the menu item to change the current settings of the menu item using any of the flag values from Table 13.2. You must pass a set of replacement flags for the menu item you want to change.

You can (optionally) pass the new menu ID as the third parameter (or the existing ID to leave it unaltered), and pass the fourth parameter a pointer to a text string to change the menu item text.

For example, to set the check mark on the menu item associated with ID_MENU_YELLOW (shown in the previous section), you could add the following line after the menu item has been added:

```
menuPopup.ModifyMenu(ID_MENU_YELLOW,
MF_BYCOMMAND | MF_CHECKED | MF_STRING | MF_MENUBARBREAK,
             ID_MENU_YELLOW,"&Yellow");
```

You can quickly change individual attributes such as the check mark and enable status by calling the CheckMenuItem() and EnableMenuItem() functions. These functions take two parameters. The first identifies the menu item to be changed by its ID, or-zero based index position.

The second parameter uses either MF_BYCOMMAND or MF_BYPOSITION to indicate that the first parameter is an ID or index value. For the CheckMenuItem() function, you can add the MF_CHECKED and MF_UNCHECKED to set or clear the check mark, respectively. The EnableMenuItem() function lets you add MF_ENABLED and MF_DISABLED to enable and disable the menu items.

For example, you could simplify the ModifyMenu() example to set the check mark by using the CheckMenuItem() function like this:

```
menuPopup.CheckMenuItem(ID_MENU_YELLOW,
MF_BYCOMMAND | MF_CHECKED);
```

Dynamically Removing Menu Items

You can remove menu items from a CMenu object by calling RemoveMenu(), which takes two parameters. The first is the ID or index value to identify the menu item to delete. The second parameter should be passed the MF_BYCOMMAND or MF_BYPOSITION flag to indicate the type of value position you passed as the first parameter.

chapter 14

Working with Toolbars and Status Bars

Creating, customizing, and using toolbars ●

Using dialog bars to use standard dialog
controls such as combo boxes ●

Customizing the status bar and showing
application-specific indicators ●

Understanding the new Internet
Explorer–style rebars ●

Customizing the Standard Framework Toolbar

Most applications use toolbars to help the user select often-used application commands. Usually toolbar buttons are provided as a shortcut to corresponding menu options and provide a graphical association with the command. For example, if the user wants to print a document, the printer icon is an obvious choice.

If you create an SDI- or MDI-based project, accepting the default toolbar settings on Step 4 of the AppWizard as shown in Figure 14.1, a normal docking toolbar is added to your new application framework.

FIGURE 14.1

MFC AppWizard Step 4 includes a Normal Docking toolbar option.

AppWizard generates code to create the toolbar window, load the toolbar's button images from a Toolbar resource, and attach it to the application's frame window. The AppWizard-generated toolbar shows buttons corresponding to the default **File**, **Edit**, and **Help** menu options as shown in Figure 14.2.

SEE ALSO

➤ *For more information about creating SDI applications, see page 267*

➤ *To create an MDI application, see page 530*

FIGURE 14.2

The standard SDI AppWizard–generated toolbar.

Understanding the Standard Toolbar

The default framework implements the toolbar by adding a CToolbar object, m_wndToolBar, to the CMainFrame class definition with a line like this:

```
CToolbar m_wndToolBar;
```

The CToolbar class is derived from CControlBar, which in turn is derived from CWnd. The CControlBar extends the basic CWnd window functionality by adding support for docking the window to a frame window or letting it float as a normal window. Toolbars, status bars, and dialog bars then extend CControlBar in different ways to specialize this docking window support for each type of control bar. The CToolbar class adds the support for a bitmap and an array of buttons to present a Toolbar interface to the user, like the standard one shown in Figure 14.2.

SEE ALSO

➤ *For details about the* CMainFrame *class, see page 271*

Creating the Standard Toolbar

Recall that the CMainFrame class is responsible for handling the frame window of the SDI- and MDI-based applications. When the frame window is created, the CMainFrame's OnCreate() member function is called. The AppWizard-generated code uses this function to create the Toolbar window as a child of the frame window and load the toolbar's associated Toolbar resource (IDR_MAINFRAME) with these lines of code:

```
if (!m_wndToolBar.CreateEx(this, TBSTYLE_FLAT, WS_CHILD |
    WS_VISIBLE | CBRS_TOP | CBRS_GRIPPER |
    CBRS_TOOLTIPS | CBRS_FLYBY | CBRS_SIZE_DYNAMIC)
    || m_wndToolBar.LoadToolBar(IDR_MAINFRAME))
{
```

```
        TRACE0("Failed to create toolbar\n");
        return -1;      // fail to create
    }
```

You can see this code in the MainFrm.cpp implementation module. The Toolbar window creation and resource loading are both combined in the `if` condition so that -1 is returned from the frame window's `OnCreate()` function if either fails.

The `CreateEx()` function is used to create the toolbar's associated window. This member function is new in the Visual C++ 6.0 implementation of toolbars, and is used to set the borders for the new flat-look toolbars. The first parameter it passes is a pointer to the parent window; by passing the C++ `this` keyword, the calling frame window object is set as the parent.

The AppWizard implementation passes the `TBSTYLE_FLAT` flag as the second parameter, which defines the style of the toolbar. You can change this parameter to pass zero if you want the old-look "raised buttons" style.

You can modify the control bar style flags passed to the third parameter of `CreateEx()` by combining any of the flag values shown in Table 14.1. However, you must remember to combine the child window flag `WS_CHILD` and the window visible flag `WS_VISIBLE`.

Using `CreateEx()` for toolbars like Microsoft Internet Explorer 4

The `CreateEx()` function enables you to set new toolbar style flags. To create a toolbar in the style of Microsoft's Internet Explorer 4 you should set the `dwCtrlStyle` equal to `TBSTYLE_FLAT ¦ TBSTYLE_TRANSPARENT`.

TABLE 14.1 Control bar style flags

Flag Value	Description
CBRS_TOP	Docks the toolbar at the top of the frame window and draws a border below it
CBRS_BOTTOM	Docks the toolbar at the bottom of the frame window and draws a border above it
CBRS_LEFT	Docks the toolbar at the left of the frame window and draws a border to its right
CBRS_RIGHT	Docks the toolbar at the right of the frame window and draws a border to its left
CBRS_ALIGN_ANY	Docks the toolbar anywhere
CBRS_FLOAT_MULTI	Multiple control bars can be floated in one miniframe window

Flag Value	Description
CBRS_TOOLTIPS	Displays ToolTips for the control bar
CBRS_FLYBY	Updates the message text when the ToolTips are updated
CBRS_GRIPPER	Adds a gripper bar for moving the toolbar
CBRS_SIZE_DYNAMIC	Lets the user resize the floating toolbar
CBRS_SIZE_FIXED	Doesn't let the user resize the floating toolbar

After the toolbar window is created, the next part of the condition loads the toolbar resource by calling the LoadToolBar() member function, and passes the ID of the toolbar to be loaded. For the default toolbar, this is set to IDR_MAINFRAME. The toolbar resource holds the bitmaps for the toolbar buttons and can be found under the Toolbar heading in the **ResourceView** tab (see Figure 14.3).

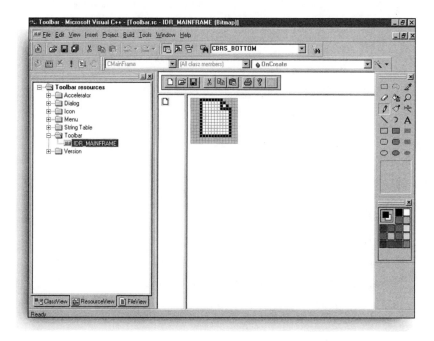

FIGURE 14.3
The default SDI/MDI toolbar shown in the resource editor.

If the `LoadToolBar()` function loads the resource correctly, a `TRUE` value is returned and the frame window's `OnCreate()` continues normally.

SEE ALSO

➤ *For more information about the resource editor, see page 34*

Docking the Standard Toolbar

After creating the default status bar, the `OnCreate()` function proceeds to dock the standard toolbar. Toolbars can be allowed to float like normal windows, or dock to a side of a frame window. *Docking* involves connecting the toolbar to the frame window seamlessly so that the toolbar doesn't display a frame of its own. The first of the docking lines you'll see in the frame window's `OnCreate()` implementation is the following:

```
m_wndToolBar.EnableDocking(CBRS_ALIGN_ANY);
```

This line enables the toolbar to dock to any edge of the frame window. If you want the toolbar to float (like a small Controls palette window), you should comment out this line by prefixing the `//` line comment syntax. Alternatively, you can specify that the toolbar can dock only to specific edges by combining the flag values as shown in Table 14.2. You can combine these flag values with the logical OR operator |. For example, you can allow the standard toolbar to be docked to only the left or right edges by changing the `EnableDocking()` call as shown:

```
m_wndToolBar.EnableDocking(CBRS_ALIGN_LEFT |
➥CBRS_ALIGN_RIGHT);
```

TABLE 14.2 Control bar docking flags

Docking Flag Value	Description
CBRS_ALIGN_ANY	Allows docking at every edge of the frame window
CBRS_ALIGN_TOP	Allows docking at the top edge of the frame window
CBRS_ALIGN_BOTTOM	Allows docking at the bottom edge of the frame window
CBRS_ALIGN_LEFT	Allows docking at the left edge of the frame window
CBRS_ALIGN_RIGHT	Allows docking at the right edge of the frame window

Notice that the next line in the standard frame window `OnCreate()` implementation calls the `EnableDocking()` member function of the frame window like this:

```
EnableDocking(CBRS_ALIGN_ANY);
```

This line enables all the edges the frame window to act as a *docking site* for control bars. You can pass the same combination of flags as shown in Table 14.2 to set or restrict the docking sites available on the frame window itself.

On the last line of the standard `OnCreate()` implementation, the frame window's `DockControlBar()` member function is called to dock the control bar initially to the frame window with the following call:

```
DockControlBar(&m_wndToolBar);
```

You can pass `DockControlBar()` three parameters. The first mandatory parameter is a pointer to the control bar that you want to dock. You can pass a flag to specify where the control bar should dock for the second parameter from the values shown in Table 14.3, or zero to specify that the control bar can be docked on any side of the frame window (default value). The third parameter lets you specify an exact position for docking by passing a pointer to a `RECT` structure holding the screen coordinates of the docking position on the frame window.

TABLE 14.3   Flag values to specify the docking edge for a toolbar docked with *DockControlBar()*

Docking Edge Flag	Description
`AFX_IDW_DOCKBAR_TOP`	Docks the control bar at the top of the frame window
`AFX_IDW_DOCKBAR_BOTTOM`	Docks the control bar at the bottom of the frame window
`AFX_IDW_DOCKBAR_LEFT`	Docks the control bar at the left of the frame window
`AFX_IDW_DOCKBAR_RIGHT`	Docks the control bar at the right of the frame window

Rather than docking the control bar, you could leave it floating by replacing the call to `DockControlBar()` with a call to the frame window's `FloatControlBar()` member function. `FloatControlBar()` also requires three parameters (two mandatory and one optional). The first is a pointer to the control bar object. You can pass a `CPoint` coordinate-holding object for the second parameter to specify where the top left of the control bar should be positioned in screen coordinates. The optional third parameter orientates the control bar. You can pass the third parameter `CBRS_ALIGN_TOP` (the default setting) for a vertical control bar, or `CBRS_ALIGN_LEFT` for a horizontal control bar.

For example, you can start the toolbar floating at position (50,50) by changing the `DockControlBar()` line in the frame window's `OnCreate()` function to the following:

```
FloatControlBar(&m_wndToolBar,CPoint(50,50));
```

After either `DockControlBar()` or `FloatControlBar()` have been called, the toolbar is displayed, and the application initialization continues as normal.

Adding Toolbar Buttons with the Resource Editor

You can add buttons to the standard toolbar from the resource editor by using the following set of steps to edit the standard `IDR_MAINFRAME` toolbar.

Adding a toolbar button

1. Select the ResourceView pane of the Project Workspace view.

2. Open the resource tree in the ResourceView pane to show the Toolbar resources, and double-click the toolbar to be edited.

3. You should see the toolbar resource displayed in the editor window as shown in Figure 14.3.

Third-party toolbar extension classes

Some software vendors provide class libraries that greatly extend the default MFC toolbar functionality to provide advanced docking and customization features as seen in Visual Studio itself. For example, the ability to drag and drop toolbar buttons as can be seen by clicking **Tools** and selecting the **Customize** option isn't provided by the normal MFC classes. However, this extended functionality is offered by third-party class library vendors.

4. To add a new button, select the blank button shown at the right of the toolbar, and start editing the button's bitmap.

5. When you start editing, you'll notice that a new blank button appears to the right of the button you are currently editing. If you want to add any further buttons, you can repeat the process from step 4.

6. For each new button, you should set a command ID and prompt string. You can set these from the Toolbar Button Properties dialog box (as shown in Figure 14.4) that can be invoked by selecting the button and pressing Alt+Enter, or clicking the **View** menu and selecting **Properties**.

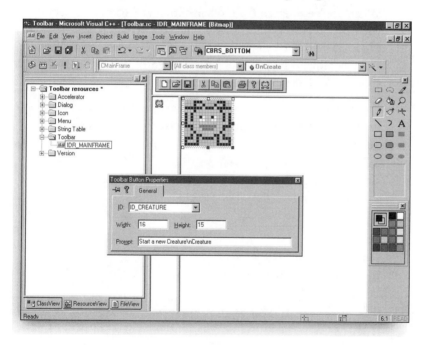

FIGURE 14.4
Setting the toolbar button properties.

7. You can set the command ID to a unique value by typing a new ID identifier into the **ID** combo box. Alternatively, you set the button to the same command ID as another object (such as a menu ID) by selecting the required ID from the combo box's drop-down list.

8. You can set a string to be displayed on the status line by entering the required string into the **Prompt** edit box. A ToolTip can also be added by adding the ToolTip string after a \n separator code in the **Prompt** edit box.

9. The toolbar button will be displayed when you next build and run the program. However, the button is disabled and grayed until you add a corresponding handler function. A handler function can be added just like a menu handler by following the "Adding a Menu Command Handler Function with ClassWizard" set of steps (which can be found in Chapter 13, "Working with Menus").

> **Mapping accelerator keys to toolbar buttons**
>
> You can create keyboard shortcuts for toolbar buttons by adding accelerator table entries in the resource editor to associate the command ID for the button with the keyboard shortcut. For example, the default framework associates the Ctrl+N key with `ID_FILE_NEW` (the ID for the first default toolbar button).

When you've inserted the toolbar button and handler function, you can add your application-specific code to run when the button is clicked. You can also share the handler function with a menu command ID as is often done when the toolbar provides a shortcut for a menu option.

For example, a simple view-based (`CToolbarView`) toolbar handler function that displays a message box where clicked might look like this:

```
void CToolbarView::OnCreature()
{
    AfxMessageBox("Creature");
}
```

SEE ALSO

➤ *Details of bitmap editing can be found on page 240*

➤ *For more details about the accelerator table, see page 34*

Moving and Removing Buttons, and Adding Separators

You can move toolbar buttons by selecting the required button to move and dragging it into the correct position. Separators can be added or removed by dragging the buttons a little way to the left or right.

You can delete a button by selecting it, and then dragging the button down to the image editing area and dropping it there. The button will then be removed from the toolbar.

Enabling and Disabling Toolbar Buttons

You can enable and disable toolbar buttons by adding a user interface (UI) handler function. The toolbar button UI handler function works just like a menu UI handler, but fewer `CCmdUI` functions, such as `SetText()`, are applicable.

To control the enabled/disabled state of a toolbar button, you can pass a controlling member variable to the `Enable()` function of the `CCmdUI` object passed to the corresponding UI handler as a pointer with code such as the following:

```
void CToolbarView::OnUpdateCreature(CCmdUI* pCmdUI)
{
    pCmdUI->Enable(m_bEnableCreature);
}
```

You can control the push in/pop out state of the button by passing `TRUE` or `FALSE` to the `CCmdUI` object's `SetRadio()` function. A `TRUE` value makes the button appear pushed in permanently, a `FALSE` value displays the normal popped out style.

SEE ALSO

➤ *For information about user interface handler functions, see page 304*

Adding Your Own Toolbar

It might be fine for smaller applications to merely modify the standard AppWizard-generated framework. However, for larger applications, you might want to offer several toolbars for various aspects of the application. You might also want to let the user show or hide any of the toolbars independently.

You can create the bitmaps for the toolbar buttons by creating a new toolbar resource. Your new resource can then be loaded into a new `CToolbar` object embedded in the frame window.

> **Why toolbar buttons are sometimes disabled**
>
> The MFC library functionality ensures that toolbar buttons are automatically disabled if they don't have either a corresponding COMMAND or UPDATE_ COMMAND_UI handler function.

Adding a New Toolbar Resource

Control bars and current input focus

A CControlBar-derived window such as CToolbar doesn't normally take the input focus from the active view unless it includes an edit box or combo box control. In this case you might find that the focus is not returned to the view when it is clicked on. The way to correct this is to provide an override in your view class for OnMouseActivate() to specifically set the focus to the view.

Inserting a new toolbar resource

1. Select the ResourceView pane to display the project resources.

2. Right-click the top-level item and select the **Insert** option from the drop-down menu to display the Insert Resource dialog box.

3. Select **Toolbar** from the list of new resource types.

4. Click the **New** button to insert the new toolbar resource.

5. You should see the new toolbar appear under the Toolbar Resource heading, and a blank toolbar button appear in the editor window.

6. Right-click the toolbar and select the **Properties** context menu option to display the menu properties.

7. You can now change the default IDD_ resource **ID** name to a more appropriate name for your dialog box.

8. Resize the blank toolbar button to change the default size of the toolbar and its buttons (if required).

9. You can start editing the blank toolbar button, and insert new buttons as described in the "Adding a Toolbar Button" set of steps earlier in this chapter.

Adding the Toolbar to the Frame Window

After you've added the toolbar resource, you'll need to add a CToolbar object to handle the new toolbar into the frame window class (CMainFrame). You can add the new toolbar declaration to the CMainFrame class definition (in the MainFrm.h module) after the other control bar entries.

For example, after adding a new toolbar declaration for a toolbar called m_wndColorSwipeBar, part of your CMainFrame class declaration would look like this:

```
protected:  // control bar embedded members
    CStatusBar   m_wndStatusBar;
    CToolBar     m_wndToolBar;
    CToolBar     m_wndColorSwipeBar;    // ** New Toolbar
```

You can then add the code to create the toolbar in the frame window's `OnCreate()` function after the standard toolbar in a similar fashion to the standard toolbar's `CreateEx()` function, like this:

```
if (!m_wndColorSwipeBar.CreateEx(this, TBSTYLE_FLAT,
    WS_CHILD | WS_VISIBLE | CBRS_LEFT | CBRS_GRIPPER |
    CBRS_TOOLTIPS | CBRS_FLYBY | CBRS_SIZE_DYNAMIC) ||
    !m_wndColorSwipeBar.LoadToolBar(IDR_COLORSWIPE))
{
    TRACE0("Failed to create color swipe toolbar\n");
    return -1;       // fail to create
}
```

These flags will create a flat-style toolbar that initially docks to the left of the frame window and offers the user a gripper bar for repositioning. The toolbar buttons and their images are loaded from the `IDR_COLORSWIPE` toolbar resource.

If your new toolbar is created successfully, you can add the lines to enable docking and to dock the toolbar to the frame:

```
m_wndColorSwipeBar.EnableDocking(CBRS_ALIGN_ANY);
DockControlBar(&m_wndColorSwipeBar);
```

You can then add the appropriate command message and UI handler functions for your new toolbar.

For example, Figure 14.5 shows an additional toolbar docked to the left of an SDI application's frame window. The modified standard framework toolbar is docked at the top.

Adding floating toolbars

Rather than docking your new toolbar, you can provide a floating toolbar like the Controls Palette window seen in the Resource Editor by calling `FloatControlBar()`.

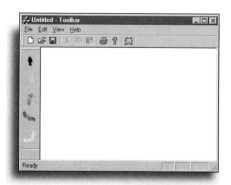

FIGURE 14.5
An SDI application showing a second, larger, left-frame docked toolbar.

SEE ALSO

➤ *For details about the* CMainFrame *class, see page 271*

Locating a toolbar from within the application

Normally toolbars are embedded as public members of the CMainFrame class. To locate this object you can use the global function AfxGetMainWnd(). Note you will need to cast the returned pointer to your application-specific main frame class, usually (CMainFrame*).

Hiding and Showing the Toolbar

You can hide or show a toolbar using the frame window's ShowControlBar() function. ShowControlBar() needs three parameters. The first is a pointer to the control bar you want to hide or show. The second is a Boolean value that should be set TRUE to show the control bar, or FALSE to hide the control bar. You should pass the third parameter a FALSE value to display the control bar immediately, or TRUE to delay showing the control bar.

For example, you might want to implement a menu option to toggle the toolbar visibility and display a check mark on the menu option when visible. The command message handler function for the menu might look like this:

```
void CMainFrame::OnViewColorswipebar()
{
    m_bColorVisible = !m_bColorVisible;

ShowControlBar(&m_wndColorSwipeBar,m_bColorVisible,FALSE);
}
```

The state of the CMainFrame object's embedded m_bColorVisible variable is then toggled between TRUE and FALSE by the =! operator combination. The toolbar is then made visible or invisible by passing the m_bColorVisible variable to the ShowControlBar() function.

You can also implement the following menu UI function to toggle the check mark on the menu depending on the toolbar's visibility state:

```
void CMainFrame::OnUpdateViewColorswipebar(CCmdUI* pCmdUI)
{
    pCmdUI->Enable();
    pCmdUI->SetCheck(m_bColorVisible);
}
```

SEE ALSO

➤ *To learn more about user interface handler functions in menus, see page 301*

Storing and Loading the Toolbar Positions

You can save and load the positions of all the application's toolbars in single function calls by using the `SaveBarState()` and `LoadBarState()` frame window functions. Both functions require just one parameter, which is a string value that specifies the name of an initialization key for the entry in your system's Registry. You can pass any unique string value to save the control bar positions (usually when the application is closed). You must then pass the same string to load that last saved state when starting the application again. These settings will be stored under the default Registry key for your application's details (in HKEY_CURRENT_USER\Software*yourcompanyname**yourappname*).

For example, you could save the current bar state when the frame window is destroyed by adding a handler function for the `WM_DESTROY` message, and saving the state before the base class `OnDestroy()` handler is called:

```
void CMainFrame::OnDestroy()
{
    SaveBarState("MyToolBarSettings");
    CFrameWnd::OnDestroy();
}
```

(See the "Adding a Handler for the `WM_DESTROY` Message" step by step in Chapter 15, "Understanding Drawing in Device Contexts," to add this handler function.)

Then, to reload the settings after creating the toolbars, you can add a line to the end of the frame window's `OnCreate()` function:

```
LoadBarState("MyToolBarSettings");
```

When the application is restarted, the user's previous toolbar docking state and position preferences will be restored.

Using Dialog Bars

Dialog bars are a type of toolbar based on modeless dialog boxes. You can add any controls you like to a dialog template, and then use that template to display the dialog bar. Normally

---

Keyboard accelerators work for disabled buttons

A keyboard accelerator will send the command message regardless of whether the toolbar button it references is disabled. In this situation you must cater for your command handler functions being called even if you've disabled the toolbar button.

the `IDD_DIALOGBAR` default template is used because it provides a bar-shaped template with no modal **OK** and **Cancel** buttons.

You can see a dialog bar in use in the standard framework print preview. The dialog bar provides the row of buttons for **Print**, **Next Page**, **Prev Page,** and so on.

A `CDialogBar` object can be embedded in the frame window like a toolbar to load and create the dialog bar. `CDialogBar` is derived from `CControlBar`, so it inherits all the docking functionality to enable dialog bars to dock and act like toolbars.

The main advantage of using dialog bars is that different controls are easier to add and maintain than toolbars.

SEE ALSO

➤ *To learn about modeless dialog boxes, see page 229*

➤ *For more details about printing and print preview, see page 562*

Adding the Dialog Bar Resource

You can add a dialog template resource for a dialog bar by following the "Inserting a New Dialog Template Resource" step by step (found in Chapter 10, "Using Dialog Boxes"), picking the `IDD_DIALOGBAR` dialog resource template from the Insert Resource dialog box.

After you've inserted the new dialog template resource and changed its ID and properties as required, you can start adding controls to the dialog template as you would for a normal dialog box.

You should assign IDs to any of the controls that you add so that these can be accessed *programmatically*.

Figure 14.6 shows such a dialog template for a dialog bar. The template has two controls, one button (marked **Apply Color**), and a drop-down list combo box initialized with a list of colors.

SEE ALSO

➤ *To learn about editing dialog templates, see page 44*

Using bitmap buttons in dialog bars

It is harder to add "normal" toolbar buttons (with images) to dialog bars. If you want to add buttons with images, you should add bitmap buttons using the `CBitmapButton` class, as discussed in the "Creating Bitmap Buttons" section of Chapter 11.

Disabling the layout guides while editing a dialog bar

If you use the default `IDD_DIALOGBAR` template, you might want to turn off the dialog box layout **Rulers and Guides** lines to make the most use of the limited room in a toolbar. You can do this by clicking the **Layout** menu and selecting the **Guide Settings** option to display the Guide Settings dialog box. You can then change the Layout Guides setting to **None** to help edit the dialog bar template.

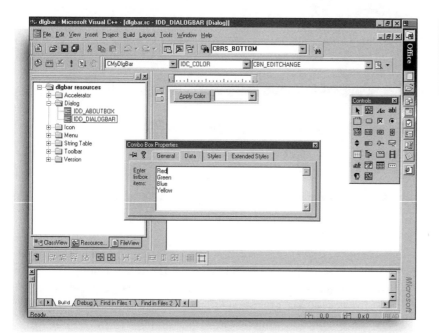

FIGURE 14.6

Editing a dialog bar resource template.

Adding the Dialog Bar to the Frame Window

You can add a dialog bar to a frame window like a toolbar by declaring a CDialogBar object in the CMainFrame class. For example, to declare a CDialogBar object with public access called m_wndColorDlgBar, you might add the following lines to the CMainFrame class definition:

```
public:
    CDialogBar m_wndColorDlgBar;
```

You could add these lines directly with the editor or via the Add Member Variable dialog box.

The new dialog bar can be created by adding code to call the CDialogBar object's Create() function from the frame window's OnCreate() function. The dialog bar's Create() function needs four parameters. The first specifies the parent window for the dialog bar (normally the frame window passed via the C++ this pointer from the frame's OnCreate()). You can pass your dialog bar resource template as the second parameter to specify which template the dialog bar should load and display. You can set the initial docking style by passing one of the alignment flags shown in Table 14.4.

TABLE 14.4 Dialog bar alignment flag values

Flag Value	Description
CBRS_TOP	Docks the dialog bar at the top of the frame window
CBRS_BOTTOM	Docks the dialog bar at the bottom of the frame window
CBRS_LEFT	Docks the dialog bar at the left of the frame window
CBRS_RIGHT	Docks the dialog bar at the right of the frame window
CBRS_NOALIGN	The dialog bar isn't repositioned when the frame window is resized

The fourth parameter lets you assign an ID to the dialog bar itself. You can assign values for this from the range defined by AFX_IDW_CONTROLBAR_FIRST and AFX_IDW_CONTROLBAR_LAST. The first few IDs are used in conjunction with print previewing, so you should preferentially use incremental values subtracted from AFX_IDW_CONTROLBAR_LAST to avoid possible conflicts.

For example, to create the dialog bar window for the m_wndColorDlgBar object, you could add the following lines to your frame window's OnCreate() function:

```
if (!m_wndColorDlgBar.Create(this,IDD_DIALOGBAR,
CBRS_TOP, AFX_IDW_CONTROLBAR_LAST-1))
{
    TRACE0("Failed to create dialog bar\n");
    return -1;      // fail to create
}
```

If the creation succeeds, you can proceed to dock the dialog bar as you would any other control bar with the following lines:

```
m_wndColorDlgBar.EnableDocking(CBRS_ALIGN_ANY);
DockControlBar(&m_wndColorDlgBar);
```

SEE ALSO

➤ *For details about the* CMainFrame *class, see page 271*

Handling the Dialog Bar Controls

You can handle messages from the dialog bar controls by adding corresponding message map entries and handler functions in either the frame window class or child view classes.

You can use ClassWizard to add these entries by selecting the appropriate dialog bar control from the resource editor and invoking ClassWizard by pressing Ctrl+W and following the normal steps to add a handler function for a control. This process differs from a normal dialog box in that your handler functions should be implemented in the appropriate view or document class rather than in a specific dialog class (like a menu or toolbar handler).

For example, Listing 14.1 shows the message map entries and handler functions for the dialog bar controls shown in Figure 14.6. The button control is identified by the IDC_APPLY_COLOR ID and the drop list-combo box is identified by the IDC_COLOR ID. The code lets the user change the color of the view's background by picking a color from the drop list and clicking the **A**pply button to redraw the window as shown in Figure 14.7.

LISTING 14.1 LST15_1.CPP—Implementing Dialog Bar Control Handler Functions to a View Class

```
1   BEGIN_MESSAGE_MAP(CDlgbarView, CView)
2       //{{AFX_MSG_MAP(CDlgbarView)
3       ON_WM_ERASEBKGND()
4       //}}AFX_MSG_MAP
5       // Standard printing commands
6       ON_COMMAND(ID_FILE_PRINT, CView::OnFilePrint)
7       ON_COMMAND(ID_FILE_PRINT_DIRECT,CView::OnFilePrint)
8       ON_COMMAND(ID_FILE_PRINT_PREVIEW,
        ➥CView::OnFilePrintPreview)
9       ON_COMMAND(IDC_APPLY_COLOR, ApplyColor)
10      ON_CBN_SELCHANGE(IDC_COLOR,ColorChange) ──────(1)
11  END_MESSAGE_MAP()
12
13  afx_msg void CDlgbarView::ApplyColor()
14  {
```

(1) Manually added message map entry to respond to the dialog bar's combo box selection change message.

continues...

LISTING 14.1   Continued

(2) The combo box control is found on the status bar and dynamically mapped to a control class to get the current selection status.

(3) Depending on the current list selection, a COLORREF value will be selected to fill the view's background when a WM_ERASEBKGND message is sent.

```
15          Invalidate();
16      }
17
18      #include "MainFrm.h"
19      afx_msg void CDlgbarView::ColorChange()
20      {
21          CMainFrame* pMainFrame =
22              (CMainFrame*)GetParentFrame();
23          CComboBox* pColSel = (CComboBox*) ──────── (2)
24              (pMainFrame->
25                  m_wndColorDlgBar.GetDlgItem(IDC_COLOR));
26          if (pColSel) m_nColor = pColSel->GetCurSel();
27      }
28
29      BOOL CDlgbarView::OnEraseBkgnd(CDC* pDC)
30      {
31          COLORREF rf = RGB(255,255,255);
32          switch(m_nColor)
33          {
34          case 0: rf = RGB(0,0,255); break;
35          case 1: rf = RGB(0,255,0); break;         (3)
36          case 2: rf = RGB(255,0,0); break;
37          case 3: rf = RGB(255,255,0); break;
38          }
39          CRect rcClient;
40          GetClientRect(&rcClient);
41          pDC->FillSolidRect(&rcClient,rf);
42          return TRUE;
43      }
```

Line 9 of Listing 14.1 shows the message-map entry for the button control (with an ID of IDC_APPLY_COLOR). This message map entry associates the button command message with the ApplyColor() handler function (just like a normal toolbar button would). The message-map entry on line 10 shows how you can associate a handler function (ColorChange()) with the CBN_SELCHANGE message, which is sent when the combo box selection is changed. After adding this message map entry (line 10), selection change notifications from the dialog bar's drop list combo will result in the ColorChange() handler function being called.

The ApplyColor() handler function implemented on lines 13 through 16 forces the window to redraw by calling Invalidate() on line 15 to redraw the view.

The ColorChange() handler function implemented on lines 19–27 changes the color index holding member variable m_nColor, depending on the list option the user chooses. After retrieving a pointer to the frame window on line 21, the combo box is dynamically mapped from its associated window pointer retrieved from the dialog bar by passing GetDlgItem(), the IDC_COLOR ID to identify the combo box control. If a valid pointer is set to the control, the current color selection is retrieved by calling the control's GetCurSel() function.

Notice that the MainFrm.h module is included on line 18 to tell the compiler about the m_wndColorDlgBar object declared in the CMainFrame definition.

Lines 29–43 provide a handler function for the WM_ERASEBKGND message. The appropriate color is set up by lines 31–38, and the background is erased by calling the FillSolidRect() function on line 41.

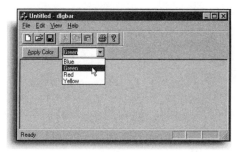

FIGURE 14.7
An SDI application displaying a dialog bar with combo box.

SEE ALSO

➤ *To understand combo box notification messages, see page 126*

➤ *For more detail about colors and the RGB macro, see page 385*

➤ *For more information about painting rectangles with brushes, see page 409*

Customizing the Status Bar

You can add your own custom *indicators* to an SDI or MDI application's status bar. The standard framework provides indicators that show the status of the CAPS lock, NUM lock and SCRL lock keys at the bottom of the frame window. These are shown as small indented boxes called *indicator panes*.

You can create, access, and maintain these panes by using a CStatusBar object declared in the main frame window. CStatusBar is another CControlBar derived class and hence supports all the docking functionality associated with control bars.

SEE ALSO

➤ *For more detail about SDI and MDI applications, see page 534*

Understanding the Standard Status Bar

The standard AppWizard-generated framework code for status bar support is very similar to the toolbar code. In the CMainFrame class definition, you'll see a declaration for a CStatusBar object call m_wndStatusBar:

```
CStatusBar      m_wndStatusBar;
```

The status bar window is then created from the frame window's OnCreate() function by calling the CStatusBar's Create() function. You can pass three parameters to the status bar Create() function. Only the first parameter, a pointer to the parent frame window, is required. The second parameter lets you pass style flags to specify the docking position and any required Windows style flags. You can pass any positioning values from those in Table 14.4 (for the dialog bar). If you omit this second parameter, the WS_CHILD, WS_VISIBLE, and CBRS_BOTTOM flags are passed by default. The third parameter lets you specify an ID for the status bar similar to that for the dialog bar, and by default this ID is set to AFX_IDW_STATUS_BAR.

In the standard framework, you will see that the status bar is created under the toolbar in the frame's OnCreate() function with the following lines:

```
if (!m_wndStatusBar.Create(this) ||
    !m_wndStatusBar.SetIndicators(indicators,
    sizeof(indicators)/sizeof(UINT)))
{
    TRACE0("Failed to create status bar\n");
    return -1;        // fail to create
}
```

If the Create succeeds, the status bar's SetIndicators() function is called to initialize the indicator panes. You must pass this function a pointer to an array of UINT (unsigned integer) values as the first parameter, and a count of the indicators passed as the second parameter. The standard framework code as shown previously passes an array called indicators, and uses the sizeof() operator to determine the number of entries by dividing the overall size of the indicators array by the size of one element.

You can see the indicators array defined at the top of the MainFrm.cpp implementation module above the OnCreate() and frame window constructor functions. The default AppWizard-generated code for declaring the indicators array looks like this:

```
static UINT indicators[] =
{
    ID_SEPARATOR,             // status line indicator
    ID_INDICATOR_CAPS,
    ID_INDICATOR_NUM,
    ID_INDICATOR_SCRL,
};
```

The first entry, ID_SEPARATOR, specifies a separator that generates a normal (non-indented) part of the status bar. By default, the first entry in the array stretches to fill up the space left by the other indicators. Because this first entry is a separator, your application displays a blank piece of normal window stretched up to the other indicators. This normal pane is then used to display the menu option and toolbar button prompt text displayed when you move over a toolbar button or menu option.

The second entry, ID_INDICATOR_CAPS, is an AppWizard ID that is handled by the default framework to display the current status of the Caps Lock key. ID_INDICATOR_NUM and ID_INDICATOR_SCRL do

Enabling tooltips for a status bar

To support tooltips in a status bar, you must set the style flags of the underlying CStatusBarCtrl. This can be done by using CreateEx() of CStatusBar in place of Create(). The second parameter of CreateEx() is dwCtrlStyle to which you can pass the SBT_TOOLTIPS flag, which enables tooltips.

the same for the Num Lock and Scroll Lock keys. These AppWizard IDs can be found in the application's string table resource. Each entry has associated text (as shown in Figure 14.8) that is displayed in each indicator frame, if that frame is enabled. The panes themselves can be enabled or disabled by command UI handler functions, just like those for menus or toolbar buttons. When enabled, the associated text is displayed; when disabled, the text is hidden. The default framework automatically enables or disables these AppWizard-generated indicators to show the associated text (CAPS, NUM, or SCRL) whenever the Caps Lock, Num Lock, or Scroll Lock keys change state.

FIGURE 14.8

Highlighted string table entries show the AppWizard-generated status bar indicators.

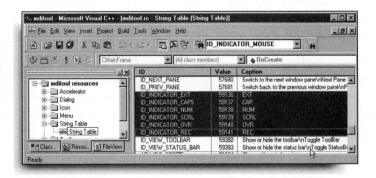

You can add, remove, or modify these default array entries to change the status bar's default indicators as discussed in the next section. When the `SetIndicators()` function is passed the `indicators` array, these values are used to change the appearance and functionality of the status bar. After the `Create()` and `SetIndicators()` functions have been called, the status bar will appear, docked to the bottom of the frame window by the default flag values in the `Create()` function.

SEE ALSO

➤ *For an explanation of string tables, see page 34*

Adding Indicators and Separators

To add your own custom indicators to the status bar, you must first add a unique ID as a string table entry. The text associated with the string table entry will be displayed in the status bar indicator when the indicator is enabled. The indicator can be enabled by passing TRUE to the CCmdUI object's Enable() function passed to a command UI function for the indicator. You can also change this text if required by calling the SetText() function of the associated CCmdUI object (like you can for a menu option).

Unfortunately, you can't use ClassWizard to create these command UI handler functions, so you must manually add the entries into the message map and declare and implement the function handler code yourself.

A working example to display the current mouse position in a status bar indicator can clarify this procedure and required entries. You could use AppWizard to generate a normal SDI framework (called StatusMouse in the sample code).

First you might use your string table entry for the new indicator, such as the ID_INDICATOR_MOUSE string entry (see Figure 14.9).

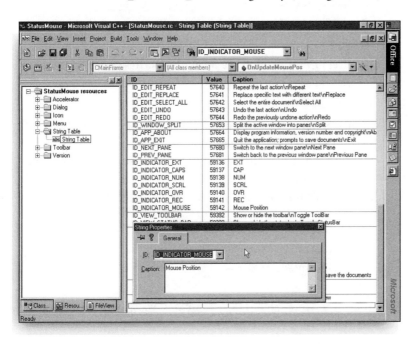

FIGURE 14.9
Adding a new string table entry for a mouse position.

Add a new string resource to a string table

1. Select the ResourceView pane to display the project resources.

2. Click the plus sign(s) to open the tree of resources until the appropriate String Table resource can be seen in the Resource View (refer to Figure 14.9).

3. Double-click the **String Table** entry to display the string table entries in the main editor window.

4. Scroll up or down the String Table list to find the appropriate string table section for your new string table entry.

5. Click the last string table entry for the specific section to select it, and then press Insert to start inserting a new string table entry. The String Properties dialog box should appear.

6. Enter the text for your new string table entry in the **C̲aption** box.

7. Click in the **I̲D** box of the String Properties dialog to change the IDS_STRING ID to your required custom ID.

8. Press Enter to close the String Properties dialog box. You should see your new string table entry appear in the list of string table entries.

After you have created a unique ID as a string resource (such as ID_INDICATOR_MOUSE), you can add it to the status bar array of indicators to appear after the initial prompt string separator like this:

```
static UINT indicators[] =
{
    ID_SEPARATOR,            // status line indicator
    ID_INDICATOR_MOUSE,
    ID_INDICATOR_CAPS,
...
```

Your new string table ID (ID_INDICATOR_MOUSE) will then identify the status bar indicator pane.

To add a command UI handler function for the new ID, you must first add a new frame window (to the MainFrm.cpp

module) message map entry to associate the ID with a handler
function like this:

```
ON_UPDATE_COMMAND_UI(ID_INDICATOR_MOUSE, OnUpdateMousePos)
```

This line associates the `ID_INDICATOR_MOUSE` ID with the
`OnUpdateMousePos()` handler function. You should place manually
edited message map entries after the ClassWizard-generated
entries (that is, after the closing `//}}AFX_MSG_MAP` comment). Your
UI handler function might then look like this:

```
void CMainFrame::OnUpdateMousePos(CCmdUI* pCmdUI)
{
    pCmdUI->Enable();
}
```

The `Enable()` function sets the default TRUE enable state, causing
the associated text to appear and resulting in a status bar with a
new indicator displaying the **Mouse Position** text (from the
string resource). If you wanted to merely turn this indicator on
or off, you could pass a Boolean member variable to the `Enable()`
function (like the "Enabling and Disabling Toolbar Buttons" section earlier in this chapter). Rather than graying the indicator
like a toolbar button or menu option UI handler might, the text
for a status bar indicator disappears when disabled.

Because the UI handler function has been manually added, you
must add a corresponding function declaration to the `CMainFrame`
class declaration (held in the MainFrm.h module). The corresponding declaration for the preceding sample handler would
look like this:

```
afx_msg void OnUpdateMousePos(CCmdUI* pCmdUI);
```

(The `afx_msg` prefix is used by the message map macros.)

The new indicator pane would then appear displaying the
Mouse Position text along with the original indicator panes (see
Figure 14.10).

FIGURE 14.10

A new status bar indicator showing the **Mouse Position** text.

(1) A new status bar indicator showing the **Mouse Position** text.

You can add ID_SEPARATOR entries to the indicator map to create separators between the individual panes. For example, if you were to add an ID_SEPARATOR to the indicators map after the new ID_INDICATOR_MOUSE entry:

```
ID_SEPARATOR,            // status line indicator
ID_INDICATOR_MOUSE,
ID_SEPARATOR,            // ** New Seperator
ID_INDICATOR_CAPS,
```

You would see a new indicator pane appear that separates the **Mouse Position** and **CAP** indicator panes (see Figure 14.11).

FIGURE 14.11

The effect of adding a new separator pane after the **Mouse Position** indicator.

(1) The new separator pane.

However, you would probably want to resize the new separator from its large initial default size, and change its appearance as discussed in the next section.

SEE ALSO

➤ *To learn more about user interface handler functions in menus, see page 301*

➤ *For an explanation of string tables, see page 34*

Dynamically Changing the Pane Size, Style, and Text

The CStatusBar class has several functions to let you change the size, style, and text contents of a status bar. These functions are SetPaneInfo(), SetPaneStyle(), and SetPaneText(), respectively. Each function identifies the specific pane by its zero-based index position in the indicators array (as passed to SetIndicators()).

It isn't always wise to use this index position directly because you might have to change lots of code when you insert a new indicator in the middle of your status bar (the existing index numbers will change). To help with this, a `CommandToIndex()` member function will return the index position of an indicator when you pass that indicator's ID as its only parameter.

For example, the following line will assign 1 to `nIndex` when the `CommandToIndex` function returns (when using the sample `indicators` array given earlier).

```
int nIndex =
        m_wndStatusBar.CommandToIndex(ID_INDICATOR_MOUSE);
```

You can then insert new items before the `ID_INDICATOR_MOUSE` entry, and the `nIndex` value will change to reflect the valid position of the required indicator that you can subsequently pass to the `SetPane...()` functions.

The `SetPaneText()` function takes the index position of the pane whose text you should change as the first parameter. The second parameter is a pointer to the new text for the pane, which can be held as a null-terminated string or `CString` object. The third (optional) parameter requires a Boolean value to indicate whether the pane should be invalidated to display the new text immediately (if passed the default `TRUE` value), or left until the window is next repainted (when `FALSE` is passed).

For example, you can code the following line to change the text of the indicator at the `nIndex` position:

```
m_wndStatusBar.SetPaneText(nIndex,"My New Pane Text");
```

A corresponding `GetPaneText()` function returns a `CString` variable, holding the current text of the pane specified by an index parameter.

You can change the style of the indicator pane by calling the `SetPaneStyle()` function and passing a style flag (from those in Table 14.5) as the second parameter, after identifying the index position as the first parameter.

For example, you can make the **Mouse Position** indicator appear popped out by coding the following lines:

```
int nIndex = CommandToIndex(ID_INDICATOR_MOUSE);
m_wndStatusBar. SetPaneStyle(nIndex, SBPS_POPOUT);
```

TABLE 14.5 Status bar style flags used to set the indicator pane style

Style Flag Value	Description
SBPS_NORMAL	A plain pressed-in style pane
SBPS_POPOUT	The pane should appear popped out rather than the usual pressed-in style
SBPS_DISABLED	Don't draw the indicator text
SBPS_STRETCH	Stretch the pane to fill spare status bar space (only one status bar pane can have this flag set)
SBPS_NOBORDERS	No 3D border should be drawn around the pane

A corresponding GetPaneStyle() function returns a UINT value holding the current style flags of the pane specified by an index parameter.

You can change the ID, style, and width of the pane all at once by calling the SetPaneInfo() function. As usual, the first parameter specifies the index position of the pane to be altered. You can pass an ID value to the second parameter to change the indicator's ID (or pass the same value to preserve it). The third parameter lets you pass any style flags shown in Table 14.5 to change the style. Finally, the fourth parameter lets you change the default width of the pane by passing an integer value specifying the new pixel width for the indicator pane (ignored if you have the SBPS_STRETCH style flag set for the pane).

For example, you can change the width of the **Mouse Position** indicator to 100 pixels by coding the following lines:

```
int nIndex = CommandToIndex(ID_INDICATOR_MOUSE);
m_wndStatusBar.SetPaneInfo(nIndex,ID_INDICATOR_MOUSE,
                    GetPaneStyle(), 100);
```

Notice that the GetPaneStyle() function is used to preserve the style passed as the third parameter of the SetPaneInfo() function.

Listing 14.2 brings these functions together in a frame window–based sample function that sets the **Mouse Position** indicator to a specified string value. The width of the pane is then adjusted to the width of the text, and the frame style is set to normal.

The text to update the status bar indicator with the current mouse position can be generated by a view-based function such as that shown in Listing 14.3. When built and run, the project will display the mouse position, updated as you move the mouse (see Figure 14.12).

LISTING 14.2   LST15_2.CPP—Dynamically Changing a Status Bar Indicator Pane's Text, Style, and Size

```
1    void CMainFrame::SetMousePosText(CString strText)
2    {
3        // ** Find the index position for ID_INDICATOR_MOUSE
4        int nIndex =
5         m_wndStatusBar.CommandToIndex(ID_INDICATOR_MOUSE);
6
7        // ** Set the pane text to the passed value
8        m_wndStatusBar.SetPaneText(nIndex,strText);
9
10       // ** Measure the width of the text
11       CWindowDC dc(&m_wndStatusBar);
12       CSize sizeText = dc.GetTextExtent(strText);  ———①
13
14       // ** Set the indicator's width to the text width
15       m_wndStatusBar.SetPaneInfo(nIndex,
16           ID_INDICATOR_MOUSE, SBPS_NORMAL, sizeText.cx);
17   }
```

① GetTextExtent() measures the width of the text so that the status bar pane can be adjusted accordingly.

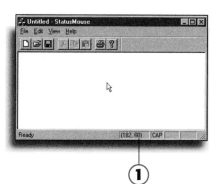

FIGURE 14.12

Displaying the current mouse position in a status bar indicator pane.

① The pane now shows the current mouse position.

Lines 4 and 5 of Listing 14.2 return the index position of the ID_INDICATOR_MOUSE indicator from the status bar's indicator array. This index is then used to set the pane set to the passed strText string on line 8.

Lines 11 and 12 measure the size of the displayed text using `GetTextExtent()`, which is then passed to the `SetPaneInfo()` function in line 15 to set the new pane width. The style is also set to `SBPS_NORMAL` and the ID preserved as `ID_INDICATOR_MOUSE` by this function call.

If you implement the code shown in this listing, you should also remember to add the relevant function declaration to the `CMainFrame` class definition with public access:

```
public:
    void SetMousePosText(CString strText);
```

LISTING 14.3   LST15_3.CPP—Creating a Text String to Show the Current Mouse Position for the Status Bar Indicator

① The mouse position is formatted as a (x,y) style coordinate for the status bar.

② When the mouse position has been formatted into a string, the status bar pane update function in Listing 14.2 is called.

```
1    #include "MainFrm.h"
2    void CStatusMouseView::OnMouseMove(UINT nFlags,
3                                          CPoint point)
4    {
5        // ** Setup a mouse position string
6        CString strMousePosition;
7        strMousePosition.Format("(%d, %d)", ────①
8                                      point.x,point.y);
9
10       // ** Get the SDI application frame window
11       CMainFrame* pMainFrame =
12                       (CMainFrame*)GetParentFrame();
13
14       // ** Set the indicator pane text
15       pMainFrame->SetMousePosText(strMousePosition); ────②
16
17       CView::OnMouseMove(nFlags, point);
18   }
```

Line 1 of Listing 14.3 includes the relevant class definition for `CMainFrame()`. The `OnMouseMove()` handler function called in response to mouse movements is passed a `point` variable that holds the new mouse cursor position. Line 7 formats this string into an (x, y) style text string `strMousePosition`, which is declared in line 6.

Lines 11 and 12 retrieve a pointer to the parent frame of the current view object. The new `SetMousePosText()` member function of the frame window (shown in Listing 14.2) can then be passed the new formatted `strMousePosition` string to update to the indicator pane.

If you implement this function, you should create the function and its related message map and class definition by using ClassWizard or the New Windows Message and Event Handlers dialog box.

SEE ALSO

➤ *For more details about handling mouse movement messages, see page 182*

➤ *For information about device contexts, see page 356*

Understanding Internet Explorer–Style Rebars

A *rebar* is one of the new IE4 common controls that works like a container for toolbars, dialog bars, and other controls. If you use Internet Explorer 4.0, you'll find a rebar control at the top that lets you slide toolbars, dialog bars, and combo boxes over each other. These sliding areas are called bands; a rebar control can have multiple bands shown as horizontal strips.

You can also set background bitmaps for rebars to display. Even though the user can slide the toolbars and dialog bars around within the rebar band, the displayed background bitmap remains unaltered.

The MFC provides a wrapper class for a docking rebar called `CReBar`, which inherits from `CControlbar` to provide the standard docking functionality. The `CReBarCtrl` class wraps the underlying rebar common control that implements the docking rebar. You can retrieve a `CReBarCtrl` object reference from a `CReBar` object by calling its `GetReBarCtrl()` member function.

Rebars are a large and complex subject; unfortunately, space here is too limited to offer more than a scant overview of their capabilities and the framework support for rebars.

SEE ALSO
➤ *To learn about using IE4 inside a view, see page 503*

What does rebar stand for?

A *rebar* is one of the controls that came into being with Internet Explorer 4. It simply stands for resizable toolbar. You may also see a rebar called a coolbar.

Using the AppWizard Framework Rebar

If you want to use a rebar control to group your toolbars and dialog bars, you can get AppWizard to generate a rebar control by picking the **Internet Explorer Rebars** toolbar look from the MFC AppWizard Step 4 dialog box (refer to Figure 14.1). AppWizard will then add a CReBar object called m_wndReBar to your CMainFrame class definition, and generate the following code in your frame window's OnCreate() function to create and initialize the rebar:

```
if (!m_wndReBar.Create(this) ¦¦
    !m_wndReBar.AddBar(&m_wndToolBar) ¦¦
    !m_wndReBar.AddBar(&m_wndDlgBar))
{
    TRACE0("Failed to create rebar\n");
    return -1;      // fail to create
}
```

The CReBar Create() function takes four parameters. The first is a mandatory pointer to the parent window. You can pass a set of style flags (see Table 14.6) to the second parameter to specify the rebar control style; this parameter defaults to RBS_BANDBORDERS to draw borders around the bands. The third parameter specifies the window and docking style for the rebar; this defaults to the WS_CHILD, WS_VISIBLE, WS_CLIPSIBLINGS, and CBRS_TOP flags so that a top-docked visible child window is created that clips the contained toolbars and dialog bars to the area of the rebar. The last parameter specifies an ID for the rebar, which defaults to AFX_IDW_REBAR.

TABLE 14.6 Style flags for rebars

Flag Value	Description
RBS_AUTOSIZE	The layout of each band is automatically adjusted when the rebar size or position changes.
RBS_BANDBORDERS	Draws separating borders between the bands.
RBS_FIXEDORDER	Maintains the same ordering of bands.

Flag Value	Description
RBS_VARHEIGHT	Normally the bands are all shown as the same height as the tallest band; by passing this flag, each band is shown just as tall as required by the controls or tool-bars it contains.
RBS_VERTICALGRIPPER	The sizing gripper bar is displayed vertically rather than horizontally when in a vertical rebar.
RBS_DBLCLKTOGGGLE	Maximizes or minimizes a rebar band only when the user double-clicks a band (rather than the default single click).
RBS_REGISTERDROP	Allows OLE drag-and-drop notification via an RBN_GETOBJECT message.

Notice that after creating the rebar, the standard toolbar and an AppWizard-generated dialog bar are added to the rebar by calling its AddBar() function. The normal toolbar docking calls are omitted, and the rebar assumes responsibility for docking and displaying both control bars within its own bounds, as shown in Figure 14.13.

FIGURE 14.13
An AppWizard-generated standard Rebar application.

You can customize the toolbar and dialog bar as shown in the earlier sections in this chapter. Additional control bars can be added with the AddBar() function.

SEE ALSO

➤ For more details about using AppWizard to build an SDI framework, see page 267
➤ To learn about clipping, see page 363

Rebar embedded controls and dialog bar messages

Messages sent from the rebar's embedded controls and dialog bars will be sent to your parent frame window. You can then add handler functions for these controls in your frame window, view, or document classes as you did for dialog bar controls.

Setting a Title and Background Bitmap for the Rebar

The CReBar object's AddBar() function needs only one mandatory parameter, which is a pointer to the control or toolbar to add. The second optional parameter lets you add some text to the rebar by passing a pointer to a null-terminated string, or left blank passing a NULL pointer (the default setting is blank). You can also set a background bitmap by passing a CBitmap pointer to a valid loaded bitmap as the third parameter.

For example, the following lines add some text to the toolbar and a background bitmap for both bars added to the rebar:

```
static CBitmap myBitmap;
myBitmap.LoadBitmap(IDB_MYREBAR_BM);
if (!m_wndReBar.Create(this) ||
  !m_wndReBar.AddBar(&m_wndToolBar,"My Toolbar",&myBitmap)||
  !m_wndReBar.AddBar(&m_wndDlgBar,NULL,&myBitmap))
```

Notice on the first line that the myBitmap object is declared as static so that it remains in memory after the OnCreate() function has returned. You could use a member variable instead, but must keep the bitmap valid for the duration of the rebar.

The second line loads the IDB_MYREBAR_BM bitmap resource. You can create these resources using the bitmap resource editor. The AddBar() functions for both the dialog bar and toolbar are passed a pointer to the CBitmap object as their third parameter.

When the m_wndToolBar object is added in the fourth line, some text is passed as the second parameter to set the rebar text. When the application is run, the text is displayed on the same band to the left of the toolbar itself. The dialog bar has no associated text because a NULL value is passed to its second parameter.

SEE ALSO

➤ *To learn about creating and using bitmaps, see page 245*

chapter

15

Understanding Drawing in Device Contexts

Understanding the different types of
device contexts and when to use them

Using and setting the drawing modes
and device capabilities

Using mapping modes to draw
antonyms from the thesaurus

Introduction to Device Contexts

Device context structures

Fundamentally, a device context is a Windows structure that holds attributes that describe the default drawing settings used in any graphical operation such as drawing a line. Unlike most other Windows structures, an application program can never directly access the device context structure, it can only change the settings via a set of standard access functions.

Don't be put off by the name *device context*. It is one of those ugly technical-sounding names that really disguises a simple idea and a central part of Windows. What would Windows look like if you took out the device contexts? It wouldn't look like anything. A device context provides the canvas on which all the dots, lines, squares, fonts, colors, and everything you see is drawn. The "device" in *device context* means that you can draw on a screen, printer, plotter, virtual reality headset, or any other possible two-dimensional display device without much specific knowledge of what device, make, or model you are using.

One of the best things Microsoft did for the software industry was to standardize all the different drawings and device supports into the Windows operating system. Since then the industry has rocketed, and graphical applications abound. This is probably the major—and most under-appreciated—effect of Windows.

I can now drive to my local PC store, buy the latest XYZ printer, install only one Windows driver that the manufacturer provides, and every bit of Windows software I own will print on that printer without a second thought. Device context is what glues them all together and provides all this drawing support.

Windows graphics DLLs

All the operating system code for performing graphical operations is implemented by the interaction between two DLLs. The first is always GDI.DLL, which "faces" the application program to provide the device independent set of drawing functions. The second DLL is the device dependent DLL, which can be specific to the screen, printer or plotter being used. For example, when drawing to a normal VGA monitor, VGA.DLL is used to provide the device facing implementation code for the drawing functions.

SEE ALSO

➤ *For drawing in device contexts, see page 390*
➤ *To use printer device contexts, see page 568*

Types of Device Contexts

There is a bulk standard device context, then there are device contexts for special occasions and particular jobs. Device contexts themselves are GDI (graphics device interface) objects. The *GDI* is a set of functions that live in a DLL at the heart of Windows. These functions provide the link between your drawing function calls and the device drivers that talk to the hardware to make them real blobs of light or ink.

Microsoft Foundation Classes (MFC) provides wrappers for the device contexts that simplify our interaction with the underlying GDI objects. The bulk standard device context wrapper is the CDC class. This class provides an enormous number of drawing, coordinate mapping, and clipping functions to implement your graphical display. All other, more specialized, device context classes are based on and extend this class. The following section explains each of these classes in a little more detail.

Using the *CDC* Class

The device context class that you use will always use the CDC as a base class. This class holds two handles relating to the underlying GDI object: the m_hDC handle and the m_hAttribDC handle. The m_hDC is the device context handle that links the class to the GDI object to handle all the output from the drawing functions. The m_hAttribDC is the device context handle that links all the attribute information, such as colors and drawing modes. You don't have to worry too much about these member attributes, but bear in mind that when you use functions such as GetDC() and ReleaseDC() (which get and release a device context from a window), these GDI handles are being attached and detached from your CDC class.

> **CDC drawing functions**
>
> The CDC class implements all the drawing functions available in Windows. Each of these implementations merely calls the corresponding low-level Win32 drawing functions (in GDI.DLL) passing the CDC object's embedded device context handles (m_hDC and m_hAttribDC).

The capability of the CDC class to attach and draw in a device context can be demonstrated with a very simple program. Every window has a device context that covers the entire window; this includes the desktop window that covers the entire screen. Up to now you've seen applications that behave quite responsibly; to show you the power and ease of device contexts, I'll be reckless and grab the desktop device context (DC) and draw straight at it. The only harm this can cause is to temporarily trash the Windows display, which can be refreshed when I exit the program.

By following the next set of steps you can create a device-context grabbing dialog-based application.

The AppWizard-generated ReadMe.txt file

AppWizard generates a ReadMe.txt file in the same directory as your new project. This text file explains each of the source modules that were created and their purpose in the overall application.

Creating a device-context grabbing dialog-based application

1. Click the **File** menu and select **New**.

2. In the New dialog box, select the **Projects** tab to display the different types of project.

3. Select **MFC AppWizard** and enter DCDraw as the **Project Name**.

4. Click **OK** to show the MFC AppWizard – Step 1 dialog box.

5. Select a **Dialog Based Application** from the application types.

6. Click the **Finish** button to show the skeleton project specifications.

7. Click **OK** and AppWizard will generate your project files.

You should now have a skeleton dialog-based application. Let's add a simple button and click handler to implement our device context grabbing code.

Creating a button

1. Click the ResourceView pane of the Project Workspace view.

2. Click the plus sign to open the DCDraw resources.

3. Click the plus sign next to Dialog to view the dialog box template resources.

4. Double-click **IDD_DCDRAW_DIALOG** to edit the main application dialog box.

5. Click **TODO: Place Dialog Controls Here** in the main dialog template and press Delete to remove it.

6. Select a button from the **Controls** palette, drop it on the dialog box, and stretch it out to make it fairly large in size.

7. Press Alt+Enter together to change the Push Button Properties and change the **Caption** to Draw!.

8. Change the button **ID** to IDC_DRAWIT.

9. Press Enter to close the Push Button Properties dialog box.

Now you should have a button on the dialog box, so you can add a handler to handle the clicked event.

Adding a *BN_CLICKED* handler with ClassWizard

1. Click on your new dialog button (**Draw!** in the example) to highlight it.

2. Press Ctrl+W to start the MFC ClassWizard.

3. You should see the MFC ClassWizard Message Maps page. The new **IDC_DRAWIT** button should be selected. If it isn't, select this ID from the **Object <u>I</u>D** list.

4. Double-click the **BN_CLICKED** message in the **<u>Messages</u>** list to add a new handler function.

5. Click **OK** on the Add Member Function dialog box to add the default OnDrawit name of the handler function.

6. Click the **<u>E</u>dit Code** button to start editing the button-click handler code.

Now you can implement device context grabbing and drawing code in the button-click handler as shown in Listing 15.1.

> **Shortcut for adding a**
> BN_CLICKED **handler**
>
> An easier way to add the button-clicked handler is to simply double-click the control you want to add the handler for from the resource editor. This adds the same message map and handler function code, but bypasses the ClassWizard steps, taking you straight to step 5 and then to the code itself.

LISTING 15.1   LST16_1.CPP—Drawing with the Desktop Device Context

```
1   void CDCDrawDlg::OnDrawit()
2   {
3       // TODO: Add your control notification handler code
4
5       // ** Get a pointer to the desktop window
6       CWnd* pDeskTop = GetDesktopWindow();         ①
7
8       // ** Get a pointer to it's device context
9       CDC* pDC = pDeskTop->GetWindowDC();          ②
10
11      // ** loop through 300 pixels horizontally
12      for(int x=0;x<300;x++)
13      {
14          // ** loop through 300 pixels vertically
15          for(int y=0;y<300;y++)
16          {
17              // ** set each pixel to a different color
18              pDC->SetPixel(x,y,x*y);              ③
19          }
20      }
21      pDeskTop->ReleaseDC(pDC);
22  }
```

① This line finds the desktop (or whole screen) window.

② This line finds the main device context for the desktop window.

③ Each pixel in the rectangle is set to a color calculated from the coordinates.

Moiré fringes

A moiré fringe is an interference pattern caused by two similar overlaid templates with transparent sections. This was originally observed in the very fine moiré watered silk fabric, hence its name. You can see a similar effect in net curtains where one layer of fabric is slightly rotated from the other. A similar interference pattern is used as the basis of holography.

In this listing I've obtained a pointer to the Main Windows desktop window using the GetDesktopWindow() function in line 6. From this CWnd pointer, I can grab its main window device context using the GetWindowDC() function as shown in line 9. Lines 12 through 20 are responsible for the arty image shown in Figure 15.1. Lines 9 through 12 iterate through 300 pixels across and 300 pixels down in the two x and y for loops. For each pixel where the SetPixel() function is called, the first two parameters specify the horizontal and vertical pixels (with 0,0 at the top left). The third parameter is the color expressed as a color reference (discussed in detail in Chapter 16, "Using Pens and Brushes"). The color is set to the cofactor of the x and y coordinates, which yields the surprisingly lovely, colored *moiré fringe* effect. Finally, you must release the device context using the ReleaseDC() function as shown in line 21.

FIGURE 15.1

Grabbing and drawing with the desktop device context.

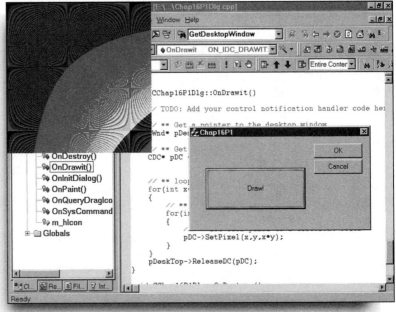

Because DCDraw is so reckless and draws straight into the desktop like this, you must make reparations and clean up. You can catch the WM_DESTROY Windows message with the OnDestroy() handler. The OnDestroy() handler is called when the dialog box is destroyed; this is a good place to put the cleanup code.

Adding a handler for the *WM_DESTROY* message

1. Select the ClassView pane of the Project Workspace view.

2. Open the list of DCDraw classes by clicking the plus sign.

3. Right-click the CDCDrawDlg class to display the pop-up context menu.

4. Select the menu option **Add Windows Message Handler**.

5. Select the WM_DESTROY message from the list of **New Windows Messages/Events**.

6. Click the **Add and Edit** button to add this handler to the CDCDrawDlg class and start editing the implementation.

Now you can add the cleanup code to the OnDestroy() handler. To do this, tell the desktop window to redraw itself and ask it to tell all its child windows (your applications) to redraw. The code to do this is shown in Listing 15.2. In line 8, the RedrawWindow() member function of the desktop window (which is found by calling GetDesktopWindow()) forces a desktop redraw. RedrawWindow() is passed three parameters; the first two are the rectangle and region to be redrawn. By passing NULL for both, RedrawWindow() assumes correctly that you want to redraw the whole area. The third parameter is a set of flag settings: RDW_ERASE (to erase everything) is passed, along with RDW_INVALIDATE (to tell it to redraw afterward), RDW_ALLCHILDREN (to make all the child applications redraw) and RDW_ERASENOW (to do it right away).

LISTING 15.2   LST16_2.CPP—Redrawing the Desktop and all Application Windows with *RedrawWindow()*

```
1   void CDCDrawDlg::OnDestroy()
2   {
3       CDialog::OnDestroy();
4
5       // TODO: Add your message handler code here
6
7       // ** Redraw the desktop and all child windows
8       GetDesktopWindow()->RedrawWindow(NULL,NULL,      (1)
9           RDW_ERASE+RDW_INVALIDATE+
10          RDW_ALLCHILDREN+RDW_ERASENOW);
11  }
```

(1) Force the whole Windows desktop and all the application windows to redraw themselves.

If you build and run this program after adding these changes, you should get a rectangle of color as shown in Figure 16.1. Of course there are an awful lot of drawing functions in the device context class, all more sophisticated than SetPixel(). However, these are too complex and numerous to mention here and are covered in depth in Chapter 16, "Using Pens and Brushes" and Chapter 17, "Using Fonts."

SEE ALSO

➤ *To draw with pens and brushes, see page 390*

➤ *To write text into a device context, see page 418*

Using Client Device Contexts

Accessing the client DC associated window handle

You might need to access the window associated with a client device context. The CClientDC class stores the handle of the associated window in its m_hWnd member variable. You can pass the m_hWnd, window handle (HWND) to the Attach() function of a CWnd object to access the associated window functions.

The CClientDC class automates the GetDC() and ReleaseDC() for you. When you construct a CClientDC object you pass a window pointer as a parameter and the class will then use this pointer to attach to the window's device context for you. When the class is destroyed it automatically calls the ReleaseDC() for you, so you never have to worry about it. Client refers to the normal drawing area of the window; there is a corresponding class CWindowDC that gives you access to the title bar and borders of the window as well, but this is rarely used because most well-behaved applications will draw only in their client areas.

You can change your sample project to use a CClientDC object rather than a CDC pointer. If you double-click the OnDrawit() function in the ClassView pane of the Project Workspace view, you can make the editor jump straight back to the button-handler code.

Make the changes to your OnDrawit() function as shown in Listing 15.3. Instead of using the desktop window, you will just draw over the dialog box device context. To do this, the CClientDC object dlgDC is passed the this pointer (a pointer to its holding class) to the dialog box itself. Because the dialog box is a form of CWnd, this is fine and the dlgDC object now contains a handle to the dialog box's own device context. You can do the usual drawing in lines 9 through 17 with one slight difference; in line 15, `dlgDC` uses an object call rather than a pointer call to `SetPixel()`. Finally, notice that no `ReleaseDC()` is called at the end of the `OnDrawit()` function; instead, the device context handle will be automatically released by the destructor of `CClientDC` when the `dlgDC` object is destroyed at the end of the function.

LISTING 15.3 LST16_3.CPP—Using a *CClientDC* class to Grab the Dialog Box Device Context

```
1   void CDCDrawDlg::OnDrawit()
2   {
3       // TODO: Add your control notification handler code
4
5       // ** Construct a client DC from the dialog window
6       CClientDC dlgDC(this);  ————①
7
8       // loop through 300 pixels horizontally
9       for(int x=0;x<300;x++)
10      {
11          // loop through 300 pixels vertically
12          for(int y=0;y<300;y++)
13          {
14              // ** set each pixel to a different color
15              dlgDC.SetPixel(x,y,x*y);
16          }
17      }
18  }
```

① Construct a device context to use the proper client area of the dialog box.

If you build and run the application again after making these changes, you should see that only the dialog box device context is drawn on when you press the **DrawIt** button, as shown in Figure 15.2.

Using Paint Device Contexts

The `CPaintDC` class is a special device context wrapper that helps handle the `WM_PAINT` message from Windows. The `WM_PAINT` message is sent to windows when part or all of them have been uncovered by another window; it tells your application that it should repaint the uncovered region.

Forcing a window to repaint

Normally `WM_PAINT` messages are sent only when a specific area of a window needs updating. However, you can use the `CWnd` class's `RedrawWindow()` function to force a `WM_PAINT` message to be sent to the window. The parameters to this function let you specify a specific area to repaint, and whether the window's background should also be erased.

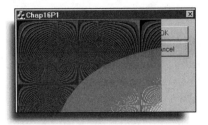

FIGURE 15.2

Capturing the dialog box's device context with `CClientDC`.

Instead of repainting the entire window every time a small portion is uncovered, Windows passes you a rectangle with the coordinates of the uncovered bit. You can then use this information to redraw only the affected portion and not waste valuable processor time drawing things that the user can't see anyway. You don't have to notice this rectangle; if you try to draw outside the changed area nothing will happen because the device context is also set up to clip your drawing area to the rectangle. However, relying on this clipping isn't wise because all your drawing code will still be executed and hence slow down everything. Sometimes this is unavoidable—when you are drawing complex text and line diagrams it's too hard to work out where to cut off the text or lines. You can let Windows take care of the *clipping*. My pixel drawing is the kind of drawing where you can use the paint information.

You can convert the test program to draw from the `OnPaint()` handler whenever a paint message is sent and to draw only the uncovered region. Double-click the `OnPaint()` function in the ClassView pane of the Project Workspace view. This takes you straight to the `OnPaint()` handler function. Notice that you didn't have to create this with the ClassWizard; the AppWizard put this code in automatically when it created the application framework. The entire `OnPaint()` function is shown in Listing 15.4. Line 24 is the line you need to add to call your `OnDrawit()` function.

Other interesting things created by AppWizard are shown in this listing. `IsIconic()` is called on line 3 and returns TRUE if your window is minimized (that is, just sitting on the taskbar). If this is the case, the application icon is drawn in the middle of the minimized window rectangle at line 18. You can use the FALSE case of `IsIconic()` to implement your `OnPaint()` code, and at line 24 call your `OnDrawit()` function.

LISTING 15.4 LST16_4.CPP—Modifying the *OnPaint()* Handler for the Dialog-Based Application

```
1   void CDCDrawDlg::OnPaint()
2   {
3       if (IsIconic())
4       {
5           CPaintDC dc(this); // device context for painting
6
7           SendMessage(WM_ICONERASEBKGND,
            ➥(WPARAM) dc.GetSafeHdc(), 0);
8
9           // Center icon in client rectangle
10          int cxIcon = GetSystemMetrics(SM_CXICON);
11          int cyIcon = GetSystemMetrics(SM_CYICON);
12          CRect rect;
13          GetClientRect(&rect);
14          int x = (rect.Width() - cxIcon + 1) / 2;
15          int y = (rect.Height() - cyIcon + 1) / 2;
16
17          // Draw the icon
18          dc.DrawIcon(x, y, m_hIcon);
19
20      }
21      else
22      {
23          // ** Call our drawing function
24          OnDrawit();
25      }
26  }
```

① Erases the background of the minimized icon window.

② Draws the icon in the middle of the minimized window.

③ The additional line, used to call the fancy color-filling function.

Now make the changes to the `OnDrawit()` function to use the `CPaintDC`. These changes are shown in Listing 15.5. Notice that at line 6 a `CPaintDC` class is used to construct the `paintDC` object from the dialog window. This works properly only when the window is responding to the `WM_PAINT` message. In this case, you call this function from the `OnPaint()` handler so it's okay. Because this is still the button-handler code, you will still be able to call this code by clicking the **DrawIt** button, but now nothing will happen because the window will not have any invalid areas—it will be totally clipped from the drawing.

The next change is at line 9 where a RECT pointer is declared and set to the address of the *rcPaint* rectangle in the *m_ps* member of the *paintDC* object. This rectangle holds the area to be repainted and is used in lines 12 and 15 so that only the invalid rectangle is iterated through by the loops. This will speed the drawing up significantly when only a small portion of the window needs repainting. SetPixel() becomes quite slow when called lots of times; the original 300×300 pixel area calls SetPixel() 90,000 times! If the uncovered region is only 50×30 pixels, you'll need to call SetPixel() only 1,500 times, which should update the window 60 times faster—well worth doing.

Notice one other change: SetPixel() is now called from the paintDC object in line 18. SetPixel() is implemented in the CDC class, so all the drawing functions are still available from any of these specialist-derived device context classes.

① Note that this time only the paint rectangle is used to draw in.

LISTING 15.5 LST16_5.CPP—Using the *CPaintDC* Class to Handle *WM_PAINT* Requests

```
1   void CDCDrawDlg::OnDrawit()
2   {
3       // TODO: Add your control notification handler code
4
5       // ** Construct a paint DC from the dialog window
6       CPaintDC paintDC(this);
7
8       // ** Make a short cut pointer to the rectangle
9       RECT* pRect = &paintDC.m_ps.rcPaint;     ──①
10
11      // ** loop through the horizontal paint rectangle
12      for(int x=pRect->left; x < pRect->right ;x++)
13      {
14          // ** loop through the vertical rectangle
15          for(int y=pRect->top; y < pRect->bottom ;y++)
16          {
17              // ** set each pixel to a different color
```

```
18          paintDC.SetPixel(x,y,x*y);
19       }
20    }
21  }
```

Build and run the application after making these changes and we'll examine the behavior of the paint device context. First you should see the dialog box with the colored background but with the buttons visible; when the window first appears, a WM_PAINT message is sent to completely draw the window and then the buttons are drawn on top obscuring the painted area underneath. To see the paint message in action, cover half the dialog box with another window (the Windows Calculator will do). You can start the Calculator from the main **Start** button; select **P**rograms, **A**ccessories and from there select the **Calculator**. The arrangement is shown in Figure 15.3.

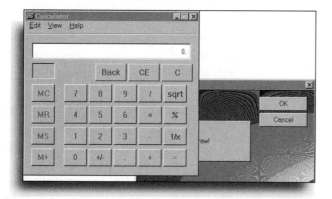

FIGURE 15.3
Experimenting with the WM_PAINT message by uncovering windows.

When you've positioned the calculator halfway over the DCDraw dialog box, click the dialog box so that it comes to the front. You'll see that the newly uncovered portion is redrawn. It takes quite a while to redraw—half a second on my old P166. Now reselect the calculator and drag it slightly up and left. Let go and the uncovered area of the dialog box should be redrawn a bit quicker. If you keep doing this, you'll notice that the dialog box is redrawn faster and faster. With only a small portion of the top left of the dialog box covered by the calculator, reselect the dialog box and watch how long it takes to refresh—much quicker. This is because the uncovered portion is quite small and because we are only refreshing that invalid rectangle. Fewer SetPixel() calls are required, so the whole thing is drawn much faster. You can move these two windows across each other and get a feel for the effect of the paint message. All Windows applications must respond to this message, although quite often it is tucked away inside a control or view class so you won't have to worry about it.

You might remember the m_ps member of the CPaintDC class. This is a PAINTSTRUCT structure that holds the rcPaint rectangle you used to determine the area to be repainted. There are some other useful members too.

The PAINTSTRUCT structure is defined as the following:

```
typedef struct tagPAINTSTRUCT {
    HDC  hdc;
    BOOL fErase;
    RECT rcPaint;
    BOOL fRestore;
    BOOL fIncUpdate;
    BYTE rgbReserved[16];
} PAINTSTRUCT;
```

The hdc member is the handle of the underlying GDI device context. There is an fErase flag, which Windows sets TRUE if you should erase the background before drawing. You saw the rcPaint member used to get an invalid rectangle to repaint in Listing 15.5. The last three members are declared as *reserved* by Windows in the Microsoft documentation, so it is probably best not to fiddle with them.

Handling the WM_ERASEBKGND message

Another way you can determine whether the background needs erasing is to add a handler function for the Windows WM_ERASEBKGND message. Your new handler function OnEraseBkGnd() will then be called whenever the background needs erasing. A pointer to the relevant device context object (a CDC object) is passed into the OnEraseBkGnd() handler function as the first parameter.

You might be wondering where all this information comes from when it is passed to your CPaintDC object. The answer is a function called BeginPaint() in the CWnd class. Remember that the CDialog class is derived like most other controls and viewed from CWnd. Therefore all the basic window functionality is available to these derived classes, and they all use BeginPaint() to set up this PAINTSTRUCT when you declare a CPaintDC object. When your CPaintDC object is destroyed, a corresponding function EndPaint() in CWnd is called to tell Windows that you've dealt with the WM_PAINT message and performed your task of redrawing the damaged region of your window.

Using Memory Device Contexts

A *memory device context* is a device context without an associated device. You might think this is strange at first, but it is actually very useful. Typically you would use one of these in conjunction with a normal device context to copy and paste image areas around the screen. You can create a memory device context that is compatible with a display device context. Then you can copy images into memory when they are not being displayed, and back on to the real device context to display them.

There isn't an MFC wrapper class for a memory device context; you don't need one because CDC will do just fine. Because it is a normal CDC device context class, you can use it to draw with as usual; the only difference is that you are drawing in memory, so the user won't see it unless you copy it back into a displayed window device context.

You can create a memory-compatible device context and change your drawing code to draw in memory rather than onscreen. After you've drawn the image in memory, you can use the BitBlt() function to copy it back onto the display. The modifications shown in Listing 15.6 are fairly extensive because you should not only create a memory device context, but also a bitmap for the memory device context. Unlike display device contexts, which are linked to windows, the memory device context doesn't automatically have a screen-compatible bitmap.

The paint device context has been changed back to a client device context and the memory device context declared at line 9 of Listing 15.6 to the memDC object. The CreateCompatibleDC() member of the device context is called at line 10. This function is passed the clientDC object, which it uses as a guide to create the size and other device context attributes to make the memory device context compatible with the screen window.

At line 17 a bitmap is declared and will be used as a memory device context for drawing. This bitmap is created using the

> **Bitmap sizes in memory device contexts**
>
> A bitmap in a memory device context can be much smaller or larger than an associated screen device context. By creating a large bitmap, you could create a drawing surface with a much higher resolution than the standard screen. However, you must bear in mind that the larger the bitmap, the more system memory is used. If the bitmap consumes more than the available RAM, your machine will slow considerably as virtual memory is used to compensate for the lack of RAM. Virtual memory is slow because large sections of memory called pages are continuously swapped between RAM and disk.

`CreateCompatibleBitmap()` member function in line 18. The `clientDC` is passed to show `CreateCompatibleBitmap()` the kind of device context it'll be using the bitmap with; it uses this as a reference to see how many colors the bitmap should support. The width and height of the client rectangle found in line 14 are passed as parameters to specify the required bitmap size. In line 22 the bitmap is inserted into the device context using the `SelectObject()` member function. Any drawing in the memory device context will now use this supplied bitmap.

You can then draw the arty background as normal; however, it is now drawn in memory rather than straight out to the screen. In line 36, `BitBlt()` is used to copy the bitmap back into the screen device context. `BitBlt()` is an image-copying function and gets its rather ugly name from an old hardware term called *bit blitting* that describes a chip circuit capable of quickly copying memory from one place to another. In some rare cases, you might have a video card that does exactly this when you call this function, but usually the CPU will do the copying. `BitBlt()` copies from `memDC` into `clientDC` when you pass the width, height, and starting offsets to copy from and to as parameters.

An interesting parameter to this function is the `SRCINVERT` flag, which tells `BitBlt()` that the copied image should be color inverted. This produces a different set of colors in the destination window that will prove that you really are drawing in memory and copying the image into the dialog box's device context. You can change this flag to `SRCCOPY` if you want an unadulterated copy of the memory device context image.

Make these changes as shown in Listing 15.6, and remove the `OnDrawit()` call from the `OnPaint()` handler (otherwise you'll get some very strange effects); then build and run. When you click the **DrawIt** button, you'll notice a short delay while the pixel image is being drawn in memory. Then the color-inverted image is copied over the dialog box device context.

Using compatible memory device contexts with bit blitting

If you want to copy colored sections of the screen to or from memory device contexts, you must always create and select a bitmap compatible with a real onscreen device context.

LISTING 15.6 LST16_6.CPP—Drawing in a Memory Device Context

```
1   void CDCDrawDlg::OnDrawit()
2   {
3       // TODO: Add your control notification handler code
4
5       // ** Construct a paint DC from the dialog window
6       CClientDC clientDC(this);
7
8       // ** Create a compatible memory device context
9       CDC memDC;
10      memDC.CreateCompatibleDC(&clientDC);
11
12      // ** Find the Client Rect
13      CRect rcClient;
14      GetClientRect(&rcClient);
15
16      // ** Create a compatible bitmaps
17      CBitmap memBitmap;
18      memBitmap.CreateCompatibleBitmap(&clientDC,
19          rcClient.Width(),rcClient.Height());
20
21      // ** Select it into our memory device context
22      memDC.SelectObject(&memBitmap);
23
24      // ** loop through the horizontal client rectangle
25      for(int x=0; x < rcClient.Width() ;x++)
26      {
27          // ** loop through the vertical client rectangle
28          for(int y=0; y < rcClient.Height() ;y++)
29          {
30              // ** set each pixel to a different color
31              memDC.SetPixel(x,y,x*y);
32          }
33      }
34
35      // ** Copy the memory image back to the client
36      ➥// device context
36      clientDC.BitBlt(0,0,
37          rcClient.Width(), rcClient.Height(),
38          &memDC,0,0,SRCINVERT);
39  }
```

① A memory device context is created to be compatible with an onscreen device context.

② The bitmap must also be compatible with the capabilities of the onscreen device context.

③ The drawing is all done in memory; nothing is at this point.

④ Finally the whole image is copied to the screen for the user to see.

Using Mapping Modes

Mapping modes are another very useful tool provided by device contexts. A mapping mode basically means that you can draw to the screen or printer in units like inches or millimeters rather than pixels and get a pretty reasonable scale representation.

When you use mapping modes you'll see terms like *logical units* and *device units*. Put simply, a device unit is a pixel, or the smallest indivisible unit a device is capable of representing. A logical unit can be an imperial, metric, or font-related measurement.

By default the device context uses a mapping mode called MM_TEXT. This strange name just means that one logical unit equals one device unit, so there is no conversion and all the coordinates you specify to a drawing command will be represented using that many pixels. There are several mapping modes, as shown in Table 15.1.

Coordinate spaces and the vertical axis

All the device context drawing functions need parameters that specify a position in the overall coordinate space. The coordinate space is a two-dimensional surface with two perpendicular axes based on Cartesian geometry. Each point has a vertical and horizontal component passed as individual parameters to the drawing functions.

When the MM_TEXT mapping mode is used, lower vertical values will be placed at the top of the screen and lower horizontal values are placed to the left. However, the other mapping modes place lower vertical values at the bottom of the screen while lower horizontal values are still placed to the left.

TABLE 15.1 Supported mapping modes

Mapping Flag	One Logical Unit Is Equivalent To
MM_TEXT	One pixel
MM_LOMETRIC	0.1 of a millimeter
MM_HIMETRIC	0.01 of a millimeter
MM_LOENGLISH	0.01 of an inch
MM_HIENGLISH	0.001 of an inch
MM_TWIPS	1/1440 of an inch or 1/20 of a point (as used in fonts)
MM_ISOTROPIC	User-defined value, but always equal in X and Y
MM_ANISOTROPIC	User-defined value

These mapping modes are set by a device context function, SetMapMode(), which simply takes one of these flags. After being set, the coordinates you pass in any drawing functions are converted to device units (or pixels) by the GDI's internal mapping for each mode. So if you have the mapping mode set to MM_LOMETRIC and pass a value of 100 to a drawing function, the mapping mode will know you want 100×0.1 of a millimeter, which is 1 centimeter. It will then calculate how many pixels the screen or printer can display in one centimeter and use that conversion.

The `MM_ISOTROPIC` and `MM_ANISOTROPIC` allow you to set these scales using the `SetWindowExt()` and `SetViewPortExt()` functions to describe the scaling. There are also `SetWindowOrg()` and `SetViewPortOrg()` functions to change the origin (or 0,0) coordinate. Another thing to remember is that all the mapping modes except `MM_TEXT` treat the y coordinate as up. This can be very confusing when you are used to dealing with pixel coordinates and can end up with things being drawn upside down or off the top of the screen. Negative coordinates are quite common, especially when you change the window origin.

You can put some of this knowledge to use in a small sample program using the view of an SDI application. Create an SDI application by following the steps to Create an SDI Application shown in Chapter 12, "Using Documents, Views, and Frames." You should accept all the default settings except the step 1 option for an SDI application, and name the project MapMode.

The `MapMode` view class has an `OnDraw()` member function that you would normally use to implement your drawing code. To get to the `OnDraw()` function follow the steps listed in the next step by step.

Finding and editing the view's *OnDraw()*

1. Select the ClassView pane of the Project Workspace view.
2. Click the plus sign to open the view of project classes.
3. Click the plus sign next to the `MapModeView` class to see the views.
4. Double-click the `OnDraw()` function of the view class to start editing.

You can add the new lines to the `OnDraw()` function as shown in Listing 15.7. First, you might notice that on line 9 the mapping mode is set to `MM_LOMETRIC`, which means each coordinate is 0.1mm. In line 10, the client rectangle is sought with `GetClientRect()`. No matter what the mapping mode, this always gives you pixel (or device) coordinates, so in line 16 you can use the device context function `DPtoLP()` to convert them into logical coordinates.

DPtoLP() stands for Device Points to Logical Points and can convert CPoint objects or CRect objects when passed as pointers. There's a reverse LPtoDP() function that converts logical points into device points. In the loop on lines 19–21, the x variable is looped from the left to the right of the client rectangle after being converted to logical points. The loop skips every 100 logical units, which should be every centimeter in MM_LOMETRIC mapping. The three SetPixel() calls draw marks in the middle of the window across at every 1cm interval.

LISTING 15.7 LST16_7.CPP—Using the *MM_LOMETRIC* Mapping Mode

(1) Here a metric mapping mode is set so that coordinates represent 0.1 of a millimeter each.

(2) DPtoLP converts device points in pixels to logical points (now 0.1mm).

(3) Three calls to the SetPixel() function are used to draw a small vertical mark.

```
1   void CMapModeView::OnDraw(CDC* pDC)
2   {
3       CMapModeDoc* pDoc = GetDocument();
4       ASSERT_VALID(pDoc);
5
6       // TODO: add draw code for native data here
7
8       // ** Set the mapping mode to 0.1 mm
9       pDC->SetMapMode(MM_LOMETRIC); ———(1)
10
11      // ** Find the client rectangle (in device coords)
12      CRect rcClient;
13      GetClientRect(&rcClient);
14
15      // ** Convert Device Coords to logical coords
16      pDC->DPtoLP(&rcClient); ———(2)
17
18      // ** Loop for every 100 logical units
19      for(int x=rcClient.TopLeft().x;
20              x<rcClient.BottomRight().x;
21              x+=100)
22      {
23          // ** Set threes pixels at the y coordinate
24          pDC->SetPixel(x,rcClient.CenterPoint().y-1,0); ———(3)
25          pDC->SetPixel(x,rcClient.CenterPoint().y,0);
26          pDC->SetPixel(x,rcClient.CenterPoint().y+1,0);
27      }
28  }
```

Notice that `OnDraw()` was passed a pointer to a device context that is used for all the drawing. The application framework has set this device context up for you. In Chapter 22, "Printing and Print Previewing," you'll see how this device context gets set up for either screen or printer. If you build and run the application you should see a horizontal row of regularly spaced marks. If you get your ruler out you should see that these marks are spaced every centimeter.

Try changing the `MM_LOMETRIC` flag to `MM_LOENGLISH`. When you build and run the program, the dots will be spaced farther apart and should represent one-inch spacing.

> **Mapping accuracy in screen displays**
>
> Don't count on the screen mapping to be perfect; differences in monitor sizes and VDU height and width settings make this inaccurate. Printer output is much more accurate and reliable.

Free-Scaling Mapping Modes

You can set your own mapping ratios, which paves the way to making zoom modes easily by using the tragically named `MM_ANISOTROPIC` mapping mode. Tragically named because *anisotropic* means having different properties in different directions; although it's undoubtedly true of this mapping mode, it is misleading because the mapping mode allows differential scaling in each axis. My dog is anisotropic, but he doesn't scale easily like this mapping mode does. Despite the strange naming, the mapping mode is incredibly powerful because it lets you set the conversion between logical units and device units.

Listing 15.8 shows this conversion by setting the device units with the `SetViewportExt()` function to the client rectangle's width across and by 500 device pixels up. Then in line 19 the logical width is set to 10,000 units across by the `SetWindowExt()` function, but still 500 logical pixels up. This means that the window is exactly 10,000 logical units across. The loop in lines 23–30 will draw exactly 100 horizontal marks across the page, each at 100 logical units across. However, in the vertical axis each logical unit is equal to one pixel (like `MM_TEXT`).

If you build and run after making the changes to the `OnDraw()` function shown in Listing 15.8, you should see 100 evenly spaced marks drawn across the window. If you try resizing the window, you should see that the marks are expanded or contracted so that there are always 100 spaced evenly across.

LISTING 15.8 LST16_8.CPP—Using the *MM_ANISOTROPIC* Mapping Mode

```
1    void CMapModeView::OnDraw(CDC* pDC)
2    {
3        CMapModeDoc* pDoc = GetDocument();
4        ASSERT_VALID(pDoc);
5
6        // TODO: add draw code for native data here
7
8        pDC->SetMapMode(MM_ANISOTROPIC);
9
10       CRect rcClient;
11       GetClientRect(&rcClient);
12
13       // ** Set the device extent to the client extent
14       // ** across and 500 pixels down
15       pDC->SetViewportExt(CSize(rcClient.BottomRight().
         x,500));
16
17       // ** Set the logical extent to the 10,000 units
18       // ** across and 500 pixels down
19       pDC->SetWindowExt(CSize(10000,500));
20
21       pDC->DPtoLP(&rcClient);
22
23       for(int x=rcClient.TopLeft().
24               x;x<rcClient.BottomRight().x;
25               x+=100)
26       {
27           pDC->SetPixel(x,rcClient.CenterPoint().y-1,0);
28           pDC->SetPixel(x,rcClient.CenterPoint().y,0);
29           pDC->SetPixel(x,rcClient.CenterPoint().y+1,0);
30       }
31   }
```

① MM_ANISOTROPIC allows each axis to be set to an arbitrary scaling system.

② The SetViewportExt() function sets the device width and height in pixel coordinates.

③ The SetWindowExt() function sets the logical width and height of the window in logical coordinates.

The MM_ISOTROPIC mapping mode is probably more aptly named and I suspect is where its MM_ANISOTROPIC sister's name is derived from. *Isotropic* means having the same properties in different directions. You can use the same SetWindowExt() and SetViewportExt() functions to set the scaling, but the GDI always adjusts your differential ratios so that one logical unit of the horizontal axis is always equal to one logical unit of the vertical axis. This mode is useful if you are trying to preserve the aspect ratio of your drawing.

SEE ALSO

➤ *To use mapping modes in printing, see page 568*

Retrieving the Device Capabilities

The device context can be interrogated directly to examine which capabilities the associated device supports. In most common cases, just about all the standard drawing and font output can be supported. But some devices—pen plotters for example—can only support line drawing. Printers might be only black and white, or they might support a narrow range of colors. One function, GetDeviceCaps(), tells you everything you might need to know about a particular device. As you might have guessed, for this function to tell you so much, there is a long list of flags that it can be passed to interrogate different technology aspects. The GetDeviceCaps() member function of the device context is passed only one parameter, which is a flag to specify the information required. These flags are grouped into different sets depending on what information is required.

The TECHNOLOGY flag inquires on the technology type of the associated device; this can return any of the values shown in Table 15.2.

> **Use of** SetWindowExt() **and** SetViewportExt() **functions**
>
> The SetWindowExt() and SetViewportExt() functions are used only in the MM_ISOTROPIC and MM_ANISOTROPIC mapping modes; in all other modes they will be ignored.

TABLE 15.2 *GetDeviceCaps()* returned values for *TECHNOLOGY*

Returned Value	Description
DT_RASDISPLAY	Normal video card and monitor
DT_RASPRINTER	Normal bitmap printer
DT_PLOTTER	Line drawing plotter device
DT_RASCAMERA	Bitmap input device
DT_CHARSTREAM	Sequence of characters, such as a keyboard
DT_METAFILE	File that holds instructions on how to draw a diagram
DT_DISPFILE	Display file

The driver version can be obtained using the DRIVERVERSION flag.

Several flags can be used to obtain the device dimensions shown in Table 15.3.

Drawing-specific capabilities

There are a whole set of flag values that show the curve drawing capabilities (CURVECAPS), line drawing capabilities (LINECAPS), polygon drawing capabilities (POLYGONCAPS), and text drawing capabilities (TEXTCAPS). These flags have particular relevance to plotter devices that might or might not support particular drawing operations.

TABLE 15.3 *GetDeviceCaps()* flags for retrieving physical dimensions

Passed Flag	Description of Returned Value
HORZRES	The width of a device in pixels
VERTRES	The height of a device in pixels
HORZSIZE	The width of a device in millimeters
VERTSIZE	The height of a device in millimeters
ASPECTX	The relative height to width of a device in pixels
ASPECTY	The relative width to height of a device in pixels
ASPECTXY	The diagonal length of a device in pixels

There are also several flags used to obtain color and drawing capabilities, as shown in Table 15.4.

GetDeviceCaps()
parameters

There are many more flags you can use than are shown here. These are mostly involved in finding whether the device can support specific drawing operations. For most common screen and printer devices, the drawing operations are applicable and will work fine.

TABLE 15.4 *GetDeviceCaps()* flags passed for retrieving color and drawing capabilities

Passed Flag	Description of Returned Value
NUMCOLORS	The number of individual colors a device can support
PLANES	The number of color planes a device can support
BITSPIXEL	The number of bits used to represent one pixel
NUMPENS	The number of pens supported by the device
NUMBRUSHES	The number of brushes supported by the device
NUMFONTS	The number of fonts supported by the device
COLORRES	The color resolution of a device as bits per pixel, if applicable
SIZEPALETTE	The number of palette entries in the system palette, if applicable

Let's use `GetDeviceCaps()` to find the attributes of your video display. The About dialog box in your `MapMode` project would be a good place to show this information in a list box.

Adding a list box control to the About dialog box

1. Select the ResourceView pane of the Project Workspace view.

2. Open the folders to show the `IDD_ABOUTBOX` dialog box.

3. Double-click `IDD_ABOUTBOX` to edit it.

4. Stretch the size of the dialog box and add a list box.

5. Press Alt+Enter to change the list box properties.

6. Set the **ID** on the **General** tab to `IDC_DEVCAPS`.

7. Click the **Styles** tab and uncheck the **Sort** option.

8. Press Enter to close the Properties dialog box.

9. Add a `Static` control above the list box and enter `Device Capabilities` as a caption.

You should now see an About dialog box with the list box properties set like the one shown in Figure 15.4.

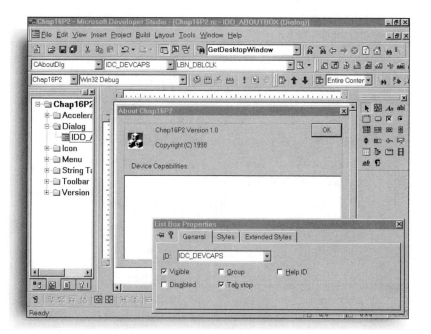

FIGURE 15.4

Editing the About dialog box in project MapMode.

Now you must map a list box control variable to your list box so that you can easily add a string to it.

Mapping a variable to the list box control using ClassWizard

1. Click the list box so that it is highlighted in the resource editor.

2. Press Ctrl+W to start ClassWizard. This should display the IDC_DEVCAPS highlighted in the Control ID's list of the **Member Variables** tab.

3. Click the **A̲dd Variable** button to display the Add Member Variable dialog box.

4. Drop the **C̲ategory** combo box and replace the **Value** entry with **Control**.

5. Enter a **Member Variable** name of m_listDevCaps.

6. Click **OK** to close the dialog box.

7. Click **OK** to close ClassWizard.

You have now mapped a CListBox variable to the list box control in the CAboutDlg class. Now you must enter the code to interrogate a device context using GetDeviceCaps() and display the results in the list box. To do this you must add an OnInitDialog() handler to the CAboutDlg dialog class to initialize the list box when it is opened.

Adding the *OnInitDialog()* handler function

1. Select the ClassView pane of the Project Workspace view.

2. Right-click the CAboutDlg entry to view the pop-up context menu.

3. Select the **Add Windows Message H̲andler** option.

4. From the list of **N̲ew Windows Messages/Events** select the **WM_INITDIALOG** message.

5. Click the **A̲dd and Edit** button to add the handler function and start editing.

You can now add the code shown in Listing 15.9 to add the results from GetDeviceCaps() to the list box in the About dialog box. In this listing a CClientDC is used at line 8 to catch the About box's device context. This device context holds the device information pertaining to the video display. In lines 14 and 15 the value associated with the HORZRES horizontal resolution flag is formatted into a readable string.

In line 16 this string is added to the list box so that it will be displayed. I've repeated the same process for each of the capabilities required.

LISTING 15.9 LST16_9.CPP—Displaying the Results From *GetDeviceCaps()* in the About Dialog Box

```
1   BOOL CAboutDlg::OnInitDialog()
2   {
3       CDialog::OnInitDialog();
4
5       // TODO: Add extra initialization here
6
7       // ** Capture the about dialog's device context
8       CClientDC dcDev(this);
9
10      // ** Declare a string
11      CString strCap;
12
13      // ** Capture and format the device cap results
14      strCap.Format("Horizontal Resolution = %d pixels",
15          dcDev.GetDeviceCaps(HORZRES));
16      m_listDevCaps.AddString(strCap);
17
18      strCap.Format("Vertical Resolution = %d pixels",
19          dcDev.GetDeviceCaps(VERTRES));
20      m_listDevCaps.AddString(strCap);
21
22      strCap.Format("Horizontal Size = %d cm",
23          dcDev.GetDeviceCaps(HORZSIZE) / 10);
24      m_listDevCaps.AddString(strCap);
25
26      strCap.Format("Vertical Size = %d cm",
27          dcDev.GetDeviceCaps(VERTSIZE) / 10);
28      m_listDevCaps.AddString(strCap);
29
30      strCap.Format("Supported Colors = %d colors",
31          dcDev.GetDeviceCaps(NUMCOLORS));
32      m_listDevCaps.AddString(strCap);
```

(1) GetDeviceCaps() is used to find out different capabilities of the device connected to the device context. The result is added to the list box.

continues...

LISTING 15.9 Continued

```
33
34      return TRUE;  // return TRUE unless you set
        ➥the focus to a control
35      // EXCEPTION: OCX Property Pages should
        ➥return FALSE
36   }
```

If you build and run the application after making these changes, and then click the **Help** menu and select **About Map Mode...**, you should see your video display capabilities as shown in Figure 15.5. Don't worry if you think your display should be supporting more colors than is shown in the list box. This is because the device context is showing you the number of colors in its *system palette*, which is 20 by default. This can be increased by assigning a bigger display palette to the device context, as high as the capabilities of your display.

FIGURE 15.5

Displaying the device capabilities returned from GetDeviceCaps().

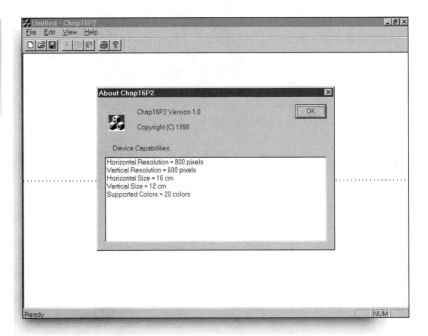

SEE ALSO

➤ *To obtain printer device capabilities, see page 570*

chapter

16

Using Pens and Brushes

Using pens to draw a variety of lines and shapes in many styles

Painting filled shapes with brushes to draw with different colors and textures

Exploiting the drawing functions to make drawing complex shapes easy

Creating Pens

Pens and filled shapes

Pens are used to draw lines and curves. When drawing filled shapes, pens are still used to draw a border around the shape, while a brush fills the interior. You might not want to fill the interior of the shape, and just draw with the outline pen. This can be achieved by using a transparent or hollow brush with any of the filled shape drawing functions. This technique is discussed later in this chapter.

Pens are one of the basic GDI (graphics device interface) objects; they live right down in the depths of Windows and have been there pretty much since day one. Before drawing anything, you must create or select your own custom pens specific to the task in hand.

Using the *CPen* Class

Fortunately MFC provides a wrapper class named CPen to make wielding the pen (drawing object) simple. This class holds the underlying GDI object and takes care of its allocation and deallocation.

To create a pen you must declare it and pass some initialization parameters. The following code line creates a solid red pen:

```
CPen penRed(PS_SOLID,3,RGB(255,0,0));
```

Setting the Pen Type

The first parameter, PS_SOLID, is the pen type, which you can use to specify a variety of pens using the style types. Table 16.1 shows some of the styles available.

TABLE 16.1 Pen type values

Pen Type	Type of Lines Drawn
PS_SOLID	Simple solid lines
PS_DASH	Dashed lines
PS_DOT	Dotted lines
PS_DASHDOT	Alternating dashed and dotted lines

Limitations to the dot and dash style

Note that the dot and dash styles work only with a pen width of 1; any greater width would create a solid line. Figure 16.1 shows different pen styles and widths in action.

Changing Pen Widths

You can adjust the width or thickness of the pen with the second parameter. A value of 1 in this parameter will give you a pen with a width of only one pixel—the thinnest available. If you set this parameter to 30 you will get a chunky, thick pen.

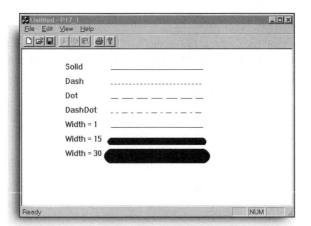

FIGURE 16.1
Pen widths and styles.

Changing Pen Colors

The third parameter you can specify when you construct the pen is the color. The value required here is a COLORREF. In its raw form, a COLORREF is just a 32-bit number that represents the red, green, and blue components that make up a color. Specifying COLORREF values directly is a bit tricky; for example, the value for bright purple is 16711935. Fortunately, there is a macro named RGB to help. Here is the RGB macro in use in the code:

```
COLORREF rgbPurple = RGB(255,0,255);
CPen penDashDotPurple(PS_DASHDOT,1,rgbPurple);
```

The RGB macro takes three parameters for the red, green, and blue brightness components of the desired color. You can set the values of each of these parameters to any value between 0 and 255 where 0 is no color and 255 is full color. You can specify a huge range of colors and hues (16.7 million) by setting these values—as long as your video card supports them. Listing 16.1 shows some examples of different colored pens and the RGB values they use.

Hardware color limitations

Although 24-bit color (called True Color) lets you specify 16.7 million colors and shades, the actual colors displayed will depend on the capabilities of your video hardware and monitor. If your current video mode supports less colors (for example, 16, 256, or 65536) Windows will attempt to compensate by allocating a color palette to best represent the colors currently displayed by the system. Sometimes it will mix two colors in a checkered pattern of pixels to produce the closest mix from the color set available.

LISTING 16.1 LST17_1.CPP—More Colored and Styled Pens

```
1   // Solid Dark Green Pen
2   CPen penSolidDullGreen(PS_SOLID,1,RGB(0,128,0));          ①
3
4   // Thick Yellow Pen
5   CPen penSolidYellow30(PS_SOLID,30,RGB(255,255,0));        ②
6
7   // Dotted Red Pen
8   CPen penDashRed(PS_DOT,1,RGB(255,0,0));                   ③
9
10  // Dasheded Blue Pen
11  CPen penDotBlue(PS_DASH,1,RGB(0,0,255));                  ④
12
```

① A solid green pen is created with a thickness of 1.

② A solid yellow pen is created with a thickness of 30.

③ A dotted red pen is created with a thickness of 1.

④ A dashed blue pen is created with a thickness of 1.

Using the NULL pen

The NULL_PEN style might seem a bit odd at first because it won't actually draw any visible lines or curves; it just leaves the background untouched. However, you'll need a NULL pen to draw filled shapes (such as ellipses and rectangles) with no outlining.

Using Stock Pens

You don't always have to specify the pen details because Windows keeps several *stock pens* hanging around. These are pre-configured with default settings that are commonly used in drawing the desktop and controls. To use one of these stock pens you declare a CPen object, but you don't have to pass any parameters. You must then call CreateStockObject(), which sets the pen defaults to the specified stock object. The following lines use CreateStockObject() to create a stock black pen:

```
CPen stockBlackPen;
stockBlackPen.CreateStockObject(BLACK_PEN);
```

Several default pen styles are available, as shown in Table 16.2.

TABLE 16.2 Stock pen types

Pen Name	Drawing Effect
BLACK_PEN	Draws black lines
WHITE_PEN	Draws white lines
NULL_PEN	Draws in the current background color

Selecting Pens into Device Contexts

Before you can draw with the pens you have created, you must select them into a device context. As discussed in Chapter 15, "Understanding Drawing in Device Contexts," the OnDraw method of a View class provides such a mechanism.

The device context has a slot for pens that can hold only one pen at a time. This is your default drawing pen. When you select a new pen into a device context, the previous pen falls out. You can use the SelectObject() method to drop your new pen into place. As you do, the old pen drops out, and you must catch it. Listing 16.2 shows how this is typically done.

LISTING 16.2 LST17_2.CPP—Selecting Pens

```
1   void MyView::OnDraw(CDC* pDC)
2   {
3       CPen penSolid(PS_SOLID,5,RGB(0,200,0)); // Green pen
4       CPen *pOldPen = NULL;
5
6       pOldPen = pDC->SelectObject(&penSolid); ————————(1)
7
8       // . . . Draw with the green pen
9
10      pDC->SelectObject(pOldPen); ————————(2)
11  }
12
```

(1) Line 6 selects the new green pen and stores the device context's original old pen.

(2) Line 10 reselects the device context's original old pen.

You can pass SelectObject() a pointer to the new pen (note the use of the & in line 6 of Listing 16.2), and it will return a pointer to the previously selected pen. You can then perform some drawing in the device context. When finished, you must put the old pen back; otherwise, Windows might start drawing buttons and controls with your pen!

If you have two pens, you must also use SelectObject() to swap between them in order to draw with them, as shown in Listing 16.3.

Line 11 swaps the new blue pen with the currently selected new green pen (selected in line 7).

LISTING 16.3 LST17_3.CPP—Selecting Between Two Pens

```
1   void MyView::OnDraw(CDC* pDC)
2   {
3       CPen penGreen(PS_SOLID,5,RGB(0,255,0)); // Green pen
4       CPen penBlue(PS_SOLID,3,RGB(0,0,255));  // Blue pen
5       CPen *pOldPen = NULL;
6
7       pOldPen = pDC->SelectObject(&penGreen); // Swap pens
8
9       // ... Draw with the green pen
10
11      pDC->SelectObject(&penBlue);            // Swap pens
12      // The green pen will be returned.
13
14      // ... Draw with the blue pen
15      pDC->SelectObject(pOldPen);             // Restore pen
16  }
```

When you want to draw with different pens as in Listing 16.3, you must store only the default pen. You don't need to store the returned pointers as you subsequently select your own pens because you created them in the first place and, hence, have references to them. Finally you must reselect the original pen to ensure that your custom pens have all been dropped from the device context.

Deleting Pens

When you've finished with your custom pens you must delete them. This frees up the underlying GDI object and releases precious system resources. The CPen class will automatically do this for you when it is deleted. You might want to do this manually if you want to reuse the same CPen object with different settings (by calling CreatePen()).

Alternatively, if you've created many pens and know that you're finished with some, you might want to free up system resources before the pen is deleted at the end of the function.

DeleteObject() is the member function that removes the underlying GDI object. Listing 16.4 shows the same pen object being created, used, deleted, and then re-created again.

Graphic object handles

Although MFC provides nice wrapper classes like **CPen** for the graphics objects, the objects themselves are identified by handles (32-bit integer values) that are member variables of the MFC wrapper classes. Whenever you call a **SelectObject()** or **DeleteObject()** function on a device context object, one of these graphic object handles is actually being selected or deleted at the Win32 level.

LISTING 16.4 LST_17_4.CPP—Using *DeleteObject()* and *CreatePen()*

```
1   void MyView::OnDraw(CDC* pDC)
2   {
3       CPen penMainDraw(PS_DASH,1,RGB(128,255,255));
4       CPen *pOldPen = NULL;
5
6       pOldPen = pDC->SelectObject(&penMainDraw);
7
8       // Draw with the dashed pen...
9
10      pDC->SelectObject(pOldPen);
11
12      penMainDraw.DeleteObject();
13      penMainDraw.CreatePen(PS_SOLID,5,RGB(200,20,5));
14
15      pOldPen = pDC->SelectObject(&penMainDraw);
16
17      // Draw with the solid pen...
18
19      pDC->SelectObject(pOldPen);
20  }
21      // Delete Object will be automatically called when
22      // penMainDraw is deleted as the function ends
```

① Line 12 deletes the underlying GDI object, the CPen object can then be reused to create another pen as shown on line 13.

In Listing 16.4 the pen penMainDraw is created at the beginning of OnDraw() on line 3, and then selected and drawn with as normal. You must never call DeleteObject() on a pen that is still being used by the device context. In the listing the old pen is selected back into the device context so that DeleteObject() can be called on the main "dashed" pen.

After it is deleted, the underlying GDI object is released and you can reuse the CPen class to create another pen. CreatePen() is then called to create a new solid pen. This member function takes the identical parameters as the constructor: CreatePen (nPenStyle, nWidth, crColor) to specify the style, width, and color reference.

Be careful using DeleteObject()

If you call a pen's DeleteObject() function while that pen is still selected in a device context, the underlying GDI object will be destroyed, and any subsequent drawing operations involving that pen might cause the application to crash or give unexpected results.

Drawing Lines and Shapes with Pens

To draw anything with pens (or any other GDI Object) you'll need a device context in which to draw. As you read in Chapter 15, the device context provides a mechanism for drawing with the same objects across a whole range of devices so that the output on each is identical.

Creating a Device Context for Drawing

Choosing the drawing device context

You can use the drawing functions to draw into any valid device context. This means you could grab another application's window, call `GetDC()` to obtain its device context, and start drawing into it. Alternatively, you could grab a device context for the entire Windows desktop and draw at it. However, most well behaved programs open their own window and confine their drawing operations to that window. Windows then clips the drawing functions so that they don't leak out over and into other windows.

The view of an SDI application would make an ideal canvas for your artistic endeavors. The following shows how to create an SDI application that uses a simple drawing-oriented view (using the `CView` base class).

Creating a device context using an SDI application

1. Click the **File** menu and select **New**.

2. Select the **Projects** tab. From the list of project types, select **MFC AppWizard (exe)**.

3. Now click the **Project Name** box and enter the project name, (such as MyDraw as shown in the sample listings).

4. Click **OK**. You should see the MFC AppWizard – Step 1 dialog box.

5. Select **Single Document** and click **Finish**. This will automatically create an SDI application framework that uses the simple `CView` base class to derive your new application's main view class.

6. Click **OK** on the New Project Information dialog box and AppWizard will create the new project and source files.

Now you're ready to do some drawing.

Moving the Pen Position

The device context holds a current coordinate position for the pen. When you draw lines, they will be drawn from the current position to the specified position, after which the specified position becomes the new current position.

The device context has a member function, `MoveTo()`, that sets this current position. You can call `MoveTo()` with two parameters to specify the X and Y positions.

Select the ClassView pane of the Workspace view. You should see the `CMyDrawView` class. Click the plus symbol to open the member's view for this class. You can use the `OnDraw()` member function to implement your drawing code. Double-click `OnDraw()` and you should see the implementation in Listing 16.5.

Finding the current drawing position

You can retrieve the current drawing position by calling the device context's `GetCurrentPosition()` function, which returns the current position in a `CPoint` object.

LISTING 16.5   LST17_5.CPP—The Standard *OnDraw()* Function

```
1  // CMyDrawView drawing
2
3  void CMyDrawView::OnDraw(CDC* pDC)
4  {
5      CMyDrawDoc* pDoc = GetDocument();
6      ASSERT_VALID(pDoc);
7
8      // TODO: add draw code for native data here
9  }
```

As you can see, this `OnDraw()` function is passed a pointer to a device context, which represents the client area of the SDI's main view. It then gets a pointer to the document class in line 5; this is because most applications will be drawing from data held in the document. Nothing is actually drawn. If you click the **Build** menu and select **Execute MyDraw.exe**, the project will build and then display a blank view.

You can start adding drawing code by moving the graphic's cursor position. To do this add the `MoveTo()` line in Listing 16.6 after the `//TODO: add draw code` comment as shown in line 8.

LISTING 16.6 LST17_6.CPP—Using *MoveTo()*

① Line 8 changes the device context's current graphics cursor position with the MoveTo() function.

```
1   void CMyDrawView::OnDraw(CDC* pDC)
2   {
3       CMyDrawDoc* pDoc = GetDocument();
4       ASSERT_VALID(pDoc);
5
6       // TODO: add draw code for native data here
7
8       pDC->MoveTo(50,100);    // ** New MoveTo Line **  ──①
9   }
```

Although nothing is drawn, the device context default graphics cursor position is now set to 50 pixels across and 100 pixels down the view by your new MoveTo() call in line 8.

Drawing Lines

Just like the MoveTo() member function, the device context has a LineTo() function. This takes the same parameters and draws a line from the last position to the specified position.

If you add the lines shown in Listing 16.7 to your OnDraw() function, these code lines will draw a triangle with the dotted pen using the LineTo() function.

LISTING 16.7 LST17_7.CPP—Drawing Lines

```
1    void CMyDrawView::OnDraw(CDC* pDC)
2    {
3        CMyDrawDoc* pDoc = GetDocument();
4        ASSERT_VALID(pDoc);
5
6        // TODO: add draw code for native data here
7
8        // Create a Pen
9        CPen penRed(PS_DOT,1,RGB(255,0,0));
10       // Declare a pointer to hold the Old Pen
11       CPen *pOldPen = NULL;
12
13       // Select the Red Pen
14       pOldPen = pDC->SelectObject(&penRed);
```

```
15
16      pDC->MoveTo(50,100);
17
18      // Draw 'base' line
19      pDC->LineTo(100,100);      ──────(1)
20      // Draw first 'side' line
21      pDC->LineTo(75,50);
22      // Draw second 'side' line
23      pDC->LineTo(50,100);
24
25      // Reselect the old pen
26      pDC->SelectObject(pOldPen);
27   }
```

(1) Lines 19 through 23 draw the three lines comprising the triangle with the LineTo() function.

As before, you must create a pen (red and dotted) and then select it into the device context. You can then move to the graphic coordinate (50,100) using MoveTo() as shown in line 16. The next LineTo() function (line 19) will draw a line from (50,100) to (100,100). This will draw a horizontal line from 50 across to 100 across; the y-coordinate stays the same (50 down). The next two LineTo() functions (lines 21 and 23) will draw from (100,100) to (75,50) and then to (50,100), respectively.

To build and run the triangle drawing changes, click the **Build** menu and select **Execute**, and then click **Yes** to the Files Out of Date - Would You Like to Build Them? prompt. If all goes well, you should have a small dotted triangle that looks like the one shown in Figure 16.2.

Drawing with Point Coordinates

You saw the point class being used to hold and pass coordinate pairs in Chapter 8, "Responding to Mouse Events." Using the CPoint class is a handy way to hold and manipulate both the x and y coordinates together. The device context's MoveTo() and LineTo() functions understand CPoint objects as parameters, so you can draw with them instead of passing x and y coordinates individually. Another useful function is GetCurrentPosition(), which returns a CPoint indicating the current graphics cursor position (where the last MoveTo() or LineTo() ended up).

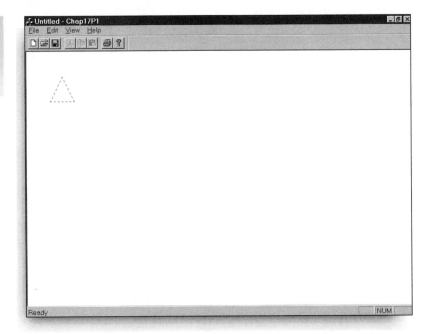

FIGURE 16.2

Sample triangle drawn with `LineTo()`.

Finding the whole window rectangle

If you want to find the coordinates for the whole window, you can use the `GetWindowRect()` function passing a pointer to a `CRect` object. The screen coordinates of the window will then be stored in the passed `CRect` object. However, if you draw using the device context passed to the `OnDraw()` function, your drawing operations will still be clipped to the client rectangle.

There is also a `CRect` class that holds two `CPoint` objects; one for the top left of a rectangle and the other for the bottom right. You can use `GetClientRect()` to get the bounding rectangle of the view window and hold the result in a `CRect` class. `CRect` also provides some useful member functions for manipulating rectangle information. One of these member function is `CenterPoint()`, which returns a `CPoint` object holding the x and y values for the middle of the rectangle. For your client rectangle, this is the center of the SDI view window itself.

`CRect` can also provide the width and height of the rectangle with the `Width()` and `Height()` member functions.

You can remove the triangle drawing lines and add the following new lines so that your `OnDraw()` looks like Listing 16.8 to produce the line pattern shown in Figure 16.3.

LISTING 16.8 LST17_8.CPP—Drawing with the *CPoint* and *CRect* classes

```
1   void CMyDrawView::OnDraw(CDC* pDC)
2   {
3       CMyDrawDoc* pDoc = GetDocument();
4       ASSERT_VALID(pDoc);
```

```
5
6        // TODO: add draw code for native data here
7
8        // Create a Pen
9        CPen penRed(PS_DOT,1,RGB(255,0,0));
10       CPen *pOldPen = NULL;
11
12       pOldPen = pDC->SelectObject(&penRed);
13
14       // Find the drawing area co-ordinates
15       CRect rcClient;
16       GetClientRect(&rcClient);
17
18       for(int x=0; x < rcClient.Width(); x+=5)
19           for(int y=0; y < rcClient.Height(); y+=5)
20           {
21               CPoint ptNew(x,y);
22               pDC->MoveTo(rcClient.CenterPoint());
23               pDC->LineTo(ptNew);
24           }
25
26       pDC->SelectObject(pOldPen);
27   }
```

(1) Lines 18 through 24 iterate through the height and width skipping every five pixels to draw lines from the center out to each grid position in the client area.

Notice how the view is asked to fill in the `rcClient` variable in lines 15 and 16 with the client rectangle information using `GetClientRect()`. This makes it easy to loop through the width and height of the rectangle with the two `for` loops. First every five points across the rectangle is set to `x` as it loops. Then for each of these `x` points, `y` will be set for every five pixels down the rectangle. This will form a grid; lines are drawn from the middle (found with `CenterPoint()` in line 22) to the changing point position created in `ptNew` in line 21 and passed to the `LineTo()` function in line 23.

You could build and run the program after making these changes. With these few lines of code, you can create a work of modern art (see Figure 16.3).

FIGURE 16.3

Drawing lines with points and rectangles.

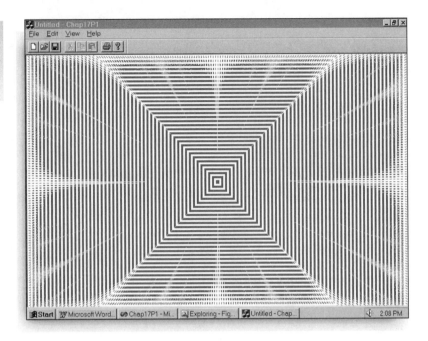

Drawing Circles and Ellipses

A circle is really just an ellipse with the same height and width, so one device context member function draws them both. The Ellipse() function comes in two forms. The first form takes a rectangle specified by passing a CRect object. The second form wants four parameters for the top-left x- and y-coordinates and the bottom-right x- and y-coordinates.

Change your OnDraw() function as shown in Listing 16.9. This will then draw circles within circles (see Figure 16.4).

LISTING 16.9 LST17_9.CPP—Drawing Circles with the Ellipse Function

```
1   void CMyDrawView::OnDraw(CDC* pDC)
2   {
3       CMyDrawDoc* pDoc = GetDocument();
4       ASSERT_VALID(pDoc);
5
6       // TODO: add draw code for native data here
7
```

```
8       // Create a Pen
9       CPen penRed(PS_DOT,1,RGB(255,0,0));
10      CPen *pOldPen = NULL;
11
12      pOldPen = pDC->SelectObject(&penRed);
13
14      // Don't fill the ellipse
15      pDC->SelectStockObject(NULL_BRUSH);
16
17      CRect rcClient;
18      GetClientRect(&rcClient);
19
20      // Declare a center-positioned rectangle object
21      CRect rcEllipse(rcClient.CenterPoint(),
22                      rcClient.CenterPoint());
23
24
25      // Keep going until the ellipse fills the area ────①
26      while(rcEllipse.Width() < rcClient.Width()
27          && rcEllipse.Height() < rcClient.Height())
28      {
29          // Increase the ellipse size by 10 pixels
30          rcEllipse.InflateRect(10,10);
31          pDC->Ellipse(rcEllipse);
32      }
33
34      pDC->SelectObject(pOldPen);
35  }
```

① The while loop in line 25 keeps iterating lines 28 through 30 drawing ever larger circles until the diameter reaches the size of the height or width of the client rectangle

The first change you'll notice is the `pDC->SelectStockObject(NULL_BRUSH)` on line 15; this is called because by default the `Ellipse()` function in line 30 will fill the area with the current brush. (Brushes are covered in the "Creating Brushes" section later in this chapter.) Note that this function instructs the device context not to fill the ellipse, just to draw the outline.

A rectangle is then created (`rcEllipse`) and used to draw the ellipse and initialize its top-left and bottom-right points with the center of the client window. The `while` loop in lines 25, 26, and 27–31 can be iterated through until the ellipse rectangle becomes wider or higher than the window.

In this loop, another CRect member function InflateRect() is used in line 30 to inflate the rectangle by 10 pixels for both width and height. This has the effect of stretching a rectangle away from the middle. An ellipse is then drawn inside this "growing" rectangle to draw circles within circles within circles.

You can see the effect of these changes by building and running the program to see your masterpiece, which should look like Figure 16.4.

FIGURE 16.4

Drawing circles with Ellipse().

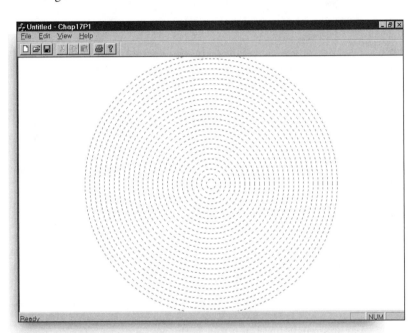

Speed implications of curve drawing

Because of the extra calculations required to draw curvy lines they take significantly longer to draw than normal straight lines. You probably wouldn't notice this speed difference when drawing just a few curves, but it might become significant if your application must draw several curvy lines.

Drawing Curves

PolyBezier() is a function named after the mathematician Bézier who reduced curves to *cubic splines*. The spline is the curvy line, and the cubic part means it has beginning and end points and two control points that pull the curve toward them by interpolation between the points. The Poly part means that we can draw several of these splines connected to each other. You must pass the function an array of CPoint objects (at least four) and the number of points in the array.

You could change your OnDraw() function between the GetClientRect() and the final SelectObject() functions so it looks like Listing 16.10 to draw the Bézier curves shown in Figure 16.5

LISTING 16.10 LST17_10.CPP—Drawing Curves with *PolyBezier()*

```
1   GetClientRect(&rcClient);
2
3   // Create an array to hold the points
4   CPoint ptBezierAr[4];
5   CPen penBlue(PS_SOLID,3,RGB(0,0,255));
6
7   pDC->SelectObject(&penBlue); ──────①
8   for(int i=0; i < 4 ;i++)
9   {
10     // Setup an array of random points
11     ptBezierAr[i] =
12     CPoint(rand()%rcClient.Width(),
13            rand()%rcClient.Height());
14
15     // Draw a label ──────②
16     CString strPointLabel;
17     strPointLabel.Format("%d.",i+1);
18     pDC->TextOut(ptBezierAr[i].x,
19                  ptBezierAr[i].y,
20                  strPointLabel);
21
22     // Draw the co-ordinates as blue dots
23     CRect rcDot(ptBezierAr[i],ptBezierAr[i]);
24     rcDot.InflateRect(2,2);
25     pDC->Ellipse(rcDot);
26   }
27
28   // Draw a red Bezier curve
29   pDC->SelectObject(&penRed);
30   pDC->PolyBezier(ptBezierAr,4); ──────③
31
32   pDC->SelectObject(pOldPen);
33
```

① The blue pen is selected in line 7 to draw the dots in blue (line 26).

② Lines 16 through 20 create a CString object, which is formatted with the point number. This string is then drawn at the position of the dot to label it with the TextOut() function in line 18.

③ Line 30 draws the Bézier curve using the PolyBezier() function with the red pen selected in line 29.

In Listing 16.10, an array of CPoints is declared as ptBezierAr in line 4, and all four points are filled in the array to random coordinates inside the client rectangle (lines 12 and 13). Then at line 18 the device context TextOut() function is used to draw a label at the point (you'll learn more about this in Chapter 17, "Using Fonts").

The Ellipse() function in line 25 is quite handy for drawing a blue blob (with the new pen) to illustrate each point. Finally, after selecting the red dotted pen again, PolyBezier() is called in line 30 and passed the array of points and telling it there are 4 points to use. This will then draw a curve from points 1 to 4 controlled by points 2 and 3.

You could build and run the program to see the PolyBezier() function drawing curves. Figure 16.5 illustrates the function of each point in the curve quite clearly. Resize the window and watch it draw a different curve each time.

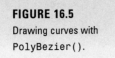

FIGURE 16.5

Drawing curves with PolyBezier().

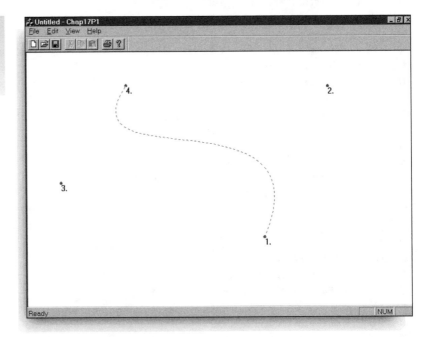

Drawing Polygons

`Polyline()` is identical to `PolyBezier()` in its parameter requirements. It takes an array of `CPoint`s and the number of points in the array. Rather than drawing the curve, it simply links the points in a series of straight lines. You can specify any number of points—but must have at least two—which can be quite useful when drawing preformed objects held in `CPoint` arrays. There is also a `PolyLineTo()` and `PolyBezierTo()`, which set the default coordinates to the last point drawn.

If you were to just change the `PolyBezier()` in your `OnDraw()` function to `Polyline()` and build and run the application. You would get linked lines instead of the Bézier curve (see Listing 16.11).

LISTING 16.11   LST17_11.CPP—Drawing Lines with *Polyline()*

```
1    // Select the red pen
2    pDC->SelectObject(&penRed);
3
4    // Draw the Polyline with 4 points
5    pDC->Polyline(ptBezierAr,4);
6
7    // Reselect the old pen
8
9    pDC->SelectObject(pOldPen);
10
```

If you want to draw polygons with `Polyline()` (as in line 5), you must set the last point in the array to the same coordinate as the first point.

Creating Brushes

Pens work well for drawing the borders of shapes, but we need a brush to color them in. Most of the GDI drawing functions use both a pen and a brush. They use the pen to draw the perimeter and a brush to draw the body of various shapes. This enables you to set a pen with one color and style and a brush with another color and draw a complete shape in a single function call.

Using the *CBrush* Class

The MFC wrapper for the brush GDI object is CBrush. A brush can be a solid color, hatched, or come from a bitmap or pattern. It therefore has constructors that can take these different types of parameters, or you can just create an uninitialized object and then call one of the many create functions to create it later.

Creating Colored and Hatched Brushes

The easiest brush to create is one of solid color. Simply declare a CBrush object and pass it a color reference for the color you require as its only parameter. This will then give you a brush that will paint areas only in that color like this:

```
CBrush brYellow(RGB(192,192,0));
```

You can create cross-hatching techniques by constructing the brush with one of the cross-hatching flags as the first parameter and the color as the second parameter, as in the following:

```
CBrush brYellowHatch(HS_DIAGCROSS,RGB(192,192,0));
```

A selection of hatching flags are available. They are described in Table 16.3.

TABLE 16.3 Brush hatching flags

Hatching Flag	Effect
HS_CROSS	A vertical and horizontal criss-cross
HS_DIAGCROSS	A diagonal criss-cross
HS_HORIZONTAL	Horizontal lines
HS_VERTICAL	Vertical lines
HS_BDIAGONAL	Diagonal lines (top left to bottom right)
HD_FDIAGONAL	Diagonal lines (bottom left to top right)

Coloring the Window Background

You can use brushes to change the background of your window by handling the Windows erase background message (WM_ERASEBKGND).

Adding a handler function to change a window's background color when the background is erased.

1. Right-click the Wizard bar—that's the one with three combo boxes. The first combo box should show your view class (for example, CMyDrawView) and the second should say **(All class members)**.

2. You should see a context menu appear with an **Add Windows Message Handler** option. Select this option. The message-handler dialog box should appear as in Figure 16.6.

3. Select the **WM_ERASEBKGND** message and click the **Add and Edit** button. This should add a handler function called OnEraseBkgnd().

4. By overriding the default implementation of this handler function, you can customize screen background. Listing 16.12 shows an example of the modifications required which result in a yellow hatched background.

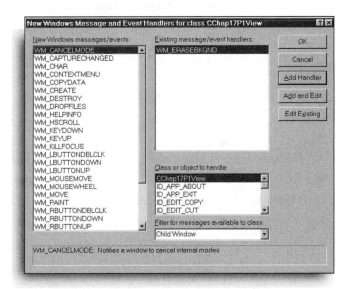

FIGURE 16.6
The Message and Event Handler dialog box.

① When handling the WM_ERASEBKGND message, you are responsible for erasing the background as shown in line 7 with FillRect(), then by returning a TRUE value as in line 9, you indicate that your handler has performed this task.

LISTING 16.12 LST17_12.CPP—Modifying the Background with *OnEraseBkGnd()*

```
1   BOOL CMyDrawView::OnEraseBkgnd(CDC* pDC)
2   {
3       CBrush brYellowHatch(HS_DIAGCROSS,RGB(192,192,0));
4
5       CRect rcClient;
6       GetClientRect(&rcClient);
7       pDC->FillRect(rcClient,&brYellowHatch); ──────①
8
9       return TRUE;
10  }
```

If you compile and run the application after making the changes shown in Listing 16.12, the hatched yellow background should appear.

By overriding OnEraseBkGnd(), you can create a hatched yellow brush (line 3), get the client rectangle (line 5), and then use FillRect() (in line 7) to fill the rectangle with our specialized brush. The return TRUE in line 9 tells Windows we have taken care of the job of erasing the background and it doesn't need to bother doing it itself.

Creating Brushes from Patterns and Images

Being able to create brushes from images is quite a nice feature of Windows. By doing this, you can paint areas of the screen with tiled images. Some applications use this to display cool-looking bitmaps on their toolbars.

Creating an image for use in a brush

1. Select the ResourceView pane from the Workspace view.

2. Click the plus sign to open up your project's (for example, MyView) resources.

3. Right-click this heading and select the **Insert** option from the context menu.

4. Choose **Bitmap** from the Insert Resource dialog box.

5. A new bitmap resource named IDB_BITMAP1 should appear. Click the grid and then press Alt+Enter to display the Properties dialog box for the bitmap, or click the **View** menu and select **Properties**.

6. Set the bitmap name to an appropriate name (for example, IDB_INVADER for the example) and the width and height both to 8. Then draw the required brush image (such as a space invader figure as shown in Figure 16.7).

Compiled bitmap resources

When your application is compiled, these bitmap resources are bundled into your final executable program (.exe file). You can open .exe files specifying the **Open As** type as Resources to view bundled bitmaps. If you want to include lots of large bitmaps in your application, it might be better to load these in from files (or resource only DLLs) than greatly increase the size of your .exe program file.

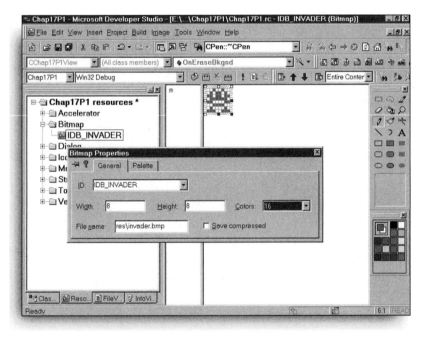

FIGURE 16.7

Designing a brush bitmap.

Now you must implement the code to construct a brush from your new bitmap. To do this, you should close the bitmap editor window and change the code for OnEraseBkgnd as shown in Listing 16.13.

LISTING 16.13 LST17_13.CPP—Using a Bitmap Brush

```
1   BOOL CMyDrawView::OnEraseBkgnd(CDC* pDC)
2   {
3       // Declare an invader bitmap
4       CBitmap bmInvader;
5
6       // Load the bitmap resource
7
8       bmInvader.LoadBitmap(IDB_INVADER);  ————(1)
9       // Create a brush from the bitmap
10
11      CBrush brInvader(&bmInvader);  ————(2)
12
13      CRect rcClient;
14      GetClientRect(&rcClient);
15
16      // Fill the rectangle from the bitmap brush
17      pDC->FillRect(rcClient,&brInvader);  ————(3)
18
19      return TRUE;
20  }
```

(1) The bitmap is loaded with the LoadBitmap() function from the IDB_INVADER resource.

(2) A CBrush object can be constructed from a CBitmap object to perform textured fills using the bitmap.

(3) A normal FillRect() using the bitmap brush can be used to erase the background.

Bitmap brush limitations

Windows 95 can draw only 8×8 pixel brushes, whereas Windows NT is unlimited.

If you compile and run the program after making the changes shown in Listing 16.13, you should see that the background pattern is made up of many little invader characters. The CBitmap class is used to hold the bitmap (line 4), and it is loaded with the invader resource using the LoadBitmap() function (line 8). When CBrush is constructed with an initialized bitmap (line 11), this brush can then be used for any of the normal drawing operations, such as the FillRect() function called in line 17.

Using Stock Brushes

Like pens, there are several stock brushes that you can pick up from Windows at any time. Table 16.4 describes these brushes.

TABLE 16.4 Stock brushes

Stock Brush	Effect
BLACK_BRUSH	Black paint
WHITE_BRUSH	White paint

Stock Brush	Effect
DKGRAY_BRUSH	Dark gray paint
LTGRAY_BRUSH	Light gray paint
GRAY_BRUSH	Gray paint
NULL_BRUSH	Transparent (doesn't fill shapes)

You can use `SelectStockObject()` to select these directly into a device context as you saw with the `NULL_BRUSH` in Line 15 of Listing 16.9.

More of the system colors can be assigned to a brush by using the `CreateSysColorBrush()`. A whole range of different system colors can be assigned by passing the relevant flags to this function. A list of these flags is shown in Table 16.5.

Using the `CreateSysColorBrush()` function

You should always use the `CreateSysColorBrush()` function when trying to emulate some of the Windows desktop colors in your application. If you emulate a color by a fixed **COLORREF** value corresponding to one of the Windows colors, you might find a user has changed their desktop colors while your application still displays the fixed color.

TABLE 16.5 System colors flags available to *CreateSysColorBrush()*

System Color Flag	Description
COLOR_DESKTOP	The desktop background color
COLOR_BTNTEXT	Color of the text on buttons
COLOR_GRAYTEXT	Color of grayed-out or disabled text
COLOR_HIGHLIGHT	The background highlight color of selected items
COLOR_HIGHLIGHTTEXT	The text color of selected items
COLOR_ACTIVEBORDER	The color of a border on an active window
COLOR_INACTIVEBORDER	The color of a border on an inactive window
COLOR_INFOBK	The background color of ToolTips
COLOR_INFOTEXT	The text color of ToolTips
COLOR_WINDOW	The window background color
COLOR_WINDOWFRAME	The color of a window's frame
COLOR_WINDOWTEXT	The color of text in a window
COLOR_3DDKSHADOW	Shadow color for buttons
COLOR_3DFACE	The face color for buttons
COLOR_3DHILIGHT	The highlight color for buttons
COLOR_3DLIGHT	The bright edge color of a button

Try changing the `OnEraseBkGnd()` function to create such a brush (see Listing 16.14).

LISTING 16.14 LST17_14.CPP—Creating a System Color Brush

> ① You can use the `CreateSysColorBrush()` member function to create a brush with one of the standard system colors.

```
1   BOOL CMyDrawView::OnEraseBkgnd(CDC* pDC)
2   {
3       CBrush brDesktop;
4
5       brDesktop.CreateSysColorBrush(COLOR_DESKTOP);  ————①
6
7       CRect rcClient;
8       GetClientRect(&rcClient);
9       pDC->FillRect(rcClient,&brDesktop);
10
11      return TRUE;
12  }
```

If you compile the changes and run the program, you should see the current desktop background color displayed in the window background.

Selecting Brushes into Device Contexts

You can use the `SelectObject()` member of the device context to select the new brush. It works just like it did for pens and will return a pointer to the previous brush when it returns. You should also keep this returned pointer as you did for pens and reselect it after use. This can be demonstrated by changing the `OnEraseBkGnd()` as shown in Listing 16.15.

LISTING 16.15 LST17_15.CPP—Selecting Brushes into a Device Context

```
1   BOOL CMyDrawView::OnEraseBkgnd(CDC* pDC)
2   {
3       CBrush brDesktop;
4       brDesktop.CreateSysColorBrush(COLOR_DESKTOP);
5
6       CRect rcClient;
7       GetClientRect(&rcClient);
8
```

```
9        CBrush* pOldBrush = pDC->SelectObject(&brDesktop);
10
11       pDC->Ellipse(rcClient);
12
13       pDC->SelectObject(pOldBrush);
14       return TRUE;
15   }
```

(1) The ellipse drawn by line 11 will be filled with the standard desktop color setting.

Because this example uses an ellipse to fill the background, some very strange things happen when this program is run. The brush is selected and an elliptical area is set to the desktop color, but because the ellipse doesn't fill the whole area, a transparent section is created where you can see the desktop underneath.

If you compile and run after making these changes, you should see these odd effects. This transparency effect would also happen when you use NULL_BRUSH to paint the background.

Deleting Brushes

Just like pens, you can delete brushes to free the underlying resource and then use one of the Create functions to create another one. The Create functions available are CreateSolidBrush(); CreateHatchBrush(); CreateBrushIndirect(), which is passed a LOGBRUSH structure; CreatePatternBrush(), which takes a bitmap; and CreateSysColorBrush(), which we've just seen. These are all passed parameters equivalent to their constructor counterparts.

Deleting bitmap or pattern brushes

When you delete a bitmap brush, you should remember to also delete the associated bitmap (which isn't deleted automatically). You must also ensure that the bitmap is deleted after the brush is deleted so you don't delete an object that is still in use.

Drawing Filled Shapes with Brushes

A whole load of drawing functions draw filled shapes with brushes. You can draw many different types of polygons, chords, pie sections, and rectangles.

Drawing Rectangles and Rounded Rectangles

You can use Rectangle() and RoundRect() to draw rectangular shapes (as well as FillRect(), which you've already seen). Rectangle() takes parameters identical to Ellipse(); that is, a CRect or four integers for the top-left and bottom-right coordinates.

RoundRect() needs one more set of coordinates, which it takes either as a CPoint or two more integers. This coordinate pair specifies the width of the ellipse that is drawn on each corner of the rectangle.

If you change OnEraseBkGnd() so that it calls Rectangle() instead of Ellipse() as shown in the following line of code, then, like FillRect(), the background is set to the desktop color:

```
pDC->Rectangle(rcClient);
// ** Draw a rectangle with the desktop colored brush
```

Notice, however, that FillRect() needed a pointer to a brush, whereas Rectangle() uses the currently selected device context brush.

You can draw rectangles with rounded edges with the RoundRect() function. If you then change the OnDraw() member again and replace the Polyline() code as shown in Listing 16.16, you'll see a rounded rectangle rather than the normal square-edge rectangle.

LISTING 16.16 LST17_16.CPP—Drawing with *RoundRect()*

```
1   void CMyDrawView::OnDraw(CDC* pDC)
2   {
3       CMyDrawDoc* pDoc = GetDocument();
4       ASSERT_VALID(pDoc);
5
6       // TODO: add draw code for native data here
7
8       CPen penRed(PS_SOLID,5,RGB(255,0,0));
9       CPen *pOldPen = NULL;
10
11      pOldPen = pDC->SelectObject(&penRed);
12
13      CRect rcClient;
14      GetClientRect(&rcClient);
15
16      CBrush brBlue(RGB(0,0,255));
17      CBrush *pOldBrush = NULL;
```

```
18
19        pOldBrush = pDC->SelectObject(&brBlue);
20
21        rcClient.DeflateRect(50,50);
22        pDC->RoundRect(rcClient,CPoint(15,15));
23
24        pDC->SelectObject(pOldBrush);
25        pDC->SelectObject(pOldPen);
26    }
```

(1) Line 22 shows how the RoundRect() function is used to draw rectangles with an edge radius of 15 pixels.

Notice here that we have changed the red dashed pen to a wide solid red pen (in line 8) to show the boundary clearly. A blue brush is declared at line 16 and then selected into the device context at line 19. The client CRect is deflated at line 21 to draw a smaller round rectangle (line 22) with elliptical corners and a width of 15 pixels.

If you compile and run these changes, you should see a rounded blue rectangle with a thick red border on the desktop colored background.

Drawing Filled Ellipses and Circles

You've already seen ellipses in action when erasing the background in Listing 16.15. The Ellipse() function that you used with the pens is the same for brushes except you had the brush set to NULL_BRUSH to stop it drawing. You could add the following lines after the RoundRect() line to draw an Ellipse():

```
// Deflate the rectangle some more
rcClient.DeflateRect(25,25);
// Draw a smaller ellipse in the rectangle
pDC->Ellipse(rcClient);
```

When you compile and run after adding these lines, you should see a smaller ellipse inside the rounded rectangle. It will have a red border because of the selected pen.

A handy trick for creating ellipses from a point

You'll often want to create an ellipse with a specific diameter from a specific point. A quick way to do this is to construct a CRect object from the same CPoint object for its top-left and bottom-right coordinates. For example, CRect rcElllipse (ptCenter, ptCenter);.

You can then use the InflateRect() function to specify the diameter of the circle and then pass this rectangle to the Ellipse() function to draw it.

Drawing Chords and Wedges

A *chord* is an ellipse that has had a straight line drawn across it and then been cut along that line into two pieces; each of those pieces is now a chord. That's exactly how we use the Chord() function. It needs a rectangle object (CRect) to specify the coordinates just like an ellipse would. Then we supply two coordinate pairs to define the beginning and end points of an imaginary line that would chop it into two pieces. The drawn section depends on which coordinate is given first.

Make the changes in Listing 16.17 between the brush selection line in OnDraw().

LISTING 16.17 LST17_17.CPP—Drawing Chord Sections with *Chord()*

① The chord will be drawn intersected by a line from the top left to the bottom right.

```
1   pOldBrush = pDC->SelectObject(&brBlue);
2
3   CRect rcChord = rcClient;
4   rcChord.DeflateRect(50,50);
5
6   pDC->Chord(rcChord,          ①
7       rcClient.TopLeft(),
8       rcClient.BottomRight());
9
10  pDC->SelectObject(pOldBrush);
```

The first thing you might notice is that the declaration of the rcChord object at line 3 is also initialized from the client rectangle. You can then Deflate() the rectangle by 50 pixels in line 4 and use this to draw your chord in lines 5, 6, and 7. The chopping line is made from the top-left and bottom-right coordinates of the client rectangle. This will give you a nice diagonal line running from the top left of the window, chopping the chord in half to the bottom-right corner.

If you compile and run after these changes, you should get a chord like Figure 16.8.

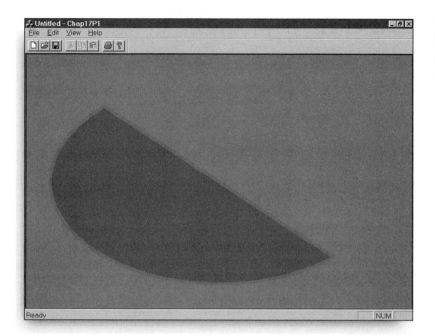

FIGURE 16.8
A filled chord.

Drawing Polygons

The Polygon() function takes identical parameters as the
Polyline() and PolyBezier() functions. It needs a set of points
for each coordinate pair and the number of coordinates in the
list. It then draws a filled polygon linking the points. Unlike
Polyline() we don't have to make the last coordinate the same as
the first in order for the object to be closed because this is done
automatically.

There is one complication to bear in mind—the fill mode.
A function named SetPolyFillMode() lets us specify either
ALTERNATE or WINDING. If it is set to ALTERNATE, the polygon
will be filled as the lines are encountered from left to right.
The WINDING mode uses the direction of the line relative to
its predecessor.

Make the changes in Listing 16.18 to the OnDraw() to draw the
polygons.

Finding the current polygon filling mode

You can find the current polygon
filling mode by calling the device
context's
GetPolyFillMode()
function. This will return either
ALTERNATE or WINDING
depending on the current fill mode
set in that device context.

LISTING 16.18 LST17_18.CPP—Drawing Stars with *Polygon()*

(1) On the first iteration, the w is zero, so the WINDING mode is used. On the second iteration the star is drawn with the ALTERNATE mode.

(2) The points of the star are calculated and stored in the ptPolyAr array of points.

(3) The polygon can be drawn from the array of points and the number of elements in the array using the Polygon() function.

```cpp
1   #include "math.h"
2   void CMyDrawView::OnDraw(CDC* pDC)
3   {
4       CMyDrawDoc* pDoc = GetDocument();
5       ASSERT_VALID(pDoc);
6
7       CPen penRed(PS_SOLID,5,RGB(255,0,0));
8       CPen *pOldPen = NULL;
9
10      pOldPen = pDC->SelectObject(&penRed);
11
12      CRect rcClient;
13      GetClientRect(&rcClient);
14
15      CBrush brBlue(RGB(0,0,255));
16      CBrush *pOldBrush = NULL;
17
18      pOldBrush = pDC->SelectObject(&brBlue);
19
20      for(int w=0;w<2;w++)
21      {
22          const int nPoints = 5;
23          double nAngle = (720.0/57.295)/(double)nPoints;
24          int xOffset = (w ? 1 : -1)*rcClient.Width()/4;
25          pDC->SetPolyFillMode(w ? ALTERNATE : WINDING);  ──────① 
26          CPoint ptPolyAr[nPoints];
27          for(int i=0;i<nPoints;i++)   ──────②
28          {
29              ptPolyAr[i].x = xOffset +
30                  (long)(sin((double)i * nAngle) * 100.0);
31              ptPolyAr[i].y =
32                  (long)(cos((double)i * nAngle) * 100.0);
33              ptPolyAr[i] += rcClient.CenterPoint();
34          }
35          pDC->Polygon(ptPolyAr,nPoints);   ──────③
36
37      }
38
39      pDC->SelectObject(pOldBrush);
40      pDC->SelectObject(pOldPen);
41  }
```

You must also add a line at the top to #include "math.h" to make sin and cos work.

Two stars are built up in the point arrays at line 26 and are drawn using the Polygon() function in line 35. The first, on the left, uses the WINDING fill mode, whereas the second uses the ALTERNATE fill mode. Because the lines making up the star shape criss-cross each other, the WINDING version fills the entire shape, whereas the ALTERNATE mode leaves an unfilled area in the middle of the shape.

When compiled and run, the polygons produced should look like Figure 16.9.

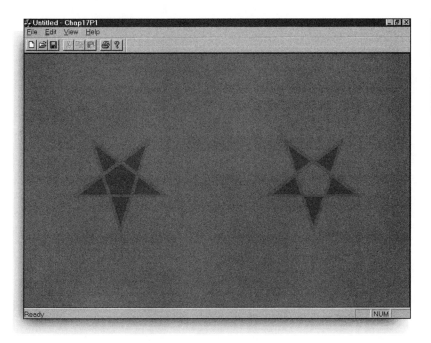

FIGURE 16.9
Polygons drawn with ALTERNATE and WINDING fill modes.

chapter 17

Using Fonts

Displaying text in a variety
of colors and styles

Using fonts to enhance
your application

Since William Caxton's invention of the printing press, the printed word has become ubiquitous in our lives. Fonts formerly designed for newsprint have multiplied and now surround us in endless variety. The correct choice of fonts can have an important effect on the presentation and style of your application. Windows provides comprehensive support for displaying text in a variety of fonts and styles.

Text-Drawing Functions

A central goal of the Windows GDI designers was to provide a mechanism that could consistently support high-quality graphical displays across a range of devices. *WYSIWYG* (what you see is what you get) was an '80s buzzword—now it is taken for granted. The rendering of text in a range of fonts across different screens and printers is one of the most challenging aspects of maintaining consistency. Fortunately, the designers succeeded, and through a powerful set of font selection and text output functions, you can render text with the knowledge that it will be accurately represented on many different devices.

SEE ALSO

➤ *For more information on device contexts, see page 356*

➤ *To retrieve device capabilities, see page 377*

Drawing Simple Text

Other TextOut() functions

The TextOut() function has several similar functions. TabbedTextOut() can expand tab characters to a series of tab positions specified in an array. PolyTextOut() can display an array of text strings in a single function call. ExtTextOut() lets you specify extended rendering options to change how the text string is drawn.

The TextOut() member function of the device context is probably the quickest and easiest way to draw text. It requires x- and y-coordinate parameters to specify positions and then a CString to hold the text to be displayed.

You can use an SDI view again to provide a blank sheet to draw on. Create an SDI framework by using AppWizard, accepting all the project defaults as you learned in Chapter 12, "Using Documents, Views, and Frames." You can use this SDI application to try out some of the text-drawing functions.

Select the ClassView pane of the Workspace view. You will see the **CSimpTextView** class. Click the plus symbol (**+**) to open the members view for this class. Double-click **OnDraw()**, and add the lines in Listing 17.1 to the default implementation. These lines will draw a simple line of text.

LISTING 17.1   LST18_1.CPP—Drawing Text with *TextOut()*

```
1    void CSimpTextView::OnDraw(CDC* pDC)
2    {
3        CSimpTextDoc* pDoc = GetDocument();
4        ASSERT_VALID(pDoc);
5
6        // TODO: add draw code for native data here
7
8        CString strText = "Water under the bridge.";
9        pDC->TextOut(100,100,strText);
10   }
```

(1) TextOut() draws the string variable text at 100 pixels across and 100 pixels down.

In Listing 17.1, text is assigned to the strText string and then passed to the TextOut() function to be displayed. TextOut() also requires a coordinate position specified as 100 pixels across and 100 down in line 9. If you compile and run these changes, you will see the text displayed in the default font and colors (black on white) near the top left of the window.

Setting the Text Alignment

You can align the text around the specified point several ways by using the SetTextAlign() function. This device context member function takes a number of flags to set the default alignment and to set how the cursor position should be updated after drawing the text.

The flags refer to where the specified point should appear in relation to the text; this might appear confusing at first. You might expect TA_RIGHT to align the text to the right of the point, but, in fact, the text is aligned to the left with the point on the right. Table 17.1 shows the flags you can pass to SetTextAlign().

Find the current text alignment setting

The current text alignment settings for a device context can be found from the value returned by calling the GetTextAlign() function. This return value is composed of the same flag settings you would use to set the text alignment when calling SetTextAlign().

TABLE 17.1 Text alignment flags for *SetTextAlign()*

Alignment Flag	Effect on Drawing Text
TA_LEFT	Text is aligned to the right of the point.
TA_RIGHT	Text is aligned to the left of the point.
TA_CENTER	Text is centered over the point.
TA_TOP	Text is aligned under the point.
TA_BOTTOM	Text is aligned above the point.
TA_BASELINE	Text is aligned so that its baseline lies on the point.
TA_UPDATECP	The *graphics cursor position* is updated after each TextOut(), the specified coordinates are ignored, and new text is displayed directly after the previous position.
TA_NOUPDATECP	The graphics cursor position isn't updated after each TextOut().

You can see the alignment in action by drawing a cross at the coordinate (200,200) and setting the various text alignments around that point by passing the various alignment flags. To try these alignment settings, change your OnDraw() implementation as shown in Listing 17.2.

LISTING 17.2 LST18_2.CPP—Setting the Text Alignment

① Text is aligned Right by default anyway, but set here for clarity.

```
1   void CSimpTextView::OnDraw(CDC* pDC)
2   {
3       CSimpTextDoc* pDoc = GetDocument();
4       ASSERT_VALID(pDoc);
5
6       // TODO: add draw code for native data here
7
8       // ** Align point to the right of the text
9       pDC->SetTextAlign(TA_RIGHT); ────────────────① 
10
11      // ** Draw the Text
12      pDC->TextOut(200,200,"<-Right->");
13
14      // ** Align point to the left of the text
15      pDC->SetTextAlign(TA_LEFT);
16      pDC->TextOut(200,200,"<-Left->");
```

```
17
18          // ** Align point to the center and below the text
19          pDC->SetTextAlign(TA_CENTER + TA_BOTTOM);
20          pDC->TextOut(200,200,"<-Center->");
21
22          pDC->MoveTo(150,200);    // ** Move
23          pDC->LineTo(250,200);    // ** Draw horizontal line
24          pDC->MoveTo(200,150);    // ** Move
25          pDC->LineTo(200,250);    // ** Draw vertical line
26
27      }
```

(2) You can combine flags where appropriate. Here the text is centered and above the specified position.

Each TextOut() call is positioned at the same coordinates, but the alignment is changed each time so that the text appears around the point indicated by the cross. If you compile and run this, you will see the text appear around the cross, as shown in Figure 17.1.

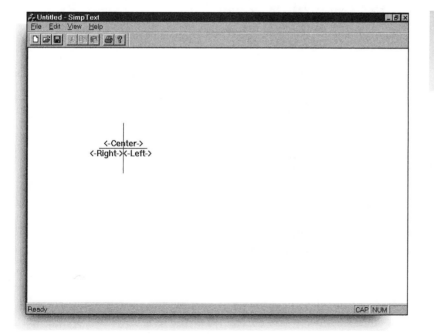

FIGURE 17.1
Various text alignment settings.

SEE ALSO

➤ *For details on drawing lines and shapes, see page 390*

Changing the Foreground and Background Colors

The default text colors are black on white, but these can be changed by the SetTextColor() and SetBkColor() functions in the device context. Both take only one parameter: a color reference value (COLORREF) for the desired text or background color. They also return a COLORREF that indicates the previous text or background color.

You can add color to your OnDraw() implementation by adding the SetTextColor() and SetBkColor() calls before the TextOut() functions are called. This can be seen in Listing 17.3.

Finding the current text colors

You can find the current text colors using the GetTextColor() and GetBkColor() functions, which return the current foreground and background color settings for a device context. Both functions return a COLORREF value to indicate the current color.

LISTING 17.3 LST18_3.CPP—Setting the Text Color with *SetTextColor()* and *SetBkColor()*

```
1   // ** Set the Foreground to Blue
2   pDC->SetTextColor(RGB(0,0,255));
3   pDC->TextOut(200,200,"<-Right->");
4
5   pDC->SetTextAlign(TA_LEFT);
6
7   // ** Set the Foreground to Red
8   pDC->SetTextColor(RGB(255,0,0));          (1)
9   pDC->TextOut(200,200,"<-Left->");
10
11  // Align point to the center and below the text
12  pDC->SetTextAlign(TA_CENTER + TA_BOTTOM);
13
14  // ** Set the Foreground to Yellow
15  pDC->SetTextColor(RGB(255,255,0));
16
17  // ** Set the Background to Dark Blue
18  pDC->SetBkColor(RGB(0,0,128));            (2)
19  pDC->TextOut(200,200,"<-Center->");
```

(1) This line sets the foreground color when text is drawn.

(2) This line sets the background color when text is drawn.

In Listing 17.3, the SetTextColor() in line 2 changes the text color to blue, in line 8 to red, and in line 15 to yellow. In line 18, the background color is set to dark blue.

If you compile and run after adding these lines, you will see the same text as before but in different colors and backgrounds.

SEE ALSO

➤ *For more details on color references and the RGB macro, see page 385*

Drawing Opaque and Transparent Text

Sometimes you might want the text that you draw to obscure the area underneath. At other times you might want to merge the text over the current drawing. SetBkMode() lets you switch between these options. It takes one parameter that is a flag for OPAQUE (the default value) or TRANSPARENT (for transparent text), indicating the desired mode. If you call SetBkMode() with OPAQUE, both background and foreground colors will be used to draw the text. When you set to TRANSPARENT, only the foreground color will be used.

You can change OnDraw() to show transparent and opaque drawing modes, as in Listing 17.4.

LISTING 17.4 LST18_4.CPP—Setting Opaque and Transparent Modes for Drawing Text

```
1    void CSimpTextView::OnDraw(CDC* pDC)
2    {
3        CSimpTextDoc* pDoc = GetDocument();
4        ASSERT_VALID(pDoc);
5
6        // TODO: add draw code for native data here
7
8        pDC->Ellipse(160,160,240,240);
9        pDC->SetTextAlign(TA_CENTER);
10
11       // ** Set Transparent Mode
12       pDC->SetBkMode(TRANSPARENT);
13
14       // ** Display some Text
15       pDC->TextOut(200, 180, "Transparent");          (1)
16
17       // ** Set Opaque Mode
18       pDC->SetBkMode(OPAQUE);          (2)
19
20       // ** Display some Text
21       pDC->TextOut(200, 220, "Opaque");
22   }
```

(1) In transparent mode, the circle can be seen under the letters of the text.

(2) In opaque mode, the text is drawn with a background obscuring the circle.

In Listing 17.4, any text displayed after line 12 will have a transparent background. The OPAQUE mode set in line 18 changes text to display on an opaque-colored background.

If you compile and run after making these changes, you will see that the ellipse is obscured by the word Opaque. However, it is visible under the word Transparent. If a current background color is set, it won't be used when drawing in transparent mode.

Clipping Text to Rectangles

Often it is necessary to *clip* text so that it doesn't spill out of a holding rectangle. Even though you might chop out part of the text, this is sometimes preferable to text sprawling over the rest of a diagram.

ExtTextOut() is a more sophisticated form of TextOut(). You can pass it an ETO_CLIPPED flag to make it clip your text. ExtTextOut() takes x- and y-coordinates, like TextOut() for the first two parameters. You can pass a couple of flag values for the third parameter, such as the ETO_CLIPPED value for clipping. You can also combine the ETO_CLIPPED flag value with the ETO_OPAQUE flag value, which lets you use opaque text even when transparent mode has been set. If you don't want either clipping or opaque text, you can pass zero to this third parameter (as shown in line 13 of Listing 17.5). The fourth parameter requires a CRect object, and if the clipping flag has been set, this rectangle will clip the text. You can pass the text to be drawn as the fifth parameter (held in a CString object). Finally, a character-spacing array can be passed as the sixth parameter, or it can be left to the default spacing by passing NULL.

You can clip your text by changing your OnDraw() function, as shown in Listing 17.5.

> **Using the TA_UPDATECP flag with ExtTextOut()**
>
> You can use the TA_UPDATECP text alignment flag as set with the SetTextAlign() function in conjunction with the ExtTextOut() function. When this flag is set, the coordinates for the first TextOut() or ExtTextOut() function are used as normal. However, all subsequent calls to these functions ignore the supplied coordinates and render the text after the current graphics cursor position.

LISTING 17.5 LST18_5.CPP—Clipping Text with *ExtTextOut()*

```
1   void CSimpTextView::OnDraw(CDC* pDC)
2   {
3       CSimpTextDoc* pDoc = GetDocument();
4       ASSERT_VALID(pDoc);
```

```
5
6        // TODO: add draw code for native data here
7
8        CRect rcClipBox(CPoint(100,100),CPoint(250,120));
9        pDC->Rectangle(rcClipBox);
10       pDC->SetBkMode(TRANSPARENT);
11
12       // ** Draw the unclipped text
13       pDC->ExtTextOut(100,100,0,rcClipBox,
14               _"This text won't fit in there!",NULL);
15
16       rcClipBox.OffsetRect(0,40);
17       pDC->Rectangle(rcClipBox);
18
19       // ** Draw the clipped text
20       pDC->ExtTextOut(100,140,ETO_CLIPPED    ,rcClipBox,
21           _"This text won't fit in there!",NULL);
22   }
```

① The ExtTextOut() function clips the text to the specified box when the ETO_CLIPPED flag is specified.

In Listing 17.5, a rectangle is declared in line 8. This will be used for both positioning and clipping the text. The ExtTextOut() in line 13 is called without the ETO_CLIPPED, so the text will spill from the rectangle. The ExtTextOut() in line 20 is clipped, so the spilled text won't be visible.

If you compile and run Listing 17.5, you will see the two rectangles, with the text spilling from one but clipped in the other.

SEE ALSO

➤ *For details on drawing and clipping, see page 363*

Creating Various Fonts

So far, you've displayed text using the default device context font. Like brushes and pens, fonts are also represented by GDI objects and can be selected in and out of a device context. You can create and tailor fonts, as required, by using the variety of functions provided by the Windows GDI and their MFC wrappers.

Using the *CFont* Class

CFont is the wrapper class for the GDI font object. Unlike some of the other wrapper classes, CFont can't simply be constructed with some defaults and used. Instead, you must declare a CFont object and then use one of the Create functions to specify the many possible parameters.

The Create functions can't always give you exactly the font you specify. Instead, the font mapper looks at your requests, tries to find the font closest to your requirements, and then tailors that font to resemble what you ask for, as best it can (it usually does quite a good job).

Creating Fonts with *CreatePointFont()*

CreatePointFont() is the easiest way to quickly create a font. It requires three parameters: the size of the point in tenths of a point, the typeface name of the font (for example, Arial), and, finally, the device context in which you must use the new font. Change your OnDraw() function to use CreatePointFont(), as shown in Listing 17.6, to draw some text in a new large Arial font.

LISTING 17.6 LST18_6—Creating Fonts with *CreatePointFont()*

① CreatePointFont() is a quick and easy way to create a sized font in the specified typeface.

```
1   void CSimpTextView::OnDraw(CDC* pDC)
2   {
3       CSimpTextDoc* pDoc = GetDocument();
4       ASSERT_VALID(pDoc);
5
6       // TODO: add draw code for native data here
7
8       // ** Create a 36 point Arial font
9       CFont fnBig;
10      fnBig.CreatePointFont(360,"Arial",pDC);  ——①
11
12      CFont* pOldFont = pDC->SelectObject(&fnBig);
13
14      pDC->TextOut(50,50,"** 36 Pt Arial Font **");
15
16      pDC->SelectObject(pOldFont);
17  }
```

Notice that in line 10, `360` is passed into `CreatePointFont()`. The point size passed here is specified in tenths of a point. This gives you flexibility in the size of the desired font. When you compile and run this, you will see a large (36-point) Arial font used to draw the text in line 14.

Creating Fonts with *CreateFont()*

`CreateFont()` is probably one of the trickiest functions you'll find in the MFC, largely because it requires 14 parameters, most of which are complex flag combinations. Even so, there isn't a way to tweak all the possible options that make up a font, so you must go with it. The prototype for `CreateFont()` can be found in Listing 17.7.

LISTING 17.7 LST18_7.CPP—Parameters for the *CreateFont* Function

```
1    BOOL CreateFont( int nHeight, int nWidth,
2      int nEscapement, int nOrientation, int nWeight,
3      BYTE bItalic, BYTE bUnderline, BYTE cStrikeOut,
4      BYTE nCharSet, BYTE nOutPrecision,
5      BYTE nClipPrecision, BYTE nQuality,
6      BYTE nPitchAndFamily, LPCTSTR lpszFacename );
```

Setting the Font Height and Width

The first two parameters of `CreateFont()` deal with the height and width of the required font. The first parameter, `nHeight`, can be negative or positive. If you specify positive values, the font mapper will try to match the height you specify against its list of available fonts and choose the nearest match, based on the cell height of the font. If you specify a negative value for `nHeight`, the font mapper will try to match the height against the character height of the font.

The difference between a *cell* and a *character* is that a cell has some blank gaps above and below the actual character, whereas the character height is the cell height with these blanks ignored. A value of zero will cause the mapper to pick a sensible (you hope) default value.

> **Height matching rules**
>
> When matching heights of fonts, the font mapper will choose the largest font smaller than the height you specify.

The nWidth parameter specifies the average width required (proportionally spaced fonts have narrow and wide characters). You can set this parameter to zero, and the mapper will work out a good default based on the height and the aspect ratio.

Setting the Font Escapement and Orientation

Escapement and *orientation* refer to the slope the text is printed at (normally, horizontal) and the rotation of the characters themselves:

- The nEscapement parameter lets you draw slanted text by specifying the angle of the text from the x-axis in tenths of a degree. A value of 900 here will give you vertical text.

- The nOrientation parameter specifies the angle of the characters' baselines and the x-axis—again, in tenths of a degree.

Setting Bold, Italic, Underline, and Strikeout

The next four parameters deal with the weight (which you can set for bold or thin styles) and let you set modes such as italics, underline, and strikeout.

- The nWeight parameter lets you change the thickness of the characters, from 0 (thin) to 1000 (chunky). There are some predefined values you can use, as shown in Table 17.2.

Equivalent font weight flags

You might see other flag values, such as FW_ULTRALIGHT, FW_REGULAR, FW_DEMIBOLD, FW_ULTRABOLD, and FW_BLACK. These are equivalent to the FW_EXTRALIGHT, FW_NORMAL, FW_SEMIBOLD, FW_EXTRABOLD, and FW_HEAVY flags, respectively.

TABLE 17.2 Font weight flags

Flag	Weight Value
FW_DONTCARE	0
FW_THIN	100
FW_EXTRALIGHT	200
FW_LIGHT	300
FW_NORMAL	400
FW_MEDIUM	500
FW_SEMIBOLD	600
FW_BOLD	700
FW_EXTRABOLD	800
FW_HEAVY	900

- The bItalic parameter draws the font in *italic*, if set to TRUE.

- The bUnderline parameter draws the font <u>underlined</u>, if set to TRUE.

- The bStrikeOut parameter draws the font ~~strikedout~~, if set to TRUE.

Setting Quality and Precision

The quality and precision parameters let you set how the font is chosen and rendered for and on the target device. There are also provisions for choosing styles, such as fixed pitch or proportional spacing, and for indicating whether serifs are preferred.

- The nCharSet parameter lets you specify a character set. Normally, you would set this to ANSI_CHARSET to get the standard ANSI characters. Sometimes you might set it to SYMBOL_CHARSET for symbols instead of normal characters.

- The nOutPrecision parameter lets you specify how the font mapper chooses a particular font instead of another. Normally, you would specify OUT_DEFAULT_PRECIS here, but if you want to insist on a TrueType font, you can specify OUT_TT_PRECIS.

- The nClipPrecision parameter lets you specify the clipping precision. Normally, CLIP_DEFAULT_PRECIS would be set here.

- The nQuality parameter lets you set the trade-off between character appearance quality and matching the other parameters you have specified. You can set DEFAULT_QUALITY, DRAFT_QUALITY, or PROOF_QUALITY here.

- The nPitchAndFamily parameter lets you set two things at once. Because of this, it's very easy to specify two parameters and receive a compile error saying that CreateFont() doesn't take 15 parameters. If you receive this message, check that these values are combined (with + or ¦) and not separated by a comma.

The possible pitch values are shown in Table 17.3.

> **Alternative clipping precision flags**
>
> These flags change the way in which a font is clipped when part of it falls outside a clipping region. Other possible flag values are CLIP_EMBEDDED (should be used for embedded read-only fonts) and CLIP_LH_ANGLES (can be used when the orientation of the font is changed). You might see other flags used in older code; however, many of these are no longer used and can be ignored.

TABLE 17.3 Pitch settings

Pitch Flag	Description
DEFAULT_PITCH	Whatever the font normally does
VARIABLE_PITCH	A variable pitch font only
FIXED_PITCH	A fixed pitch font only, useful for terminal emulators

You can combine the pitch flags shown in Table 17.3 with the font family flags shown in Table 17.4 for the nPitchAndFamily parameter. For example, you might specify DEFAULT_PITCH | FF_SCRIPT for a default pitched handwriting font.

Using the TrueType fonts

You can use the TMPF_ TRUETYPE flag in combination with one of the family flags to request a specific family member of a TrueType font.

TABLE 17.4 Font family settings

Family Flag	Description
FF_DECORATIVE	Novelty fonts
FF_DONTCARE	As it says
FF_MODERN	Fixed pitch or constant stroke-width fonts
FF_ROMAN	Proportionally spaced fonts with variable stroke width
FF_SCRIPT	Handwriting styles
FF_SWISS	Proportional spacing but no serifs
TMPF_TRUETYPE	A TrueType version required

The *TrueType* fonts are fonts drawn as a series of curves and hints. Because of the way they are drawn, they are much better than raster fonts when scaled up.

Setting a Specific Font Name

The lpszFacename parameter lets you specify the name of one of the currently installed fonts, such as Times New Roman.

Creating a Font with the *CreateFont()* Function

You can try an example to create and use a font while changing some of the settings. To do so, you must make the changes to the OnDraw() view member function, as shown in Listing 17.8. This listing displays a line of text that is spun around a central point by changing its orientation through 360 degrees.

LISTING 17.8   LST18_8.CPP—Creating Fonts with *CreateFont()*

```
1    void CSimpTextView::OnDraw(CDC* pDC)
2    {
3        CSimpTextDoc* pDoc = GetDocument();
4        ASSERT_VALID(pDoc);
5
6        // TODO: add draw code for native data here
7
8        // ** Declare a CRect to hold the client rect
9        CRect rcClient;
10       GetClientRect(&rcClient);
11
12       // ** Find the mid point
13       CPoint ptCentre = rcClient.CenterPoint();
14       pDC->SetBkMode(TRANSPARENT);
15
16       // ** Loop through 360 degrees
17       for(int i=0 ; i <360 ; i+=18)
18       {
19           CFont fnBig;
20
21               // ** 30 high, default width
22           fnBig.CreateFont(30,0,
23                   // ** Change Orientation
24               i*10,i*10,
25                   // ** Increase the weight
26               i/4,
27               FALSE,
28               TRUE, //** Underlined
29               FALSE,
30               ANSI_CHARSET,
31               OUT_DEFAULT_PRECIS,
32               CLIP_DEFAULT_PRECIS,
33               PROOF_QUALITY,
34               DEFAULT_PITCH + FF_DONTCARE,
35               "Arial"
36               );
37
38           CFont* pOldFont = pDC->SelectObject(&fnBig);
39
40           // ** Draw the text
```

① CreateFont() lets the font mapper pick and create a sophisticated font, but can be difficult to use with all these parameters.

continues...

431

LISTING 17.8 Continued

```
41              pDC->TextOut(ptCentre.x,ptCentre.y,
42                  ".....Beautiful Fonts");
43
44              pDC->SelectObject(pOldFont);
45          }
46      }
```

② This simple
TextOut() can
draw the rotated font
text.

Creating the font once to speed up your application

In a real application, you would probably create the font once and then hold it as a member variable of the view class, thus reducing the time overhead for creating the font.

In Listing 17.8, lines 17–44 spin the text around the central point found in line 13. The huge CreateFont() function starting at line 22 is passed an ever-increasing font weight parameter at line 26. The angle is passed to the orientation and escapement in line 24, causing the font to slope through all the angles iterated through by the loop.

If you compile and run this version, you will see the text spun around the center of the window, as illustrated in Figure 17.2.

FIGURE 17.2

Spinning text by using CreateFont().

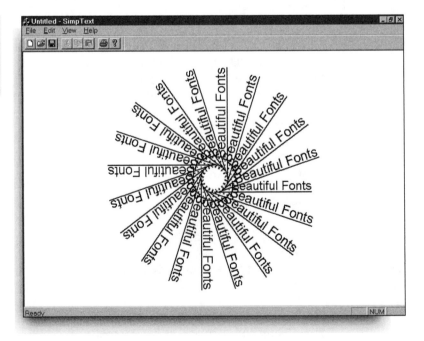

Selecting and Choosing Fonts

The modern Windows user is accustomed to selecting from a wide range of available fonts. Many applications, not just word processors, now offer this as a standard capability. To incorporate this flexibility in your applications, you need a way to get at the list of installed fonts and their settings. The GDI offers this capability through a set of font enumeration functions and special selection dialog boxes.

Enumerating Fonts

How can your program obtain a list of the currently available fonts and all their settings? Answer: The `EnumFontFamilies()` function and its associated *callback function*.

Callback functions work by setting up a function that is called with each item in the list and then telling a callback *enumerator* the name of your callback function. The enumerator works down the list of items (in this case, fonts) and calls your callback function for each of those items.

You can set up such an enumerator to walk through your list of fonts and fetch the information associated with each one. It then passes all the details it knows about each font to your callback function.

For example, you can obtain a list of the installed fonts, each displayed in its own font settings, as shown in Figure 17.3. The code in Listing 17.9 and following explanation shows how `EnumFontFamilies()` can be used to accomplish this task.

To draw the font list (shown in Figure 17.3), you must add the following callback function above the `OnDraw()`. Note that it is a global function and, therefore, has no class scope before its name. You must put it above the `OnDraw()`; otherwise, you would need to add a function declaration somewhere before the `OnDraw()`. Also add the `EnumFontFamilies()` function to the `OnDraw()`, as shown in Listing 17.9.

Enumerator functions in C++

Enumerator functions were common in the straight C world of WIN32. However, callback techniques have no way of passing the object context normally supplied by the C++ **this** keyword. This means they must be global functions that don't sit nicely with the object-oriented world of C++. However, because the MFC C++ classes must utilize the WIN32 subsystem like any Windows program (regardless of its language), they must accept global callback functions for these special cases.

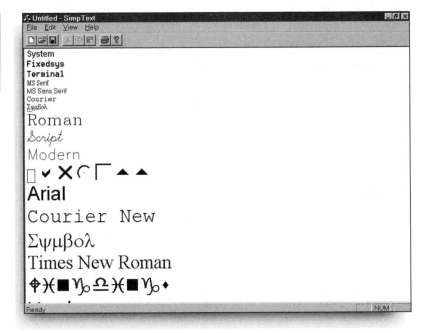

FIGURE 17.3

Enumerated fonts with
EnumFontFamilies().

LISTING 17.9 LST18_9—Enumerating and Displaying the Installed Fonts

① Your callback function will be called for each of the installed fonts in the system. Their details are passed as parameters.

② The CreateFont Indirect() function is just like the CreateFont() function, but the parameters are passed as members of the LOGFONT structure.

```
1   // ** The Font Callback function
2   int CALLBACK FontCallBack(ENUMLOGFONT FAR* lpelf,          ①
3                             NEWTEXTMETRIC FAR *lpnt,
4                             int FontType,
5                             LPARAM lParam)
6   {
7       // ** Pick the DC pointer from the lParam
8       CDC* pDC = (CDC*)lParam;
9       CFont fnEnum;
10
11      // ** Create the font indirectly
12      fnEnum.CreateFontIndirect(&lpelf->elfLogFont);          ②
13
14      CFont* pOldFont = pDC->SelectObject(&fnEnum);
15
16      // ** Get the current Cursor position
17      int nYPos = pDC->GetCurrentPosition().y;
18
19      // ** Draw the font name
20      pDC->TextOut(5,nYPos,CString(lpelf->elfLogFont.
        ➥lfFaceName));
```

```
21
22        //** Move down by the height of the font
23        pDC->MoveTo(0,nYPos + lpelf->elfLogFont.lfHeight);     ──③
24
25        pDC->SelectObject(pOldFont);
26
27        // ** return TRUE to keep on going
28        return TRUE;
29    }
30
31
32
33    //////////////////////////////////////////////////////
34    // CSimpTextView drawing
35
36    void CSimpTextView::OnDraw(CDC* pDC)
37    {
38        CSimpTextDoc* pDoc = GetDocument();
39        ASSERT_VALID(pDoc);
40
41        // TODO: add draw code for native data here
42
43        // ** Setup the enum callback calling your
44        //     function
44        EnumFontFamilies(pDC->GetSafeHdc(),NULL,──────④
45              (FONTENUMPROC)FontCallBack,(LPARAM)pDC);
46    }
```

③ This MoveTo() function is called to set up the graphics cursor ready for the next font.

④ The address of your callback function is passed to EnumFontFamilies( ) so that it can call it with each of the installed fonts.

In Listing 17.9, the first function shown in lines 1–29 is the callback function. For every font installed on your machine, this function will be called, with the details of each font passed as its parameters. So, what is happening here? In the OnDraw(), the callback enumerator is set up.

The LParam parameter is a user-defined value that has been set up as the device context pointer by the callback initialization function in line 44. This device context is then used to draw each of the different fonts that are compatible with that device (in this case, the device is the screen).

The CreateFontIndirect() function in line 12 is like CreateFont() but takes a structure holding all the parameters, as shown later in Listing 17.11.

The second parameter to the enumerator function on line 44 is the font family. By passing NULL, you'll have all the font families. You could have passed one of the families such as Arial or Courier, and you'd have only the fonts in that family.

The third parameter is the name of your callback function, which you can cast into a (FONTENUMPROC) to keep the compiler from complaining.

Finally, you can pass some user information in the long parameter provided. Because you want to draw the fonts, the device context (which you'll draw with) is probably the most useful thing to pass.

As you can see, the enumerator finds the list of installed fonts, starts calling your callback function FontCallBack(), and passes it several parameters. The first is an ENUMLOGFONT structure. Listing 17.10 shows how this is defined.

LISTING 18.10   LST17_10.CPP—The *ENUMLOGFONT* Structure

```
1   typedef struct tagENUMLOGFONT {
2      LOGFONT    elfLogFont;
3      BCHAR      elfFullName[LF_FULLFACESIZE];
4      BCHAR      elfStyle[LF_FACESIZE];
5   } ENUMLOGFONT;
```

The ENUMLOGFONT passed holds the name elfFullName and style elfStyle of the font, but probably the most useful thing is the LOGFONT structure it holds. The LOGFONT is a structure version of all the parameters that you can pass into CreateFont(). As you saw in line 12 of Listing 17.9, it can be used with CreateFontIndirect(). Listing 17.11 shows how this structure is defined by Windows.

LISTING 17.11   LST18_11.CPP—The *LOGFONT* Structure

```
1   typedef struct tagLOGFONT { // lf
2      LONG lfHeight;
3      LONG lfWidth;
4      LONG lfEscapement;
5      LONG lfOrientation;
```

```
6      LONG lfWeight;
7      BYTE lfItalic;
8      BYTE lfUnderline;
9      BYTE lfStrikeOut;
10     BYTE lfCharSet;
11     BYTE lfOutPrecision;
12     BYTE lfClipPrecision;
13     BYTE lfQuality;
14     BYTE lfPitchAndFamily;
15     TCHAR lfFaceName[LF_FACESIZE];
16   } LOGFONT;
```

You can access any of these LOGFONT details by interrogating the LOGFONT structure via the ENUMLOGFONT structure pointer lpelf pass to your callback function (as shown in line 2 of Listing 17.9). It's first used in line 12 (by using the &lpelf->elfLogFont code to find the address of the LOGFONT structure).

The next parameter passed to your callback function in Listing 17.9 is a NEWTEXTMETRICS structure. This is used for holding details about character sizes and details of how the font will appear when mapped to a specific device context.

You are then passed a FontType. This tells you whether the font is a TRUETYPE_FONTTYPE, a RASTER_FONTTYPE, or a DEVICE_FONTTYPE. Finally, you're passed your device context pointer as an LPARAM, which you immediately cast back to the lovable CDCX form.

After creating and selecting the font, you obtain the current graphics position from the device context by using GetCurrentPosition(), as shown in line 17 of Listing 17.9. You can obtain the name of the font from the LOGFONT structure (as shown in line 20 of Listing 17.9) and display it with a call to TextOut().

The graphics cursor position can be updated by the height of the font and set with a MoveTo() call, as in line 23. After reselecting the old font, you must return a TRUE value for the *enumerator* to continue. Alternatively, a FALSE would indicate that you don't want to be called again.

> **The TEXTMETRICS structures**
>
> As you might have already guessed, the NEWTEXTMETRICS structure had a predecessor called TEXT-METRICS. There are in fact many different versions of the WIN32 structures and different functions can require slightly different versions. To add to the confusion, there is also a NEWTEXTMETRICSEX, TEXTMETRICW, and TEXTMET-RICA that deal with font signatures, Unicode, and non-Unicode, respectively.

Using the Choose Font Dialog Box

Windows provides a standard dialog box for choosing a font and its settings. Lots of applications incorporate it, and you've already used it probably countless times.

You can add the Choose Font dialog box to the sample application by first adding a new menu option to select the Choose Fonts dialog box. You can do this by adding a new menu subitem with the Choose Font caption text (as shown in Figure 17.4) and a corresponding ID of ID_CHOOSEFONT. The "Insert a New Submenu Item" step by step described in Chapter 13, "Working with Menus," explains how to do this.

Then you'll need to add a COMMAND message handler function called OnChoosefont() for your new menu option (ID_CHOOSEFONT) to the CSimpTextView class (as shown in Figure 17.5) by following the "Adding a Menu Command Handler Function with ClassWizard" step by step also found in Chapter 13.

FIGURE 17.4
Inserting a Choose Font menu option.

FIGURE 17.5
Adding an OnChoosefont menu handler with ClassWizard.

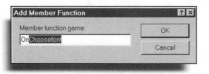

You now have a menu and associated handler function in which you can add and use the CFontDialog class, as shown in Listing 17.12.

LISTING 17.12 LST18_12.CPP—Implementing the *OnChooseFont()* Menu Handler

```
1    void CSimpTextView::OnChoosefont()
2    {
```

```
3        // TODO: Add your command handler code here
4
5        // ** Declare the CFontDialog ──────⬤①
6        CFontDialog dlgChooseFont;
7        if (dlgChooseFont.DoModal() == IDOK)
8        {
9            m_fnCustom.DeleteObject();
10           m_fnCustom.CreateFontIndirect(
11               dlgChooseFont.m_cf.lpLogFont);
12           Invalidate();
13       }
14   }
```

① The CFontDialog wraps the systems standard CHOOSEFONT dialog box and provides an easy but sophisticated method of letting the user pick a specific font and style.

In Listing 17.12, a CFontDialog object is declared as dlgChooseFont in line 6. You can then start the dialog box by calling DoModal(), as in line 7. The user can select the new font, and if he or she clicks **OK** you must call DeleteObject() on your existing font to free any GDI object. Then you can create the new font from the CFontDialogs m_cf member that has a pointer to the LOGFONT structure. Then call Invalidate() (line 12) to force the view to redraw and redisplay your OnDraw() message.

Next, you must add that m_fnCustom font variable to the view class. Click the **ClassView** tab of the Project Workspace view, and then double-click the **CSimpTextView** header to obtain the view class declaration. Add the following font member under the // Attributes comment, as shown in Listing 17.13.

LISTING 17.13   LST18_13.CPP—Adding a *CFont* Member to the View Class

```
1    // Attributes
2    public:
3    // ** Your New Added Font Member
4    CFont    m_fnCustom;
5
6    CSimpTextDoc* GetDocument();
```

Finally, you should change the OnDraw() implementation to draw a message using the selected font. Listing 17.14 shows you the code to use.

LISTING 17.14   LST18_14.CPP—Drawing with the Custom Font

```
1   void CSimpTextView::OnDraw(CDC* pDC)
2   {
3       CSimpTextDoc* pDoc = GetDocument();
4       ASSERT_VALID(pDoc);
5
6       // TODO: add draw code for native data here
7
8       CFont* pOldFont = pDC->SelectObject(&m_fnCustom);
9       pDC->TextOut(20,20,
10          _"Bah bah black sheep, have you any wool");
11      pDC->SelectObject(pOldFont);
12  }
```

The font is selected in line 8 of Listing 17.14 and the test text drawn with TextOut() in lines 9 and 10.

Compile and run. If all went well, you will now be able to change the font of the displayed message by clicking the **Edit** menu and selecting your new **Choose Font** option. Change the settings in this dialog box, and the message will be redisplayed, as illustrated in Figure 17.6.

FIGURE 17.6

The Font dialog box in action.

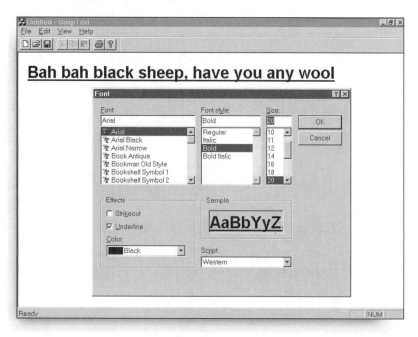

SEE ALSO

➤ *To add and implement various menus and menu styles, see page 294*

Drawing Formatted and Multiline Text

Because various size fonts make a big difference to the area on the view they will use, writing code that draws text which is formatted correctly for a specific box would be a significant task. Fortunately, Windows provides a function that helps with this task. DrawText() takes three parameters: The first is a CString holding the text to be displayed. The second is a rectangle to draw in the text. Last (but certainly not least) is a flag value to specify exactly how the text should be drawn and formatted.

These flags can be combined in various ways to set different options. Table 17.5 presents these combinations.

Using DrawTextEx()

There is an extended version of DrawText() called DrawTextEx(). This is available only as a global WIN32 function, so you must pass the device context handle for the destination device context as its first parameter. The extended form takes the normal parameters (after the device context handle parameter), but also allows a pointer to a DRAWTEXTPARAMS structure as its last parameter. This structure can be used to specify tab stop positions and left and right margins.

TABLE 17.5 *DrawText()* formatting flags

Flag Value	Description
DT_LEFT	Align text flush left in the box.
DT_RIGHT	Align text flush right in the box.
DT_CENTER	Center the text in the box.
DT_VCENTER	Center the text vertically.
DT_WORDBREAK	Break whole words (like a word processor) into lines.
DT_CALCRECT	Don't draw the text; calculate the bounding rectangle.
DT_EXPANDTABS	Expand tab characters into spaces (8 by default).
DT_NOPREFIX	Turn off prefixing; otherwise, & characters are used to draw shortcuts.
DT_TOP	Display the text at the top (single line only).
DT_BOTTOM	Display the text at the bottom (single line only).

You can modify the OnDraw() in your Choose Font program to use DrawText() rather than TextOut() by using the code in Listing 17.15.

① By passing the DT_
WORDBREAK and
DT_CENTER flags to
DrawText(), the text
is word-wrapped and
centered inside the
specified rectangle.

LISTING 17.15 LST18_15.CPP—Drawing Formatted Text with *DrawText()*

```
1    void CSimpTextView::OnDraw(CDC* pDC)
2    {
3        CSimpTextDoc* pDoc = GetDocument();
4        ASSERT_VALID(pDoc);
5
6        // TODO: add draw code for native data here
7
8        CFont* pOldFont = pDC->SelectObject(&m_fnCustom);
9
10       CRect rcSmall(CPoint(20,20),CPoint(200,100));
11       pDC->Rectangle(rcSmall);
12       pDC->SetBkMode(TRANSPARENT);
13       // ** Call DrawText with the message in the rect
14       // ** Word Breaking and centralized
15
16       pDC->DrawText(
17           "Bah bah black sheep, have you any wool",
18               rcSmall, DT_WORDBREAK + DT_CENTER);         ①
19
20       pDC->SelectObject(pOldFont);
21   }
```

In line 16 of Listing 17.15, you can see the DrawText() function
used to draw the sample text in the rectangle rcsmall. If you
compile and run these changes, you will see the text neatly centered and word-wrapped in the rectangle, as in Figure 17.7. By
choosing the font, you can see the effect of a resized font on the
formatting of the text in the rectangle.

SEE ALSO
➤ *To obtain text input from a user with edit controls, see page 97*

Deleting Fonts

As with the other wrapper classes, the underlying GDI fonts are
automatically deleted when the wrapped objects go out of scope.
You could do this manually by calling DeleteObject() (as long as
the font isn't currently selected in a device context). Thereafter,
you could use the wrapper class again by calling one of the
Create functions.

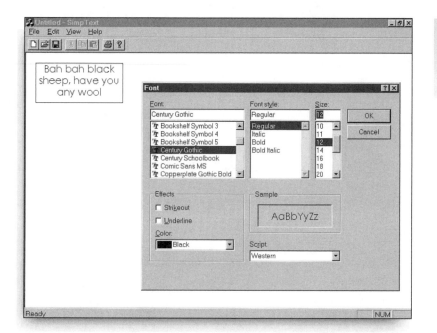

FIGURE 17.7
Text formatted with
DrawText().

Of all the GDI objects, the fonts are probably some of the most memory-hungry, so whenever possible, it is well worth deleting fonts that won't be reused. If you will reuse them, it's best to make them member variables of the view class so that you can select them in and out rather than re-create them every time you draw, thus hindering program performance.

SEE ALSO

➤ *For more details on GDI objects, see page 356*

chapter

18

Sizing and Scrolling Views

Finding out when the user has stretched
your window and how your program
should respond

Setting limits on the smallest
and largest sizes of your window

Drawing text and diagrams larger than
the physical screen or window and
using scrollbars to view the
different parts

Resizing windows is one of the most common things we do in the Windows environment. We take this flexibility for granted, usually without much thought about the consequences for the applications we resize. However, from the application's point of view—or the programmer's—resizing can be a major task. Controls might need to be repositioned and resized; scrollbars might need to be added or removed; diagrams or text might need to be redrawn or resized accordingly.

The MFC classes provide a great deal of help, but we are still responsible for deciding how our application should respond to resizing—if at all.

Handling Window Resizing

> **Find the current window state and position**
>
> You can always find a window's current state and position information by calling the associated `CWnd` object's `GetWindowPlacement()` function. This function then fills in a `WINDOWPLACEMENT` structure (passed by pointer as the first parameter) with the details of the window's current position, minimized, maximized, shown or hidden states. A corresponding `SetWindowPlacement()` function lets you programmatically change the state of a window.

Whenever you grab and resize a window several things happen. First, when you grab the window Windows will lock your window so that you can't draw in it. As you resize the window, your frame window receives lots of sizing messages (`WM_SIZING`).

When you let go of the mouse button your application will receive a final message (`WM_SIZE`) indicating that your window should resize to the size you've indicated.

Handling the Sizing Event

You can use an SDI application with a Form view to examine some of these sizing issues. A Form view displays a dialog template in a view that enables us to add controls to the view, just like a dialog box.

The following step by step shows how a Form view-based application can be created with AppWizard.

Create a Form view-based SDI application

1. Click the **File** menu and select **New**.

2. Select the **Projects** tab and from the list of project types, select **MFC AppWizard (exe)**.

3. Now click the **Project Name** box and enter the project name, SizeForm.

4. Click **OK**. Now you should see the MFC AppWizard – Step 1 dialog box.

5. Select **Single Document**, and click **Next** until you reach the checkered flag finish page.

6. Click the `CSizeFormView` class in the list of AppWizard-created classes.

7. You should see the **Base Class** combo box become enabled. Click the drop-down arrow to open the list of possible base classes for the view.

8. Select `CFormView` as shown in Figure 18.1.

9. Click **Finish**.

10. Click **OK** on the New Project Information dialog box and AppWizard will create the new project and source files.

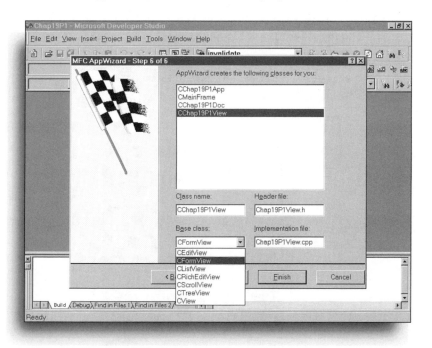

FIGURE 18.1
Selecting CFormView as the main view, from the AppWizard.

Handling the Sizing Event

You can watch and catch the Windows sizing event message (`WM_SIZING`) to display the changing size on the window's title.

The window is locked for the sizing operation, so you must also unlock and relock the window during this operation. The following (SizeForm) example shows how you can accomplish these tasks in a Form view-based SDI application. Add an `OnSize()` handler function.

Use the Event Wizard to insert a *WM_SIZING* handler function

1. Click the plus sign next to the **SizeForm Classes** entry in the ClassView pane of the Project Workspace view. This should open the list of project classes.

2. The window frame deals with the sizing messages, so the `CMainFrame` class is where we will add our handler to catch the messages. Right-click the `CMainFrame` class to open the context menu, and select the **Add Windows Message Handler** option.

3. You should then see the New Windows Message and Event Handlers for Class CMainFrame dialog box.

4. Scroll down the messages in the **New Windows Messages/Events** list box until you see the `WM_SIZING` event.

5. Select this event and then click the **Add and Edit** button, as shown in Figure 18.2.

FIGURE 18.2

Adding a handler for the `WM_SIZING` event.

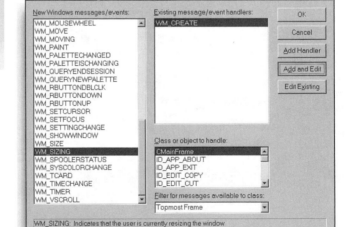

448

You should now see the new handler code for the OnSizing() function. Add the lines as shown in Listing 18.1 to display the sizing details in the title bar.

LISTING 18.1 LST19_1.CPP—Displaying the Sizing Rectangle

```
1    void CMainFrame::OnSizing(UINT fwSide, LPRECT pRect)
2    {
3        CFrameWnd::OnSizing(fwSide, pRect);
4
5        // TODO: Add your message handler code here
6
7        // ** Construct a CRect from the structure pointer
8        CRect rcSize(pRect); ─────────────────────────────────── (1)
9
10       // ** Create a String to hold our message
11       CString sizeMsg;
12
13       // ** Display the Sizing information
14       // ** From the Sizing Rectangle
15       sizeMsg.Format("Sizing: width = %d, height = %d", ───── (2)
16           rcSize.Width(),rcSize.Height());
17
18       // ** Turn off Window Locking
19       UnlockWindowUpdate(); ───────────────────────────── (3)
20
21       // ** Update the Title Bar Text
22       SetWindowText(sizeMsg);
23
24       // ** Turn Locking back on
25       LockWindowUpdate();
26   }
```

(1) The RECT structure is easier to use when converted to a CRect class.

(2) The current stretching size is formatted into a CString ready for setting to the window title.

(3) Because Windows locks the window during sizing, you must temporarily unlock it.

This handler will now be called every time the mouse is moved while the window is being resized. You are passed a flag indicating the side(s) of the window being moved (fwSide) and a pointer to a rectangle holding the coordinates (pRect). First you must convert this RECT structure into a friendlier CRect object as shown in line 8. You can then drop the width and height of the sizing rectangle into a string ready for display. Finally you might set the window title to this string to display the coordinates using the SetWindowText() function as shown in line 22.

Notice the `UnlockWindowUpdate()` and `LockWindowUpdate()` functions around the `SetWindowText()` (lines 19 and 25). These are needed because Windows automatically locks you out from drawing in the window while it is resizing. That's a good thing normally; otherwise the window display would go berserk. It would try to draw everything while you are dragging the sizing rectangle around.

If you build and run the application after making these changes, you should see the width and height of the window displayed in the title bar as you resize the window.

Handling the Final Size Event

The sizing event probably isn't as useful as the final size event. You can use the sizing event to manipulate that rectangle structure you were passed, but this is rarely done. The final size event is more useful. This indicates that the user has decided the proper size for the window and has released the mouse button. You could catch this message in the frame like you did with the sizing event, but then the message is passed down to the view window where it is probably more relevant. Now add this handler function.

Add a view handler for the size event

1. Select the `CSizeFormView` class from the ClassView pane in the Project Workspace.

2. Right-click this class and then select **Add Windows Message Handler**.

3. You should see the New Windows Message and Event Handlers dialog box for the view class.

4. Select the `WM_SIZE` event from the **New Windows Message/Events** list.

5. Click the **Add and Edit** button to add the handler code.

You could add the modifications shown in Listing 18.2 to display the final width and height in the title bar.

LISTING 18.2 LST19_2.CPP—Implementing a Size Event Handler

```
1   void CSizeFormView::OnSize(UINT nType, int cx, int cy)
2   {
3       CFormView::OnSize(nType, cx, cy);
4
5       // TODO: Add your message handler code here
6
7       // ** Declare a string object
8       CString strTitle;
9
10      // ** Setup and display the Document Title
11      strTitle.Format("Final Width = %d,
        ➡Height = %d",cx,cy);
12      GetDocument()->SetTitle(strTitle);
13  }
```

(1) strTitle.Format("Final Width = %d, ———— (1)

(1) The width is formatted and then set to the document title (which is displayed in the window title bar).

The OnSize() handler as shown in Listing 18.2 will be called whenever the window is resized. Windows passes you a flag value in the first nType parameter passed to the OnSize() handler function. This flag value indicates why the window was resized. This code can be set to one of the flag values shown in Table 18.1.

TABLE 18.1 Sizing event flags

Flag Value	Description
SIZE_RESTORED	The window was resized
SIZE_MAXIMIZED	The window was maximized
SIZE_MINIMIZED	The window was minimized

The other two parameters passed to OnSize() in Listing 18.2 are integers for the new width cx and height cy. You could format a string to display these values as shown in line 8 and then use the document's SetTitle() function as in line 9 to set the window title bar.

If you build and run the program after adding this handler, you should see the sizing messages as you stretch the window about, and then the final size message when you've finished sizing it.

You might be wondering when and why you would want to know about window resizes. A typical case might be when you are resizing controls in a Form view. Imagine that you have written a small text editor with a multiline edit control. When the user resizes the application window, you would want the edit control to size accordingly. The following shows how to add such an edit control.

Adding a multiline scrollable edit control to your existing form view project

1. Click the Resources pane of the Project Workspace view.

2. Click the plus sign next to your project's **Resources** to open the project resources.

3. Click the plus sign next to **Dialog** to open the Project dialog box.

4. You should see a dialog box entry labeled with the project name (such as IDD_SIZEFORMFORM). This dialog box is the dialog template for the form view.

5. Double-click this entry and you should see a blank dialog box with the message **TODO: Place Controls Here.**

6. Delete this message by clicking it and pressing Delete.

7. From the Controls palette, drag an edit box control onto the empty dialog template and drop it there.

8. Now resize the edit box control so that it fills the dotted blue area of the dialog template.

9. Press Alt+Enter to show the Edit Properties dialog box.

10. Click the **Styles** tab and then check the **Multiline, Horizontal Scroll, Auto HScroll, Vertical Scroll, Auto VScroll**, and **want Return** flags.

11. Select the **General** tab and change the resource ID to IDC_SIZEABLE_EDIT, as shown in Figure 18.3.

12. Press Enter to close the Properties dialog box

You have now added your edit control, but there is no associated program variable to map to the control to communicate with it. The next task is to map a variable to the control with ClassWizard.

Using the scrolling options

The **Horizontal** and **Vertical Scroll** options will add horizontal and vertical scrollbars to the edit control, respectively. The **Auto HScroll** and **Auto VScroll** options will cause the edit control, to automatically scroll at the end of a line, or when the user presses Return at the end of the control, respectively. If the **Auto HScroll** option isn't set, the control text will be automatically wrapped to the next line of the edit control.

FIGURE 18.3
Adding the multiline edit
control.

Mapping a variable to an edit control with ClassWizard

1. Carefully click the edit control border.

2. Press Ctrl+W to start ClassWizard (or click the **View** menu and select **Classwizard**).

3. You should now see the ClassWizard dialog box with the **Member Variables** tab selected.

4. Select the appropriate control ID from the **Control IDs** list (such as IDC_SIZEABLE_EDIT). Click **Add Variable** to display the Add Member Variable dialog box.

5. You can now add a variable to represent the edit control.

6. Select **Control** from the **Category** combo box; notice this should automatically show a **Variable Type** of CEdit.

7. Click in the **Member Variable Name** edit box and enter the name of your new mapping variable (such as m_SizeableEdit), as shown in Figure 18.4.

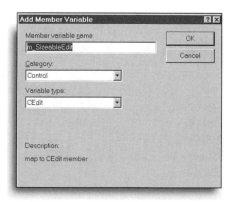

FIGURE 18.4
Adding a CEdit variable
to map the Sizeable Edit
control.

8. Click **OK** to add the member variable to the view class.

You now have a variable `m_SizeableEdit` that maps to the control. This enables you to set and retrieve text between the program and the control. You can also use this variable to send the sizing messages to the control.

The next thing you must do is handle the `WM_SIZE` message so that you know when to resize the edit control and by how much. You'll already have an existing handler function, and you can find it straight from ClassWizard as shown in the following step by step.

Finding a member/handler function from within ClassWizard

1. Select the **Message Maps** tab of the ClassWizard and ensure that the relevant **Class Name** (such as `CSizeFormView`) is selected.

2. Scroll down the list of **Member Functions** to find the appropriate message (such as `ON_WM_SIZE`), or member function (such as `OnSize()`).

3. Double-click this entry and you should find yourself back at your member function (such as `OnSize()`) in the `CSizeFormView` Form view class.

You currently don't have any code in here to resize the edit control when the window is stretched. If you build and run the application you'll notice that the edit control now appears in the view. Try resizing the window and you'll see that the edit control stays the same size. You can type text into the control like a mini text editor, but any text editor worth its salt would size the edit region to be as large as the window allows.

Close the application and return to the `OnSize()` function in the Form view (`CSizeFormView`). Add the lines shown in Listing 18.3 to the end of the `OnSize()` handler function.

LISTING 18.3 LST19_3.CPP—Resizing the Edit Control When the Window Is Resized

```
1  void CSizeFormView::OnSize(UINT nType, int cx, int cy)
2  {
3      CFormView::OnSize(nType, cx, cy);
4
```

Finding a member function via the ClassView pane

Another way to do this is to find the `OnSize()` function entry in the ClassView pane of the project workspace window. The member function should be listed under the `CSizeFormView` and can be automatically displayed in the main editor window just by double-clicking the `OnSize()` function. Alternatively, clicking the right mouse button while over the function will let you choose whether you want to see the function's definition or declaration via the **Go to Definition** or **Go to Declaration** menu options.

```
5        // TODO: Add your message handler code here
6
7        CString strTitle;
8        strTitle.Format("Final Width = %d,
   ➥Height = %d",cx,cy);
9        GetDocument()->SetTitle(strTitle);
10
11       // ** Check the Edit Box is 'Alive'
12       if (m_SizeableEdit.GetSafeHwnd())
13
14           // ** Size to the new window size
15           m_SizeableEdit.SetWindowPos(this,0,0, ────────(1)
16                                       cx-40,cy-40,
17                   // ** Only Resize
18                   SWP_NOMOVE+SWP_NOZORDER+SWP_SHOWWINDOW+
19                                       SWP_NOACTIVATE);
20   }
```

(1) The edit control is sized to just less than the window width and height. The flags indicate that only resizing is required.

You must call the edit control's GetSafeHwnd() member function to check that the edit control has been initialized as shown on line 12 of Listing 18.3 (otherwise you mustn't do anything with the uninitialized window). The SetWindowPos() member in line 15 is an "all singing, all dancing" function that lets you reposition, resize, activate, or hide the window. In this case you'll only want to resize it, so you can pass the new cx and cy window sizes (minus 40 pixels). The flag values passed as the last parameter to SetWindowPos() tells the function what actions to perform and which parameters are valid. These flag values and their meanings are shown in Table 18.2.

TABLE 18.2 *SetWindowPos()* flags

Flag Value	Description
SWP_NOMOVE	Don't move the window; ignores the second and third (x and y) parameters
SWP_NORESIZE	Don't resize the window; ignores the fourth and fifth (cx and cy) window size parameters
SWP_NOZORDER	Don't place the widow above or below any others (ignores the first pWndInsertAfter parameter)
SWP_NOACTIVATE	Don't activate the window
SWP_SHOWWINDOW	Make the window visible

Build and run the application after adding these lines and you should have a resizable text editor as shown in Figure 18.5.

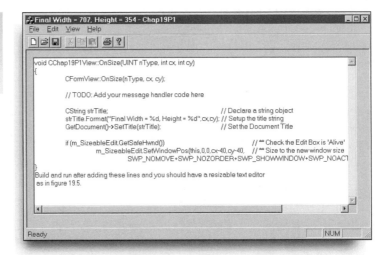

```
Final Width = 707, Height = 354 - Chap19P1

File   Edit   View   Help

void CChap19P1View::OnSize(UINT nType, int cx, int cy)
{
        CFormView::OnSize(nType, cx, cy);

        // TODO: Add your message handler code here

        CString strTitle;                              // Declare a string object
        strTitle.Format("Final Width = %d, Height = %d",cx,cy); // Setup the title string
        GetDocument()->SetTitle(strTitle);             // Set the Document Title

        if (m_SizeableEdit.GetSafeHwnd())                       // ** Check the Edit Box is 'Alive'
                m_SizeableEdit.SetWindowPos(this,0,0,cx-40,cy-40,    // ** Size to the new window size
                               SWP_NOMOVE+SWP_NOZORDER+SWP_SHOWWINDOW+SWP_NOAC1
}
Build and run after adding these lines and you should have a resizable text editor
as in figure 19.5.
```
```
Ready                                                            NUM
```

Setting Size Limitations

You might want to prevent the user from sizing the window larger or smaller than a certain size. You can do this by handling the window's WM_GETMINMAXINFO with an OnGetMinMaxInfo() handler function in the frame window. You can catch this message as it is passed through the frame window and set your own maximum and minimum size limits.

Adding a handler function to control the maximum and minumum allowable window sizes

1. Right-click the CMainFrame class in the ClassView pane of the Project Workspace. A context menu will pop up.

2. Select **Add Windows Message Handler** from this menu. You should now see the New Windows and Event Handlers for Class CMainFrame dialog box.

3. From the list of **New Windows Messages/Events**, select the WM_GETMINMAXINFO message and click the **Add and Edit** button to add the new handler.

You can add the lines shown in Listing 18.4 to the frame's new OnGetMinMaxInfo() handler function. These will limit the maximum and minimum allowable window sizes to stop the user from exceeding the limits.

LISTING 18.4 LST19_4.CPP—Setting the Minimum and Maximum Window Sizes with *OnGetMinMaxInfo()*

```
1   void CMainFrame::OnGetMinMaxInfo(MINMAXINFO FAR* lpMMI)
2   {
3       // TODO: Add your message handler code here and/or c
4
5       // ** Set Min Size
6       lpMMI->ptMinTrackSize = CPoint(200,200);
7
8       // ** Set Max Size
9       lpMMI->ptMaxTrackSize = CPoint(500,400);
10
11      CFrameWnd::OnGetMinMaxInfo(lpMMI);
12  }
```

If you build and run the application after adding these lines, try sizing the window. You should notice that you can't stretch it smaller than 200×200 pixels or larger than 500×400 pixels. By changing the `ptMinTrackSize` in line 6 and `ptMaxTrackSize` in line 9 in the `MINMAXINFO` structure, you've set minimum and maximum window sizes.

The `MINMAXINFO` structure is defined in Listing 18.5.

LISTING 18.5 LST19_5.CPP—The *MINMAXINFO* Structure

```
1   typedef struct tagMINMAXINFO {
2   POINT ptReserved;
3   POINT ptMaxSize;
4   POINT ptMaxPosition;
5   POINT ptMinTrackSize;
6   POINT ptMaxTrackSize;
7   } MINMAXINFO;
```

The POINT data type

The `POINT` data type is a WIN32 structure with an x and y member that holds a single point coordinate. You might be more familiar with the `CPoint` class, which encapsulates the `POINT` structure and also adds several useful member functions and overloaded operators.

There are two other points we could adjust here. One is `ptMaxSize` in line 3, which lets you set the maximized width and height of the window. The other is `ptMaxPosition` in line 4, which lets you set the left and top position for the maximized window.

Creating Resizable Dialog Boxes

You can very easily make a dialog box resizable. The following section describes how to make our application's About dialog box resizable.

Making the About box resizable

1. Click the ResourceView pane of the Project Workspace view.

2. Open the Dialog Resources by clicking the plus sign on the project's (such as SizeForm) **Resources** and **Dialog** categories.

3. Double-click the IDD_ABOUTBOX dialog box to start editing it.

4. Press Alt+Enter to modify the Dialog properties.

5. Drop the **Border** style list and select the **Resizing** option.

6. Build and run the application.

7. Click the Application's **Help** menu and select the About menu option (such as **About SizeForm**).

You should now be able to resize the dialog box from the window stretch gadget on the bottom right of the dialog box border. If you wanted, you could handle the OnSize() messages in exactly the same way as the edit control in the Form view example.

Scrolling Windows

Sometimes it isn't always possible to display your entire image or dialog box form in the current window size. Occasionally you might even want to draw on a surface bigger than the screen and enable the user to scroll around this area. The MFC provides a handy view class that makes all these cases possible by using the CScrollView class. You've probably used many applications that provide scrollbars and enable you to scroll around the viewable region of a window. You can build an SDI application that provides such a scrollable region using CScrollView with the AppWizard.

The steps are almost identical to those for the `CFormView`, as shown in the "Create a Form View-Based SDI Application" step by step. Rather than selecting a `CFormView` from the **Base Class** combo box on the last page of the AppWizard, you should select a `CScrollView`.

The following examples show aspects of a `CScrollView`-based application called PanSDI.

Setting the Scroll Sizes

If you build and run such an AppWizard-generated `CScrollView` SDI project, you'd see nothing different from an SDI with a `CView` main view. That is because the default total size for the default scroll view application framework is 100×100 pixels. You can change that default size to make the entire view size bigger than the screen by changing the defaults in the view's `OnInitialUpdate()` function, as shown in the following.

Finding the view's *OnInitialUpdate()* to change the scroll view sizes

1. Select the ClassView pane from the Project Workspace view.

2. Open the project (such as PanSDI) classes by clicking the plus symbol.

3. Open the `CScrollView`-derived class (such as `CPanSDIView`) by clicking its own plus sign. Near the bottom of the list of member functions, you should see an `OnInitialUpdate()` member function.

4. Double-click this function and you should see the default implementation, as shown in Listing 18.6.

5. You can change the default sizes for the scroll view by changing the `sizeTotal.cx` and `sizeTotal.cy` sizes.

The `OnInitialUpdate()` **function**

`OnInitialUpdate()` is a good place to perform any once off initialization of the view because it is called once when the view window is being initialized. It is similar to a dialog box's `OnInitDialog()` function.

LISTING 18.6   LST19_6.CPP—Standard Scroll View Implementation for *OnInitialUpdate()*

```
1   void CPanSDIView::OnInitialUpdate()
2   {
3       CScrollView::OnInitialUpdate();
4       CSize sizeTotal;
```

continues...

LISTING 18.6 Continued

```
5
6      // TODO: calculate the total size of this view
7      sizeTotal.cx = sizeTotal.cy = 100;
8      SetScrollSizes(MM_TEXT, sizeTotal); —————————(1)
9  }
```

① By default the total scroll view size is set to just 100×100 pixels, usually too small to actually scroll.

The OnInitialUpdate() function (as shown in Listing 18.6) is called once, just before the view is displayed for the first time but after it has been attached to the document. You can use it to implement any one-off initialization of the view before it is first displayed.

A CSize class is initialized to 100×100 in line 7 of Listing 18.6; then it's passed to the SetScrollSizes() function. This function sets the total size of the view in a specific mapping mode. The MM_TEXT mode means consider the size as pixels. (Mapping modes are covered in more detail in Chapter 15, "Understanding Drawing in Device Contexts.") So the View size is set to 100×100 pixels; this is normally smaller than the window size, so no scrollbars are displayed.

You might want a very large view size, larger even than the screen itself. If so, you can change the size from 100×100 pixels to 2000×2000 pixels by changing the 100 to 2000 as shown in Listing 18.7. These changes will increase the size of your scroll view beyond the size of the screen (unless you have a very high resolution display!).

LISTING 18.7 LST19_7.CPP—Setting the View Size Larger than the Screen

```
1  void CPanSDIView::OnInitialUpdate()
2  {
3      CScrollView::OnInitialUpdate();
4      CSize sizeTotal;
5
6      // TODO: calculate the total size of this view
7      sizeTotal.cx = sizeTotal.cy = 2000; // ** New Size
8      SetScrollSizes(MM_TEXT, sizeTotal);—————————(1)
9  }
```

① 2000×2000 pixels is a bigger area than the screen will display, so the scroll view is forced to scroll to show the user a section of the entire view at any time.

You might draw something big in the view to see the scrolling in action. You could add the new lines as shown in Listing 18.8 to draw an ellipse. You can find the OnDraw() function by double-clicking the OnDraw() function in the ClassView pane of the Project Workspace view.

LISTING 18.8 LST19_8.CPP—Drawing Larger than the Screen in a Scroll View

```
1    void CPanSDIView::OnDraw(CDC* pDC)
2    {
3        CPanSDIDoc* pDoc = GetDocument();
4        ASSERT_VALID(pDoc);
5
6        // TODO: add draw code for native data here
7
8        // ** Select a Gray Brush
9        CBrush* pOldBrush =
10       (CBrush*)pDC->SelectStockObject(LTGRAY_BRUSH);
11
12       // ** Make a CRect
13       CRect rcTotal(CPoint(0,0),GetTotalSize());
14
15       // ** Draw Ellipse
16       pDC->Ellipse(rcTotal); ──────────( 1 )
17
18       // ** Reselect the old brush
19       pDC->SelectObject(pOldBrush);
20   }
```

(1) The ellipse will be drawn bigger than the window and hence will be clipped to the visible window portion.

Notice in Listing 18.8 that the scroll view function GetTotalSize() is used (in line 13) to obtain the size of the total scroll area, as set by the SetScrollSizes() in OnInitialUpdate(). A CRect can be constructed from this information and used to draw a 2000×2000 pixel ellipse. A light gray stock brush (LTGRAY_BRUSH) is used (in line 10) to draw the ellipse.

If you were to build and run your application after making these changes, you would see a window containing part of a huge circle (as shown in Figure 18.6). By moving the scrollbars you should be able to see more of the circle. You might try resizing the window and notice how the scrollbars change to represent what you can see.

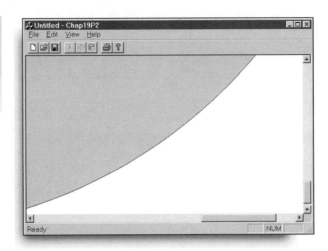

Changing the Page and Line Scroll Amounts

The line and page scroll values

Normally the line and page scroll values are specified in pixels by the MM_TEXT mapping mode flag. However, the scroll values can be set in any of the mapping modes to provide real-world scrolling values. For example, you could set the scrollbars to scroll up and down by 1cm as a line amount, and by 10cm as a page amount.

If you click the arrows at the end of the scrollbars, you'll notice that the image scrolls by a small amount; this is known as the *line scroll amount*. If you then click in the gap between the end arrow and the scrollbar's knob, you'll notice that the image is scrolled by a larger amount. This is the *page scroll amount*. The names are obviously named in relation to text-based applications like word processors, but they work equally well for anything displayed in the view.

You can alter the distances moved when these elements of the scrollbar are used by adding parameters to the SetScrollSizes() function. If left out, the line and page scroll amounts default to some sensible defaults. You can pass a CSize object to change each of these values for both the horizontal and vertical scroll-bars. The CSize holds a cx and cy member. The cx amount changes the line or page scroll for the horizontal scrollbar; the cy amount changes the vertical scrollbar movements.

The SetScrollSizes() function can be initialized when the view is first displayed in the OnInitialUpdate() function. You can double-click the OnIntialUpdate() function in the ClassView pane of the Project Workspace to edit the OnInitialUpdate() member function in the view class.

You could add the `CSize` objects to the parameters of the `SetScrollSizes()` function to change the scroll amounts for the page and line movements, respectively (see Listing 18.9).

LISTING 18.9 LST19_9—Setting the Page and Line Scroll Amounts with *SetScrollSizes()*

```
1  void CPanSDIView::OnInitialUpdate()
2  {
3      CScrollView::OnInitialUpdate();
4      CSize sizeTotal;
5      // TODO: calculate the total size of this view
6      sizeTotal.cx = sizeTotal.cy = 2000;  //  New Size
7      SetScrollSizes(MM_TEXT, sizeTotal,
8          CSize(200,10), // ** Page Scroll (X,Y) ─────── ①
9          CSize(20,1));// ** Line Scroll (X,Y)
10  }
```

① SetScrollSizes() can also change the page and line increments for each scrollbar.

Notice that the horizontal scroll amounts are much larger than the vertical scroll amounts for both page and line. If you build and run the application, then click the scrollbar arrows and gaps, you should see a marked difference between the horizontal and vertical scrollbar movements.

Using the Current Scroll Position

You might want to know which portion of the view is currently visible and where it's located in the big picture. For example, what should you do if you want to draw cross hairs in the middle of the window? Could you use `GetClientRect()` and the `CRect`'s `CenterPoint()` function as you've done before? Well, that would give you the middle of the window if your window was sitting right up at the top left of the view. However, if the scrollbars were set to look at the middle of the view, the middle of the client `RECT` would still be at the top left, and that's where your cross hairs would stay. The scroll view's `GetScrollPosition()` function will tell you where the top left of the visible portion is in the whole view. If you then add that to the result of `CenterPoint()` from the client `RECT`, you should be able to draw where the visible portion is sitting.

Finding the device scroll position

The `GetScrollPosition()` will return the current scroll position in logical units. These units will therefore depend on the mapping mode you've set. If you always want the scrollbar positions in device units (pix-els), you should use the `GetDeviceScrollPosition()` function instead. These will be equivalent when the `MM_TEXT` mapping mode is used.**Finding the device scroll position**

The `GetScrollPosition()` will return the current scroll position in logical units. These units will therefore depend on the mapping mode you've set. If you always want the scrollbar positions in device units (pix-els), you should use the `GetDeviceScrollPosition()` function instead. These will be equivalent when the `MM_TEXT` mapping mode is used.

You could add the lines after the `Ellipse()` function in our `OnDraw()` in Listing 18.10 to draw the cross hairs at the middle of the visible region.

LISTING 18.10 LST19_10.CPP—Drawing Cross Hairs at the Scroll Position with *GetScrollPosition()*

```
1   // Make a CRect
2       CRect rcTotal(CPoint(0,0),GetTotalSize());
3
4       // Draw Ellipse
5       pDC->Ellipse(rcTotal);
6
7       // ** Get Client Rect
8       CRect rcClient;
9       GetClientRect(&rcClient);
10
11      // ** Get Scroll Pos
12      rcClient += GetScrollPosition();              ①
13
14      // ** Find Middle
15      CPoint ptCenter = rcClient.CenterPoint();
16
17      // ** Top Left to Bottom Right Line
18      pDC->MoveTo(ptCenter + CPoint(-30,-30));
19      pDC->LineTo(ptCenter + CPoint(+30,+30));
20
21      // ** Top Right to Bottom Left Line
22      pDC->MoveTo(ptCenter + CPoint(+30,-30));
23      pDC->LineTo(ptCenter + CPoint(-30,+30));
24
25      // Reselect the old brush
26      pDC->SelectObject(pOldBrush);
27  }
```

① The client RECT will hold the correct width and height of the visible region. But the GetScrollPosition() must be used to add the current scroll offsets in order to draw to the correct position of the scroll view.

Other than adding the `GetScrollPosition()` to `rcClient` in line 12, this drawing function is fairly routine. You can then add the `rcClient.CenterPoint()` (found in line 15) into the `MoveTo()` and `LineTo()` functions' coordinates as shown in lines 18 to 23 to draw cross hairs.

This looks pretty complete, but there is one hidden problem that will stop it from working properly. If you build and run the program after making these changes, you'll see the cross hairs appear and everything looks fine. But when you try to scroll around, the cross hairs will disappear.

This happens due to something known as *clipping*. Windows tries to minimize the amount of work it must do in order to speed things up. When you move the scrollbar around the scroll view, Windows thinks "Ah well, I only have to redraw the new bit of the exposed window." So it only redraws a sliver along the side that was exposed and shifts the rest along. This works well if you are only drawing the nonmoving circle, but your cross hairs move. Therefore you must explicitly tell Windows that its ideas about the invalid region of the window are wrong. To do this, a set of functions tells Windows to invalidate parts of, or the entire, window. Invalidate() is a handy function that tells Windows to trash all its clipping rules and redraw the whole area.

So you must call Invalidate(), but where? You might think of the OnDraw() function, but that would be disastrous. Windows relies on OnDraw() to redraw the invalid area; if you call Invalidate() it will then try to draw everything again, and again, and again....

Instead you must know what causes the redraw, and tell it to redraw everything. That situation occurs when the scrollbar is moved. Therefore you must catch scrolling messages and call Invalidate() from there.

> **Invalidating a specific rectangle or region**
>
> You can invalidate a specific rectangle using the InvalidateRect() function by passing a rectangle to invalidate as its first parameter. Alternatively, you can use the InvalidateRgn() function to invalidate more complex shapes specified by a CRgn object passed as its first parameter. These functions will update the list of clipping rules so that Windows redraws the areas you specify.

Handling Scrollbar Messages

The OnScroll() virtual function is called whenever the scrollbar is used. You can catch and override this function to add our application-specific code for handling scrollbar movements.

Adding the *OnScroll()* override

1. Right-click the CScrollView-derived class (such as **CPanSDIView**) in the ClassView pane of the Project Workspace. You should see a context menu displayed.

2. Select the **Add Virtual Function** option from this menu. The New Virtual Override for Class CPanSDIView dialog box should pop up.

3. Scroll down the list of **New Virtual Functions** until you see the OnScroll() function as shown in Figure 18.7.

4. Click **OnScroll()** and then click the **Add and Edit** button to add the new virtual function override.

5. Add your OnScroll() application code (such as the Invalidate() function call under the // TODO: comment, as shown in Listing 18.11.).

FIGURE 18.7
Adding the OnScroll virtual override with the New Virtual Override dialog box.

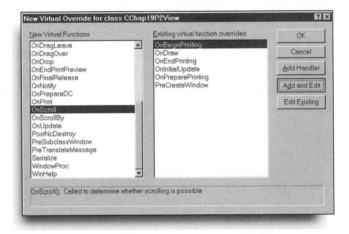

LISTING 18.11 LST19_11.CPP—Forcing a Complete Redraw When the View Is Scrolled with *Invalidate()*

```
1   BOOL CPanSDIView::OnScroll(UINT nScrollCode, UINT nPos,
    ➥BOOL bDoScroll)
2   {
3
4
5       // ** Invalidate the whole window
6       Invalidate();
7
8       return CScrollView::OnScroll(nScrollCode,
9                                    nPos, bDoScroll);
10  }
```

This completes your additions to draw the cross hair. The `Invalidate()` call in line 6 tells Windows that the whole client area is invalid and must be redrawn. Your `OnDraw()` drawing won't be clipped and you'll see the cross hairs drawn whenever the view is scrolled.

You can build and run the program after adding this line; you should now be able to scroll around the big circle with the cross hairs permanently displayed in the center of the window, as shown in Figure 18.8.

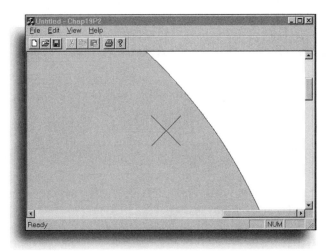

FIGURE 18.8
Redrawing the cross hairs whenever the view is scrolled.

You can also intercept the individual horizontal or vertical scrollbar messages and add code to them, or manipulate the values before they are used to update the window by the scroll view. This is done by catching WM_HSCROLL and WM_VSCROLL messages with an `OnHScroll()` or `OnVScroll()` handler function, respectively.

Adding an *OnHScroll()* handler function to catch *WM_HSCROLL* or *WM_VSCROLL* messages

1. From the ClassView pane in the Project Workspace view, right-click the `CScrollView`-derived class (such as **CPanSDIView**). You should see the context menu again.

2. Select the **Add Windows Message Handler** option. The New Windows Message and Event Handlers for Class CPanSDIView dialog box should be displayed.

3. Select the WM_HSCROLL message from the list of **New Windows Messages/Events**.

4. Click the **Add and Edit** button to add a handler for the Horizontal Scroll message.

You should now see the new OnHScroll() handler for the WM_HSCROLL message. This message is sent to your view whenever the horizontal scrollbar is moved. There is a corresponding OnVScroll() handler for the WM_VSCROLL message, which is sent for movements of the vertical scrollbar.

Line 6 in the OnHScroll() handler shown in Listing 18.12 reverses the position returned from the scrollbar before it is passed into the scroll view.

① By changing the nPos position before the base class OnHScroll() function is called, the value is modified and reversed.

LISTING 18.12 LST19_12.CPP—Reversing the Scrollbar Position Message in *OnHScroll()*

```
1   void CPanSDIView::OnHScroll(UINT nSBCode, UINT nPos,
    ↪CScrollBar* pScrollBar)
2   {
3       // TODO: Add your message handler code here
4
5       // ** Reverse view position
6       nPos = GetScrollLimit(SB_HORZ) - nPos;          ①
7
8       CScrollView::OnHScroll(nSBCode, nPos, pScrollBar);
9   }
10
```

The GetScrollLimit() function is used in line 6 to find the limit of the scrollbar and passed the SB_HORZ flag to specify the horizontal scrollbar. You can subtract the current scrollbar position nPos from the horizontal scrollbar limit to reverse the action of the horizontal scrollbar. The modified nPos position is then passed into the scroll view's base implementation of OnHScroll() at line 8, where it happily deals with the scroll message as it normally would. However, the horizontal scrollbar now acts in reverse!

You can build and run the program after adding this modification and watch the weird behavior of the horizontal scrollbar. The vertical scrollbar still acts in the normal way (although you could also change this by catching the WM_VSCROLL message in the same way).

chapter 19

Using List, Tree, Rich Edit, and HTML Views

What Are the List, Tree, and Rich Edit Views?

The *List*, *Tree*, and *Rich Edit* views are all based on the controls that can be used in dialog boxes. They work largely by embedding one of these control classes inside the view itself. Even so, when used as views they can become very powerful central elements to an application.

Creating and Using a List View

Many applications focus their activities around a list of items. One obvious example is the Windows Explorer, which uses a List view in the right pane. List views give you a fair bit of control over how the list-based data is displayed. Items can be displayed as large or small icons and as columns that show different details. They can be set to automatically sort the data and enable single or multiple selections. All this functionality is ready-to-use, enabling you to focus on your application rather than the dreary job of writing code to draw your list of data items.

SEE ALSO

➤ *To use a list control in a dialog box, see page 113*

➤ *To create multiple views like Windows Explorer uses, see page 508*

➤ *To change the default font using* `SetFont()`, *see page 433*

Using AppWizard to Create a List View Application

You can use AppWizard to automatically create an SDI framework that supports a List view rather than the standard view class. Let's create such a project to build a basis for examining List views.

Creating an SDI framework with a List view

  1. Click the **File** menu and select **New**.

  2. Select the **Projects** tab; from the list of project types, select **MFC AppWizard (exe)**.

3. Click the **Project Name** box and enter the project name: ListV.

4. Click **OK**. You should now see the MFC AppWizard – Step 1 dialog box.

5. Select **Single Document**, and keep clicking the **Next** button until you reach the checkered flag finish page.

6. Click the CListView class in the list of AppWizard-created classes.

7. You should see the **Base Class** combo box become enabled. Click the drop-down arrow to open the list of possible base classes for the view.

8. Select the CListView class as the view's base class.

9. Click **Finish**.

10. Click **OK** on the New Project Information dialog box and AppWizard will create the new project and source files.

You should now have an SDI application framework with a CListView as its main view. You could build and run the application now, but because there are no items in the list control you wouldn't see anything different from an SDI application with a CView-based view. Before anything is displayed you must insert some items into the list.

Inserting Items

Any real-world application should keep its data separate from the view in the document class (or in a class of its own). Your view should be used mainly for any specifically view-related operations. The CDocument-derived class CListVDoc is the correct place to hold a list of data items. Let's make up some data in the form of a list of strings; these can be the names of chemical elements. MFC provides the CStringList class specifically for this purpose. You can add one of these to the document by following these steps.

Inserting a member variable with *ClassView*

1. Select the **ClassView** tab in the Project Workspace view.

2. Open the ListV classes to show the CListVDoc class.

Collection classes

The CStringList class provided by MFC is an example of what is termed a collection class. A collection class manages a set of data of a particular type. In the case of CStringList this data is rather obviously a list of CString objects.

3. Right-click this class to show the class context menu.

4. Select the **Add Member Variable** menu option to display the Add Member Variable dialog box.

5. Enter a **Variable Type** of CStringList; then press the Tab key to move to the next field.

6. Enter m_listElements as the **Variable Declaration**.

7. Select the **Private Access** option and click **OK** to add the new string list member variable.

You now have a string list object embedded in the document class. I told you to select private access for this variable so that it can be directly modified only from the document class's member functions. This is to stop accidents from happening and another class's member function inadvertently changing this list variable. Of course, that's unlikely to happen in a small example like this, but in a large application you would typically do this to restrict access to the list to trusted functions in the document. Public access here would mean that any other class can access the variable. Protected mode works much like private mode except that derived classes won't see private member variables, but they could see protected members.

This is an *object-orientated design* issue and I don't want to digress too much, but this becomes relevant when you access the embedded list control from the CListView class. As with our member variable, the variable can't be accessed from outside the document. That will present a problem now because you must fill the list view from the contents of the document's string list. The answer to this is to provide an access function. The job of an access function is to provide trusted access to a private member variable. If you know that the only access can be through a particular function, you can track the use of this function to see where things might be going wrong.

Let's add such a member function to the document to access this string list. Follow these steps to add an access function that returns the m_listElements string list.

Preventing accidents with access functions and private members

Remember that when you're writing computer software, anything that can go wrong most certainly will—especially if you're demonstrating your new program to your CEO. Protecting member variables and using access functions help stop accidents from happening.

Inserting a member function with *ClassView*

1. Right-click the `CListVDoc` class to show the class context menu.

2. Select the **Add Member Function** menu option to display the Add Member Function dialog box.

3. Enter a **Function Type** of `const CStringList&` and then press the Tab key to move to the next field.

4. Enter `GetElements()` as the **Function Declaration**.

5. Click **OK** to add the new `GetElements()` member function.

When you click **OK** you'll be shown the new `GetElements()` function. Add the following line to return a reference to the list of elements:

```
return m_listElements;
```

Because this function is returning a `const CStringList&`, any function accessing this list from outside the document will only be able to read the string list. The read-only access is specified by the `const` keyword. This means that the view class can access the list, but won't be able to modify it. That's fine because you only want to be able to modify the list from the document.

You'll need some data to test the List view, so in the constructor of the document class you can add some elements into the element list object. To edit the constructor of the document class, double-click the member function under `CListVDoc` named `CListVDoc` (the constructor function name is the same as the class name). Add the test element names as shown in Listing 19.1.

LISTING 19.1   LST20_1.CPP—Adding Element Names to the Document Constructor Class *CListVDoc*

```
1  CListVDoc::CListVDoc()
2  {
3      // TODO: add one-time construction code here
4      // ** Add Element names to the String List
5      m_listElements.AddTail("Carbon");
6      m_listElements.AddTail("Uranium");
```

continues...

LISTING 19.1 Continued

```
7         m_listElements.AddTail("Gold");
8         m_listElements.AddTail("Osmium");
9         m_listElements.AddTail("Oxygen");
10        m_listElements.AddTail("Lead");
11    }
```

On lines 5 to 10 in Listing 19.1, different elements are added to the m_listElements list by passing string values to the CStringList's AddTail() member function, which adds this string to the tail of the list of strings.

The next thing you'll need to do is load this test data into the List view when the view is first displayed. The only access to the string list from the view is via the GetElements() access function, so you must use this in the OnInitialUpdate() method of the view. OnInitialUpdate() is called once when the view is first displayed. To find OnInitialUpdate() you can use the ClassView pane of the Project Workspace view and double-click the OnInitialUpdate() function shown as a member of the CListVView class. You can add the lines shown in Listing 19.2 to copy the items from the document's list into the List view.

LISTING 19.2 LST20_2.CPP—Inserting Items into a List View with *InsertItem()*

① Your document can always be found using the GetDocument() function from the view.

```
1    void CListVView::OnInitialUpdate()
2    {
3        CListView::OnInitialUpdate();
4
5        // TODO: You may populate your ListView with items
6        //   its list control through GetListCtrl().
7
8        // ** Get a pointer to the document
9        CListVDoc* pDoc = GetDocument(); ─────────①
10       // ** make sure it is a valid document
11       ASSERT_VALID(pDoc);
12
13       // ** Find the head position of the string list
14       POSITION pos =
15           pDoc->GetElements().GetHeadPosition();
16
```

```
17      // ** While the position is not NULL, add elements
18      while(pos)
19      {
20          // ** Get the next element in the list
21          CString strElement =
22                  pDoc->GetElements().GetNext(pos);
23
24          // ** Insert it into the list view
25          GetListCtrl().InsertItem(0,strElement);──(2)
26      }
27  }
```

(2) This is where the item is added to the list with InsertItem().

You can obtain a pointer to the document as shown in line 9 by using the view's GetDocument() function, which returns the document that owns this view.

The ASSERT_VALID() macro in line 11 checks that the object pointed to is valid (in this case the CListVDoc document).

Lines 14 and 15 use your new GetElements() access function to get to the string list and calls the CStringList function GetHeadPosition() to set the POSITION variable pos to the head of the list. The while loop in line 17 keeps looping through lines 20 to 23 while the pos variable isn't zero, indicating that there are more elements in the list.

Inside the loop in line 21, the strElement string is set to the string returned from the GetNext() function, which will return the next string (or the first one when at the head of the list). If the last item has been retrieved, the pos variable will be set to zero and the while loop will end the next time around.

At last the new string is inserted into the list control using InsertItem(), which takes as parameters a position (zero in this case) and the string to be added. Notice that I got the embedded list control from the view by using GetListCtrl(), which is analogous to my GetElements() function in that it returns a reference to an embedded *private member* to protect the member from accidents.

If you build and run the application after making the changes shown in Listing 19.2, you should see the List view display the element names very crudely as shown in Figure 19.1.

Using the ASSERT macros to catch problems before they start

The ASSERT() and ASSERT_VALID() macros help you detect bugs early in their formation. You can use ASSERT to make sure the condition is True. For example, ASSERT(a>10) will give you a big warning message if a is less than 10.

FIGURE 19.1

A simple list view display from the elements data.

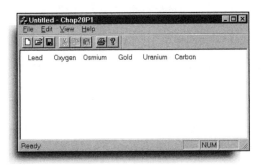

FIGURE 19.1

A simple list view display from the elements data.

Highlighting the entire row of a list control

By default in report mode, when a list control item is selected only the text of the first column is shown highlighted. You can highlight the entire row by setting the LVS_EX_FULLROWSELECT flag. This also means that the row can be selected by clicking any of the subitems.

Changing the List Styles

The display of this list is very crude. The default List view style shows the items across the page. You can set a different style to produce better-looking output from the list. If you want to display the items in a vertical list, you can use the LVS_LIST style. Four styles are available, as shown in Table 19.1.

TABLE 19.1 List view styles

List View Style	Description of Style
LVS_LIST	A plain, list-oriented style
LVS_REPORT	Like LVS_LIST, but with column headings
LVS_ICON	Large icons, arranged from left to right and then down
LVS_SMALLICON	Small icons, arranged from left to right and then down

Listing 19.3 shows the additions that are required to change the style to a list-oriented style (LVS_LIST) from the default icon arranged style (LVS_ICON). This is done by getting the style values associated with the window, changing their values, and then setting them back to the window.

LISTING 19.3 LST20_3.CPP—Changing the Default List View Style Using *GetWindowLong()* and *SetWindowLong()*

① Line 6 gets the current style from the list control.

```
1    GetListCtrl().InsertItem(0,strElement);
2    }
3
4    // ** Get the current style flags
5    DWORD dwStyle =
6        GetWindowLong(GetListCtrl().GetSafeHwnd(),
```
——①

```
 7    GWL_STYLE);
 8
 9      // ** Remove the current style flags
10      dwStyle &= ~LVS_TYPEMASK;
11
12      // ** Add the List style
13      dwStyle |= LVS_LIST; ──────────── ②
14
15      // ** Set it back into the list view
16      SetWindowLong(GetListCtrl().GetSafeHwnd(), ──────── ③
17      GWL_STYLE,dwStyle);
18
19      // ** Redraw the list view
20      SetRedraw(TRUE);
21    }
```

② The style is modified here.

③ Line 16 sets the modified style back to the list control.

The lines shown in Listing 19.3 should be added to the end of OnInitialUpdate() after the while loop. To set the style, you must first retrieve the current style from the window, which you do with the GetWindowLong() function. By passing the GWL_STYLE flag, you can indicate that you need the style bit settings from the window style parameters. GetWindowLong() retrieves many flags associated with a window. You must change only the LVS_ style flags, so the rest of the style flag value should be preserved. The value returned is stored in a DWORD type of variable named dwStyle in line 5. The code in line 10 then removes the existing style flags using the C++ &= and ~ bitwise operators. You can use the C++ ~ operator in front of the LVS_TYPEMASK to invert the bits of the mask value (make the 1s become 0s and the 0s become 1s).

Because the mask value stores all the possible settings for the List view style, inverting these will give you a mask where all the bit's values are set except these. Then, by using the &= operator, you can perform a logical AND operation between the existing bits and the style mask. This has the effect of removing any current settings of the List view style.

Then you should logically OR the required style, as shown in line 13, with the |= operator. This has the effect of adding this flag into the current flag setting. When the proper style is set, you

Changing the List view colors

You can use `SetTextColor()` and `SetTextBkColor()` to change the text foreground and background colors of the List view text and `SetBkColor()` to change the entire background color of the List view.

must write it back into the window's style settings, which can be done with the `SetWindowLong()` function. `SetWindowLong()` requires the window handle, a context flag (`GWL_STYLE`), and your modified style setting as its parameters. This is shown in line 16. Finally, the `SetRedraw()` in line 20 tells the List view to redraw itself.

You can build and run the program after making these changes and you should now get a list of the elements, which looks like Figure 19.2.

FIGURE 19.2

The element List view using an `LVS_LIST` style.

SEE ALSO

➤ *To add icons and images to the List view items, see page 258*

Adding Columns and Column Headers

You can easily add resizable column headers and columns by using the `LVS_REPORT` style. You can make the program more interesting by adding extra columns to show the chemical symbol of each element and its atomic number.

The first change you need is to add extra data items to the display. In a large application you might consider creating and using your own class to collect this information. To keep things easy here, the information has been added to the end of the strings with commas separating them, as shown in Listing 19.4. To edit the document's *constructor function*, you can double-click the `CListVDoc` member function listed under the `CListVDoc` class in the ClassView pane of the Project Workspace view.

LISTING 19.4 LST20_4.CPP—Adding the Chemical Symbol and Atomic Number to the String Data

```
1   CListVDoc::CListVDoc()
2   {
3       // TODO: add one-time construction code here
4
5       // ** Elements names with symbols
6       m_listElements.AddTail("Carbon,C,6");
7       m_listElements.AddTail("Uranium,U,92");
8       m_listElements.AddTail("Gold,Au,79");
9       m_listElements.AddTail("Osmium,Os,76");
10      m_listElements.AddTail("Oxygen,O,8");
11      m_listElements.AddTail("Lead,Pb,82");
12  }
```

Now that the data is changed, you must insert the column headers for these new data items. You can do this in the OnInitialUpdate() function of your (CListView) derived class (CListVView), which is getting quite large now as shown in Listing 19.5.

LISTING 19.5 LST20_5.CPP—The *OnInitialUpdate()* Function with Column Support

```
1   void CListVView::OnInitialUpdate()
2   {
3       CListView::OnInitialUpdate();
4
5       // TODO: You may populate your ListView with items
6       //  its list control through a call to GetListCtrl()
7
8       // ** Insert the columns and headings
9       GetListCtrl().InsertColumn(0,"Element Name",
10                                  LVCFMT_LEFT,120);
11      GetListCtrl().InsertColumn(1,"Symbol",
12                                  LVCFMT_CENTER,70);
13      GetListCtrl().InsertColumn(2,"Atomic Number",
14                                  LVCFMT_RIGHT,130);
15
```

continues...

LISTING 19.5   Continued

```
16     // Get a pointer to the document
17     CListVDoc* pDoc = GetDocument();
18     // make sure it is a valid document
19     ASSERT_VALID(pDoc);
20
21     // Find the head position of the string list
22     POSITION pos =
23         pDoc->GetElements().GetHeadPosition();
24
25     // While the position is not NULL, add elements
26     while(pos)
27     {
28         // Get the next element in the list
29         CString strElement =
30             pDoc->GetElements().GetNext(pos);
31
32         // ** Find the name part of the string
33         CString strName =
34             strElement.Left(strElement.Find(","));
35
36         // ** Find the symbol & Number part
37         CString strSymbol =
38             strElement.Mid(strElement.Find(",")+1);
39
40         // ** Find the atomic number part
41         CString strAtomicNumber =
42             strSymbol.Mid(strSymbol.Find(",")+1);
43
44         // ** Cut the atomic number from the end
45         strSymbol =
46             strSymbol.Left(strSymbol.Find(","));
47
48         // ** Insert it into the list view at 0
49         GetListCtrl().InsertItem(0,strName);
50
51         // ** Set the second column text to the symbol
52         GetListCtrl().SetItemText(0,1,
53                                 strSymbol);
54
55         // ** Set the third column text to the symbol
56         GetListCtrl().SetItemText(0,2,
```

(1) This section cuts the string down by the commas to break it into a string for each column.

```
57                        strAtomicNumber);
58
59   }
60
61   // Get the current style flags
62   DWORD dwStyle =
63        GetWindowLong(GetListCtrl().GetSafeHwnd(),
64                                   GWL_STYLE);
65
66   // Remove the current style flags
67   dwStyle &= ~LVS_TYPEMASK;
68
69   // ** Add the List style
70   dwStyle |= LVS_REPORT; ──────────②
71
72   // Set it back into the list view
73   SetWindowLong(GetListCtrl().GetSafeHwnd(),
74                              GWL_STYLE,dwStyle);
75
76   // Redraw the list view
77   SetRedraw(TRUE);
78   }
```

② The LVS_REPORT style adds the sizeable column headers to the normal List view.

In Listing 19.5, the columns are inserted using the InsertColumn() member of the list control in lines 9, 11, and 13. This function is passed the column number to insert the heading name, a formatting flag, and the desired width of the column in pixels. Each column can be formatted so that the text is left-, center-, or right-aligned. To do this you can pass the LVCFMT_LEFT, LVCFMT_CENTER, or LVCFMT_RIGHT flags to format the text as shown in these lines.

Now that you have the column headings you must insert the text against each column. Before you can do this, you must do a bit of string chopping as shown in lines 29 through 46. These lines find the commas and then chop out the relevant strings into three separate strings, each holding its specific column's data: strName, strSymbol, and strAtomicNumber, respectively, and are then set into each column. Notice that the first column is still

Deleting columns

You can delete columns after inserting them with the DeleteColumn() function by passing it the column number to remove.

inserted with the InsertItem() function at line 49, but the subsequent columns are set using the SetItemText() function, which takes the item position, the column, and the text to set as its three parameters.

Finally, you must use the LVS_REPORT style to display the column headings, which are changed in line 70 from the previous LVS_LIST style.

You can build and run the program after making these changes and you should see the list displayed with sizable columns, as shown in Figure 19.3.

FIGURE 19.3

The List view with columns.

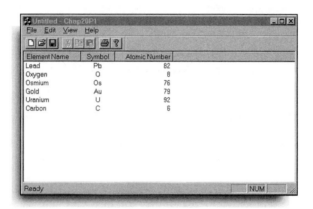

SEE ALSO

➤ *For inline editing of* ListViews, *see page 495*

Retrieving the Selected List

One common use of the List view is to enable the user to specify a selection of items. You can use the GetNextItem() function to find items with specific flags set. GetNextItem() takes two parameters, the first of which is the starting index of the desired search. This lets you start searching from an arbitrary item, or you can pass –1 to start at the top of the list. The second parameter is a flag value to specify which particular items you want to find. A list of these flag values is shown in Table 19.2. As you can see from this table, there are many geometrical relationships such as LVNI_TOLEFT. This is because in the icon view styles, figuring out which item is directly to the left of a specified item is tricky. This function handles all these cases including the one you need for finding selected items. The LVNI_SELECTED flag value indicates that the function should find the next selected item for you. When you call GetNextItem() with its last returned index as a start position, it will find the next item that matches your search criteria.

After you have an index from GetNextItem(), you can use another of the list control functions to get the text for that item GetItemText(). This takes the index and the column for the requested text and returns a CString holding the text that you request.

TABLE 19.2   Flag values used in *GetNextItem()*

Flag Value	Description
LVNI_SELECTED	The item is currently selected
LVNI_FOCUSED	The item has a dotted focus rectangle around it
LVNI_ALL	Just get the next item—this is the default flag
LVNI_ABOVE	Get the item above the specified index
LVNI_BELOW	Get the item below the specified index
LVNI_TOLEFT	Get the item left of this one
LVNI_TORIGHT	Get the item right of this one

You could write some code that uses these functions to display the list of currently selected items in the application's title bar. First you'll need to consider when this list should be updated. An obvious choice for this update is when the user has clicked in the list. That will be a likely time for the selection to have changed. You can catch a notification message that the list has been clicked and use ClassWizard to write the skeleton handler function.

Add a notification message handler

1. Press Ctrl+W to start ClassWizard.

2. Select the **Message Maps** tab and ensure that the **Class Name** combo box displays the appropriate class (such as CListVView). If it's not displayed, select it.

3. Ensure that CListVView is selected in the **Object IDs** list box.

4. Now find the =NM_CLICK message in the long list of messages in the **Messages** list box.

5. Double-click =NM_CLICK to show the Add Member Function dialog box showing OnClick as the new member function.

6. Click **OK** to add the new handler function.

7. Click **Edit Code** to start editing this new handler function.

You should now have an OnClick() handler that will be called whenever the user clicks anywhere inside the List view.

You can add the lines as shown in Listing 19.6 to find the selected items and display them in the title bar.

The GetNextItem() searches for the specified relationship. Here LVNI_SELECTED specifies the next selected item.

LISTING 19.6 LST20_6.CPP—Finding the Selected Items Using *GetNextItem()*

```
1   void CListVView::OnClick(NMHDR* pNMHDR,
    ➥LRESULT* pResult)
2   {
3       // TODO: Add your control notification handler
4
5       *pResult = 0;
6
7       // ** String to hold selected items
8       CString strSelectedItems;
9
10      // ** Initial GetNextItem() index must be zero
11      int nSelected=-1;
12      do
13      {
14          // ** Find the next selected item
15          nSelected = GetListCtrl().GetNextItem(
16              nSelected,LVNI_SELECTED);
17
```

```
18          // ** Is there a selected item
19          if (nSelected != -1)
20          {
21              // ** Add its text to the list
22              strSelectedItems += _" " +
23                  GetListCtrl().GetItemText(nSelected,0); ─②
24          }
25      } while(nSelected != -1);
26
27      // ** Set the document title to the selected items
28      GetDocument()->SetTitle(
29          "Selected:" + strSelectedItems);
30  }
```

② Add the selected item to the list of selected items.

The string declared at line 8, strSelectedItems, will be used to hold the list of selected items. Notice at line 11 the nSelected integer is declared and set to –1. This variable is then used as an index to the GetNextItem() function that is called in line 15. The LVNI_SELECTED flag is then passed to GetNextItem() to tell it that you're interested in finding the next selected item.

The first time through, nSelected is set to –1, so the function will start the search from the top of the List view. If there are any selected items, the index of the next one will be returned and set to nSelected. An if conditional check at line 19 tests to see whether nSelected isn't –1 (if it is –1, there are no more selected items). If it does find a selected item, GetItemText() is called at line 23 and passed the index value and a column value of 0 (the first column). The text found at this position is then added (along with a space) to the list already in the strSelectedItems string.

The while test on line 25 will repeat the whole do loop again if a selected item was found. Otherwise all the selected items must have been found and you can set the document title to the selected item, as shown in line 28.

If you build and run the program after adding these lines to the handler function, you should have the selected items displayed in the title bar, as shown in Figure 19.4.

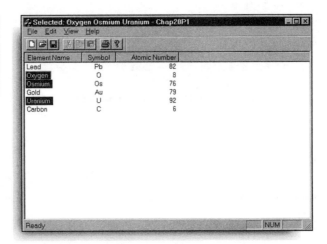

Creating and Using a Tree View

List views are great for displaying and manipulating ordinary lists of items. Sometimes more hierarchical data must be displayed; for this you need a Tree view. An excellent example of a Tree view is the left pane of the Windows Explorer. This displays the Explorer as a collection of folders that can be opened to show yet more folders or files.

SEE ALSO

➤ *To use a tree control in a dialog box, see page 117*

➤ *To create multiple views like Windows Explorer, see page 508*

➤ *To change the default font using* SetFont(), *see page 433*

Using AppWizard to Create a Tree View Application

You can use AppWizard to automatically create an SDI framework that supports a Tree view. The steps are very similar to the List view except at the end where you choose a CTreeView rather than a CListView view class. You can follow the step by step titled "Creating an SDI Framework with a List View," earlier in this chapter, and substitute CTreeView for CListView. If you want to follow the sample code, don't forget to call your project TreeV.

Changing the Tree Styles

Like List views, Tree views also have a range of style flags. Unlike List views, these flags are used for adding different possible components to the Tree view display. These components are the lines that link the parent and child items and the buttons that open and close hierarchies. There are also flags that disable drag-and-drop and enable you to edit the items directly. A list of these flags is shown in Table 19.3.

TABLE 19.3   Tree view style flags

Flag Value	Description
TVS_HASLINES	Draws lines between the child items and their parents
TVS_LINESATROOT	Draws lines between the overall parent and the child items
TVS_HASBUTTONS	Draws small buttons to allow the hierarchies to be expanded or contracted
TVS_SHOWSELALWAYS	Retains the selected item even when another window is selected
TVS_DISABLEDRAGDROP	Disables dragging items from the tree in drag-and-drop operations

Highlighting the entire row of a tree control

By default when a tree item is selected only the text of the item is shown highlighted. You can highlight the entire row including any image by setting the TVS_FULLROWSELECT style flag. Note that this style and the TVS_HASLINES style are mutually exclusive.

Most trees combine several of these styles to present the familiar Explorer-style Tree view. As with the List view, these styles can be set by using the GetWindowLong() function to retrieve the current setting, modifying the style bits, and finally setting them again with SetWindowLong(). Notice that in Listing 19.7 the style is set with the TVS_HASLINES + TVS_HASBUTTONS + TVS_LINESATROOT flags in lines 55 to 63, which will add the lines to child items, expand and contract buttons and the lines to the root items, respectively.

Inserting Items

The best way to think of a Tree view is as a list of expandable lists. There is an access function to retrieve the control from the view GetTreeCtrl(). After you have the control, you can call the control's InsertItem() function to add an item to the tree. There

Associating a tree item with application data

Sometimes it is handy to associate each item within a tree with a pointer to an object. This can be done using the SetItemData() and GetItemData() functions.

489

are several forms of InsertItem() that take various parameters; the simplest form takes only three. These parameters are the string to be inserted, a handle for the parent of the new item, and a handle for the position after which to insert the new item. You must pass in only the string to be inserted; the other two parameters will default to inserting the string at the root level and at the end of the list. However, doing this would be pointless because you would end up with a list rather than a tree.

The InsertItem() function returns a handle to the newly inserted item. You can use this handle in subsequent insertions to be the parent or the insert after item. When you start the tree, the first item must have a parent of TVI_ROOT; this flag specifies the tree's root as a parent. Subsequent insertions can specify a previous item as the parent, in which case a branch is formed and the new item becomes a child of a previously inserted item.

The third parameter to InsertItem() enables you to specify the order of the new insertion; by default this parameter is set to TVI_LAST, which indicates that the new item should be placed at the end of the list. However, you can specify a previously inserted item to insert the new item after, or you can specify TVI_SORT, which puts the new item in its correct alphabetical order within the current sublevel.

You can add some code that uses these different flags to insert items into different places in the Tree view as shown in Listing 19.7. An OnInitialUpdate() function has been inserted by AppWizard when the project was created. You can use this function to add the items to the Tree view just before it is displayed.

Deleting tree items

The DeleteItem() member function can be used to remove inserted tree items; this takes a HTREEITEM handle from an inserted item.

LISTING 19.7 LST20_7.CPP—Inserting Items into a Tree View

```
1    void CTreeVView::OnInitialUpdate()
2    {
3        CTreeView::OnInitialUpdate();
4
5        // TODO: You may populate your TreeView with items
6        //  its tree control through a call to GetTreeCtrl()
7
8        // ** Declare a shortcut to the tree control
9        CTreeCtrl& tree = GetTreeCtrl();
```

```
10
11      // ** Insert a root level item
12      HTREEITEM hAnimals = tree.InsertItem("Animals");
13
14      // ** Insert a sub item, the root item is parent
15      HTREEITEM hVerts =
16          tree.InsertItem("Vertibrates",hAnimals);
17
18      // ** Insert sub items, hVerts sub item is parent
19      tree.InsertItem("Whales",hVerts,TVI_SORT);
20      tree.InsertItem("Dogs",hVerts,TVI_SORT);
21      tree.InsertItem("Humans",hVerts,TVI_SORT);
22
23      // ** Insert a sub item,root item is parent
24      HTREEITEM hInverts =
25
26
27      // ** Insert sub items, hInverts sub item is parent
28      tree.InsertItem("Jellyfish",hInverts,TVI_SORT);
29      tree.InsertItem("Worms",hInverts,TVI_SORT);
30      tree.InsertItem("Snails",hInverts,TVI_SORT);
31
32      // ** Insert a root level item after hAnimals
33      HTREEITEM hPlants =
34      tree.InsertItem("Plants",TVI_ROOT,hAnimals);
35
36      // ** Insert a sub item, root item is parent
37      HTREEITEM hFruit =
38      tree.InsertItem("Fruit",hPlants);
39
40      // ** Insert sub items, hFruit sub item is parent
41      tree.InsertItem("Apples",hFruit,TVI_SORT);
42      tree.InsertItem("Plums",hFruit,TVI_SORT);
43      tree.InsertItem("Pears",hFruit,TVI_SORT);
44
45      // ** Insert a sub item,root item is parent
46      HTREEITEM hCereal =
47      tree.InsertItem("Cereal",hPlants);
48
49      // ** Insert sub items, hCereal sub item is parent
```

continues...

LISTING 19.7 Continued

```
50      tree.InsertItem("Wheat",hCereal,TVI_SORT);
51      tree.InsertItem("Rye",hCereal,TVI_SORT);
52      tree.InsertItem("Rice",hCereal,TVI_SORT);
53
54      // ** Get the current style flags
55      DWORD dwStyle =
56              GetWindowLong(GetTreeCtrl().GetSafeHwnd(),
57                                          GWL_STYLE);
58
59      // ** Add the List style
60      dwStyle |= TVS_HASLINES +
                    ➥TVS_HASBUTTONS + TVS_LINESATROOT;
61
62      // ** Set it back into the list view
63      SetWindowLong(GetTreeCtrl().GetSafeHwnd(),
64          GWL_STYLE,dwStyle);
65
66      // ** Redraw the list view
67      SetRedraw(TRUE);
68  }
```

On line 9 of Listing 19.7, a tree object that is a CTreeCtrl& reference is declared. This creates a shortcut that stops you from having to use GetTreeCtrl() to get the embedded tree control each time.

The first item inserted on line 12 only needs to specify one parameter, "Animals". The second parameter defaults to TVI_ROOT, which is where this needs to go. The third parameter defaults to TVI_AFTER; because this is the first item, its sequence isn't relevant.

The "Vertibrates" item inserted on line 16 specifies hAnimals as its parent item—this now becomes a child item of the "Animals" item.

The vertebrate animals are inserted next in lines 19–21. Notice that these now specify the hVerts handle as their parent item and also use the TVI_SORT flag as the sequencing parameter to sort them alphabetically.

(1) Setting the style flags.

More items are inserted in lines 23 through 52; these show more items and subitems to produce the hierarchical Tree view. The required style flags, as mentioned previously, are set in lines 56 to 66.

If you build and run after adding these lines, you should see the Tree view as shown in Figure 19.5. You will need to expand all the branches to see these inserted items.

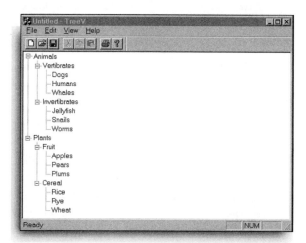

FIGURE 19.5
The expanded Tree view.

Retrieving the Selected Node

You can find the selected node of a Tree view by using the tree control's GetSelectedItem() member function, which returns the HTREEITEM handle of the selected item. Alternatively, there is a GetNextItem() function that is analogous to the List view's GetNextItem(). The Tree view's version takes two parameters: the first is an HTREEITEM and the second is a flag value to specify the relationship that you want to search for. Possible values for this flag are shown in Table 19.4. GetNextItem() will then return the item related to the specified item or a NULL handle if there are no requested items.

TABLE 19.4 *GetNextItem()* flags for the Tree view

Flag Value	Description
TVGN_CARET	Returns the currently selected item
TVGN_ROOT	Returns the root item of the specified item
TVGN_PARENT	Returns the immediate parent of the specified item
TVGN_CHILD	Returns the first child item; specified item must be NULL
TVGN_NEXT	Returns the next child
TVGN_PREVIOUS	Returns the previous child
TVGN_PREVIOUS_VISIBLE	Returns the first visible item before the specified item
TVGN_FIRST_VISIBLE	Returns the first visible item

You can also set an item from the program by calling the SelectItem() function and passing the HTREEITEM handle for the item you want to select. After you have an HTREEITEM handle returned from a GetSelectedItem() or a GetNextItem() function, you can use GetItemText() to get the text associated with that item.

The code to retrieve the current selected item and its text is shown in Listing 19.8. Like the List view, the OnSelchanged() handler is used to catch the TVN_SELCHANGED *reflected notification message* in the view class, which can be added from the **ClassWizard Message Maps** tab.

LISTING 19.8 LST20_8.CPP—Retrieving Text from the Currently Selected Item

```
1    void CTreeVView::OnSelchanged(NMHDR* pNMHDR,
     ➥LRESULT* pResult)
2    {
3        NM_TREEVIEW* pNMTreeView = (NM_TREEVIEW*)pNMHDR;
4
5        // ** Find the handle of the selected item
6        HTREEITEM hSelected =
7                        GetTreeCtrl().GetSelectedItem();
8
```

```
 9          // ** Ensure there is a selected handle
10          if (hSelected >= 0)
11          {
12              // ** Get the text from the selected item
13              CString strSelected =
14                      GetTreeCtrl().GetItemText(hSelected);
15
16              // ** Set the title to the Windows' title bar
17              GetDocument()->SetTitle(strSelected);
18          }
19
20          *pResult = 0;
21      }
```

The GetSelectedItem() function is used to get the selected handle at line 6 of Listing 19.8 and then check that this is a valid handle in line 9. If so, GetItemText() in line 14 retrieves text from the selected item and sets the document title to this text in line 17.

If you add this code and build and run the program, you should see the selected item displayed in the title bar.

Handling Inline Editing

You might have seen applications that enable you to change the text in a Tree view by clicking a text item and changing it in place. This is known as *inline editing*. You can implement this quite easily by adding a TVS_EDITLABELS style flag and handling a couple of notification messages. These messages are the TVN_BEGINLABELEDIT and TVN_ENDLABELEDIT flags for which you can add corresponding OnBeginlabeledit() and OnEndlabeledit() handler functions with ClassWizard.

Inline editing in List views

You can also use the LVS_EDITLABELS style to perform the same inline editing in the List view.

When you've added a TVS_EDITLABELS style to a Tree view, the user can start editing the label by slowly double-clicking any of the text items in the tree. Your OnBeginlabeledit() handler is then called and from here you can use a GetEditControl() function to modify a dynamic edit control added to the tree to allow the inline edit. You might use this edit control pointer to set things like the text color or to limit the amount of text entered.

The user can then change the text and press Enter or click out of the edit control to end editing. At this point your `OnEndlabeledit()` handler function will be called. You must now use the `GetEditControl()` function to get to the edit control once more, this time retrieving the modified text. At this point you can validate the text and optionally set it back into the tree. If the text isn't set back to the tree at this point, the edited changes will be lost and the item text will revert to the way it was before the editing. The `SetItemText()` function can now be used to set this text back to the tree item.

The `TVS_EDITLABELS` style can be added to the existing tree style items like this:

```
// ** Add the List style
dwStyle |= TVS_HASLINES + TVS_HASBUTTONS + TVS_LINESATROOT
                + TVS_EDITLABELS;    // ** Add Edit Labels
```

The handler implementation for the `OnBeginlabeledit()` and `OnEndLabeledit()` functions is shown in Listing 19.9.

If you add these handlers and the edit labels style, and then build and run the application, you should be able to double-click the labels to edit them inline as shown in Figure 19.6.

Starting the inline edit

Making a Tree view start inline editing is a bit tricky; you must double-click an item but pause between the two clicks.

① Limiting the text size of the edit control.

LISTING 19.9 LST20_9.CPP—Implementing *OnBeginlabeledit()* and *OnEndLabeledit()* Handlers for Inline Editing

```
1    void CTreeVView::OnBeginlabeledit(NMHDR* pNMHDR,
2                                        LRESULT* pResult)
3    {
4        TV_DISPINFO* pTVDispInfo = (TV_DISPINFO*)pNMHDR;
5        // TODO: Add your control notification handler
6
7        GetTreeCtrl().GetEditControl()->LimitText(20); ————①
8
9        *pResult = 0;
10   }
11
12   void CTreeVView::OnEndlabeledit(NMHDR* pNMHDR,
     ⮑LRESULT* pResult)
13   {
14       TV_DISPINFO* pTVDispInfo = (TV_DISPINFO*)pNMHDR;
```

```
15        // TODO: Add your control notification handler
16
17        // ** Get the modified text from the edit control
18        CString strText;
19        GetTreeCtrl().GetEditControl()->
20                      GetWindowText(strText);
21
22        // ** Might do some text validation here
23
24        // ** Check string isn't empty
25        if (strText.GetLength()>0)
26        {
27           // ** Get the selected item handle
28           HTREEITEM hSelected = pTVDispInfo->item.hItem;
29
30           // ** Set the modified text ────────（2）
31           GetTreeCtrl().SetItemText(hSelected,strText);
32        }
33
34        *pResult = 0;
35    }
```

（2） Setting the modified text back to the tree item.

The OnBeginlabeledit() handler is quite simple and the only non-ClassWizard generated code is at line 7, where the edit control's input limit is set to 20 characters.

The OnEndlabeledit() is more sophisticated; lines 19 and 20 get the window text from the edit control. If the string isn't zero length (checked at line 25), the current selected item is found from the TV_DISPINFO structure pointer passed into the handler. This selected handle is then used to set the modified text from the edit control into the selected item at line 31.

Creating and Using a Rich Edit View

A Rich Edit view enables you to present a very powerful customizable text-editing interface to the user for very little programming effort. The view is fully *OLE-enabled*, which means that you can drop pictures, video clips, and sound recordings in the text. This is an involved topic, so I won't be able to cover it all here, but hopefully I can give you a taste.

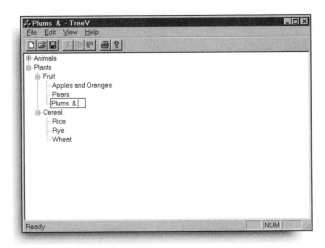

Creating the Rich Edit View

You can use AppWizard to create an SDI application with the `CRichEditView` as the application's standard view class in just the same way as you did with the Tree and Edit views. Again, you must choose `CRichEditView` from the drop-down list of views on the last tab of the AppWizard.

You can create an SDI application named `RichV` to experiment with the Rich Edit view's capabilities.

The Edit view

There is a simpler Edit view that is based on multiline edit controls. It doesn't have all the editing and OLE capabilities of the Rich Edit view, but might be more appropriate when you don't need the power of the Rich Edit view. This view is `CEditView` and can be specified from the AppWizard Finish page.

When you click **Finish** you'll be presented with a dialog box asking you to click **OK** to add OLE container support to your project. You must click **OK** to add this support because the Rich Edit view works as an OLE container. You can bypass this prompt by specifying **Container** at the **What Compound Document Support Would You Like to Include?** question in MFC AppWizard – Step 3.

You can now build and run the Rich Edit view without any modifications and obtain sophisticated text-editing capabilities without any coding.

SEE ALSO

➤ *OLE containers are covered in more detail starting on page 647*

Loading and Saving View Text

Try entering some text into your new Rich Edit view application and then click the **File** menu and select **Save**. You can enter a filename and save this text. Then close the application and run it again. Click the **File** menu and select the **Open** option, select the saved file, and click **OK**. You can see that the editor even saves and loads files without any modifications on your part. Printing and print preview are also implemented for you. These work because the OLE container merges its file options with your options. When the Rich Edit view is active, the file options are those from the view and are implemented automatically for you.

SEE ALSO

➤ *For more details about saving and loading files, see page 607*

➤ *For an overview of OLE containers, see page 671*

Formatting Paragraphs

Notice that there is no support for paragraph formatting. The Rich Edit view offers some of the more basic word processing functions as standard, but it leaves you to customize the user interface and call these functions.

You can add the user interface to format the currently selected paragraphs. Three new toolbar buttons are used to represent formatting paragraphs flush left, centered, and flush right. Add these buttons to your standard toolbar following the steps in the "Customizing the Toolbar" section of Chapter 14, "Working with Toolbars and Status Bars."

You can design your own graphic to represent each of these paragraph alignment options. My not-so-artistic attempts at toolbar button design can be seen in the toolbar in Figure 19.7. My more artistic friend has created a lovely bitmap image (.bmp) that shows how easily the rich content can be inserted into the Rich Edit view. You can insert images along side the text by clicking the **Edit** menu and selecting the **Insert New Object** option.

FIGURE 19.7

The Rich Edit View in action.

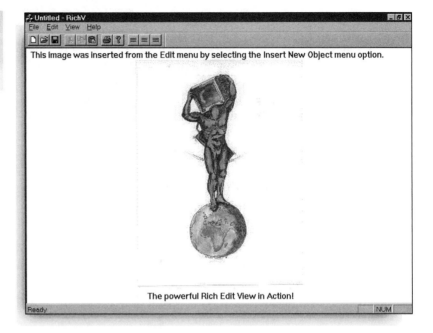

When you've added the new toolbar icons, assign the IDs ID_ALIGNLEFT, ID_ALIGNCENTER, and ID_ALIGNRIGHT against each toolbar button. You can then use ClassWizard to insert command handlers for each called OnAlignLeft(), OnAlignCenter(), and OnAlignRight(). You should create these in the CRichVView class.

The code for formatting the paragraphs is fairly trivial (as shown in Listing 19.10). The Rich Edit view uses a PARAFORMAT structure to specify several formatting operations. The mask flag member *dwMask* is set to the specific operation as shown in line 6. The operations available are shown in Table 19.5; these are mostly concerned with indentation. The mask flags represent each member variable of the PARAFORMAT structure that is valid. This enables you to set one variable at a time (as in the example) or many in conjunction by adding the relevant flags together.

TABLE 19.5 Mask values for the *dwMask* member of *PARAFORMAT*

Mask Flag Setting	Operation Performed
PFM_ALIGNMENT	Selected paragraph is left-, center-, or right-aligned by the flag in wAlignment
PFM_NUMBERING	Selected paragraph is autonumbered starting at the value set in wNumbering
PFM_TABSTOPS	Tab stop positions can be set by the count in cTabStop and the rgxTabs array
PFM_OFFSET	The dxOffset value specifies the indentation of lines relative to the first line
PFM_OFFSETINDENT	The dxStartOffset value specifies the indentation width when formatting
PFM_RIGHTINDENT	The dxRightIndent value specifies the indentation width from the right margin
PFM_STARTINDENT	The dxStartIndex value specifies the width added to each changed paragraph

LISTING 19.10 LST20_10.CPP—Paragraph Formatting Implementation in a Rich Edit View

```
1    void CRichVView::OnAligncenter()
2    {
3        // TODO: Add your command handler code here
4
5        PARAFORMAT pf;
6        pf.dwMask = PFM_ALIGNMENT;  ————①
7        pf.wAlignment = PFA_CENTER;
8        SetParaFormat(pf);
9    }
10
11   void CRichVView::OnAlignleft()
12   {
13       // TODO: Add your command handler code here
14
15       PARAFORMAT pf;
16       pf.dwMask = PFM_ALIGNMENT;  ————②
17       pf.wAlignment = PFA_LEFT;
```

① Set the center paragraph alignment flags.

② Set the left paragraph alignment flags.

continues…

501

③ Set the right paragraph alignment flags.

LISTING 19.10 Continued

```
18        SetParaFormat(pf);
19    }
20
21    void CRichVView::OnAlignright()
22    {
23        // TODO: Add your command handler code here
24
25        PARAFORMAT pf;
26        pf.dwMask = PFM_ALIGNMENT;
27        pf.wAlignment = PFA_RIGHT;          ③
28        SetParaFormat(pf);
29    }
```

Only the PFM_ALIGNMENT flag is set and the corresponding wAlignment member variable of the structure in lines 6 and 7. Then this structure is passed to the formatting member function SetParaFormat(), which formats the selected paragraph according to the values set in the structure as represented by the dwMask values, as shown in line 8.

Notice that the OnAlignleft() and OnAlignright() implementations are almost identical except that they pass the PFA_LEFT and PFA_RIGHT flags rather than the PFA_CENTER flag.

If you build and run the program after adding these changes, you should be able to format paragraphs by selecting them and then clicking one of your three new toolbar buttons.

Inserting OLE Objects

Because the Rich Edit view supports OLE containment, you can insert pictures and media clips by using the standard OLE menu options. To try this, click the **Edit** menu and select the **Insert New Object** option. You should be presented with the standard Insert Object dialog box. Notice that a wide range of OLE types is supported, and you can drop any of these into the Rich Edit view.

SEE ALSO

➤ *For an overview of OLE and COM, see page 647*

Creating and Using an HTML Browser View

Like the Rich Edit view, the HTML view is very powerful and can add the full capabilities of the Microsoft Internet Explorer 4 Web browser to your application. You are responsible for adding the user interface components and hooking them up to the browser; from there all the work is done for you. Again this is a huge topic in itself and I have room for only a taster.

Creating the HTML View

You can use AppWizard to create an application based on the CHtmlView by selecting this **Base class** from the final page of AppWizard like you did for the Rich Edit view. AppWizard will then generate a standard framework where your main view class is derived from CHtmlView. The following sections show how you can use the variety of functionality associated with this view class.

Setting the Universal Resource Locator

To start browsing, call the CHtmlView's Navigate2() function by passing the desired *URL*.

The browser will now find this page if possible and display it in your view. You can call the GoForward(), GoBack(), GoSearch(), GoHome(), Stop(), or Refresh() functions from your own toolbar buttons to implement the common browser functionality. These functions then perform the same actions as the corresponding buttons in a full navigator would.

There is also an ExecWB() function that takes various OLE commands (some of these are shown in Table 19.6) to change font sizes or to print the current page view. This function takes several command flags and a COleVariant variable to pass the required parameter.

For example, to change the font size, you might implement the following function call:

What does HTML stand for?

HTML is an acronym for Hypertext Markup Language. This is the standard language used to present information on Internet Web pages. The language uses tags to specify formatting information and supports graphics and tabulation.

Understanding URLs

A URL can be an Internet Web page address such as http://chaos1.demon.co.uk. It could also be a local HTML page that you generated in your program, a text file, FTP archive, or any of the other supported browser resources.

```
COleVariant vaFontSize(9);
ExecWB(OLECMDID_ZOOM, OLECMDEXECOPT_DONTPROMPTUSER,
        & vaFontSize, NULL);
```

A COleVariant is a type of object that can hold string values, integers, dates, or floating-point numbers in one variable. These are used quite extensively in COM and OLE to pass unknown data types through a common function. ExecWB() can be passed a whole range and variety of commands and values to perform any of the browser functions.

TABLE 19.6 OLE command flags for the *CHtmlView ExecWB()* function

OLE Command Flag	Description
OLECMDID_SAVEAS	Save the current page
OLECMDID_PRINT	Print the current page
OLECMDID_ZOOM	Set the zoom value
OLECMDID_FIND	Find text on the current page
OLECMDID_STOP	Stop downloading page
OLECMDID_COPY	Copy the page into the Clipboard
OLECMDID_ENABLE_INTERACTION	Enable or disable user interaction

Handling Browser Events

You will probably want to perform certain application-specific tasks when different browser events occur, such as the user clicking a hyperlink. You can override several virtual functions to catch these events.

OnBeforeNavigate2() is passed the URL string. You can validate this string or use the event to start a progress display (such as the famous spinning globe). The prototype for this function is

```
void OnBeforeNavigate2(LPCTSTR lpszURL, DWORD nFlags,
    LPCTSTR lpszTargetFrameName, CByteArray& baPostedData,
    LPCTSTR lpszHeaders, BOOL* pbCancel);
```

Unlike other virtual functions, overriding this function doesn't require you to call a base class, but you can cancel the navigation by setting *pbCancel = TRUE; when this function is called.

The corresponding navigation event is `OnNavigateComplete2()` whose prototype is defined as

```
virtual void OnNavigateComplete2(LPCTSTR strURL);
```

If you had started a progress display or animation from the `OnBeforeNavigate2()` override, this is the place to stop that progress display.

You can get the status text that is normally displayed at the bottom of the browser window from `OnStatusTextChanged()`, which is defined as

```
virtual void OnStatusTextChange(LPCTSTR lpszText);
```

Notice that the `lpszText` parameter holds a pointer to the text of the new status message.

The `OnProgressChange()` function is called whenever the loading progress has increased. The virtual function is defined as

```
virtual void OnProgressChange(long nProgress,
                              long nProgressMax);
```

This passes you an `nProgress` variable as the amount of the total `nProgressMax` loaded so far. You can set the maximum progress range using the `ExecWB()` function and passing the `OLECMDID_SETPROGRESSMAX` flag along with a maximum progress setting.

There are `OnDownloadBegin()` and `OnDownloadComplete()` functions that are called when you start or complete a file download. You can use this to display your specific warning messages or take hold of the downloaded file.

Many more possible overridable event notification functions let you hook into the browser functionality to catch or validate commands before they happen and let you know when tasks have completed. Unfortunately, space is too limited to cover them all here, but hopefully you have an idea of the power of `CHtmlView`.

chapter 20

Creating Multiple Views

Working with dynamic and static
splitter windows

Producing applications with a Windows
Explorer–style interface

Creating and managing multiple
views without splitters

Understanding Multiple Views

The document/view architecture brings numerous advantages to development. The greatest of these is the comprehensive functionality built in to the MFC classes that support document/view, dramatically easing the programmer's workload. As illustrated in previous chapters, these classes handle the creation and management of the document, view, and frames. They also deal with mapping menu command messages, docking toolbars, displaying the status bar, and much more.

Separating the data (document) handling code from the user interface (view) code also provides a flexible structure. It makes it possible to show several views of the same data. This can be used, for example, to display two separate sections of a large document or schematic drawings at the same time, or to display tabulated figures next to a pie chart representation of those figures. You are not limited to two views either—any number of views can be associated with a single document.

Several methods are used to create multiple views. Splitter windows can be used to divide a frame into panes, each pane containing a separate view. Many applications take this approach. Windows Explorer uses a splitter window to show a tree view of drives and folders on the left and a list view of files on the right. Several styles of tab controls can also be used to overlay views and enable the user to switch between them. MS Excel uses tabbed views to toggle worksheets.

Using Splitter Windows

Using splitter windows is a very common method of presenting multiple views within a single frame window. A splitter window is embedded within the frame and is used to create panes. Each pane contains its own view, which can be of the same or different classes. Within a multiple document application, each MDI view is contained within a frame window; therefore, splitters can be implemented for each MDI child window.

Frame windows can be split horizontally, vertically, or both ways and there might be any number of panes created. The user can alter the size of the panes by dragging a splitter bar with the mouse. There are two types of splitter window, static and dynamic. The `CSplitterWnd` class implements both types.

Creating Dynamic Splitter Windows

A frame with a dynamic splitter window is not shown separated into panes until the user selects a splitter box within the splitter window's scrollbar. Initially, the first view (top-left pane) fills the entire client area. After the splitter box is dragged into the view area, a splitter bar is shown and the frame window is separated into panes showing two or more views. Splitting the frame causes the necessary view objects to be constructed. The panes can be removed by dragging the splitter bar to either end of the scrollbar. When a pane is removed, its view object is destroyed.

Dynamic splitter window panes are normally used to show two or more different areas of the same view and therefore usually have the same view class. The text editor window within Developer Studio is an example and has both horizontal and vertical dynamic splitter windows.

There are three methods by which you can add dynamic splitter windows to your application. If splitters are part of the initial design, you can use AppWizard to incorporate them. To add dynamic splitters to an existing application, you can either write the code yourself or insert the Splitter Bar component from the Components and Controls Gallery. The easiest way is to use AppWizard. This has the slight advantage that it will automatically add a **Split** menu option to the **View** menu that selects the splitter box, allowing the user to size the view panes.

Use AppWizard to create a new SDI-based project called DSplit. On the Step 4 dialog box, click the **Advanced** button and select the **Window Styles** tab. Check the **Use Split Window** option shown in Figure 20.1. On step 6, select `CScrollView` as the base view class.

AppWizard adds a Split menu option

If you select the **Use Split Window** option of AppWizard an option called **Split** is added to the **Window** menu. If you add splitter windows to an existing application the **ID** of this option is `ID_WINDOW_SPLIT`.

FIGURE 20.1

AppWizard's Advanced Options dialog box.

If you want to add dynamic splitter windows to an existing SDI or MDI application, use the following steps. Please note this procedure is for reference only; it isn't necessary for the DSplit example.

Adding the Splitter Bar component

1. Open the project to which you want to add dynamic splitter bars in Developer Studio.

2. From the **Project** menu select **Add to Project**, and on the submenu select **Components and Controls**. The Components and Controls Gallery dialog box appears.

3. Double-click the **Visual C++ Components** folder.

4. From the list of components, select **Splitter Bar** as shown in Figure 20.2. At this stage, you can click the **More Info** button to see information about the component you are adding.

5. Click the **Insert** button. Click **OK** in the **Insert the Splitter Bar Component** message box. The Splitter Bar options dialog box appears (see Figure 20.3).

6. Select the type of splitters you require; then click **OK**.

7. Close the Components and Controls Gallery dialog box.

SEE ALSO

➤ *For details of how to create an SDI-based application, see page 267*

➤ *For detailed information on the* CSrollView *class, see page 458*

➤ *For more information on the component gallery, see page 196*

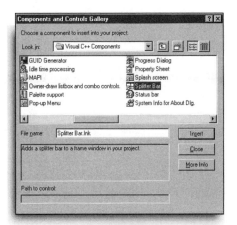

FIGURE 20.2
The Components and Controls Gallery dialog box.

FIGURE 20.3
The Splitter Bar component options dialog box.

Initializing Dynamic Splitter Windows

Whether AppWizard or the component gallery is used to insert dynamic splitter windows, the code added is identical. A CSplitterWnd class object is embedded as a member of CMainFrame (in an MDI application, this would be CChildFrame). The splitter object takes over the client area of the frame window and controls the creation and destruction of view windows. In the DSplit example, you'll find the following as a protected member variable of CMainFrame:

```
CSplitterWnd m_wndSplitter;
```

The splitter window is created in the override function CMainFrame::OnCreateClient, as shown in Listing 20.1. This function is called during the frame window creation process from within CFrameWnd::OnCreate. The default implementation creates the view object and sizes it to occupy the client area of the frame. The override first creates the splitter window itself, which then initializes itself by creating a `View` object. Further views are created when the user splits the frame.

Listing 20.1 LST21_1.CPP—Creating Dynamic Splitter Windows in *OnCreateClient*

```
1   BOOL CMainFrame::OnCreateClient(LPCREATESTRUCT /*lpcs*/,
2                CCreateContext* pContext)                      ①
3   {
4       return m_wndSplitter.Create(this,
5                2, 2,            // TODO: adjust  rows and columns
6                CSize(10, 10), // TODO: adjust minimum pane size   ②
7                pContext);
8   }
```

① Override
OnCreateClient to
create splitter windows.

② Create the splitter window passing the number of rows and columns.

The splitter window `Create` function (line 4) can be passed up to seven parameters. The first is a pointer to the parent window `this`. The second and third are the maximum number of rows and columns, respectively (line 5). The `CSplitterWnd` class only supports the creation of one horizontal and one vertical dynamic splitter, so the row and column numbers must be either 1 or 2. For example, 1 row and 2 columns result in a vertical splitter only.

The fourth parameter is a `CSize` that sets the minimum row height and column width (line 6). A view is created only when the pane is made larger than the minimum settings and is removed as soon as the pane is made smaller. These settings can be altered at runtime using `SetRowInfo` and `SetColumnInfo`. The fifth parameter is a pointer to a `CCreateContext` object; this contains runtime information about the document, view, and frame classes. The `pContext` structure has already been initialized, and is just passed on to `Create` (line 7).

Creating windows at runtime

It is easy to add controls to dialog templates but to conditionally place, say, an edit box on a dialog box at runtime, use `CEdit::Create`. Using the `Create` function you can dynamically bring into being any type of window. Runtime window generation is always a two-stage process. First you construct an object of the window's class (for example, `CEdit`, `CComboBox`) then call its `Create` function passing the window's style, its initial size, its parent window, and a control identification number.

The final two parameters are optional. For the sixth you can pass window style settings. The default styles are `WS_CHILD ¦ WS_VISIBLE ¦ WS_HSCROLL ¦ WS_VSCROLL ¦ SPLS_DYNAMIC_SPLIT`. The last parameter is the child window ID. Unless you are embedding splitter windows within each other, the default `AFX_IDW_PANE_FIRST` should be used. To illustrate the use of dynamic splitter windows, edit the two `CDSplitView` functions as shown in Listing 20.2.

Listing 20.2 LST21_2.CPP—Demonstrating Dynamic Splitters by Displaying 50 Text Lines

```
1   void CDSplitView::OnDraw(CDC* pDC)
2   {
3       CDSplitDoc* pDoc = GetDocument();
4       ASSERT_VALID(pDoc);
5
6       // TODO: add draw code for native data here
7       TEXTMETRIC tm;
8       int nLineHeight;
9
10      // ** Get metrics of the current font & calculate the line
        ➥height
11      pDC->GetTextMetrics(&tm);
12      nLineHeight = tm.tmHeight + tm.tmExternalLeading;        ①
13
14      // ** Output 50 lines of text
15      CString str;
16      for(int nLine = 1; nLine < 51; nLine++)
17      {
18          str.Format("Line %d - I must NOT feed my homework to my
            ➥dog.", nLine);
19          pDC->TextOut(5, nLine * nLineHeight, str);          ②
20      }
21  }
22
23  void CDSplitView::OnInitialUpdate()
24  {
25      CScrollView::OnInitialUpdate();
26
27      CSize sizeTotal;
28      // TODO: calculate the total size of this view
29
30      // ** Initialize the total scroll size to 1000 x 1000
31      sizeTotal.cx = sizeTotal.cy = 1000;
32      SetScrollSizes(MM_TEXT, sizeTotal);                     ③
33  }
```

① Calculates the height for a line of text using the current font.

② Outputs text to the screen.

③ Setting the scroll size to 1000 by 1000 pixels forces scroll-bars to be displayed.

The only editing necessary in CDSplitView::OnInitialUpdate is to alter line 31 to read 1000 instead of 100. This makes the logical view size larger than the physical view, causing scrollbars to be added. The override of OnDraw displays 50 lines of text. To calculate the height of the device context's currently selected font, a TEXTMETRIC structure is declared in line 7 and initialized using the CDC::GetTextMetrics function in line 11.

Build and run the application. Select the splitter boxes and try scrolling the views. Note that the scrollbars serve both the horizontal and vertical views. Figure 20.4 shows an example of the DSplit example.

FIGURE 20.4

The DSplit example.

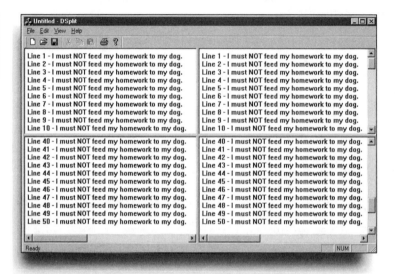

SEE ALSO

➤ *For more information about MDI classes, see page 534*
➤ *For information on device contexts, see page 356*

Creating Static Splitter Windows

A frame with a static splitter window is shown separated into panes immediately after the frame is created. The number of panes, their initial positioning, and the view class are specified during frame creation. The view objects are also created at this time. Unlike dynamic splitter windows, the user can't remove statically split panes; therefore, the view objects persist and are not constructed and destroyed. The splitter bar is always visible and when dragged, will stop when the minimum pane size is reached.

If you want to develop an application with a design similar to Windows Explorer, which uses a static splitter window with a tree view in the left pane and a list view in the right, AppWizard can give you a helping hand. If the Explorer style fits your needs, see the section "Creating a Windows Explorer–Type Application" later in this chapter. The only other way to add static splitters is to write some code. To illustrate the necessary code, use AppWizard to create a new SDI-based project called SSplit. Choose `CEditView` as the base view class in step 6.

Initializing Static Splitter Windows

Depending on the application, static splitter window panes can show different types of views and therefore can maintain differing view classes. Use AppWizard to create a new SDI-based project called SSplit. On step 6 of AppWizard, select `CEditView` as the base view class.

To this project you'll add code that implements a static splitter window and a second view class. The static splitter will be vertical with a `CEditView`-derived view in the left pane and a `CView`-derived view in the right pane. After you have generated the project, use the following steps.

Deriving a custom view class with ClassWizard

1. Press Ctrl+W to start ClassWizard, or from the **View** menu select **ClassWizard**.

2. Click the **Add Class** button and from the displayed list select **New**. The New Class dialog box appears.

3. Enter a **Name** for the new class. For this example use `CArtView`.

4. In the **Base Class** combo box, select **CView**. Then click **OK** to add the class.

5. Click **OK** to close the ClassWizard dialog box.

Now that the new view class is created, you can implement the static splitter window code. First add a protected member variable of type `CSplitterWnd` to the `CMainFrame` class. Use `m_wndSplitter` for the name of the member variable. Now use

> **Customizing the display of splitter bars**
>
> To customize how splitter bars appear you can derive your own subclass of `CSplitterWnd` and override the virtual function `OnDrawSplitter()`. The function is passed an enumerator that indicates which element of the splitter is to be drawn. The types are `splitBox`, `splitBar`, `splitIntersection`, and `splitBorder`.

the following steps and then edit the CMainFrame::OnCreateClient function as shown in Listing 20.3.

Implementing a static splitter window

1. Press Ctrl+W to start ClassWizard, or from the **View** menu select **ClassWizard**.

2. Select the **Message Maps** tab.

3. Select CMainFrame in the **Class Name** combo box.

4. Select CMainFrame in the **Object IDs** list box.

5. Select OnCreateClient in the **Messages** list box, and then click the **Add Function** button.

6. Click the **Edit Code** button.

① Creates a static splitter with 1 row and 2 columns (split vertically).

② Create a view for each pane of the splitter window.

③ Tidy up if creation was unsuccessful.

Listing 20.3 LST21_3.CPP—Creating Static Splitter Windows in *OnCreateClient*

```
1   BOOL CMainFrame::OnCreateClient(LPCREATESTRUCT lpcs,
    ➥CCreateContext* pContext)
2   {
3       // TODO: Add your specialized code here and/or call the base
        ➥class
4       // ** Create the static splitter window ─────────①
5       if (!m_wndSplitter.CreateStatic(this, 1, 2))
6           return FALSE;
7
8       // ** Create two views and insert in to the splitter panes
9       if (!m_wndSplitter.CreateView(0, 0, RUNTIME_
        ➥CLASS(CSSplitView), CSize(150, 100), pContext) ||
10          !m_wndSplitter.CreateView(0, 1, RUNTIME_CLASS(CArtView),─②
            ➥CSize(100, 100), pContext))
11      {
12          m_wndSplitter.DestroyWindow(); ─────────③
13          return FALSE;
14      }
15
16      // ** Return successful
17      return TRUE;
18  }
```

Please note that you'll need to add the following #include directives at the top of the MainFrm.cpp file:

```
#include "SSplitView.h"
#include "ArtView.h"
```

You also must add a forward class declaration for the document class in the SSplitView.h file above the class definition line. This is necessary due to the order in which header files are now being included. Add the following line:

```
class CSSplitDoc;
```

above the line:

```
class CSSplitView : public CEditView
```

To create a static splitter, `CreateStatic` is called rather than `Create`, which is used for dynamic splitters.

The splitter window `CreateStatic` function can be passed up to five parameters. The first is a pointer to the parent window `this`. The second and third are the maximum number of rows and columns, respectively. The one row and two columns passed in line 5 result in two panes split vertically. The final two parameters are optional. For the fourth you can pass window style settings. The last parameter is the child window ID. Unless you are embedding splitter windows within each other, the default `AFX_IDW_PANE_FIRST` should be used.

For each pane, a view object must be created by calling the `CreateView` function as shown in lines 9 and 10. The first two parameters are the row and column position into which the view is placed. The third parameter is a pointer to the runtime class information of the view class. This class must be a derivative of `CWnd` but is most commonly derived from `CView`. The fourth parameter is a `CSize` that sets the minimum row height and column width. These settings can be altered at runtime using `SetRowInfo` and `SetColumnInfo`. The fifth parameter is a pointer to a `CCreateContext` object. This contains runtime information about the document and frame classes. The `pContext` structure has already been initialized when passed to `CFrameWnd::OnCreateClient`, and so can simply be passed on to `CreateView`.

At the end of the function, the call to the base class has been removed and it simply returns `TRUE` (line 17) if the splitter window and views were created successfully.

Static splitter limit

Unlike dynamic splitters, which are limited to a maximum of two rows and two columns, static splitters have a 16-row and 16-column limit. However, using that number might bring about a user-unfriendly interface.

To illustrate the use of static splitter panes having differing view classes, edit the `CArtView::Ondraw` function as shown in Listing 20.4.

Listing 20.4 LST21_4.CPP—Overriding *OnDraw*

① Call the view's GetDocument() to retrieve a pointer to the application document class.

② Retrieve a pointer to the brush currently selected in the device context pDC.

③ Create a brush that will draw in a solid blue color.

④ Select the new brush into the device context.

⑤ Draw the large ellipse.

⑥ Detach the brush from the device context.

⑦ Create a yellow brush that will draw in a 45 degree diagonal pattern.

⑧ Draw the small ellipse.

⑨ Reselect the original device context brush.

```cpp
1   void CArtView::OnDraw(CDC* pDC)
2   {
3       CDocument* pDoc = GetDocument();                      ①
4
5       // TODO: add draw code here
6       // ** Save the current brush
7       CBrush* pOldBrush = pDC->GetCurrentBrush();           ②
8
9       // ** Create a solid blue brush
10      CBrush br;
11      br.CreateSolidBrush(RGB(0,0,255));                    ③
12
13      // ** Select the blue brush in to the device context
14      pDC->SelectObject(&br);                        ④
15      pDC->Ellipse(1, 1, 300, 300);                     ⑤
16      br.Detach();                          ⑥
17
18      br.CreateHatchBrush(HS_FDIAGONAL, RGB(255,255,0));    ⑦
19      pDC->SelectObject(&br);
20      pDC->Ellipse(50, 50, 200, 200);                  ⑧
21
22      // ** Restore the current brush
23      pDC->SelectObject(pOldBrush);                   ⑨
24  }
```

The `CArtView::OnDraw` function is called when the right splitter pane requires redrawing. The code draws two ellipses, one with a solid brush and one with a hatched brush. The positional parameters passed to drawing functions such as `CDC::Ellipse` in lines 15 and 20 are relative to the view area within each pane.

Build and run the application. Figure 20.5 shows an example of SSplit.

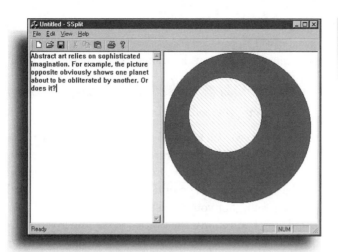

FIGURE 20.5
The SSplit example.

Creating a Windows Explorer–Type Application

Windows Explorer is an excellent example of a multiple view application. A vertical static splitter window separates two view types—a tree view on the left and a list view on the right. This general design can be made to fit many purposes. We have used this style while developing a production scheduling system. Our tree shows the names of employees and machines and the right view shows details of tasks to be performed. AppWizard now directly supports generating a project with the Windows Explorer style. The options necessary to do this are shown in the following steps.

Creating an Explorer-type project

1. Create a new MFC AppWizard (exe) project.

2. On the MFC AppWizard Step 1 dialog box, select either the **Single Document** or **Multiple Documents** radio button.

3. Ensure **Document/View Architecture Support?** is checked.

4. On the MFC AppWizard step 4 dialog box, select the **Windows Explorer** radio button.

Setting the AppWizard options to **Windows Explorer Style** creates a skeleton application with two view classes: a CLeftView

519

that is derived from CTreeView and an application view class derived from CListView. The static splitter window is automatically embedded in the frame and the necessary code to create the view is added in the override OnCreateClient. Both view classes are associated with the same document and have GetDocument functions provided.

AppWizard also adds four icons to the toolbar that switch the view type of the list control to small icons, large icons, list, and details. A dialog bar is also added and positioned under the toolbar. Explorer uses an optional dialog bar to show titles above each view, but you can use it for any purpose. To remove the dialog bar, remove the CMainFrame member variable m_wndDlgBar and the code in CMainFrame::OnCreate that refers to m_wndDlgBar.

The left pane's view class CLeftView is always derived from CTreeView and can't be altered via AppWizard, but the base view class of the right pane can be changed. On AppWizard's Step 6 dialog box, you can choose the view class of the right pane from those listed in the **Base Class** combo box. After the skeleton code has been generated, you are responsible for populating the tree control and implementing the view class of the right pane.

SEE ALSO

> *For more details on the* CTreeView *class, see page 488*
> *For more details on the* CListView *class, see page 472*

At the heart of a tree view is a tree control

The CTreeView class is really only a wrapper class for a CTreeCtrl that is used on dialog boxes. The view version is sized to fit the client area of the frame window and is automatically resized when the size of the frame changes. You can also add message handler functions to CTreeView to process menu and toolbar commands. To access the underlying tree control, use the GetTreeCtrl() function.

Creating Multiple Views to Order

The document/view architecture permits endless flexibility in the way data can be presented to the user. You have already seen how splitter windows can be used, but these are not always ideal, especially if there are many different visual representations of the data. The MFC framework provides versatility by supplying methods to construct a view dynamically and associating it with an existing document. After the association is made, the new view interacts with the document in the same fashion as a document template view.

Adding and Removing Views

Views can be constructed at any time during execution. A document can be associated with a newly constructed view object by passing a pointer to the view to CDocument::AddView. A view is disassociated from a document by calling CDocument::RemoveView, again passing a pointer to the view that is to be removed. Note these functions don't instantiate or delete the view object. The view must exist before calling AddView and must be destroyed only after calling RemoveView. The document maintains a list of views; these two functions simply manage this list.

AddView and RemoveView are also called from within CView::OnCreate and CView::~CView, respectively, when views are created via document templates. Both functions call the virtual function OnChangedViewList after performing their own implementation. CDocument::OnChangedViewList checks to see whether the document's view list is empty and if so, closes the document with a call to OnCloseDocument. You can override OnChangedViewList if you don't want this behavior—for example, if you want the document to remain open when no views are attached.

> **A view is limited to one document**
>
> A view can be associated with a document only once; attempting a second **AddView** with the same view pointer results in an assert in the MFC code.

Controlling View Creation and Activation

Adapting when and which views are shown to the user can be achieved easily by hooking into the underlying document/view functions. These enable you to add and remove views in response to user actions, customizing the interface. In this section you'll develop an application that allows the user to swap between two views that fill the entire client area. First, use AppWizard to create a new SDI-based project called VPick, choosing CEditView as the base view class on step 6. The VPick example is based on the previous example SSplit, to demonstrate a different approach from using splitters. After you have generated the project, follow the set of steps "Deriving a Custom View Class with ClassWizard" that you used earlier in this chapter.

The view the user wants to see is selected from the menu. Add the two new menu items to the view menu using

ID_SHOW_ARTVIEW and ID_SHOW_EDITVIEW for the IDs, and add meaningful captions. Now add command handlers for these two options. The command handlers are implemented in CMainFrame in this SDI example; in an MDI this would be the CChildFrame class.

Adding menu command handlers

1. Press Ctrl+W to start ClassWizard, or from the **View** menu select **ClassWizard** and select the **Message Maps** tab.

2. Select CMainFrame in the **Class Name** combo box.

3. Select ID_SHOW_EDIT in the **Object IDs** list box.

4. Select COMMAND in the **Messages** list box, and then click the **Add Function** button. Click **OK** on the Add Member Function dialog box.

5. Select UPDATE_COMMAND_UI in the **Messages** list box, and then click the **Add Function** button. Click **OK** on the Add Member Function dialog box.

6. Select ID_SHOW_ART in the **Object IDs** list box.

7. Select COMMAND in the **Messages** list box, and then click the **Add Function** button. Click **OK** on the Add Member Function dialog box.

8. Select UPDATE_COMMAND_UI in the **Messages** list box, and then click the **Add Function** button. Click **OK** on the Add Member Function dialog box.

9. Click **OK** to close the ClassWizard dialog box.

Much of the code for the OnShowEdit and OnShowArt functions is common. Rather than duplicating code unnecessarily, create a helper function that is called from both handlers by following these steps. The function parameters are described later in this section.

Creating a helper function

1. On the ClassView pane, select the CMainFrame class, and then from the context menu select **Add Member Function**.

2. Enter void in the **Function Type** edit box.

3. Enter `CreateActivateView(CRuntimeClass *pNewView, UINT nID)` in the **Function** **Declaration** edit box.

4. Select the **Private Access** radio button. Click **OK**.

All that remains now is to write the code. The idea is that the user can choose to see the edit view or art view by selecting the appropriate menu option. The selected view is displayed occupying the entire window area, while the deselected view is hidden. The menu options are also enabled and disabled according to which view is currently active. Edit the `CArtView::OnDraw` override as shown in Listing 20.4, earlier in the chapter. This is taken from the previous sample SSplit, and is used only to illustrate the different view classes. Edit the `CMainFrame` member functions as shown in Listing 20.5.

Please note you will need to add the following `#include` directives at the top of the MainFrm.cpp file:

```
#include "VPickView.h"
#include "ArtView.h"
```

You will also need to add a forward class declaration for the document class in the VPickView.h file above the class definition line. This is necessary because of the order in which header files are now being included. Add the following line:

```
class CVPickDoc;
```

above the line:

```
class CVPickView : public CEditView
```

Listing 20.5 LST21_5.CPP—Implementing Menu Options to Create and Activate Views

① Menu command handler

```
1   void CMainFrame::OnShowEdit()        ①
2   {
3       // ** Call helper function passing a pointer to the
4       // ** views runtime class and a unique ID
5       CreateActivateView(RUNTIME_CLASS(CEditView), 1);
6   }
7
8   void CMainFrame::OnUpdateShowEdit(CCmdUI* pCmdUI)
9   {
10      // ** Enable/Disable the menu option according to the
```

523

② Disables the menu option if CEditView is active; otherwise, this enables it.

③ Menu command handler.

④ Disables the menu option if CArtView is active; otherwise, this enables it.

⑤ Iterates the document's views to find a specific view class.

Listing 20.5 Continued

```
11      // ** active view's class
12      pCmdUI->Enable(
13          !GetActiveView()->IsKindOf(RUNTIME_CLASS(CEditView)));   ──②
14  }
15
16  void CMainFrame::OnShowArt()   ────────────③
17  {
18      // ** Call helper function passing a pointer to the
19      // ** views runtime class and a unique ID
20      CreateActivateView(RUNTIME_CLASS(CArtView), 2);
21  }
22
23  void CMainFrame::OnUpdateShowArt(CCmdUI* pCmdUI)
24  {
25      // ** Enable/Disable the menu option according to the
26      // ** active view's class
27      pCmdUI->Enable(
28          !GetActiveView()->IsKindOf(RUNTIME_CLASS(CArtView)));   ──④
29  }
30
31  void CMainFrame::CreateActivateView(
32                          CRuntimeClass *pNewViewClass,
33                          UINT nID)
34  {
35      // ** Retrieve a pointer the active view
36      CView* pOldView = GetActiveView();
37      CView* pNewView = NULL;
38
39      // ** Retrieve a pointer to the active document then
40      // ** iterate the document's views looking for a view
41      // ** object of the same runtime class that was passed
42      // ** to the function
43      CDocument* pDoc = GetActiveDocument();
44      POSITION pos = pDoc->GetFirstViewPosition();
45      while(pos && !pNewView)
46      {
47          CView* pView = pDoc->GetNextView(pos);   ────⑤
48          if(pView->IsKindOf(pNewViewClass))
49              pNewView = pView;
50      }
51      // ** Check to see if a view object was found.
52      // ** If not construct, create and initialize one.
```

```
53      if(pNewView == NULL)
54      {
55          // ** Initialize a CCreateContext variable with
56          // ** a pointer to the document
57          CCreateContext context;
58          context.m_pCurrentDoc = pDoc;
59
60          // ** Construct the view object using the runtime
61          // ** class and create the view window.────6
62          pNewView = (CView*)pNewViewClass->CreateObject();
63          pNewView->Create(NULL, NULL, 0,
64                              CFrameWnd::rectDefault,
65                              this, nID, &context); ──7
66          pNewView->OnInitialUpdate();
67      }
68      // ** Set the new view as the active viewand show it's
69      // ** window. Hide the window of the old view.
70      SetActiveView(pNewView);
71      pNewView->ShowWindow(SW_SHOW);
72      pOldView->ShowWindow(SW_HIDE);────8
73
74      // ** Swap the two window IDs because the ID of the active
75      // ** view window must be set to AFX_IDW_PANE_FIRST.
76      pOldView->SetDlgCtrlID(pNewView->GetDlgCtrlID());──9
77      pNewView->SetDlgCtrlID(AFX_IDW_PANE_FIRST);
78
79      // ** Reposition control bars and size the view window.
80      RecalcLayout();
81  }
```

6 Dynamic construction of a runtime object.

7 Creates the view and calls OnInitialUpdate.

8 Shows the new view and hides the view that's being replaced.

9 Swaps the window IDs.

You can see the two menu handlers OnShowEdit (line 1) and OnShowArt (line 16) immediately delegate to the helper function CreateActivateView (shown in line 31). They pass two parameters, a pointer to the runtime information of the view class and a unique ID. The first parameter, m_pNewViewClass, is used to distinguish the kind of view being selected. The second parameter is used to identify the view window.

The OnUpdateShowEdit (line 8) and OnUpdateShowArt (line 23) functions are called each time the menu items are drawn. These check the class of the active view using the CObject::IsKindOf function. If the active view class matches the runtime class passed to `IsKindOf`, `FALSE` is passed to `CCmdUI::Enable` to disable the option. This means the hidden view's option is always enabled while the visible view's option is always disabled.

`CreateActivateView` on line 31 first calls `GetActiveView` and stores a pointer to the view in `pOldView` because this is the view that is being replaced. Its next task is to determine whether a view already exists of the kind of `pNewViewClass` associated with the active document. The combination of `GetFirstViewPosition` and `GetNextView` (lines 44 through 50) iterate through all the document's views. If a view of the `pNewViewClass` kind is found, `pNewView` is set to point to it in line 49. The `if` in line 53 checks whether the view was found; if it was, it must be reactivated, if not, it must be constructed and activated.

The construction and creation of new view objects is performed between lines 57 and 67. The `CCreateContext` variable `context` is a structure that is initialized with a pointer to the document. The structure is later passed to the `Create` function in line 65 to form the document/view association. The view object is instantiated in line 62; the `pNewViewClass` in this circumstance can be either a `CEditView` or a `CArtView`. Because these classes support dynamic creation, the `CreateObject` function will call the appropriate constructor and return a pointer to the new object. The `Create` function on line 63 creates the view window and attaches it to the `CView`-derived object. When the view is fully created, a call is made to the virtual function `OnInitialUpdate()` so it can perform self initialization.

Whether construction was required or not, the selected view is passed to `SetActiveView` in line 70, which activates the view and gives it input focus. Note that when views are activated or deactivated, they receive an `OnActivateView` message with the `BOOL` parameter `bActivate`, indicating the state. Line 71 shows the selected view and line 72 hides the replaced view.

The active view must always have its ID set to `AFX_IDW_PANE_FIRST` because this is hard-coded within `RecalcLayout`, but only one window must have this ID. For this reason, line 76 sets the window ID of `pOldView` to that of `pNewView` before setting `pNewView`'s ID to `AFX_IDW_PANE_FIRST` in

The `ASSERT_KINDOF()` macro

In addition to the `IsKindOf()` function an object of any class derived from `CObject` can be passed to the `ASSERT_KINDOF()` macro. The macro parameters are a class name and a pointer to a class object. The macro checks whether the object is of the correct class; if not, the MFC Assert dialog box appears. The macro is performed only in a debug version of a project and is ignored in a release version.

line 77. The call to `RecalcLayout` in line 80 is responsible for sizing the view window and repositioning toolbars and control bars around the frame window.

Build and run the application. Try selecting each view. Figure 20.6 shows the VPick application.

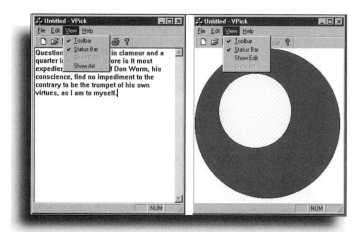

FIGURE 20.6
The VPick example.

SEE ALSO

➤ *For more details on menus, see page 294*

➤ *For more information on MDI classes, see page 530*

➤ *For information on runtime class information, see page 592*

chapter 21

Developing Multiple Document ApplicationsUse Proofing Tools

Creating a multiple document
interface application

Navigating between the application,
document, view, and frame classes

Developing an application using the
MFC multiple Document/View
architecture

Many of the most popular and widely used software applications today are based on the *Document/View* architecture or variants of it. This architecture provides a modular programming structure that separates data management code from user-interface code. Data is managed within the document, and the user interface is managed within the view. The document normally relates directly to a disk file.

The MFC library framework provides two types of Document/View applications: *SDI (single document interface)* and *MDI (multiple document interface).*

SDI applications are described in Chapter 12, "Using Documents, Views, and Frames." Chapter 12 covers the fundamentals of the Document/View architecture, which is primarily the same for both SDI and MDI applications. If you're unfamiliar with the Document/View paradigm, read Chapter 12 in conjunction with this chapter. We have deliberately used the same sample code in these chapters to enable easier comparison of the two application types.

The difference between single and multiple document applications is pretty much self explanatory by their names. SDI applications allow only one document to be open at a time. MDI applications allow one or more documents to be open concurrently, each having a separate user interface view window.

SEE ALSO

➤ *For more information about SDI applications, see page 265*

Creating a Multiple Document Interface Application

There have been many debates about whether applications should be developed using the SDI or MDI composition. Many protagonists have written for some years now that the software world should adopt a strict document-centric approach and make SDI a standard. However, software is developed for users, and users dictate by their purchases how they want software products to perform. MDI applications such as MS Word and Excel are bought by more people than most others. For certain types of software packages, the capability to see and manage several documents (or files) within the same instance of an application is more convenient than executing the program several times.

Generating an MDI project is simply a matter of selecting the right AppWizard options. You should be aware, however, that after the project has been created, changing between SDI and MDI isn't a simple task. Depending on how much development has taken place, it might well be easier to start again and create a new project. It is wise to consider carefully which interface type best suits your particular application before starting.

In this section you will create an MDI application that will then be used to explore the generated classes and how the document/view architecture operates. Create a new project named MDICoin by following these steps.

Creating an MDI application with AppWizard

1. Select **New** from the **File** menu; then, on the **Projects** tab of the New Project dialog box, select **MFC AppWizard (exe)**.

2. Enter a name for the project (use MDICoin for this example) and then click **OK**.

3. On the MFC AppWizard Step 1 dialog box, select the **Multiple Documents** radio button and ensure that **Document/View Architecture Support?** is checked (see Figure 21.1). Click **Next**.

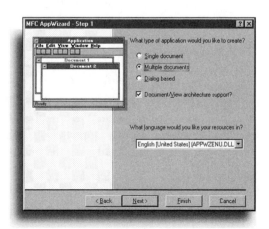

FIGURE 21.1
AppWizard Step 1.

4. On the Step 2 dialog box, select the **None** radio button. The options on this step allow for various types of database support that are not necessary for this example. Click **Next**.

5. On the Step 3 dialog box, select the **None** radio button and check the **ActiveX Controls** option. The other options on this step deal with adding OLE automation features that are not necessary for this example. Click **Next**.

6. On the Step 4 dialog box, check the following options: **Docking Toolbar, Initial Status Bar, Printing and Print Preview,** and **3D Controls**. Select the **Normal** radio button for the toolbar style. (See Figure 21.2 for the correct settings.) Click **Next**.

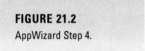

FIGURE 21.2
AppWizard Step 4.

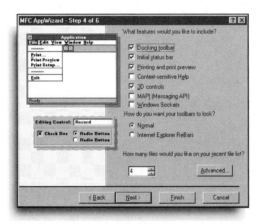

7. On the Step 5 dialog box, select **MFC Standard** for the project style, select **Yes** to generate source file comments, and select **As a Shared DLL** for how to use the MFC library. Click **Next**.

8. On the Step 6 dialog box, click **Finish**. The New Project Information dialog box appears as shown in Figure 21.3. This dialog box includes some useful information about the generated classes and names of source files. You can also check the list of features. Click **OK**. The new project should now be created and open in Developer Studio.

FIGURE 21.3
The New Project
Information dialog box.

You will develop this application so that it displays a stack of coins. Menu options will enable a coin to be added or removed from the stack. The data is simply the number of coins held in the document class and accessed by the view class in order to display the stack. The MDICoin example is based on the SDICoin sample program in Chapter 12, and the coding is very similar. However, MDICoin will allow several Document/View windows to be opened simultaneously. The MDICoin example will be enhanced to manage a new type of document that displays notes rather than coins. Whereas a single document Interface application has one document class derived from MFC's CDocument, a multiple document interface application can have as many CDocument-derived classes as necessary.

Each document class is associated with a view class. The view class can be used by different documents or can be unique to a particular document. The base view class is chosen on Step 6 of AppWizard; the choices are CView, CSrollView, CListView, CTreeView, CEditView, CRichEditView, CFormView, CRecordView, and CHtmlView. The MDICoin example uses the default CView class.

SEE ALSO

> *For an overview of MFC view classes, see Table 12.1 on page 270*
> *For information on the CListView class, see page 472*

Documents encapsulate application data

The document class is derived from **CDocument** and its member variable contain the application data. The member functions of your **CDocument**-derived class provide the means to act on the data. For example, the **Serialize()** function is used to both load and store the data to disk.

➤ *For information on the* CTreeView *class, see page 488*

➤ *For information on the* CRichEditView *class, see page 497*

➤ *For information on the* CHtmlView *class, see page 503*

➤ *For information on the* CSrollView *class, see page 458*

➤ *For information on the* CFormView *and* CRecordView *classes, see page 643*

➤ *For information on file handling with the Document/View architecture, see page 591*

➤ *For information on including database support, see page 633*

➤ *For information on OLE automation, see page 657*

Understanding the Classes of an MDI Application

The class structure you see on the ClassView pane of a multiple document application looks virtually identical to that of a single document application. The only visible difference is the addition of a new class CChildFrame. However, there are more subtle differences behind the scenes. The inheritance of the AppWizard-generated classes is shown in Figure 21.4.

FIGURE 21.4
Class hierarchy of an MDI application.

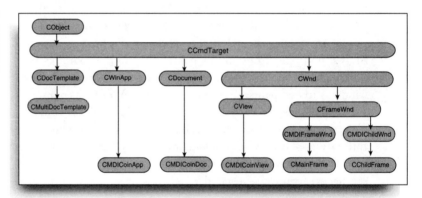

The overall structure of SDI and MDI applications is very similar. The CWinApp-derived class CMDICoinApp manages the initialization of the application. The base class CWinApp maintains the association between the document, view, and frame classes.

It also receives Windows messages and dispatches them to the appropriate target window.

The CDocument-derived class CMDICoinDoc is a container for the document data and is responsible for serializing the data to and from persistent storage, such as a disk file. Unlike SDI applications where there is only one instance of the document class, an MDI application can have many document objects allocated concurrently. Each document object is responsible for holding the data pertaining to one file. The creation of a document object will always create a new view window, associate it with the document, and create a new frame window to contain the view. Because there might be several document instances, the MDI framework introduces the concept of an *active document*. A document is made active when the user interacts with any of its associated views.

The CMDICoinView class is responsible for rendering the visual representation of the document's data to the user and enabling the user to interact with the data. In the MDICoin example, the view will draw a stack of coins. Each view can be interfaced with only one instance of a document, whereas a document can be interfaced with several view objects. The view class accesses the data it requires via *public member functions* of the document class.

The role of the CMainFrame class is to supply a window for the application to use. The implementation of frame windows differs between SDI and MDI applications. MDI applications derive CMainFrame from CMDIFrameWnd, which creates a separate frame window for the application (often called the main frame window) and one for each view window. The main frame window contains the toolbar(s) and status bar and performs window management functions. For example, the CFrameWnd::RecalcLayout function is responsible for positioning the toolbar and status bar and sizing the view window.

Each view window is contained within its own frame window, and the CChildFrame class provides this. You can see from Figure 21.4 that CChildFrame is derived from CMDIChildWnd. To support the additional functionality of the MDI architecture, this class actually utilizes a special Windows system window, MDIClient.

> **The active view and document**
>
> A view window becomes the active view when the user begins interacting with it. Whenever the active view changes, the OnActivate() function is called. First OnActivate() is called for the window being deactivated and then the window being activated has OnActivate() called. A parameter indicates the window's new state and is set to one of the following values: WA_INACTIVE, WA_ACTIVE, or WA_CLICKACTIVE. The document object associated with the active view is termed the active document.

When an MDI frame window is created an `MDIClient` window is also created as a child window, and the MDI child windows are children of `MDIClient`, making them grandchildren of the main frame window.

SEE ALSO

➤ *To learn more about the difference between MDI and SDI classes, see page 271*

The Visual Elements of an MDI Application

Chapter 12 explained that AppWizard generates the resources required for an SDI application such as a menu, toolbar, and so on, and these were all given the same ID, `IDR_MAINFRAME`. For an MDI application, AppWizard generates those resources and a few extras. The additional resources are necessary for two reasons. First, because an MDI application can handle several types of documents, and second, because an SDI application must always have a document object, whereas an MDI application doesn't. Figure 21.5 shows the resources within the MDICoin example.

FIGURE 21.5

MDI application resources.

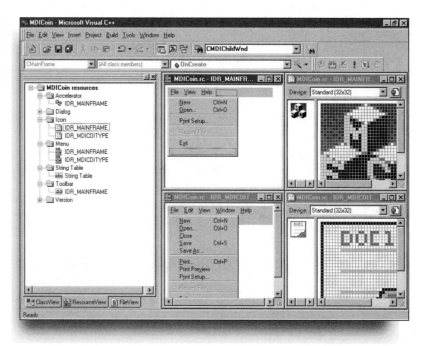

In addition to the `IDR_MAINFRAME` resources, AppWizard has created an icon, menu, and string table entry specific to the document type and given them all the `IDR_MDICOITYPE` ID. This enables you to customize these resources on a per-document basis.

The document icon `IDR_MDICOITYPE` is displayed on the left of the menu when the view window is maximized and in the title bar of the view window otherwise.

The menu resource associated with the document type automatically becomes active when the document object is activated. If there is no active document, which is perfectly valid for an MDI application, the `IDR_MAINFRAME` menu is activated. You can see in Figure 21.5 the difference between the main **File** menu and the document **File** menu: The MDI also adds a **Window** menu that enables the user to arrange the view windows with **Tile** and **Cascade** options. This menu also has a **New Window** option that automatically adds support for the user to see multiple views, each inside a separate MDI frame window.

There is also a string table entry `IDR_MDICOITYPE` resource, which informs the framework of seven separate aspects of the document and is utilized for displaying window titles automatically, among other uses.

An overview of the visual elements of an MDI application is shown in Figure 21.6. The following explains the different parts of the elements:

- `CMainFrame` is derived from `CMDIFrameWnd` and provides the application's main frame window.

- `CToolbar` implements toolbars docked to the main frame window.

- `CChildFrame` is derived from `CMDIChildWnd` and implements a frame window for each view.

- `CMDICoinView` implements the view as a child of the MDI frame window.

- `CStatusBar` implements the status bar attached to the main frame window.

Document-specific menus

Each type of document handled within an MDI application has its own IDR_ menu resource that is shown automatically when an associated document object becomes active. It is possible in an MDI program to have no active document, in which case the `IDR_MAINFRAME` menu resource is shown.

■ The MDI view windows override the client area of the main frame window.

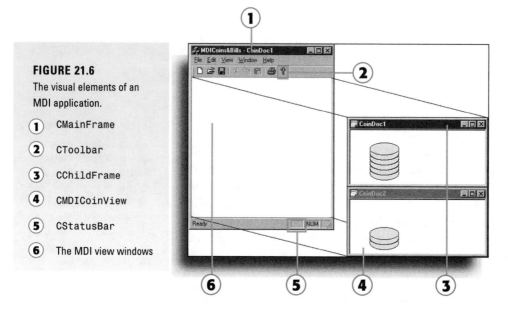

FIGURE 21.6

The visual elements of an MDI application.

(1) CMainFrame

(2) CToolbar

(3) CChildFrame

(4) CMDICoinView

(5) CStatusBar

(6) The MDI view windows

SEE ALSO

➤ For information on menus, see page 294

➤ For information on toolbars, see page 320

Understanding MDI Document Templates

At the heart of the Document/View architecture are document templates. Although these are also used in SDI applications, they play a more significant role when you are developing MDI applications. A document template binds together the document, view, and frame set of a particular document type. In a single document interface project, you don't usually need to interfere with the AppWizard-generated code that deals with document templates. In a multiple document project, however, you might need to create new document types and associate different frame and view classes with them, which means implementing the document template code yourself.

Fortunately, coding additional document types isn't difficult, particularly when you realize that AppWizard has already generated all the code necessary for the first document, view, and frame, giving you a relatively easy example to follow. If you refer to Figure 21.4, which shows the class hierarchy of an MDI application, you will see it includes `CMultiDocTemplate`, which is the document template class used by multiple document interface applications.

About halfway down the `CMDICoinApp::InitInstance` function (which is called by the MFC framework to initialize the application), you'll see the following code:

```
1      // Register the application's document
       ➥templates. Document templates
2      //   serve as the connection between documents,
       ➥frame windows, and views.
3      CMultiDocTemplate* pDocTemplate;
4      pDocTemplate = new CMultiDocTemplate(        ①
5          IDR_MDICOITYPE,
6          RUNTIME_CLASS(CMDICoinDoc),
7          RUNTIME_CLASS(CChildFrame),
8          RUNTIME_CLASS(CMDICoinView));
9      AddDocTemplate(pDocTemplate);                ②
10
11     // Create main MDI Frame window            ③
12     CMainFrame* pMainFrame = new CMainFrame;
13     if (!pMainFrame->LoadFrame(IDR_MAINFRAME))   ④
14         return FALSE;
15     m_pMainWnd = pMainFrame;
```

① Instantiates a multiple-document template object and passes the associated resource ID and the runtime class of its document, view, and frame.

② Registers the newly created document template with the application class.

③ Instantiates the application's frame window.

④ Informs the main frame window which set of resources to load (such as a menu or toolbar).

A `CMultiDocTemplate` object is created and passed four parameters (line 4). The first parameter is the resource ID `IDR_MDICOITYPE` (line 5). This identifies three separate resources, all associated with the document `CMDICoinDoc`: an icon, a menu, and a string table entry. The next three parameters are all pointers to run-time class information for the document, frame, and view classes, respectively (lines 6, 7, and 8). The `RUNTIME_CLASS` macro is used to generate these pointers. This is possible because AppWizard included support for dynamic creation of these classes by incorporating the DECLARE_DYNCREATE and IMPLEMENT_DYNCREATE macros.

There are some differences between SDI and MDI document templates. Both CSingleDocTemplate and CMultiDocTemplate classes are derived from the same base class CDocTemplate. Whereas CSingleDocTemplate maintains only one document object, CMultiDocTemplate maintains a list of pointers to documents (in this case CMDICoinDoc objects).

The document, view, and frame objects themselves are not created at this time. This code initializes the CMultiDocTemplate object with the information needed in order to be able to load the resources and allocate documents, views, and frames on demand.

The application class maintains a list of document templates. The AddDocTemplate function call in line 9 adds the document template object to this list. You can call AddDocTemplate as many times as you want to register several document templates. This enables a single application to handle different types of document, view, and frame associations.

The CWinApp class retains the CMultiDocTemplate object until it is destroyed itself, which happens only when the application is terminated. During its destruction, the CWinApp class will tidy up any memory allocated for document templates as long as they have been added to the applications list via a call to the AddDocTemplate function. Document templates use a trivial amount of memory, so there is no problem in them hanging around for the entire life of the application.

In line 12 the main frame window is created via the CMainFrame constructor. The LoadFrame function on line 13 is passed the ID of the resources to load and attach to the frame window IDR_MAIN-FRAME. You may pass a second optional parameter to LoadFrame specifying the window style flags. By default the window styles are WS_OVERLAPPEDWINDOW and FWS_ADDTOTITLE. The WS_OVERLAPPEDWINDOW style combines the style settings shown in Table 21.1. The FWS_ADDTOTITLE flag is specific to MFC and causes the name of the active document to be displayed in the title bar. Normally the application name is displayed first, followed by the active

---

The new document dialog box

If more than one type of document is registered within the application class, selecting **New** from the **File** menu will cause a dialog box to appear asking the user to choose the kind of document he wants to create. The description shown in the dialog box is taken from the string table IDR_ entry related to the document.

document name. This order can be swapped by adding the style flag FWS_PREFIXTITLE.

Table 21.1 Main frame window styles included by **WS_OVERLAPPEDWINDOW**

Style	Description
WS_OVERLAPPED	Creates an overlapped window
WS_CAPTION	Adds a title bar to the window
WS_SYSMENU	Adds the default system menu to the title bar
WS_MINIMIZEBOX	Adds a minimize box to the title bar
WS_MAXIMIZEBOX	Starts a DDE session
WS_THICKFRAME	Enables sizing of the window

SEE ALSO
➤ *To learn more about runtime class information, see page 591*

The Document, View, and MDI Frame Creation Sequence

As mentioned in the previous section, the initialization of the document template object doesn't construct any document, view, or MDI child window objects. The document templates simply retain the runtime class information for each document/view/frame set. This runtime information is used to create the objects and store pointers to them in the application object only when the user chooses to create a new document or open an existing one.

Following the creation and initialization of the CMultiDocTemplate object and after the successful creation of the main frame window in the CWinApp::InitInstance function is the following code:

```
1  // Parse command line for standard shell commands, DDE,
➥file open
2  CCommandLineInfo cmdInfo;
3  ParseCommandLine(cmdInfo);
```

```
4   // Dispatch commands specified on the command line
5   if (!ProcessShellCommand(cmdInfo))
6       return FALSE;
7   // The one and only window has been initialized,
    ➥so show and update it.
8   m_pMainWnd->ShowWindow(SW_SHOW);
9   m_pMainWnd->UpdateWindow();
```

The CCommandLineInfo class aids in handling arguments passed to the application from the command line. By default, the command-line options are initialized to create a new document when the application starts. The actual construction of the document, view, and MDI frame windows takes place behind the scenes within the CWinApp::ProcessShellCommand function shown in line 5. Listing 21.1 gives an overview of the creation sequence. Note the code contained in Listing 21.1 is paraphrased and has been condensed in order to focus specifically on the creation sequence.

Listing 21.1 LST22_5.CPP—Document, View and MDI Frame Window Creation Sequence

① Called by InitInstance function.

② Also the message handler for the **File**, **New** option.

```
1   BOOL CWinApp::ProcessShellCommand(CCommandLineInfo& rCmdInfo) ┐
2   {                                                              │ ①
3       if(rCmdInfo.NewFile)
4       {
5           OnFileNew();
6       }
7       if(rCmdInfo.OpenFile)
8       {
9           OpenDocumentFile(rCmdInfo.strFileName);
10      }
11      ...
12  }
13  void CWinApp::OnFileNew() ─────────────────────────────── ②
14  {
15      m_pDocManager->OnFileNew();
16  }
17  void CDocManager::OnFileNew()
18  {
19      pTemplate = m_templateList.GetHead();
```

```
20      if(m_templateList.GetCount() > 1)
21      {
22          // more than one document Template
23          // bring up dialog prompting user
24          pTemplate = dlg.m_pSelectedTemplate;
25      }
26      pTemplate->OpenDocumentFile(NULL);
27  }
28  CMultiDocTemplate::OpenDocumentFile(LPCTSTR lpszPathName)
29  {
30      pDocument = CreateNewDocument();
31      pFrame = CreateNewFrame(pDocument);
32      ...
33      if(lpszPathName == NULL)
34      {
35          SetDefaultTitle(pDocument);
36          pDocument->OnNewDocument();
37      }
38      else
39          pDocument->OnOpenDocument();
40      InitialUpdateFrame(pFrame, pDocument);
41  }
```

(3) pTemplate is a pointer to the CMultiDocTemplate object.

(4) If more than one document type is registered, a dialog box prompts the user to select one.

(5) Document and frame objects are constructed using runtime class information in the template. CreateNewFrame also constructs the view.

(6) OnNewDocument and OnOpenDocument are virtual functions that are overridden to perform document initialization.

(7) Activates the view and sends a WM_INI-TIALUPDATE message that causes CView::OnInitialUpdate to be called.

The difference between the creation sequence of the SDI and MDI structure is that the MDI model creates a new document object each time OpenDocumentFile is called (line 26), whereas the SDI model creates one document object and reuses it. The CreateNewDocument function called in line 30 uses the template runtime class information to construct your application-specific document object. The function also adds the document to the list of current documents. After the document has been created, the frame and view are also created by a further template function, CreateNewFrame.

The CreateNewFrame function called in line 31 uses the template runtime class information to construct both the frame window and view objects. After creating the frame, the CFrameWnd::LoadFrame function is called and passed the resource ID that was specified in the template constructor. For an MDI application, the resource ID is document specific. For example, the

MDICoin example passes `IDR_MDICOITYPE` as the resource ID. `LoadFrame` loads each resource (menu, toolbar, icon, accelerator table, and string) and attaches them to the frame window. Please note that if the loading of any of the resources fails, the `LoadFrame` function will fail and produce a trace message:

`Warning: CDocTemplate couldn't create a frame.`

Finally, in the creation sequence the template function `InitialUpdateFrame` is called (line 40). This sets the newly created view as active and then sends the message `WM_INITIALUPDATE` to the frame window's children, which includes the view window. On receiving this message, the virtual function `CView::OnInitialUpdate` is called. Overriding this function to perform specific view initialization is a very common practice. Please note that it is normally necessary to ensure that the base class version of `OnInitialUpdate` is also called.

SEE ALSO

➤ *For information on command-line parameters, see page 277*

Navigating Between the Document/View Objects

When developing with the Document/View paradigm, you will often need to interrelate the various class objects. The two components that interact most often are the document and its associated view, but numerous circumstances arise that require interaction between other classes. For example, you might have member variables within the application class that you want to access from within a view class. Table 21.2 shows the functions provided by the MFC library for navigating between the objects of an MDI application.

Table 21.2 MDI navigation functions

Class	Function	Returns
Global	AfxGetApp	A pointer to the `CWinApp` object.
Global	AfxGetMainWnd	A pointer to the main frame window (`CWnd`) object.
CMDIFrameWnd	MDIGetActive	A pointer to the active MDI child window (`CMDIChildWnd`) object.

Class	Function	Returns
CWnd	GetParentFrame	A pointer to the parent frame window (CFrameWnd) object.
CFrameWnd	GetActiveView	A pointer to the current active view (CView) object.
CFrameWnd	GetActiveDocument	A pointer to the current active document (CDocument) object.
CView	GetDocument	A pointer to the view's associated document (CDocument) object.
CDocument	GetFirstViewPosition	The position of the first view from the list of views associated with the document. Used to iterate through a document's views.
CDocument	GetNextView	A pointer to the next view (CView) object from the list of views associated with the document.

AfxGetApp and AfxGetMainWnd are global functions that can be called from anywhere. The pointers returned by these two functions can be safely cast to your own application-specific classes, as shown in the following examples:

```
CMDICoinApp* pApp = (CMDICoinApp*)AfxGetApp();
CMainFrame* pFrame = (CMainFrame*)AfxGetMainWnd();
```

A view is associated to one particular document, so it is enough for the view class to have one GetDocument function. The pointer returned from this function is cast automatically to your application-specific document class by the AppWizard-generated code.

A document can have one or more views associated with it, and there can be more than one document object. To find the active document or view, it is necessary first to find the active MDI child window and then call either GetActiveDocument or GetActiveView, as shown in the following example:

```
// Find the active MDI child window
CMDIChildWnd* pChild =
        ((CMDIFrameWnd*)AfxGetMainWnd())->MDIGetActive();
```

```
// Get the active document
CMDICoinDoc* pDoc =
        (CMDICoinDoc*)pChild->GetActiveDocument();


// Get the active view
CMDICoinView* pView =
        (CMDICoinView*)pChild->GetActiveView();
```

A view can see only one document

A document object can have several views but a view can be associated with only a single document.

If you have a requirement to perform a task on some or all the views associated with a particular document, use the document class functions GetFirstViewPosition and GetNextView to iterate through each of the document's views, as shown in the following example:

```
void CMyDoc::DoTaskForAllViews()
{
    POSITION pos = GetFirstViewPosition();
    while (pos != NULL)
    {
        CMyView* pMyView = GetNextView(pos);
        pMyView->DoTask();
    }
}
```

Developing a Sample MDI Application

At the beginning of this chapter you created the MDICoin sample project. So far the purpose it has served is to provide examples of code generated by AppWizard to help explain how the MDI framework operates. In this section you'll develop the example, first to display a stack of coins graphically with menu options that add or remove a coin. Then you'll create a second document type to display bills. The second document type will require its own specific document and view classes and its own resources. It will also require a document template object to be created, initialized, and registered within the application.

Adding Member Variables to the Document

The sample document class CMDICoinDoc requires only one member variable that is a count of the current number of coins in the stack. In order for the view class `CMDICoinView` to access this variable you will add a function to the document class that returns it. Follow these steps to add the necessary code.

Implementing the document data storage and access methods

1. On the ClassView pane, select the `CMDICoinDoc` class; then from the context menu select **Add Member Variable**.

2. Select the **Member Variables** tab. Enter `int` in the **Variable Type** edit box. Enter `m_nCoins` in the **Variable Name** edit box and select the **Protected Access** radio button. Click **OK**.

3. With the `CMDICoinDoc` class still highlighted, select **Add Member Function** from the context menu.

4. Enter `int` in the **Function Type** edit box. Enter `GetCoinCount` in the **Function Declaration** edit box and select the **Public Access** radio button.

5. Enter the following line of code in the body of the `GetCoinCount` function:

   ```
   return m_nCoins;
   ```

6. On the ClassView pane, double-click the `CMDICoinDoc` constructor function item.

7. Enter the following line of code after the `TODO` comments in the constructor function:

   ```
   m_nCoins = 1;
   ```

The `CMDICoinDoc` now has a protected member variable `m_nCoins`, which is initialized in the constructor function. Note that initializing variables in the document constructor is safe for MDI but not necessarily for SDI applications. In an MDI application a new document object instance is allocated whenever a document is created or opened and destroyed when it is closed. In an SDI application the document object is allocated only once and then reused for all subsequent documents; it is destroyed when the application terminates.

You have also added an access member function `GetCoinCount`, which will be used by the view to retrieve the value of `m_nCoins`.

Protecting document variables

Your document class should contain *protected member variables* that are accessed via public member functions.

SEE ALSO

➤ *For more information on initialization within SDI applications, see page 283*

Accessing Document Data from the View

In order for the view to retrieve data from the document, it must first be capable of accessing the document object. The MFC framework provides for this automatically by adding a GetDocument function to your application-specific view class. This function returns a pointer to the document object to which the view was attached with the document template.

The CMDICoinView class displays the stack of coins with the OnDraw function. The MFC framework calls the OnDraw function whenever the view must be rendered to the screen. Edit the CMDICoinView::OnDraw function as shown in Listing 21.2.

Listing 21.2 LST22_1.CPP—Accessing Document Data to Render the View Image

```
1   void CMDICoinView::OnDraw(CDC* pDC)
2   {
3       CMDICoinDoc* pDoc = GetDocument();
4       ASSERT_VALID(pDoc);
5
6       // TODO: add draw code for native data here
7       // ** Save the current brush
8       CBrush* pOldBrush = pDC->GetCurrentBrush();
9
10      // ** Create a solid yellow brush
11      CBrush br;
12      br.CreateSolidBrush(RGB(255,255,0));
13
14      // ** Select the yellow brush in to the device context
15      pDC->SelectObject(&br);
16
17      // ** Retrieve the number of coins from the document
18      // ** and draw two ellipses to represent each coin
19      for(int nCount = 0; nCount < pDoc->GetCoinCount();
        ➥nCount++)
20      {
```

```
21              int y = 100 - 10 * nCount;
22              pDC->Ellipse(40, y, 100, y-30);
23              pDC->Ellipse(40, y-10, 100, y-35);
24          }
25
26          // ** Restore the current brush
27          pDC->SelectObject(pOldBrush);
28      }
```

The first two lines in the function (lines 3 and 4) are automatically provided by AppWizard. The GetDocument function returns a pointer to the document object associated with this view. The pointer to the document is used in the for loop on line 19 to retrieve the current number of coins by calling GetCoinCount.

SEE ALSO

➤ *For information on device contexts, see page 356*

➤ *For information on drawing graphics, see page 409*

Modifying Document Data and Updating the View

To modify the number of coins, you must add two menu options to the MDICoin example—one to add a coin and one to remove a coin. When selected, these options will each call a function within the document class that will either increase or decrease the coin count and then ensure all views associated with that document are updated. Add the options to the menu resource IDR_MDICOITYPE because this is specific to the coin document type. To add the menu options, follow these steps.

Adding menu options

1. On the ResourceView pane, expand the Menu folder and double-click **IDR_MDICOITYPE**. The menu resource appears in the resource editor.

2. Click the **Edit** menu item within the resource editor. The drop-down menu appears.

3. Double-click the blank item at the bottom of the drop-down list. The Menu Item Properties dialog box appears as shown in Figure 21.7.

4. Enter an **ID** for the menu item. For this example use
   `ID_EDIT_ADD_COIN`.

5. Enter a **Caption** for the menu item. For this example use
   `Add a Coin`.

6. Enter a **Prompt** for the menu item. For this example use
   `Increase the number of coins`.

7. Double-click the blank item at the bottom of the drop-down
   list.

8. Enter an **ID** for the menu item. For this example use
   `ID_EDIT_REMOVE_COIN`.

9. Enter a **Caption** for the menu item. For this example use
   `Remove a Coin`.

10. Enter a **Prompt** for the menu item. For this example use
    `Decrease the number of coins`.

11. Press Ctrl+W to start ClassWizard or from the **View** menu
    select **ClassWizard**.

12. Select the **Message Maps** tab.

13. Select `CMDICoinDoc` in the **Class Name** combo box.

14. Select `ID_EDIT_ADD_COIN` in the **Object IDs** list box.

15. Select `COMMAND` in the **Messages** list box; then click the **Add
    Function** button. Click **OK** on the Add Member Function
    dialog box.

16. Select `ID_EDIT_REMOVE_COIN` in the **Object IDs** list box.

17. Select `COMMAND` in the **Messages** list box, and then click the
    Add Function button. Click **OK** on the Add Member
    Function dialog box.

18. Click the **Edit Code** button.

An alteration to the document data should be reflected within its
associated views. This is achieved by calling functions that
redraw the view. Edit the two new command handler functions
`OnEditAddCoin` and `OnEditRemoveCoin`, as shown in Listing 21.3.

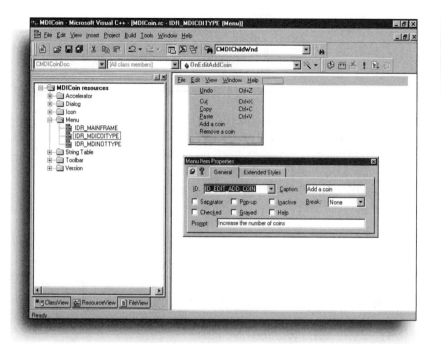

FIGURE 21.7

The Menu Item
Properties dialog box.

Listing 21.3 LST22_2.CPP—Updating Associated Views from the Document

```
1   void CMDICoinDoc::OnEditAddCoin()
2   {
3       // TODO: Add your command handler code here
4
5       // ** Increment the number of coins
6       m_nCoins++;
7
8       // ** Update view to redraw coin stack
9       UpdateAllViews(NULL);
10  }
11
12  void CMDICoinDoc::OnEditRemoveCoin()
13  {
14      // TODO: Add your command handler code here
15
16      // ** Decrement the number of coins
17      if(m_nCoins > 0)
18          m_nCoins--;
19
```

continues...

> **Listing 21.3**   Continued

```
20        // ** Update view to redraw coin stack
21        UpdateAllViews(NULL);
22   }
```

Better performance when updating views

You can pass application-specific hint information to the `UpdateAllViews` function. This is passed on to the `OnUpdate` function and can be interpreted to determine exactly what requires updating.

As you can see, each function either increases or decreases `m_nCoins` (line 6 and 18, respectively). Then a call is made to `UpdateAllViews`, passing `NULL` as a parameter (lines 9 and 21). The `NULL` parameter means all views attached to the document are to be updated. Each view is updated by calling its `OnUpdate` function. This invalidates the client area of the view window and causes the `OnDraw` function to be called.

Now build and run the MDICoin project. Try selecting **New** on the **File** menu to create a new document window, and then select the **Add a Coin** and **Remove a Coin** menu options. The view should be similar to Figure 21.8. You should also be able to create a second view of the same document by selecting **New Window** on the **Window** menu.

FIGURE 21.8
The MDICoin application.

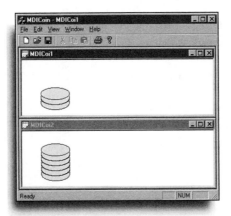

Adding New Document Templates

The advantage of using the MDI model over SDI isn't only giving the user the convenience of working with more than one open document, but also having the capability to handle several types of documents within one application. To cater to this, you'll need to create your own document and view classes, insert resources, and add code that creates and initializes a

`CMultiDocTemplate` object. In this section, you'll add a new document type to the MDICoin example that will display bills rather than coins. Then, to generate the new document and view classes, follow these steps.

Creating new document and view classes

1. Press Ctrl+W to start ClassWizard, or from the **View** menu select **ClassWizard**.

2. Click the **Add Class** button and from the displayed list select **New**. The New Class dialog box appears.

3. Enter a **Name** for the new class. For this example use `CMDIBillDoc`.

4. In the **Base Class** combo box, select `CDocument`. Then click **OK** to add the class.

5. Click the **Add Class** button and from the displayed list select **New**.

6. Enter a **Name** for the new class. For this example use `CMDIBillView`.

7. In the **Base Class** combo box, select `CView`. Then click **OK** to add the class.

8. Click **OK** to close the ClassWizard dialog box.

9. On the ClassView pane select the `CMDIBillDoc` class; then from the context menu select **Add Member Variable**.

10. Select the **Member Variables** tab. Enter `int` in the **Variable Type** edit box. Enter `m_nBills` in the **Variable Name** edit box and select the **Protected Access** radio button. Click **OK**.

11. With the `CMDIBillDoc` class still highlighted, select **Add Member Function** from the context menu.

12. Enter `int` in the **Function Type** edit box. Enter `GetBillCount` in the **Function Declaration** edit box and select the **Public Access** radio button. Click **OK**.

13. Enter the following line of code in the body of the `GetBillCount` function:

    ```
    return m_nBills;
    ```

14. On the ClassView pane, double-click the `CMDIBillDoc` constructor function item.

15. Enter the following line of code after the `TODO` comments in the constructor function:

    ```
    m_nBills = 1;
    ```

16. On the ClassView pane, select the `CMDIBillView` class; then from the context menu select **Add Member Function**.

17. Enter `CMDIBillDoc*` in the **Function Type** edit box. Enter `GetDocument` in the **Function Declaration** edit box and select the **Public Access** radio button. Click **OK**.

18. Enter the following line of code after the `TODO` comments in the constructor function:

    ```
    return (CMDIBillDoc*)m_pDocument;
    ```

You now have the new document and view classes. The document has a member to store the data an access method. The view class has a method to retrieve its document. Please note you will need to add the following `#include` directive at the top of the MDIBillView.cpp file before the `#include` of MDIBillView.h:

```
#include "MDIBillDoc.h"
```

The next step is to insert a menu resource. To create a new menu resource by copying an existing one, follow these steps.

Creating a document menu

1. On the ResourceView pane, expand the **Menu** folder and select the `IDR_MDICOITYPE` item. Press Ctrl+C and then press Ctrl+V. A copy of the selected menu is inserted with the ID `IDR_MDICOITYPE1`.

2. Select `IDR_MDICOITYPE1` on the ResourceView pane; then select **Properties** from the context menu. The Menu Properties dialog box appears.

3. Enter an **ID** for the menu. For this example use `IDR_MDIBILTYPE`. Close the Menu Properties dialog box.

4. On the ResourceView pane, double-click `IDR_MDIBILTYPE`. The menu is displayed in the resource editor.

5. Click the **Edit** menu item within the resource editor. The drop-down menu appears.

6. Double-click the **Add a Coin** item. The Menu Item Properties dialog box appears.

7. Enter an **ID** for the menu item. For this example, use `ID_EDIT_ADD_BILL`.

8. Enter a **Caption** for the menu item. For this example, use `Add a Bill`.

9. Enter a **Prompt** for the menu item. For this example, use `Increase the number of bills`. Then double-click the **Remove a Coin** item.

10. Enter an **ID** for the menu item. For this example, use `ID_EDIT_REMOVE_BILL`.

11. Enter a **Caption** for the menu item. For this example, use `Remove a Bill`.

12. Enter a **Prompt** for the menu item. For this example, use `Decrease the number of bills`.

13. From the **File** menu select **Save**. Then from the **File** menu select **Close**.

14. Press Ctrl+W to start ClassWizard or from the **View** menu select **ClassWizard** and select the **Message Maps** tab.

15. Select `CMDIBillDoc` in the **Class Name** combo box.

16. Select `ID_EDIT_ADD_BILL` in the Object **IDs** list box.

17. Select `COMMAND` in the **Messages** list box; then click the **Add Function** button. Click **OK** on the Add Member Function dialog box.

18. Select `ID_EDIT_REMOVE_BILL` in the **Object IDs** list box.

19. Select `COMMAND` in the **Messages** list box; then click the **Add Function** button. Click **OK** on the Add Member Function dialog box.

20. Click **OK** to close the ClassWizard dialog box.

Now you have two new command handler functions in the `CMDIBillDoc` class, `OnEditAddBill` and `OnEditRemoveBill`. These two functions must increment and decrement `m_nBills`.

Using the code shown in Listing 21.3 as an example, edit the two new functions (replacing m_nCoins with m_nBills). After the two functions are complete, the next step is to create a resource string for the document.

Creating a document string

1. On the ResourceView pane, expand the String Table folder, and then double-click **String Table**. The string table appears in the resource editor.

2. To insert the new string below the IDR_MDICOITYPE string, select IDR_MDICOITYPE on the String Table and from the context menu select **New String**. The String Properties dialog box appears.

3. Enter an **ID** for string. For this example use IDR_MDIBILTYPE.

4. Enter the string **Caption**. For this example use the following string:
   ```
   \nMDIBil\nBills\n\n\nMDIBill.Document\nMDIBil Document
   ```

5. Edit the IDR_MAINFRAME string to read
   ```
   MDICoins&Bills.
   ```

6. Edit the IDR_MDICOITYPE string to read
   ```
   \nMDICoi\nCoins\n\n\nMDICoi.Document\nMDICoi Document
   ```

7. Close the String Properties dialog box.

The document string has a strict format, identical for both SDI and MDI applications. The string is broken into seven substrings delimited by the \n (newline) character. The purpose of each substring is described in Table 21.3.

Table 21.3 The document string resource

String Example	Description
1	Left blank in MDI. In SDI this is the application title. In MDI the application title is held separately in IDR_MAINFRAME.

String Example	Description
2 MDICoi	Default document name. An identifying number is automatically appended for each new document. For example, in MS Word the string is Document and the first new document defaults to Document1, the second Document2, and so on.
3 Coins	Document title. Used to display the list of available documents to the user. You can leave this substring blank to hide its existence from the user.
4 Coin Viewer (*.coi)	Document type and filter description. Used on the common File Open dialog box in the **Files of Type** combo box.
5 .coi	File extension associated with the document. Note wildcards should not be included in this string.
6 MDICoi.Document	Explorer registration name. Used to associate the document type with Explorer so the application is launched when an associated file is run.
7 MDICoi Document	Registry and OLE identity name. This string is stored in the Registry to enable OLE support. Users see this string when selecting the OLE command **Insert Object**.

Everything is now in place for you to start utilizing the new document and view classes within the MDICoin example. You can let the MFC framework do all the work of instantiating the objects and managing the view and frame windows. To do this you simply must register your document/view and frame set with your application by creating a second document template. Document templates are registered in the applications override of CWinApp::InitInstance. To create and add the document template, add the code in lines 16 through to 25, shown in Listing 21.4. Please note you will need to add the following include directives at the top of the MDICoinApp.cpp file:

```
#include "MDIBillDoc.h"
#include "MDIBillView.h"
```

① Original document template object added by AppWizard.

② Add a second document template object to the application.

Listing 21.4 LST22_3.CPP—Creating and Initializing the Document Template

```
1   BOOL CMDICoinApp::InitInstance()
2   {
3       // ** Note: some lines removed for brevity
4
5       // Register the application's document templates.
            Document templates
6       //  serve as the connection between documents,
            frame windows, and views.
7
8       CMultiDocTemplate* pDocTemplate;
9       pDocTemplate = new CMultiDocTemplate(
10          IDR_MDICOITYPE,
11          RUNTIME_CLASS(CMDICoinDoc),                          ①
12          RUNTIME_CLASS(CChildFrame), // custom MDI child frame
13          RUNTIME_CLASS(CMDICoinView));
14      AddDocTemplate(pDocTemplate);
15
16      // ** Instantiate a second document template and
17      // ** initialize by passing the document resource ID and
18      // ** runtime information for the document, frame,
            and view classes.
19      // ** Then call AddDocTemplate to register with
            the application.
20      pDocTemplate = new CMultiDocTemplate(
21          IDR_MDIBILTYPE,
22          RUNTIME_CLASS(CMDIBillDoc),
23          RUNTIME_CLASS(CChildFrame), // custom MDI child frame  ②
24          RUNTIME_CLASS(CMDIBillView));
25      AddDocTemplate(pDocTemplate);
26
27      // create main MDI Frame window
28      CMainFrame* pMainFrame = new CMainFrame;
29      if (!pMainFrame->LoadFrame(IDR_MAINFRAME))
30          return FALSE;
31      m_pMainWnd = pMainFrame;
32
33      // ** Note: some lines removed for brevity
34  }
```

Finally, you must implement some code in the view class to display the dollar bills according to the count in the document. Edit the CMDIBillView::OnDraw function as shown in Listing 21.5.

Listing 21.5 LST22_4.CPP—Implementing the Draw Code in the View

```
1   void CMDIBillView::OnDraw(CDC* pDC)
2   {
3       // ** Retrieve a pointer to the document
4       CMDIBillDoc* pDoc = GetDocument();        (1)
5       ASSERT_VALID(pDoc);
6
7       // ** Save the current brush
8       CBrush* pOldBrush = pDC->GetCurrentBrush();
9
10      // ** Create a solid green brush
11      CBrush br;
12      br.CreateSolidBrush(RGB(0,128,32));
13
14      // ** Select the green brush into the device context
15      pDC->SelectObject(&br);
16
17      // ** Retrieve the number of bills from the document
18      // ** and draw a rectangle and a $ to represent each bill
19      for(int nCount = 0; nCount < pDoc->GetBillCount();   (2)
    ➥nCount++)
20      {
21          int x = 40 + 20 * nCount;
22          pDC->Rectangle(x, 40, x+100, 90);
23          pDC->TextOut(x + 5, 45, "$");
24      }
25
26      // ** Restore the current brush
27      pDC->SelectObject(pOldBrush);
28  }
```

(1) Retrieves a pointer to the document object.

(2) Calls the document access function that returns the current number of bills.

The GetDocument function returns a pointer to the document object, which is stored in pDoc. The pointer is used in the for loop in line 19 to retrieve the current number of bills by calling the access method GetBillCount. The actual drawing code produces only a cheap imitation of dollar bills using a solid green brush to fill a rectangle and the $ sign as simple text.

Build and run the project. If you select **New** from the **File** menu, the New dialog box should appear. Try opening both document types and switching between them; notice the **Edit** menu changes according to the active document. Notice also the application and document title bars are constructed using the string resource associated with the document type. An example of the MDICoin application is shown in Figure 21.9.

FIGURE 21.9
The MDICoin application.

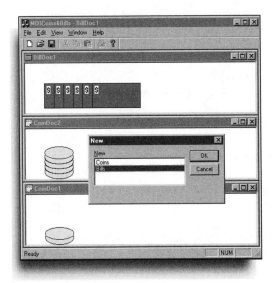

SEE ALSO
➤ *For more information on menus, see page 294*
➤ *For more information about device contexts, see page 356*
➤ *To learn more about drawing graphics, see page 409*

22

Printing and Print Previewing

- Customizing the standard framework to easily implement printing and print previewing

- Implementing multiple page reports

- Handling different aspect ratios and device dimensions

- Printing directly to the Windowss printing mechanism, bypassing the standard framework

Using the Framework's Functionality

The SDI and MDI frameworks created by AppWizard add the hooks for printing and previewing by default. These can be turned off by unchecking the **Printing and Print Preview** option in Step 4 of the MFC AppWizard, but generally they are useful to include in any project and add very little overhead. Most of the real work of printing is taken care of by the device context and GDI (as covered in Chapter 15, "Understanding Drawing in Device Contexts"). The framework presents you with a device context for a print document page; you can treat it pretty much as if it's a normal window device context.

SEE ALSO

➤ *For more information on the SDI framework, see page 267*

➤ *For a detailed understanding of device contexts, see page 356*

Using Default Print Functionality

The SDI (single document interface) framework supports printing images from views based on information held in the document. Because this information is already displayed in your applications views, you can probably print this information by modifying the view to add printing support.

The framework calls your OnDraw() function in the view to display an image. There is a corresponding OnPrint() function that it calls to let your view handle printing the information. Often this task is simply a case of using the same drawing code as you've implemented in your OnDraw() function. If this is so, you don't actually need to implement the OnPrint() function; the framework does this by default in the CView base class and calls OnDraw(). The printer is then treated just like it would be for a screen because it offers a device context for the drawing functions to use, as a substitute for the usual screen device context. Your OnDraw() function can determine whether the device context it is passed is a screen or printer device context, but because the drawing functions will work in the same way on both, even this knowledge isn't necessary.

You can explore the printing functionality added by the standard framework by creating a standard SDI application with AppWizard. Leave the **Printing and Print Preview** option in Step 4 checked (this means you can click **Finish** on Step 1) and name the project PrintIt.

The first thing you'll need is a graphic to print. You can create a graphical test display in the OnDraw() function of my CPrintItView class (just a normal CView) as shown in Listing 22.1. This test displays a line-art style picture with some centralized text in a large font (see Figure 22.1). The test image isn't too important, but it will make a useful comparison between printed output and screen display.

Standard print framework support

The standard print and print preview support is available only in SDI and MDI applications. Dialog-based applications must implement their own printing support.

LISTING 22.1 LST23_1.CPP—Drawing in *OnDraw* to Produce a Print Sample

```
1   void CPrintItView::OnDraw(CDC* pDC)
2   {
3       CPrintItDoc* pDoc = GetDocument();
4       ASSERT_VALID(pDoc);
5
6       // TODO: add draw code for native data here
7
8       // ** Set metric mapping
9       pDC->SetMapMode(MM_LOMETRIC);           (1)
10
11      // ** Declare and create a font 2.2cm high
12      CFont fnBig;
13      fnBig.CreateFont(220,0,0,0,FW_HEAVY,FALSE,FALSE,0,
14          ANSI_CHARSET,OUT_DEFAULT_PRECIS,
15          CLIP_DEFAULT_PRECIS,DEFAULT_QUALITY,
16          FF_SWISS+VARIABLE_PITCH,"Arial");
17
18      //** Select the new font and store the original
19      CFont* pOldFont = pDC->SelectObject(&fnBig);
20
21      //** Declare a client rectangle
22      CRect rcClient;
23      GetClientRect(&rcClient);
24
25      // ** Convert to logical units
```

(1) MM_LOMETRIC mapping mode is set, so logical coordinates are 1/10th of a millimeter.

continues...

563

LISTING 22.1 Continued

② These lines draw the string and peg background.

③ Line 61 draws the Sample Print text in the center of the window.

```
26        pDC->DPtoLP(&rcClient);
27
28        // ** Set up some drawing variables
29        const int nPoints = 50;
30        int xm = rcClient.Width();
31        int ym = rcClient.Height();
32        double dAspW = xm/(double)nPoints;
33        double dAspH = ym/(double)nPoints;
34
35        // ** Select a black pen
36        CPen* pOldPen =
37            (CPen*)pDC->SelectStockObject(BLACK_PEN);
38
39        // ** Draw the lines
40        for(int i=0;i<nPoints;i++)
41        {
42            int xo = (int)(i * dAspW);
43            int yo = (int)(i * dAspH);
44
45            pDC->MoveTo(xo,0);
46            pDC->LineTo(xm,yo);
47            pDC->LineTo(xm-xo,ym);
48            pDC->LineTo(0,ym-yo);
49            pDC->LineTo(xo,0);
50        }
51
52        // ** Reselect the old pen
53        pDC->SelectObject(pOldPen);
54
55        // ** Draw the text on top
56        pDC->SetTextAlign(TA_CENTER+TA_BASELINE);
57        pDC->SetBkMode(TRANSPARENT);
58
59        // ** Set gray text
60        pDC->SetTextColor(RGB(64,64,64));
61        pDC->TextOut(xm/2,ym/2,"Sample Print");
62
63        // ** Reselect the old font
64        pDC->SelectObject(pOldFont);
65    }
```

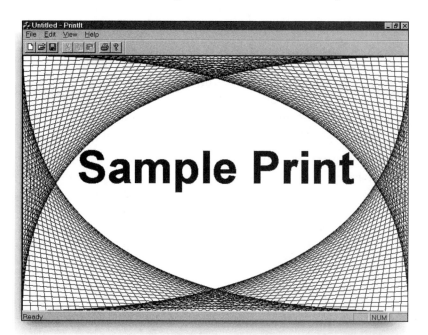

FIGURE 22.1

Graphical test output of
PrintIt in a window.

Although there is a fair bit of code in this OnDraw() function, none of it is unusual. It just draws lines inside the client rectangle and writes some text in the middle. Notice at line 9, the mapping mode is set to MM_LOMETRIC; this sets the logical coordinates to tenths of a millimeter (see Chapter 15, "Understanding Drawing in Device Contexts").

A 2.2cm high font is created at line 13 and used to draw the sample text at line 61. Lines 40 to 50 draw the arty "peg and string" frame using the client rectangle coordinates. I'll let you decipher the details; the important thing here is to investigate the business of printing.

If you build and run the program after adding these lines to the OnDraw() function of Listing 22.1, you should see a graphical display in your application window, as shown in Figure 22.1.

So the big question is: What must you do to print this image output? Surprisingly little because the standard framework tries to print this by calling your OnDraw() function and passing the device context for the printer rather than for the window.

Using mapping modes with screen displays

You might notice that when displayed on the screen, the font isn't exactly 2.2cm high. This is because it is difficult for Windows to know the exact dimensions of every monitor type (even if it is set properly in the Control Panel). However, printer device drivers have a much more accurate idea of proper sizes, and when printed the font should appear exactly 2.2cm high.

If you click the **File** menu of the PrintIt application and choose **Print Preview**, you'll see a small representation of the image in the top-left corner, although the font is too big for the line drawing. This isn't the framework's fault; it has done its best to represent your window, but it was passed the wrong coordinates for the device context. The problem lies with the GetClientRect() used in line 23.

Notice that GetClientRect() is a member of the view, not of the device context. This works fine for the window because the device context is the same size as the window rectangle. Now you're passing the window rectangle to the printer device context (which is small in comparison) but creating a 2.2cm high font that is always the same size (because of the mapping mode).

SEE ALSO

➤ *For more detail about overriding* OnDraw( ), *see page 373*

➤ *For more information about drawing lines, see page 392*

➤ *For more information about drawing text, see page 418*

Overriding *OnPrint()*

To fix the client rectangle coordinate size problem, you must pass the correct rectangle for the printer rather than the window. Fortunately, the framework calls a virtual function that you can override in your view and use to find all the information you need. As you read earlier, this function is named OnPrint() and is analogous to OnDraw(). When drawing in a window, OnDraw() is called; when drawing on a printer, OnPrint() is called. You might be wondering how the drawing code in OnDraw() was executed to print preview the sample graphical display. The default CView implementation of OnPrint() simply calls OnDraw(), passing its printer device context.

Your OnPrint() doesn't have to call OnDraw(); you can override OnPrint() to make it draw something entirely different, but many applications must print out what the user sees. These applications reuse their OnDraw() code with the printer device context.

Virtual functions and polymorphism

A virtual function is a function that is defined in a base class and usually implemented with code that performs a default action. When a class then inherits from that base class, it can optionally implement its own version of the virtual function to perform a more specific action. Whenever the function is called, even from a base class pointer to the derived object, the function in the derived class will be called; this technique is called virtual function overriding. The overriding function can also call down to its base class version by explicitly calling the overridden function with base class scope. This way the overriding function can also use the base class functionality. Virtual functions are one of the main ways that C++ programmers can implement polymorphism in their objects.

Overriding the *OnPrint()* Virtual Function

1. Click the **ClassView** tab of the Project Workspace view.

2. Click the top plus sign to open the view of the project classes.

3. Right-click the view class to which you want to add the OnPrint() override (such as CPrintItView in the PrintIt example) to display the context menu.

4. Select the **Add Virtual Function** option to display the New Virtual Override dialog box.

5. You should see an OnPrint virtual function in the **New Virtual Functions** list.

6. Click the **Add and Edit** button to start editing the OnPrint() virtual function.

The standard override for OnPrint() looks like this:

```
void CPrintItView::OnPrint(CDC* pDC, CPrintInfo* pInfo)
{
    // TODO: Add your specialized code here
    CView::OnPrint(pDC, pInfo);
}
```

The first thing you'll notice that's different from OnDraw() is the second parameter, the pointer to a CPrintInfo object pInfo. This is where you'll find the details about the current print, specifically the rectangle coordinates for the printer device context you require. There are lots of useful CPrintInfo member variables. Some of these are shown in Table 22.1.

> **Using the CView class's default OnPrint()**
>
> Notice that the standard Wizard-generated code for your OnPrint() override calls the CView base class's own OnPrint() function. Investigating the MFC source code shows how the magical framework print support works automatically. You'll find that in the ..\MFC\SRC\VIEWCORE.CPP source module under your Visual C++ directory is the implementation for CView::OnPrint(), which merely calls OnDraw() passing the pDC device context pointer.

TABLE 22.1   *CPrintInfo* member variables specific to print information

Variable Name	Description of Contents
m_nCurPage	The current page number for multipage prints
m_nNumPreviewPages	Either 1 or 2, depending on the preview pages shown
m_rectDraw	The coordinates of the print page rectangle
m_pPD	Pointer to a CPrintDialog class if the Print dialog box is used
m_bDirect	TRUE if the Print dialog box has been bypassed

continues...

567

TABLE 22.1 Continued

Variable Name	Description of Contents
m_bPreview	TRUE if currently in print preview
m_strPageDesc	A format string to help generate the page number
m_lpUserData	A pointer that can be used to hold user data

Some other member variables in CPrintInfo are covered later in this chapter, but first you'll need to find the printing rectangle coordinates rather than the window's rectangle. The m_rectDraw member holds the coordinate rectangle of the current print page. You can use these coordinates with the printer device context in the OnDraw() function. There is a problem though, in that this structure isn't passed to the OnDraw(), but you can copy the coordinates into a member variable held in your CPrintItView class.

Add the following lines to store the rectangle after the // TODO comment, but before the CView::OnPrint() call:

```
// ** copy the print rectangle from the pInfo
    if (pInfo) m_rcPrintRect = pInfo->m_rectDraw;
```

This will store the printing rectangle in the m_rcPrintRect member of the CPrintItView class. You must therefore declare this member variable, which is easily done by right-clicking the CPrintItView class in the ClassView pane of the Project Workspace view, and choosing the **Add Member Variable** option. The **Variable Type** is a CRect, and the declaration is obviously m_rcPrintRect. Access should be private because you don't need or want any other classes to know about this internal rectangle.

SEE ALSO

➤ *For more detail about view classes and* CView, *see page 282*

Using the Printer Device Context

The device context passed to OnPrint() differs slightly from the display context in that it may have fewer colors, and is probably larger that your display. Other than these attributes, you can use it to draw in exactly the same way as the screen device context.

Public, private, and protected access

Every member function and member variable in a class definition may be designated as having public, private or protected access. This affects how other classes and derived classes can access those member functions and variables. Public access lets any class access the member variable or function. Private access only lets the member functions of the same class access the specified class member. Protected access is similar to private access, except that classes that have been derived with public access from the base class can also access those protected base class members.

These techniques let C++ programmers enforce safety by only allowing access to their objects through the proper "public" access methods. By doing this, it is much harder to accidentally access the wrong member variable or function and cause the software to crash.

This is how you can use the same OnDraw() to print as well as view in a window. The base class call CView::OnPrint() implements code that does exactly this.

The device context holds a flag that you can interrogate via the IsPrinting() function to determine whether you are drawing to a screen-based device context or a printer-based device context. You might use this difference to change the printed output from the screen output, or more subtly to adjust the coordinates used to produce the printed output.

For the sample program it only remains to use the m_rcPrintRect coordinates when printing in the OnDraw() function. The code necessary to use the IsPrinting() function to determine whether the window's client rectangle or the printer's rectangle should be used is shown in Listing 22.2. The output produced is shown by the print preview in Figure 22.2.

LISTING 22.2 LST23_2.CPP—Adding Printing Rectangle Support to the Standard *OnDraw()* Implementation

```
1   // Declare a client rectangle
2   CRect rcClient;
3
4   // ** Check the device context for printing mode
5   if (pDC->IsPrinting())
6   {
7       // ** Printing, so use the print rectangle
8       rcClient = m_rcPrintRect;
9   }
10  else
11  {
12      // ** Not printing, so client rect will do
13      GetClientRect(&rcClient);
14  }
15
16  // Convert to logical units
17  pDC->DPtoLP(&rcClient);  ———(1)
```

(1) This line converts from device coordinates in pixels to logical coordinates in 1/10 of a millimeter.

Notice in Listing 22.2 that an If statement is used in line 5 to call the device context's IsPrinting() function. This function returns TRUE if this is a printer device context (or preview) and

569

FALSE for any other device contexts. In the printing case, you can assign the stored print page rectangle to rcClient, as shown in line 8. In the normal screen window case you can just use the standard GetClientRect() to find the window's rectangle, as shown in line 13.

Because you've used a mapping mode, you must convert both printing and display rectangle coordinates from device units to logical units. This is done by the DPtoLP() function in line 17. If you change and add lines 4–14 to your existing OnDraw() function, and then build and run the application, you should be able to run the print preview as before, with better results (see Figure 22.2).

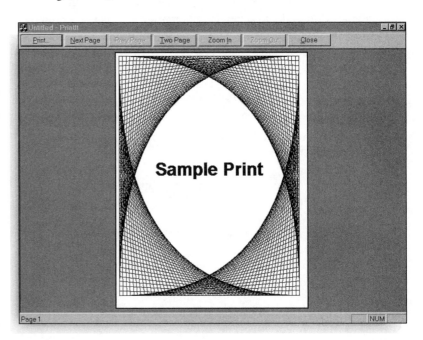

FIGURE 22.2
Print preview using the full print page rectangle coordinates.

SEE ALSO
➤ *To understand mapping modes in detail, turn to page 372*

Maintaining the Aspect Ratio

As you can see from Figure 22.2, because the paper is much longer and thinner than the window, the printed output becomes stretched. The relationship between the width and the height is the *aspect ratio*. To stop the image from stretching one way or another, you must keep the same aspect ratio as the image in the window. The code in Listing 22.2 doesn't try to maintain aspect ratios, which isn't very satisfactory in most cases, so you would need to add some code to maintain the aspect ratio of the printed output.

The best tactic to use in this case is to find out whether setting either the width or the height to the full width or height of the paper will give maximum coverage, and then shorten the other dimension to maintain the aspect ratio.

To do this, you need some information about the paper dimensions and its own aspect ratio. There is a device context function that retrieves these details (and many more) named `GetDeviceCaps()`. By passing the `ASPECTX` or `ASPECTY` flags to `GetDeviceCaps()`, you can find the relationship between the width of a pixel and its height. If the relationship is 1:1 the pixel is square; otherwise, it is oblong and might differ from the screen's own aspect ratio. If it differs you can decide which axis will give you the largest image, while maintaining the same aspect ratio as the screen. That way you can avoid a stretched-looking image.

Code that does just that in the `OnDraw()` function is demonstrated in Listing 22.3.

> **Device aspect ratios**
>
> For most printers, you'll probably find that the aspect ratio is 1:1. But if you look closely at thermal printer output like those in fax machines, you can see a very distinctive aspect ratio difference in their pixels.

LISTING 22.3   LST23_3.CPP—Maintaining the Aspect Ratio While Producing the Largest Printed Representation

```
1    //** Declare a client rectangle and get the client rect
2    CRect rcClient;
3    GetClientRect(&rcClient);
4
5    // ** Check the device context for printing mode
6    if (pDC->IsPrinting())
7    {
8      // ** Find the Print width : Window width ratio
9      double dWidthRatio=(double)m_rcPrintRect.Width()/
10                         (double)rcClient.Width();
11
```

continues...

LISTING 22.3 Continued

① Calculate the Width and Height ratios between the window and the printer page sizes.

② This line calculates the printer's own aspect ratio differences by information retrieved from the device context capabilities.

③ Depending on whether the printed area is longer or wider can help you make the most use of the paper to print the largest possible image.

```
12    // ** Find the Print height : Window height ratio
13    double dHeightRatio=(double)m_rcPrintRect.Height()/ ────── ①
14                        (double)rcClient.Height();
15
16    // ** Calculate the device's aspect ratio
17    double dAspect=(double)pDC->GetDeviceCaps(ASPECTX)/ ────── ②
18                   (double)pDC->GetDeviceCaps(ASPECTY);
19
20    // ** Find the new relative height
21    int nHeight=(int)(rcClient.Height() *
22                      dWidthRatio * dAspect );
23
24    // ** Find the new relative width
25    int nWidth=(int)(rcClient.Width() *
26                     dHeightRatio * (1.0 / dAspect) );
27
28    // ** Set the whole rectangle
29    rcClient=m_rcPrintRect;
30
31    // ** Determine the best fit across or down the page
32    if (nHeight > nWidth) ─────────────────────────────── ③
33    {
34        // ** Down is best, so adjust the width
35        rcClient.BottomRight().x=
36            m_rcPrintRect.TopLeft().x + nWidth;
37    }
38    else
39    {
40        // ** Across is best, so adjust the height
41        rcClient.BottomRight().y=
42            m_rcPrintRect.TopLeft().y + nHeight;
43    }
44  }
45
46  // Convert to logical units
47  pDC->DPtoLP(&rcClient);
```

Notice that both the screen window and printed case use the window coordinates that are found from the GetClientRect() in line 3. In the onscreen window case, nothing else is done and the code continues as normal.

However, a lot now happens when printing, if the `IsPrinting()` test in line 6 returns `TRUE`. First, you must find the ratios of the window width to the paper width and the window height to the paper height. You can find these ratios as shown in lines 9 and 13 by dividing the paper dimensions by the window dimensions.

The next thing you must calculate is the device's own aspect ratio peculiarities. You can use the `GetDeviceCaps()` function in line 17 to find the ratio of width to height in the device itself and store the result in `dAspect`.

Using these values, you can now calculate the device's comparative width and height coordinates in terms of the opposing window dimension, as shown in lines 21 and 25. This calculation, which includes the device aspect ratio for each dimension, will yield the adjusted height for the full page width or vice versa. Now you must decide whether you can best fit the full width or height of a page and adjust the other dimension. The condition on line 32 makes this decision based on the bigger width or height. This means that if you have a tall, thin window, it is better to use the full height of the paper and adjust the width; conversely, if you have a short, wide window, it is better to use the full width and adjust the height. Depending on what is better, the adjustment is made on line 35 or 42 by setting the bottom-right point's x- or y-coordinate to the adjusted width or height.

Notice that all the other dimensions are set to `rcClient` from the paper in the assignment on line 29, so the adjustment is the only change required. After this section, the program continues and will use the adjusted rectangle to do its drawing.

If you build and run the application after adding the lines in Listing 22.3 to the `OnDraw()` function, you should see that printing or previewing the window will now maintain the same aspect ratio as the onscreen window. If you stretch the window to make it higher than it is wide, the printed output will use the full height of the page rather than the full width, but still maintain the correct aspect ratios.

SEE ALSO

➤ *For more detail on device capabilities, see page 377*

Common application printing options

Many graphics-oriented applications offer several options that either maintain or ignore the aspect ratio. The sample program implements an option commonly called Best Fit. Another common option is Size to Page, which means that the image is stretched to the full printer page size (thus losing the Aspect Ratio). You might also find options such as Original Image Size that maintain the aspect ratio but display the image (usually centered) at its onscreen size (usually looks quite small on a high-resolution printer).

Pagination and Orientation

Printing a single image over multiple pages

Sometimes you might want to print a single image split over multiple pages. To do this you'll need to render a portion of the image in the device context for each page. The **CScrollView** class can help with this because it supports **ScrollToPosition()** and allows variable scaling. However, some work is still required to prepare and position the printer device context between pages.

Printing a single page to represent the view in a window is a common requirement, but largely the printing process is concerned with printing large and complex multipage documents from the user's sophisticated data. The framework comes to the rescue again and simplifies this process by providing a common Print Setup dialog box and a page enumeration system to print and preview the specified range of pages.

Setting the Start and End Pages

The first considerations for a multipage document are the start and end pages, which also indicate how many pages you are going to print. A framework virtual function in the view class is called first when printing begins. This function is OnPreparePrinting() and it supplies one parameter, the CPrintInfo object pInfo. This is the first time you'll see the CPrintInfo and this is where you can first change it to customize the print to your requirements. The OnPreparePrinting() function is supplied automatically from AppWizard when you created the SDI, so you don't have to add it yourself. You can see the default implementation by double-clicking the OnPreparePrinting() member of the CPrintItView class in the ClassView pane.

It should look like this:

```
BOOL CPrintItView::OnPreparePrinting(CPrintInfo* pInfo)
{
    // default preparation
    return DoPreparePrinting(pInfo);
}
```

By default, the DoPreparePrinting() function is called and passed the pInfo pointer to the CPrintInfo object for the print. DoPreparePrinting() sets up the required device context and calls the standard Print dialog box if you are printing (not previewing). This dialog box is covered in more detail in the next section, but first you can set up a range of pages to print by modifying the CPrintInfo object before the DoPreparePrinting().

To do this, add the following lines before the // default preparation comment:

```
pInfo->SetMinPage(2);
    pInfo->SetMaxPage(8);
```

These two member functions of the CPrintInfo class will modify the CPrintInfo object pointed at by pInfo to set the starting page at page 2 via SetMinPage() and the ending page at page 8 via SetMaxPage().

Now when the document is printed, the OnPrint() function will be called six times. The only difference between each of these calls will be the pInfo->m_nCurPage member variable that will hold the current page as it iterates between 2 and 8.

Depending on the kind of application you write, the technique you'll use to determine the number of pages will vary. If you are selling music compact discs and want to print a brochure of your product range, you would probably fit the cover picture and review of each CD on one printed page, so if you sell 120 different CDs, you need 120 pages. However, if you are printing a complex government tender with different bill elements and formatted items, you'll probably need to measure the height of all the different parts and calculate a page count after performing your own pagination. Either way, when you have the page count, OnPreparePrinting() is where you'll set it into the CPrintInfo object.

To emphasize the difference between a full report and a window print, you can implement a completely different drawing in the OnPrint() function than OnDraw(), as shown in Listing 22.4. In this OnPrint(), the base class CView::OnPrint() function isn't called at all, which means that the default call of OnDraw() isn't performed. So in this implementation, the printing output and the display output are entirely different.

Bypassing the Print dialog box when printing

You don't always need to bother the user with the Print dialog box; this can be bypassed by setting the pInfo->m_bDirect variable to TRUE in OnPreparePrinting().

LISTING 22.4 LST23_4.CPP—Implementing Page-Specific Drawing in *OnPrint()*

① Create a 72 point font using CreatePointFont().

② Find the current page number from the CPrintInfo object.

③ Set up the array points for the diamond background.

④ Draw using the text with the current page number.

```cpp
1   void CPrintItView::OnPrint(CDC* pDC, CPrintInfo* pInfo)
2   {
3       // TODO: Add your specialized code here
4
5       // ** Create and select the font
6       CFont fnTimes;
7       fnTimes.CreatePointFont(720,"Times New Roman",pDC);          ①
8       CFont* pOldFont=(CFont*)pDC->SelectObject(&fnTimes);
9
10      // ** Create and select the brushe
11      CBrush brHatch(HS_CROSS,RGB(64,64,64));
12      CBrush* pOldBrush =
13          (CBrush*)pDC->SelectObject(&brHatch);
14
15      // ** Create the page text
16      CString strDocText;
17      strDocText.Format("Page Number %d",
18                          pInfo->m_nCurPage);                       ②
19
20      pDC->SetTextAlign(TA_CENTER+TA_BASELINE);
21
22      // ** Set up some useful point objects
23      CPoint ptCenter=pInfo->m_rectDraw.CenterPoint();
24      CPoint ptTopLeft=pInfo->m_rectDraw.TopLeft();
25      CPoint ptBotRight=pInfo->m_rectDraw.BottomRight();
26
27      // ** Create the points for the diamond
28      CPoint ptPolyArray[4]=
29      {
30          CPoint(ptTopLeft.x,ptCenter.y),
31          CPoint(ptCenter.x,ptTopLeft.y),                           ③
32          CPoint(ptBotRight.x,ptCenter.y),
33          CPoint(ptCenter.x,ptBotRight.y)
34      };
35
36      // ** Draw the diamond
37      pDC->Polygon(ptPolyArray,4);
38
39      // ** Draw the text
40      pDC->TextOut(ptCenter.x,ptCenter.y,strDocText);               ④
```

```
41
42       // ** Unselect the fonts
43       pDC->SelectObject(pOldFont);
44       pDC->SelectObject(pOldBrush);
45   }
```

In lines 6–12 of Listing 22.4, the resources for the print (a font and a brush) are set up. Note that there is a better place to do this, as explained later in this chapter in the section "Adding GDI Objects with `OnBeginPrinting()`."

You can use the current page number to draw the different textual content of each page by its position in the printed document, as shown in line 17. In a real application you would probably use this page number to reference the document and look up a specific item of data. In the compact disc scenario mentioned earlier, this page number might be used to reference a specific CD and the drawing functions would then use that data. I don't have space to demonstrate anything quite so sophisticated here, so I've just used the current page number from `pInfo->m_nCurPage` to illustrate the point.

Lines 22–37 set up a diamond-shaped polygon to draw as the background and line 40 draws the text containing the current page in the middle of the page. Lines 43–44 reselect the old font and brush.

If you build and run the program after making these changes to `OnPrint()`, and then click the test application **File** menu and choose **Print Preview**, you should be able to preview multiple pages using the **Next Page** and **Prev Page** buttons shown in Figure 22.3. If you have a printer attached, you'll also be able to print the multipage document.

SEE ALSO

➤ *To understand how to select objects into device contexts, see page 356*

➤ *To learn about drawing with different brush types, see page 401*

The MFC print preview implementation

The MFC framework implements print preview using a special undocumented class called `CPreviewDC`. This special device context acts like a printer device context to the application, but renders the image on the screen like a normal screen device context. It must do this to simulate printer-specific concepts such as pagination. Although it's undocumented, you can examine the source code for `CPreviewDC`, which is implemented in the MFC\SRC\DCPREV.CPP source module under your Visual C++ directory.

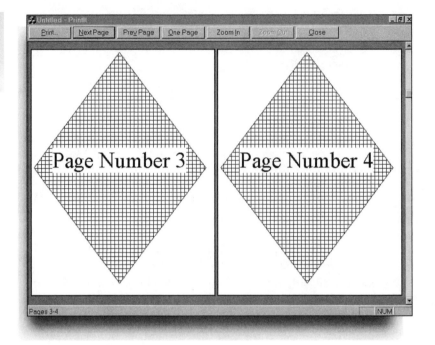

Using the Print Dialog Box

Notice that when you print a multipage document you are first presented with a dialog box that enables you to customize the print settings, as shown in Figure 22.4. This is the standard Print dialog box; it is called from the `CView::DoPreparePrinting()` function that was called from within the `OnPreparePrinting()` override. This dialog box lets you set the page ranges to print, the number of copies, collation flags, the destination printer, and a whole host of things specific to the printer properties.

The user can change the print options from this dialog box, which will then update the settings in the `CPrintInfo` object before it is passed to your application. You can customize this dialog box to a small or great degree depending on the amount of customization you require and the work you're prepared to put into the job.

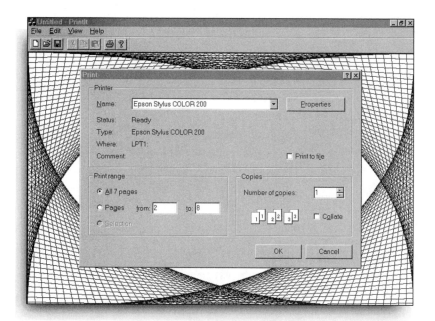

FIGURE 22.4
The standard Print dialog box.

From the `CPrintInfo` class members in Table 22.1, recall that there is an `m_pPD` pointer. This points to a `CPrintDialog` class that is an MFC wrapper class for the Print dialog box. This class also holds an `m_pd` member, which is a `PRINTDLG` structure holding the default settings that are displayed in the Print dialog box. There are many members of this structure, as shown in Listing 22.5. This allows complete customization of the dialog box defaults, even to the level of specifying a completely different dialog box template than the default template (if you want a challenge). There isn't enough space here to describe all these members in detail; one of the more obvious members is the `nCopies` member variable. You could change the default number of copies displayed in this dialog box by setting the `nCopies` member of this structure directly before calling the `CView::DoPreparePrinting()` function. To do this, add the following line to your `OnPreparePrinting()` function:

```
pInfo->m_pPD->m_pd.nCopies = 15;
```

When you open the Print dialog box after adding this line, the number of copies will default to 15 (if your printer or printer driver supports multiple copies). You can set the other default values in the `PRINTDLG` accordingly.

Using the DevMode **structure**

The DevMode structure holds many useful attributes that describe the technical capabilities and configuration of the device. The structure pointer is returned by the GetDevMode() function in the CPrintDialog class.

579

LISTING 22.5 LST23_5.CPP—The *PRINTDLG* Structure

```
1    typedef struct tagPD {
2    DWORD      lStructSize;
3    HWND       hwndOwner;
4    HANDLE     hDevMode;
5    HANDLE     hDevNames;
6    HDC        hDC;
7    DWORD      Flags;
8    WORD       nFromPage;
9    WORD       nToPage;
10   WORD       nMinPage;
11   WORD       nMaxPage;
12   WORD       nCopies;
13   HINSTANCE  hInstance;
14   DWORD      lCustData;
15   LPPRINTHOOKPROC lpfnPrintHook; ─────────①
16   LPSETUPHOOKPROC lpfnSetupHook;
17   LPCTSTR    lpPrintTemplateName;
18   LPCTSTR    lpSetupTemplateName;
19   HANDLE     hPrintTemplate;
20   HANDLE     hSetupTemplate;
21   } PRINTDLG;
```

① The last six items in this structure let you customize the print dialog by replacing the normal print dialog with your own custom dialog template. This is a very sophisticated feature that lets you have full control over the interface your application presents to the user.

After the user has confirmed **OK** in the Print dialog box, you can retrieve the changes by using the CPrintDialog class access functions shown in Table 22.2. So if you wanted to find the number of copies specified by the user before printing, you could catch the value after it is returned from the CView::DoPreparePrinting() function, as shown in Listing 22.6.

Obviously, any of the values in the PRINTDLG structure pInfo-> m_pPD->m_pd can be tested here also.

TABLE 22.2 *CPrintDialog* access functions

Function Name	Description
GetCopies()	Returns the number of copies set by the user
GetFromPage()	Returns the starting page as specified
GetToPage()	Returns the last page as specified
GetPortName()	Returns the selected printer port, for example, LPT1:

Function Name	Description
GetDriverName()	Returns the selected print driver (destination printer)
GetPrinterDC()	Returns a device context for the printer
PrintAll()	Returns TRUE if all pages are selected
PrintCollate()	Returns TRUE if collation is required
PrintRange()	Returns TRUE if a range is specified
PrintSelection()	Returns TRUE if a specific selection of pages is chosen

LISTING 22.6 LST23_6.CPP—Validating the Standard Print Dialog Box for a Specific Number of Copies

```
1   BOOL CPrintItView::OnPreparePrinting(CPrintInfo* pInfo)
2   {
3       pInfo->SetMinPage(1);
4       pInfo->SetMaxPage(10);
5
6       pInfo->m_pPD->m_pd.nCopies = 3;
7
8       do
9       {
10          // ** Check if user has cancelled print
11          if (DoPreparePrinting(pInfo) == FALSE) ————(1)
12              return FALSE;
13
14          // ** Warn the user if too many copies
            ➥are specified
15          if (pInfo->m_pPD->GetCopies()>5)
16              AfxMessageBox("Please choose less than
                ➥5 copies");
17
18          // ** Keep looping until they specify a
            ➥valid number
19      } while(pInfo->m_pPD->GetCopies()>5); ————(2)
20      return TRUE;
21  }
```

(1) You must let the user out of the loop if they have clicked the Cancel button, otherwise they have no option other than to print.

(2) This unusual condition makes the user stay in the loop unless they have specified five or less copies. This demonstrates the validation control over the details entered into the Print dialog box.

In Listing 22.6 the CView::DoPreparePrinting() returns FALSE if the user has pressed Cancel in lines 11 and 12. Otherwise, the number of copies set is checked in line 15 and a warning is issued if more than five copies have been selected (my arbitrary criteria). The loop is repeated at line 19 until the user enters a valid number of copies or presses **Cancel**.

Using Portrait and Landscape Orientations

Varying paper sizes

The user may specify different paper sizes from envelopes to A3. You don't need to do any special processing to handle these options because the device context passed to your application will be automatically sized for the specified paper selection by Windows. The `CPrintInfo` object's `rectDraw` member variable will be set to the coordinates that represent the device context dimensions.

If you click the **File** menu from the application and chose the **Print Setup** option, you can change the printers orientation defaults. You can choose either **Portrait** or **Landscape** from the dialog. You don't need to make any code changes to handle Landscape printing; if you choose this option and then run a print preview, you should notice that the device context is now drawn to the shape of the paper turned on its side. As long as your application takes note of the `rectDraw` member of the `CPrintInfo` object, it should be able to cope with landscape printing automatically.

Adding GDI Objects with *OnBeginPrinting()*

As I mentioned earlier, the code in Listing 22.4 works fine, but there is a better way to allocate the resources needed. Currently every time a page is printed, `OnPrint()` is called to draw the page and all the resources are created from scratch. That probably won't slow things down too much for this simple output, but in a large, complex report you might want to set up a number of resources and other calculations just once at the start of the report. Then you can print a number of pages and clean up the resources at the end of the report.

The `OnBeginPrinting()` virtual function is an ideal place to do this initialization, and its sister function, `OnEndPrinting()`, is the place to clean up these resources. `OnBeginPrinting()` is called after `OnPreparePrinting()` and is the first place where a printer device context is passed in. This device context is the one that is used during the printing process, so you can set up all the GDI objects and printer page coordinates at this point. The default code supplied automatically by ClassWizard just gives you an empty function:

```
void CPrintItView::OnBeginPrinting(CDC* /*pDC*/,
➡ CPrintInfo* /*pInfo*/)
{
    // TODO: add extra initialization before printing
}
```

Take a close look at that function definition. Notice the parameters are actually commented out to the compiler, throwing warning messages about unused parameters when you compile. You'll have to remember to uncomment these parameters before you start using them.

You can now add the GDI object creation calls to this function to avoid doing it on every page:

```
m_fnTimes.CreatePointFont(720,"Times New Roman",pDC);
m_brHatch.CreateHatchBrush(HS_CROSS,RGB(64,64,64));
```

Notice that the fnTimes and brHatch objects have been prefixed by an m_; this is a naming convention to indicate that the objects have class scope (are embedded in the class) rather than local scope (are embedded in the function). Because you'll need to access these GDI objects in OnPrint(), you can add them to the class declaration. You can do this by adding the font and brush objects to the class declaration like this:

```
protected:
    CFont    m_fnTimes;
    CBrush   m_brHatch;
```

You can add these either by double-clicking the CPrintItView class in the ClassView and adding them directly or by using the Add Member Variable dialog box.

Also notice that the hatched brush is created with the CreateHatchBrush() function rather than with the constructor. This is because the brush will exist as long as the view does, but you must call DeleteObject() in the OnBeginPrinting() function so that the underlying GDI resource is freed between prints. You can add the code to delete both the font and brush GDI objects in OnEndPrinting(), as shown in these lines:

```
m_fnTimes.DeleteObject();
m_brHatch.DeleteObject();
```

Color and mono printing

Notice that the COLORREF value supplied by the RGB(64,64,64) macro sets the brush to a dark gray color. Most mono printers will deal with shades of gray quite well by a dithering technique. You can also specify real TrueColor color 24-bit COLORREF values; the device context will then automatically transform the color into the closest match that the printer can offer. Color printers might be able to represent the actual color specified, whereas mono printers will convert the color to a shade of gray.

All that remains is to remove the local GDI objects from the `OnPrint()` function itself and replace their references with the member variable versions. You can do this by replacing the `CFont fnTimes` and `CBrush brHatch` local variables and their creation functions and just select the precreated font and brush:

```
CFont* pOldFont = (CFont*)pDC->SelectObject(&m_fnTimes);
CBrush* pOldBrush = (CBrush*)pDC->SelectObject(&m_brHatch);
```

If you were to build and run the application after making these changes, you'd probably notice no difference. Functionally it's the same, but the print and preview should be a little faster. If you had a large, complex 100-page report using lots of GDI resources, you'd definitely find this technique useful in speeding up the printing.

SEE ALSO
➤ *To learn about GDI brush creation, see page 401*
➤ *To learn about GDI font creation, see page 425*
➤ *To learn about inserting a member variable with* `ClassView`, *see page 473*

Using coordinates from
`OnBeginPrinting()`

You might be tempted to also store the coordinates from `OnBeginPrinting()`. This won't work because `CPrintInfo`'s `m_rectDraw` member hasn't been initialized by that stage, and random coordinates will be used.

Customizing Device Context Preparation

Before both `OnDraw()` and `OnPrint()` are called, the `OnPrepareDC()` virtual function is called and can be overridden in your view class to perform any device context modifications that might be common to both `OnDraw()` and `OnPrint()`. You might want to set mapping modes or set certain common draw modes to the device context for both onscreen and printing modes. The override isn't supplied by AppWizard, but can easily be added from the Add Virtual Function dialog box. One thing common to both `OnDraw()` and `OnPrint()` in the example is the `SetTextAlign()` device context function. You could add this to an `OnPrepareDC()` function like this:

```
void CPrintItView::OnPrepareDC(CDC* pDC, CPrintInfo* pInfo)
{
    pDC->SetTextAlign(TA_CENTER+TA_BASELINE);
}
```

There might be times, especially when preparing WYSIWYG printouts, that it is advantageous to set mapping modes and window extents in a common function before the draw or print function is called. `OnPrepareDC()` is the place to put any device context–specific initialization code.

SEE ALSO

➤ *To learn about device context settings, see page 357*

➤ *To understand font alignment, see page 418*

Aborting the Print Job

Another use of `OnPrepareDC()` is to call printer escapes or other print document–specific functions. If you had a particularly long report, you might want to give the user the option of terminating the printing process and aborting the print. The `AbortDoc()` device context function aborts the printing document for a printer device context. You can try this by adding the following lines to `OnPrepareDC()` and aborting the document after three pages:

```
if (pDC->IsPrinting())
    if (pInfo->m_nCurPage==3) pDC->AbortDoc();
```

Direct Printing Without the Framework

So far in this chapter, I've shown you the SDI and MDI framework support for printing. This support melds nicely into the Document/View architecture but there are times when you just want quick and easy access to a printer or don't have the framework available—in a dialog-based application, for example.

The framework support hides lower-level printing support that is the bedrock for all the printing operations. This section explains how this support works and shows it in use in a dialog-based application example.

Invoking the Print Dialog Box Directly

You saw in the previous section, "Using the Print Dialog Box," how the CPrintDialog class provides a wrapper for the common PRINTDLG dialog and how this was called from CView::DoPreparePrinting().

The same dialog box and class can be used directly to set up the destination printer and its default settings just like you'd use a normal modal dialog box. You can use the same access functions to set the page numbers and copy defaults as you used from inside the framework's DoPreparePrinting() function.

Listing 22.7 shows this dialog box being used directly to configure the printer for dialog-based printing and then prints a small document from the defaults set by the dialog box.

The direct printing mechanism works via the StartDoc() and EndDoc() functions shown in this listing and is explained in the next section.

You can use AppWizard to create a dialog-based application named DlgPrint and create an OnOK() handler with ClassWizard to implement the printing code as shown in Listing 22.7.

Using the special CreateDC mode

Instead of displaying the Print dialog box, you can use its built-in functionality to just create a printer device context configured with the default settings. You can then print to this device context as normal. To use this technique, there is a CreatePrinterDC() member function of the CPrintDialog class. You can also change the default settings by modifying the values in the associated DEVMODE and DEVNAMES structures. Pointers to these structures can be obtained from the GetDevMode(), and the DEVNAMES structure can be found from the m_pd PRINTDLG member variable.

LISTING 22.7 LST23_7.CPP—Implementing a Direct Document Print in *OnOK* of a Dialog-Based Application

```
1    void CDlgPrintDlg::OnOK()
2    {
3        // TODO: Add extra validation here
4
5        // ** Construct a CPrintDialog object
6        CPrintDialog dlgPrint(FALSE,PD_ALLPAGES,this);
7
8        if (dlgPrint.DoModal()==IDOK)
9        {
10            // ** Attach the printer DC from the dialog
11            // ** to a CDC object
12            CDC dcPrint;
13            dcPrint.Attach(dlgPrint.GetPrinterDC());
14
15            // ** Create and fill a DOCINFO structure
16            DOCINFO myPrintJob;
```

```
17          myPrintJob.cbSize = sizeof(myPrintJob);
18          myPrintJob.lpszDocName = "MyPrintJob";
19          myPrintJob.lpszOutput = NULL;
20          myPrintJob.lpszDatatype = NULL;
21          myPrintJob.fwType = NULL;
22
23          // ** Start the printing document
24          if (dcPrint.StartDoc(&myPrintJob)>=0)
25          {
26              // ** Start a page
27              dcPrint.StartPage();
28
29              // ** Start drawing
30              dcPrint.TextOut(0,0,"My Small Print Job");
31
32              // ** Throw the page
33              dcPrint.EndPage();
34
35              // ** Close the document
36              dcPrint.EndDoc();
37          }
38
39          // ** Delete the printer device context
40          dcPrint.DeleteDC();
41      }
42
43      // ** Carry on with the standard OnOK
44      CDialog::OnOK();
45  }
```

(1) Set up the DOCINFO structure with the minimum information required to start a print job.

(2) The only printed output line, inside the StartPage() and EndPage() calls.

(3) You must delete the device context that the Print dialog box created for us.

Listing 22.7 declares a CPrintDialog object dlgPrint at line 6 that takes three parameters in its constructor. The first parameter is a flag that can be set as TRUE to display the Print Setup dialog box, or FALSE to display the Print dialog box. The second parameter is a set of combinable flags that customize the settings of the dialog box (too numerous to cover here). The third parameter is a pointer to the parent window; in this case the C++ this pointer indicates that the dialog box is the parent.

On line 8, dlgPrint.DoModal()is called to display this dialog box. If the user clicks **OK**, the print begins; otherwise, the block is skipped.

When the user has clicked **OK** in the Print dialog box, a device context for the printer is created and attached to a CDC object in line 13 to make it easier to use. You must remember to delete the device context itself, as shown in line 40.

You can add the listing lines and handler, build and run it, and click **OK** of the dialog box application to run the new code.

Using *StartDoc()* and *EndDoc()*

The CDC device context has many printer-specific functions. To start a new print, Windows must create a spool document to store the print job and submit it to the printer when it is complete. The StartDoc() function tells Windows to start spooling and the EndDoc() function tells it that the document is complete and can be sent to the printer. You saw the AbortDoc() function earlier that will abort the print and cancel the print job rather than send to the printer.

Listing 22.7 calls the StartDoc() member of the printer device context object dcPrint at line 24, passing a pointer to a DOCINFO structure. This structure holds the details of the print job. The only detail you must specify is a name for the spool document, which is assigned at line 18. Notice that it has an unusual cbSize member that holds the size of the structure. This is assigned the value from sizeof(myPrintJob) at line 17. You see this sort of strange action going on a lot down at the Win32 API level because DOCINFO is an old C-style structure; the cbSize is used because there are a few different forms of DOCINFO and the only way to tell them apart is the size.

When StartDoc() is called, it will try to start the print job and return a positive value if it succeeds. There are many reasons why it might fail, such as low disk space or memory, or a corrupt printer driver, so it's a good idea to carry on with the print only after checking the return code.

After the document is printed, you should call EndDoc() as shown on line 36 to start printing the document.

Watching the Windows spooler

You can watch the print document as it builds up by placing a breakpoint in the OnPrint() function or after a StartDoc() function and opening your printer status icon from the **Printers** group available from the main Windows Start menu under the **Settings** option.

SEE ALSO

➤ *To understand APIs and the Win32 API, see page 732*

Using *StartPage()* and *EndPage()*

Another pair of printer device context functions are StartPage() and EndPage(). The StartPage() function is used to initialize the device context ready for printing a new page. This will reset some of the device context settings such as the current graphics cursor position, and set the document spooling information for starting a new page.

Typically, you'd call StartPage(), do some drawing in the device context for the details to be printed on that page, and call EndPage() to write the page away to the spool file to add it do the print document.

In Listing 22.7, StartPage() is called on line 27, followed by a solitary TextOut() function to draw something on the printer page, followed by a call to EndPage() on line 33.

When EndPage() is called, the special printer codes for throwing a Form Feed are sent to the spooler and the spool document registers another print page. You can repeat this StartPage() and EndPage() sequence for all the document pages before calling EndDoc() to complete the printing process. You can use the printer device context for drawing in just the same way as the OnPrint() was used in the SDI application in between the StartPage() and EndPage() calls. The same functions were called in the SDI framework, but the framework hides it from you, only calling your OnPrint() between start and end page calls.

Sending device specific escape codes

Theoretically you should never need to know anything about the connected printer, but there is still a way you can bypass all the Windows device context mechanisms to send character sequences straight to the printer.

The **CDC** class's **Escape()** function lets you do just this, letting you send specific printer escape codes directly to the connected device. These escape functions are identified by a function code, and are either device specific (passed directly to the device) or Windows specific (translated by the Windows device driver).

You might need to do this if a specific feature of the device isn't supported by the standard Windows mechanisms.

chapter 23

Saving, Loading, and Transferring Data

Saving and loading document data •

Creating, reading, and writing files •

Transferring data to and from •
the Clipboard

Using Serialization

Serialization is a technique that can be used to turn your application's data into a sequenced list of individual data elements and then store them on disk or transfer them to another program. When a program reloads or accepts an incoming transfer of serialized data, it can read in a stream of these data elements and reconstitute them into structured and interacting memory-based objects.

The SDI and MDI frameworks provide serialization and file handling support—the only work you must do is to make your data serialize itself when the framework requests it.

Creating a File-Handling SDI Framework

You can use the normal AppWizard New Project procedure to create an SDI application to create, hold, and *serialize* data objects stored in your CDocument-derived class. The only things relevant to serialization that you should consider when creating the new project are the document template strings for your default document type.

You can set these document template strings from the MFC AppWizard by clicking the **Advanced** button in step 4. The Advanced Options dialog box (see Figure 23.1) is then displayed, letting you set the document template-specific strings:

- **File Extension**—You can specify the file extension by changing **File Extension** dialog box contents to specify any alphanumeric filename extension. The files created when your document is saved or loaded by the framework are then suffixed by this file extension.

- **File Type ID**—Lets you specify a document type that will be registered in the system registry so that applications can associate your application executable with files of that type. Normally you would leave this to the default setting that is based on the application name. Your application can then be automatically launched to load a file in response to a user double-clicking the file on the desktop or in Windows Explorer.

File handling in dialog-based applications

Dialog-based applications wouldn't normally need to use serialization—direct file handling using the CFile class would normally suffice (discussed later in this chapter). However, dialog-based applications can use serialization via the CArchive class. To do this you must implement a specific user interface from your dialog box to initiate the serialization process.

- **Filter Name**—You can specify a default file filter for your filename extension.

- **File Type Name**—Associated with the **File Type ID** because this is the text equivalent name that will be displayed when other applications describe your document type. You can see these registered names when you right-click the desktop and select the **New** option from the desktop. The list of registered file types is then displayed. This registration is covered in more detail later in the "Registering Document Types" section of this chapter.

- **File New Name**—You can specify the default name that will be used when unnamed files are saved.

You could use AppWizard to create a sample SDI project called Persist to demonstrate serialization. If you create such a project, accept the MFC AppWizard defaults in Steps 1 to 3, clicking the **Next** button to step through until you reach Step 4. Click the **Advanced** button to show the Advanced Options dialog box and set the **File Extension** name for the Persist example to blb to create files with a .blb suffix as shown in Figure 23.1.

Framework file filter options

The options available on the Advanced Options dialog box are stored as a string resource `IDR_MAINFRAME`. You can change the settings after you create the project by editing the `IDR_MAINFRAME` string from the **ResourceView** tab of the Project Workspace view.

FIGURE 23.1
Setting the file filter name in the Advanced Options dialog box.

SEE ALSO

➤ *For more information on creating SDI applications, see page 267*

➤ *To edit string resources, see page 34*

Creating Serializable Data Objects

Any class you derive from the CObject MFC base class has a Serialize() virtual function that can be overridden in your derived class to let you load and store the object's member variables to a disk file. When the user chooses **File Save** or **File Open** from an SDI or MDI application, the document's Serialize() function will be automatically called by the framework to save or load the document's data objects.

The MFC CArchive class is responsible for serializing your CObject-derived objects into or from an embedded file member variable of the CArchive class.

A CArchive object is constructed by the framework and attached to the file that the user is loading or storing. You can override the Serialize() function in your document (which is itself derived from CObject). When saving or loading, your documents' overridden Serialize() function is passed a reference called ar, which is the framework-created CArchive object. This CArchive object contains the embedded file variable connected to the physical disk file being saved or loaded. From your documents' Serialize() function, you must write code for calling Serialize() for each of your application's objects and passing each object the CArchive object (ar) that was passed to you from the framework into your document's Serialize() function.

When the document data is being saved, data is read from each object being serialized and stored in the file associated with the archive. When the document data is being loaded, data is read from a disk file associated with an archive object and then set back to each data object by calling each object's own Serialize() function.

Using CArchive to transfer data across networks

You can use the CArchive class in conjunction with the CSocket and CSocketFile classes. This lets you transfer data between two machines across local area networks, or even across a wide area network such as the Internet.

The disk file created by the serialization process is called a serialized archive file, and it stores a copy of the data from each application object along with the type and version of the object. The version number lets you change the object's data and track different versions of the stored object when your application evolves. This version and type information is often called a *schema*.

You can derive your own application classes from CObject, and then use the serialization functionality just by adding a DECLARE_SERIAL macro to the class definition and a corresponding IMPLEMENT_SERIAL macro to your class implementation. These macros replace the normal DECLARE_DYNCREATE and IMPLEMENT_DYNCREATE macros used in CObject derived classes, to add some syntax required for the serialization to work smoothly.

Declaring the Serializable Class

If your application requires specific data objects, you'll need to create your own application-specific classes to describe and handle that data. You can then add the serialization macros and functionality to save and load the data from each object to your new *class definitions*.

You can create a new header (.h) and implementation (.cpp) file to store the class definition and implementation code, respectively.

Creating a new header file for a class definition

1. Click the Developer Studio's **File** menu and select **New** as you would for a new project.

2. On the **Files** tab of the New dialog box, you can select **C/C++ Header File** to create a new file.

3. Enter a **File Name** for the new header file. (In this example, you can use blob.h.)

4. If the **Add to Project** check box is clicked (which it is by default), the new empty header file is automatically added to the project and is shown in the editor pane. Make sure this check box is checked.

> **Serialization schemas and database schemas**
>
> Although the terminology is the same, serialization schemas are very different from database schemas. Database schemas hold the details of each field in a database table. However, serialization schemas only hold the class type and a version number.

5. Click **OK** to add the new header file to the project and start editing it.

Listing 23.1 shows a class definition for a simple serializable object. The class is a normal CObject-derived class, but the DECLARE_SERIAL macro adds the specific MFC requirements for serialization.

LISTING 23.1   LST24_1.CPP—blob.h, the Blob Data Object Class Definition

① The DECLARE_SERIAL macro expands to include all the support needed for framework serialization.

② Attributes needed to draw a single blob object.

```
1    // ** Ensure the class isn't declared twice
2    #ifndef _BLOB_H
3    #define _BLOB_H
4
5    // ** Derive a CBlob class from CObject
6    class CBlob : public CObject
7    {
8        // ** Include the Serialization functions
9        DECLARE_SERIAL(CBlob); ────────①
10
11   public:
12
13       // ** Declare two constructors
14       CBlob();
15       CBlob(CPoint ptPosition);
16
17       // ** Declare a drawing function
18       void Draw(CDC* pDC);
19
20       // ** Declare the attributes
21       CPoint    m_ptPosition; ─────②
22       COLORREF  m_crColor;
23       int       m_nSize;
24       unsigned  m_nShape;
25   };
26
27   #endif // _BLOB_H
```

On line 6, you can see that the new CBlob class is derived from CObject. It is a good idea to derive all your classes from CObject when writing MFC-compatible applications because CObject provides a common base class including other useful MFC features such as runtime type information. This information helps MFC identify to which type of class an object belongs. This information is saved along with your object's data so that when the data is reloaded, objects of the right class can be automatically created for you.

The DECLARE_SERIAL() macro on line 9 adds the code needed to make serialization work. On lines 14 and 15 there are two constructors. The first on line 14 takes no parameters and will be used by the framework to make these objects on the fly while it is loading them from a disk file. The constructor on line 15 can be used to create an object instance and automatically initialize its position member from a CPoint. This is so you are able to create these objects from mouse click positions, as you'll see later in this section.

The Draw() function is declared on line 18 for a corresponding drawing function in the implementation.

The variables on lines 21 to 23 will have to be serialized when the object is loaded or saved.

Implementing the Serializable Class

After you've defined your new class, you'll need to write some corresponding implementation code to construct (initialize) and manipulate the data declared in your class definition.

Creating a new .cpp file for a class implementation

1. Click Developer Studio's **File** menu and select **New** as you would for a new project.

2. On the **Files** tab of the New dialog box, you can select **C/C++ Implementation File** to create a new file.

3. Enter the **File Name** for the new implementation file. (You can use blob.cpp for this example.)

4. If the **Add to Project** check box is checked (which it is by default), the new empty header file is automatically added to the project and is shown in the editor pane. Make sure this check box is checked.

5. Click **OK** to add the new implementation file to the project and start editing it.

> **Developing with Visual SourceSafe**
>
> If you are using an integrated source control application such as Visual SourceSafe, you will be asked if you want to add your new source to the SourceSafe project (and you should). Source control software lets you track different versions and changes to source modules and revert to older versions if necessary. They are especially useful when several programmers are working in the same project because they stop two developers from changing the same source file at the same time and thus overwriting each others work.

A serializable class must have a generic constructor—that is, a constructor with no arguments. This is for when the objects are being created from the disk file during serialization. The MFC can then call a common constructor for all types of objects to create them when loading from a file. By implementing a generic constructor with no arguments it can create an instance of an object of any serializable class and then rely on your Serialize() function implementation to fill in the new object's member variables.

You can also add any customized constructors so that you can create an instance of a new object of your class with whatever initialization data you need.

Your implementation code module for every serializable object must also contain an IMPLEMENT_SERIAL macro. This macro needs three parameters. The first is the class name itself, the second is the base class, and the third (wSchema) is a UINT value that represents a version number. If you add new member variables to your class and want to serialize them, you can increment the version number and optionally check it to maintain compatibility with existing older versions of the serialized archive file.

The implementation for the CBlob sample class is shown in Listing 23.2. This sample implementation shows the IMPLEMENT_SERIAL macro and the various constructors along with some code to make the object draw itself.

Versioning control

If you are writing commercial software using serialization it is very important to maintain a schema version number for each different file/object version, and to either convert or maintain compatibility with old objects. Otherwise you might find yourself in the embarrassing situation of upgrading a client's software but rendering all their existing disk-based data obsolete.

LISTING 23.2 LST24_2.CPP—blob.cpp, the Blob Data Object Class Implementation

```
1   // ** include the standard header
2   #include "stdafx.h"
3   #include "blob.h"
4
5   // ** Add the implementation for serialization
6   IMPLEMENT_SERIAL(CBlob,CObject,1)
7
8   // ** Implement the default constructor
9   CBlob::CBlob()
10  {
11  }
```

```
12
13   // ** Implement the position constructor
14   CBlob::CBlob(CPoint ptPosition) ——————(1)
15   {
16       // ** Set the random seed
17       srand(GetTickCount());
18
19       // ** Set the position to the specified position
20       m_ptPosition = ptPosition;
21
22       // ** Set the attributes to random values
23       m_crColor= RGB(rand()%255,rand()%255,rand()%255);
24       m_nSize  = 10 + rand()%30;
25       m_nShape = rand();
26   }
27
28   void CBlob::Draw(CDC* pDC) ——————(2)
29   {
30       // ** Create and select a colored brush
31       CBrush brDraw(m_crColor);
32       CBrush* pOldBrush = pDC->SelectObject(&brDraw);
33       CPen* pOldPen =
34           (CPen*)pDC->SelectStockObject(NULL_PEN);
35       // ** See the random generator to the shape
36       srand(m_nShape);
37       for(int n=0;n<3;n++)
38       {
39           // ** Set the blob position and random shift
40           CPoint ptBlob(m_ptPosition);
41           ptBlob+=CPoint(rand()%m_nSize,rand()%m_nSize);
42
43           // ** Create and draw a rectangle
44           CRect rcBlob(ptBlob,ptBlob);
45           rcBlob.InflateRect(m_nSize,m_nSize);
46           pDC->Ellipse(rcBlob);
47       }
48
49       // ** Reselect the GDI Objects
50       pDC->SelectObject(pOldBrush);
51       pDC->SelectObject(pOldPen);
52   }
```

(1) You can use this constructor to create a blob object from a mouse click position and set its values to randomly picked numbers.

(2) The Draw() function lets each Blob object draw itself when passed a device context pointer from the view's OnDraw() function..

The `#include` files on lines 2 and 3 tell the compiler about the class definition and the MFC class definitions. The `IMPLEMENT_SERIAL()` macro on line 6 complements the `DECLARE_SERIAL()` macro in the class definition.

The default constructor is declared on line 9. When a file is being loaded the serialization mechanism can create these objects with the default constructor and then fill instances of these objects with the data from the file.

A custom constructor is implemented on line 14 to create these objects from mouse click positions with some random attributes set. The `Draw()` function on line 28 can then draw these objects when passed a view's device context pointer.

Holding Document Data

After you've defined your application's classes you must create instances of those classes to represent the user's data as individual objects. If you create any objects you must keep track of them so that you can manipulate their data, save and load them, and ultimately destroy them. Whenever you load or save the document data you must iterate through all the stored data and serialize each object in turn.

Some MFC classes help track these objects and support serialization, so they will automatically iterate through the object instances they are tracking. One of these is the `CObArray` class. `CObArray` is one of the *MFC Collection Classes*. It is a growable array designed to hold `CObject`-derived classes, and hence any data objects you define. Moreover it knows all about serialization and will help when you serialize the document data.

You can add a `CObArray` object to the `CPersisDoc` document class definition under the `//Attributes` comment and `public:` access definition like this:

```
// Attributes
public:
    CObArray m_BlobArray;
```

This new `m_BlobArray` object can then hold and track the `CObject`-derived objects (such as `CBlob`).

Besides holding objects, the document must destroy them all when you close the application. You can implement this by adding a function as shown in Listing 23.3, with the corresponding function declaration in the class definition:

```
void DeleteBlobs();
```

LISTING 23.3 LST24_3.CPP—Implementation and Use of the *DeleteBlobs()* Function to Remove All Allocated Blob Objects

```
1    void CPersistDoc::DeleteBlobs()                (1)
2    {
3        // ** Delete the allocated blobs
4        for(int i=0;i<m_BlobArray.GetSize();i++)
5            delete m_BlobArray.GetAt(i);
6        m_BlobArray.RemoveAll();
7    }
8
9    CPersistDoc::~CPersistDoc()
10   {
11       DeleteBlobs();
12   }
13
14   BOOL CPersistDoc::OnNewDocument()
15   {
16       if (!CDocument::OnNewDocument())
17       return FALSE;
18
19       // TODO: add reinitialization code here
20       // (SDI documents will reuse this document)
21
22       DeleteBlobs();                (2)
23
24       return TRUE;
25   } DeleteBlobs( )
```

(1) The `DeleteBlobs()` function runs through all the blobs, deleting the memory allocated for each object instance and finally clears the holding array.

(2) A new document must destroy the old blobs because the SDI framework reuses the same document object.

The implementation of this function is shown in Listing 23.3 (lines 1 to 7). The `DeleteBlobs()` function iterates through the `CObArray` of `CBlob` objects and deletes each one in turn. The array itself is then cleared by calling its `RemoveAll()` function.

When the document itself is destroyed its destructor function is called, and you should use your cleanup function to delete any existing data objects as shown in line 11. The user can create a new document while an existing document is open; if he does this, the framework just reuses the existing document. In this case, you must clear any data objects being held in the document. You can do this in the `CPersistDoc::OnNewDocument()` function by calling the `DeleteBlobs()` function as shown in line 22.

That covers holding and deleting the data objects but you will also need a mechanism that allows the user to create new objects and then insert them into the document. The mechanism to do this is likely to vary from application to application and will depend on your user interface implementation. After you've created the new data object, you can then insert it into a container like the `CObArray`. `CObArray` has an `Add()` function that needs only one parameter, a pointer to the new object.

The simplest way to create these objects in the sample program is to let the user click anywhere in the view and create a `CBlob` object positioned at that mouse click. To do this you'll need an `OnLButtonDown()` Windows message-handler function. You can create one of these with the wizard as shown in the step by step called "Add a Notification Message Handler" in Chapter 19, "Using List, Tree, Rich Edit, and HTML Views."

Add the following lines to the new `OnLButtonDown()` handler to create and add a new blob from the `point` parameter and add this to the `m_BlobArray` in the document (after the `// TODO` comment):

```
GetDocument()->m_BlobArray.Add(new CBlob(point));
Invalidate();
```

The `Invalidate()` function will then redraw the view, and hence the new objects, using the code shown in Listing 23.4.

> **Using the `CObArray`**
>
> Instead of adding objects with the `Add()` member function, `CObArray` also lets you insert objects at a specific position using the `InsertAt()` member function (specifying the position at which to insert the object and a pointer to the object to be inserted). There is also a corresponding `RemoveAt()` function to remove objects from a specific position. The `SetAt()` and `GetAt()` functions can be used to change or retrieve existing array elements by their index.

LISTING 23.4 LST24_4.CPP—Drawing the Blobs from *OnDraw()*

```
1   void CPersistView::OnDraw(CDC* pDC)
2   {
3       CPersistDoc* pDoc = GetDocument();
4       ASSERT_VALID(pDoc);
5
```

```
6          // TODO: add draw code for native data here
7
8          for(int i=0;i<pDoc->m_BlobArray.GetSize();i++)
9          {
10           CBlob* pBlob=(CBlob*)pDoc->m_BlobArray.GetAt(i);
11           pBlob->Draw(pDC);
12         }
13     }
```

(1) The view merely iterates through the array of blobs and tells each one to draw itself.

In Listing 23.4, the objects are iterated through in lines 8 to 12 calling each blob object's Draw() function as shown in line 11.

The compiler will also need the object's class definition:

```
#include "blob.h"
```

You can add this line after the other #includes in PersistView.cpp.

If you build and run the Persist application, you should be able to click in its view and add new blobs as shown in Figure 23.2.

FIGURE 23.2
Displaying the blob objects from the Persist application.

SEE ALSO

➤ *To learn more about documents and their data, see page 283*

➤ *To understand how to draw filled shapes in device contexts, see page 409*

Serializing the Data Objects

To serialize your data objects you must add a `Serialize()` function to your class in order to turn all your member variables into a sequential list that can be saved to or loaded from a file. The following is the definition of the `Serialize()` virtual function:

```
// ** Add the Serialize Override
virtual void Serialize(CArchive& ar);
```

You would add the `Serialize()` function declaration shown above to your class definition held in the relevant .h header file (for example, Blob.h) . A corresponding implementation for the `Serialize()` function must then be added to your corresponding class implementation .cpp file (for example, Blob.cpp).

The disk file is embedded in the `CArchive` object that is passed to your `Serialize()` function from the framework.

The `CArchive` object helps turn the data into a list and holds the direction of the transfer, either storing or loading. When the user chooses to load or save the document, the framework automatically creates an archive object and opens the file ready for transfer. It then calls the document's own `Serialize()` function, passing in the archive object.

`CArchive` also has several functions declared as operators << and >>. These are used in transferring the data to or from the archive and are used like this to store a value:

```
ar << m_MyVar
```

They are used like this to load a value from the file:

```
ar >> m_MyVar
```

When you write your object's `Serialize()` function, you can determine whether the object is being saved or loaded using the

---

Adding virtual functions to your own classes

If you have used the New Virtual Override dialog box to add virtual functions via the ClassView context menu previously, you'll notice that this feature can't be used to add virtual functions to your own classes. Instead, you must manually add the function declaration and implementation code to your class definition (.h) and implementation files (.cpp) using the text editor.

IsLoading() or IsStoring() member functions of the CArchive
object. Typically, you'll then have several lines that use the << or
>> operators to save and load each of the member variables you
must store or load. This is shown with the sample CBlob object
in Listing 23.5.

LISTING 23.5   LST24_5.CPP—Adding the Serialize Implementation to the *CBlob*
Class

```
1    void CBlob::Serialize(CArchive& ar)
2    {
3        CObject::Serialize(ar);
4        if (ar.IsStoring())
5        {
6            ar << m_ptPosition; ──────①
7            ar << m_crColor;
8            ar << m_nSize;
9            ar << m_nShape;
10       }
11       else
12       {
13           ar >> m_ptPosition; ──────②
14           ar >> m_crColor;
15           ar >> m_nSize;
16           ar >> m_nShape;
17       }
18   }
```

① When storing, the member variables are added to the archive.

② When loading, the archive is broken down and assigned to each member variable.

In line 4 of Listing 23.5, the IsStoring() member of CArchive is
called to find out whether the archive is saving or loading the
data. If the archive is saving you must send your data to the
archive. If it is loading you must retrieve your data from the
archive. In lines 6 through 9, the archive is saving the data. The
<< operator passes each member attribute of the blob class to the
archive where it is added to the disk file.

In lines 13 to 16 the reverse is happening, and the >> operator
takes a member variable and fills it with data from the archive.

You must call Serialize() on each of your document's objects to
save or load each one. You can do this by modifying the document's own Serialize() implementation and calling Serialize()
on each object.

Holding the objects in a `CObArray` such as the `m_BlobArray` in the example makes this process much simpler. The `CObArray` is serialize aware, and it will iterate through all the objects it is holding and save them. Alternatively, when loading a new document from disk it will see how many objects it should be holding and their type, create them for you (with the default constructor), and then call `Serialize()` on each object to load it. That means all you must do is call one `Serialize()` on the holding array like this:

```
void CPersistDoc::Serialize(CArchive& ar)
{
    m_BlobArray.Serialize(ar);
}
```

You could add these changes to the sample program then build and run the application at this point to see how the blob objects are loaded and saved by the serialization code. The following paragraphs explain how to save and load the blobs in the sample program.

Draw some blobs by clicking in the window. Click the **File** menu and select **Save As**. The framework automatically presents you with the Save As common dialog box and will let you change the default filename of Untitled.blb to a blob file of your choice. If you change this and click **Save**, all that serialization takes place and the blobs are now saved on disk.

You can prove this by closing the application, starting it again, and clicking the **File** menu and choosing **Open**. Because of the .blb filter you specified in AppWizard, you'll see only blob files by default, so your saved file should be the only one visible. You can select it and click the **Open** button to load it again. Presto!—you should see the original blobs in their same old positions. You can now add new blobs and resave it, or create a new document and save it under a different name and do all standard file-handling operations that most applications support. You can turn off your PC, come back after two weeks, and the blob file will still be there with the same blobs in the same positions with the same shapes and colors.

Serializing document data

Most applications would obviously store much more sophisticated data than this simple example. However, the document's `Serialize()` function provides an entry point for serializing the application's data. You will probably need to add many arrays and other more sophisticated collection objects to the document's `Serialize()` function to load or store all your application's data.

Using the Most Recently Used File List

Another bit of functionality the framework throws in for free is the most recently used file list. If you save several differently named blob files, you should notice that under the **File** menu are the most recently used files. You can select these straight from the menu to open the stored files quickly and easily.

Registering Document Types

You have probably seen how just double-clicking a document file associated with a particular type can launch Windows applications. These are registered file types; just by adding a couple of lines of code to your application, you can make the same association. The following two lines should be placed in the `InitInstance()` member function of your application class, directly after the `AddDocTemplate(pDocTemplate);` line:

```
RegisterShellFileTypes();
EnableShellOpen();
```

SEE ALSO

➤ *To learn more about documents and their data see page 265*

File Handling

Document serialization is very useful for SDI and MDI applications that must store their document data, but there are times when you must directly create, read, and write files.

MFC provides a wrapper class for a disk file called `CFile`. This encapsulates all the file operations and attributes associated with the file on disk. By creating and using `CFile` objects you can create, open, read, and write disk files through functions provided by the `CFile` class.

If you are serializing data from a document or writing a file directly, you'll still end up using the `CFile` class or one of its derivatives. The `CArchive` class used in serialization actually connects to a `CFile` object to finally read or write the document data. This section explains how `CFile` works and covers some of the more specialized versions of the `CFile` class.

Using the `CRecentFileList` class

The standard SDI and MDI application frameworks use the `CRecentFileList` class to implement the recently used file list. You can use this class directly (rather than via the framework) to implement your own recently used file lists and attach them to custom menus. The `CRecentFileList` class lets you specify a display name and full path name for each file. It can also automatically update a menu to add or remove the files in the list.

Using the *CFile* Class

You can construct a CFile object in one of three ways. The simplest constructor takes no parameters and simply creates an unopened file object that you call Open() on later to create or open a real disk file. The second version of the constructor that takes one parameter is an hFile handle that should be a valid open file. You might use this version to attach a CFile object to an already open file. The third constructor version needs two parameters: the first is a string holding the name and path of a disk file you want to open or create, and the second is a combination of the possible file opening flags.

Opening Files

One of the most important operations in file handling is the initial file open. By specifying various flags you are declaring in advance how you want to deal with the specified filename. You might want to always create a new file, open a file for reading only, or open a file for both reading and writing operations. The Open() function lets you specify a wide range of modes to access a file by passing any of the flags in nOpenFlags in Table 23.1 as its second parameter. The first parameter to open is the filename of the file you need to open or create. You can also combine some of the flag values where appropriate like this:

```
CFile fileMyFile;
fileMyFile.Open("MyFile.txt",
        CFile::modeCreate + CFile::modeNoTruncate);
```

These flags will open the file called MyFile.txt if it exists; otherwise, they will create a new empty file with the same name. If you were to specify just the CFile::modeCreate flag, an empty file would be created even if one already existed, so the CFile::modeNoTruncate flag modifies the CFile::modeCreate flag so that existing files aren't truncated to zero length. I've used the + operator to combine these flags, but you might often see the logical OR operator ¦, used like this:

```
fileMyFile.Open("MyFile.txt",
    CFile::modeCreate ¦ CFile::modeNoTruncate);
```

This is equally valid because these flags are bit values and will be combined by a logical OR in the same way as adding them together.

If the file open is successful, the `Open()` function will return a TRUE value; otherwise, a FALSE is returned to indicate that the file open failed. An optional CFileException pointer can be passed as a third parameter to the open, if the file fails to open this CFileException object will hold details indicating the cause of the open failure.

TABLE 23.1 Combinable open mode flags that can be passed to *CFile::Open()*

Flag Name	Description
CFile::modeCreate	Always creates a new file (even if the filename exists).
CFile::modeNoTruncate	This flag can be combined with CFile::modeCreate to create a new file if one doesn't exist or to open any existing file with the specified filename.
CFile::modeRead	The file will be opened for reading only; no data can be written back to the file.
CFile::modeWrite	The file will be opened for writing only; no data can be read back from the file.
CFile::modeReadWrite	The file will be opened for both reading and writing operations.
CFile::shareDenyNone	The file can be read from and written to by other processes.
CFile::shareExclusive	No other processes can read or write to the file while open in the current processes.
CFile::shareDenyRead	No other processes can read from the file while open.
CFile::shareDenyWrite	No other processes can write to the file while open.
CFile::typeText	Used for specific text processing in some of the derived classes.
CFile::typeBinary	Does no special processing on the characters when read and written to the file. This flag is required only in some of the derived classes.

Using the CFileException **object**

If an error occurs while opening a file, a pointer to the CFileException object is passed. The cause of the error can be read from the CFileException object's m_cause member variable (for a CFileException enumerated list), or from the m_IOsError member variable (which returns operating system specific error codes). or example, some common m_cause codes are CFileException:: fileNotFound, CFileException:: accessDenied, and CFileException:: diskFull.

Reading and Writing a File

After the file is open you can perform the specific read or write operations allowed by the current open mode. The CFile class has functions called Read() and Write() to perform these operations. Associated with these reading and writing operations is a current file position. When the file is opened, this file position is set to the start of a file. If you read 200 bytes from the file, the file position is updated so that the next Read() function will read from after the first 200 bytes. The section "Manipulating the Current File Position," later in this chapter, explains how to manipulate this current position. A typical file Read() function might look like this:

```
CFile myFile("MyFile.txt",CFile::modeRead);
char arMyReadBuffer[200];
UINT uBytesRead =
    myFile.Read(arMyReadBuffer,sizeof(arMyReadBuffer));
```

The Read() function is passed two parameters. The first is the address of a destination buffer. Any data read will be written to this buffer. The second parameter tells the Read() how many bytes you want to read; this can be just a few bytes or the size of your buffer as in the preceding example.

Reading past the end of the buffer

You must be careful to never request a Read() operation to read more bytes than your buffer can take. If you do, the read overwrites sensitive areas of your program and is a sure way to cause a crash or unpredictable problems.

When the Read() function has completed, the number of bytes actually read is returned. This number can be the same number of bytes as you requested, or if the end of the file has been reached it might be less, indicating that the remaining available file bytes have all been read. If a zero is returned, no more bytes in the file are left to read.

You can put this knowledge to practice to create a simple dialog-based editor application. By adding code to the OnInitDialog() of the dialog box, you could read text from a disk file, edit it, and then save it again when the **OK** button is pressed.

You can create a sample dialog-based application called FileEdit by following the steps in Chapter 5, "Using Text Controls," and add a large edit control to the main dialog box with the **MultiLine** style set. Then you can use ClassWizard to map a CString variable called m_EditBox to the edit control (also shown in Chapter 5).

By adding the lines in Listing 23.6 to the `OnInitDialog()` in the `CFileEditDlg` class, you can read the text from the fixed filename C:\MyFile.txt.

LISTING 23.6 LST24_6.CPP—Reading the Contents of a File into an Edit Control

```
1    // TODO: Add extra initialization here
2
3    // Declare and open a file object for reading
4    CFile fileEditText;
5    if(fileEditText.Open("C:\\MyFile.txt",CFile::modeRead))
6    {
7        // Declare a large buffer for reading the text
8        char cBuf[512];
9        UINT uBytesRead;
10
11       // Continue reading until no more data is read
12       while(uBytesRead =          ①
13             fileEditText.Read(cBuf,sizeof(cBuf)-1))
14       {
15           // Null terminate after the last character
16           cBuf[uBytesRead] = NULL;
17
18           // Add the buffer to the mapped CString
19           m_EditBox += CString(cBuf);
20       }
21
22       // Close the file
23       fileEditText.Close();
24
25       // Send the m_EditBox string to the edit control
26       UpdateData(FALSE);
27   }
```

Using the special backslash character

Notice that there are two backslash characters in the filename on line 5. This isn't a typo; the backslash is a special introducer character so that you can do things like \n, \r, or \b for newline, return, or backspace characters. To specify a backslash character you must include a \\ for each \ character you require.

① This while loop is repeated until the Read() function returns a value indicating that no bytes were read; this is the end of the file.

In Listing 23.6, `fileEditText`, a `CFile` object, is declared at line 4 and opened at line 5 with the hard-coded filename C:\MyFile.txt.

The buffer declared on line 8 is used in the `Read()` at line 13 to store the bytes as they are read from the file. The second parameter to the read specifies that the required number of bytes is one less than the size of this buffer. This is done so that a NULL character can be added to the end of the data read from the file, to make a *null terminated string*. After it is terminated with a NULL character, the buffer can be converted into a CString object and added to the end of the m_editBox CString at line 19.

If the file is longer than the buffer in the first pass, the whole section will be repeated, thus repeating the read until no more bytes are available from the file. When uBytesRead is set to zero from the read, the while loop ends and the file is closed on line 23 by calling the Close() function. The m_editBox mapped to the edit control is updated to the control by calling UpdateData(FALSE) at line 26.

This completes the read side of the file editor. If you build and run the program after adding these lines you can see that text from the C:\MyFile.txt file is displayed. You can create this file by running the Windows NotePad program to write some text and saving that text as a file named C:\MyFile.txt.

After the user presses **OK** after changing the text, you must write the changes back to a file. You can do this by always creating the new file (and overwrite any existing data), then using the Write() function to store the contents of the edit control's mapped CString object back to the file.

You can use ClassWizard to add a BN_CLICKED handler for the **OK** button called OnOk() to implement the code to save the edit box contents as shown in Listing 23.7. If you need some help on how to add a BN_CLICKED handler please refer to the "Adding a Button Click Handler Function" step by step outlined in Chapter 4, "Using Button Controls."

LISTING 23.7 LST24_7.CPP—Writing the Edit Control Data to a Disk File

```
1    void CFileEditDlg::OnOK()
2    {
3        // TODO: Add extra validation here
4
5        // Set the m_EditBox string from the edit control
6        UpdateData(TRUE);
7
8        // Declare and open a file object for writing
```

```
9        CFile fileEditText;
10       if (fileEditText.Open("C:\\MyFile.txt",
11           CFile::modeCreate + CFile::modeWrite))
12       {
13           // Write out the full string
14           fileEditText.Write(
15               (LPCSTR)m_EditBox,m_EditBox.GetLength());  —①
16
17           // Close the file
18           fileEditText.Close();
19       }
20
21       CDialog::OnOK();
22   }
```

① The whole edit control text can be written out in one Write() function call because the length is known in advance.

In Listing 23.7, UpdateData() is called at line 6 to set the m_EditBox member variable to the current contents of the edit control. The file object declared on line 9 is opened on lines 10 and 11 with the CFile::modeCreate and CFile::modeWrite flags specified to create and overwrite any previous files (or create a new file if none already exists). The Write() function on line 14 writes out the entire contents of the m_EditBox string after casting it to a (LPCSTR) buffer. This is considerably easier than the Read() because the whole string can be written at once because you already know exactly how many bytes to write. The file is then closed with the Close() function on line 18 to finish the file writing operation.

SEE ALSO

➤ *For more information on edit controls and string mapping, see page 97*

➤ *For details on designing dialog boxes, see page 90*

➤ *For details on transferring data between dialog box controls and member variables, see page 223*

Manipulating the Current File Position

As mentioned earlier, a current file position is maintained so that Read() and Write() functions continue from the present file position. This position can be manipulated, a technique often used when writing fixed-size record-based information to various places on a file. This current position can be retrieved by calling the GetPosition() function on a file object to return a DWORD value holding the present position of the file position pointer.

You can also change this position by using the seek functions, Seek(), SeekToBegin(), and SeekToEnd(), which seek to a specific position—the beginning or end of a file, respectively. The only one of these that needs parameters is the Seek() function, which takes two parameters. The first is a LONG value lOff, which specifies the number of bytes to move by. The second parameter can be any of the flag values shown in Table 23.2 to indicate whether the seek is relative to the start, end, or current file position.

TABLE 23.2 Possible flag values for the *CFile::Seek()* function

Flag Value	Seek Operation
CFile::begin	Position set to lOff bytes from the start of the file
CFile::end	Position set to lOff bytes from the end of the file
CFile::current	Position set to lOff bytes from the current file position

CFileException **causes on** Seek() **failure**

A CFileException is thrown when a Seek() function fails for any reason. The cause code for a seek (held in m_cause) will normally be CFileException:: badSeek because the file position isn't valid for the file. You might also get a CFileException:: invalidFile for trying to perform a Seek() operation on a file that isn't open.

Negative values can be passed into Seek if you must move relative to the end or current positions. For example, to move backward by 50 bytes from the current file position, you would add the following line:

```
LONG lOffSet = fileMyFile.Seek(-50, CFile::current);
```

Seek also returns the new current position relative to the beginning of the file if the seek succeeds. An exception is thrown if the Seek() function fails (usually because you have tried to move past the end or beginning of the file).

Finding File Information

One set of functions returns details about the current open file. GetLength() returns a DWORD value that tells you the current length of the whole file (an associated `SetLength()` truncates or extends the file to the specified size parameter). `GetStatus()` returns the information about creation and modification times along with read and write attribute information. It has two forms. One works with an already open file and fills in a `CFileStatus` object passed by reference. The other requires a filename string as its first parameters and will obtain the details about the specified file in the `CFileStatus` object passed by reference as its second parameter. For example, if you wanted to find details about the C:\MyFile.txt file such as the last modification time, you could add the following lines after the file writing section in the `OnOk()` handler:

```
CFileStatus statusEditText;
CFile::GetStatus("C:\\MyFile.txt",statusEditText);
AfxMessageBox(_T("Last Modified on")+
statusEditText.m_mtime.Format("%A, %B %d, %Y"));
```

The `GetStatus()` function is called with the `CFile::` scope operator because it is a static function and doesn't require an object when called with a filename. If you had an open file, you'd use the `fileMyOpenFile.GetStatus(statusEditText)` version instead. The details are stored in the `statusEditText` object. One of the members `m_mtime`, which holds the last modification time and date, is then formatted to display a string such as `Last Modified on Saturday, February 28, 1998` by the `CTime::Format()` function.

If you build and run after adding these lines, you should see the message displayed after clicking **OK** as in Figure 23.3.

FIGURE 23.3

Showing the last modification date of the file in the simple text editor example.

The other members of the `CFileStatus` class that you can use are shown in Table 23.3.

TABLE 23.3 File status member attributes from the *CFileStatus* class

Attribute and Type	Description
CTime m_mtime	Last modified date and time
CTime m_atime	Last time the file was read
CTime m_ctime	The creation date and time
LONG m_size	The size of the file in bytes
BYTE m_attribute	Read, write, and other attributes (see Table 23.4)
char m_szFullName	The full filename and path

Windows path names length limitations

Many of these Windows structures define the full filename and path as a character array with MAX_PATH characters. Currently MAX_PATH is defined as 260 characters, hence the Windows path and filename must not exceed 260 characters.

Most of the members are self explanatory, but the m_attribute holds several flag values that can be tested by using the logical AND operator &. The flag values are shown in Table 23.4 and can be tested like this:

```
if (statusEditText.m_attribute & CFile::readOnly)
AfxMessageBox("File is Read Only!");
```

In these lines the file is tested for a read-only attribute set; all the other flags are ignored because the ampersand logical AND operator strips all the bits except the CFile::readOnly bit (value of 1). If the flag is set, then the result will be nonzero and hence TRUE; otherwise, it is zero or FALSE.

TABLE 23.4 Flag values for the *m_attribute* member of *CFileStatus*

Flag Name	Hex Value	Description
normal	0x00	Just a normal file, no special attributes are set
readOnly	0x01	The file can only be read, not written to
hidden	0x02	The file is hidden
system	0x04	The file is a system file
volume	0x08	The file is a disk volume
directory	0x10	The file is a disk directory
archive	0x20	The file is an archive

Other functions to retrieve file information are GetFileName(), which returns just the filename (no directory path).

`GetFilePath()` returns the full name and path of the current file. `GetFileTitle()` returns the filename without path or extension, so `GetFileTitle()` returns C:\MyFile.txt as just `MyFile`.

Renaming and Removing Files

Two static functions are provided to rename and remove files: `Rename()` and `Remove()`. `Rename()` takes two parameters, the old filename and the new filename. Because it is static, you don't need to open any files, just use the `CFile::` scope operator to call it like this:

```
CFile::Rename("C:\\MyFile.txt","C:\\NewName.txt");
```

The `Remove()` function is also static and just takes the filename of the file to be removed like this:

```
CFile::Remove("C:\\MyFile.txt");
```

Both of these functions will throw an exception if they fail for any reason.

Other *CFile*-Derived Classes

`CFile` provides the base class file handling functionality. However, for more specialized functionality there are several derived classes. There isn't enough room to cover each in detail, so I'll just mention some of the types available and what they are used for.

- `CMemFile` provides a memory-based file. This can be quite useful when you need some of the file access functionality but want the speed of dealing with memory rather than disk.

- `CSharedFile` is a special case of `CMemFile` that allocates and attaches to shared memory. This is usually used in inter-process communications such as Clipboard transfer. See "Transferring Data with the Clipboard," later in this chapter, for an example.

- `COleStreamFile` is the base class for OLE-based stream operations. Several classes are derived from this for OLE linking, embedding, and automation types such as `CMonikerFile`, `CAsyncMonikerFile`, `CDataPathProperty`, and `CCachedDataPathProperty`.

> **C++ static functions**
>
> A static function is a C++ class member function that doesn't need an object context. Whereas most C++ member functions need a `this` pointer that points to the object itself to reference local member variables, a static function doesn't use any of the object's member variables and can be called without a memory instance of the object itself.

- CSocketFile lets you treat network connections as though they were files to aid in network transfer of document data via serialization (when used with a CArchive object).

- CStdioFile wraps the old C-based concepts of stdin and stdout to allow command line-based redirections. It uses those text mode open flags to convert between <CR> and <CR><LF> combinations (carriage return and line feed characters). This is further specialized by CInternetFile, which adds base functionality for the CHttpFile, which helps with *HTML World Wide Web* style documents; and CGopherFile, which helps with the now nearly extinct Internet *Gopher server* format.

- Not derived from CFile but associated with it is the CRecentFileList, which provides the most recently used file functionality described in the serialization section of this chapter. You can use the class directly to implement your own recently used file menus and lists.

SEE ALSO
➤ *For more information on Internet support classes, see page 503*

Transferring Data with the Clipboard

> **The new and old Clipboard transfer methods**
>
> With the advent of OLE the old DDE (Dynamic Data Exchange) Clipboard mechanisms have been superseded by OLE data sources and data objects. You should always use the OLE methods in preference to DDE because these are better supported, more flexible, and lead to easier drag-and-drop implementation.

Cutting and pasting data from one application to another has become one of the stalwart principles securing the Windows common user interface paradigm. By registering the supported data types an application can offer and accept data from another instance of that application or an entirely different application that supports a common data format.

Setting the Clipboard Data Formats

The first thing you must do before you can transfer data to or from the Clipboard is make your application register the data formats that your application can support. These can either be a number of standard formats, some of which are shown in Table 23.5, or you can register your own special unique format with the RegisterClipboardFormat() function. Either way the format is a UINT value.

TABLE 23.5 Standard Clipboard formats

Format Flag	Description of Format
CF_TEXT	Probably the most common format, used to transfer text with <CR> and <LF> (carriage return and line feed characters) marking the end of each line.
CF_BITMAP	The data is a handle to a bitmap.
CF_DIB	The data is an image stored as a device-independent bitmap.
CF_TIFF	The data is an image in tagged image format.
CF_WAVE	The data is a standard pulse code modulated (PCM) wave audio format.
CF_PALETTE	The data is the handle to a color palette.
CF_METAFILEPICT	The data is a metafile picture defined by the METAFILEPICT structure.

You could add cut-and-paste support to the Persist example shown earlier in this chapter to support a user-defined blob file format. You can utilize all the code to do serialization and reuse it for the Clipboard transfer as well. Because a blob file isn't a supported Clipboard format (yet!), you must register the format by calling RegisterClipboardFormat().

RegisterClipboardFormat() is passed one parameter, a string to uniquely identify the data format, and returns a UINT value that represents the registered format. The first program that registers the string will get a unique value; subsequent programs registering the same format string will be returned the same value. This ensures that multiple instances of the same application will have a common Clipboard format, so they will know that they can support the specified format.

You can add the RegisterClipboardFormat() call to the constructor of CPersistDoc so that the format is registered as soon as the document is created.

```
CPersistDoc::CPersistDoc()
{
    // TODO: add one-time construction code here
    m_uClipFormat =
        RegisterClipboardFormat("PersistClipFormat");
}
```

Clipboard formats

A Clipboard format is an agreed data type that lets programs that understand that data type find out whether data they can deal with exists on the Clipboard. You can also use CountClipboardFormat(), which returns an integer indicating how many different formats are currently registered with the Clipboard. Another function, EnumClipboardFormats(), returns each registered format in turn. To start with you must pass zero to EnumClipboardFormats() to get the first format. Then by passing this format back to a subsequent EnumClipboardFormats() call you can retrieve the next registered format in turn.

Notice that the returned format is stored in a member variable for use later in the document object. You can insert this member variable after the `m_BlobArray` blob container in the document class definition:

```
CObArray m_BlobArray;
UINT m_uClipFormat;      // ** New Format Member
```

That's all the code you need to register your unique `PersistClipFormat` Clipboard type. If you were supporting one of the standard types such as `CF_TEXT` you wouldn't need to register at all; `CF_TEXT` would be the format identifier you pass to the Clipboard transfer functions.

Copying Data to the Clipboard

Dynamic data exchange Clipboard transfer

Before the advent of OLE, dynamic data exchange (DDE) was the primary method of Windows Clipboard data transfer (using shared memory segments). The DDE functions still exist to provide backward compatibility, but nowadays OLE should be used in preference to DDE because OLE provides more flexibility and makes drag-and-drop operations simpler and more standard between different applications.

The next thing you must implement is the cut-and-copy side of Clipboard transfer. Cut is really just a special case of copy where the document data is deleted after use. You can implement the copy code in a menu handler for the **Edit** menu's **Copy** option. Use ClassWizard to add an `OnEditCopy()` handler for this menu option to the document class and another for the Cut option called `OnEditCut()`. If you need some help in doing this, you can find step-by-step instructions in Chapter 13, "Working with Menus," in the "Adding Command Handler Code with ClassWizard" section.

After you have the handler functions in place, you can add the Clipboard code as shown in Listing 23.8. The three-phase process is used fundamentally to create an OLE data source object, serialize the document data into a shared memory file, and offer that data on the Clipboard.

LISTING 23.8 LST24_8.CPP—Serializing the Document Data into the Clipboard to Implement the Edit/Copy Option

```
1    void CPersistDoc::OnEditCopy()
2    {
3      // Create a data source object
4      COleDataSource* pDataSource = new COleDataSource;
5
6      // Create a shared file and attach a CArchive
```

```
7    CSharedFile fileClipCopy;
8    CArchive arClipCopy(&fileClipCopy,CArchive::store);
9
10   // Serialize the document into this archive
11   Serialize(arClipCopy);
12   arClipCopy.Close();
13
14   // Grab the global memory handle from the mem file
15   HANDLE hGlobalMem = fileClipCopy.Detach();
16   if (hGlobalMem)
17   {
18       // Globally cache the data with the unique format
19       pDataSource->CacheGlobalData( ———(1)
20                   m uClipFormat, hGlobalMem);
21       // Offer it on the clipboard
22       pDataSource->SetClipboard();
23   }
24   else AfxMessageBox("Can't alloc memory for copy");
25   } ———(2)
```

(1) The CacheGlobalData() is one of many ways to set a data reference to the CDataSource object.

(2) You don't need to delete the allocated data source object because the Clipboard will do this automatically.

The first thing you must do is simply create a COleDataSource object as in line 4. This OLE object has the job of offering all sorts of data for transfer in several different applications—not just Clipboard transfer but drag-and-drop and many other types of data transfer.

A CSharedFile as declared on line 7 is a special type of memory-based file. The simple constructor automatically opens the memory file and allocates some global shared memory for its contents.

Lines 8 and 11 do the clever job of utilizing the same document serialization you've already implemented in the CBlob class and document to store the data directly into the shared memory file. This is done by creating a local CArchive object at line 8 and attaching it to the shared memory file with the CArchive::store flag, which will make the IsStoring() archive function return TRUE and store the archive data.

The archive is closed on line 12 to flush the contents into the file so that the global memory is fully set with the document contents. If you need more shared memory, the CShareFile automatically allocates more as required.

Lines 15 and 16 detach the handle for the shared memory from the file and if successful you can use it in the data source.

At line 19, the `CacheGlobalData()` function of the `CDataSource` object is passed the global memory handle along with the unique format identifier. Your source data is ready to be offered to the Clipboard, and this is done at line 22 with the `SetClipboard()` member of the data source object.

You'll need a couple extra `include` files to define the OLE objects and Clipboard functions. These can be put just above the document class definition in the PersistDoc.h header file, as in the following:

```
#include <afxadv.h>     // ** New required Header file
#include <afxole.h>     // ** New required Header file
class CPersistDoc : public CDocument
{ ...
```

Because you are now using OLE, you must initialize the OLE and COM libraries. This is easily done by adding the following `AfxOleInit()` function call after the `AfxEnableControlContainer()` call in the `InitInstance()` member function of the `CPersistApp` class:

```
BOOL CPersistApp::InitInstance()
{
    AfxEnableControlContainer();
    AfxOleInit();      // ** New OLE Library initilization
```

AfxOleInit() return codes

For simplicity the return codes of `AfxOleInit()` aren't checked here. However, if the OLE initialization fails a zero value is returned from `AfxOleInit()`; this usually indicates that the versions of DLLs installed on your system are invalid. Because most other software will have already failed if this is the case it is often assumed that `AfxOleInit()` will probably succeed.

That has completed the copy to Clipboard option. You can easily reuse this functionality for the cut code by calling the **Copy** menu handler function from the **Cut** menu handler function and removing all the document data after copying to the Clipboard. So your `OnEditCut()` handler just must look like this:

```
void CPersistDoc::OnEditCut()
{
    OnEditCopy();
    DeleteBlobs();
    UpdateAllViews(NULL);
}
```

Pasting Data from the Clipboard

The other side of Clipboard transfers is to implement the pasting function. This uses a corresponding OLE object called the COleDataObject. This object can check whether the correct type of data is available on the Clipboard and if so, retrieve it. From there it is just a case of running the serialization backward to drop the blobs from the Clipboard into another document via another CArchive and CSharedFile combination as shown in Listing 23.9.

LISTING 23.9 LST24_9.CPP—Pasting Data from the Clipboard Into the Document by Serializing Data Delivered by a *CDataObject*

```
1    void CPersistDoc::OnEditPaste()
2    {
3      // Create a data object and attach to clipboard
4      COleDataObject oleTarget;
5      oleTarget.AttachClipboard();
6      if (oleTarget.IsDataAvailable(m_uClipFormat))
7      {
8        // Get the global memory handle
9        HANDLE hGlobalMem =
10            oleTarget.GetGlobalData(m_uClipFormat);
11       if (hGlobalMem)
12       {
13         // Unwind the data into the document
14         CSharedFile fileTarget;
15         fileTarget.SetHandle(hGlobalMem);
16         CArchive arTarget(&fileTarget,CArchive::load);  ──①
17         DeleteBlobs();
18
19         // Run the serialize and update the display
20         Serialize(arTarget);
21         UpdateAllViews(NULL);
22       }
23     }
24   }
```

① The paste operation is essentially the reverse of the copy operation with the data loaded back from the shared memory.

In this listing, the COleDataObject oleTarget is declared at line 4 and attached to the Clipboard at line 5. If the IsDataAvailable()

function of the data object returns TRUE when it tests for the unique format m_uClipFormat in line 6, the correct format is on the Clipboard and can be transferred.

The global shared memory handle is extracted from the COleDataObject at line 9, and on line 14 another shared memory file fileTarget is declared and set to the extracted handle. Then a CArchive object arTarget is created at line 16 and set to load. Any current blobs are wiped at line 17 and loaded from the memory file by line 20. Finally, on line 21 the display is updated with the new transferred data.

You can easily add a user interface handler (see Chapter 13, "Working with Menus," "Enabling and Disabling Menu Options" section) for the **Paste** menu option so that it is enabled only if valid data exists on the Clipboard:

```
void CPersistDoc::OnUpdateEditPaste(CCmdUI* pCmdUI)
{
  COleDataObject oleTarget;
  oleTarget.AttachClipboard();
  pCmdUI->Enable(oleTarget.IsDataAvailable(m_uClipFormat));
}
```

The AttachClipboard() function

AttachClipboard() connects your COleDataObject to the existing Clipboard data. The data is locked on the Clipboard until you call the COleDataObject's Release() function. This is automatically called by the destructor of the COleDataObject class when the object falls out of scope at the end of the function.

This checks whether the data is available and enables the menu item if the IsDataAvailable() function returns TRUE; otherwise, the pCmdUI's Enable() function is set to FALSE so the menu item becomes grayed out.

That completes the code you must add to perform cut-and-paste operations. You can build and run the application and test it by running two instances, creating some blobs, copying or cutting from one and pasting into the other as shown in Figure 23.4. The file serialization will still work if you want to load a previous blob file or save one after pasting.

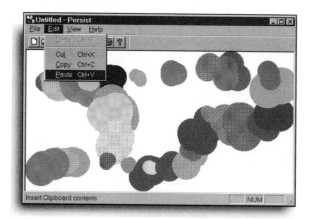

FIGURE 23.4
Cutting and pasting blob objects between two persist program instances.

SEE ALSO

➤ *For details about enabling and disabling menu options, see page 304*

➤ *For more information on OLE and COM support, see page 657*

chapter 24

Using Databases and Record Views

Configuring an ODBC data source •

Connecting to databases within
MFC applications •

Querying record sets and
accessing the results •

Adding, removing, and editing
records on a database •

Developing a record view–based
project •

Using Databases

Business organizations amass a great deal of information during their day-to-day commercial activities. They record details about their customers and suppliers, their sales and stock requirements, and so on. The vast majority of corporations choose to store this vital data in databases or more correctly in a *DMS (database management system)*. A database management system is a software product that stores data in a well-organized structure and provides the means to access and update the data efficiently.

There are two different types of databases, relational databases and object databases. The difference between them is in the conceptual way they handle data. Relational databases are centered around recognized simple data types (characters, strings, integers, and so on) and don't allow the creation of new data types. Object databases deal with data types at a higher level, enabling creation of definable data types. These objects mirror those created in an object-oriented programming language; for example, an object stored in an object database could be a person or a vehicle. This chapter concentrates on the use of relational databases because these have been around longer and are by far the most widely used.

Using Relational Databases

Before the advent of database management software, applications were written with proprietary file structures. Only the developers that designed and programmed the system really knew how the data was arranged. This meant that when users of the system required the data to be manipulated in a specific manner, they usually had to request further development, which was often time-consuming.

Relational databases eliminated much of this problem by standardizing the design of a system's data storage. Their data is organized into tables, columns, and rows. Typically a database might have a Customer table with columns such as Trading Name and Telephone Number. The rows are the actual entries in the table for one specific entity. For example, a Customer table would have a row for Macmillan Publishing and another for Microsoft. The design of these tables and columns are retained in the *database schema*. The schema defines the data type of each column and the manner in which the tables are interrelated.

Using Open Database Connectivity

You can purchase a relational database from one of many different vendors. Each database has its own specific structure and consequently its own set of API calls. This can mean a steep learning curve attempting to understand the specifics of a database from a particular vendor. More and more, applications are required to be database agnostic. To develop applications that utilize a relational database no matter which company actually supplies it you need a generic programming method. Such a method exists and is termed ODBC (Open Database Connectivity).

ODBC enables a common programming interface to use different breeds of relational database. To make this possible, middleware must exist that interprets the ODBC standard function calls into database-specific function calls. This middleware is the ODBC driver, which is supplied by the database vendor or a third-party company specializing in such connectivity products. ODBC has been adopted as a standard, and ODBC drivers are now available for all well-known databases. You will need to install the ODBC driver for the particular database you are using. The setup procedure of Microsoft applications such as Office and Visual Studio allow you to install the most common Microsoft ODBC drivers; to use other databases contact the database vendor about the availability of an ODBC driver. Figure 24.1 shows how a database is connected to your application through an ODBC driver.

Distributing ODBC applications

If you develop database applications using ODBC there are some additional files you will need to distribute along with your C++ executable file. These additional files can be found in the OS\System directory of the Visual C++ CD. Read the REDISTRB.WRI in that directory for more information.

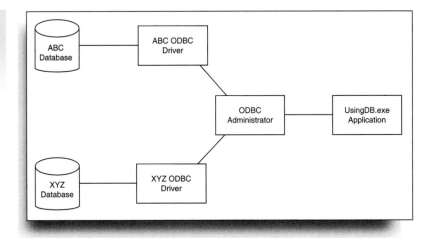

FIGURE 24.1
Connecting to databases via ODBC.

Structured query language

Structured query language (SQL) is a text-based language used by relational databases as a standard for retrieving, updating, and managing data.

Commands are issued to the ODBC driver and passed on to the database using SQL (Structured Query Language). This language was designed specifically for accessing databases and is now the *de facto* standard. There are almost as many flavors of SQL as there are databases, with each vendor adding their own enhancements. There are minimum requirements ensuring each ODBC driver must at least support a stipulated set of commands. This doesn't stop drivers from supporting nonstandard commands because ODBC has a pass-through method that allows direct execution of SQL statements. However, incorporating nonstandard statements means your application loses the capability to connect to other vendor's databases, which is ODBC's big advantage.

SQL has three types of language commands, DDL, DML, and DCL. DDL (Data Definition Language) commands are used to create and modify the database schema. Examples of DDL statements include CREATE DATABASE and CREATE TABLE. DML (Data Manipulation Language) commands are used to query and manipulate values. There are four main DML statements: SELECT, INSERT, UPDATE, and DELETE. Each is given parameters to specify which table(s) and column(s) are to be affected. DCL (Data Control Language) commands are used to grant specific access rights to certain users.

Configuring a Data Source

The first task to exploiting ODBC is to configure a data source. A data source tells your program where to locate the physical files of the database and which ODBC driver to use to translate the API calls. Configuring data sources is done using the ODBC data source administrator, located in the control panel.

To configure a data source that will be used later in this chapter's sample application, follow the steps given in "Creating and Configuring an ODBC Data Source." The sample application uses the stdreg32.mdb file, which is an Access database supplied as a sample on the Visual C++ CD. At the time of this writing, the exact location of this file on the CD is unknown. You'll need to find this file and copy it from the CD to your hard disk. The following procedure assumes the file is located in the C:\Databases\ directory.

Creating and configuring an ODBC data source

1. From the **Start** menu on the desktop select the **Settings** menu, then select **Control Panel**.

2. Double-click (or select and then press Enter) the icon labeled **32bit ODBC**. The ODBC Data Source Administrator dialog box appears as shown in Figure 24.2.

> **Using the correct ODBC administrator program**
>
> You may find two ODBC applet icons in the control panel; if you do, use the one that has a 32 on the image for configuring 32-bit database connections. The other applet is for 16-bit database connections.

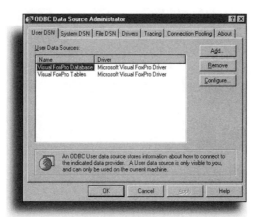

FIGURE 24.2
The ODBC Data Source Administrator dialog box.

3. Select the **User DSN** tab and click the **Add** button. The Create New Data Source dialog box appears as shown in Figure 24.4. You can alter the settings of an existing data source by selecting its name in the **User Data Sources** list and clicking **C**onfigure.

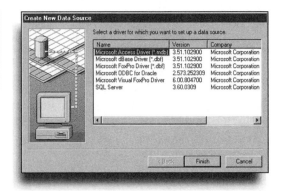

4. Select the name of the ODBC driver for which you want to create a data source. Note that this must match the type of database. Select **Microsoft Access Driver (*.mdb)** for this example. Click **Finish**. The ODBC Microsoft Access Setup dialog box appears as shown in Figure 24.4.

5. Enter a name for the data source in the **Data Source Name** edit box. Enter Student Registration for this example. You can enter any name you want but should avoid having two data sources with identical names.

6. Optionally, enter a description of the data source in the **Description** edit box. For example, you could enter Course enrollment and administration for this example.

7. Click the **Select** button; the Select Database dialog box appears.

8. Enter the name of the database file in the **Database Name** edit box or select the filename using the **Directories** folder list. Select the stdreg32.mdb file for this example. Click **OK**. The location and name of the selected database are displayed on the setup dialog box.

9. Click **OK** to close the ODBC Microsoft Access Setup dialog box; Student Registration should now appear in the **User Data Sources** list.

10. Click **OK** to close the ODBC Data Source Administrator dialog box and close the Control Panel window.

Note that the dialog box in Figure 24.4 shows the ODBC configuration options specifically for a Microsoft Access database. Other databases will show their own setup dialog boxes at this step and might require additional options to be set.

Note also that you can configure two types of data source: User DSNs (the default) and System DSNs. A user data source is available only to the user who added it, whereas a system data source becomes available to any user who logs on to the computer.

> **Troubleshooting a database connection**
>
> If you experience problems with a database connection, try swapping the data source type. For example, if you have selected **User DSN** switch it to **System DSN** and vice-versa.

Generating an Application with Database Support

The way to write an application that requires access to a database depends very much on some fundamental governing factors. For example, does the application need access to more than one database or do other file types need to be supported also? All these configurations are possible and require consideration because the easiest method to incorporate database support is at project creation time using AppWizard options. If you recall, after they are generated the AppWizard options cannot be revisited, and you can alter them only by editing code or creating the project from scratch.

Including Database Support with AppWizard

AppWizard Step 2 enables you to choose one of four options that build in varying degrees of support for databases (see Figure 24.5).

FIGURE 24.5

AppWizard's database support options.

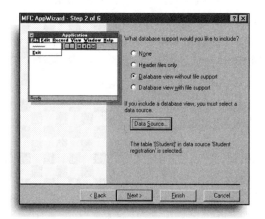

The first support (**None**) is obvious. It excludes any support for databases.

The second (**Header Files Only**) simply adds an `#include` directive to your project for the header file containing the MFC classes `CDatabase` and `CRecordset`. These are the classes used to connect to databases and access their data.

Adding database support to an existing project

You can add database support to a project that was originally created by AppWizard with no database support simply by including two header files in stdafx.h: afxdb.h and afxdao.h.

The third (**Database View Without File Support**) and fourth (**Database View With File Support**) both require a data source to be specified for the project and will automatically create classes based on further options. The difference between them is that "with file support" adds the **File** menu to the application and "without file support" does not.

Use AppWizard to create an SDI application called UsingDB and on step 2, select the **Database View Without File Support** radio button. Then follow these steps.

Connecting to a data source with AppWizard

1. On the Step 2 dialog box select the **Database View Without File Support** radio button if the application does not require a **File** menu; if it does, select the **Database View With File Support** radio button. Select **Database View Without File Support** for this example. Note that this selection forces the project to be an SDI application.

2. Click the **Data Source** button. The Database Options dialog box appears as shown in Figure 24.6.

3. Select the appropriate connectivity radio button option. Select **ODBC** for this example.

4. Select the data source name in the **Datasource** combo box. Select **Student Registration** for this example. If this doesn't appear, you must create and configure the data source. See the "Creating and Configuring an ODBC Data Source" set of steps earlier in this chapter.

5. Select the **Recordset Type**. Select **Snapshot** for this example.

6. Click **OK**. The Select Database Tables dialog box appears as shown in Figure 24.7.

7. Select the table or tables for which you want to create a recordset. Select the **Student** table for this example.

8. Click **OK**. You have added database support to the project; you can now continue with the further AppWizard steps.

Snapshots and dynasets

A snapshot is a recordset that buffers all data fields and does not take account of updates performed by other users.

A dynaset is a recordset that buffers only the key fields. Moving through the records of a dynaset will take account of updates and deletions performed by other users.

635

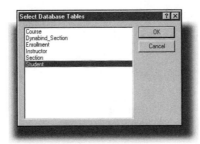

FIGURE 24.7

The Select Database Tables dialog box.

Data access objects (DAO)

An alternative to using CDatabase and CRecordset is to use CDaoDatabase and CDaoRecordset. The difference between these classes is that the DAO classes work only in conjunction with databases based on the Microsoft Jet engine whereas the non-DAO classes are based on database driven via ODBC.

Connecting to a Database

Connecting to a database and accessing its data is handled by two MFC classes that work in conjunction: CDatabase and CRecordset. The CDatabase class is responsible for opening the connection to the database. You can use CDatabase objects within your program to establish connections to several databases or connect to the same database several times. Because opening database connections is a somewhat lengthy process and takes a great deal of system resources, you should reuse connections rather than opening another for each record set. One way to do this would be to embed the CDatabase object within your document class that establishes the connection and then create a GetDatabase() function that returns a pointer to the CDatabase. You can pass a pointer to a CDatabase object in the constructor of CRecordset to have the record set use an existing connection. You connect to a particular database by calling the CDatabase::OpenEx function. The prototype of the OpenEx function is shown in Listing 24.1.

LISTING 24.1 LST25_1.CPP—Parameters for the *OpenEx* Function

```
1      virtual BOOL OpenEx( LPCTSTR lpszConnectString,
2                           DWORD dwOptions = 0);
```

Frequently, only the first parameter is supplied. The lpszConnectString is a pointer to a string that contains the data source name and any additional information required to connect to the database in question, such as a username and a password. ODBC data sources are configured using an administrator program run from an applet within Control Panel. For details about how to configure a data source, refer to "Configuring a Data Source" earlier in this chapter. The second parameter, dwOptions, is a bitmask used to specify a combination of the connection options shown in Table 24.1. The default value 0 will open the database with write access, the ODBC cursor library will not be loaded, and the connection dialog will display only if the connection string doesn't include enough details to successfully connect.

TABLE 24.1 Possible settings for the *dwOptions* parameter of *CDatabase::OpenEx()*

Setting	Description
OpenReadOnly	Open the data source as read only.
useCursorLib	Load the ODBC cursor library DLL. This overrides some of the ODBC driver functionality. For example, dynasets cannot be used when the cursor library is loaded.
noOdbcDialog	Prevents the ODBC connection dialog box from being displayed.
forceOdbcDialog	Displays the ODBC connection dialog box.

An example of using the CDatabase::OpenEx() function would be the following:

```
CDatabase db;
db.OpenEx("ODBC;DSN=Student Registration;UID=TinyTim;PWD=
➥CASTLE", CDatabase::openReadOnly ¦
➥CDatabase::noOdbcDialog));
```

Earlier in this chapter, I mentioned that it's possible to issue direct SQL statements. This is useful if your database provides extensions to the ODBC SQL standards; for example, to call stored procedures in the database. You issue a statement directly by calling CDatabase's ExecuteSQL function. The function takes a pointer to a string containing the statement.

Querying Database Values

The CRecordset class handles the task of accessing the data within the tables and columns of a database. CRecordset is an abstract class, so you must derive your own classes from it. Through Crecordset, SQL queries are performed. The results of a query are stored in a record buffer. The class maintains a current record pointer (also known as a cursor) and enables iteration through the records via the member functions Move, MoveNext, MovePrev, MoveFirst, and MoveLast.

The CRecordset-derived class maintains a member variable for each column (field) within the query. These variables are updated with the value of the column they represent every time a call is made that alters the current record. AppWizard created a CRecordset derivative called CUsingDBSet within the UsingDB project. The CUsingDBSet class definition and implementation is shown in Listing 24.2.

LISTING 24.2 LST25_2.CPP—*CUsingDBSet* Class Definition

(1) You can optionally pass in a pointer to an existing CDatabase object in the CRecordset.

(2) ClassWizard added variables for each field in the record-set.

```
1      class CUsingDBSet : public CRecordset
2    {
3    public:
4        CUsingDBSet(CDatabase* pDatabase = NULL);        (1)
5        DECLARE_DYNAMIC(CUsingDBSet)
6
7    // Field/Param Data
8        //{{AFX_FIELD(CUsingDBSet, CRecordset)
9        long     m_StudentID;
10       CString m_Name;                                   (2)
11       int      m_GradYear;
12       //}}AFX_FIELD
13
14   // Overrides
15       // ClassWizard generated virtual function overrides
16       //{{AFX_VIRTUAL(CUsingDBSet)
17       public:
18       virtual CString GetDefaultConnect();
19       virtual CString GetDefaultSQL();
20       virtual void DoFieldExchange(CFieldExchange* pFX);
21       //}}AFX_VIRTUAL
22
23   // Implementation
24   #ifdef _DEBUG
25       virtual void AssertValid() const;
```

```
26          virtual void Dump(CDumpContext& dc) const;
27      enndif
28      };
29      CUsingDBSet::CUsingDBSet(CDatabase* pdb)
30          : CRecordset(pdb)
31      {
32          //{{AFX_FIELD_INIT(CUsingDBSet)
33          m_StudentID = 0;
34          m_Name = _T("");
35          m_GradYear = 0;
36          m_nFields = 3;
37          //}}AFX_FIELD_INIT
38          m_nDefaultType = snapshot;
39      }
40
41      CString CUsingDBSet::GetDefaultConnect()
42      {
43          return _T("ODBC;DSN=Student registration");
44      }
45
46      CString CUsingDBSet::GetDefaultSQL()
47      {
48          return _T("[Student]");
49      }
```

① ClassWizard added initialization for each field in the recordset and the CRecordset m_nFields variable.

② Gets called by the framework to supply the connection string when the recordset is opened.

③ Gets called by the framework to supply the table name when the recordset is opened.

You'll find the document class CUsingDBDoc has a member variable m_usingDBSet of type CUsingDBSet and that the view class CUsingDBView has a member variable m_pSet that is a pointer to the document's recordset object. The view's pointer, m_pSet, is initialized in the OnInitialUpdate function.

The definition of the CUsingDBSet class has been assembled according to the selections made within AppWizard. You selected the Student table, which has three columns StudentID, Name, and GradYear. You can see the class has three corresponding variables (lines 9–11). The data types and variable names have been obtained using information supplied by the database itself. These variables are initialized to default values in the constructor (lines 33–35). The constructor also initializes the m_nFields variable to 3 (line 36), which informs the recordset how many columns there are.

When instantiated, the CUsingDBSet constructor can be passed a pointer to a CDatabase object (line 29); if this is NULL (as it is in the example) the base class CRecordset will create a CDatabase object and call the CDatabase::Open function to connect to the database. Before calling CDatabase::Open, a call to the virtual function GetDefaultConnect (line 41) is made, which returns the connection string (line 43). This informs the database object which data source to connect to.

The GetDefaultSQL function in line 46 is called from within CRecordset::Open. The CRecordset::Open constructs a default SQL SELECT statement and performs the query on the database. The constructed SQL statement in this case will be "SELECT * FROM Student", which retrieves all the rows from the Student table and stores them in the record buffer. After Open has been performed, you can start moving through the retrieved records and accessing the column data. CRecordset also has a Requery function that performs the query again to refresh the records in the buffer without the need for closing and reopening.

Two flags indicate whether the current record (cursor) is positioned at the start or end of the set. You can test for these flags by calling IsBOF (beginning-of-file) and IsEOF (end-of-file). Listing 24.3 shows some sample code that iterates through each record until the end of the file is reached.

LISTING 24.3 LST25_3.CPP—Iterating Through a Recordset

① Instantiates a CRecordset-derived class object.

② Opens the recordset connection.

③ Ensures the recordset is not empty (has no records)

④ Loops until the end of the recordset is reached.

```
1    void CMyView::OnIterateSet()
2    {
3        // ** Open a recordset
4        CMyRecordSet rs(NULL); ————①
5        rs.Open(); ————②
6
7        // ** Check if the recordset is empty
8        if(rs.IsBOF()) ————③
9            return;
10
11       // ** Iterate through each record
12       // ** calling a Process function
13       while(!rs.IsEOF()) ————④
```

```
14        {
15            DoSomeFunction(&rs);
16            rs.MoveNext();
17        }
18    }
```

Updating Database Values

Being able to query a database and extract the values is all well and good, but this won't get you very far. You also must be able to add, delete, and modify records. Thankfully, CRecordset handles almost all the work involved in these operations.

Adding a new record is accomplished in three stages. First, call AddNew, which puts the recordset into Add mode and sets the field values to NULL. Next, update the fields with the values you want to store on the database for the new record. This simply means assigning values to the member variables of your recordset class. Finally, call Update, which creates the new record on the database and ends the recordset Add mode. Note that for snapshot record sets you'll need to call Requery to access the newly added record.

Modifying an existing record is also accomplished in four stages. First, position the current record on the record you want to modify. Next call Edit, which puts the recordset into Edit mode. Next you update the field values. Finally, call Update, which stores the values on the database, updates the recordset, and ends the Edit mode.

Deleting a record is accomplished in a single stage. Simply call Delete to remove the current record. The record is removed from the recordset and from the database. You must move from a deleted record because trying to access it will trigger an assert.

> **Database exceptions**
>
> Be aware that many CRecordset functions such as Open(), AddNew(), Edit(), and Update() can throw a CDBException if a problem is encountered. Calls to these functions should therefore be encased within try/catch statements. Help can be gained when debugging database exceptions by checking the **Database Tracing** option from the **Tools**, **MFC Tracer** menu.

Binding Fields to Database Tables

Each time an update or scroll operation is performed, data must be exchanged between the record buffer and the database. You have already seen that the recordset class has a member variable for each column in the query. Which member variable is designated to which column is specified within the DoFieldExchange function. Listing 24.4 shows the DoFieldExchange function of the CUsingDBSet class in the UsingDB sample.

The DoFieldExchange function is called automatically whenever it's necessary to both retrieve and store field values. Macros supplied by MFC and prefixed RFX (Record Field Exchange) are used to handle the exchange of each specific data type from the column on a database table to a record set's member variable and vice versa. The second parameter passed to the RFX macro is the database table's column name. The third parameter is the member variable that is designated to store its value. Note the special comments (line 3 and 8). Don't edit or remove these because ClassWizard uses them.

① DoFieldExchange() is called by the framework to retrieve or update the recordset's column values.

② Indicates the following data members are output fields as opposed to input parameters.

③ Exchanges the data between the recordset member variables and the database table.

LISTING 24.4 LST25_4.CPP—The *DoFieldExchange* Function

```
1      void CUsingDBSet::DoFieldExchange(CFieldExchange* pFX)   — ①
2      {
3          //{{AFX_FIELD_MAP(CUsingDBSet)
4          pFX->SetFieldType(CFieldExchange::outputColumn);   — ②
5          RFX_Long(pFX, _T("[StudentID]"), m_StudentID);
6          RFX_Text(pFX, _T("[Name]"), m_Name);               ③
7          RFX_Int(pFX, _T("[GradYear]"), m_GradYear);
8          //}}AFX_FIELD_MAP
9      }
```

Creating and Using a Record View

If you choose to include database support when you create a project with AppWizard, the view class of your application will by default be derived from CRecordView. CRecordView is a subclass of CFormView, which implements a view based on a paper form. A borderless and captionless dialog template is used to represent the form and fills the client area of the view window. CRecordView adds the ability to connect the form type view with database records within a CRecordset subclass. Controls added to the dialog box template can be linked directly to member variables that are updated from fields on a database. AppWizard also adds a

Record menu and toolbar icons that enable the user to scroll through the records within the recordset, automatically updating the view for each record.

Editing the Record View Template

Record view dialog templates might look different from other dialog boxes because there is no border and no caption, but controls are added and edited within the resource editor the same as any dialog box. Normally, a control is added for each data field that is to appear on the form. The controls are then attached to a member variable of the CRecordset subclass.

The UsingDB example requires two fields to be added to the record form view, one for the student name and one for the graduation year. To design the UsingDB record view, follow these steps.

Designing a record view dialog box template

1. On the ResourceView pane, expand the **Dialog** folder and double-click IDD_USINGDB_FORM. The dialog template appears in the resource editor.

2. Click the **TODO: Place Form Controls Here** text, and then press the Delete button to remove it.

3. Select the static text image on the Controls toolbar. Add a text control at the top left of the dialog box as shown in Figure 24.8.

4. Enter the static text caption. Enter Student &Name for this example.

5. Select the edit box image on the Controls toolbar. Add an edit box control to the right of the **Student Name** text control.

6. Enter IDC_NAME in the **ID** combo box.

7. Select the static text image on the Controls toolbar. Add a text control under the **Student Name** text control.

8. Enter the static text caption. Enter Graduation &Year for this example.

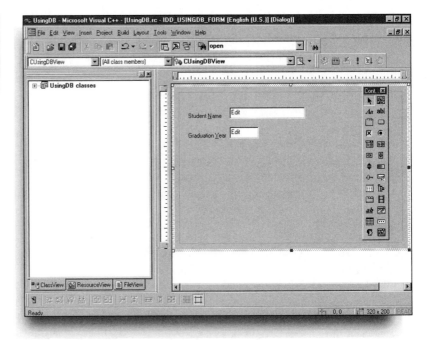

9. Select the edit box image on the Controls toolbar. Add an edit box control to the right of the **Graduation Year** text control.

10. Enter IDC_YEAR in the **ID** combo box. Your dialog template should now look like Figure 24.8.

Attaching Edit Controls to Recordset Fields

Each of the edit controls on the record view dialog template can be associated with a database field. This association is achieved by attaching a variable to the edit control that points directly to a member variable of the recordset class. The view class CUsingDBView holds a pointer to the CUsingDBSet object in its member variable m_pSet. ClassWizard can be used to associate a member of m_pSet with an edit control.

To attach the record view name and year edit boxes with the student database fields, follow these steps.

Attaching controls to recordset fields with ClassWizard

1. On the ResourceView pane expand the **Dialog** folder and double-click `IDD_USINGDB_FORM`. The dialog template appears in the resource editor.

2. Select the first edit box control and then press Ctrl+W to start ClassWizard, or from the context menu select **Class<u>W</u>izard**.

3. Select the **Member Variables** tab.

4. Select the edit control ID in the **Control <u>I</u>Ds** list box; select `IDC_NAME` for this example, and then click the **Add Variable** button. The Add Member Variable dialog box appears. You can also add a member variable for a control by double-clicking the control's ID.

5. Expand the list of the **Member Variable <u>N</u>ame** combo box; the choice of recordset variables is displayed as shown in Figure 24.9. Select the name of the member variable to attach to the edit control. Select **m_pSet->m_Name** for this example.

FIGURE 24.9

Attaching a recordset variable to an edit control.

6. Select the **<u>C</u>ategory**; use **Value** for this example.

7. Select the **Variable Type**; use **CString** for this example.

8. Click **OK**.

9. Select `IDC_YEAR` in the **Control <u>I</u>Ds** list box, and then click the **Add Variable** button.

10. Expand the list of the **Member Variable <u>N</u>ame** combo box. Select **m_pSet->m_GradYear** from the list.

11. Select the **<u>C</u>ategory**; use **Value** for this example.

12. Select the **Variable Type**; use **int** for this example.

13. Click **OK** to close the Add Member Variable dialog box.

14. Click **OK** to close the ClassWizard dialog box.

Now build and run the project. The application should automatically connect to the Student Registration data source and the record view initial update should position you at the first record in the Student table. Try scrolling through the records. Figure 24.10 shows the UsingDB example.

FIGURE 24.10

The UsingDB example.

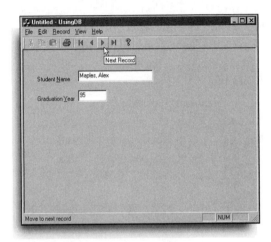

SEE ALSO

➤ *For more information on designing dialog boxes, see page 44*

➤ *For further details about the* CFormView *class, see page 458*

chapter 25

Understanding OLE and COM Programming

Understanding the principles of the
Component Object Model

Creating your own OLE
Automation server

Learning about OLE servers
and containers

Component-Based Programming

COM+, the future of COM

The next step in the evolution of COM will be COM+. Microsoft promises that COM+ will greatly simplify the coding required for COM so that COM objects work more like C++ objects and can be created and released using the C++ `new` and `delete` keywords. At the time of this writing, Visual C++ 6.0 does not support COM+, but a COM+ SDK or service pack might be released subsequently.

The rising complexity of software development in sophisticated environments such as Windows, with its many application programming interfaces (APIs), and the need for standards, version control, development speed, and distributed computing has given rise to a technology called *component-based programming*.

Components are small software entities (like class instances) that perform specific tasks through well-defined interfaces. Unlike class instances, they have no strong loyalties to one program instance or host machine. They can be written in many languages and still talk happily through their interfaces to programs and components implemented in other languages.

Microsoft has evolved this technology to its present state, which is now called the Component Object Model (COM). You might see other terms such as Object Linking and Embedding (OLE) and ActiveX Controls. You should bear in mind that these are just specific implementations in COM programming. COM itself is a language- and platform-independent standard that defines how different objects can communicate with each other using a common agreed protocol.

The most important thing about COM objects are their interfaces; the objects themselves are just black box implementations of specific functionality. However, for you to be able to use this functionality, your program and others must have a well-defined contract for passing parameters and getting results. This contract between client program and object is called an *interface*.

Whole APIs can be defined and designed in terms of interfaces. If you are writing a client application, you can write your program to talk to a server via these agreed interfaces, and it doesn't matter whose server software you use. Alternatively, you might decide to write server components that conform to the interface definitions, and market your component as a competitive alternative to other vendors' components.

The Messaging API (MAPI) is a good example of COM in use. MAPI is a set of standard interfaces to COM objects. Anyone is free to write the COM objects that perform tasks such as storing messages, transporting messages, and providing an address book of message recipients. Microsoft Exchange is a particular implementation of these server components, but there are many other implementations. The actual coding might differ wildly between implementations, but all the COM objects conform to the same interface specifications. That means that clients of these services such as Microsoft Outlook can use any vendor's MAPI-compliant components to send, receive, and store its messages. Similarly, any vendor can provide its own client programs (and many do) that use Exchange, or any other MAPI server components, without even knowing whose components it is using. The only requirement of the client and server components is that they call each other via these agreed interface definitions, called MAPI.

SEE ALSO

➤ *To use ActiveX controls in your application, see page 196*

➤ *To create ActiveX controls, see page 676*

➤ *For more information on MAPI, see page 754*

COM Interfaces

An interface is a definition for a collection of functions and their parameters. Every COM object has at least one interface, but often offers many, each having its own unique set of functions.

You can write a COM object in any language that has a way of supporting these interfaces. Some are better suited for this than others. For example, Java works very well because each Java object can have multiple interfaces and so maps naturally to each COM object. A COM object puts the actual code behind these interfaces, so a program calling a function that lives on an interface will find an implementation that performs the task defined by that function on the specific interface.

By some not-so-strange quirk of fate, the standard COM interface structure is exactly the same as the Visual C++ virtual function table structure. This means you can use the virtual function table mechanism to define and implement COM interfaces.

> **Interface naming conventions**
>
> COM interfaces are named like most things according to their function. However, they are conventionally distinguished by prefixing the letter `I` to the beginning of the name. Some COM interfaces that follow this rule are `IUnknown`, `IDispatch`, `IMoniker`, and `IMessageFilter`.

Virtual function tables

Every instance of a C++ object in memory has an appended virtual function table (although some may have no entries and so be zero length). Each entry in the table stores a pointer to the code that implements a virtual function. Whenever one of the object's virtual functions is called, the appended table provides the correct address for either the base class's function or derived class's function.

You would normally use virtual functions to provide a way of overriding a base class function in a derived class (using the `virtual` prefix in the base class function declaration). When you do this, a table of virtual functions associated with that class—a `vtable`—is declared.

You can declare a C++ class that contains only pure virtual functions. This is called an abstract base class. You can't create an instance of one of these abstract classes, but it can be used to create a C++ compatible COM interface definition and might look like this:

```
class IUnknown
{
public:
    virtual HRESULT QueryInterface(REFIID riid, LPVOID FAR*
    ➥ppvObj)=0;
    virtual ULONG AddRef()=0;
    virtual ULONG Release()=0;
}
```

Microsoft provides these C++ definitions for all the interfaces to COM objects that they supply, although you might see the functions wrapped in a macro that expands to the same thing:

```
STDMETHOD(QueryInterface)(THIS_ REFIID riid, LPVOID FAR*
➥ppvObj) PURE;
STDMETHOD_(ULONG, AddRef)(THIS) PURE;
STDMETHOD_(ULONG, Release)(THIS) PURE;
```

Every COM object must implement the `IUnknown` interface comprising these three methods (or functions), and every interface must implement these three functions before its own custom functions. The role of these functions is as follows:

- `AddRef()`—When a client gains a pointer to an interface, an internal reference count is incremented to represent the number of client references that are currently active.

- `Release()`—When a client releases a pointer to an interface, the internal reference is decremented, until it reaches zero when the object is destroyed (usually by itself).

- `QueryInterface()`—A client with a pointer to one interface can ask for a pointer to another COM object interface by passing the ID (`riid` in the preceding example) of the required interface. If such an interface exists, `AddRef()` is called on a pointer to the requested interface and returned in the `ppvObj` pointer. The requested interface ID (`riid`) is explained in detail in the next section.

Because every interface is guaranteed to implement these common functions, you can write a client program that asks for an instance of a COM object (which automatically calls `AddRef()` for you). Navigate around the object's interfaces using `QueryInterface()`. When you've finished, call `Release()` on each interface pointer that you've obtained to let the object destroy itself (unless of course something else is using it). The same functions work universally across all COM objects.

Collaterally, if you implement a COM object you must provide the code that maintains this count and passes back a pointer to the requested interface, or `NULL` if there is no such interface.

An interface that supports only these three functions would be fairly pointless, so normally more sophisticated interfaces inherit this definition as a base and then define more specific functions to form a customized and useful interface.

There are many ways to implement the code behind the `vtable`. One of the simplest is just to inherit a real (non-abstract) C++ class from the interface definition class. Then implement the methods in your derived class.

> **Freeing memory in COM objects**
>
> Because the COM object is responsible for its own reference count, it must also be responsible for freeing the memory it uses when all its clients have released it and the reference count has fallen to zero. You can do this in C++ by deleting the C++ `this` pointer, which will then delete the memory for the calling object. After your object has deleted itself, it should return from the final function without any further processing. You must be especially careful not to try to use any of the objects' member variables because the object no longer owns the memory for these variables.

Interface IDs, Class IDs, and GUIDs

As you saw in the previous section, the `QueryInterface()` function will return a pointer to another interface that lives on the particular COM object when you pass it the ID of the interface you need. Each interface has its own unique ID called `IID`, as does each COM class called `CLSID`. These IDs are 128-bit long numbers that are guaranteed to be unique to every interface and every COM object anywhere in the world. They're called globally unique IDs (GUIDs).

When you write a new COM object or define a new interface you can use a program called guidgen.exe to generate these globally unique numbers. You should find this program in your ...Visual Studio\VC98\Tools\Bin\ directory. When you run guidgen.exe, it generates a new GUID and lets you choose between four different ways of expressing it (see Figure 25.1). You can pick the format closest to your requirements and click the **Copy** button to copy that number to the Clipboard. If you click **New GUID**, guidgen.exe will pick another unique number for you. Don't worry about getting duplicates—you won't unless you live to be very, very, very old.

FIGURE 25.1
Guidgen.exe generating a new globally unique number.

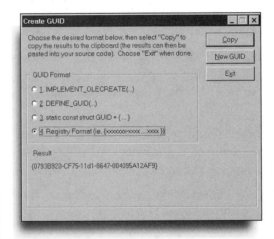

Locating and using the guidgen.exe program

You may find that the location of guidgen.exe changes in different versions and editions of the Visual C++ compiler. You can use the Windows Explorer's **Find** (**Files or Folders**) option from the **Tools** menu to locate guidgen.exe on your machine.

Once located, you can add the tool to your Visual Studio **Tools** menu using the **Tools**, **Customize** option and selecting the **Tools** tab from the Customize dialog box to add guidgen.exe to your list of tools.

A typical GUID looks like this when in Registry format:

```
{0793B920-CF75-11d1-8647-004095A12AF9}
```

You might see them coded differently when used for different purposes. For example, in C++ code, the same number might be defined like this:

```
// {0793B920-CF75-11d1-8647-004095A12AF9}
DEFINE_GUID(<<name>>,
    0x793b920, 0xcf75, 0x11d1, 0x86, 0x47, 0x0, 0x40, 0x95,
    ➥ 0xa1, 0x2a, 0xf9);
```

Remembering 128-bit numbers isn't a common talent, so we also tend to associate readable nicknames to interfaces and classes. For example, the IUnknown interface would be known as IID_IUnknown and the DEFINE_GUID macro can be used to associate these names with the 128-bit number to produce a static structure that you can pass to QueryInterface() as the interface ID. For example, the following code will set the pIDD2 pointer to the IID_IDirectDraw2 interface from an existing pIDraw interface pointer to a direct draw object:

```
IDirectDraw2* pIDD2 = NULL;
    HRESULT hr = pIDraw->QueryInterface(IID_IDirectDraw2,
                                (LPVOID *)&pIDD2);
```

> **Range of 128-bit numbers**
>
> With 128 bits, you can represent every integer value between 0 and the excess of 340282366920938460000000000000 00000000000!

(DirectDraw is just a sample COM object and isn't important here. If you want to see it being used, see the "Using DirectDraw" section of Chapter 28, "Working with APIs and SDKs.")

COM classes have a similar prefix, CLSID. The DirectDraw object that implements the IID_IDirectDraw2 interface may be known as CLSID_DirectDraw.

However, behind the scenes, both the interface and class IDs are just GUIDs, and the real numbers can be found in the DDRAW.h header file declared as

```
DEFINE_GUID( CLSID_DirectDraw,
    0xD7B70EE0,0x4340,0x11CF,0xB0,0x63,0x00,
    0x20,0xAF,0xC2,0xCD,0x35 );
DEFINE_GUID( IID_IDirectDraw2,
    0xB3A6F3E0,0x2B43,0x11CF,0xA2,0xDE,0x00,
    0xAA,0x00,0xB9,0x33,0x56 );
```

SEE ALSO

➤ *For an example of using* DirectDraw *with* CoCreateInstance(), *or to see* DirectDraw *in use, see page 734*

Creating Instances of COM Objects

When you create an instance of a COM object, a running server process will start and maintain it. The server process can be your own client program, an attached DLL, an .exe executable on the local machine, or a program on a remote machine. Each of these different cases is called a context and they are shown in Table 25.1.

TABLE 25.1 Different contexts for running COM code

Context Name	Associated Flag	Description
Inproc Server	CLSCTX_INPROC_SERVER	The code runs in the same process as the calling client program.
Local Server	CLSCTX_LOCAL_SERVER	The code runs in another .exe program in a different process on the same machine as the client program.
Remote Server	CLSCTX_REMOTE_SERVER	The code runs on an entirely different machine than the calling program.

The Windows Registry is used to associate the CLSID GUID of the class with a .dll, or an .exe that will create and manage the COM object when requested. All the COM classes registered on your system have entries under HKEY_CLASSES_ROOT\ CLSID identified by their GUID. They then have a key entry for each of the various types of servers registered—either InprocServer32, LocalServer32, or RemoteServer32 (and some others). Under each of these keys, you'll see the filename of the .dll or .exe that holds the code to create and manage them.

For example, Figure 25.2 shows the Registry Editor expanded to show the DirectDraw object's CLSID and its in-process handler DLL, ddraw.dll.

FIGURE 25.2

Registry Editor displaying a CLSID registration entry.

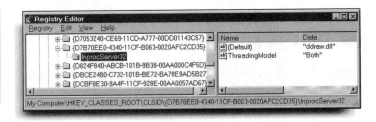

These servers implement a special COM object called a Class Object. These are like any other COM object but implement the standard `IClassFactory` interface. By calling the `CreateInstance()` function on this interface, a class of the required type can be created. Usually you would do this by using the COM library function `CoCreateInstance()` to create a single instance, or `CoGetClassObject()` to get a pointer to the class factory object. These class factories should really be called object factories because they churn out objects, not classes. (Programmers are class factories!)

`CoCreateInstance()` is defined as:

```
STDAPI CoCreateInstance(REFCLSID rclsid,
    LPUNKNOWN pUnkOuter, DWORD dwClsContext,
    REFIID riid,  LPVOID* ppv);
```

The first parameter, `rclsid`, is a reference to a GUID for the class ID (`CLSID`) of the class you need to instance. You should normally pass a `NULL` value as the second parameter `pUnkOuter`, which is used only in an advanced COM technique called aggregation. You should normally pass the `CLSCTX_SERVER` flag value to `dwClsContext`, which is used to specify the type of server required. `CLSCTX_SERVER` is just a combination of some of the flags shown in Table 25.1. The fourth parameter, `riid`, is a reference to a GUID for the interface that you require on the new COM object. The last parameter, `ppv`, is a pointer to your client's interface pointer, which will receive a pointer to the specified interface on the new object.

For example, to create an instance of the `DirectDraw` object and receive a pointer to the `IDirectDraw2` interface, you might code the following:

```
IDirectDraw2* pIDirectDraw2 = NULL;
HRESULT hr = CoCreateInstance(&CLSID_DirectDraw, NULL,
    CLSCTX_ALL, &IID_IDirectDraw2, (void**)&pIDirectDraw2);
```

If the function succeeds, a new `DirectDraw` object is created, and `pIDirectDraw2` will point to the `IDirectDraw2` interface on the new COM object.

Creating objects on remote machines

To create objects on remote machines you must use the `CoCreateInstanceEx()` function. This uses Distributed COM (DCOM), which allows communication over networked machines via Remote Procedure Calls (RPC). Client machines must be configured with the DCOMCNFG.EXE utility to register these remote COM servers.

Proxy DLLs and Marshalling

Distributing proxy DLLs

If you are marshalling between machines with DCOM, you must ensure that the same version of the proxy DLL exists on both the client and host machine.

When your client program obtains a pointer to an interface on the COM object, it doesn't care where the actual object is located. However, if the COM object is running outside your client process, the pointer can't point directly to the vtable of functions in the interface; instead, a stub is created in your process space that looks to your client like a local interface pointer. When you then call functions on that interface pointer, a technique called marshalling is performed behind the scenes to link your client and the COM object by another DLL called a proxy.

Each interface is also registered in the Windows Registry under HKEY_CLASSES_ROOT\Interface identified by their GUID. These then store keys such as ProxyStubClsid32, which hold the CLSID that identifies the location of the proxy DLL that can marshal the interface's functions. The proxy DLL is responsible for bundling the parameters into a machine-independent form for transmission. It might then use remote procedure calls (RPC) to call a function on a remote COM object. Proxy DLLs can be generated automatically by writing definitions in Interface Definition Language and passing them through the Microsoft IDL compiler (MIDL). The compiler will churn out RPC and marshalling code suitable for inclusion in a proxy DLL.

Interface Versioning

The old problem of maintaining correct software versions is solved by a simple rule. After you have released your COM object into the big wide world for people to use, you must leave its interfaces unaltered in future versions. This means that newer versions of the COM object must implement additional interfaces, leaving the original ones unaltered. Any old client programs that know how to use only the old style interface will just request that interface, whereas client programs that know about the new features can request the newer version of the interface.

The standard naming technique for these new interfaces is to add a version number after the interface. For example, the original IClassFactory interface has been upgraded to support licensing, so as well as the original, class factories can implement `IClassFactory2` with its extra methods. Client programs can then request `IClassFactory` and use `QueryInterface()` to request the more sophisticated `IClassFactory2` interface. If the COM class factory object doesn't offer this interface, a `NULL` value is set as the interface pointer from the `QueryInterface()` call, and an `S_FALSE` code is returned.

Because only the interface definition matters, COM objects are free to use the same implementation code to implement functions that remain the same on the old and new versions of the interfaces.

OLE Automation

Object Linking and Embedding (OLE) was a term originally designed to describe the capability to insert objects of various types into documents of another, such as inserting Excel worksheets into Word documents.

The documents that support linking and embedding operations are called compound documents. If you click the **Insert** menu of many applications, you'll see common **Object** menu options. Applications that support this option hold these compound documents and let you insert objects from a list of registered OLE servers.

Inserted objects can either be embedded, which means they will be saved in the current document, or linked, which means a reference to another file (called a Moniker) is inserted into the current document. These two operations gave rise to the original term OLE.

However, this term has grown to include OLE drag and drop and OLE Automation, which is where one program can call methods held in another program that runs invisibly so that the user is unaware of any interaction.

Understanding the Dispatch Interface

The automation capabilities arise from one main COM interface definition, `IDispatch`. A COM object offering a dispatch

> **Microsoft Word: automation server**
>
> If you have Microsoft Outlook and Microsoft Word installed on your machine you might find that while composing an email message with Outlook, the same spell checking features you see in Word also work in Outlook. This is an example of Word working as an automation server for Outlook. Word still does the spell check while running invisibly in the background and invoked by Outlook.

Dual interfaces

You may see the term dual interfaces used in conjunction with COM and OLE. A COM object can support dual interface by providing access to its interface functions by a direct COM interface and from a dispatch interface. This provides client programs with the best of both worlds; fast C++ programs can access the object directly via the fast direct COM interface and Visual Basic and scripting languages can access the functions via the slower dispatch interface.

interface holds a table of named methods (functions), events (functions that register client callbacks for specific notifications), and properties (functions that get or set a specific variable in the COM object). Client programs can access this type of information dynamically (called late binding) while running to discover details about the automation object.

The dispatch interface extends IUnknown by these four functions:

- GetTypeInfoCount()—Lets the client program know whether type information is available.

- GetTypeInfo()—Retrieves type information.

- GetIDsOfNames()—Returns a set of array positions (called dispatch IDs) that corresponds to the names of methods, events, or properties requested.

- Invoke()—Calls one of the functions in the dispatch array when passed the dispatch ID with a number of VARIANT parameters and sets a VARIANT result on returning (the VARIANT structure is explained in the next section).

This dispatch interface is used extensively throughout OLE in things like ActiveX controls, OLE documents, and Visual Basic Scripting. This system of looking up functions from an internal table at runtime is far slower than directly calling methods in an interface, but does allow some flexibility. Whole libraries of this type information can be produced as .tlb files; these allow Visual C++ to quickly construct skeleton classes (called dispatch drivers) that can be called with methods that look just like a local version of the automation object. These skeleton classes accept the correct parameters, then turn them into an array of VARIANTs and call the Invoke() function to call the actual OLE automation object.

Using Variants

Because the single Invoke() function is called for many different OLE automation functions, it must have a way of passing different types of parameters to the various functions being called. It does this by passing a DISPPARAMS structure that points to an array of VARIANT structures. A VARIANT structure just holds a C++

union of many different data types that can be marshaled by OLE. It also holds a variant type flag (VARTYPE) called vt that indicates which type is used. Table 25.2 shows some of the many data types that the VARIANT structure can hold. VARIANT can also hold pointers to each object that is indicated by prefixing a p to the name (such as plVal) and adding a VT_BYREF flag value to the type flag (such as VT_I4¦VT_BYREF).

Passing arrays of variant data

You can pass whole arrays of variant data to OLE functions using the COleSafeArray class. This class lets you define the type of element, number, and dimensions of the array so that you can pass large blocks of data in single calls. You should see the standard Microsoft documentation for more details about using COleSafeArray.

TABLE 25.2   Some of the available variant data types

Data Type	Name	Type Flag	Description
unsigned char	bVal	VT_UI1	A one-byte unsigned value
short	iVal	VT_I2	A two-byte signed value
long	lVal	VT_I4	A four-byte signed value
float	fltVal	VT_R4	A four-byte floating-point value
double	dblVal	VT_R8	An eight-byte floating-point value
BOOL	boolVal	VT_BOOL	A four-byte TRUE or FALSE value
SCODE	scode	VT_ERROR	A COM error code value
DATE	date	VT_DATE	A floating-point date value compatible with COleDateTime
BSTR	bstrVal	VT_BSTR	A Visual Basic–compatible string value that can be converted to and from CString
IUnknown	punkVal	VT_UNKNOWN	A pointer to an IUnknown interface
IDispatch	pdispVal	VT_DISPATCH	A pointer to an IDispatch interface

The data types held by the variant are language-independent and can be understood by any OLE-compatible language. To convert between BSTR (Visual Basic string type) and an MFC CString object, you can use CString's AllocSysString() and SetSysString() functions, which allocate a new BSTR and set an existing BSTR from the CString's contents, respectively. The reverse translation can be performed by using the (char*) and (const char*) casts to turn the BSTR into a null-terminated string.

COleDateTime can also accept a VARIANT structure directly as a constructor parameter, or a DATE type extracted by using the (DATE) cast.

Variant types aren't solely used by the dispatch interface; they can pop up in many places in OLE as a useful way of holding and transferring various types of data.

Creating an Automation Server

Many applications, such as Word, Excel, and Developer Studio itself, are automation servers. These applications offer client applications a dispatch interface that can be used to invoke their functions to provide specialist services such as spell checking.

VB Scripting (Visual Basic Scripting), the tool used to write macros, uses these methods to create and manipulate automation server documents. Whenever you write a macro for one of these programs, you are actually writing a cut-down form of Visual Basic, which can call the functions from the dispatch interface of each automation server.

Automation servers are usually associated with a human readable name that can be used to find their CLSID. These names are held in the Registry under HKEY_CLASSES_ROOT and have subkeys that refer to the CLSID for the automation server. For example, Microsoft Visual Studio has the following entry that associates it with its relevant CLSID:

```
HKEY_CLASSES_ROOT\MSDEV.APPLICATION\CLSID =
    {FB7FDAE2-89B8-11CF-9BE8-00A0C90A632C}
```

A client can then use the `CLSIDFromString()` function, passing the human readable string version of the CLSID (`MSDEV.APPLICATION`) and a pointer to a CLSID structure to be filled with the full numeric CLSID (`FB7FDAE2-89B8-11CF-9BE8-00A0C90A632C`).

The client program can then use `CoCreateInstance()` to create an invisible background running instance of Developer Studio, requesting a pointer to its dispatch interface. Automation server's .exe programs can be launched with the `/Automation` command-line flag to stop them from displaying their normal windows. When run in this mode, interaction with the server must be via a dispatch interface. Word, Excel, and all the other automation servers behave in this way, allowing client programs to use their functionality without the user being aware of the inter-program communication.

You can use the AppWizard to create an application framework for an automation server by checking the **A<u>u</u>tomation** option on Step 3 of the MFC AppWizard (see Figure 25.3).

> **Viewing the Running Object Table**
>
> Running automation servers often register themselves in a Running Object Table, so that automation clients can connect to the running instance. They perform this registration using a hook called a moniker, which is a sophisticated name that can identify programs, compound documents or sections of data. You can see these register running objects using a utility called ...\Microsoft Visual Studio\ Common\IRotview.exe. When run, IRotview.exe will display the current running (and registered) objects. Visual Studio registers its class ID as a moniker like `!(FB7FDAE2-89B8-11CF-9BE8-00A0C90A632C)`. If you load a Microsoft Word document, you'll see the name of the document registered in the Running Object Table.

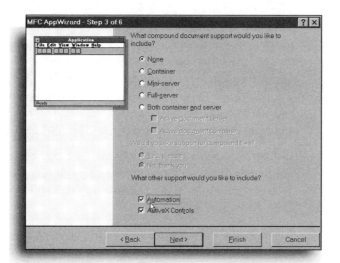

FIGURE 25.3
Adding Automation support with AppWizard.

When you create an automation framework project, you'll notice that a couple of additional files appear. One of the additional files is a .reg file that holds the registration entries required for your new automation server. You'll need this file only if you plan to install your automation server on other machines with an installation program. Your server will also create the required Registry entries automatically when you run it normally without the /Automation command-line flag.

AppWizard automatically picks a new CLSID GUID for your document, which can be seen in the new .reg file. For example, if you create an automation server framework called Autoserver, the following .reg Registry entries are generated:

```
HKEY_CLASSES_ROOT\Autoserver.Document = Autose Document
HKEY_CLASSES_ROOT\Autoserver.Document\CLSID =
    {D11ED783-CFD8-11D1-931D-444553540000}
HKEY_CLASSES_ROOT\CLSID\{D11ED783-CFD8-11D1-931D-4445535400
➥00} =
    Autose Document
HKEY_CLASSES_ROOT\CLSID\{D11ED783-CFD8-11D1-931D-4445535400
➥00}\ProgId = Autoserver.Document
HKEY_CLASSES_ROOT\CLSID\{D11ED783-CFD8-11D1-931D-4445535400
➥00}\LocalServer32 = AUTOSERVER.EXE
```

Type libraries MkTypLib and MIDL

Formerly, type libraries were compiled from object definition language (.odl) files with the MkTypLib tool. The similar interface definition language (.idl) file type was used to define interface specifications, but couldn't create type libraries. Microsoft has since rationalized this situation by extending the .idl file capabilities so that they can also specify type library information. The new Microsoft IDL compiler (MIDL) can compile both .idl and .odl files (rendering MkTypLib obsolete). Also, although .odl files still are used they aren't strictly necessary for producing type libraries because the required specification can be declared in .idl files.

The other additional file is an .odl file. This holds the object definition language that will be used to generate a type library for your new automation server. When you add new methods or properties to your automation server, new entries will be written to this file to describe the parameters used by the new functions. You don't have to worry about maintaining or compiling this file yourself because the file is entirely maintained by ClassWizard and compiled automatically when you build the project.

Listing 25.1 shows a sample .odl file for the Autoserver automation server. It has only one method, SquareRoot(), which is declared on line 26 in the IAutoserver dispatch interface, declared in lines 13 to 28.

The Autoserver example shown here implements the SquareRoot() method that simply returns a double value, representing the square root result of a double input value.

LISTING 25.1 LST26_1.ODL—An Object Definition Language File for an Automation Server Called Autoserver with One Method

```
1   //autoserver.odl:type library source for autoserver.exe
2
3   // This file will be processed by the MIDL compiler to
4   // produce the type library (autoserver.tlb).
5
6   [ uuid(D11ED784-CFD8-11D1-931D-444553540000),
    ➥version(1.0) ]
7   library Autoserver
8   {
9       importlib("stdole32.tlb");
10
11      //  Primary dispatch interface for CAutoserverDoc
12
13      [ uuid(D11ED785-CFD8-11D1-931D-444553540000) ]
14      dispinterface IAutoserver
15      {
16      properties:
17  // NOTE - ClassWizard will maintain property information
18  //    Use extreme caution when editing this section.
19          //{{AFX_ODL_PROP(CAutoserverDoc) ─────────①
20          //}}AFX_ODL_PROP
21
22      methods:
23  // NOTE - ClassWizard will maintain method information
24  //    Use extreme caution when editing this section.
25          //{{AFX_ODL_METHOD(CAutoserverDoc) ───────②
26          [id(1)] double SquareRoot(double dInputVal);
27          //}}AFX_ODL_METHOD
28      };
29
30      //  Class information for CAutoserverDoc
31
32      [ uuid(D11ED783-CFD8-11D1-931D-444553540000) ] ──────③
33      coclass Document
34      {
35          [default] dispinterface IAutoserver;
36      };
37      //{{AFX_APPEND_ODL}}
38      //}}AFX_APPEND_ODL}}
39  };
```

① ClassWizard adds OLE properties here as get/set methods.

② ClassWizard adds OLE methods here.

③ This section declares the document as a class with one dispatch interface.

The AppWizard also adds various source code to the standard framework to enable OLE automation. The InitInstance() function in the application class (CMyServerApp) must initialize the OLE and COM libraries, which it does by a call to AfxOleInit().

You'll also see an additional line to connect your application's document template to a new COleTemplateServer member variable called m_server:

```
m_server.ConnectTemplate(clsid, pDocTemplate, TRUE);
```

This template server is derived from COleObjectFactory, which is OLE's own class factory implementation. Client applications will use this class factory when they want to create a new instance of your automation server's document object via either CoCreateInstance() or CoGetClassObject() and CreateInstance().

If the application is being called as an automation server from a client application, it can register any OLE automation objects as being ready for use by the following additional lines in InitInstance():

```
if (cmdInfo.m_bRunEmbedded || cmdInfo.m_bRunAutomated)
{
    COleTemplateServer::RegisterAll();
    return TRUE;
}
```

Otherwise, you can run your automation server as a normal application and the following lines will create the required Registry entries in the Window Registry:

```
m_server.UpdateRegistry(OAT_DISPATCH_OBJECT);
COleObjectFactory::UpdateRegistryAll();
```

If you look at the AppWizard-generated document class, you'll see that there are also some additions to make the document itself an automation object.

The ID of the dispatch interface for the document is declared as a static const GUID value:

```
static const IID IID_IAutoserver =
    { 0xd11ed785, 0xcfd8, 0x11d1, { 0x93, 0x1d, 0x44, 0x45,
    ➥ 0x53, 0x54, 0x0, 0x0 } };
```

Embedded and automation command-line arguments

When a client application calls functions from an automation server .Exe application, the automation server (such as Word) must run silently in the background. OLE accomplishes this by launching the server program with a /Automation flag as a command-line argument. The ParseCommandLine() function called from the server's InitInstance() function sets the CCommandLineInfo object's m_bRunAutomated flag. The application can then test this flag, which indicates that the program is being run as an automation server from a client application rather than as a standalone application in its own right. If the program is launched with the /Embedded command-line argument, the application knows that it is being used to handle an embedded object in a *compound document*.

The dispatch interface itself is implemented with the help of some AppWizard-generated macros:

```
BEGIN_INTERFACE_MAP(CAutoserverDoc, CDocument)
  INTERFACE_PART(CAutoserverDoc, IID_IAutoserver, Dispatch)
END_INTERFACE_MAP()
```

The methods in the dispatch map are automatically added via another set of macros that maintain the dispatch map. For example, a new `SquareRoot()` method added to the Autoserver document would look like this:

```
BEGIN_DISPATCH_MAP(CAutoserverDoc, CDocument)
  //{{AFX_DISPATCH_MAP(CAutoserverDoc)
  DISP_FUNCTION(CAutoserverDoc, "SquareRoot", SquareRoot,
  ➡ VT_R8, VTS_R8)
  //}}AFX_DISPATCH_MAP
END_DISPATCH_MAP()
```

The `"SquareRoot"` string provides the dispatch interface with the method name, and the `VT_R8` and `VTS_R8` flags provide the parameter and return types (that is, the floating-point `double` values).

You shouldn't alter these macro entries yourself; ClassWizard will do this for you when you add new automation methods.

Adding an automation server method with ClassWizard

1. Press Ctrl+W or click the **View** menu and select the **ClassWizard** option to invoke ClassWizard.

2. Select the **Automation** tab and ensure that the document class is selected in the **Class Name** combo box.

3. Click the **Add Method** button to add the new method.

4. Enter an external name for the name of the method visible to client applications, such as `SquareRoot` for the `CAutoserverDoc` server, as shown in Figure 25.4.

5. You should see the internal function name to call the event shown below. This name can be modified if required, but it's usually left as the default.

6. Pick a data type to return from the new method from the **Return Type** drop-down combo box. (This should be a double for the Autoserver example.)

The `DISP_FUNCTION` macro parameters

The first parameter to the `DISP_FUNCTION` macro provides the class name of the class that implements the function. The second parameter specifies an external name for the function—this name will be seen by automation clients examining the server's dispatch interface. The third parameter provides the name of the implementing function. The fourth parameter specifies the `VARIANT` data type returned from the function. The last parameter is a space-separated list of the `VARIANT` parameter data types to be passed to the function. These parameters are defined (in AFXDISP.H) as a string of binary character values that are later converted to indexes specifying the `VARIANT` data type.

FIGURE 25.4

Adding a new method to an automation server object using ClassWizard.

7. Enter a name in the **Parameter List** such as dInputVal for the first parameter to be passed by the firing event to its owner application.

8. Select a type of variable to pass from the drop-down list under the **Type** column against the new parameter. (This should be a double for the Autoserver example.)

9. Repeat steps 6 and 7 for subsequent parameters that should be passed from a client application to the new automation server function.

10. Click **OK** to add the new method, which should then appear in the list of external names displayed in the **Automation** tab of Class Wizard.

11. Click the **Edit Code** button to start editing the new automation method code.

When you've added a new method, you can add implementation code to the method to perform whatever task your automation server should perform.

The SquareRoot() method of the Autoserver example simply returns the square root of the input value by calling the sqrt() math function:

```
#include "math.h"
double CAutoserverDoc::SquareRoot(double dInputVal)
```

```
{
    return sqrt(dInputVal);
}
```

The ClassWizard steps and your own implementation code are all you need to add a new automation method. ClassWizard automatically adds lines to the dispatch map and .odl file to generate the required OLE automation server type information for the new method.

If you build your new automation server, you'll see that the .odl file is compiled along with your normal implementation source code. In the Debug (or Release) output directory, an additional .tlb file will be generated that holds the type information library definitions for your new dispatch methods.

You can use this type library to generate an OLE dispatch driver class in a client program (as shown in the next section). You might want to distribute your type library files to other developers who want to call your automation server. For example, you can download type libraries for Word from the Microsoft Web pages (www.microsoft.com) and build client programs that can call methods from Word.

Creating an Automation Client

You can create instances of automation servers and call their methods from any type of client application. The first thing you must do is initialize the OLE libraries. This is simply done by adding a call to `AfxOleInit()` to your application's `InitInstance()` function:

```
BOOL CAutoclintApp::InitInstance()
{
    AfxOleInit();
```

You can then get ClassWizard to create an OLE dispatch driver class from a type library (.tlb file) in order to simplify calling the automation server's methods.

Adding a dispatch driver class from a type library with ClassWizard

  1. Press Ctrl+W or click the **View** menu and select the **ClassWizard** option to invoke ClassWizard.

> **Type libraries**
>
> Remember that whereas static libraries (.lib) and dynamic link libraries (.dll) store real executable code, type libraries (.tlb) store only the parameter and return type definitions for an OLE automation server. The executable code for an automation server resides on the automation server itself. For example, if you download the type library for Microsoft Word, you'll only have the information required to pass parameters to Word's functions and know what results are returned. To actually call these functions requires an installed version of Word itself.

2. Select the **Automation** tab.

3. Click the **Add Class** button and select the **From a Type Library** option from the drop-down menu.

4. Browse for the required type library file, which might be held in .tlb, .olb, or .dll files.

5. When you have found the required file, you can double-click the file and select **Open** to display the Confirm Classes dialog box.

6. You can change the default class names and implementation files to be generated from each imported class by selecting the class and changing the **Class Name**, **Header File**, or **Implementation File** edit boxes.

7. Click **OK** to import the selected classes; these will then be added to your project.

You could use the type library produced in the previous server example (autoserver.tlb) to generate autoserver.cpp and autoserver.h files that contain the IAutoserver dispatch driver class. The dispatch driver class has dummy function entries that call the invoke function (via a helped function) to call the corresponding function by table ID on the automation server's dispatch interface.

For example, the Autoserver SquareRoot() function looks like this in the dispatch driver class:

```
double IAutoserver::SquareRoot(double dInputVal)
{
    double result;
    static BYTE parms[] = VTS_R8;
    InvokeHelper(0x1, DISPATCH_METHOD, VT_R8,
    ➥(void*)&result,
        parms, dInputVal);
    return result;
}
```

The first parameter to the InvokeHelper() function above (0x1) is the ID of the SquareRoot() function in the automation server's dispatch interface's function array. The second parameter is a flag that specifies that a method call, rather than an event or

---

Dispatch driver class names

It is unfortunate that the OLE dispatch driver class produced by ClassWizard defaults to a name prefixed with the letter I. This confuses the class name with a COM interface definition (which it isn't). The OLE dispatch driver class just provides a handy wrapper for calling the IDispatch interface's Invoke() method an automation server object. You shouldn't confuse these dispatch driver class names with COM interface names.

property call, is being made. The third parameter is the returned value, which will be stored in `result`. The fourth parameter, `parms`, specifies the format of the parameter values. The following parameters are the passed parameter values that will be packed into a `DISPPARMS` parameter array by the `InvokeHelper()` function, ready for the `Invoke()` function call.

Before you can call these automation server functions, you must obtain a valid dispatch pointer to the object. If you look at the class definition header file for the dispatch driver class, you'll see that it is derived from the `COleDispatchDriver` class. This class has member functions that help with creating the dispatch interface pointer.

You can call the `CreateDispatch()` method on the dispatch driver class and pass the OLE readable string association for the required class (for example, `"Autoserver.document"`). The `CreateDispatch()` function will then find the associated CLSID from the Registry and create an instance of the required automation server class. If successful, a `TRUE` value is returned and the methods in the driver class can then be called.

Listing 25.2 shows a fragment of code that creates an instance of the new imported dispatch driver class, and then creates a dispatch interface and calls one of the automation server's methods.

You could create a dialog-based application called Autoclient to test the automation server code. You can add the code fragment shown in Listing 25.2 to the end of the dialog application's `OnInitDialog()` function (in the autoclientDlg.cpp source code-module). The `#include` in line 1 should be inserted at the top of the autoclientDlg.cpp source module.

If you then build and run the application, you should see the message box shown in Figure 25.2, the automation server program is automatically loaded behind the scenes to provide the square root functionality.

Automation object Registry entries

You'll find these automation objects listed under the **HKEY_CLASSES_ROOT** Registry key. Under each automation is a **CLSID** key that holds a default string value indicating the 128-bit GUID value identifying each auto-mation class.

LISTING 25.2   LST26_2.CPP—Initializing and Calling a Function on an
Automation Server Through a Dispatch Driver Class

```
1   // Include the dispatch driver class header file
2   #include "autoserver.h"
3
4   //.. Function declaration
5
6   // ** Initialize the dispatch driver class
7   IAutoserver IAutoserver;
8
9   // ** Create an instance of the server and connect
10  // ** to ites dispatch interface
11  if (IAutoserver.CreateDispatch("Autoserver.document"))      ①
12  {
13      // ** Call the SquareRoot method on the server program
14      double dNumber = 36.0;
15      double dRoot = IAutoserver.SquareRoot(dNumber);
16
17      // ** Display the result
18      CString strMsg;
19      strMsg.Format("Root of %f = %f\n",dNumber,dRoot);
20      AfxMessageBox(strMsg);
21  }
```

① The Create
Dispatch()
finds the CLSID for
the specified name
and the calls
CoCreateInstanc
e(), requesting the
dispatch interface.

Line 2 of Listing 25.2 includes the header file definition for the dispatch driver class (created from the type library). Lines 6 through 21 show a fragment of code that calls the automation server. An instance of the dispatch driver class is declared on line 7. The CreateDispatch() member is called on line 11 to create an instance of the automation server document object and store its dispatch interface pointer (as the m_lDispatch member). If the connection succeeds, the SquareRoot() method is called on line 15 and its resulting return value, dRoot, is displayed in the message box on line 20, as shown in Figure 25.5.

When the IAutoserver class falls out of scope, the dispatch interface will be automatically released by the class's destructor function.

Alternatively, you can call the dispatch driver's ReleaseDispatch() member function to release the dispatch driver. It also has

`AttachDispatch()` and `DetachDispatch()` methods to dynamically attach and detach a dispatch interface pointer already connected to an automation server object.

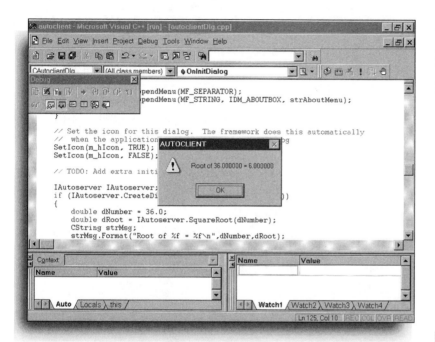

FIGURE 25.5
The operation of the OLE automation example.

OLE Containers, Servers, and Mini-Servers

An OLE server is an application that can be launched from within the window of a container application. For example, Excel worksheets can be inserted and edited from Word. In this situation, Word is acting as an OLE container application and Excel is acting as an OLE server application.

Applications can be both OLE containers and OLE servers, in which case they can act in either role. Word and Excel are good examples of this because you can run Excel and insert Word documents, and vice versa.

A full server can run as an application in its own right or as an inserted object, whereas mini-servers can be launched only from a container program.

Active documents

You may see the term Active Documents used in conjunction with OLE servers and containers. These are relatively new ActiveX-related technologies that extend the OLE container/server architecture to allow embedded objects to take control of the whole client area of the container (rather than a small frame) and directly manipulate the container's frame, menus, and toolbars. You can find more information about Active Documents in the standard Microsoft documentation by searching for `IOleDocument` and its related interfaces.

671

OLE containers support the **Insert/Object** menu option. The Windows WordPad application is an OLE server. You can use WordPad to test OLE servers by clicking the **Insert** menu and then selecting the **Object** option. You'll see a list of registered OLE servers that can be inserted into the WordPad document.

When an OLE server object is inserted, it can be edited inside a rectangular area described with a thick black hashed border called an in-place frame. This process is called in-place activation and is initiated by passing flag values, called verbs, from the container to the server. When inactive, the border disappears and the image displayed is the last image rendered while active (stored and played by a metafile device context). When active, the border is shown and menu items from the in-place server object are added to the container's own menu.

The data for the embedded document can be serialized by the container document using the standard document serialization functions. The server documents are passed a `CArchive` object from the container's document to serialize each server item's own specific data.

You can use AppWizard to create the basic framework for OLE servers and OLE containers; however, there is some sophisticated cooperation between the container and server that must be implemented to ensure that both work properly.

The basic framework for OLE servers is extended by two additional classes to support in-place editing. One of the classes is a server item class that is a derivation of `COleServerItem`. This is used to represent the embedded item that is shown in the container and supports `OnDraw()` functions to draw the embedded item on request from the container. It also has an `OnDoVerb()` function that handles requests to show, open, or hide the embedded item from the container application. The container can also communicate with the server via an `IOleObject` interface offered by the server item.

The other class is an in-place frame window, which is a derivation of `COleIPFrameWnd`. This class is used to implement the server's own toolbars and menu options in place of the container's own menu options when the server is activated.

Compound documents: embedding and linking

Although the embedded document is stored completely inside the client application's *compound document*, linked objects are simply stored as monikers. A *moniker* is a small object that uniquely identifies where the real data resides and how it should be displayed when viewed inside the client application.

The framework generated for a container just adds one additional class, which is a derivation of `COleClientItem`. This new class has numerous functions that help create and maintain linked or embedded items in a compound document. It also provides the container side link to the server item, communicating through verbs via a `DoVerb()` function and several functions designed to maintain the correct position of the server item and its activation status.

By customizing the two server classes and the additional container class, you can support fairly sophisticated capabilities of in-place editing while running inside the frame of a container application's window. Neither the server nor container need to know what sort of object it is embedded in or is containing. As long as the server and client items follow the same standards, container and server can be seamlessly integrated to appear to the user as a single application.

chapter 26

Creating ActiveX Controls

Active Template Library ActiveX controls

This chapter covers Microsoft Found-ation Classes (MFC)–based ActiveX controls, but you can also create ActiveX controls developed with the Active Template Library (ATL). ActiveX controls built using ATL are generally faster and need less memory than MFC-based ActiveX controls. However, you can't easily mix and match MFC classes with ATL classes. ATL is itself a huge and complex subject and therefore beyond the scope of this book. If you require very fast, sophisticated, and memory light ActiveX controls, you should con-sider investigating ATL and the ATL COM AppWizard options instead of the MFC route.

Creating an ActiveX Framework with the ActiveX Control Wizard

A special AppWizard is available specifically for writing ActiveX control frameworks. This wizard helps with the code generation, licensing, and help support for your new control. You can invoke this wizard by clicking the **File** menu and selecting **New** to display the New dialog box. If you select the **Projects** tab, you should see an **MFC ActiveX ControlWizard** option. Select this option to insert a new control called **Rotary (Project Name)**.

Specifying the Number of Controls, Licensing, and Help

The first step of the MFC ActiveX ControlWizard (shown in Figure 26.1) lets you add various levels of support to the new ActiveX control project.

FIGURE 26.1
MFC ActiveX ControlWizard - Step 1 of 2.

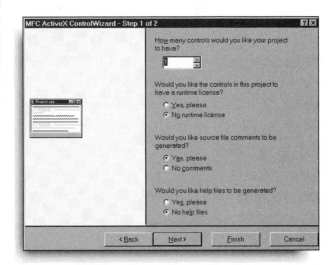

- The first question asks **How many controls would you like your project to have?**. If you increase this from the default value of 1, it will generate a control class and property page classes for each control.

676

- The next question asks **Would you like the controls in this project to have a runtime license?**. If you answer yes to this question, license-checking functions will be added to your classes and a default .lic license file will be generated. Your control can then be distributed only with a valid license file.

- The next question, **Would you like source file comments to be generated ?**, adds source code comments to the framework as with the SDI and MDI AppWizards.

- The last question on the Step 1 of 2 page is **Would you like help files to be generated?**. If you answer yes to this, context help files will be generated with the project.

Specifying the Class Names and Usage Options

Step 2 of 2 lets you specify a whole range of settings that affect how your control appears and is used (see Figure 26.2).

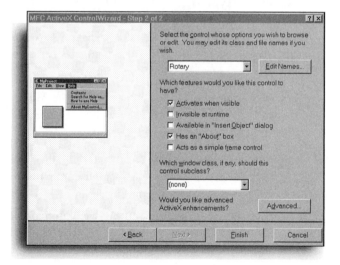

FIGURE 26.2
MFC ActiveX
ControlWizard - Step
2 of 2.

The initial combo box and **Edit Names** button lets you override the default file and class names for the control selected in the combo box. When you click the **Edit Names** button, you'll see a list of files and class names that will be generated for that control as shown in Figure 26.3.

FIGURE 26.3

The Edit Names dialog box lets you modify the default framework class and filenames.

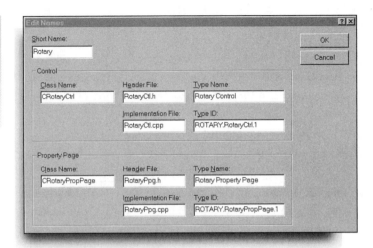

There is a class for the control itself (`CRotaryCtrl`) and a class for its associated property page `CRotaryPropPage`. Because ActiveX controls are COM/OLE objects, you'll see the associated **Type Name** and **Type ID** listed on the right side of the Edit Names dialog box. These names will be used from Visual Basic, Scripting, or other languages that want to use the ActiveX control. Any of these class, file-, or type names can be changed at this point.

If you close this dialog box and return to the MFC ActiveX ControlWizard - Step 2 of 2 dialog box (Figure 26.2), you'll see a list of features available to the control.

- **Activates when Visible.** This is normally checked and requests that the control container automatically activates the control when it becomes visible.

- **Invisible at Runtime.** You can write ActiveX controls that don't actually display anything, but can be included in OLE containers to add some functionality.

- **Available in "Insert Object" Dialog.** If you want a user to be able to include your control in a Word, Excel, or HTML file, you would tick this box.

- **Has an "About" Box.** Adds an About dialog box to the project.

- **Acts as a Simple Frame Control.** Sets the status information that allows this control to contain other Windows controls.

Subclassing Existing Controls to Gain Functionality

You can use the last combo box on the page to pick a control from which you want to subclass (or base) the ActiveX control. This lets you extend the functionality of a normal Windows control. For example, if you're improving the standard scrollbar, you could subclass from the scrollbar to build upon the scrollbar functionality.

Using Advanced ActiveX Features

You can click the **Advanced** button to display the Advanced ActiveX features. These features let you set the following options:

- **Windowless Activation.** Set this option so that your control uses the containers window rather than a window of its own that is faster but requires some work to implement.

- **Unclipped Device Context.** If your control is well-behaved and won't draw outside its own region, this will provide a small speed gain.

- **Flicker-Free Activation.** Controls normally redraw themselves when activated or deactivated, but if there is no difference in the display of both states, you can check this flag to cancel the redraw requests.

- **Mouse Pointer Notifications When Inactive.** Setting this option enables an interface to process mouse movement notifications even when the control is inactive.

- **Optimized Drawing Code.** Some containers might support a mode that preserves the handles for the GDI objects used in the controls. You can test this and if supported, write drawing code that reuses these handles.

Handling reflected control messages

One of the main tasks involved in subclassing an existing Windows control is to handle messages that would normally be sent from the Windows control to its parent window. To stop these messages from being sent directly to the container window, the derived control class (COleControl) creates a dummy window that acts like the control's parent window and receives the messages sent from the control. You must then intercept relevant messages from the control and where necessary fire an ActiveX event from your control.

> ■ **Loads Properties Asynchronously.** If your control is embedded in a Web page, you can implement asynchronous downloading to get the user interface running as soon as possible. You can leave images and other properties that are slower to download and less important until the more important properties have loaded.

SEE ALSO

➤ *For more information on using ActiveX controls, see page 196*

Implementing the Control

ActiveX control project classes

Whenever you create an MFC-based ActiveX control with AppWizard, you'll see several classes created to implement the ActiveX control framework. One application class has an `InitInstance()` and `ExitInstance()` implementation derived from the `COleControlModule` class. Another class maintains the control's property pages and is derived from `COlePropertyPage`. Finally the main control class is derived from `COleControl`, which brings together the various aspects of an ActiveX control. Also note that `COleControl` itself is derived from `CWnd` to provide the normal functionality associated with a window. This helps provide the familiar environment associated with the `CWnd` member functions and event handlers you've already seen in dialog boxes and views.

The business of an ActiveX control is to provide interaction with the user. To do this it must usually draw a user interface, handle event messages from keyboard, mouse, or other input devices, and be able to transform those events into a representation that the user will understand and that the application using the control can access and use. Usually properties can be set by the application to change the default appearance or behavior of the control. The control is therefore a mini-application in its own right and should be thought of as such. If you have written Windows message handling applications, you'll recognize the standard MFC architecture used to implement ActiveX controls.

For a sample exercise, you can write a rotary knob control that behaves like a volume or brightness control. You should leave all the AppWizard project settings as the default for the Rotary ActiveX sample.

Drawing the Control

The drawing code should be pretty familiar to you if you've implemented any other MFC-based drawing such as in SDI/MDI and dialog-based applications. The `OnDraw()` function of the control's main `CRotaryCtrl` is called to render the control. However, the parameters passed are slightly different than the normal `OnDraw()`. The first parameter is the normal pointer to a device context. The next parameter is a rectangle reference holding the bounds of the control, and the third a rectangle reference holding the invalid region that must be redrawn.

To draw the rotary control, you can convert a mouse click or move position into an angle that corresponds to the position of the click as a vector from the center point of the control. A small circle can be drawn at a position 90 percent of the height and width from the center, and a larger circle can represent the body of a rotary control. A line from the center to the notch position should provide a clear directional position very much like a familiar volume or brightness knob.

Listing 26.1 LST27_1.CPP—Implementing the ActiveX Control *OnDraw()* Function

```
1   void CRotaryCtrl::OnDraw(CDC* pdc,
2     const CRect& rcBounds,const CRect& rcInvalid)
3   {
4     // ** Set up the background and foreground brushes
5     CBrush brForeGnd(RGB(0,255,0));
6     CBrush brBackGnd(TranslateColor(AmbientBackColor()));
7
8     // ** Draw the control background
9     pdc->FillRect(rcBounds, &brBackGnd);
10
11    CBrush* pOldBrush = pdc->SelectObject(&brForeGnd);
12
13    // ** Calculate the relative positions and midpoint
14    CPoint ptRelative = m_ptClicked - rcBounds.TopLeft();
15    CPoint ptMid(rcBounds.Width()/2,rcBounds.Height()/2);
16
17    // ** Find offset from the middle
18    double dRelX = ptRelative.x - ptMid.x;
19    double dRelY = ptRelative.y - ptMid.y;
20
21    // ** Use trig to find the angle by T=O/A
22    double dAngle = atan2(dRelY,dRelX);
23    double dRadX = (double)ptMid.x * 0.9;
24    double dRadY = (double)ptMid.y * 0.9;
25
26    // ** Find a point on the radius of the knob
27    int nXPos = ptMid.x + (int)(cos(dAngle) * dRadX);
28    int nYPos = ptMid.y + (int)(sin(dAngle) * dRadY);
29
```

(1) The container's ambient background color setting is used so that the control's background color matches the container window.

(2) Trigonometry is used to find the angle from

continues...

681

③ The main rotary ellipse draws the large circle indicating the control, while the small ellipse draws a notch mark at the radius.

Listing 26.1 Continued

```
30   // ** Set the notch point position
31   CPoint ptKnob=CPoint(nXPos,nYPos)+rcBounds.TopLeft();
32
33   // ** Set a rect and draw the notch circle
34   CRect rcPoint(ptKnob-CSize(4,4),CSize(8,8));
35   pdc->Ellipse(rcPoint); ———③
36
37   // ** Draw the main rotary circle
38   pdc->Ellipse(ptMid.x-(int)dRadX,ptMid.y-(int)dRadY,
39               ptMid.x+(int)dRadX,ptMid.y+(int)dRadY);
40
41   // ** Draw a line from the center to the notch
42   pdc->MoveTo(ptMid);
43   pdc->LineTo(ptKnob);
44
45   pdc->SelectObject(pOldBrush);
46 }
```

Setting ambient properties

There are a number of ambient properties common to all ActiveX controls. These properties let the control blend in with its parent application. Because you can't possibly know in what type of application your control may be used, you should implement as many of these ambient properties as possible. **Spell check doesn't work?**

The OnDraw() implementation in Listing 26.1 implements just such rendering. Lines 5 and 6 construct a foreground and background brush in the colors RGB(0,255,0) (Green) and AmbientBackColor(). There is also a corresponding AmbientForeColor() function. These functions return two of the ambient properties common to all controls. When used in a container, these properties will inherit their values from the container itself, but you can also set these properties from the container application programmatically or by making them available in the accompanying property sheet. I've hard coded the foreground color to green because the AmbientForeColor() isn't always supported. The background color is then used in line 9 to draw the background; in production code you'd probably optimize this so that the main knob circle isn't drawn over by this rectangle to reduce flicker.

Because the rectangles passed hold the coordinate space of the control in its container, coordinates relative to the control's top-left point must be calculated to transform the mouse position m_ptClicked into relative coordinates in line 14. Line 15 calculates the relative midpoint of the control.

Lines 17 through 28 use trigonometry to calculate an angle from the mouse position relative to the center of the control, and then convert the angle back into a position 90 percent from the center of the control to draw the notch (line 35). To use the trig functions, you'll need to add an include file for the math function declarations after the other includes at the top of RotaryCtrl.cpp like this:

```
#include "math.h"
```

In Line 38 the larger main circle is drawn to represent the rotary control itself and is drawn over the notch circle so that the notch becomes a bump on the main circle's circumference.

Lines 42 and 43 then draw a line from the center to this bump to represent the angular position of the rotary control.

You must also add the `m_ptClicked` position as a `CPoint` member variable of the `CRotaryCtrl` class. You can do this by using the Add Member Variable dialog box that can be invoked from the context menu over the `CRotaryCtrl` class in the ClassView pane. This will add the variable to the `CRotaryCtrl` class definition like this:

```
CPoint m_ptClicked;
```

SEE ALSO

➤ *For detail on drawing lines and circles, see page 384*

➤ *If you're unsure how to add the* `CPoint m_ptClicked` *member variable, see page 183*

Handling User Events and Input

The mouse position `m_ptClicked` is used in Listing 26.1 to convert the user input into an angle. You must add code to set up this member variable whenever the user clicks the control or moves the mouse with the left button held down. You can add a Windows message handler function to catch the `WM_LBUTTONDOWN` message, store the clicked position, and start the mouse capture mode as shown in Listing 26.2.

Using the math.h header file

Although all the mathematics functions are linked with your code in the standard C++ runtime library, you'll need to include the math.h header file to declare the function prototypes for the compiler. These functions include a wide range of common mathematical functions to provide trigonometry, logarithms, rounding support, and several double and float type conversion functions.

① The clicked position is stored for later to draw the control indicator in OnDraw( ).

Listing 26.2 LST27_2.CPP—Implementing the *OnLButtonDown()* Handler to Store the Mouse Position and Start Mouse Capture

```
1   void CRotaryCtrl::OnLButtonDown(UINT nFlags, CPoint point)
2   {
3       // ** Call the base class
4       COleControl::OnLButtonDown(nFlags, point);
5
6       // ** Start Mouse Capture
7       SetCapture();
8
9       // ** Store the clicked point
10      m_ptClicked = point;              ①
11
12      // ** Redraw the control
13      InvalidateControl();
14  }
```

In Listing 26.2, the mouse capture is started by the SetCapture() function on line 7. The new class member variable m_ptClicked is used on line 10 to store the mouse click position. Finally, the InvalidateControl() is analogous to an Invalidate() function in a normal window in that it marks that the whole control needs redrawing. You could also pass a rectangle to InvalidateControl() to indicate that just a portion held in the rectangle needs redrawing.

When the user has pressed the mouse button, the control position must be rotated to represent the position of the mouse when moved. To do this, you should add a handler for the WM_MOUSEMOVE message. You can use the wizard again to do this and produce an OnMouseMove() handler function as shown in Listing 26.3.

Listing 26.3 LST27_3.CPP—Implementing the *OnMouseMove()* Handler Function to Store and Move the Control Position

```
1   void CRotaryCtrl::OnMouseMove(UINT nFlags, CPoint point)
2   {
3       // ** Check whether the left mouse button is held down
4       if (nFlags & MK_LBUTTON)
```

684

```
5    {
6        // ** Store the moved position
7        m_ptClicked = point;
8
9        // ** Redraw the control
10       InvalidateControl();  ——————( 1 )
11   }
12
13   // ** Call the base class function
14   COleControl::OnMouseMove(nFlags, point);
15 }
```

(1) If the left mouse button is held down, the control position is updated and redrawn as the mouse moves.

Line 4 of Listing 26.3 checks that the left mouse button is held down by testing the nFlags parameter for the MK_LBUTTON flag. If set, the point position can be updated and the control redrawn to reflect the movement.

Finally, you'll need to catch the WM_LBUTTONUP message with the wizard-generated OnLButtonUp() handler function to release the mouse capture. When you've added this handler, you only need to add the ReleaseCapture() function before the base class call, like this:

```
ReleaseCapture();
```

SEE ALSO

➤ *For a detailed explanation of mouse events and mouse capture, see page 176*

Quick Partial Testing of the Control

At this point, enough code exists to build the control. If you build the control at this point, you'll notice the extra automatic build step:

```
Registering ActiveX Control...
```

This step registers the control using the regsrvr32.exe program, which actually only calls a global function in your control DllRegisterServer(void), which does the work of registering the control. You can see this function and its companion unregister function DllUnregisterServer(void) in the Rotary.cpp implementation.

685

You can't run the control directly because it's designed to be used in a container application. But if you remember from Chapter 9, "Using ActiveX Controls," you can add ActiveX controls to a dialog box. Now that your new control is registered, you can use the resource editor to add the control to the ActiveX control's own About dialog box (IDD_ABOUTBOX_ROTARY). You can do this by first selecting the IDD_ABOUTBOX_ROTARY into the dialog resource editor for editing (by double-clicking IDD_ABOUTBOX_ROTARY from the dialog resources list in the Project Workspace view). Then you can add the control to the About dialog as normal by right-clicking and choosing the **Insert Active<u>X</u> Control** option.

You can then use Ctrl+T or click the **<u>L</u>ayout** menu and choose **<u>T</u>est** to try out your new control (see Figure 26.4). From the resource editor's dialog tester, you should be able to click the new rotary control and move the mouse to reposition it to point to any angle.

FIGURE 26.4
Quick and dirty testing using the project's own About dialog box.

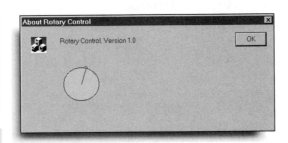

When you've finished testing it, remember to delete the control from the About dialog box because it doesn't belong there and could cause all sorts of nasty problems.

SEE ALSO
➤ *To add an ActiveX control to a dialog box, see page 201*

Implementing Event Firing

A control must inform its owner application that the user has changed its state in some way. An ActiveX control is no exception, and you should add a handler to the Rotary control to inform the owner application when it has been repositioned. This process is called *event firing*, and you can use ClassWizard to add an ActiveX event by following these steps.

Adding an ActiveX control event with ClassWizard

1. Press Ctrl+W or click the **View** menu and select the **ClassWizard** option to invoke ClassWizard.

2. Select the **ActiveX Events** tab.

3. Click the **Add Event** button to add the new event.

4. Enter an external name for the name of the event visible to owner applications in the **External Name** combo such as Repositioned for the Rotary Control (see Figure 26.5).

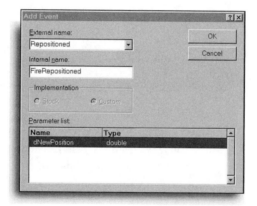

5. You should see the internal function name to call (which fires the event) shown in the **Internal Name** box; this name can be modified if required but is usually left as default.

6. Enter a name in the **Parameter List** such as dNewPosition for the first parameter to be passed by the firing event to its owner application.

7. Select a type of variable to pass from the drop list under the **Type** column against the new parameter.

8. Repeat steps 6 and 7 for subsequent parameters that should be passed to the owner application when informed of the new event.

9. Click **OK** to add the new event, which should then appear in the list of **External** names as shown in the **ActiveX Events** tab (see Figure 26.6).

FIGURE 26.6
The **ActiveX Events** tab of ClassWizard shows the control's current output events.

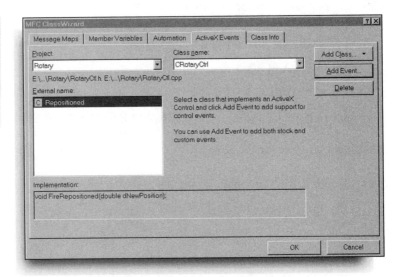

When you've completed these steps, you should have a new function, `FireRepositioned()`, listed under the `CRotaryCtrl` class in the ClassView pane. This will fire the external `Repositioned` event, which will be visible to external applications using this ActiveX control.

Now you should add code to fire this event when the user releases the left mouse button (which indicates that the rotary control has been moved). Before you can do this, you must store the current position in the control class. You can add a new member variable to the class by using the New Member Variable dialog box, or by adding the following line directly to the `CRotaryCtrl` class definition:

```
double m_dCurrentPosition;
```

This `double` will store an angle in the range 0° to 360° to represent the position of the rotary control from East (0°) through North (90°), West (180°) and back to East (360/0°). You can set this value from the angle calculated in the `OnDraw()` function by adding the following line to the end:

```
m_dCurrentPosition = dAngle * 57.2978 + 180.0;
```

This will convert the calculated angle from radians to degrees and store the result in the new `m_dCurrentPosition` member variable.

You can then fire the event to inform the application that the user has moved the control inside the `OnLButtonUp()` function. To do this, you should add a call to the new event firing function (`FireRepositioned()`). This can be added after the `ReleaseCapture()` function in the `OnLButtonUp()` handler and passed the current position variable, like this:

```
FireRepositioned(m_dCurrentPosition);
```

Now whenever the user changes the control position and releases the mouse button, the application will receive a `Repositioned` event from your control. This event can be implemented easily using ClassWizard as you saw when using ActiveX controls in Chapter 9, "Using ActiveX Controls."

SEE ALSO
➤ *For an explanation of Windows messages and events, see page 69*
➤ *For information on adding an ActiveX event handler function, see page 208*

Creating the Properties Interface

Your ActiveX control will, like any other, probably have several properties that you or a developer can change during the design phase of a control—that is, while designing a dialog box using the control. The developer using your control should also be able to change these properties from the application programmatically.

These properties are associated with OLE automation functions so that the control can be used and changed from Visual C++ applications, Visual Basic applications, a Web browser, or any other program that knows how to talk to dispatch interfaces.

SEE ALSO
➤ *For information on OLE automation, see page 657*

Implementing the Stock Properties

When you add a property to a control, you are really adding new entries in the control's OLE dispatch interface. These entries are

The three types of properties

The ActiveX control's properties can be divided into three main categories. Ambient properties are those properties inherited from the control's container to help it blend into the client application more naturally. Stock properties are shared by all controls, such as colors, fonts, and enabled statuses. Custom properties are those that you must add to your control, and are specific to its operation.

689

associated with a unique word so that other languages will be able to find the property associated with that word in the control's OLE dispatch interface. Several stock properties, as shown in Table 26.1, are common to all ActiveX controls. The foreground and background colors are two such stock properties, and are called `BackColor` and `ForeColor`. You can add these stock properties to your control with ClassWizard. Follow these steps to add a `ForeColor` stock property that will let applications change the foreground color of the rotary control.

Adding an ActiveX control stock property with ClassWizard

1. Press Ctrl+W or click the **View** menu and select the **ClassWizard** option to invoke ClassWizard.

2. Select the **Automation** tab.

3. Click the **Add Property** button to display the Add Property dialog box.

4. Pick a stock property name from the **External Names** combo box's drop list such as `ForeColor` for the Rotary control (see Figure 26.7). You should see the other boxes disabled after choosing a stock property.

5. Click **OK** to add the stock property, which should then appear in the list of **External Names** in ClassWizard's **Automation** tab.

FIGURE 26.7

Adding a stock property with the ClassWizard Add Property dialog box.

Table 26.1   Stock properties available to an ActiveX control

Property Name	Accessed By	Description
BackColorGet	GetBackColor() SetBackColor()	Maintains the background color
ForeColor	GetForeColor() SetForeColor()	Maintains the foreground color
Font	GetFont() SetFont() InternalGetFont()	Maintains the current font
Caption	InternalGetText()	Maintains caption text
Text	InternalGetText()	Same as Caption
BorderStyle	m_sBorderStyle	ccNone or ccFixedSingle (single border)
Appearance	m_sAppearance	1 for 3D effect, 0 for flat look

After you've added the ForeColor stock property, you'll see ForeColor appear under the _DRotary interface entry in the ClassView pane of the Project Workspace view. You can change OnDraw() to set the foreground brush to this foreground color using the GetForeColor() function:

```
CBrush brForeGnd(TranslateColor(GetForeColor()));
```

Adding the Stock Color Property Page

When using the control at design time, you can help the developer using your control set the foreground stock color more easily by adding the stock color property page to your control. This page is identified by a CLSID_CColorPropPage and there is another for fonts called CLSID_CFontPropPage. In your CRotaryCtrl class implementation file, RotaryCtrl.cpp, you should be able to find a // Property Pages section. This holds a table of the current property pages associated with your control. When adding your control to a dialog box in the resource editor, the user/developer can right-click the control to change the properties. Doing this will display the pages held in this table along with the **General** and **All** tabs as discussed in Chapter 9. Currently, your rotary control will just hold the one ClassWizard-generated property page:

OLE_COLOR and TranslateColor()

Use the TranslateColor() function to change between the OLE_COLOR data type returned from the OLE-specific functions to the COLORREF data types used by the standard Windows functions. OLE_COLOR extends the COLORREF data type's 24-bit color specification with a set of flags that indicate alternative methods of storing the color information. One alternative is to store indexes for standard system colors that can be used with GetSysColor() to get the local machine's system color settings. Alternatively, it can also specify colors as palette indexes rather than just a 24-bit TrueColor value as in COLORREF.

Changing the property page count

Don't forget to change the count of pages when adding new property pages; otherwise, Developer Studio will crash when you display the control properties from the resource editor.

```
BEGIN_PROPPAGEIDS(CRotaryCtrl, 1)
    PROPPAGEID(CRotaryPropPage::guid)
END_PROPPAGEIDS(CRotaryCtrl)
```

You can add the stock color page just by adding the following entry after your default page (CRotaryPropPage::guid) and updating the number of pages to two in the BEGIN_PROPPAGEIDS macro:

```
BEGIN_PROPPAGEIDS(CRotaryCtrl, 2)
    PROPPAGEID(CRotaryPropPage::guid)
    PROPPAGEID(CLSID_CColorPropPage)
END_PROPPAGEIDS(CRotaryCtrl)
```

You can build the control after making these changes and test it by adding a rotary control to the project's IDD_ABOUTBOX_ROTARY dialog box in the resource editor. The control will appear completely black with the foreground color set to the default value (zero). If you press Alt+Enter to change its properties, you'll see your new ForeColor stock property in the **All** tab with the OLECOLOR value it holds shown against it (see Figure 26.8). By clicking the ... button, you can select a color from the Colors page to use as the color value. The new color is displayed automatically as shown in Figure 26.9. When you've chosen a new color, close the properties dialog box and your control should be drawn in the new foreground color.

FIGURE 26.8
The **All** tab of the control's property sheet showing the new ForeColor property.

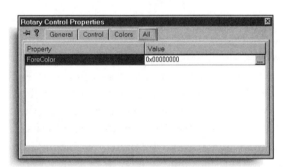

Adding Custom Properties

You can add your own custom properties to the control, and add property page controls to maintain them. For example, you could add tick marks to the rotary control to let the user judge its position better, and let the dialog box designer specify the number of tick marks to add.

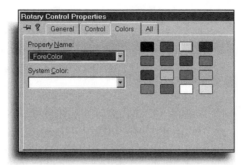

FIGURE 26.9
The stock **Colors** tab of the control's property sheet.

You can add two custom properties using ClassWizard from the **Automation** tab in a similar fashion to the stock properties. Instead of picking a stock property from the **External Names** combo box, you can enter your own custom property such as TicksEnable to enable tick marks around the control. As you enter, you'll see that a variable name of m_ticksEnable appears as the **Variable Name** and a **Notification Function**, OnTicksEnableChanged, is automatically generated for you. Rather than using a member variable, you can change the methods to Get and Set methods by clicking the **Get/Set Methods** radio button. This will then show a **Get Function** and a **Set Function** name of GetTicksEnable and SetTicksEnable. From the **Type** combo box, choose BOOL for this Boolean value as shown in Figure 26.10.

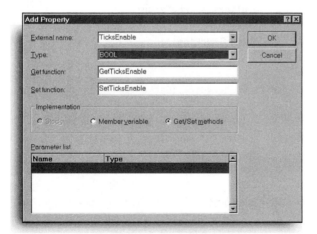

FIGURE 26.10
Adding a custom property with the Add Property dialog box.

693

You can click **OK** to add these new methods and insert another property, called NumTicks, for the number of tick marks to be displayed, again choosing the **Get/Set Methods** radio button and specifying a **Type** of short to store the number of check marks.

To implement these functions, you can select the **External Name** for each property, and click the **Edit Code** button (from the ClassWizard **Automation** tab) to start editing the property's new Get and Set functions. Whenever a Set method is called, you'll want to store the passed new property value in the class to use when drawing. Whenever the corresponding Get method is called, you can return that stored property. These changes are shown in Listing 26.4.

> **External property names**
>
> These external property names are just like the external names used in OLE Automation. They will be stored in the lookup table of an **IDispatch** interface so that a client program (such as the ActiveX control test container) can determine the available properties at runtime.

Listing 26.4 LST27_4.CPP—Implementing the Custom Property *Get/Set* Functions

```
1   BOOL CRotaryCtrl::GetTicksEnable()
2   {
3       // TODO: Add your property handler here
4       return m_bTicks;
5   }
6
7   void CRotaryCtrl::SetTicksEnable(BOOL bNewValue)
8   {
9       // TODO: Add your property handler here
10      m_bTicks = bNewValue;
11
12      SetModifiedFlag();
13  }
14
15  short CRotaryCtrl::GetNumTicks()
16  {
17      // TODO: Add your property handler here
18
19      return m_sNumTicks;
20  }
21
22  void CRotaryCtrl::SetNumTicks(short nNewValue)
23  {
24      // TODO: Add your property handler here
25
```

```
26      m_sNumTicks = nNewValue;
27
28      SetModifiedFlag();
29  }
```

In Listing 26.4, two new member variables from the CRotaryCtrl class are used (m_bTicks and m_sNumTicks) to store the enable state and the number of ticks respectively. In the Get/Set methods for tick marks shown in lines 1 through 13, this value is returned or set. The same thing happens for the m_sNumTicks value for the NumTicks property in lines 15 through 29. You should add these member variables to the class definition directly or by the Add Member Variable dialog box to add these two definitions to the CRotaryCtrl definition:

```
short m_sNumTicks;
BOOL m_bTicks;
```

and set up default values for these member variables in the CRotaryCtrl constructor function CRotaryCtrl::CRotaryCtrl() like this:

```
// TODO: Initialize your control's instance data here.
m_bTicks = TRUE;
m_sNumTicks = 20;
```

If you open the _DRotary interface entry in the ClassView pane, you should see entries for the new TicksEnable and NumTicks properties.

Adding Property Page Controls for the Custom Properties

The new Get and Set methods will let an application using your control change the custom properties, but you should also add a user interface for dialog designers to change the properties from the resource editor.

Select the ResourceView pane of the Project Workspace view and find the IDD_PROPPAGE_ROTARY dialog box. You can add controls for the new custom properties to this dialog box. The TicksEnable property can be represented by a check box labeled

Property page properties

By designing a property page for your custom properties, you are providing the implementation of the user interface to maintain these control-specific properties. When a developer adds your control to his dialog box and presses Alt+Enter to change the control properties, your custom property page will appear between the **General Properties** tab and **Stock Properties** tab of the control just like any ordinary Windows control.

Show Tick Marks with an ID of IDC_TICKS_ENABLED. You can use a numeric edit control with an ID of IDC_NUM_TICKS to represent the number of tick marks. A spin control with the buddy flags (**Auto Buddy** and **Set Buddy Integer** from the **Styles** tab of the Spin Properties dialog box) can be added to this edit control to let the designer easily change the number of tick marks as shown in Figure 26.11.

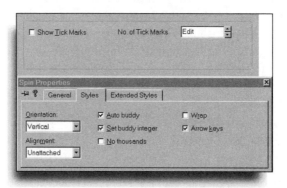

FIGURE 26.11
Adding controls to the ActiveX control's property page.

There is an easy way to map the control values to the custom properties using ClassWizard. You can map the **Show Tick Marks** check box to the TicksEnable property by following the "Mapping Custom Properties with ClassWizard" steps.

Mapping custom properties with ClassWizard

1. Select the control you want to map (the **Show Tick Marks** check box on the IDD_PROPPAGE_ROTARY dialog box in the Rotary ActiveX control example) and press Ctrl+W to invoke ClassWizard and ensure that the **Member Variables** tab is selected.

2. Select the **IDC_TICKS_ENABLED** ID from the **Control IDs** list.

3. Click the **Add Variable** button to add the new mapped property. You should see the **Add Member Variable** dialog box displayed as shown in Figure 26.12.

4. Enter m_bTicksEnabled for the **Member Variable Name**.

5. Enter TicksEnabled for the **Optional Property Name** as shown in Figure 26.12.

6. Click **OK** to add the new mapped name.

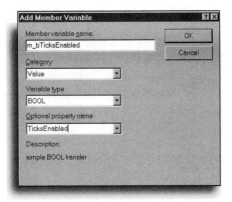

FIGURE 26.12

Mapping a custom property to the control in the Add Member Variable dialog box.

You could repeat the preceding steps to map the `IDC_NUM_TICKS` **Control ID** to a member variable called `m_sNumTicks`, with a **Variable Type** of `short`. You can also map the variable to a custom property (called `NumTicks`) by specifying the **Optional Property Name** as `NumTicks`. When you click **OK** to the Add Member Variable dialog box, the code for these maps will be created, and the new entries will be added to the list of mapped variables in the ClassWizard **Member Variables** tab.

You can set a validation range for mapped integer variables, allowing the user to only enter values in a specific range (such as between 1 and 100). To do this, you should select your new mapped integer (`m_sNumTicks`) from the list in the **Member Variables** tab; when selected, two edit controls appear at the bottom of the **Automation** tab to let you specify the validation range. You can enter 1 for the **Minimum Value** and 100 as the **Maximum Value** as shown in Figure 26.13 to set an allowable number of tick marks between 1 to 100.

ClassWizard maps these property sheet properties to the OLE interfaces by adding these special `DDP` macro entries to the `CRotaryPropPage` class's `DoDataExchange()` function like this:

```
DDP_Check(pDX, IDC_TICKS_ENABLED, m_bTicksEnabled,
➥ _T("TicksEnable") );
DDP_Text(pDX, IDC_NUM_TICKS, m_sNumTicks, _T("NumTicks") );
```

Now whenever the designer sets the control settings, he will be updated to your ActiveX control's custom `Get` and `Set` methods.

FIGURE 26.13

Setting the Validation range for the m_sNumTicks member variable.

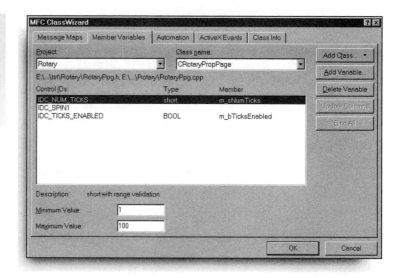

Making Properties Persistent

When you set properties in a control from the resource editor, those properties stay set when you use or redesign the control. These properties are serialized into a *persistent* storage for each instance of the control so that the properties you set when adding a control to a dialog box will stay set when you next edit that dialog box.

To do this, the control has a DoPropExchange function, which is called whenever the control properties need to be loaded or saved. You can add PX_ property exchange macros to serialize your custom properties as shown in Listing 26.5.

Listing 26.5 LST27_5.CPP—Making Custom Properties Persistent with *PX* Entries in *DoPropExchange*

```
1   /////////////////////////////////////////////////////////
2   // CRotaryCtrl::DoPropExchange - Persistence support
3
4   void CRotaryCtrl::DoPropExchange(CPropExchange* pPX)
5   {
6       ExchangeVersion(pPX, MAKELONG(_wVerMinor,_wVerMajor));
7       COleControl::DoPropExchange(pPX);
```

```
8
9        // TODO: Call PX_ functions for each persistent cust
10
11       // ** Serialize the Enabled Ticks Option
12       PX_Bool(pPX,_T("TicksEnable"),m_bTicks,TRUE);
13
14       // ** Serialize the Number of Ticks Option
15       PX_Short(pPX,_T("NumTicks"),m_sNumTicks,20);
16   }
```

(1) — at line 12

① The PX_ macros are used to associate an interface property with a member variable of the control class.

In line 12 the `m_bTicks` property is made persistent with the `PX_Bool` macro and the `m_sNumTicks` property is made persistent with the `PX_Short` macro in line 15. The first parameter to these macros is a pointer to the `CPropExchange` object `pPX`. The second parameter is the OLE property name. The third parameter is your local value setting passed by member variable. The last parameter specifies a default value if the storage is being created. There are `PX_` macros for just about all the types of data you might want to set, such as `PX_Double`, `PX_Color`, and `PX_String`.

You can also see that version numbers are stored in the `ExchangeVersion()` function called in line 6. You can test these version numbers if you add extra properties to your control in a later version after distributing the control. That way you only exchange the properties relevant to each version and thus maintain compatibility with old versions of the control properties when the user upgrades the control to a newer version.

You can now add the code to draw the tick marks to the end of your `OnDraw()` function as shown in Listing 26.6.

Listing 26.6 LST27_6.CPP—Add the Code to Draw the Tick Marks to the End of the *CRotary* Control's *OnDraw()* Function

```
1  // Check whether the ticks are enabled
2  if (m_bTicks)
3  {
4      // Iterate in radians from -2*PI to +2*PI
5      const double dPi = 3.14185;
6      double r = -2.0 * dPi;
7      for(int i=0;i<m_sNumTicks;i++)
```

continues...

① Tick marks are drawn outside the main circle of the control radiating outward.

Listing 26.6   Continued

```
8      {
9          // Move to a position outside the main circle
10         nXPos = ptMid.x + (int)(cos(r) * dRadX * 1.05);
11         nYPos = ptMid.y + (int)(sin(r) * dRadY * 1.05);
12         pdc->MoveTo(CPoint(nXPos,nYPos));
13
14         // Draw a line even further out for a tick mark
15         nXPos = ptMid.x + (int)(cos(r) * dRadX * 1.15);
16         nYPos = ptMid.y + (int)(sin(r) * dRadY * 1.15);
17         pdc->LineTo(CPoint(nXPos,nYPos)); ———①
18
19         // Increment the angle
20         r += dPi / (m_sNumTicks / 2.0);
21     }
22  }
```

In the listing, the m_bTicks member is tested to ensure that the tick marks are enabled in line 2. Then the loop in line 7 iterates lines 9 through 20 by the number of ticks specified by m_sNumTicks. Lines 10 through 12 move to a position depending on the angle held in r, which is incremented from −2PI to 2PI by line 20. Lines 14 through 17 extend this point into a line following the path of the angle, thus drawing tick marks all around the outside of the main rotary circle.

SEE ALSO

➤ *For details on drawing lines and circles, see page 384*

➤ *For information on OLE automation, see page 657*

Compiling and Registering the Control

The files used and produced when compiling an ActiveX control are slightly different from a plain dialog-based or SDI/MDI application because of the COM/OLE interfaces exposed by the control. The control code is generated in an .ocx file, which is really a .dll in all but name. Therefore, the source code includes the normal .dll initialization and registration functions and definition files. You can aggregate many controls into a single .dll file to make distribution easier.

Although the build step runs through all this automatically, you should know what files are being used and which are produced and should be used when distributing the control.

The Various Source Files

If you select the FileView pane of the Project Workspace view for the Rotary ActiveX control project, you'll see the following files under the Source Files folder:

- *Rotary.cpp.* This holds the version numbers, the globally unique ID for the control. It also implements the `DllRegisterServer()`, `DllUnregisterServer()`, `InitInstance()`, and `ExitInstance()` needed to run and register the control.

- *Rotary.def.* This holds the DLL's Export function definitions.

- *Rotary.odl.* This file holds the Object Definition Language entries that define the COM/OLE interfaces used by the control, which will produce the type library output file so that various applications and languages can use the control.

- *Rotary.rc.* The resource file that holds the custom property pages and other project resources.

- *RotaryCtl.cpp.* The C++ source file that holds your control implementation code.

- *RotaryPpg.cpp.* The C++ source file that holds your control's property page implementation code.

The first step of the compilation uses the MIDL (Microsoft Interface Definition Language) compiler to compile the .odl file. As mentioned previously, this produces the interface definitions and the associated type library. Then the source files are compiled in the normal way. Finally, the regsrvr32.exe program is executed to set the system Registry entries for the control and its interfaces.

Registering the control during compilation

The registration step using regsrvr32.exe updates the Registry on your machine to register the various CLSIDs required for your new control. This step is included in the compilation as a convenience because you'll probably want to run the control on your machine to test it. You should also remember that this registration is also required on your end users' machines before they can use the control, and would usually be included in the installation /setup script.

Creating the Type Library and License Files

After compilation, if you look in your output Rotary/Debug directory, you'll see a Rotary.tlb file. The compiler generates this file, which will be used to generate the dispatch or interface classes when your control is incorporated into an application project. When you distribute the control, you should distribute this .tlb file along with the .ocx holding the code. You might also want to distribute the .lib and .exp DLL definition files and the .lic file produced if you've specified Licensing support.

SEE ALSO
➤ *For information on type libraries, see page 660*

Registering the Control

When you distribute the control to end users, the only file you'll need to send is the .ocx file and the regsvr32.exe program, which can be freely distributed with the consent of Microsoft. You should then register the control on the user's machine by running regsvr32.exe like this (which registers the Rotary control):

```
regsvr32.exe /s Rotary.ocx
```

The /s option just specifies silent operation; otherwise, you'll get a message box to confirm that the control has been registered successfully.

Testing with the ActiveX Control Test Container

Although adding the control to your About dialog box provides a very crude but simple way to test the control, a far better way is to use the ActiveX Control Test Container program provided with the compiler. This program is fairly sophisticated and enables you to set all the properties associated with the control, log events from the control, and test the property's user interface.

You can invoke the ActiveX Control Test Container by clicking the **Tools** menu and selecting the **ActiveX Control Test Container** option.

Licensing ActiveX controls

When a licensed developer adds your control to his application, a unique license key is generated and embedded in the control and stored in the application program. To generate this key and the associated copyright messages, the licensed developer must have the correct .lic file. He can then distribute to an end user his application that uses your control. When the end user runs the application the control container must make a call to the `CreateInstanceLic()` function to create a license instance. The application passes its own license key, which is tested against the control's embedded license key to see if they match, in which case the application can continue as normal.

Selecting and Inserting the Control

You can insert your new ActiveX control into the test container by clicking the **Edit** menu and selecting **Insert OLE Control** or by clicking on the first toolbar button. This will display the Insert OLE Control dialog box from which you can select your control. Select the Rotary Control from this list (near the bottom) and click **OK** to display the control.

You should see the rotary control appear all in black (the default ForeColor setting is zero). You can resize and reposition the control anywhere in the container's view.

Testing the Control Properties

If you click the **Edit** menu after inserting your control, you'll see a new option has appeared at the bottom: **Properties...Rotary Control Object**. Select this option to display the control's property pages. You should see the custom page that allows tick marks to be turned on and off, and the number of marks specified. These and the ForeColor can be set to test different properties as shown in Figure 26.14.

You should also be able to interact with the control by pressing the left mouse button over it and dragging the direction indicator around to reposition it.

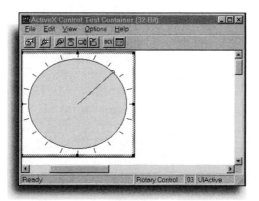

FIGURE 26.14
Testing the Rotary control properties in the ActiveX test container tool.

Testing the Ambient Properties

You can also set the container's ambient properties by clicking the **Edit** menu and selecting the **Set Ambient Properties**

703

option. This will display the Ambient Properties dialog box shown in Figure 26.15. You can select the ambient property to change from the **S̲tandard Property** combo box. Then you can set the property using the controls on the right. If you select the BackColor ambient property supported by your Rotary control, and then click the **C̲hoose** button, a list of colors is displayed and a new ambient background color can be selected. When you've selected the new color, click the **Close** button to close the dialog box. The control should have the new background color. (To see this, you might have to place another window over the test container to obscure it and then uncover the control to force a repaint.)

FIGURE 26.15
Setting the ActiveX test container's ambient properties.

Logging Fired Events

You can ensure that the events are firing properly by clicking the **V̲iew** menu and selecting the **Event Log** option to display the Event Log dialog box. You can then reposition the control and when you release the left mouse button, the new position angle is shown in the Event Log dialog box as the Repositioned event fires (see Figure 26.16).

FIGURE 26.16
Logging control events as they are fired with the event log.

chapter 27

Using the Integrated Debugger

Building programs with debugging
information or optimized in
release mode

Tracking down errors by single
stepping through code

Spying on windows and
their messages

Creating Debugging and Browse Information

A large part of application development is actually *debugging* your program. All software development is a tight cycle of application design, implementation, and debugging.

Visual C++ has an extensive debugging environment and a range of debugging tools that really help with program development. You can quickly identify problems, watch the contents of variables, and follow the flow of programs through your own code and the MFC code.

Tools like the Spy++ program can show you the messages passed between Windows and your application and let you spy on applications to see which user interface controls and Windows styles they use.

Using Debug and Release Modes

Setting the active project configuration

The active project configuration is the set of configuration instructions that the compiler will use to produce the output program. After you've developed your application using the Debug configuration, you'll want to set the Release configuration to produce a small fast executable to release to your end users.

You can do this by clicking the **Build** menu and choosing the **Set Active Configuration** option. The Set Active Project Configuration dialog box will then be displayed showing you the list of Project configurations. You can then double-click the Release configuration to instruct the compiler to use that configuration rather than the Debug configuration.

There are two main compiler configurations that you can set to build your application: Debug and Release mode. You can change these configurations by clicking the **Project** menu and selecting the **Settings** option or by pressing Alt+F7, which will display the Project Settings dialog box (see Figure 27.1). The main project settings are shown at the top level and can be changed by selecting the options listed in the combo box. When one setting is selected, changes that you make to any options on the tabs on the right will be set against that configuration. When you build the application, it will be built using your current configuration settings, or you can select **All Configurations** to build and make changes to all configurations simultaneously.

Both Release and Debug configurations are supplied whenever you create a new project; they produce very different object code. When configured for Debug mode, your build will produce a large and fairly slow executable program. This is because lots of debugging information is included in your program and all the compiler optimizations are disabled.

When you compile the same program in Release mode, you'll see a small, fast executable program but you won't be able to step through its source code or see any debugging messages from it.

Normally, when developing an application you leave the compiler set to Debug mode so that you can easily spot and debug problems that arise in your code. When you've finished your application and are preparing to release it, you can set the configuration to Release mode and produce a small, fast program for your users.

SEE ALSO

➤ For more information on project management and configuration, see page 40

Setting Debug Options and Levels

You can set a variety of debugging options and levels from the **C/C++** tab of the Project Settings dialog box. This dialog page is available from the **Project** menu by selecting the **Settings** option (or by pressing Alt+F7) and then selecting the **C/C++** tab.

With the **General Category** selected, the following items are available:

- **Warning Level.** This is the level of compiler warning messages given during compilation. You can set it to any of the

Release mode testing

You should always fully test your application after rebuilding it in Release mode before sending it to users. Bugs can arise from things like leaving proper program code in **ASSERT** macros (discussed later this chapter), which are then removed, or because of the effect of some speed and memory optimizations.

values shown in Table 27.1. The default level is **Level 3**, which is quite sensitive, although many good C++ programmers insist on using **Level 4** to get the most warning of potential problems from the compiler. **Level 1** and no warnings (**None**) should be used only in special circumstances because they indicate only severe warnings (or none at all).

- **Warnings as Errors.** By checking this, warning messages are shown as errors that then stop the compiler.

- **Generate Browse Info.** When you check this, the compiler generates information that can be used to help you locate functions, symbols, and class relationships shown in a Browse window (discussed in the next section). Unfortunately, generating this useful information increases the compilation time quite a bit for large projects (where you most need it).

- **Debug Info.** This lets you specify the level of debugging information generated by the compiler, as shown in Table 27.2.

- **Optimizations.** In Debug mode, you would normally leave these disabled because they interfere with the debugging process and take longer to compile. However, in Release mode you can decide whether to **Maximize Speed** or **Minimize Size** of your application (or a default that compromises to get the best of both).

- **Preprocessor Definitions.** This specifies manifest definitions that are defined when your program is compiled. You can use these definitions in conjunction with the #ifdef, #else, and #endif preprocessor commands to compile sections of code in specific configurations. The _DEBUG definition is set by default when in Debug mode. You can use this to compile Debug mode–only code in your application like this:

```
int a = b * c / d + e;
#ifdef _DEBUG
CString strMessage;
strMessage.Format("Result of sum was %d",a);
AfxMessageBox(strMessage);
#endif
```

The message box code is then compiled and run when your application is built in Debug mode. When you switch to Release mode, the code isn't compiled into your executable.

- **Project Options.** The compiler itself runs as a console-based application and converts your Developer Studio options into several flags to be passed on the command line. You can add additional flag settings for more obscure compiler settings that don't have a user interface switch directly into this edit box.

TABLE 27.1 Compiler warning levels

Level	Warnings Reported
None	None
Level 1	Only the most severe
Level 2	Some less severe messages
Level 3	Default level (all reasonable warnings)
Level 4	Very sensitive (good for perfectionists)

TABLE 27.2 Debug info settings

Setting	Debugging Information Generated
None	Produces no debugging information—usually reserved for Release modes.
Line Numbers Only	This only generates line numbers that refer to the source code for functions and global variables. However, compile time and executable size are reduced.
C 7.0–Compatible	This generates debugging information that is compatible with Microsoft C 7.0. It places all the debugging information into the executable files and increases their size, but allows full symbolic debugging.
Program Database	This setting produces a file with a .pdb extension that holds the maximum level of debugging information, but doesn't create the Edit and Continue information.
Program Database for Edit and Continue	This is the default and usual debug setting. It produces a .pdb file with the highest level of debugging and creates the information required for the new Edit and Continue feature.

Effect on compiler flags

Each project setting is translated into a long list of compiler command-line flags that are passed to the command-line based compiler. For example, the Debug info settings translate into different /Z command line options. These are /Zd for line numbers only, /Z7 for C7 compatible, /Zi for program database, and /Zl for edit and continue mode. If you change the Debug info setting, you'll also see the changes displayed in the Project Options box.

Creating and Using Browse Information

You can use the Source Browser tool to inspect your source code in detail. This tool can be invaluable if you are examining someone else's code or coming back to your own code after you haven't viewed it for awhile.

To use the Source Browser, you must compile the application with the **Generate Browse Info** setting checked, in the **C/C++** tab of the Project Settings dialog box. To run the tool, press Alt+F12 or click the **Tools** menu and select the **Source Browser** option (the first time you run the tool, it will ask you to compile the browser information).

The first dialog box the Source Browser presents requests an **Identifier** to browse for (as shown in Figure 27.2). This identifier can be a class name, structure name, function name, or global or local variable name in your application. After you have entered an identifier, the **OK** button is enabled and you can browse for details about that identifier.

FIGURE 27.2
The Browse dialog box requesting a symbol to browse.

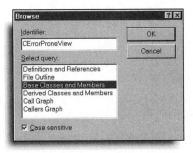

Select Query offers various options for details pertaining to your chosen symbol. You can choose from any of the following:

- **Definitions and References.** This option shows you all the files that have references to the specified identifier and whether they are references to the identifier (places where it is used in the code) or definitions (places where the identifier is defined), as shown in Figure 27.3. The line numbers are listed along with the filenames in each file. By double-clicking one of the references or definitions, the code to which it refers will be loaded and shown in the Developer

Studio editor at that specific position. This is very useful for tracking all the places that a specific variable or function is used.

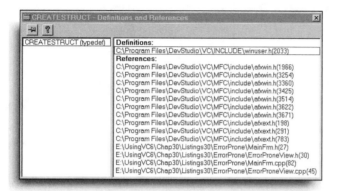

FIGURE 27.3
Source Browser showing definitions and references.

- **File Outline.** This option shows you all the classes, data, functions, macros, and types that are defined in the specified filename (identifier), as shown in Figure 27.4. You can filter each type in or out by pressing relevant buttons along the top of the browser window.

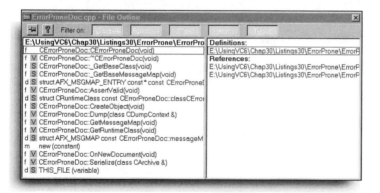

FIGURE 27.4
The file outline display of the source browser.

- **Base Classes and Members.** This arguably is one of the most useful options of the source browser. By specifying a class as the identifier, all the classes' hierarchy and member functions and variables at each hierarchy level are displayed (see Figure 27.5). You can also set the filter options to show only certain types of member functions and variables.

FIGURE 27.5
The Base Classes and Members view of the source browser.

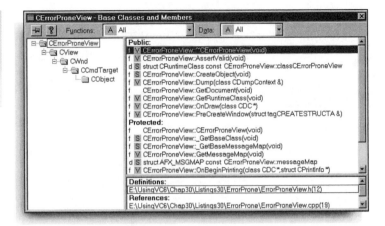

- **Derived Classes and Members.** This view is also very useful and shows all the classes that are derived from the specified class, along with their own member functions and variables. You can also use the browser with the MFC classes to gain more insight into the MFC implementation, as shown with the MFC CWnd class in Figure 27.6.

FIGURE 27.6
The Derived Classes and Members view of Source Browser showing CWnd-derived classes.

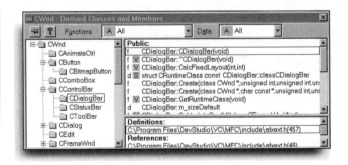

- **Call Graph.** The call graph option shows you all the functions that are called by a specified identifier and the files in which they are defined and implemented. This lets you quickly track the potential flow of a program.

- **Callers Graph.** The corresponding Callers Graph option shows you all the functions that call the specified identifier. You can use this to track the possible callers of your specified function.

Using Remote and Just-in-Time Debugging

The debugger includes tools that let you debug a program running on a remote machine (even over the Internet via TCP/IP). This can be useful if you want to test your application in a different environment other than your development machine. To do this, you must have exactly the same versions of the .dll and .exe files on both machines. After loading the project, you can debug it via a shared directory from the remote machine by changing the **Executable for debug session** edit box to the path and filename of your local .exe file (located in the Project Settings dialog box under the **Debug** tab).

You must also add a path to the .exe file in the **Remote Executable Path and File Name** edit box at the bottom of the **Debug** tab, leaving the **Working Directory** blank. You can then start the remote debugger monitor on the remote computer by running the MSVCMON.EXE program and connecting to it by clicking the **Build** menu and selecting the **Debugger Remote Connection** option.

From the Remote Connection dialog box you can choose **Local** for a shared directory debug session, or **Remote** to debug via a TCP/IP connection. (You can set the address by clicking **Settings**.) This will connect to the remote monitor that will start the remote debugging session.

Just-in-time debugging lets you debug a program that was run normally (not through the debugger) and then developed a problem. If you have Visual C++ installed on a machine and this option is enabled, any program that develops a fault will be loaded into a new Developer Studio session ready for debugging and show the code that caused the crash.

This often raises a chuckle when Developer Studio itself crashes and then proceeds to load another session of itself, offering you an assembly code view of where the crash took place in the original for you to debug. It can be very useful to debug your own applications when they crash unexpectedly (usually in a demonstration to your boss). You can enable this option by clicking the **Tools** menu and selecting **Options** to display the Options dialog box. Then select the **Debug** tab and ensure that the **Just-in-Time** debugging check box is checked.

> **Installing the remote debugger files**
>
> You will also need the following files to run the remote debugger monitor on the remote machine: MSVCMON.EXE, MSVCRT.DLL, TLN0T.DLL, DM.DLL, MSVCP50.DLL, and MSDIS100.DLL. These files can be found in your installed ...\Microsoft Visual Studio\Common\MSDev98\bin subdirectory.

The **OLE RPC** debugging option on this tab is also very useful when developing *COM* and *DCOM* applications because it lets the debugger traverse a function call into another out-of-process program or .dll and let another debugger take over for the other process. It then hands control back when returning from the remote function and works across networks and different computers.

SEE ALSO

➤ *For more details about COM and OLE, see page 648*

Tracing and Single Stepping

Conditional breakpoints

You can set conditions against breakpoints, making them very powerful and sophisticated debugging tools. These conditions can check whether certain program variables are within specific ranges, or they can be set to skip a breakpoint so many times before stopping at the specific program line.

One of the most useful features of the Visual C++ debugging environment is the interactive single stepping. This feature lets you step through the code one line at a time and examine the contents of variables as you go. You can also set *breakpoints* so that the program runs until it reaches a breakpoint and then stops at that point, letting you step from that point until you want to continue running.

Trace statements and assertions are also very useful tools for finding program faults. Trace statements let you display messages and variables from your program in the output window as it runs through trace statements. You can use assertions to cause the program to stop if a condition isn't TRUE when you assert that it should be.

Using the *TRACE* Macro

You can add TRACE macros to your program at various places to indicate that various parts of the code have been run, or to display the contents of variables at those positions. The TRACE macros are compiled into your code in the debug configuration and displayed in the Output window on the **Debug** tab, when you run your program through the debugger.

You can safely leave in the TRACE macros when you perform a release build because these macros are automatically excluded from the destination object.

You can display simple messages or output variable contents by passing a format string as the first parameter to the TRACE macro. This format string is exactly the same as you would pass to a printf() or CString::Format() function. You can specify various special formatting codes such as %d to display a number in decimal, %x to display a number in hexadecimal, or %s to display a string. The following parameters should then correspond to the order of the formatting codes. For example, the following code:

```
int nMyNum = 60;
char* szMyString = "This is my String";
TRACE("Number = %d, or %x in hex and my string is: %s\n",
        nMyNum, szMyString);
```

will result in the output trace line:

```
Number = 60, or 3c in hex and my string is
➥This is my String
```

Listing 27.1 shows the TRACE macro used to display the contents of an array before and after sorting by a very inefficient but simple sort algorithm.

If you want to try the code shown in Listing 27.1, you can use AppWizard to build a simple SDI framework. Simply add the code above the OnNewDocument() member function of your document class and then call it by adding a DoSort() call into your OnNewDocument() function.

You can run the application through the debugger (click **Build**, select **Start Debug**, and choose **Go** from the pop-up menu) to see the output trace.

You must ensure that the output window is visible (click the **View** menu and select **Output**) when the tabbed output window is shown (same as the compiler output). Ensure that the **Debug** tab is selected.

Shortcut key for debugging

A faster way to start the debugging process is by pressing the F5 key. This will start running the program through the debugger immediately if the executable is up to date, or prompt you to build the latest files if required before debugging commences.

(1) The Swap() function swaps two variables from a position in the array.

(2) The TRACE macro is used to dump the number before sorting.

(3) Each pair of numbers is checked and if in the wrong sequence, they are swapped.

(4) The TRACE macro is used again to dump the numbers after sorting.

LISTING 27.1   LST30_1.CPP—A Simple Sort Routine to Demonstrate Debugging Techniques

```
1    void Swap(CUIntArray* pdwNumbers,int i) ————(1)
2    {
3        UINT uVal = pdwNumbers->GetAt(i);
4        pdwNumbers->SetAt(i, pdwNumbers->GetAt(i+1));
5        pdwNumbers->SetAt(i+1,uVal);
6    }
7
8    void DoSort()
9    {
10       CUIntArray arNumbers;
11       for(int i=0;i<10;i++) arNumbers.Add(1+rand()%100);
12
13       TRACE("Before Sort\n"); ————(2)
14       for(i=0;i<arNumbers.GetSize();i++)
15           TRACE("[%d] = %d\n",i+1,arNumbers[i]);
16
17       BOOL bSorted;
18       do
19       {
20           bSorted = TRUE;
21           for(i=0;i<arNumbers.GetSize()-1;i++) ————(3)
22           {
23               if (arNumbers[i] > arNumbers[i+1])
24               {
25                   Swap(&arNumbers,i);
26                   bSorted = FALSE;
27               }
28           }
29       } while(!bSorted); ————(4)
30
31       TRACE("After Sort\n");
32       for(i=0;i<arNumbers.GetSize();i++)
33           TRACE("[%d] = %d\n",i+1,arNumbers[i]);
34   }
```

Listing 27.1 sorts an array of random numbers (between 1 and 100), generated in line 11. Lines 13 to 15 then print out the contents of the array before sorting by TRACE statements. Lines 17 through 29 sort the array by swapping pairs of numbers that are in the wrong order (by calling the Swap() function in line 25). The Swap() function (lines 1 to 6) takes a pointer to the array and a position, and then swaps the two numbers at that position.

After sorting, the contents of the array are again printed in the output window by the TRACE statements in lines 31 to 33.

The trace output of this program appears in the Output window of Developer Studio, as shown in Table 27.3.

TABLE 27.3 Output from the sorting program

Before Sort	After Sort
[1] = 42	[1] = 1
[2] = 68	[2] = 25
[3] = 35	[3] = 35
[4] = 1	[4] = 42
[5] = 70	[5] = 59
[6] = 25	[6] = 63
[7] = 79	[7] = 65
[8] = 59	[8] = 68
[9] = 63	[9] = 70
[10] = 65	[10] = 79

Sorting algorithms

Although this sorting technique makes a simple and effective debugging example it probably is one of the least efficient of the possible sorting algorithms. If you must implement a fast efficient sort, you should investigate the quick-sort algorithm, which is implemented by the qsort() function from the C++ runtime library.

Using the *ASSERT* and *VERIFY* macros

You can use the ASSERT macro to ensure that conditions are TRUE. ASSERT is passed one parameter that is either a TRUE or FALSE expression. If the expression is TRUE, all is well. If the expression is FALSE, your program will stop and the Debug Assertion Failed dialog box will be displayed (see Figure 27.7), prompting you to **Abort** the program, **Retry** the code, or **Ignore** the assertion. It also shows the program, source file, and line number where the assertion failed. If you choose **Abort**, the debugging session is terminated. **Retry** is probably the most useful option because the compiler will then show you the code where the ASSERT macro has failed, enabling you to figure out what went wrong. If you already know or don't care about the assertion, you can choose **Ignore** and continue running the program, which might then result in a more fatal error.

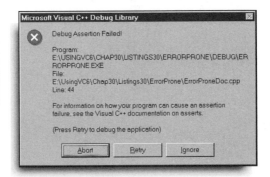

FIGURE 27.7
The Debug Assertion Failed dialog box helps you track down bugs.

A common use of ASSERT is to ensure that input parameters to functions are correct. For example, you could make the Sort() function (shown in Listing 27.1) more robust by checking its input parameters. To check the input parameters, add ASSERT macros at the top of the Sort() function like this:

```
ASSERT(pdwNumbers);
ASSERT(i>=0 && i<10);
```

This will ensure that the pointer to the numbers array isn't zero and that the position to swap is between 0 and 9. If either of these is incorrect, the Debug Assertion Failed dialog box is displayed. This technique helps you track down errors caused by passing faulty parameters to functions. It is a good practice to use the ASSERT macro to check that the values passed to each of your functions conform to your expectations.

Another macro, ASSERT_VALID, can be used with CObject-derived classes such as most MFC classes. This performs a more thorough check on the object and its contents to ensure the entire object is in a correct and valid state. You can pass a pointer to the object to be checked like this:

```
ASSERT_VALID(pdwNumbers);
```

Another ASSERT macro is ASSERT_KINDOF, which is used on CObject-derived classes to check that they are of the correct class type. For example, you could check that a pointer to your view object is of the correct view class like this:

```
ASSERT_KINDOF(CYourSpecialView,pYView);
```

The Assertion Failed dialog box will be displayed if it isn't of the correct class type or any of its derivatives.

You must be careful not to put any code that is needed for normal program operation into ASSERT macros because they are excluded in the release build. A common source of release mode errors that are hard to track down is coding like this:

```
int a = 0;
ASSERT(++a > 0);
if (a>0) MyFunc();
```

In the debug build, this code will increment the integer a in the ASSERT line, and then call MyFunc() in the following line because a is greater than zero. When your sales team is eager to demonstrate your new application, you might think it works fine because there aren't any Debug mode problems. So you recompile it in Release mode and hand it over to your sales department, who demonstrates it to a customer, whereupon it crashes badly. It crashes because the ++a isn't performed—the release mode excludes ASSERT lines.

The VERIFY macro helps with this problem. VERIFY works like ASSERT and in Debug mode it throws the same Assertion Failed dialog box if the expression is zero. However, in Release mode the expression is still evaluated, but a zero result won't display the Assertion dialog box. You would tend to use VERIFY when you always want to perform an expression and ASSERT when you only want to check while debugging. Therefore, replacing ASSERT in the previous example with VERIFY, as shown in the following example, will enable the release build to work properly:

```
VERIFY(++a > 0);
```

You are more likely to use VERIFY to check return codes from functions:

```
VERIFY(MyFunc() != FALSE);
```

Other assertion macros

Some less used assertion macros are **ASSERT_ POINTER**, which takes a pointer and the data/object type that it refers to. **ASSERT_ POINTER** will then assert that the pointer isn't **NULL**, occupies a valid memory address, and that the memory it occupies is valid for the whole size of the object. A companion assertion test is **ASSERT_NULL_OR_POINTER**, which allows **NULL** pointers but not pointers to objects that would inhabit an invalid memory address for the current process.

Using Breakpoints and Single Stepping the Program

The use of single stepping and breakpoints is probably the most effective debugging tool for tracking down the majority of problems. The support for various types of breakpoints and the single-stepping information available is very sophisticated in Visual C++; I can only hope to give you a taste of the power of this debugging tool.

The key to single stepping is breakpoints. You can set a breakpoint anywhere in your code, and then run your program through the debugger. When the breakpoint is reached the code will be displayed in the editor window at the breakpoint position, ready for you to single step or continue running.

You can add a breakpoint by selecting the specific code line (clicking the editor cursor onto the line in the editor window) and then either clicking the Breakpoint 🔘 icon in the Build MiniBar (see Figure 27.8) or by pressing F9. Alternatively, most sophisticated breakpoints can be added or removed by clicking the **Edit** menu and selecting the **Breakpoints** option to display the Breakpoints dialog box (see Figure 27.9). When you add a breakpoint, it's displayed as a small red circle next to the line you have specified. Breakpoints can be set only against valid code lines, so sometimes the Developer Studio will move one of your breakpoints to the closest valid code line for you.

FIGURE 27.8

Adding a breakpoint to your code via the Build MiniBar toolbar or the F9 key.

① Compile (Ctrl+FT)

② Build (F7)

③ Stop Build (Ctrl+Break)

④ Go (F5)

⑤ Insert/Remove Breakpoint

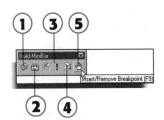

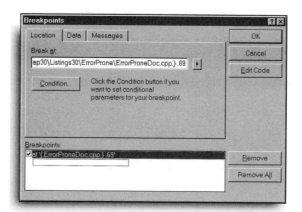

FIGURE 27.9
Adding a breakpoint
using the Breakpoints
dialog box.

You can toggle the breakpoint on or off by clicking the
Breakpoint (hand shaped) icon, or remove it by clicking the
Remove or **Remove All** buttons on the Breakpoints dialog box.
You can leave them in position but disable them by clicking the
check mark to the left of each breakpoint listed in the
Breakpoints dialog box. Clicking there again will show the check
and re-enable the breakpoint.

When you have set your breakpoint(s), you can run the code
through the debugger by choosing **Build**, **Start Debug**, **Go**.
Alternatively, you can use the shortcut by clicking the Go
icon (to the left of the Breakpoint icon on the Build Minibar
toolbar—refer to Figure 27.8) or by pressing the F5 key.

The program will run as normal until it reaches the breakpoint,
where it will stop and display an arrow against the line with the
breakpoint. At that point, you can use the Debug toolbar to control the single stepping process, as shown in Figure 27.10.

FIGURE 27.10
The debugger stopped at
a breakpoint ready for
single stepping with the
Debug toolbar.

Single stepping speed/run to cursor

If you perform some single stepping operations such as Step Out and Run to Cursor, you might experience a short delay, especially if the debugger must run through a large iterative loop first. This shows the semi-interpreted nature of the debugger, which must stop after each instruction to check that the point in the code you've specified has been reached.

When stopped in the debugger, you can see the contents of most variables merely by moving the cursor over them in the editor window. Their contents are then displayed in a ToolTip at the cursor position. More detailed contents are shown by dragging the variables into the Watch window, as discussed in detail in the next section.

You can single step through the code using the four curly brace icons shown on the Debug toolbar 〔{}〕 〔{}〕 〔{}〕 〔{}〕 or by clicking the **Debug** menu and choosing one of the step options. The available step options are shown in Table 27.4. You can find these on the **Debug** menu and the Debug toolbar.

TABLE 27.4   Step options available in single stepping

Icon/Step Option	Shortcut Key	Effect When Selected
Step Into	F11	The debugger will execute the current line and if the cursor is over a function call, it will enter that function.
Step Over	F10	Like Step Into except when over a function call line; it will run that function at normal speed and then stop when it returns from the function, giving the effect of stepping over it.
Step Out	Shift+F11	The debugger will run the rest of the current function at normal speed and stop when it returns from the function to the calling function.
Run to Cursor	Ctrl+F10	The debugger will run until it reaches your specified cursor position. You can set this position by clicking the line you want to run to.
Go	F5	Continue running the program at normal speed until the next breakpoint is encountered.
Stop Debugging	Shift+F5	This stops the debugger and returns to editing mode.
Restart	Ctrl+Shift+F5	This option restarts the program from the beginning, stopping at the very first line of code.

Icon/Step Option	Shortcut Key	Effect When Selected
Break Execution		This option stops a program running at normal speed in its tracks.
Apply Code Changes	Alt+F10	This option lets you compile the code after making changes during a debugging session, and then continue debugging from where you left off.

By using these options, you can watch the flow of your program and see the contents of the variables as they are manipulated by the code. The yellow arrow in the Editor window will always show the next statement to be executed.

The next sections describe some of the debugging windows you can use when you are stopped in the debugger.

Using Edit and Continue

A great new feature of Visual C++ 6.0 is the capability to Edit and Continue. This means that you can change or edit the code while you are stopped in the debugger. After editing, you'll notice the **Debug** menu's **Apply Code Changes** option becomes enabled (as well as the corresponding debug toolbar icon). You can then select the **Apply Code Changes** option (or toolbar button) to compile your new code changes, and then continue debugging the new changed code. By using this new feature, you can fix bugs while debugging and continue the debug run from the same place in the code with the same variable settings, which can be very useful when debugging large and complex programs.

Watching Program Variables

The Watch and Variables windows are shown in Figure 27.11. These windows display the contents of variables when stopped in the debugger. You can view these windows by clicking the **View** menu and selecting them from the **Debug Windows** pop-up menu, or by clicking the or icon from the toolbar.

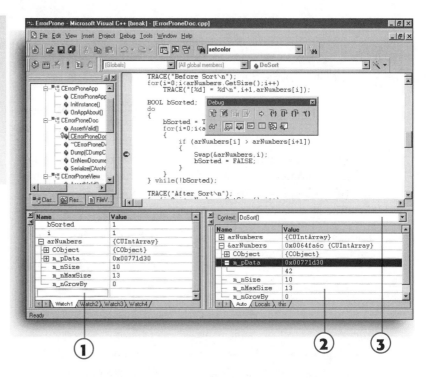

The Variables window always shows the local variables of the function displayed in the **Context** combo box at the top of the window. To get to your current function, you can drop this combo box list to display all the functions that were called in turn. This is the *Call Stack* and shows your current context within the program by showing the list of functions that have been called in order to get to the program's currently executing function where the debugger has stopped. When you select a different function, the relevant local variables are shown for that function level.

You can expand any object pointers shown by clicking the plus symbol next to the pointer name. The special C++ `this` pointer is always shown for class member functions and can be opened to show all the member variables for the current object.

The Watch window lets you enter variable names from the keyboard or drag variable names from the editor window (after selecting and inverting them with the mouse point). The values that are held in the displayed variables are shown until they go out of scope (that is, aren't relevant to the function currently being debugged).

You can also enter simple casts and array indexes in the Watch window to show related values. Right-clicking the mouse can switch the displayed values between hexadecimal and decimal display. As you step through the program, the values shown in the Watch and Variable windows are updated accordingly so that you can track how the program changes the variables.

Other Debugger Windows

Other debugging display windows are available by clicking the **View** menu and selecting them from the **Debug Windows** pop-up menu or alternatively by clicking the various icons shown to the right of the Debug toolbar. These windows are

- **QuickWatch.** By clicking a variable in the listing and choosing **QuickWatch** or pressing Shift+F9, you can display the contents of the select variable. You can also enter variables directly and then click the **Add Watch** button to transfer them into the main Watch window.

- **Registers.** The Registers window displays the current values in your CPU's register set. This probably isn't too useful to you unless you are tracking machine or assembly code-level problems.

- **Memory.** The Memory window displays the memory from the application's address space in columns that represent the address, the hex values, and the character values for each 8 bytes. You can change this display to show Byte, Short, or Long values by right-clicking to display the appropriate context menu options.

- **Call Stack.** The Call Stack window shows the list of functions that were called in order to get to your current function, and the parameter values that were passed to each function. This can be very useful to investigate how the program flow reached a specific function. By double-clicking any of the listed functions, you can display the position

---

Evaluating expressions with QuickWatch

You can also use the **QuickWatch** window like a calculator that lets you enter mathematical and logical expressions, including program variables with their current values. When you press the **Recalculate** button the result of the expression is displayed in the **Current Value** box.

where the function call was made in the code, shown by the Editor window.

Where source code isn't available, function entries are shown as follows:

```
KERNEL32! bff88f75()
```

If you click these entries, you'll be shown assembly code rather than C++ code.

- ▪ 🖳 **Disassembly.** By selecting the **Disassembly** toolbar button or menu option, you can toggle between displaying the C++ code mixed with assembly code or just C++ code. Where the source code is unavailable, only assembly code is shown.

Single stepping assembly code

When the **Disassembly** window is showing, the debugger steps through the assembly code instruction by instruction. The assembly code and corresponding operation codes shown are the raw bytes of your executable program and represent each CPU instruction. Stepping through the assembly code is slow and arduous, but provides the definitive answers to why your program doesn't behave how you would expect. It is also often the only way to spot faulty code produced by the bugs in the compiler itself, which can sometimes occur while you are trying to optimize and compile complex source code.

Additional Debugging Tools

Along with the integrated debugging tools are several noninte-grated but very useful tools. You can start these by clicking the **Tools** menu and selecting the specific tool option from the menu.

These tools generally let you track operating-specific items such as Windows messaging, running processes, and registered OLE objects to enhance your available information while debugging your application.

Using Spy++

Spy++ is undoubtedly one of the most useful of these tools. With Spy++ you can see the hierarchical relationships of parent to child windows, the position and flags settings for windows, and base window classes. You can also watch messages as they are sent to a window.

When you first run Spy++, it shows all the windows on the current desktop, their siblings, and the base Windows class of each object (see Figure 27.12). The view shown in Figure 27.12 has been scrolled to shown the standard Microsoft Windows CD Player. Spy++ shows you all the buttons and combo boxes, which are windows in their own right as child windows of the main CD Player window.

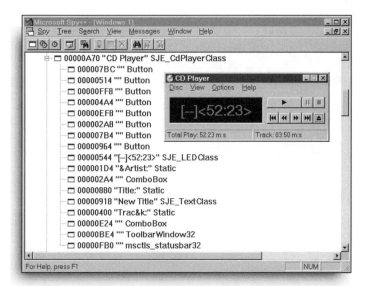

FIGURE 27.12
The Spy++ initial view of the Windows desktop showing the CD Player portion.

If you click the **Spy** menu, you are shown the following options:

- **Messages.** You might find that the Messages view is probably one of the most useful options because you can use it to watch messages that are sent to any windows (including your own application). You can also filter these messages so that you don't receive an avalanche of Mouse Movement messages.

  To use messages, select this option to display the Message Options dialog box shown in Figure 27.13. You can then drag the finder tool over any window in the system, displaying the details of the window as it moves. Spy++ also highlights the selected window so you can see frame and client windows. When you've located the window you want to view, just let go of the tool. At this point you can use the other tabs to set filtering options and output formatting options. When you're finished, click **OK** to close the Message Options box.

  The output shown in Figure 27.14 are the messages produced from using a normal SDI application's toolbar. As you can see, with no filtering you'll receive many mouse movements and cursor check messages, but you can also see the familiar WM_LBUTTONUP message with its position parameters.

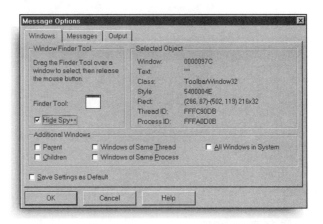

FIGURE 27.13

Using the Spy++
Message Options Finder
to locate windows.

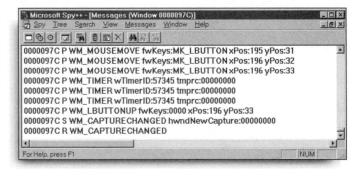

FIGURE 27.14

Windows Messages for a
toolbar logged by Spy++.

- **Windows.** The Windows view is the view shown in Figure 27.12 of the layout and structure of the Windows desktop. If you double-click any of these windows, you'll be shown a property sheet containing all the selected windows' positioning information and flag settings. To update this information, you must click the **Windows** menu and choose **Refresh**.

- **Processes.** You can view all the running programs with the Processes view. These can be opened to show each thread and any windows attached to those threads.

- **Threads.** The Threads option shows the same details without the processes level of hierarchy, so you can see every thread running on your machine and the windows that each thread owns.

Spy++ is too sophisticated to cover in its entirety here, but as a tool for understanding the structure of Windows hierarchies and messaging it is unsurpassed. You can glean a lot of valuable knowledge just by looking at commercial applications with Spy++. It is also a wonderful tool for debugging messaging problems in your own application to ensure that your windows are getting the correct messages, and to see how these messages are sequenced.

SEE ALSO

➤ *For more details about Windows messages, see page 69*

Process Viewer

You can see all the processes in more detail than shown in Spy++ with the Process Viewer (PView95.exe). You can start this application from your system's main Windows **Start** menu from **Programs** under the **Microsoft Visual Studio 6.0 Tools** option (or similar program group). This application lists the processes running on your machine and lets you sort them by clicking any of the column headers. You can then click a process to display all its threads. Figure 27.15 shows Process Viewer running with the Developer Studio application (MSDEV.EXE) selected and all its many threads displayed.

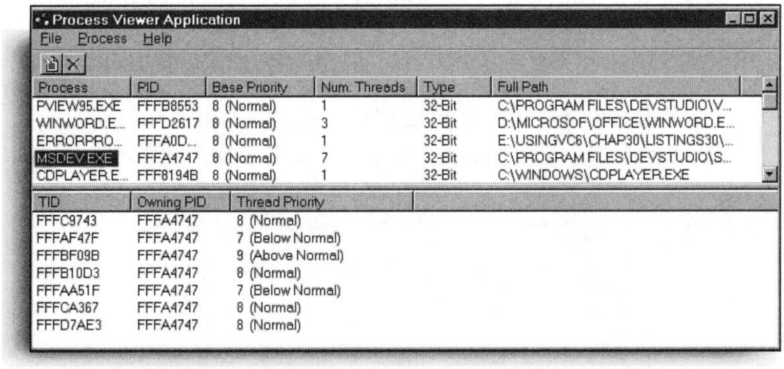

FIGURE 27.15
The Process Viewer showing MSDEV.EXE and its threads.

The OLE/COM Object Viewer

The OLE/COM Object Viewer tool shows you all the registered OLE/COM objects on your system, including ActiveX controls, type libraries, embeddable objects, automation objects, and many other categories.

You can even create instances of various objects and view their interfaces in detail. The OLE/COM Object Viewer is very useful if you are developing an OLE/COM application or looking for an elusive ActiveX control.

SEE ALSO

➤ *To learn how to use ActiveX controls in your applications, see page 196*

➤ *To create an ActiveX control, see page 676*

➤ *For more details about COM and OLE, see page 648*

The MFC Tracer

Using the MFC Tracer tool shown in Figure 27.16, you can stop the normal tracing or add specific Windows trace output to the normal program trace output. When you select this tool, you are shown a set of check boxes that you can check or uncheck to include that tracing option.

You can add Windows messages, database messages, OLE messages, and many other levels of trace output to help track down elusive problems. These messages are then generated by the MFC code for the various selected flags.

You can even turn off the standard tracing generated by your application by unchecking the **Enable Tracing** option.

FIGURE 27.16
The MFC Tracer tool options.

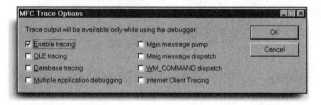

chapter

28

Working with APIs and SDKs

Learning how to use the numerous
APIs and SDKs available
to Visual C++ programmers

Creating ultra-fast sound and
graphics applications with DirectX

Sending and receiving email messages
with the MAPI architecture

Using the Media Control interface
for multimedia sound and video

Introduction to APIs and SDKs

APIs (application programming interfaces) are collections of functions normally held in dynamic link libraries (.dlls) or static libraries (.libs). These help you implement specific types of application functionality such as graphics, sound, database access, or communications by supplying a layer of code between your application and the base hardware.

There are many different APIs that simplify a vast arena of programming problems and unite them into a standard set of function calls. Whole books are dedicated to exploring individual APIs, so in this chapter I can only hope to show a few examples of common APIs and how they are used.

Modern developments in COM and OLE technology mean that many of these APIs are now implemented as COM objects, which helps enormously with versioning problems due to several versions of a .dll.

SDKs (software development kits) are APIs bundled with documentation and sample programs. They can help you develop specific kinds of applications, such as the Game SDK for game development and the OLE DB SDK to help develop OLE-based database applications.

Generally, API functions aren't included in your project's default link library settings and they require you to link with specific libraries. You can usually add all the function prototypes and API macro definitions you need by including one .h header file specific to the API you must use.

SEE ALSO

➤ *To understand the ideas and concepts of OLE and COM, see page 648*

Obtaining APIs and SDKs

Not all the APIs and SDKs are distributed with Visual C++, but most can be downloaded from the Microsoft Web site at www.microsoft.com usually at no cost. Even if the API or SDK you want to use is distributed with Visual C++, it's often best to check whether there is a more up-to-date version available before you start.

Implementing Fast Sound and Video with DirectX

The DirectX APIs were created to solve the problem of fast access to video and sound hardware. Although Windows provides sophisticated standard graphics and sound support functions, these weren't flexible or quick enough for programmers trying to write fast-moving action games or graphical presentation software. For a long time, the only solution was to write the software as a DOS application and lose the benefits of Windows hardware independence, configuration information, and other Windows services.

Microsoft has filled this gap with a set of APIs that still provide hardware independence but offer far faster and more direct access to the video, sound, and input device hardware. These APIs are `DirectSound`, `DirectDraw`, `Direct3D`, `DirectPlay`, `DirectInput`, and `DirectSetup`; together they compose the Game SDK, which has been incredibly popular with developers in the challenging games and presentation graphics industries.

These APIs are all implemented using the Component Object Model (COM) and therefore the function calls are grouped by the specific COM interface to the COM object that implements them.

The DLLs that these APIs require aren't installed with Windows, but are freely distributed and included with most modern games software. They can also be downloaded from the Microsoft Web site at `www.microsoft.com/directx`.

SEE ALSO

➤ *To understand the ideas and concepts of OLE and COM, see page 648*

Using DirectSound

You can use the DirectSound API to directly access your sound card hardware to generate sound based on the contents of a *waveform buffer*. This buffer is just a patch of memory that can be directly read by the sound card hardware, which changes the

The difficulties of high-speed graphics

The main problem with trying to write applications that use graphical animation is one of raw processor power. To fool the human eye into perceiving continuous motion rather than a series of frames an application must present about 24 frames per second. There are 480,000 pixels in a 256 color 800×600 display. To potentially change the color of each of these 24 times a second means you must perform 11,520,000 operations per second. It might take around 12 CPU clock cycles to set each pixel needing 138,240,000 clock cycles just to refresh the screen. On a modern 266Mhz processor 50% of the CPU's time could be occupied by just drawing the screen. Then, in the remaining 50% of CPU time, you must think about doing many very complex and time-consuming 3D calculations, texture mapping, bitmap scaling, and interaction with the user.

values held in the buffer to sound levels. The simplest coding technique is for each byte in the buffer to represent 256 levels of sound amplitude, which will then correspond directly to the position of the speaker cone in your sound card–connected loudspeakers.

By setting the values in the buffer to represent a waveform, you can produce a sound with a pure pitch. By changing the amplitude of this waveform at various places in the buffer, you can modulate the waveform to produce many different effects.

This waveform buffer is called the DirectSound primary buffer. You don't normally directly create a primary buffer; normally you create secondary buffers and when these secondary buffers are played they are automatically mixed to produce the primary buffer.

By using the mixing mechanism with multiple secondary buffers, you can easily produce very complex sound effects. Figure 28.1 shows the output of the sample program mixing two very different secondary buffers. The buffer shown at the top is a decaying sine wave (pure tone) and the middle buffer is set to random values (*white noise* or hiss) increasing in amplitude. The bottom waveform shows the contents of the primary buffer that is the result of these two buffers being played and hence mixed together. This results in a pure tone that quickly decays into white noise when played. You can mix tones with other tones, square waves, saw-tooth waveforms, or any other buffer contents including sampled (recorded) sound to produce any audio output you need.

The first thing you must do to use the DirectSound API is create an `IDirectSound` interface either by using a `CoCreateInstance()` call directly (see Chapter 25, "Understanding OLE and COM Programming") or by using the `DirectSoundCreate()` shortcut function.

`DirectSoundCreate()` needs three parameters; the first is a pointer to a GUID (globally unique identifier) that identifies the sound device you want to use. These sound device GUIDs can be found by setting up a callback function with `DirectSoundEnumerate()`. Alternatively, you can pass NULL to use

Using the `DirectSoundCreate()` function

If you use `DirectSoundCreate()`, you must also include the dsound.lib library on your Project Settings dialog box's **Object/Library Modules** line, available on the **Link** tab. If you use the `CoCreateInstance()` route, you won't need this library but you will need to declare the `CLSID`s (class IDs) and `IID`s (interface IDs) required.

the default sound device. The second parameter is a pointer to the DirectSound Interface object pointer, which is used to set your application pointer to the new object. The third parameter is normally set to NULL unless you must use the COM aggregation technique.

If this function succeeds, the returned pointer points to an IDirectSound interface that can be deallocated by calling its Release() function like all other COM interfaces.

After you have an IDirectSound interface, you must immediately set its cooperative level. Many DirectX APIs have cooperative levels that specify how the hardware they are using should be shared among applications. You can set the level by calling SetCooperativeLevel() on the IDirectSound interface and passing it a Window handle to identify your application. You must also pass a flag value for the required cooperation level. The normal cooperation level used is DSSCL_NORMAL to enable full cooperation with other applications.

You can then create the secondary sound buffers by using the CreateSoundBuffer() function from the IDirectSound interface. CreateSoundBuffer() needs three parameters. The first is a DSBUFFERDESC structure that describes the type of buffer you want to create. The second is a pointer to your application's IDirectSoundBuffer interface pointer for the new buffer. The third parameter is normally NULL, unless you need COM aggregation.

The DSBUFFERDESC is defined as

```
typedef struct _DSBUFFERDESC{
    DWORD           dwSize;
    DWORD           dwFlags;
    DWORD           dwBufferBytes;
    DWORD           dwReserved;
    LPWAVEFORMATEX  lpwfxFormat;
} DSBUFFERDESC, *LPDSBUFFERDESC;
```

The member variables of the DSBUFFERDESC represent the following:

- dwSize is the size of the structure (which can found by the sizeof() operator).

- `dwFlags` lets you set several options to control things like stereophonic sound, pan, and volume control. A good set of defaults can be set using the `DSBCAPS_CTRLDEFAULT` flag.

- `dwBufferBytes` describes how many bytes of data your new buffer should hold. You might need a large buffer for long samples or complex sounds; you can use a smaller buffer for short or repetitive sounds. The buffers can be played in a looping mode to reuse the contents over and over again for long repetitive sound effects.

- `lpwfxFormat` points to a `WAVEFORMATEX` structure, which holds information that tells the sound card how the effect should be played.

The `WAVEFORMATEX` structure holds details such as the speed at which the buffer should be played and how many bytes in the buffer represent each sound value. It also holds the technique for playing the sound, which is hardware-dependent, but normally most sound cards support the simple `WAVE_FORMAT_PCM` technique described earlier.

After you have a secondary buffer, you can set the values either by loading them from a .wav file or by setting them programmatically. Either way, access to the buffer is controlled by calling a `Lock()` function on the `IDirectSoundBuffer` interface, which returns the buffer address and size. You can then write the required wave values into the buffer and call the `Unlock()` function to release the buffer.

When the buffer has been set you can play it by calling the `IDirectSoundBuffer` interface's `Play()` function, which needs three parameters. The first two are reserved and must be set to zero. The third can be set to `DSBPLAY_LOOPING` to play the buffer in a loop, or zero to play just once. You can stop the playing effect by calling the `Stop()` function.

Listing 28.1 shows how DirectSound can be used to make a simple but effective keyboard-driven synthesizer sound effect from the `view` class of a simple SDI application. It creates and displays the contents of two secondary sound buffers as the top red and green lines, which are set to decaying sine and increasing noise values, respectively (see Figure 28.1).

Locking and unlocking the buffer

The sound buffer shouldn't be locked for long periods of time; otherwise, any sound currently being played might need that part of the buffer you have locked and start playing random noise. Some sound cards will have onboard buffer memory that isn't directly accessible from the main CPU's address space. If so, the `Lock()` and `Unlock()` function also transfer the memory from and then back to the onboard sound buffer after presenting it into system memory for your program to update.

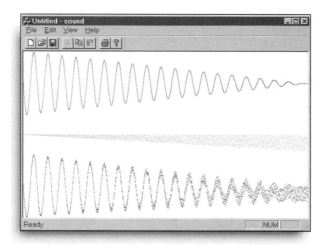

FIGURE 28.1

The SoundView example showing two buffers and their resulting mixed waveform.

Then it plays both buffers together whenever the user presses a key to produce a sine wave that becomes swamped in white noise from the primary buffer (this combined wave is displayed as the lower blue line). The pitch of the sine wave is determined by the ASCII code of the key pressed, so letters higher in the alphabet produce higher notes.

Obviously, this example requires a sound card.

LISTING 28.1 LST32_1.CPP—A Simple Synth Program Created by Mixing Two *DirectSound* Buffers Played by the Keyboard

```
1   CSoundView::CSoundView()
2   {
3     m_pDSObject = NULL;
4     m_pDSBuffer = NULL;
5     m_pDSMix = NULL;
6   }
7
8   CSoundView::~CSoundView()
9   {
10    if (m_pDSMix) m_pDSMix->Release();
11    if (m_pDSBuffer) m_pDSBuffer->Release();
12    if (m_pDSObject) m_pDSObject->Release();
13  }
```

① The DirectSound COM objects should be deallocated gracefully by calling `Release()`.

continues...

LISTING 28.1 Continued

```
14
15   void CSoundView::PlayFreq(double dFreq)
16   {
17     if (!m_pDSObject)
18     {
19       // Create the Direct Sound Object
20       if(DS_OK==DirectSoundCreate(
21                         NULL,&m_pDSObject,NULL))
22       {
23         // Set the Co-Operation level
24         m_pDSObject->SetCooperativeLevel(m_hWnd,
25                             DSSCL_NORMAL);
26
27         // Clear the direct sound buffer
28         memset(&m_DSBufferDesc,0,sizeof(DSBUFFERDESC));
29
30         // Setup a secondary buffer
31         m_DSBufferDesc.dwSize = sizeof(DSBUFFERDESC);
32         m_DSBufferDesc.dwFlags = DSBCAPS_CTRLDEFAULT;
33         m_DSBufferDesc.dwBufferBytes = 4096;
34
35         // Set a wave format for 22.0Khz, 1 byte DtoA
36         static WAVEFORMATEX sWave = {
37             WAVE_FORMAT_PCM,1,22000,22000,1,8,0 };
38
39         m_DSBufferDesc.lpwfxFormat = &sWave;
40
41         // Create the First Secondary buffer
42         m_pDSObject->CreateSoundBuffer(&m_DSBufferDesc,
43                             &m_pDSBuffer,NULL);
44
45         // Create the Second Secondary buffer
46         m_pDSObject->CreateSoundBuffer(&m_DSBufferDesc,
47                             &m_pDSMix,NULL);
48       }
49     }
50
51     // if the DirectSound object is valid ...
52     if (m_pDSObject)
53     {
54       // Declare buffer pointers
```

```
55      LPBYTE pBuffer1,pBuffer2;
56      LPBYTE pEnv1,pEnv2;
57      DWORD dwSize1,dwSize2;
58
59      // Erase the background
60      CClientDC dcClient(this);
61      CRect rcClient;
62      GetClientRect(&rcClient);
63      int yOff = (rcClient.Height()-24)/3;
64      dcClient.FillSolidRect(
65              rcClient,RGB(255,255,255));
66
67    // Lock the sound buffer
68    m_pDSBuffer->Lock(0,m_DSBufferDesc.dwBufferBytes,
69                    (LPVOID*)&pBuffer1,&dwSize1,
70                    (LPVOID*)&pBuffer2,&dwSize2,0);
71    m_pDSMix->Lock(0,m_DSBufferDesc.dwBufferBytes,
72                    (LPVOID*)&pEnv1,&dwSize1,
73                    (LPVOID*)&pEnv2,&dwSize2,0);
74
75      // Set the two buffers
76      double dRange = 128.0 / (double)dwSize1;
77      double dXRange = (double)rcClient.Width()
78                          / (double)dwSize1;
79      for(int i=0;i<(int)dwSize1;i++)
80      {
81        double dAmplitude = 1.0 + dRange * (double)i;
82        BYTE b1 = (BYTE)(127 + (128.0 - dAmplitude)
83                  * sin((double)i / (0.147 * dFreq)));
84        BYTE b2 = (BYTE)(rand()%(int)dAmplitude)>>1;
85        *(pBuffer1+i) = b1;
86        *(pEnv1+i) = b2;
87
88        BYTE b3 = b1 + b2;
89
90        // Draw the waveform
91        int x = (int)(dXRange * (double)i);
92        dcClient.SetPixelV(x,
93                  (b1>>1),RGB(255,0,0));
94        dcClient.SetPixelV(x,yOff+64+
95                  (b2>>1),RGB(0,255,0));
```

(2) The Lock()_ function locks the memory and returns pointers to the buffers for your program to use.

(3) The waveform values are also drawn so you can see the buffer contents.

continues...

LISTING 28.1 Continued

```
96           dcClient.SetPixelV(x,yOff*2+
97                       (b3>>1),RGB(0,0,255));
98       }
99
100      // Unlock the buffers and play the sound ————④
101      m_pDSBuffer->Unlock(pBuffer1,dwSize1,
102                       pBuffer2,dwSize2);
103      m_pDSMix->Unlock(pEnv1,dwSize1,
104                       pEnv2,dwSize2);
105      m_pDSBuffer->Play(0,0,0);
106      m_pDSMix->Play(0,0,0);
107      }
108  }
109
110  void CSoundView::OnKeyDown(UINT nChar,UINT nRepCnt,
111                                      UINT nFlags)
112  {
113      CView::OnKeyDown(nChar, nRepCnt, nFlags);
114
115      // Play the note with a freqency of the key value
116      if (nRepCnt==1) PlayFreq((double)nChar);
117  }
```

④ The buffers are set playing after they are unlocked.

The code shown in Listing 28.1 should be made in the view class of a normal SDI framework (named Sound) created by AppWizard. Because of these additions to the view class (in the SoundView.cpp file), you'll also need to add the following lines to the class header definition (in SoundView.h) for the new member variables that are used in Listing 28.1:

```
IDirectSound*        m_pDSObject;
IDirectSoundBuffer*  m_pDSBuffer;
IDirectSoundBuffer*  m_pDSMix;
DSBUFFERDESC         m_DSBufferDesc;
void                 PlayFreq(double dFreq);
```

These lines declare the interface pointer member variables needed for the DirectSound interface, the two sound buffers, and the buffer description structure. It also defines the PlayFreq() function that is used to implement the sound effects.

You should add the `OnKeyDown()` handler using ClassWizard to generate a handler function for the `WM_KEYDOWN` message. This will then generate the required header file and message map entries.

To tell the compiler about the required Interface pointers, the wave format structure in the implementation, and the sine function used, you should also add the following `#include` lines to the top of the view class definition header (soundview.h):

```
#include "mmsystem.h"
#include "DSOUND.H"
#include "math.h"
```

The view's constructor in lines 1 to 6 of Listing 28.1 initializes the pointers for the DirectSound object `m_pDSObject`, and the two buffer pointers `m_pDSBuffer` and `m_pDSMix`, to `NULL`. The corresponding destructor in lines 8 to 13 destroys these COM objects by calling their interface `Release()` function and thus releases their reference counts. Lines 17 to 49 of the main `PlayFreq()` function are used to initialize the required DirectSound object and buffers when the function is first called. This initialization must be performed here because the call to `SetCooperativeLevel()` in line 24 needs a valid window handle, `m_hWnd`, which won't be valid in the constructor.

If the `DirectSound` object initializes properly in line 20, the two secondary buffers are created by calling the `CreateSoundBuffer()` function after setting up the required buffer description `m_DSBufferDesc` and `WAVEFORMATEX` structure `sWave`.

The second half of the `PlayFreq()` function sets the sound buffers, draws the waveforms, and plays the sounds according to the values passed in the `dFreq` parameter. Lines 59 to 65 initialize a client device context, blank the view, and initialize a client rectangle for the whole view. Lines 68 to 73 `Lock()` the two secondary sound buffers to return their pointers. Lines 79 to 98 then implement the main loop that generates the wave values for the two buffers and draws them to the view. Line 83 calculates a sine wave value `b1`, based on the frequency and position in the buffer represented by the loop counter `i` and a fading `dAmplitude` volume value. This value is stored in the first of the two buffers

Cooperative levels

There are four cooperative levels for the DirectSound object. `DSSCL_EXCLUSIVE` gives your application exclusive access (if it is first to do so) to the sound card. Other applications will be muted. `DSSCL_NORMAL` allows full cooperation and provides smooth multitasking interaction with other running applications. `DSSCL_PRIORITY` gives your application priority over other normal applications for access to the sound card resources. `DSSCL_WRITEPRIMARY` is the highest priority setting giving your application access to the primary sound buffers and blocking any secondary sound buffers (from all applications) from playing.

in line 85 and used to draw the wave in the view with the SetPixelV() function in line 92 as a red pixel.

The random white noise value for the second of the two buffer values, b2, is found by calling the rand() function for a random number and finding its modulus by the inverted but halved dAmplitude volume value, to give an increasing level of white noise as shown in line 84. This value is then set to the buffer in line 86 and displayed in the view in line 94 as a green pixel. The third value, b3, which will be equivalent to the primary buffer contents when played, only must be calculated as a mix (accumulation) of b1 + b2, as shown in line 88, and used to display the mix waveform as a blue pixel position in line 96.

Lines 101 to 103 Unlock() the two buffers ready for playing with the Play() functions in lines 105 and 106 for each buffer. When the first Play() function is called, a primary buffer will be automatically constructed to mirror the requirements of the secondary buffer and used for writing to the hardware itself. The subsequent Play() will then cause the second secondary buffer to be mixed with this primary buffer to give the required sound effect.

Finally, an OnKeyDown() function can be added using the New Windows Message/Event handler dialog box to catch each key-press and call PlayFreq(), passing the ASCII code of the key as the frequency to make a simple keyboard-driven synthesizer effect.

Before building this application, you must remember to link with the dsound.lib library by adding dsound.lib to the **Object/Library Modules** line in the **Link** tab of the Project Settings dialog box. You can display this dialog box either by pressing Alt+F7 or by clicking the **Project** menu and selecting the **Settings** option.

When you build and run the application, you can display the waveforms by pressing different keys on the keyboard and listen to the sound effect produced.

SEE ALSO

➤ *To understand the ideas and concepts of OLE and COM, see page 648*

Mixing sound buffers

By mixing the waveforms from two concurrently played secondary sound buffers the sound produced by one waveform can be modulated by the other. This technique lets you set a high-frequency oscillating waveform in the first buffer and then modulate it with a lower-frequency oscillator in the second. This can give a vibrato or rough effect to the sound produced.

Using DirectDraw

You can use the DirectDraw API to write super-fast flicker-free graphics applications. This API lets you use the frame synchronized double buffering technique necessary for fast-action games and animation software. You can take control of the whole Windows display, change to different video modes (including the infamous ModeX reportedly used in the Doom2 game), and then flip the visible video surface to draw on a background surface while the screen displays another. This flip can be synchronized to take place when the monitor's electron beam sweeps back to the starting position of the video frame, which allows smooth flicker-free animation.

You can also retain the Windows display and use the faster drawing support directly inside the frame of a normal window. DirectDraw achieves its greatly increased drawing and bit-blitting capabilities by two software layers, the hardware abstraction layer (HAL) and the hardware emulation layer (HEL). When you use the rendering and blitting functions of a DirectDraw surface, you'll be calling the HAL.

This provides a device-independent mechanism allowing your same code to work on a multitude of different video cards. If the rendering function can be performed by the video card hardware, your function will gain the huge speed benefits of hardware implementation. If not, the HEL transparently emulates the hardware functionality so you don't have to worry about the capabilities of the video card hardware.

The DirectDraw API has only four main COM objects available via COM interfaces, as shown in Table 28.1. You can see from the table that some of the interfaces have a number 2 appended to their name. This is because these are later versions than the original COM interfaces still available to older applications. You can also see that the main business object is the DirectDrawSurface. Surfaces are created by the main DirectDraw object and then can be clipped by DirectDrawClipper objects or use the colors from a DirectDrawPalette.

> ## ModeX
>
> ModeX is an undocumented VGA video mode. Many game developers were forced to choose a low-resolution mode with plenty of colors to achieve the fast frame update rate needed for animation. As a result, the best candidate was VGA mode 0x13 (hex), which gives a resolution 320 across by 200 down. However, the exotic ModeX allowed a slightly higher vertical resolution giving 320 pixels across by 240 pixels down.

TABLE 28.1 DirectDraw objects and their functionality

DirectDraw Object	COM Interface	Functionality
DirectDraw	IDirectDraw2	Handles the video modes, device capabilities, and creates the other objects.
DirectDrawSurface	IDirectSurface2	Handles primary and secondary bitmaps, double buffering, drawing, and blitting functions. It can be clipped by the DirectDrawClipper object and can use the colors from the DirectDrawPalette object.
DirectDrawClipper	IDirectDrawClipper	Handles the clipping list information for clipping surfaces.
DirectDrawPalette	IDirectDrawPalette	Handles the palette color entries and mapping information for the colors used in a surface.

COM aggregation

Aggregation in COM is a technique employed by components that contain other components to reuse their functionality. The outer component offers an interface to client objects that is really the interface of the inner object. When a client requests a pointer to that interface, the outer component hands it a direct pointer to the interface of the inner object being aggregated. By offering this third parameter, the DirectDraw object will let other objects aggregate it. In older versions of the DirectX libraries this feature may be unsupported and the DirectDrawCreate() function will return an error code.

You can create the main DirectDraw COM object using the ddraw.lib library function DirectDrawCreate() or by directly calling CoCreateInstance().

The DirectDrawCreate() function needs three parameters. The first is a pointer to a GUID that identifies the display driver to be used. This is normally passed a NULL value to indicate the active display driver that should be used; the other drivers can be found by enumeration. The second parameter is a pointer to an IDirectDraw interface pointer to the new object. If you use this method, you should then use the COM QueryInterface() function to get a pointer to the newer IDirectDraw2 interface. The third parameter is normally set to NULL and is included for COM aggregation.

It is probably simpler to use CoCreateInstance() to create the COM object because you can access the newer IDirectDraw2 interface immediately and don't need to link with the ddraw.lib library. You can do this by passing CLSID_DirectDraw to CoCreateInstance() as the Class ID and IID_IDirectDraw2 to access the newer interface directly; these IDs are available from the DrawDlg.h header file. You must then call the `Initialize()` function to pass the GUID that identifies the display driver (usually `NULL`).

After you have a `DirectDraw` object, you must set its cooperative level using the `IDirectDraw::SetCooperativeLevel()` function. This takes two parameters; the first is a window handle identifying the owner application, and the second is a flag setting.

You can share access with other applications if you retain the normal Windows display by passing the `DDSCL_NORMAL` flag, but if you need control of the whole display, you must use the `DDSCL_EXCLUSIVE` and `DDSCL_FULLSCREEN` flags in conjunction. To do any frame synchronized double buffering, you must take control of the entire display.

You can create surfaces for rendering and blitting by calling the `DirectDraw` object's `CreateSurface()` function and passing it a `DDSURFACEDESC` structure to describe the new surface. This structure describes many types of surfaces. Usually you would create one primary surface with the `DDSCAPS_PRIMARYSURFACE` flag and a number of back buffer surfaces to blit to/from or perform page flipping (double buffering). For the page flipping technique, you can automatically create and link back buffers in the same call to `CreateSurface()` as the primary buffer by specifying a `dwBackBufferCount` and including the `DDSD_BACKBUFFERCOUNT` flag.

You can also create several `clipper` objects to define clipping lists. These are very useful when using `DirectDraw` with the normal Windows display because you can create clipping lists from a parent window to stop rendering outside your window's area. These objects can be created from the `DirectDraw` object using the `CreateClipper()` function, and then selected into a surface by the surface's `SetClipper()` function.

Palettes that support color cycling can be created from the main `DirectDraw` object using the `CreatePalette()` function; these can then be initialized with a set of `COLORREF` values and selected into a surface using the surface's `SetPalette()` function.

You can draw to the surface using the normal GDI functions by first locking it and then retrieving a device context by calling its

---

Using color cycling for animation

Color cycling can also be a useful technique for getting extra animation for free. Reducing the amount of drawing needed in animated video is always a big benefit. By using some color palette colors for color cycling you can add simple monochrome static loops of animation to areas of the screen that don't need to be subsequently redrawn. For example, if you were to draw four circles at the same point, each with subsequently larger diameters in four different colors, you could then redefine three colors as black and one as white. The white color can be shifted along the palette through the four color positions between each frame causing each circle to be illuminated in turn.

GetDC() function. When you've finished drawing to it, you must call its ReleaseDC() function. A range of fast bit blitting functions such as Blt() let you copy and color surfaces using a wide range of techniques such as stretching and texture mapping.

Primary surfaces and their back buffer surfaces can be flipped by calling the primary surface's Flip() function, which can work asynchronously and will wait for the next vertical frame refresh period. Alternatively, you can pass a flag to wait for the refresh or use the DirectDraw object's WaitForVerticalBlank() function. Other useful video-specific functions include GetMonitorFrequency() and GetScanLine().

Listing 28.2 shows a sample DirectDraw application that uses double buffering to produce an entrancing fast, flicker-free spirograph-style animation after taking control of the Windows desktop. It doesn't need to link to ddraw.lib because it uses CoCreateInstance() to create the DirectDraw object and gracefully restores the Windows display when you press Esc. The example uses a default dialog-based application framework named Draw to set up the screen in OnInitDialog() and draw the image in a background buffer in response to a normal Windows timer message in an OnTimer() function. When the fast and complex drawing is complete, the background and foreground buffers are flipped so that the new image is instantly displayed without flicker during the vertical blanking period.

> **Using the bit blit functions and GDI functions**
>
> You must be careful not to call a bit blit function while you have a valid device context from GetDC(). The GetDC() locks the device context and the bit blit function will fail; you must call ReleaseDC() before you can perform other bit blit functions.

LISTING 28.2 LST32_2.CPP—*DirectDraw* Used to Render an Entrancing Flicker-Free Spirograph Animation Using Double Buffering

```
1   CDrawDlg::CDrawDlg(CWnd* pParent /*=NULL*/)
2       : CDialog(CDrawDlg::IDD, pParent)
3   {
4       //{{AFX_DATA_INIT(CDrawDlg)
5       // NOTE: the ClassWizard will add member initializa
6       //}}AFX_DATA_INIT
7       // Note that LoadIcon does not require a subsequent
8       m_hIcon = AfxGetApp()->LoadIcon(IDR_MAINFRAME);
9
10      m_pIDraw = NULL;
11      m_pIMainSurface = NULL;
12
```

```
13        CoInitialize(NULL);  ──────①
14    }
15
16    CDrawDlg::~CDrawDlg()
17    {
18      if (m_pIMainSurface)
19      {
20        m_pIDraw->SetCooperativeLevel(m_hWnd,DDSCL_NORMAL);
21        m_pIDraw->RestoreDisplayMode();  ──────②
22        m_pIMainSurface->Release();
23      }
24      if (m_pIDraw) m_pIDraw->Release();
25      CoUninitialize();
26    }
27
28    BOOL CDrawDlg::OnInitDialog()
29    {
30      CDialog::OnInitDialog();
31
32      // ** Initialize the OLE / COM library
33      if (FAILED(CoInitialize(NULL))) return FALSE;
34
35      // ** Create a direct draw object and interface
36      HRESULT hr = CoCreateInstance(CLSID_DirectDraw,NULL,  ──────③
37        CLSCTX_ALL, IID_IDirectDraw2, (void**)&m_pIDraw);
38
39      if(!FAILED(hr))
40      {
41          hr = m_pIDraw->Initialize((struct _GUID*)NULL);
42          if (hr !=DD_OK) return FALSE;
43      }
44
45      // ** Set exclusive full screen mode
46      m_pIDraw->SetCooperativeLevel(m_hWnd,
47        DDSCL_EXCLUSIVE¦DDSCL_FULLSCREEN
48      ➡¦DDSCL_ALLOWREBOOT);
49      // ** Set up a surface description structure
50      DDSURFACEDESC DrawSurfaceDesc;
51      memset(&DrawSurfaceDesc,0,sizeof(DrawSurfaceDesc));
52      DrawSurfaceDesc.dwSize = sizeof(DrawSurfaceDesc);
```

① CoInitialize initial-
   izes the COM libraries.

② The display mode is set
   to NORMAL and the
   COM objects are
   released.

③ CoCreateInstance
   () is used to return a
   pointer to the
   IdirectDraw2 inter-
   face of a new
   DirectDraw object.

continues...

LISTING 28.2 Continued

④ A primary surface with one back buffer is described in the DrawSurfaceDesc structure.

⑤ A pointer to the back buffer surface can be found with GetAttachedSurface ().

⑥ A Blt() function can be used to fill a surface with a specified color rather than copying surfaces.

```
53   DrawSurfaceDesc.dwFlags = DDSD_CAPS                         ④
54                            | DDSD_BACKBUFFERCOUNT;
55   DrawSurfaceDesc.ddsCaps.dwCaps = DDSCAPS_COMPLEX
56 | DDSCAPS_FLIP | DDSCAPS_PRIMARYSURFACE;
57   DrawSurfaceDesc.dwBackBufferCount = 1;
58   // ** Create the primary surface
59   hr = m_pIDraw->CreateSurface(&DrawSurfaceDesc,
60       (IDirectDrawSurface**)&m_pIMainSurface,NULL);
61   if (FAILED(hr)) return FALSE;
62
63   // ** Find the back buffer
64   DrawSurfaceDesc.ddsCaps.dwCaps = DDSCAPS_BACKBUFFER;
65   hr = m_pIMainSurface->GetAttachedSurface(          ⑤
     ➥&DrawSurfaceDesc, ddsCaps,&m_pIFlipSurface);
66
67
68   SetTimer(1,50,0); // ** Start the 50ms Timer
69
70   return TRUE;
71 }
72
73 void CDrawDlg::OnTimer(UINT nIDEvent)
74 {
75     CDialog::OnTimer(nIDEvent);
76
77     static RECT rc={0,0,0,0};
78     static double dPetals=2.0;
79
80     // ** Clear the surface quickly with a blit
81     if (rc.right>0)
82     {
83         DDBLTFX dbltfx;
84         dbltfx.dwSize=sizeof(DDBLTFX);
85         dbltfx.dwFillColor=RGB(0,0,0);
86         HRESULT hr = m_pIFlipSurface->Blt(&rc,NULL,   ⑥
87                       &rc,DDBLT_COLORFILL,&dbltfx);
88     }
89     HDC hdc = NULL;
90
91     // ** Get a device context for the surface
92     if (m_pIFlipSurface->GetDC(&hdc) == DD_OK)
```

```
93          {
94              if (hdc)
95              {
96                  CDC dc;
97                  dc.Attach(hdc);
98
99                  rc.right = dc.GetDeviceCaps(HORZRES);
100             rc.bottom = dc.GetDeviceCaps(VERTRES);
101
102             double mx = (double)(rc.right>>1);
103             double my = (double)(rc.bottom>>1);
104
105             CPen psCol(PS_SOLID,1,RGB(0,255,0));
106             CPen* ppsOld = dc.SelectObject(&psCol);
107
108             double sx = mx/2;
109             double sy = my/2;
110             double sAngle = 0.0;
111
112             // ** Draw the graphical animation
113             for(int i=0;i<(int)dPetals;i++)
114             {
115                 double s1a = sin(sAngle);
116                 double c1a = cos(sAngle);
117                 double s2a = sin(sAngle * dPetals);
118                 double c2a = cos(sAngle * dPetals);
119                 int x = (int)(mx+sx*c1a+sx*c2a);
120                 int y = (int)(my+sy*s1a-sy*s2a);
121                 if (i==0)    dc.MoveTo(x,y);
122                 else    dc.LineTo(x,y);
123                 sAngle+=0.01745;
124             }
125
126         dPetals+=0.1;
127         dc.SelectObject(ppsOld);
128         dc.Detach();
129     }
130     m_pIFlipSurface->ReleaseDC(hdc);
131 }
128
133 // ** Show the newly drawn surface
```

(7) These lines of mathmatics produce two quickly swirling, complex patterns of a continuously changing spirograph.

continues...

LISTING 28.2 Continued

```
134    m_pIMainSurface->Flip(NULL,DDFLIP_WAIT);  ———⟨8⟩
135    }
```

⟨8⟩ The Flip() function waits for the video flyback period and then flips the video pages to avoid flicker caused by half-drawn pages on the monitor.

In addition to Listing 28.2, you'll also need to add and ensure that the following #include files are present at the top of the DrawDlg.cpp implementation to supply the GUID values and the cosine definitions:

```
#include <initguid.h>
#include "DrawDlg.h"
#include "math.h"
```

The definitions for the DirectDraw interfaces can be supplied by including the appropriate DirectDraw header file at the top of the DrawDlg.h class definition file:

```
#include <ddraw.h>
```

The following interface pointers should also be added to the DrawDlg.h file as member variables of the CDrawDlg class definition:

```
IDirectDraw2*           m_pIDraw;
IDirectDrawSurface2*    m_pIMainSurface;
IDirectDrawSurface2*    m_pIFlipSurface;
```

In Listing 28.2, the interface pointers are set to NULL in the CDrawDlg constructor (in lines 10 and 11) and the COM library is initialized with the CoInitialize() function in line 13.

The OnInitDialog() function is used to create the DirectDraw object by calling CoCreateInstance() on line 36. It's completed with the call to its Initialize() function on line 41, which indicates that the active display driver should be used. Line 47 then sets the cooperative level to exclusive and full screen.

The DDSURFACEDESC structure DrawSurfaceDesc is declared on line 50 and set up for a primary buffer with a single background buffer for the double buffering. The DrawSurfaceDesc structure can then be used to create the surface in the CreateSurface() call in line 59; an interface pointer to the additional background surface can then be obtained by calling GetAttachedSurface() as shown in line 65.

Finally, a timer with a 50ms interval period is set with the `SetTimer()` call in line 68 to repeatedly call the drawing function implemented in the `OnTimer()` handler in line 73. You should add this `OnTimer()` handler with ClassWizard to handle the `WM_TIMER` message. This ensures that the correct class definition and message map entries are created.

After setting some default values, the `Blt()` function is used in line 86 to quickly clear the background buffer to a black background and erase any previous drawing on the surface.

`GetDC()` is called on line 92 to obtain a device context handle from GDI drawing to the background surface. This handle can then be attached to a `CDC` class as shown in line 97. Lines 99 to 126 use normal GDI calls and a `CPen` object to draw very fast lines on the surface to render one frame of the complex animated spirograph shape. The device context is released in line 130 and then the buffers are flipped to display the newly drawn frame by calling `Flip()` and passing the `DDFLIP_WAIT` to wait for the next vertical blanking period to occur.

The destructor function in lines 16 to 25 reconstruct the normal Windows desktop by resetting the cooperative level and calling `RestoreDisplayMode()` to normalize the display. The interfaces are released with `Release()` to free them and the COM library is de-initialized gracefully.

If you make these changes to a normal dialog-based framework, you can build the application without any extra API libraries, showing the power of pure COM objects. Then run the application and enjoy the smooth and fast flickerless computer graphics that demonstrate the true power of DirectX.

You can terminate the application at any time by pressing the Esc key (which is a shortcut to the dialog box's still active Cancel button). This will then gracefully redisplay the normal desktop and close the application.

SEE ALSO

➤ *To understand the ideas and concepts of OLE and COM, see page 648*

➤ *To learn about device contexts and drawing with the GDI, see page 356*

The vertical blanking period

When your (cathode ray tube-based) monitor draws the output from the video card it scans an electron beam from left to right drawing each line in turn. The electrons hitting phosphors on the inside surface of the screen glow for a short while after being hit, illuminating the pixels. When the beam reaches the bottom right of the screen it must return to the top left again without illuminating any pixels. At this point the electron beam is turned off between frames. The video card sets a flag during this period to indicate that vertical blanking is occurring. This is the best time to change the memory that the video card is using to generate the video output because it isn't displaying anything.

Using Direct3D

You can use the Direct3D API to harness the power of modern video cards with 3D hardware capabilities. It works in conjunction with `DirectDraw` to produce smooth and fast real-world perspective graphics as seen in games and virtual reality applications.

Direct3D uses a rendering engine that is composed of three modules to support matrix transformation of coordinates, lighting effects for spot and ambient lighting, and a rasterization module to draw the resulting scene.

Several Direct3D interfaces offer all the functionality required for constructing and rendering complex three-dimensional views and are broken into two categories, immediate-mode and retained-mode.

The immediate-mode objects are the low-level and fast foundation 3D drawing objects (their interfaces are shown in Table 28.2). Built on top of the immediate-mode objects are the numerous retained-mode objects that extend the functionality to produce sophisticated high-quality real-time 3D scenes and animations.

TABLE 28.2 Direct3D interfaces and their functionality

Direct3D Interface	Functionality
IDirect3D	Initializes the environment and creates the `Light`, `Material`, and `Viewport` objects.
IDirect3DDevice	Handles configuration of the underlying 3D hardware capabilities and environment capabilities. You can obtain such an interface from a DirectDraw surface using a call to `QueryInterface()`.
IDirect3DExecuteBuffer	Execute buffers are used to store the vertex information and rendering instructions for specific elements of a 3D scene ready for rendering.
IDirect3DLight	Configures the lighting data for individual lights in a scene.

Direct3D Interface	Functionality
`IDirect3DMaterial`	Maintains the properties of materials and their reflective or transparent qualities.
`IDirect3DTexture`	Maintains a texture bitmap for overlaying on 3D surfaces.
`IDirect3DViewport`	Groups lighting, texture, and background effects into a screen position. Several viewports are then strung together, ready for the device to draw along with the vertex data.

Using DirectPlay

You can use the DirectPlay API to easily construct a fast networked multiplayer game without the hassle of implementing support for every type of network connection. The two interfaces `IDirectPlay2` and `IDirectPlayLobby` manage all the aspects of multiplayer game objects and session management, respectively.

Using DirectInput

You can use the DirectInput API to gain faster access to the mouse and keyboard input than the standard Windows APIs allow. It also supports input from multi-axis joysticks with many buttons and has functions to help calibrate them. The API is simple but flexible and is implemented by two COM interfaces. The `IDirectInput` interface manages the system's input devices and their statuses. It also lets you create instances of `IDirectInputDevice` devices to handle the configuration and input of individual devices.

Using DirectSetup

The DirectSetup API is probably the smallest API ever. It has just two functions, `DirectXSetup()`, which automates the installation and setup of all the DirectX components, and `DirectXRegisterApplication()`, which registers a game as a `DirectPlayLobby`-enabled multiplayer networked application.

> **DirectPlay network transport support**
>
> The DirectPlay API supports machines connected by serial cable, TCP/IP LANs, Dialup and Direct Internet connection, Netware, and many other types of network implementation.

Creating Messages and Email Using MAPI

The Microsoft Messaging API (MAPI) isn't really an API; it's a set of standards that compose an architecture. By following these rigid and extensive standards, software developers can focus on and create different parts of an email system.

Most developers will probably want to create custom client applications (reading and writing), whereas others develop the service providers that transport and store the messages or hold a list of recipients in an address book. Each of these components can be implemented separately and users can mix and combine solutions to provide integrated and interchangeable messaging solutions. This flexibility is often necessary in large organizations that must integrate old, new, and very different email systems together.

Extended MAPI SDK and the MDBView sample program

If you really need Extended MAPI support, prepare for a lot of hard work and learning. You will need to download the MAPI SDK. This SDK contains the excellent MDBView.exe sample program and its source code, which can greatly help in understanding the complexities of programming with extended MAPI.

When you're writing a MAPI application, you have a choice of two flavors depending on the complexity of your messaging requirements. Simple MAPI supports the minimum set of functions required to log on and create a MAPI session, send or read messages, and resolve (find closest matching) addresses from an address book. If your application will only need these fundamental capabilities, it is best to use simple MAPI. Any extra functionality will require Extended MAPI, which is implemented by the mapi28.dll and whichever service provider components you want to use. Extended MAPI is necessarily huge and complex; to work with it you'll need a good understanding of COM because it is implemented mainly via an object-oriented hierarchy of COM interfaces and objects.

SEE ALSO
➤ *To understand the ideas and concepts of OLE and COM, see page 648*

Using Simple MAPI

Simple MAPI is implemented by the mapi28.dll, and its function prototypes and flag values are defined in the mapi.h header file. Your simple MAPI session can log on to a message provider specifying a MAPI profile or accepting the default profile to start the session. You can configure these MAPI profiles using the Mail and Fax Control Panel applet shown in Figure 28.2. Each profile holds the details of the transport, message, and address book providers that a client program will use when it logs on, such as Microsoft Exchange or Lotus Notes. When you're logged on, you can then send or receive email and log off when finished.

The Mail and Fax Control Panel applet

The Mail and Fax Control Panel applet might appear different or with a different title depending on the MAPI email applications you currently have installed on your machine.

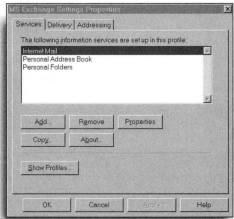

FIGURE 28.2

The Control Panel's Mail and Fax Control Panel applet configures MAPI profiles.

The simple MAPI functions are shown in Table 28.3. These functions can be called from your application either by directly linking with the mapi28.lib, which provides the export entry points for the mapi28.dll, or by using `LoadLibrary()` and `GetProcAddress()` to load and unload the DLL dynamically.

Simple and Enhanced MAPI functions

Implementation code for both Simple and Enhanced MAPI functions can be found in the MAPI32.DLL.

TABLE 28.3 Simple MAPI functions

Function	Description
MAPILogon()	Log on to a MAPI session via a profile configuration
MAPILogoff()	Log off from the MAPI session
MAPISendMail()	Send a message from a `MapiMessage` structure
MAPISendDocuments()	Send a set of document files by specifying their filenames
MAPIFindNext()	Find the first or next message and return an identifier to it
MAPIReadMail()	Read aspects of the message into a `MapiMessage` structure
MAPISaveMail()	Save the new message in an inbox if supported by the provider
MAPIDeleteMail()	Delete a message specified by the last `MAPIFindNext()` function
MAPIFreeBuffer()	Free MAPI allocated buffers
MAPIAddress()	Display the address list dialog box and enable user modifications
MAPIDetails()	Show the entries in a specific address entry
MAPIResolveName()	Change an ambiguous recipient name into an address list entry

SEE ALSO
➤ *To understand the ideas and concepts of OLE and COM, see page 648*

Using AppWizard to Add MAPI Send Mail

You can use AppWizard Step 4 to add MAPI support to an SDI or MDI framework (see Figure 28.3) by checking the **MAPI (Messaging API)** check box under the **What features would you like to include?** section. This will add the **Send** menu option to your new framework's **File** menu and the following message map entries in your document class:

```
ON_COMMAND(ID_FILE_SEND_MAIL, OnFileSendMail)
ON_UPDATE_COMMAND_UI(ID_FILE_SEND_MAIL,
➡OnUpdateFileSendMail)
```

FIGURE 28.3
Adding MAPI support to an SDI or MDI framework with AppWizard.

You can build and run this framework without any modifications and have instant send-email functionality. You can click the **File** menu and select the **Send** option to invoke the MAPI logon dialog box. When you've chosen a profile (or configured your email system), your email package will start and you can compose and send an email message. The framework will automatically serialize your current document by calling OnSaveDocument() and attaching this to the new email.

If you need more sophisticated email support in your application you must use either the simple MAPI or the Extended MAPI functions.

Listing 28.3 shows how to use simple MAPI in a MAPI SDI framework based on an Edit view to make a mail client that can send messages via the normal framework **File**, **Send** menu option and read messages via an added **File**, **Receive** menu option. The new messages are then displayed in the Edit view.

The example loads the mapi28.dll dynamically in the document constructor, logs on to a new MAPI session, and then logs off and frees the DLL in the constructor.

You can create a normal SDI framework with AppWizard and enable the MAPI option for the **Send** option. You can specify an Edit view as the base view on the last AppWizard step. You will then need to add a new menu option to the **File** menu named **Receive** via the resource editor. The code can then be simply added around a menu handler for the new menu option in the document implementation.

LISTING 28.3   LST32_3.CPP—Using Simple MAPI to Read Email Messages in a MAPI-Enabled SDI Application

① The DLL functions are found manually using the GetProcAddress() function.

② The program logs on to MAPI using the default profile.

```
1    #include <mapi.h>
2
3    HMODULE g_hMAPI;
4    LHANDLE g_hSession;
5
6    LPMAPILOGON g_lpfnLogon;
7    LPMAPILOGOFF g_lpfnLogoff;
8    LPMAPIFINDNEXT g_lpfnFindNext;
9    LPMAPIREADMAIL g_lpfnReadMail;
10   LPMAPIFREEBUFFER g_lpfnFreeBuffer;
11
12   CMailClientDoc::CMailClientDoc()
13   {
14     // ** Dynamically load the dll and functions
15     g_hMAPI = LoadLibrary("MAPI28.DLL");
16     g_lpfnLogon = (LPMAPILOGON)
17   GetProcAddress(g_hMAPI,"MAPILogon");        ——①
18     g_lpfnLogoff = (LPMAPILOGOFF)
19   GetProcAddress(g_hMAPI,"MAPILogoff");
20     g_lpfnFindNext = (LPMAPIFINDNEXT)
21   GetProcAddress(g_hMAPI,"MAPIFindNext");
22     g_lpfnReadMail = (LPMAPIREADMAIL)
23   GetProcAddress(g_hMAPI,"MAPIReadMail");
24     g_lpfnFreeBuffer= (LPMAPIFREEBUFFER)
25   GetProcAddress(g_hMAPI,"MAPIFreeBuffer");
26
27     (*g_lpfnLogon)(0,NULL,NULL,           ——②
28       MAPI_NEW_SESSION | MAPI_LOGON_UI,0,&g_hSession);
29   }
30
31   CMailClientDoc::~CMailClientDoc()
```

```
32   {
33       // ** Log off and free the session
34       (*g_lpfnLogoff)(g_hSession,0,0,0);
35       FreeLibrary(g_hMAPI);
36   }
37
38   void CMailClientDoc::OnFileReceive()
39   {
40       // ** Find the view
41       POSITION pos = GetFirstViewPosition();
42       CView* pView = GetNextView(pos);
43
44       // ** Declare the message identifiers
45       static char szSeedMessage[512];
46       static char szMessage[512];
47
48       static LPSTR pSeed = NULL;
49       static LPSTR pMsg = szMessage;
50       lpMapiMessage lpMessage = NULL;
51
52       // ** Find the next mail
53       ULONG ulResult = (*g_lpfnFindNext)(g_hSession,
54                     (ULONG)pView->m_hWnd,NULL,pSeed,
55                        MAPI_LONG_MSGID, 0L, pMsg);
56
57       // ** Read the next email
58       ulResult = (*g_lpfnReadMail)(g_hSession,
59       (ULONG)pView->m_hWnd,pMsg,MAPI_PEEK, 0L,&lpMessage);
60
61       CString strMessage;
62       CString strFmt;
63       if (ulResult == 0L)
64       {
65           // ** Store the message parts
66           strFmt.Format("From: %s\r\n",
67               lpMessage->lpOriginator->lpszName);
68           strMessage += strFmt;
69           strFmt.Format("To: %s\r\n",
70               lpMessage->lpRecips[0].lpszName);
71           strMessage += strFmt;
72           strFmt.Format("Subject: %s\r\n",
```

(3) FindNext() looks for the next email based on the seed value for the previous email.

(4) ReadMail() reads the message contents into a MapiMessage buffer.

continues...

LISTING 28.3   Continued

```
73                     lpMessage->lpszSubject);
74             strMessage += strFmt;
75             strMessage += lpMessage->lpszNoteText;
76             pSeed = szSeedMessage;
77             strcpy(pSeed,pMsg);
78
79             // ** Set the message to the edit view
80             pView->SetWindowText(strMessage);
81
82             // ** Free the allocated buffer
83             (*g_lpfnFreeBuffer)((LPVOID)lpMessage);
84         }
85     }
```

Checking the GetProcAddress() return value

After you've successfully loaded the DLL, you can find its functions by calling GetProcAddress(). The GetProcAddress() function returns the address of a named function passed as a string parameter from the DLL handle that you must also pass.

If the GetProcAddress() found the correct address, the lpfnLogon function pointer will hold the correct address; otherwise it will hold a NULL value. You should always ensure that GetProcAddress() returns a value function pointer. There is no surer way to crash your program than to transfer program flow to address zero!

The first line of Listing 28.3 includes the mapi.h header, which holds all the prototypes and flags used. The document's constructor in lines 12 to 29 loads the mapi28.dll using the LoadLibrary() function in line 15, and then finds the addresses of the functions from the DLL using the GetProcAddress() storing the addresses in global pointers declared in lines 6 to 10. Finally, line 27 logs on to a new MAPI session, storing the session handle in g_hSession.

The OnFileReceive() menu handler function at line 38 should be added to the document with ClassWizard and implements the email-reading code. Lines 41 and 42 find the Edit view that is used as the parent window handle in line 53 to find the next waiting message with FindNext(). The szSeedMessage buffer provides a key to FindNext() so it can determine the next available message based on the contents of the seed, or the first if the pSeed pointer is NULL.

Line 58 attempts to read the contents of the message identified by the lpMessage entry pointer with a ReadMail() call. If it's successful, zero is returned in ulResult and the lpMessage pointer will point to a MapiMessage structure. The message details can then be picked out from the structure using the lpMessage pointer (shown in lines 65 to 75).

After the formatted `strMessage` has been built up from the structure, you can set the message to the view using `SetWindowText()` as shown in line 80 and free the structure using the `MAPIFreeBuffer()` call via the `g_lpfnFreeBuffer` function pointer (set up in line 24), as shown in line 83.

Lines 76 and 77 copy the current message into the seed buffer ready for the next `FindNext()` call, so that it can retrieve the subsequent message when the user next selects the new **Receive** menu option.

When the document is closed, the session is logged off in line 34 and the .dll is unloaded by the `FreeLibrary()` call in line 35.

If you build and run this application, you should be able to send and receive email as shown in Figure 28.4 by clicking **File** and selecting **Send** or your new menu option **Receive**. Subsequent messages can be then be read by selecting **Receive** again.

When you first run the application, you'll be shown a MAPI Profile logon dialog box showing your default profile; you can simply click **OK** to log on with the specified profile.

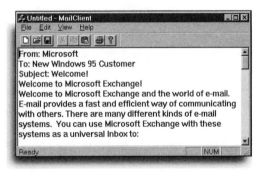

FIGURE 28.4
Reading email from an SDI Edit view application using Simple MAPI.

Using the Video and Sound Multimedia Libraries

Multimedia capabilities have transformed the stale business workhorse image of the PC. You can now play compact discs, television, sound effects, and movies through your PC and easily add these features to your application thanks to the multimedia libraries and the Media Control Interface (MCI). The MCI and its user interface mechanism, the MCIWnd window, provide a simple and centralized way to control some very sophisticated software and hardware.

Using the Media Control Interface

The MCI provides you with either a text-based or structure-based command system to control the various multimedia devices from your applications.

The text-based Command Strings system works by letting you string together control commands that are then submitted to the MCI by the mciSendString() function. The text-based system is simple and easy to use, and is helpful when debugging human readable strings.

Alternatively, you can set up the commands with normal C++ flags and structures with the Command Messages system, which uses the mciSendCommand() function to send messages to the MCI. This system might be a little faster because the strings don't need to be built up and parsed. However, the two systems are functionally identical and you can pick whichever suits your application better.

The first command you send to the MCI should be to open a specific device. You can do this by using the open string to the mciSendString() function or the MCI_OPEN flag to the mciSendCommand() function. You can open any of the device types listed in Table 28.4 that are installed on your system. Some require specialist hardware, whereas others such as waveaudio and digitalvideo have player software included standard in Windows.

MCI commands

The MCI commands are designed to be as generic as possible, which means a core set of commands can be used with every device. These basic commands let you open, close, find the status and capabilities, load data, save data, play, record, pause, resume playing or recording, stop or seek to a position on every type of media device.

TABLE 28.4 MCI device types

Device String	Device Message Flag	Description
waveaudio	MCI_DEVTYPE_WAVEFORM_AUDIO	Play/record .wav audio wave files
sequencer	MCI_DEVTYPE_SEQUENCER	MIDI sequencer

Device String	Device Message Flag	Description
cdaudio	MCI_DEVTYPE_CD_AUDIO	Plays compact discs
dat	MCI_DEVTYPE_DAT	Play/record digital audio tape
digitalvideo	MCI_DEVTYPE_DIGITAL_VIDEO	Plays .avi digital video files
vcr	MCI_DEVTYPE_VCR	Play/record video cassettes
videodisc	MCI_DEVTYPE_VIDEODISC	Plays video discs
mmmovie	MCI_DEVTYPE_ANIMATION	Plays animations
overlay	MCI_DEVTYPE_OVERLAY	Analog video input in window
scanner	MCI_DEVTYPE_SCANNER	Scan images
other	MCI_DEVTYPE_OTHER	Undefined device

As you might expect, the open command requires some parameters, and for the mciSendString() function you must send the following command string parameters after open, separated by spaces:

```
open devicename openflags notifyflags
```

The devicename parameter can be any of the device strings listed in Table 28.4. The openflags parameter can specify an alias name (this identifies the specific instance of an opened device in future string commands), and various device-specific options. The notifyflags can be set to either wait or notify to signal that the command should wait for the device to open, or continue and notify your program when the open has occurred.

You can also ask mciSendString() to return a status message by passing a return buffer and the size of the buffer. If you need notifications, you can also pass a window destination handle for the notification message.

For example, you could pass the following command string to the MCI via mciSendString() to open the compact disc player and identify it in future calls as mycd:

```
char szRetMsg[80];
mciSendString("open cdaudio alias mycd wait",
➥szRetMsg,sizeof(szRetMsg),m_hWnd);
```

MCI device names

MCI is extensible, and you can add new MCI devices by adding and registering their relevant device drivers. The registration entries on Windows 95 can be found in your C:\Windows\ System.ini file under the [mci] section. Under Windows NT, these settings are stored under the HKEY_LOCAL_MACHINE\ SOFTWARE \Microsoft\Windows NT\CurrentVersion\#SYS...\MCI key.

This command will wait until the CD player is opened properly and will return a "1" in the szRetMsg buffer if all goes well; otherwise, the CD player isn't opened and a "0" will be set to the szRetMsg buffer. If the open fails, an MCIERROR is returned; this can be turned into a message string by the mciGetErrorString() function.

The mciSendCommand() function can perform the same CD player open function by passing four parameters:

- A device identifier (not used in the open)
- A command flag (MCI_OPEN)
- The notify flags, either MCI_WAIT or MCI_NOTIFY
- A pointer to an MCI_OPEN_PARMS structure

The function will then return an MCIERROR status like the mciSendString() function.

You could pass the following command message to the MCI with mciSendCommand() to open the CD player:

```
MCI_OPEN_PARMS myCDOpen = {NULL,0,"cdaudio",NULL,NULL};
errOpen = mciSendCommand(NULL,MCI_OPEN,
    MCI_OPEN_TYPE¦MCI_WAIT,(DWORD)&myCDOpen);
```

Notice that mciSendCommand() uses an MCI_OPEN_PARMS structure passed as myCDOpen. This structure is defined as

```
typedef struct {
    DWORD       dwCallback;
    MCIDEVICEID wDeviceID;
    LPCSTR      lpstrDeviceType;
    LPCSTR      lpstrElementName;
    LPCSTR      lpstrAlias;
} MCI_OPEN_PARMS;
```

The MCI_OPEN_PARMS structure lets you pass a notification window handle in dwCallBack. The ID of the newly opened device will be returned in wDeviceID, which can be used in subsequent calls to identify the device. The lpstrElementName would be used to specify a filename if you were opening the device with an associated

---

MCI device capabilities

You can check whether an MCI device has specific capabilities using the **capabilities** string. For example, to check that a CD has record capabilities, you can use the **capabilities cdaudio can record** string and check the return code to see whether it can. The equivalent command flag is **MCI_GETDEVCAPS**.

file such as a .wav or .avi waveform audio or digital video file. You can set an alias with `lpstrAlias`, although this is less necessary when using command messages because the `wDeviceID` can be used to identify the device.

There are as many of these structures for each of the various `MCI_` command messages to identify the various command parameters as there are different string parameters for each string command.

After the device is open, you can use subsequent commands to play, record, close, or send many other multimedia commands to whichever device you have opened. A few of the many possible command messages and strings are shown in Table 28.5. For each of the possible commands, there are many possible parameters—far too many to cover here, but hopefully this has given you a taste.

TABLE 28.5 Sample command messages and strings

Command Message	Command String	Description
MCI_OPEN	open	Opens a device
MCI_CLOSE	close	Closes the device
MCI_PLAY	play	Plays the device
MCI_RECORD	record	Records from the device
MCI_STOP	stop	Stops playing or recording
MCI_SEEK	seek	Seek to a position
MCI_PAUSE	pause	Pause the device
MCI_RESUME	resume	Continue after pausing
MCI_LOAD	load	Load content
MCI_SAVE	save	Save content
MCI_STATUS	status	Retrieve status information
MCI_WINDOW	window	Display a video window
MCI_WHERE	where	Positions the display

MCI Notification Messages

When you use the `MCI_WAIT` or `wait` flags in an MCI command, the command will wait until it has finished before it returns. This is useful in some circumstances, but if you started playing a CD your application would wait on the play command until it had finished, and an hour might be a long time for a user to wait for a response! Consequently, you can pass no notification or wait flags and the command will return immediately, passing control back to your program. Alternatively, you can pass an `MCI_NOTIFY` flag so that the `play` command tells your application when it has finished playing. Your application might then display a message, eject the CD, or take some other action. Most of the MCI commands support notification.

If you specify `MCI_NOTIFY` or `notify`, the command will return immediately and send a notification message to the message loop of the window handle that you've passed. This might be a View, Dialog, or any other `CWnd`-derived class that is attached to a valid Windows window (you can pass the `m_hWnd` member of any valid `CWnd` object).

You can add a handler for the `MM_MCINOTIFY` message in an `MFC` application using an `ON_MESSAGE` macro entry in the specified window's message map as these lines show:

```
BEGIN_MESSAGE_MAP(CMciDlg, CDialog)
    ON_MESSAGE(MM_MCINOTIFY,OnMCINotify)
END_MESSAGE_MAP()
```

You could then add a handler function that is passed two parameters to identify both the device that sent the notification message and the status code returned by the command. Your handler function should resemble this:

```
void CMciDlg::OnMCINotify(WPARAM wFlags,LPARAM lDevID)
{
    AfxMessageBox("MCI notify: Your Command has finished!");
}
```

The possible `wFlags` parameter can inform your handler of any of the possible status codes shown in Table 28.6. The `lDevID` identifies the device that posted the notification. If you are using the command string methods and using aliases to identify your devices, you can still get the correct device ID for your device by calling the `mciGetDeviceID()` function and passing the alias name string as its only parameter.

TABLE 28.6 Possible status codes in a notification message

Status Code Value	Description
MCI_NOTIFY_SUCCESSFUL	The command has finished and was successful.
MCI_NOTIFY_FAILURE	An error occurred while performing your command.
MCI_NOTIFY_ABORTED	The notification for a previous command has been aborted by a subsequent command on the same device that was incompatible with the first command.
MCI_NOTIFY_SUPERSEDED	A new command has requested notification on the same device as a previous command. The commands are compatible and the previous command has now been superseded.

Checking the command function return code

You must always check the return code from the command function that requests the notification message. If the command function immediately returns an error code indicating failure, your notification message will never be sent. This can lead to situations in which your program might hang waiting for a notification message that never arrives.

Listing 28.4 demonstrates both the Command String and Command Message forms of MCI used to play 5 seconds of a compact disc, from track 3 and 12 seconds to track 3 and 17 seconds. You can add this code into any place of an MFC application (the `InitDialog()` function of a dialog-based application is a quick and easy place to try this).

To include the MCI flags and prototypes, you must add a line to include the following header file:

```
#include "mmsystem.h"
```

Applications using the MCI libraries should link with the `winmm.lib` library file. This should be placed in the **Object/Library Modules** line of your project's Project Settings dialog box in the **Link** tab.

CHAPTER 28 Working with APIs and SDK's

LISTING 28.4 LST32_4.CPP—A Sample String and Message MCI CD Player That Each Play Five Seconds of the CD

① The Command String Open sets the alias for subsequent references.

② MCI_OPEN flag is the Command Message equivalent to the open string.

```cpp
1   // Play 5 seconds of CD track 3 via the Command String
2   char szRetMsg[80];
3   char szErrorMessage[512];
4   MCIERROR errOpen;
5   errOpen = mciSendString("open cdaudio alias mycd wait",      ①
6                   szRetMsg,sizeof(szRetMsg),m_hWnd);
7   if (szRetMsg[0]!='1')
8   {
9       // Display the open error
10      mciGetErrorString(errOpen,szErrorMessage,512);
11      AfxMessageBox(szErrorMessage);
12  }
13  else
14  {
15      // set format to tracks/minutes/seconds/frames
16      mciSendString("set mycd time format tmsf",
17                  szRetMsg,sizeof(szRetMsg),m_hWnd);
18      // Play 5 seconds of track 3 from 12 seconds in
19      mciSendString(
20          "play mycd from 3:0:12:0 to 3:0:17:0 wait",
21                  szRetMsg,sizeof(szRetMsg),m_hWnd);
22      // ** Close the device
23      mciSendString("close mycd",
24                  szRetMsg,sizeof(szRetMsg),m_hWnd);
25  }
26
27  // Play 5 seconds of CD track 3 via Command Message
28  MCI_OPEN_PARMS myCDOpen={NULL,0,"cdaudio",NULL,NULL};      ②
29  errOpen = mciSendCommand(NULL,MCI_OPEN,
30              MCI_OPEN_TYPE|MCI_WAIT,(DWORD)&myCDOpen);
31  if (errOpen)
32  {
33      // Display the open error
34      mciGetErrorString(errOpen,szErrorMessage,512);
35      AfxMessageBox(szErrorMessage);
36  }
37  else
38  {
39      // set format to tracks/minutes/seconds/frames
40      MCI_SET_PARMS setParams = {NULL,
```

```
41                              MCI_FORMAT_TMSF,0};
42      errOpen=mciSendCommand(myCDOpen.wDeviceID,MCI_SET,
43              MCI_SET_TIME_FORMAT,(DWORD)&setParams);
44
45      // Play 5 seconds of track 3 from 12 seconds
46      MCI_PLAY_PARMS playParams = {NULL,
47                      MCI_MAKE_TMSF(3, 0, 12, 0),
48                      MCI_MAKE_TMSF(3, 0, 17, 0)};
49      mciSendCommand(myCDOpen.wDeviceID,MCI_PLAY,
50                      MCI_FROM ¦ MCI_TO ¦ MCI_WAIT,
51                      (DWORD)&playParams);
52      // ** Close the device
53      MCI_GENERIC_PARMS genParams = {NULL};
54      mciSendCommand(myCDOpen.wDeviceID,MCI_CLOSE,
55                      NULL,(DWORD)&genParams);
56   }
```

(3) The time range values are set up by the MCI_MAKE_ TMSF macro for Command Messages.

On line 5 of Listing 28.4, the mciSendString() function is first called to open the CD player device and create an alias named mycd. If the call fails, the relevant error message will be displayed by lines 10 and 11 using mciGetErrorString() to convert the error code into a readable error message.

Line 16 sets the time format to tmsf, which tells MCI to treat subsequent position commands as specifying the track, minute, second, and frame parameters.

Line 19 starts the CD playing with the play command, and specifies the optional from and to commands to play from 12 seconds into track 3 to 17 seconds into track 3. The wait flag tells the function to return only when finished playing the section. Line 23 then closes the device.

The same section is played using Command Messages and reopened by the MCI_OPEN message in line 29. The time format is set with the MCI_SET message by specifying the MCI_SET_TIME_FORMAT flag and set to the tmsf format by the MCI_FORMAT_TMSF member of the setParams structure.

Line 49 plays the same section, this time using the MCI_MAKE_TMSF macro to specify the CD from and to positions held in the MCI_PLAY_PARMS structure. Finally, line 54 closes the device with an MCI_CLOSE message.

Adding the MCI Window

The previous section discusses using the MCI entirely program-matically with either no user interface or with your own custom user interface, but there is a higher level standard interface that you can use instead, the MCIWnd.

The MCIWnd is a high-level control that gives the user full control over a specific MCI device. The interface of the control differs from device to device. For a digitalvideo device, you'll see video-playing controls and a video window; however, for a waveaudio device, you'll just see the play, rewind, and pause controls relevant to playing .wav files.

You can add the MCIWnd to your application with incredible ease. For example, by merely adding one function call to the end of an InitDialog() function, the fully functional .avi digitalvideo player control is added to the dialog box as shown in Figure 28.5.

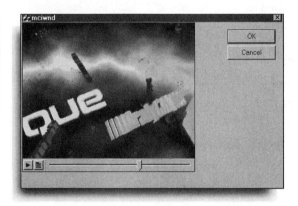

FIGURE 28.5
An MCI window attached to a standard dialog box with one MCIWND function.

The MCIWndCreate() call creates an MCIWnd initialized with an .avi file to play:

```
HWND hMCI = MCIWndCreate(m_hWnd, AfxGetApp()->m_hInstance,
MCIWNDF_SHOWALL, "C:\\Vidclip.avi");
```

The first parameter in m_hWnd is a handle to the parent window (the dialog box). The second is a handle for the application instance. The third parameter lets you specify a whole range of flags to control the creation and style of the window, as shown in Table 28.7. The final parameter lets you specify a filename with a recognized MCI extension or MCI device to open. The type of the control displayed will correspond to the specified file or device type.

If the open is successful, a valid MCI window handle is returned into hMCI; otherwise hMCI is set to NULL.

TABLE 28.7 *MCIWndCreate* creation flags

Flag Value	Description
MCIWNDF_SHOWALL	Uses all the SHOW style flags.
MCIWNDF_SHOWNAME	Displays the name of the device or file in the MCIWnd title bar.
MCIWNDF_SHOWMODE	Displays the device mode in the title bar, such as playing, stopped, not ready, seeking, open, and paused.
MCIWNDF_SHOWPOS	Displays the current play position in the title bar.
MCIWNDF_RECORD	Adds a record button if the device can record.
MCIWNDF_NOAUTOSIZEWINDOW	Won't automatically size the window if the image size changes.
MCIWNDF_NOAUTOSIZEMOVIE	Stops the image being resized to the window's size if the window size changes.
MCIWNDF_NOERRORDLG	Stops MCI-based error messages from being displayed.
MCIWNDF_NOMENU	Removes the pop-up menu button.
MCIWNDF_NOOPEN	Stops the user from opening different files.
MCIWNDF_NOPLAYBAR	Hides the user controls—can only be played programmatically.
MCIWNDF_NOTIFYALL	Notifies the parent window of any of the following messages.
MCIWNDF_NOTIFYMODE	Notifies the parent window of mode change messages.
MCIWNDF_NOTIFYMODE	Notifies the parent window of play position information.
MCIWNDF_NOTIFYMEDIA	Notifies the parent window of MCI filename or device changes.
MCIWNDF_NOTIFYSIZE	Notifies the parent window of the MCIWnd size changing.
MCIWNDF_NOTIFYERROR	Notifies the parent window of MCI errors.

Changing the MCI window styles

You can change the window styles of an existing MCI window using the MCIWndChangeStyles() function. This function needs a handle identifying the MCI window, a bitmask to indicate the styles that might change, and a value with the new flag settings for the window. A corresponding macro, MCIWndGetStlyes(), can return the current flag settings for a specified window.

When the MCIWnd is open, you can send control messages to the window by using a set of macros. These macros send messages such as MCI_PLAY and many others that correspond to the MCI commands that were shown in Table 28.5. There are many MCIWnd messaging macros; some examples that correspond to the messages that were shown in Table 28.5 are listed in Table 28.8.

Finding the current window mode

After issuing a command to an MCI window, you might want to check what its current operating mode is (playing, stopped, and so on). The MCIWndGetMode() macro lets you find this for a specified window. You must also pass it a pointer to a buffer and the size of that buffer to fill the buffer with a string or structure indicating the current mode. The possible modes are MCI_MODE_NOT_READY, MCI_MODE_OPEN, MCI_MODE_PLAY, MCI_MODE_RECORD, MCI_MODE_PAUSE, MCI_MODE_SEEK and MCI_MODE_STOP.

TABLE 28.8 The *MCIWnd* macros

MCIWnd Macro	MCI Message	Description
MCIWndOpenDialog	MCIWNDM_OPEN	Opens a new MCI device or file.
MCIWndOpen	-1	Opens a new MCI device or file.
MCIWndClose	MCI_CLOSE	Closes the MCI device or file.
MCIWndPlay	MCI_PLAY	Plays the device or file.
MCIWndRecord	MCI_RECORD	Records from the device.
MCIWndStop	MCI_STOP	Stops playing or recording.
MCIWndSeek	MCI_SEEK	Seek to a position.
MCIWndPause	MCI_PAUSE	Pause the device.
MCIWndResume	MCI_RESUME	Continue after pausing.
MCIWndPutDest	MCIWNDM_PUT_DEST	Positions the display window.
MCIWndPlayFromTo	MCI_SEEK, MCIWNDM_PLAYTO	Plays from a position to a position by sending an initial seek message, then a play to message.

You must pass the handle of the MCI window to these macros and can pass extra parameters to some macros where relevant. For example, to play from position 1 to position 5 of the .avi file, you could use the following macro after the previous MCIWndCreate() returns a valid hMCI window handle:

```
MCIWndPlayFromTo(hMCI,1,5);
```

You can destroy the window as easily as it was created by using the MCIWndDestroy macro passing the window handle:

```
MCIWndDestroy (hMCI);
```

All this really does is send the normal WM_CLOSE message to close the window.

You can try these MCIWnd macros from any application that can supply a valid parent window handle.

You will need to include the Vfw.h header file for the macro definitions and function prototypes, as shown:

```
#include "vfw.h"
```

You must link your application with the vfw28.lib to use the MCIWnd API functions by adding vfw28.lib to your **Object/Library Modules** line in the **Link** tab of the Project Settings dialog box. You can invoke this dialog box by clicking the **Project** menu and selecting the **Settings** option.

SEE ALSO

➤ *To use the* MCIWnd *as an ActiveX control, see page 200*

GLOSSARY

accelerator table A project resource containing an array of data structures that define keystroke combinations that send commands to the application.

access See *private*, *protected*, or *public access*.

ActiveX See *object linking and embedding*.

ActiveX controls Controls that can be shared among programs and have configurable properties that can be set or obtained via COM/OLE interfaces. These controls can be used in World Wide Web pages and downloaded and used dynamically or incorporated in application software to speed software development.

alignment How the text is displayed relative to a fixed point, usually left, right, or centered on the specified point.

anisotropic Having different properties in different directions.

ANSI American National Standards Institute—In programming, a character set that uses one byte to represent each character.

API See *application programming interface*.

application programming interface (API) Specialist libraries of code designed to help with a particular type of operation, usually in conjunction with specific types of hardware.

application resource See *resource*.

AppWizard A development tool that enables the creation of a Visual C++ project.

archive A backup file that contains all the data required by an application in a serial contiguous dump or file.

aspect ratio The ratio of width to height. Usually describing the ratio of a pixel's width to its height. If this differs between representations of the same data, the dimensional relationships will differ.

ASSERT A statement that a condition is always true. Assertion macros are used in debugging programs.

assertions A test used in debugging code to warn the developer if a condition defined in an ASSERT macro isn't TRUE. Usually a developer inserts ASSERT statements to ensure the assumed entry conditions for a function are correct.

asynchronously   Program control can continue without waiting for response from a remote device that's busy performing a specific task (such as waiting for the video blanking period).

attribute information   Information that holds the default colors, drawing modes, and actions that will influence the drawing functions.

background bitmap   An image displayed as a background to the application's user interface.

background color   In image editing, specifies which color to draw when the right mouse button is clicked.

base address   An address that identifies the start of an object's position in memory.

bit blitting   Quickly copying rectangular regions of pixels from one place in memory to another—usually aided by custom hardware.

bitmap   An array of data representing a colored image.

branch node   An item within a tree control that has child items.

breakpoints   Flags that can be set against a line of code to force the compiler to halt execution at the specified position when run in debug mode.

browser   An application or view that displays data in a specifically formatted fashion. For example, the Microsoft Internet Explorer 4 Web browser displays Internet World Wide Web–based hypertext pages using the HTML language.

buffer   A byte array used as temporary storage when transferring data to and from a disk file or performing an input/output operation.

calibrate   To measure a piece of equipment in test conditions so that a scale for that equipment can be ascertained for real operation.

callback function   A function that is called from another function whenever a specific event occurs or during enumeration.

catching   Writing a handler that will be called whenever a specific message or event is received.

cell   Refers to the whole rectangular area used to store a character of a font, including whitespace.

character   Refers to a single alphabetical or numeric figure as defined by a font.

character height   The height of the visible area used by the figure of a font character.

class definition   A section of code usually contained in a header file (.h) that defines the member functions and variables that compose the class. Definitions start with the class C++ keyword.

class factory A C++ programming method that enables the creation of objects to be deferred to subclasses.

class implementation See *implementation code.*

clip Chopping off a drawing so that it draws only within a specified region. Similar to drawing through a stencil.

Clipboard A Windows concept of a common interchange buffer. Users can cut or copy information to the Clipboard. Then this data can be pasted into other running programs.

clipping See *clipping functions.*

clipping functions Functions that let you define regions that will be unaffected by any drawing functions applied to them.

CLSID A COM class ID, a 128-bit globally unique number that identifies every COM object class.

collection classes Classes that handle the storage and iteration of several objects, such as arrays and linked lists.

color reference A 24-bit value that holds the red, green, and blue components of a specific color as used for drawing.

Component Gallery A list of registered controls and COM components maintained by Developer Studio that can be incorporated into a project.

COM/OLE See *component object model* and *object linking and embedding.*

component object model A programming model that extends the concepts of object orientation beyond the scope of a single program. Many different programs can communicate and use objects through well-defined interfaces without needing to know where those objects are located. Objects can be run locally, in another program, or on another machine across a network.

constructor A special C++ class function that has the same name as the class, and is used to initialize with a set of parameters when it is declared or created with the new operator.

container In OLE terminology, an application that can hold and display other applications within a framed area. Usually integrating with the embedded object by a set of standard functions.

coordinate A set of numbers that represent an exact position by relative offsets along each dimension in a frame of reference. In two-dimensional coordinates, this is usually a distance along an x axis and a y axis.

coordinate mapping See *mapping mode.*

CScrollView An MFC class that provides base functionality for views that must represent information bigger than the available window size. This functionality is implemented by the use of vertical or horizontal scrollbars attached to the view to represent the current window position over the entire view area.

cursor Image resource representing the mouse pointer. A cursor has a hotspot that determines the exact coordinates of the mouse.

.dll A dynamically linked library that contains the executable code to implement an ActiveX control, or functions available to an .exe program or icons and other compiled resources.

DAO (database access objects) A Microsoft-specific database access system that deals specifically with databases using the Microsoft Jet Engine.

database schema The design of a database's tables and field attributes.

DDE See *dynamic data exchange*.

deadlock When one task is waiting for a resource from the other, but the other task is waiting for a resource from the first, neither can proceed.

debug version A version of a project that includes debugging information to allow stepping through source code while the program is running.

debugging The process of investigating the reason for a program not running as intended and then finding a solution to the problem to fix it.

device capabilities The technical specifications of devices attached to a device context that affect the possible effects and functions that can be used while drawing.

device context A Windows object that presents a common interface between the graphics device interface and underlying two-dimensional display devices such as screens and printers.

destructor A special C++ class function that has the same name as the class, but with a ~ (tilde) character prefix. The destructor can deallocate any memory allocated during the class lifetime and implement any other cleanup code associated with the class.

dialog template An application resource that describes the layout of several dialog controls to present an interactive form to the user.

dimensions A measure of a quantity with no direct mathematical relationship to any other quantity. Usually describing width and height generically.

dispatch class A class that provides the function stubs to call invoke methods across a COM interface to call code that implements those methods in a remote object.

dispatch functions See *dispatch class*.

DLL See *dynamic link library*.

docking Connecting a control bar window such as a toolbar, dialog box, or status bar to a frame window so that the control bar appears to become part of the frame window itself.

docking site Specifies a place where a control bar can dock to the frame window.

document A collection of data.

document template A set of C++ classes that perform dynamic creation of the document, view, and frame classes of SDI and MDI applications.

Document/View   A programming paradigm. See also *single document interface* and *multiple document interface*.

double-clicking   A special action performed by the user clicking one of the mouse buttons twice in quick succession. Usually used to indicate a shortcut for selecting an item from a list.

drawing modes   Settings that affect the default rendering action drawing of the standard drawing functions.

dynamic link library   A library of compiled object code or resources that can be linked into an executable at runtime, usually as a .dll file.

dynamic data exchange   An old Windows methodology for transferring data between applications. Although it is still possible to use this mechanism, OLE should be used preferentially.

dynamic edit control   An edit control that is created temporarily to perform a function and then discarded. This normally involves allocating some memory for the control, using it, and then deleting it immediately.

dynamic splitter window   A splitter window that is dynamically created and destroyed by the user's actions.

dynamically   While the program is running, on-the-fly.

enabled state   The condition of a window, either enabled or disabled.

encapsulate   To hold data from one document within another often different document.

enhanced metafile   A file format that stores a picture in a device-independent way. The enhanced format is specifically used in Win32 applications.

enumerator   A function that iterates through a list of items such as fonts and calls a callback function for each one.

escapement   The amount of slope between one character and the next in tenths of a degree.

events   A message passed to your application by Windows to inform you that the user has interacted with the application in some way or that something has changed.

.exe   Executable code that forms the starting point for an application program.

fixed pitch   The font is displayed so that all characters are displayed with the same width. l's and I's take up just as much room as W's and M's. Often used when displaying formatted numbers.

font mapper   Windows has a set of functions that choose and create the closest font from the computer's installed fonts that best match the specified criteria.

foreground color   In image editing, specifies which color to draw when the left mouse button is clicked.

format   An agreed standard for representing data.

framework   A common piece of software that provides several support services for basing application development upon.

function pointer   A special type of C++ pointer that holds the start address of a function.

function stubs   See *dispatch class*.

GDI   See *graphics device interface*.

geometrical relationships   Spatial positioning of one item to another. Up, down, left, and right are all geometrical relationships.

global function   A function that has global scope and can be called from anywhere within a program.

global memory   A Windows concept to describe memory allocated by the operating system that is potentially visible to other applications and maintained in the operating system address space rather than in the program's local address space.

Gopher server   A popular file and document server protocol that has declined since the introduction of the World Wide Web.

graphics cursor position   A coordinate position held by the device context to store the last drawing position so that the new drawing can optionally be relative to the last position.

graphics device interface (GDI)   A set of drawing objects and methods that allow applications to draw graphical representations of their data using a common set of functions and structures.

growability   Ability to increase in size on demand.

GUID   A 128-bit globally unique number, guaranteed to be unique.

handle   A type of variable that holds a unique reference (usually a number) that identifies a specific type of object. For example, pigeons are sometimes tagged by a numbered band attached to their legs. This number is the computer equivalent of a handle and the pigeon is the object to which the handle refers.

handler   See *Windows message handler*.

hit test   Testing whether the user has clicked in a specific predefined region of the display.

HMENU   A handle to a Windows operating system level menu object.

HRESULT   See *SCODE*.

HTML   Hypertext Markup Language is a text-based language that contains special labels for specifying insertions of pictures and hyperlinks to take the user from one hypertext page to another by a mouse click. HTML is widely used on the Internet in World Wide Web pages.

icon   An image resource containing two bitmaps to allow transparency.

IID   A COM interface ID, a 128-bit globally unique number that identifies every COM object interface.

IMPLEMENT_DYNAMIC   See *runtime class information*.

implementation code   A section of code that forms the body of a class's member functions.

import library   A static link library that just holds code to identify and call functions in a DLL, usually automatically generated by the compiler.

indicators   A small pane in an application's status bar that displays text (or an icon) to indicate a specific piece of status or configuration information.

inheritance   Creating a new C++ class by extending the capabilities of an existing class. See also *subclass*.

inline editing   Editing a piece of text directly in a list or tree control. For example, renaming a file in the Windows Explorer uses inline editing.

instantiate   Create an instance of a specific class as a real object in the computer's memory.

interface class   See *dispatch class*.

inverse color   Used in icon editing to specify parts of the image that are inversed when the icon is being dragged.

isotropic   Having similar properties in different directions.

landscape   An image whose width exceeds its height.

late binding   Type information is discovered at runtime rather than when the client program is compiled (early binding).

leaf node   An item within a tree control that has no child items.

.lib   See *static link library*.

linked list   A list of data items that store pointers to the next and previous items in the list.

list view   A view that displays items of text and sometimes icons in a list format.

local variable   A variable that is scoped locally within a function.

logical coordinates   When using a mapping mode, the coordinate system can be set to represent real-world coordinates rather than pixel-based coordinates. These are called logical coordinates and their units depend on the specific mapping mode.

Mandelbrot fractal   A mathematical fractal named after its discoverer, computer scientist Benoit Mandelbrot.

Mandelbrot set   See *Mandelbrot fractal*.

mapping mode   A device context mode that converts between logical coordinates and pixel-based coordinates to provide a real-world scale representation of data. See also *logical coordinates*.

marshal   The process of packaging a function's parameters into inter-machine compatible forms for transmission between processes or machines on a network.

MCI   See *media control interface*.

MDI   See *multiple document interface*.

media control interface   An API library that provides a set of easy-to-use and standard functions to play video or audio clips to or from CDs, wave files, AVI files, and digital video devices.

megabytes   A measure of data storage. 1,048,576 bytes in decimal notation.

781

message   See *events*.

message handler   See *catching*.

message map   In MFC, a macro-driven mechanism for connecting Windows messages with specific C++ functions.

methods   A set of functions that belong to a specific class.

MFC   See *Microsoft foundation classes*.

MFC library   See *Microsoft foundation classes*.

Microsoft clip gallery   A collection of clip art images supplied with the Microsoft Office suite of programs. These images are designed to be incorporated into user's documents and spreadsheets.

Microsoft foundation classes   A set of classes provided with the Visual C++ compiler to aid and provide support for rapid application development.

Microsoft interface definition language   A language that specifies COM interface definitions and COM classes for building remote procedure call (RPC) code and passing parameters in a well-defined and compatible fashion between different applications.

Microsoft Internet Explorer 4   A hypertext browser program that displays HTML pages and navigates the user around World Wide Web pages.

Microsoft QuickView   A program distributed with Windows 95 and Windows NT that can view multiple file types.

MIDL   See *Microsoft interface definition language*.

modal message box   A message box that waits for user input before continuing.

module state   A pointer to information that describes the unique attributes and memory state of a particular object, such as a running .exe program or a dynamically linked DLL.

moiré fringe   A set of overlapping lines that cause patterns to be formed from the conjunction of the two sets of lines.

multimedia   Combination of video and sound devices in a PC environment that can record sound, scan images, and play compact discs, video clips, and audio clips.

multiple document interface   A standard base architecture that separates the concepts of data (called documents) and multiple representations of views of that data. An MDI can have many documents open concurrently, whereas an SDI has only one set of common data open at once.

newing   See *instantiate*.

notification message   A special kind of Windows message usually sent from a control to inform the program that the user has interacted with that control in some way.

null-terminated string   A standard way of encoding strings of text by adding a character of binary zero value to the ASCII coded string to indicate the end of the string. Normally ASCII codes don't venture below the value 32 (for a space), so a zero is an exceptional character value.

object linking and embedding   The capability of one program to display and use capabilities of another program within its windows. For example, a spreadsheet can be displayed in a word processor document without the word processor needing to know anything about the displayed object; the code to display and maintain the object is being delegated to the spreadsheet.

object orientation   A programming methodology that closely associates behavior and properties to a class of objects that correspond to objects in a real-world problem. This promotes faster development and more robust software by breaking the problem into discrete, testable objects that communicate with other objects through agreed interfaces.

object-oriented design   See *object orientation*.

.ocx   A file type that contains the executable code to implement an ActiveX control.

ODBC   See *open database connectivity*.

offset address   An address used in conjunction with a base address to identify a member of a particular object instance.

OLE   See *object linking and embedding*.

OLE dispatch interface   See *dispatch class*.

OLE enabled   An object or view that is capable of using object linking and embedding to manipulate, display, and share data items from other programs.

open database connectivity   A set of standard drivers that allow applications to use standard functions to access many different databases.

operator overloads   A class can implement functions that are represented by one of the normal C++ syntax operators, such as =, >, +=, %, and so on. The functions are implemented as normal, but use the keyword operator in their definition. Parameters are implied by the right-hand operand of the operator.

ordinal number   Unique numbering system for each function in a DLL.

orientation   The amount of slope for each character, in tenths of a degree.

overloaded function   A function that has more than one definition. See also *operator overloads*.

persistent   Data that is stored on disk so that settings are held permanently and can be recalled when the control is used or modified.

pixels   The smallest unit of display that can be individually modified.

pointer   A type of variable that holds the address of another variable or object so that functions can indirectly edit an object by passing its address to one another.

portrait   An image whose height exceeds its width.

preprocessor   The first stage of the compilation process that expands macro definitions and follows `#include` and `#ifdef` directives to decide what code should and shouldn't be compiled.

printer codes   Agreed numbers sent to a printer to request a specific function, such as scrolling the paper to the next sheet.

private access   A class declaration that makes it impossible to directly access a member variable or member function from another class without using access functions or friend constructs.

private member   A member variable or object that is protected so that it can be accessed directly only by methods in its own class. Other classes must access it via access member functions.

programmatically   Causing an event to happen from lines of code in the program rather than by user initiation.

proportionally spaced   The font is displayed so that thinner characters such as l's and I's are narrower than wider letters such as W's and M's.

protected access   A class declaration that makes it impossible to directly access a member variable or member function from another class without using access functions or friend constructs, but can be accessed from a derived class.

protected member function   See *protected access*.

pseudo random number generator   An algorithm that generates a list of numbers that appear to be random in nature; however, they are only pseudo random because the list can be regenerated by setting an initial seed value.

public access   A class declaration that makes it possible to directly access a member variable or member function from any other class.

public member function   See *public access*.

radio controls   A group of items where only one item from a set can be set at once. When any of the set items is selected, the others are automatically deselected.

reflected notification message   A notification message that has been sent from the parent window to a control and then reflected from the control to a specific message handler.

release version   A version of a program from which the debug information is excluded. Typically a release version is sent to the end user.

resolution   The finest individually representable unit.

resource   An additional project component to the C++ code that is stored along with the application and can be used by the code to display icons, menus, bitmaps, strings, or dialog boxes.

Rich Edit view   A view that lets the user edit text and insert OLE objects. It supports basic word processor-like operations to manipulate and format text.

root node   The base item within a tree control.

rubber banding   Selecting an item, several items, or a region by clicking a mouse button, dragging a sizable rectangle to define the selection area, and then releasing the mouse button. Usually used to select several graphical items.

runtime class information   MFC classes derived from `CObject` can hold information that identifies the specific class by implementing the `DECLARE_DYNAMIC` and associated macros. Applications can then determine an object's class by using `RUNTIME_CLASS` and `IsKindOf` macros and functions.

SCODE   A 32-bit value used to report errors arising from many OLE functions in a structured fashion.

screen color   Used in the editing of icons to represent transparency.

scrollbars   Vertically or horizontally aligned controls that have a movable bar to represent a sliding variable amount by the bar position along the entire axis of its containing control.

SDI   See *single document interface*.

SDI framework   See *single document interface*.

seeding number   See *pseudo random number generator*.

serialization   See *serialize*.

serialize   The action of turning a set of variables into a continuous stream of data or turning a stream of data back into individual variables.

shared memory   Memory available to several running applications, usually used to transfer information between running programs. Normally memory is kept separate from other running programs to stop accidental overwriting of another program's memory space.

single document interface   A standard base architecture that separates the concepts of data (called documents) and multiple representations of views of that data. An SDI has only one set of common data open at once, whereas an MDI application can have many documents open concurrently.

SQL   See *structured query language*.

standard framework   The framework used by SDI and MDI applications.

static link library   A library of compiled object code that can be linked into an executable at compile time, usually as a .lib library file.

static splitter window   A splitter window that is created on initialization and cannot be removed by the user.

string table   A project resource containing an array of strings.

structured query language (SQL)   A text-based standard protocol for retrieving or setting database data.

subclass   To extend existing functionality by using an existing implementation and building on it.

synchronize   To control the access to thread resources so that one thread can access a resource while the others wait their turn.

system palette   A common set of colors held by Windows to best represent the bulk standard colors required by running applications that don't require advanced color palette support.

TCHAR   Defines a character data type. If _UNICODE is defined, TCHAR is defined as the two-byte character type (wchar_t), or else TCHAR is defined as the one-byte character type (char).

TCP/IP (Transmission Control Protocol/Internet Protocol)   A set of standard definitions that form a protocol for low-level network and Internet communications on a packet-based network.

templates   A special addition to the C++ syntax that allow type-specific functions and classes to be generated automatically from a generic set of instruction code. Akin to macro expansion.

Tree view   A view that displays hierarchical items of text in folders that can be expanded to show child items. These child items can themselves be folders. For example, the left pane of Windows Explorer represents the disk directory structure with a tree view.

tri-state control   A check box or radio button control supporting an intermediate or indeterminate third state, usually portrayed visually by dimming the control.

type information   Information that describes the various parameters that should be passed to functions

implemented by a dispatch interface. These can be formed into libraries called type libraries.

type safety   Using specific class names in prototypes rather than their generic base classes to ensure that the compiler issues a warning if the wrong type of class is passed or returned to or from a function.

Unicode   A character set that uses two bytes to represent each character to encode all possible worldwide symbols.

URL   The Universal Resource Locator is a coded way of specifying the location of different types of resources on the Internet or local disk drives. For example, http://www.chaos1.demon.co.uk/ specifies that a hypertext protocol resource (http) is located at the Internet address www.chaos1.demon.co.uk.

user friendly   A concept in programming to describe an application interface that is easy to understand and use.

vector   Describing both direction and magnitude (or distance).

vertical blanking period   The time when a full video frame has been drawn on the monitor display and the scanning electron beam is turned off while it is repositioned at the top left for the next frame.

view   A visual representation of the program's data shown in a window.

virtual function   A C++ language concept indicated by prefixing *virtual* to a function definition. A virtual function that is implemented in a base class can have its standard functionality overridden by adding an implementation to a derived class. C++ uses virtual functions to achieve polymorphism.

virtual key codes   A device-independent value to identify a keystroke (for example, VK_ESCAPE).

vtable   A table of virtual functions created by the compiler for each class definition. Used in COM to define an interface specification.

waveform   See *waveform buffer*.

waveform buffer   A piece of memory that stores the changing amplitude values for the length of an audio wave or sound clip.

white noise   A random hissing sound, like a radio tuned to a dead channel.

Win32   See *Win32 subsystem*.

Win32 subsystem   A layer of code (Application Programming Interface) that implements the basic operating system functionality for Windows.

> **Windows environment**   Programs running under the Window operating system and its variants.

> **Windows Explorer**   A standard Windows application that lets the user view and manipulate the disk directory and file structure.

Windows message handler   A function that is called whenever the application receives an associated message. The function interprets the messages and may perform some application functionality on the function.

Windows open services architecture   A collection of standards such as TCP/IP Sockets, RPC, and MAPI that are used to integrate Windows-based systems into other network computing environments.

WYSIWYG   An acronym for "What you see is what you get." This means that the onscreen representation of some data will appear identical when printed.

Index

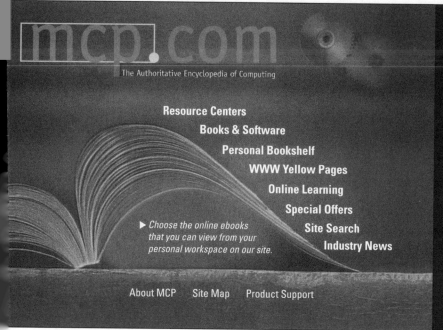

Microsoft Foundation Class Hierarchy - Version 6.0

CObject

Classes Not Derived from CObject

Graphical Drawing

CDC
- CClientDC
- CMetaFileDC
- CPaintDC
- CWindowDC

Control Support

- CDockState
- CImageList

Graphical Drawing Objects

CGdiObject
- CBitmap
- CBrush
- CFont
- CPalette
- CPen
- CRgn

Menus

CMenu

Command Line

CCommandLineInfo

ODBC Database Support

- CDatabase
- CRecordset

user recordsets

- CLongBinary

DAO Database Support

- CDaoDatabase
- CDaoQueryDef
- CDaoRecordset
- CDaoTableDef
- CDaoWorkspace

Synchronization

CSyncObject
- CCriticalSection
- CEvent
- CMutex
- CSemaphore

Arrays

- CArray(Template)
- CByteArray
- CDWordArray
- CObArray
- CPtrArray
- CStringArray
- CUintArray
- CWordArray

arrays of user types

Lists

- CList (Template)
- CPtrList
- CObList
- CStringList

lists of user types

Maps

- CMap (Template)
- CMapWordToPtr
- CMapPtrToWord
- CMapPtrToPtr
- CMapWordToOb
- CMapStringToPtr
- CMapStringToOb
- CMapStringToString

maps of user types

Internet Services

- CInternetSession
- CInternetConnection
  - CFtpConnection
  - CGopherConnection
  - CHttpConnection
- CFileFind
  - CFtpFileFind
  - CGopherFileFind
- CGopherLocator

Windows Sockets

- CAsyncSocket
  - CSocket

Internet Server API

- CHtmlStream
- CHttpFilter
- CHttpFilterContext
- CHttpServer
- CHttpServerContext

Runtime Object Model Support

- CArchive
- CDumpContext
- CRuntimeClass

Simple Value Types

- CPoint
- CRect
- CSize
- CString
- CTime
- CTimeSpan

Structures

- CCreateContext
- CMemoryState
- COleSafeArray
- CPrintInfo

Support Classes

- CCmdUI
  - COleCmdUI
- CDaoFieldExchange
- CDataExchange
- CDBVariant
- CFieldExchange
- COleDataObject
- COleDispatchDriver
- CPropExchange
- CRectTracker
- CWaitCursor

Typed Template Collections

- CTypedPtrArray
- CTypedPtrList
- CTypedPtrMap

OLE Type Wrappers

- CFontHolder
- CPictureHolder

OLE Automation Types

- COleCurrency
- COleDateTime
- COleDateTimeSpan
- COleVariant

Synchronization

- CMultiLock
- CSingleLock